Oracle Web Application Server Handbook

About the Author . . .

Established in 1991, Dynamic Information Systems, LLC, is a national technology management and implementation consulting firm headquartered in Minneapolis, Minnesota. In 1994, Dynamic saw the potential of exploiting the World Wide Web as a new database application delivery mechanism. Since then, Dynamic has implemented some of the most sophisticated enterprise-grade Web- and network-centric applications for some of the world's best-known companies. This book distills much of this hard-won experience.

Today, Dynamic continues to focus on delivering enterprise information management solutions using a combination of traditional and leading-edge technologies. In addition to general intranet strategy planning and application development, Dynamic provides specialized web practices for electronic commerce, security, Oracle applications on the Web, and web-enabled HRIS.

Dynamic Information Systems is a charter member of the Oracle Web Alliance, and its president, Barry Johnson, is a founding member of the Oracle Developer Programme Advisory Board.

Dynamic's Web site can be found at www.dynamic-info.com.

ORACLE® Oracle Press™

Oracle Web Application Server Handbook

Dynamic Information Systems, LLC

Osborne **McGraw-Hill**

Berkeley New York St. Louis
San Francisco Auckland Bogotá Hamburg London Madrid
Mexico City Milan Montreal New Delhi Panama City
Paris São Paulo Singapore Sydney Tokyo Toronto

Osborne/**McGraw-Hill**
2600 Tenth Street
Berkeley, California 94710
U.S.A.

For information on translations or book distributors outside the U.S.A., or to arrange bulk purchase discounts for sales promotions, premiums, or fund-raisers, please contact Osborne/**McGraw-Hill** at the above address.

Oracle Web Application Server Handbook

234567890 DOC DOC 901987654321098

ISBN 0-07-882215-7

Publisher	**Proofreaders**
Brandon A. Nordin	Paul Medoff
	Linda Medoff
Editor-in-Chief	Roberta Rieger
Scott Rogers	
	Indexer
Acquisitions Editor	Jack Lewis
Scott Rogers	
	Computer Designer
Project Editors	Sylvia Brown
Emily Rader	
Nancy McLaughlin	**Illustrators**
	Leslee Bassin
Editorial Assistant	Artlette Crosland
Ann Sellers	
	Series Design
Technical Editor	Jani Beckwith
John Ogilvie	
	Cover Design
Copy Editors	Lisa Schultz
Mark Woodworth	
Emily Rader	
Tim Barr	

Contents at a Glance

Contents

Foreword

I't's with great pleasure that I write this forward to the *Oracle Web Application Server Handbook.* Barry Johnson, president of Dynamic Information Systems, has worked closely with our development team to ensure that the technical information presented throughout the book is accurate and up to date. I have had the pleasure of watching the chapters evolve over the past few months into a comprehensive presentation of Oracle's state-of-the-art Web Application Server and Network Computing Architecture, and I'm certain you will find it both interesting and rewarding to read.

At the time of writing, Oracle Web Application Server 3.0 is taking the market by storm. This product provides extensibility independent of programming languages, enabling developers to deploy web applications written in Java, Perl, C, PL/SQL, or COBOL. It is the industry-leading platform for deploying shared application logic for thin-client computing and can use multiple HTTP servers from Netscape, Microsoft, and Apache to service requests from any web browser. These capabilities allow developers to develop once, deploy anywhere, and efficiently insulate application logic from proprietary HTTP server APIs and details of the underlying networking protocols. Oracle Web Application Server also introduced the industry's first transaction model for the Web. Application developers can design their web applications to take full advantage of the transactional capabilities of Oracle7 or Oracle8, even across multiple HTML pages. Finally, given Oracle's long history of providing real business solutions to our many thousands of customers, we have paid special attention to the need for embracing and integrating existing legacy applications and data. To complement our broad line of database gateway technologies, Oracle Web Application Server ships with sophisticated Java-based GUI tools that make "web-enabling" mainframes simpler than ever.

All of these nice features are provided through a cartridge architecture that is efficiently load-balanced, highly reliable, and very scalable. At the time of writing, some of the world's largest interactive web sites are being developed and deployed using Oracle Web Application Server, and it is truly changing not only the face of the Web, but the entire IT industry. Our mission is to enable the information age, which we are doing through network computing.

I hope I have managed to get you excited by now. You should be. You hold in your hand a great in-depth technical resource that will help you develop applications for the new thin-client computing paradigm. The remainder of this forward is more personal, and shares with you some of the war stories that are told around campfires when us old-timers and web veterans gather together to remember the days of NCSA Mosaic. I hope you find it entertaining—it's certainly been quite a ride!

Barry wanted me to write about the early days of Oracle Web Application Server and of my role in developing one of the key technologies: the PL/SQL cartridge. It's true, I did sort of "invent" it, and I joined the original Internet Products team that later made it into a real product. But the key word in the previous sentence is "team." Without a close-knit team this product would never have made it to market. Having said that, there are two people who deserve special recognition and my very special thanks: Jack Haverty, the granddaddy of the Internet, is such a source of inspiration and never ceases to amaze me. Jack gave birth to Oracle's Intranet, "discovered" my skunk works, and sold me his Jeep for $1,500. My second hero is Mark Jarvis, who more than anyone at Oracle realized how much the Web was going to change life as we know it. Mark pulled together the original Internet Server Products team, including me, and made this all happen. The real heroes are, of course, the hard-working and dedicated engineers who have built Oracle's Internet server products, working under Senior Director of Development Ankur Sharma's guidance.

Back in the stone age (spring of 1994) I discovered the Web. I had a lot of fun writing HTML for a few days and then I discovered CGI. That changed everything. It's hard to describe the impact of seeing my first dynamic data-driven page pop up in a browser. A simple HTML form submitting query parameters to a simple back-end SQL*Plus script changed my view of the world. Over the next month or so I wrote several CGI programs exploring a variety of methods for accessing an Oracle database from the Web, and one morning I had inspiration for a new program that I quickly hacked together in about two hours. I called it WOW. The acronym stood for "Web Oracle Web" and was meant to indicate that information was being passed from the Web into Oracle and then back to the Web again. It was different from the other prototypes because it instantly "web-enabled" Oracle-stored procedures and took advantage of their ability to execute application logic instead of simply fetching data. Well, that's how it all started.

Suddenly WOW was generating a lot of interest within Oracle's Product Division, and to make a long story short, I was asked to join a small team that would create Oracle's first commercial Internet server product. The PL/SQL Agent emerged after professional developers had reworked the WOW prototype into tight Oracle C code (which also made it portable). It did pretty much the same thing, though. It still does to this day, but with lots of performance enhancements and new features and capabilities, such as the configurable transactions introduced in release 3.0.

We were a small team at first (you could count us on one hand), but we were growing quickly. We had a fun first year. I think everybody who was starting up Internet businesses was having a lot of fun (a few were even making money). I think Oracle executives made a wise decision in letting us fool around a bit at that time because nobody was really sure where this was all going. Remember, at that time Bill Gates thought the Internet was a fad. We shipped the first version of Oracle WebServer in 1995. We made a few million in revenue, but it was insignificant compared to what Oracle's database and applications business was doing. We viewed ourselves very much as being part of the database.

Something very important happened in late 1995. Oracle's New Media Division was breaking up due to the disappointing ITV market, and our Internet team was consolidated with a team of engineers who had spent the last couple of years building CORBA-based high-tech multimedia systems. Peter Relan became VP of the team (which he still is) and Ankur Sharma took charge of the engineering team. This proved to be a very fruitful combination. A vision of a general purpose application server platform for the Web starting taking shape in our minds. Concepts like "cartridge" and "web request broker" were born in late night planning meetings over cold pizza and coffee. We made a fundamental decision to change our product strategy from being a database extension to becoming an extensible platform for web-based applications, and in May 1996 we were ready to ship our second generation Internet server: Oracle WebServer 2.0. It was quite a feat to pull off the 2.0 release because we were severely constrained by our resources at the time. It would not have happened without the extraordinary engineering contributions made by Mala, Seshu, and Shehzaad.

The key feature of Oracle WebServer 2.0 was, in addition to the PL/SQL cartridge, the Web Request Broker. This was basically a dispatch mechanism for web servers, enabling them to access server-side application logic that plugged into the Web Request Broker as "cartridges." It was an architecture far superior to the single-process plug-in model adopted by competing Internet servers. Another important fact that few people realize is that Oracle WebServer 2.0 had the industry's first fully integrated Java VM. This was before server-side Java was even considered by anybody; the Java development community was still trying to build applets that did more than just rotate.

WebServer 2.0 was a smash hit. I couldn't believe how much revenue it generated in its first month. After a slow start, we had suddenly leapfrogged the industry and were right on the bleeding edge. We even got a "coolest new product" award at InterOp! What had started out as a creative PL/SQL hack was actually slowly changing the direction of Oracle Corporation. In late 1996 Oracle presented its Network Computing Architecture, a blueprint of how thin-client computing could be implemented by combining well-known and accepted technologies from client/server computing, the Internet, and CORBA. The Web "Application" Server was becoming a strategic product and the centerpiece of NCA.

Also important to note is that we released WebServer 2.1 in late 1996. This release was strategic because it included support for third-party HTTP servers. It clearly demonstrated that Oracle was not in the web server business. Instead, our product was targeted at people who wanted to deploy applications on the Web. Existing Netscape and Microsoft web server customers could "upgrade" their web sites to become transactional and distributed by using Oracle WebServer 2.1 as the platform for hosting web applications.

In September 1995, in parallel with WebServer 2.0 development, we had started planning our biggest project to date—Web Application Server 3.0—which would be the delivery vehicle for NCA. It was an ambitious project, and Peter Relan succeeded in getting Larry Ellison to sanction it, which was no small feat, given that Oracle had previously only really endorsed client/server computing. We intended to rip out the internal plumbing of WebServer 2.0 and replace it with an industry standard CORBA-compliant ORB. This would give us the industry's first fully distributed application server for the Web. The rest is history. Thanks to the engineering team led by Ankur and with key contributors like Mala, Sam, and Joe, Oracle Web Application Server 3.0 started shipping in the first half of 1997 after going through the largest beta program in Oracle's history: over 25,000 registered beta testers had been pounding away at the product for almost six months!

That's what this book is about. Oracle Web Application Server 3.0. In it you will find a rich collection of samples and instructions to get you going quickly and smoothly. Whether you are heavily into Oracle's PL/SQL, or more on the early adopter curve of n-tier Java development, Oracle Web Application Server will satisfy your need for a robust, scalable platform.

Of course, the story doesn't end here. One of the challenges that technical authors like Barry Johnson face when writing about Internet technology is that the world moves ahead (quickly) while their manuscripts go to print. By the time you read this, chances are that we have started at least the beta program for Oracle Web Application Server 3.1. The place for you to stay in touch with us is at http://www.olab.com. We will be distributing beta versions of upcoming releases from this web site on a regular basis. Please visit us frequently!

Magnus Lonnroth
Director, Product Management
Internet Application Server Division
Oracle Corporation
Redwood Shores, October, 1997

Acknowledgments

hen I was first contacted about writing the *Oracle Web Application Server Handbook*, it sounded like a great opportunity. Today, as I type what are the last few paragraphs of this book, I would call it a great odyssey. During the course of the writing, the WebServer became the Web Application Server, thanks to a quantum upgrade between versions 2.0 and 3.0. The architecture changed, the components changed—everything changed. As a developer, this was wonderful; as an author, it was maddening. Of course, many of the interesting hacks and workarounds that had been written for version 2.0 were replaced by discussions of features added in version 3.0.

This book, like any, is a culmination of the efforts of many people who are deserving of thanks (and maybe some apologies.) Ann Sellers and Scott Rogers from Osborne both had the not entirely happy responsibility of driving this book forward. This was of course made more difficult because this book was written by practitioners quite busy with ongoing consulting engagements. I believe the book, albeit delayed, is better for having been written by experienced consultants. I am greatly thankful for the patience we were shown by Scott and Ann, as well as the assistance they provided in coordinating changing schedules.

Also at Osborne, the editorial and production staff were especially helpful. The book's final production schedule was very compressed, and Emily Rader's group, with considerable assistance from Nancy McLaughlin, Roberta Rieger, and the production staff, did an outstanding job of driving the final steps forward to completion. Mark Woodworth and Emily, herself, did an outstanding job of both editing the text as well as explaining to us the difference between "that" and "which," which hopefully will save future editors no shortage of corrections.

Of course, many people at Oracle are deserving of thanks as well. Jeff Bates originally brought up the subject of the book to me and introduced me to Scott Rogers at Osborne. Magnus Lonnroth is possibly most deserving of thanks both for creating and driving what is now the Web Application Server, as well as for his help in resolving certain technical details in the book. John Ogilvie, a former consultant with Oracle Services, technically reviewed nearly all of the content for the book, as well as provided some outstanding commentary about developing C cartridges for the Web Application Server, much of which is included in Chapter 11.

Gregg McCroskey was an enormous help during the transition from version 2 to version 3 by always making sure we had access to the latest beta versions as soon as they became available. In all, we found that everyone involved with the Web Application Server at Oracle was extremely willing to help in the completion of this book.

I would also like to thank Beatriz Infante, Senior Vice President of the Application Server Division, and Julie Gibbs, Senior Director of Oracle Publishing, for their support of this book as well as their patience. I hope it was worth the wait to be able to include material that is completely updated for version 3.0.

Most important, however, I would like to dedicate this book to our clients who support sophisticated and creative uses for web technology and the consultants who find equally sophisticated and creative solutions. It is this interaction of necessity and invention that built much of the knowledge found in this book.

Introduction

he Oracle Web Application Server is at the heart of Oracle's offerings for web development. It is a complete environment for implementing and deploying web-based applications in a variety of languages. There are three general differences between the Web Application Server and most other web development tools.

The first is that the Web Application Server, or WAS, is extremely flexible for developers. While most web development tools support only one development language, the Web Application Server supports several. Developers can create applications using C, PL/SQL, Java, or Perl for procedural programming tasks, as well as using server-side includes for less-complex development tasks.

The second is the level of sophistication of the WAS. While many tools force web developers to spend significant time focusing on things such as passing parameters, communicating with databases, and worrying about scalability, the WAS either relieves the developer of these concerns, or makes the process much easier. Even support for state management and true transaction control are built into the Web Application Server.

The third area of difference is the support the WAS provides for the deployment and administration of scalable and robust distributed systems. Because the Web Application Server uses an Object Request Broker, or ORB, to manage the communication between the web listener, or

HTTP server, and the developer's applications, administrators gain two main advantages: First, web applications, known as *cartridges* or *components,* can be distributed across multiple machines to balance machine loading and tune performance. Second, the ORB architecture works to balance the typically competing goals of high application performance and overall system stability.

The goal of this book is to provide the reader with all the information necessary to fully exploit the capabilities of the Web Application Server. Any developer with some experience with database applications should be able to follow this book through the chapters and learn how web-based applications work, how to install and administer the WAS, and how to develop applications for the WAS with a variety of languages.

Chapter 1 introduces the motivations that exist to develop applications using web-based technology. It discusses the manner in which database-enabled web applications can serve the interests of information technology and business managers, application designers, and webmasters. It should stimulate the reader's imagination with ways in which web applications may help their organization.

Chapter 2 provides a fairly comprehensive overview of the World Wide Web, including its architecture, general concepts, and the evolution of application development for the Web. For readers unfamiliar with the Web, this chapter should provide sufficient information necessary to provide context to the discussion throughout the rest of the book. In addition, it closes with a list of resources, including books and URLs, where you can find more-detailed information about the subjects discussed.

Chapter 3 introduces the architecture of the Oracle Web Application Server, or OWAS, and explains the process of installing and configuring the WAS. It is meant to complement and supplement the platform-specific installation manuals supplied by Oracle. As such, it focuses more on certain advanced installation topics and provides a road map to configuring the OWAS.

Chapters 4 and 5 explain, in progressive detail, how to develop applications for the OWAS using PL/SQL, the 4GL used throughout Oracle's tools, and the RDBMS. Chapter 4 focuses on the core functionality of the PL/SQL Web Application Server SDK, while Chapter 5 introduces several advanced techniques and third-party development tools to streamline development and produce more-sophisticated applications.

Chapter 6 describes the development of Java-based Web Application Server components. It describes how to use the classes Oracle provides for the dynamic generation of web pages, as well how to access PL/SQL-stored procedures from Java.

Chapter 7 explains Oracle's server-side include mechanism, known as LiveHTML. LiveHTML allows less technically oriented users to create dynamic web pages. It also describes how to use Oracle's Inter-Cartridge Exchange (ICX) to invoke other cartridges to insert content in LiveHTML documents.

Chapter 8 then describes the ODBC cartridge, which provides a basic but useful method for accessing data from any ODBC-supported data source. We demonstrate how using ICX to embed ODBC content inside of LiveHTML documents provides an easy way to create database-driven web pages.

Chapter 9 describes various options that the Web Application Server provides for securing content, programs, and data. It describes standard, database-controlled, and customized user authentication for securing cartridge access. It also describes the Secure Sockets Layer (SSL) and how to implement it in the Web Application Server. It closes with a number of suggestions to use in developing a web security strategy.

Chapter 10 describes the architecture and function of the Web Request Broker, or WRB. The WRB is the heart of the Web Application Server, as it is responsible for managing and invoking cartridges and components. The chapter also describes the various services provided by the WRB, such as ICX and XA-compliant transaction control and how to use the services from cartridges or components written in various languages.

Chapter 11 describes the process of writing custom WRB cartridges in the C language. In addition to describing the structure of cartridges, it provides a discussion of the core WRB API used by cartridges. It closes with some cartridge design considerations and suggestions.

Chapter 12 provides a fairly comprehensive overview of many of Oracle's web technologies. It discusses Oracle's Java initiatives such as J/SQL and the Oracle JDBC drivers. It also discusses the manner in which Oracle is web-enabling many of its tools and applications, such as Oracle Forms and Oracle Reports.

This book should serve as both a solid introduction to novices, as well as a practical reference for experienced developers. Three appendixes provide a detailed description of the PL/SQL and Java SDKs and the WRB APIs. In addition, the text identifies many tricks and techniques for all types of cartridge and component development.

Because of a relatively late change of plans, this book includes a CD containing a trial version of Web Application Server 3.0 for Windows NT. Due to production issues, this CD does not contain the source code for examples in this book. However, the source is available from two online locations: http://www.dynamic-info.com/ and http://www.oraweb.com/. We apologize if this is an inconvenience, but it will allow us to post updated examples as they are available.

CHAPTER
1

Benefits of the Web Application Server

n your hands, you hold a book describing how to integrate enterprise-grade relational database technology from Oracle with the continually emerging world of the Internet and the World Wide Web. Very likely, you already have some ideas about what to do with this technology. Or maybe you have heard from a variety of sources that web-database integration is the next big thing, or can save your company money, or make your company so much money that you will not have to worry about saving any. In any event, you may have heard some intriguing or puzzling things about the technology and would like to understand how to use it to meet certain objectives of your organization.

Many books have been written about the Web. This book is not a primer, although nearly all the basic concepts of the Web and software development using the Web are discussed in this book. Rather, this book focuses on using Oracle's new Web Application Server as a platform for developing applications serving the era of network computing, an era that for many is already upon us.

In this chapter we briefly introduce the World Wide Web, and then discuss the nature of applications developed for web deployment. We also discuss some of the reasons why people with various business responsibilities may be interested in web development to achieve certain goals. We further address some general points related to web development: when it may make sense and when it may not. This information can provide a foundation for using the application development techniques explained later in this book.

A Brief Overview of the Web

The World Wide Web was developed in research laboratories and universities, as a means by which researchers could easily share information about various research efforts. The Web was developed to run over TCP/IP, the networking protocol of the Internet, a global network that links computers and users from systems all over the world. However, in contrast to most previous Internet-based services that tended to be purely text based and confusing to novice users, the Web was designed to support richer datatypes and be easier to use.

The Web consists of a collection of computers acting as servers that use the Hypertext Transfer Protocol, or HTTP, to serve requests for information from programs on end users' computers, known as *browsers* because they let a user browse through content. These browsers are designed to interpret and display pages of information written using the Hypertext Markup Language, or HTML (although most browsers today can display many other types of data as well). These HTML pages use tags both to affect the appearance of the text on the page (whether onscreen or printed) and to allow graphics and other content to be embedded in the page. The programs on the servers that serve requests to the browsers are known either as HTTP servers or as *listeners*, because they listen for a request to which to respond.

The most critical feature of HTML is the ability to embed links to other documents inside a page. These links, when activated by the user, direct the browser software to fetch and display a new "page" of information (one or more screens deep). In most GUI web browsers, the user simply clicks the link using her mouse to jump to the new page. These links can direct the browser to fetch pages from any HTTP server on the Internet anywhere in the world. This allows the user, for example, to retrieve three different pages from three different machines on three different continents—without ever needing to know from where the information is being accessed, what the time zone is, or what language humans speak there.

Because of the simplicity of its interface, as well as the ease of setting up a basic HTTP server, the Web's popularity skyrocketed. Servers and browsers both became more feature-rich and more robust, while more people put additional content onto servers, thus encouraging yet more people to get at it with their browsers. Today, the Web has become so immensely popular that the popular press, from your local newspaper to *Time* to *Dateline NBC*, regularly discuss the subject, and many print advertisements and broadcast commercials routinely list Web addresses to contact for more information or to purchase products or services.

Some information managers saw the promise of web technology and implemented HTTP servers that were accessible only from within their own organization. Such systems have come to be known as *intranets*, in contrast to the publicly accessible Internet. Other organizations have extended their intranet to form an *extranet*, one or more web applications accessible to a select group of users external to the organization. Often, such applications are used by distributors or current customers to access data that is not truly public but that needs to be available to a wider audience than just a company's employees.

In addition to delivering relatively static documents, the Web can be used as an environment in which to implement functional applications.

These applications use HTML to display the GUI, or graphical user interface, on a remote user's screen (say, a paralegal in a large law firm with staff located in several buildings across town) while the computation and processing occur only on the server machine. This processing is carried out by programs that are executed by the HTTP listener program in response to certain requests from the browser. This book is designed for those who want to implement such applications.

The Oracle Web Application Server

Oracle's Web Application Server is a comprehensive, robust, highly scalable platform for implementing and running web applications. Actually, it is a combination of several components. First, it includes an optimized version of Spyglass' web listener, although its other components can be used with such listeners such as Netscape Enterprise Server, Microsoft Internet Information Server, and Apache. The Oracle listener is similar in most respects to other web listeners in that it is able to serve static pages and documents as well as execute server-side programs using the *Common Gateway Interface*, or *CGI*.

As its features are fully described, however, the Web Application Server rapidly begins to differ from most other web listeners. It incorporates a CORBA-based object request broker (ORB) to allow the listener to invoke server-side applications in a robust, scalable manner across one or more machines. This significantly increases both the stability and the scalability of the Web Application Server versus basic web listeners such as Netscape's or Microsoft's.

The most critical element of the system, though, is the Web Request Broker (WRB) and the cartridges Oracle has created for application development. The WRB provides a foundation for writing server-side programs in the C language; such programs are called *cartridges*. These cartridges may be specialized, in that they implement the functionality of an entire application. They may also be utility cartridges, which provide services accessible to other cartridges. A large focus of this book is cartridges that provide the capability of invoking or executing code written in languages other than C, such as PL/SQL or Java. Programs written in such a way that they are invoked by a cartridge are known as *components*.

Beyond simply providing an environment for executing programs, the Web Request Broker also provides a host of services that simplify the process of writing any web application, as well as support for more complex services such as transaction management and content services. These services are discussed in more detail in Chapter 10.

Motivations for Web-Based Application Development

Although the Oracle Web Application Server (or OWAS) can be used simply as an application server without integrating with a relational database management system (RDBMS) from Oracle or another vendor, the primary strength of OWAS lies in its ability to integrate with the database to implement web-based applications. These applications may be newly developed especially for the Web or may be designed to offer an alternate interface to data already available through a client/server application.

Many goals have motivated software strategists and programmers to merge Web technology with traditional enterprise RDBMS systems. Depending on an individual's responsibilities, these goals may include achieving certain technical as well as business ends. In this section we sketch some common reasons why four types of stakeholders—information technology managers, application architects, line of business managers, and webmasters—may wish to implement such technologies. The real driver for most of these stakeholders is typically a variation on the "better, faster, cheaper" theme.

IT Management

Information technology (IT) managers and directors in most organizations are beginning to examine web technology to understand how it may fit in their organization. For some, this examination is driven by business units that are demanding web-enabled applications. Other information managers are proactively examining ways to improve the level of service and sophistication of their applications and infrastructure. Independent of the boon that web technology can offer to the organization as a whole, which alone is a compelling reason for IT managers to investigate, these new tools offer many ways to further the missions and objectives of the IT group itself.

More-Efficient Application Distribution

Applications deployed via the Web offer some significant benefits with respect to efficiency and timeliness. A common problem organizations face is the issue of how to deploy their client/server applications effectively across a large, installed user base. Some organizations have invested heavily in network installation technologies that can automatically copy all necessary executables to client machines. However, many organizations still employ the more traditional methods of installing manually, either from removable media (floppies, tape drives) or from a network drive. Often, temporary help is brought in for large installations. When new computers are added to the network, or a new user needs the application, it must be installed on the new machines, and often the users must be trained as well.

This cost is a recurring one: every time the application is enhanced, the process of deployment must be executed. Obviously, this can add significant overhead costs to many application development efforts. It also has the impact of decreasing the frequency of updates that might otherwise be useful, because the distribution costs for each incremental version are so high.

Developing web-based applications for deployment via a corporate intranet offers one alternative to this situation. Because web applications are implemented in such a way that they typically have no client-side execution, installation need only be performed at the server, rather than on the workstations of every individual who will access the system. Even for small client-executable applications, known as applets, the object code can be downloaded dynamically at run time. Because applets written in the Java language are machine independent, any user with a web browser that supports Java can access these applications, regardless of their operating system platform.

Obviously this reduces the actual cost of deploying software, but it also allows for more frequent releases and upgrades of the application. Rather than adding enhancements in large batches, possibly every year or so, smaller changes can be rolled out more frequently. This is especially convenient if a serious program defect is found or a regulatory or legal business requirement changes: a new version can simply be deployed almost instantly, at very low cost. The upshot for many applications can be lower lifecycle costs, together with improved responsiveness.

Reduced Capital and Administrative Costs

More significant than deployment costs are the capital and administrative costs of maintaining a large application user base. Hardware is the first to be considered, and in the business world it is increasingly more powerful and laden with memory and hard disk space. Then there is the cost of managing that hardware: configuration, setup, customizing, training, updating, and so on. Moreover, help-desk and support services come into play. Web application deployment can dramatically alter all of these costs.

Because HTML-based applications execute on the server, only the display of the resulting HTML reaches the client workstation. At the time of this writing, client-executable Java applets require significant processor power to run quickly, although specialized chips are driving down the cost in this area. Help-desk resources are reduced because there are no client-installed components of the application that may conflict with another part of a user's configuration. Additionally, the standard interface of web applications acts to reduce the training and support time needed for each additional application delivered via the Web.

It is even possible to replace the typical Windows-based PCs found in most offices with lightweight Network Computers (NCs): inexpensive computers that have an embedded web browser and can execute Java applications. These machines typically have little or no long-term local storage such as a hard disk, for they access and store all data and applications at the server. In addition to applications typical of client/server architectures, these machines can even run standard productivity applications such as word processing, spreadsheet, database, and presentation graphics packages. Figure 1-1 shows a full-featured word processor running under Java. Given the estimates that Network Computers have a total cost of ownership of as little as one-tenth that of Microsoft Windows-based PCs, they may become a popular alternative. By developing web-enabled applications now, organizations can better accommodate a possible transition to "thin-client" computing (discussed shortly).

Strong Vendor and Financial Support

The management of any IT group needs to be pragmatic about technology decisions. A balance must be struck between the risk associated with any technology and the potential reward of using that technology. Often, one significant risk with many new technologies is that others may not adopt

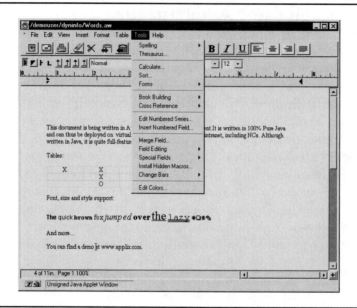

FIGURE 1-1. *A full-featured word processor written in Java*

the technology and that companies may find few if any strong vendors from which to acquire products or services supporting it.

The Web, even though it is constantly in flux, clearly does not present such a risk to organizations. Established enterprise technology vendors such as Oracle, IBM, and Sun Microsystems are pouring significant resources into web-enabling existing technologies or creating entirely new web products. In addition, venture capitalists and the financial markets have been quite generous in capitalizing smaller startups with strong Internet technology plans, such as Netscape, Marimba, NetDynamics, and others. Also, corporate demand for web tools is enormous and continues to grow, virtually guaranteeing the continued viability of the technology in the marketplace. Although no one can predict which vendors will be the major players in the web-tools market in years to come, the application developers and the users of these tools are certain to win. Of course, Oracle's financial strength combined with its proven technical track record in enterprise computing ensures customers of the continued strength of its Web Application Server platform.

Managers, directors, and CIOs can all find compelling, independent reasons for using web technology in their organizations—even without pondering the demands of the business units they support. At the same time, since web technology is new to many organizations, issues such as staffing, training, project management, and various development processes employed may need to be reexamined in light of a move to network computing.

Application Architect

Those responsible for designing the architecture of software applications have several reasons to examine the Web as an application development platform. As with any new set of tools and technologies, there exist certain problems to which the platform is well suited and other problems to which it is not ideal. In this section we discuss some of the areas in which web technology is very effective, as well as some caveats to web development. Note that our focus here is on web development that uses browser-displayed HTML as the interface, rather than Java applets, which we discuss further in Chapter 2.

Cross-Platform and Thin-Client Support

Without question, the most immediate architectural benefit of developing a web-based application is the virtually complete platform independence of the application for the client running the application. The only requirement for a user to access the application is the availability of a web browser. This is ideal for applications that may be used across an enterprise in which most users may use Windows-based PCs but that has an engineering group using Unix workstations plus a graphic design group using Macintoshes.

Dynamic User Interface Generation

A sometimes overlooked benefit of web applications is that, compared to many GUI-builder/4GL tools (such as PowerBuilder or Visual Basic), it is much easier to create a dynamic GUI in a web-based application. Because the screens created in HTML are generated on the fly as text, any aspect of the display can be customized at any time in the execution. Such aspects can range from simple things like permitting user-defined control of background colors or font sizes and styles, to more sophisticated uses such as altering the layout of individual table rows based on data in the rows.

Lightweight Interfaces Among Applications

A significant convenience of developing web applications relates to the fact that interfacing two or more such applications in a reasonably seamless manner is quite straightforward. Because HTML pages generated by server-side applications are invoked through simple text-based requests, creating a link to one application from within another application is virtually trivial: everything is text transmitted via HTTP.

A frequent use of this capability is seen in order-tracking applications, as might be used by a chip manufacturer, for example. After the order has been shipped, the database is updated with the shipper's airbill number, and the user can track the status of the shipment of chips by clicking a link on the order status page from the vendor's web site, thereby invoking a server script on the carrier's server, which in turn displays the status of the shipment to the user. Another example is an HTML-based contact database. Clicking a link on a contact detail screen could link the user directly to a Mapquest page showing local freeway and street driving directions from the user's address to the contact's address. This functionality could be especially useful in sales force automation applications, in which the users must frequently travel to appointments in new and different locations.

Remote User Support

Applications that will be used by remote users are very good targets for web deployment. Some of the reasons for this are the often-simplified interface that reduces training and support costs, as well as lowered configuration management problems resulting from the fact that the only client-side component is a web browser. In addition, the infrastructure is already in place. Any user can open an account with a local Internet service provider (ISP) to provide dial-up TCP/IP access, thereby avoiding issues such as modem banks. One caveat here is that because web-based applications require connectivity to a network, such applications are not suitable for use in situations where network access is unavailable. Some workarounds in this area include cellular modems or, less expensively, radio modems, which provide TCP/IP connectivity without being tethered to a phone line or network drop.

Query, Reporting, and Transaction-Intensive Applications

Although the Oracle Web Application Server offers an outstanding platform for the development and deployment of web applications, and although web-based applications offer many unique benefits, not every application is ideally suited to implementation as a web application. This is sometimes an issue of design. For instance, if the objective is to create an application that mirrors the behavior of an application designed in a client/server tool, an HTML interface may be inappropriate. If, however, the problem is abstracted to solving the business problem solved by the client/server application, a web application that meets the business requirements may be implemented quite effectively.

To understand some of these considerations, consider typical application functionality and think how it relates to the Web. Most applications serve one of two primary functions: putting data into a database or getting data out of one. The former include applications such as order entry, general ledger, or the employee benefits or purchasing application described above. The latter include applications for analyzing sales activity, checking product availability, or looking up employee information. Most application systems provide both types of functions.

Web delivery is often an excellent choice for query-intensive applications. The interface is very flexible and can be quite straightforward for users. An additional benefit stems from the fact that query-oriented applications tend to grow after their initial release, as users playing with their new tools say excitedly, "Gee, could we get this data *too?*" Because of the lower redeployment costs of web applications, it is possible to deliver these enhancements to users more frequently.

As for transaction-based applications that are primarily used to insert, update, or delete data from the database, web applications may be well suited, but not as universally as query-oriented applications. Because virtually all the application logic resides at the server rather than at the client, some things that are very straightforward in client/server applications are decidedly tricky in web applications. Validations that must check entered values against data already in the database require a request to the server. Because each request involves returning a page to the browser, it is very difficult to perform field level validations such as this smoothly.

Despite this drawback, such a limitation does not decrease HTML's suitability for many data entry applications. A great number of extremely useful data capture applications actually require very little data entry by the user at any one time (after all, how often is a first-time order placed, benefits changed, or a product registered?). Additionally, solutions to challenging application needs can usually be arrived at creatively. For example, pop-up windows that implement "List of Values" type functionality (as found in Oracle Forms) can be designed and executed in an HTML interface, with little difficulty.

Of course, to achieve many of the benefits of application delivery via the Web, but without the interface limitations of the request-response-redraw cycle, Java applets can be used to provide an interface more similar to traditional client/server GUI builders.

The Oracle Web Application Server has broken down one of the largest barriers to using the Web as a platform for transaction-based applications by providing the facility for robust XA-compliant transaction control across multiple HTTP requests. For example, say that an application must allow users to complete a form with some information about themselves, and after they fill out and submit the first form, they see another form displayed. The desired behavior is that if they complete and submit the second form, data (often repetitive, such as name and address) from the first and second forms are saved, while if they cancel from the second form, even the data from the first form is not saved. In traditional terminology, the first and second forms make up a transaction.

Because HTTP is a stateless protocol, that is to say that each request is unaware of any requests which have arrived previously, implementing such functionality previously required the web developer to hack together some type of state management to accomplish this. The complexity of the problem increased very rapidly, depending on how many individual web pages and data elements could be affected by the transaction, making sophisticated transactional application both difficult to develop and potentially fragile. Version 3.0 of the Oracle Web Application Server provides a true transaction manager that is configured by the developer to transparently manage the transaction control for a set of web pages. The transaction manager does all the sensible things, such as supporting commit and rollback, as well as automatically rolling back transactions after some timeout period has elapsed. This is necessary because there is no explicit logoff from a web application; instead, requests just stop being made.

Although Web Application Server 3.0 does an outstanding job of addressing data-integrity issues, HTML-based interfaces still present issues for a number of transaction-intensive applications. Many of these issues are the same that client/server systems present. The primary issue is that using a web browser as an application interface demands the use of a mouse or pointing device on most GUIs. But HTML pages cannot be configured to support hot keys to invoke particular functions from a keystroke. For high-volume data entry, then, this is not the way to go. As anyone who has seen a "heads-down" data entry shop knows, the data entry operators want to be able to perform all activities with (ideally) a ten-key entry device, but will grudgingly use the rest of the keyboard as well. A mouse slows them down far too much.

The final general application feature of reporting also presents some new challenges for web development. On one hand, web applications can be used to dramatically decrease a user base's reliance on hard-copy reporting by allowing quick access to data from their browser, a process that is often quicker than reaching into a cabinet for a paper file containing a printed report. However, some applications still demand complete print reporting capabilities. For such applications, HTML suffers under certain severe limitations. HTML was designed as a display language for nonpaged devices, that is, devices that support arbitrarily sized display areas (such as a window with scroll bars). Thus, although onscreen reports created with HTML can be very sophisticated and designed to be very readable and attractive, much of this aesthetic quality is stripped away if the page is printed. Things such as page headers and footers cannot be displayed, nor is there support for forced page breaks at certain levels in a roll-up report.

Some ways can be found to get around this limitation. In Chapter 2, we discuss Adobe Portable Document Format, or PDF, which allows pages to be transmitted electronically in such a way that they display identically on screen and when printed. In addition, PDF allows complete control over the physical formatting and layout of the pages (by contrast, HTML allows only partial control over the physical formatting). Oracle's reporting engine, Oracle Reports, which is part of the company's Developer/2000 product, supports a Web Application Server cartridge that can generate reports in PDF format, thus providing complete control over the layout and formatting. These PDF reports, which can be displayed in a browser or printed, are of the same quality that can be achieved through any client/server reporting tool.

New Application Design Challenges and Opportunities

The previous discussion of reporting underscores a crucial issue in moving to the Web. Unlike many client/server development environments, where a single tool might be used for designing database structures, forms, procedures, and reports, the Web is far more flexible. The lightweight interfaces among components mean that application architects can solve virtually any problem by combining a variety of tools or techniques that are well suited to individual tasks. At the same time, the demands on the architect increase dramatically, because rather than needing a thorough understanding of a single tool, she must now keep up with many tools, and understand how they can be interfaced.

Just as the transition from terminal/host to client/server development created a great deal of confusion on the part of software designers, in terms of how to best make use of new application display capability and logic partitioning, the transition to the Web brings with it a number of new design issues and opportunities to confront. It is incumbent on an application designer to take the initiative to thoroughly understand the manner in which web applications can be developed, as well as the way they are commonly implemented.

One of the issues that those new to web development will have to confront—although some may find them irritating!—is the importance assigned to the cosmetic appearance of web applications. Unlike client/server applications, which were purely functional, many users will have encountered extremely well designed web sites and have similar, or at least enhanced, expectations of what a web application should look like. One key point for the application developer to bear in mind with such requests is that they do serve a functional purpose, especially with many self-service applications. If users can use either traditional paper forms or the telephone rather than the web application, any enhancement to the application that entices them to use it versus the traditional methods becomes a genuinely valuable feature. At the same time, applications developers must remain conscious of the fact that they are creating a business application, not a site vying for a design award. An outstanding source of interface design information for any software developer is the Association for Computing Machinery's special interest group in Computer-Human Interaction (ACM SIGCHI), information about which can be found at the ACM's Web site: http://www.acm.org/.

Line of Business Manager

For managers of business units, applications developed for web deployment offer several advantages. Some of these advantages stem from ways in which the web can be used to deliver applications that otherwise would be very difficult to deploy to their intended user base. Also, because IT groups' expenses are often billed back directly to the business units they support, the potential cost savings and efficiency discussed earlier in the chapter impact managers from any business unit.

New Distribution Channels

Managers of sales and marketing departments are always seeking new ways to increase sales. In general terms, there are two ways to increase sales volume: sell more to existing customers, or find more customers. Web applications can help with both these strategies. With respect to finding new customers, companies can simply market to people who already use the Web. Often, these are prospects who may not have heard of the company (especially if its products were previously marketed regionally) and who represent a fresh crowd of typically affluent consumers.

For manufacturers who typically sell their products to distributors, who in turn resell them to end users, the Web offers two possible avenues to pursue. The first is to use the Web as a marketing vehicle to market directly to end users, while providing them with distributor lookup capabilities so that they can acquire the product through the traditional channel. This can be extended to provide existing customers with value-added services via the web site, such as service or support.

The second, and decidedly radical, approach that some companies may take is to not just market but to sell directly to their end users via the Internet. This is not a viable option for many products; for instance, Proctor & Gamble probably won't sell Crest or Tide via the Internet in our lifetimes. In addition, distributors often add value themselves, in areas such as installation, configuration, or optioning advice and postsales support. However, for manufacturers whose distributors are truly box-movers, direct end-user sales may be a very interesting way to exploit the profit margins. The combination of streamlined customer service and direct sales to end users can significantly alter the gross margins associated with a sale. Either these increased margins can be harvested, or the company can choose to exploit its lower-cost position by cutting prices to garner additional share.

Or, if pricing must be matched by the competition, price cuts can be used as a way to hurt competitors and their distributors.

Efficient Means of Customer Contact

In addition to using web technology to move additional products through both new and existing channels, the Web offers organizations the opportunity to increase the quality of their postsale support while decreasing the cost of providing this support. For many companies, especially firms that market complex products such as software or office equipment, both these aspects are very significant. On the one hand, the cost of providing postsale service and support can be quite high; on the other hand, the quality of this support is often critical both to word-of-mouth advertising and to repeat sales.

Web applications made available to customers offer an outstanding way to deliver around-the-clock customer service and support, while radically reducing the amount of staff required to handle the requests. In addition, customers are often much happier to access the information via their web browser than they are by waiting in a phone queue or using a long-drawn-out telephone voice response system. Applications of this sort include order status and delivery tracking, as well as online searchable technical support databases. Although there will always be questions that are not in the system, and there will be people who prefer to speak with a human, a web-based customer service department can significantly drive down costs of such service, while it increases responsiveness to the average customer.

Increased Business Unit Performance

Sales and marketing departments are hardly the only units of a company that can benefit from web-enabled applications. Virtually any business unit may benefit from the use of such applications. An increasingly popular use of self-service web-based applications is in the area of Human Resources. Managing the administrative issues associated with employees is not a trivial task. Many HR staffs are flooded in paper and mired in manual processes. Over the past several years, many organizations have attempted to streamline HR operations by implementing increasingly more sophisticated Human Resource Information Systems (HRIS) software packages, from vendors such as Oracle, PeopleSoft and others.

Interestingly, though, many companies have not yet seen the increase in efficiency or the decrease in overhead that they may have expected.

These organizations found that although the application systems were indeed effective at streamlining the HR business unit, they were not so effective at streamlining the entire HR process—for much of the time and cost in HR operations is driven by the HR department acting as an intermediary. For example, if an employee needs to change benefit elections, he or she may fill out a paper form, which is then routed to the HR department via interoffice mail. In the HR office, someone manually keys the employee's elections into their extremely sophisticated HRIS system. Thanks to the sophisticated HRIS application, the data entry clerk is interactively informed that the elections are in conflict. At least the software was able to avoid having to manually validate all the forms that might be processed.

At this point, however, the data entry clerk must call the employee to resolve the conflict in the form he submitted. The clerk calls and leaves the employee a voicemail. The two of them trade several voicemails, and finally are able to speak and resolve the issue. As it turns out, the employee's penmanship was not so good, and the data entry clerk mistook for a 9 what the employee had written as a 4. Of course, during this time, the employee was undoubtedly frustrated by the processing delay, and probably bemoaning so much time spent on the phone with the HR staff. As many people in large organizations can attest, this is hardly an uncommon scenario.

Web-enabling HRIS packages with self-service front-ends, such as is shown in Figure 1-2, cut vast amounts of time, effort, and frustration out of this equation. In no more time than it might take to fill out a paper form, employees could enter information directly into the HRIS system via a web interface. Transcription errors would be eliminated completely, and any errors users make would be announced to them immediately, allowing them to correct them on the spot. When the data is submitted properly, the information is immediately processed by the HRIS package. At this point, HR staff can validate or approve any changes, as needed, and some processes may not demand any time of HR staff.

Beyond Human Resources, any business unit that services other units can likely benefit from the creation of web-based applications. Another example would be web-based expense reporting, in which the user enters expenses directly into a web form. Small line items could be automatically approved, while larger items can make use of a web-based workflow

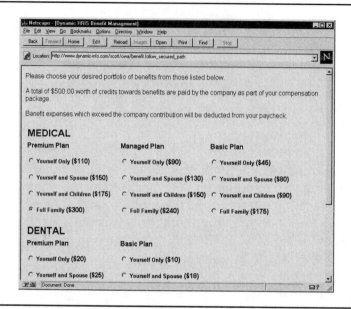

FIGURE 1-2. *An example of an online benefits enrollment form*

system through which managers or directors can approve expenses. In fact, virtually any workflow routing and control application is reasonably well suited to development for the Web.

PURCHASING Some organizations are implementing intranet solutions to streamline their purchasing processes. One method in which this is accomplished is by providing an employee-accessible interface, allowing workers to browse catalogs of available items and create purchase requisitions online. For purchases that exceed an employee's discretionary authority, web-based workflow allows a manager to view and approve requisitions of her group's members. As soon as the requisition is approved, it can be routed directly into the company's enterprise purchasing system.

The second way in which the Web can streamline purchasing is in the vendor selection process. Currently, companies frequently solicit bids, quotations, and proposals from several vendors who provide fungible products. In terms of price and other factors, the company's choices are limited primarily by the number of bidders, which in turn is limited by the number of possible bidders who are aware of the open bidding process. By publishing open bids via the Web, and accepting bids or proposals via the web site or e-mail, a company can both dramatically decrease the cost of the bidding process, as well as increase the number of potential bidders competing for the award.

Integrated Supply Chain Management

Another popular application of web technology is the creation of extranet applications. Such applications are accessible outside of a company's secured internal network , but only to select users. Most frequently, access is provided to users from organizations integral to a company's supply chain, such as vendors or distributors. Such applications are then used to improve the flow of communication among these groups. For organizations seeking peak operating efficiencies in areas such as just-in-time inventory management or negotiating the best prices from vendors, easy and efficient communication with their vendors is quite as critical as good communication with customers.

Extranet applications for supply-chain communication tend to be especially well suited to organizations that do not use standardized electronic data interchange (EDI) communication with their trading partners. Such nonuse may be attributed to the size of either party, or to the relatively high cost of implementing EDI for only one or two out of a large number of trading partners.

Integrating the various organizations that make up a company's total supply chain encompasses a very broad set of functionality. Some of the common functionality to implement in these areas includes online ordering and order tracking, as discussed earlier. However, these applications must also focus on the company's vendors. Thus, increasingly popular are such functions as providing access to a vendor's accounts payable data or to the on-hand inventory levels of components sourced from a given vendor.

Virtually any business unit will have some applications that can benefit from the sort of functionality and convenience Web-based applications can deliver. Often, the best places to look for such opportunities are areas in which staff are being used solely for entering data or answering questions that they in turn query another application for the answer. These areas are ideal candidates for self-service applications that allow both staff and management to enter or access the data themselves.

Webmaster

The webmaster is a recent title and position in the world of business. This individual is typically some combination of marketer, copywriter, programmer, and system administrator. The job is functionally defined: manage the web site. For organizations with a large web presence, the webmaster may be a manager of several people (webminions?) who serve one or more of the webmaster roles. Although there are webmasters for internal sites, a company's webmaster most typically focuses on its public Web site.

For many organizations, their public Web site has become an important conduit for flowing information between the organization and the constituencies the organization serves. For most companies, this includes both current and prospective customers. For publicly held firms (such as General Motors or Oracle), information of interest to stockholders can also be delivered via the Web, while for organizations that provide a public service (such as the Sierra Club or the International Red Cross) the Web can be used to communicate with those who need the service, or even to attract volunteers to help.

Most organizations have also realized that keeping a web site fresh, with frequent additions of new content, is important to ensuring repeat visits to their site. Just as few people would enjoy reading the same issue of a magazine over and over again, a web site that doesn't often change will not entice visitors to return frequently, if at all. This revisitation is critical to all types of sites. For web sites that are partially or wholly underwritten by advertisers, an increasing volume of visitors is necessary to increase site revenues. Likewise, for those using a corporate web site as an advertising or marketing vehicle, repeat impressions is the name of the game, as with any advertising activity. In the case of advertising and marketing, the webmaster must often also provide various details to some party about site usage and activity.

Meeting all these demands can be time consuming, and sometimes tedious, in the typical web site composed of basically static pages. Webmasters can vastly increase their efficiency, as well as freeing more of their time to add meaningful content improvements to their site, by using tools such as Oracle Web Application Server.

Providing Dynamic Content

The first way in which a web can be demonstrably improved by web-database integration is by allowing the web site to include truly dynamic content. There are a number of specific ways in which to implement this dynamic content, depending on the nature of the site. A simple example might be the inclusion of a survey of users, or a user message board. These sorts of things can add value both to the users and to the sponsors of the site. Surveys, such as the one in Figure 1-3, allow the sponsors to gauge the opinions of the visitors, and if the results are shown online, the user finds out how others have responded. The message board is often even more valuable for users because it offers them a chance to ask questions that can be answered by other users or representatives of the site's organization. Message boards, like the one in Figure 1-4, encourage return visits by creating a sense of community while providing valuable information to the visitor.

Another way in which dynamic content can be used is by maintaining information about individual users' preferences, and altering the content or format of the HTML pages displayed to the users. This can be used to control fairly simple changes; for example, whether or not the user prefers a certain layout style, such as the use of frames. It can also be used to completely customize the content of the page, such as is used in personalized web sites. As an example of this, see http://my.yahoo.com/.

Simplifying Content Administration

As we mentioned earlier, many of the webmaster's responsibilities may be tedious. For instance, changing the look of a site may sound like fun, and certainly the design can be, but it also has a downside. After the changes have been designed, they may have to be implemented across the entire site—potentially hundreds or thousands of pages. Obviously, applying these changes is a nontrivial and far from exciting task.

The Web Application Server provides LiveHTML, which implements functionality known generally as *server-side includes*, or *SSI*. This allows the administrator to insert special tags into HTML documents that are then interpreted by the server when the HTML document is requested. These LiveHTML tags allow HTML developers to do many things. One of the less exciting, but very useful, features is to embed documents into other documents. This means that a site's standard headers and footers can be coded once in files, then embedded at run time by the LiveHTML engine. If

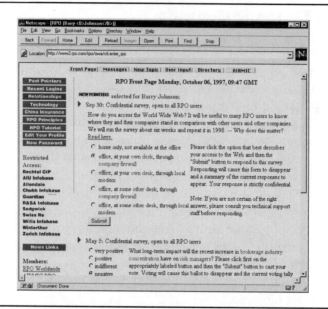

FIGURE 1-3. *Taking a survey on a Web page*

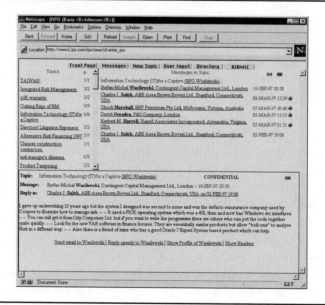

FIGURE 1-4. *Message boards give users a reason to visit again*

a change must be made to these common elements, only a single file needs to be changed. Chapter 7 explores LiveHTML in detail and discusses the variety of ways in which it can be used to easily enhance otherwise static web pages.

Improving Site Use Analysis

The success of most web sites today is primarily a function of the visitors it receives. To adequately assess the value or impact of a site, user activity must be monitored and accumulated. To support this, most HTTP listeners support some type of activity logging. In typical web installations, the logged information about requests is written to standard text files. Analyzing the information in these log files involves creating or purchasing programs that process these often large files, distilling the information in them, and presenting the results in some format to the webmaster. This is typically a batch operation, with very little in the way of ad hoc query capabilities.

In addition, most web listeners do not offer an integrated logging environment either for recording usage information or for noting application errors and warnings for both the listener and the server programs invoked by the web listener. This means that webmasters who want to monitor the web site adequately may be forced to review many logs and error files written by different components.

The Oracle Web Application Server addresses all these issues. First, it allows all log information to be written either to standard files or to an Oracle database in real time. It also implements utilities to load log files into the database for further analysis (if real-time database logging is not enabled). By capturing log information in the database, the webmaster can make use of the ad hoc reporting functionality provided with the Log Analyzer, a component of Oracle Web Application Server 3.0. As shown in Figure 1-5, the Log Analyzer allows the creation of reports containing all manner of information about the requests and errors that have been encountered. Depending on the logging configuration, these reports can be run against either real time or historical activity in the database.

The Web Application Server also supports an integrated application error and warning log system that allows all the components (both Oracle supplied and user-written) to write error messages, warnings, or debugging information to a single log destination. Components can also be configured

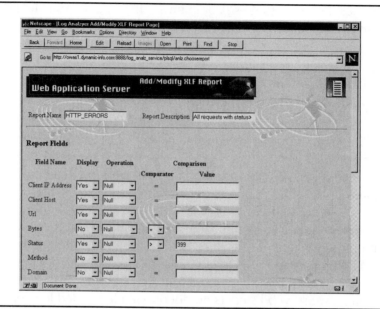

FIGURE 1-5. *Ad hoc report creation with the Log Analyzer*

to log to their own files, although integrated logging makes monitoring the site much easier.

A Technology with Enormous Opportunities

It is important to remember that no matter what your roles or responsibilities are, the web is merely a means to an end, another aid in your pursuit of other goals—whether they be improved department responsiveness, easier application interfaces, or increased market share. As with any technology, the web is not a silver bullet for any problem, and often its power can only be exploited after laying down an appropriate technical foundation in other areas. For example, although Human Resources departments can very effectively exploit the web, the best solutions are available only after all the functional aspects of the HR group have been automated.

In the next chapter, we provide a reasonably detailed discussion of many of the technologies employed in web development today, and we discuss the manner in which they may be used together to create compelling applications. In the remainder of this book we focus on creating web applications with the Oracle Web Application Server, using languages such as Java, PL/SQL, and C. This flexibility is a key strength of the Web Application Server: because of the choices available for application development languages, any application that can be implemented for the web can also be implemented against the Web Application Server.

CHAPTER
2

Introduction to Web Architecture and Components

rom Chapter 1, it should be evident that there is a significant upside to merging web and database technologies. One may wonder why everyone has not done so already. One reason is the sheer number of heterogeneous technologies and components that are brought to bear in creating web solutions. This chapter lays a groundwork of understanding about the web model and its constituent protocols, languages, and technologies.

NOTE

If you are a webmaster or are otherwise very familiar with HTML, Java, HTTP, and the manner in which web servers work, including CGI scripting and server APIs, you may wish to skip this chapter and continue on to Chapter 4, which introduces database concepts you may be less familiar with.

This chapter is divided into several sections, each examining a key component of the system that makes up the Web. By the end of this chapter, the reader should have a reasonably detailed foundation of understanding about most of the web components. This knowledge should be sufficient to understand many of the terms and concepts that are used in the remainder of the book. At the end of the chapter, there are additional resources, including books and web sites, that provide more information on these subjects.

The Web from a User's Perspective

Most readers of this book should be somewhat familiar with web technology, at least to the extent of having used a web browser, such as Netscape Navigator or Microsoft Internet Explorer, to browse for web pages. The experience of the Web, to a user, is that the browser launches and displays some content in its window. This content is known as a *page*. The page typically displays a combination of text, pictures, and possibly other active onscreen objects such as animation, sound, or even miniature applications. Web pages often contain *links*, references to other web pages or browser-accessible resources. The user can display the content of these linked pages by simply clicking, or otherwise activating, the link.

These pages are retrieved from web servers without regard for the relative location or nature of the server. While using a web browser, users can move from a web page on their Windows PCs to a page from their department's Novell server, to another page on the accounting department's AS/400, and to a Sun or HP Unix workstation in Japan, without ever needing to be aware of the differences among these servers in terms of geography, hardware, or operating systems. This transparency of access has led many to refer to the web browser as the *universal desktop.*

To many users, this is a tremendously intuitive and simple way to navigate through vast amounts of information. Users need only learn a single generalized interface, rather than different applications or configurations, to access different servers. Thus they are allowed to focus solely on the task at hand: accessing information. Needless to say, users love this.

Understanding Basic Web Architecture

Figure 2-1 presents a very basic sketch of web architecture. The Web is based on a stateless request/response protocol, the Hypertext Transfer Protocol (HTTP). The typical chain of events in this model is as follows: An HTTP server, often called an HTTP daemon, waits for incoming requests on a TCP port, typically port 80. An HTTP (web) client, typically a browser, opens a network connection to the server's port and makes a request for a resource on a remote server. This request is sent to the remote server, which in turn retrieves the resource requested and returns it to the web client. The server then closes the network connection and displays the returned resource to the user. This returned resource may contain embedded content, such as pictures, which cause the browser to make other requests for these embedded resources. The HTTP server can simultaneously serve several client requests in this fashion.

Based on this description, then, you can break the Web down into three main areas. One is the *client browser,* which is the user's window into the Web and which is responsible for displaying content from servers and

FIGURE 2-1. *A basic HTTP transaction*

assisting the user's navigation. The *web server* is also critical, as it is responsible for fulfilling the user requests sent by the browser. Of course, the *protocol* itself, HTTP, is the bedrock foundation on which the Web was built. The following sections describe the various components of the high-level web architecture and how they fulfill their appointed roles. Because of its foundational role, the discussion begins with the protocol.

The Protocol Explained

The entire point of the World Wide Web is to allow straightforward access to large volumes of information and services over a network. Given that the network is the precondition for the Web's existence, a brief discussion of the network environment is in order. HTTP is an application-layer protocol that runs over a TCP/IP network. TCP/IP is the industry standard network transport protocol for all open system (i.e., Unix) vendors, and today even the IBM AS/400 provides native support for TCP/IP.

The more relevant protocols to be concerned with are the application-layer protocols. In the case of the Web, the protocol that started everything is HTTP. HTTP was invented by Tim Berners-Lee while he was at the European Particle Physics Lab. The goal of HTTP was to provide a network application protocol to allow researchers to quickly and easily share information in a variety of formats, including text, images, and even audio and video.

HTTP has several characteristics that are important to understand:

- *It is easy to implement.* A minimal HTTP server can be implemented in only a few hundred lines of C code. A fairly sophisticated implementation of the entire protocol can be implemented in less than 10,000 lines.

- *It is stateless.* Every HTTP request a client makes to the server is independent from any other request that client makes. The server maintains no information about previous client activity, except for logging.

- *It is transient.* Even though clients frequently make multiple requests from a given server, each request is made on a different network connection (according to the standard).

- *It is content neutral.* The HTTP server itself does not need to have knowledge about the material it is serving.

All of these statements add up to one thing: HTTP is a simple protocol. It has some limitations and flaws due to its simplicity, but ultimately that simplicity is what allowed its near-universal adoption. Complex protocols, even if superior, have difficulty achieving ubiquity because fewer implementations exist, and they are usually more expensive. HTTP on the other hand, was simple enough to be implemented by many people. Consequently, web servers were developed for almost every platform, and many were and remain freely available.

All HTTP transactions consist of a request by the client directed to the server, and a response to that request returned from the server. All communication between the client and server takes place in this environment, or channel. This differs from protocols such as File Transfer Protocol (FTP), which typically has two channels between client and server—one that is used for sending control messages back and forth (for example: "get this file" or "show contents of this directory") and a second for sending actual content, such as the content of a file or the directory listing, back and forth.

The formal details of this request/response protocol are detailed in RFC 1945 by Tim Berners-Lee, et al. This document contains a complete and thorough description of all data structures in the protocol. It is very dry reading, and much of its content is unnecessary for most web developers, unless they wish to create a web browser or server. This section attempts to hit on the main features of the protocol used by developers creating applications for the Web.

Requests are made by specifying a uniform resource locator, or URL (sometimes pronounced "earl"), either in a link or by directly typing it in the browser, typically in a field labeled Location. A URL specifies a service to use, such as HTTP, FTP, e-mail, telnet, or gopher. After establishing the service, it specifies the resource to access. The following are some examples of URLs:

http://www.dynamic-info.com/index.html	An HTTP request to the Dynamic Information Systems web server for the file index.html
ftp://ftp.oracle.com/	An FTP request to Oracle's FTP server
mailto:webmgr@dynamic-info.com	Displays an e-mail form to let the browser's user send e-mail
telnet://foo:bar@127.0.0.1:1234/	A request to connect via telnet to the local host machine on port 1234 using the account name foo and password bar

One of the responsibilities of the web browser is to decipher this URL and choose a meaningful action based on its service type. The service type instructs the browser as to what type of protocol to use when communicating with the system, how to interpret the rest of the URL, and provides information about the default port. This book concentrates primarily on URLs that use the HTTP service. HTTP URLs have the following specific format:

```
http://{{username}{:password}@}host{:port}uniform_resource_identifier
```

The curly braces indicate optional elements of the URL. That is, neither *username, password,* nor *port* are required in the URL. Also, a username can be specified without a password. If a port is not specified, port 80 (the well-known port for HTTP) is used. The following are three valid URLs requesting the same resource:

```
http://scott:tiger@www.oracle.com:80/foo/bar.html
http://scott@www.oracle.com:80/foo/bar.html
http://www.oracle.com/foo/bar.html
```

In addition, one other service, SHTTP, is of interest. It is identical in virtually all respects to HTTP. The only differences are that the SHTTP service instructs the browser to connect using the HTTP protocol wrapped in the Secure Sockets Layer and has a well-known TCP/IP port of 443.

This URL is not part of the HTTP protocol. However, from a well-formed URL, the browser or other user agent is able to extract the information necessary to formulate and submit an HTTP request for the intended resource. It combines this information with other user preferences or usage information to create the complete request to be sent to the server. The generalized basic format of the request is as follows:

```
Command[space]Uniform_Resource_Identifier[space]HTTP/version[CRLF]
(Header_field_name:Header_field_value][CRLF])*
[CRLF]
optional_body_content
```

The *uniform_resource_identifier,* or *URI,* is the name of the resource being requested from the server. The URI is basically the URL with the host and port information stripped away. The *command* portion of the HTTP request specifies a method the server should apply to the resource specified by the URI. For all URL-extracted HTTP requests, this command is GET, as in "get this for me." There are other commands that are part of HTTP (originally only POST and HEAD were defined in version 1.0 of HTTP), although others such as DELETE have been added with various levels of support in proposed newer versions. GET simply requests that some content be returned. HEAD is similar to GET, except it requests that only the response headers be returned, not the body. POST, like GET, usually expects a complete body as a response but is primarily used for sending data, the request body, to the server. This data is then processed by the server or another application. Application developers typically need only be concerned with POST and GET commands, as HEAD commands are handled by the web server directly.

```
GET / HTTP/1.0
Accept: text/html, text/plain
Accept: image/gif, image/jpeg, application/pdf
Accept: */*
User-Agent: SuperWebBrowser 1.0
Referer: http://www.dynamic-info.com/main/links.html
[this line is the second carriage return/line feed pair]
```

After receiving the request from the user agent, the server attempts to service the request. This is commonly merely a matter of translating the requested URI into a file system path name and returning the file with that path name. In the applications developed in the book, the server will do much more than that. However, regardless of how the server fulfills the request, it must respond to the request in some way.

As with the client request, a server response is composed of a head and an optional body. The structure of the response header is very similar to the client request. The following text describes its general structure:

```
Protocol/Version[space]Result_Code[space]Reason_Phrase[CRLF]
Server_software_name_and_version[CRLF]
(Header_field_name:Header_field_value[CRLF])*
[CRLF]
optional_body_content
```

The following is a header returned in the event that the requested method is not supported for the requested URL. For instance, with most web servers, trying to perform a POST to a standard HTML page or graphic image will result in this response:

```
HTTP/1.0 405 Method Not Allowed
Date: Monday, 30-Sep-96 15:13:41 GMT
Server: SuperServer/0.0.1a
MIME-version: 1.0
Content-type: text/html
Last-modified: Tuesday, 16-Jul-96 14:33:00 GMT
Content-length: 248
```

The HTTP standard defines a collection of request and response headers. These are enumerated in Table 2-1. Many of the headers have little significance to most developers; however, many can be used to more creatively and effectively solve unique data processing problems. For example, knowing that the *username* and *password* fields are transmitted in the header of every request within a realm allows a developer to more

Header Name	Type	Description
Allow	Response	Infrequently used. Specifies methods (GET, POST, etc.) that can be applied to the resource.
Authorization	Request	Optional. Provides the credentials of *username* and *password.*
Content-Encoding	Response	Rarely used. Specifies additional encoding applied to the response body. After reversing the encoding process, the body will be of type Content-Type.
Content-Length	Response	Optional. States the length in bytes of the content body.
Content-Type	Either	Required. Describes the nature of the content body, which affects how the user agent (browser) will display or process it. Requests include this header only if making a POST request.
Date	Response	Optional. The date the response was generated.
From	Request	Optional, rarely seen. Identifies the Internet e-mail address of the user running the browser or user agent.
If-Modified-Since	Request	Optional. Used to implement a conditional GET request, in which the server will not return the requested object if it has not been modified.
Last-Modified	Response	Optional. Specifies the last time the resource being returned was modified. The browser uses this combined with the conditional GET feature to implement caching.
Location	Response	Optional. Specifies the exact URL of the requested resource. This is used to redirect the browser to another location when combined with 3xx response codes.
Pragma	Either	Optional. Used to specify the use of implementation or product-specific features. For example, the "no-cache" header instructs certain browsers and proxy servers not to cache the results of the returned page.

TABLE 2-1. *Common HTTP Request and Response Headers*

Header Name	Type	Description
Referer	Request	Optional. Specifies the URL from which the user agent requested the current URL. This can be used to see how many hits are coming from a given search engine or web site.
Server	Response	Optional. Identifies the server software being used.
User-Agent	Request	Optional. Identifies the browser or user agent software being used. This allows a server to customize its response based on the capabilities of a specific browser (for instance, not including images in a text-only browser).
WWW-Authenticate	Response	Optional. If the server refuses access to a resource, the response should use this header to describe the type of credentials that must be supplied to access the system.

TABLE 2-1. *Common HTTP Request and Response Headers* (continued)

easily manage user authentication within a database application. At the same time, knowing the referring page, the page from which the user made the current request, allows different information to be presented to users based on their likely interests.

Table 2-2 lists the response codes, with reason phrases, that are part of version 1.1 of HTTP. Most of these are part of the HTTP 1.0 standard as well. These are useful for both application debugging and development. Some tools manage most of the response codes and header fields for the developer; some do not. Moreover, the developer can get additional control over the application by returning certain response codes that instruct the browser to perform some additional actions. Most common among these uses are the 302, "Moved Temporarily" code, which redirects the browser to another URL, and the 401, "Unauthorized" code, which can be used for implementing customized security features.

Response Code	Reason
100	Continue
101	Switching Protocols
200	OK
201	Created
202	Accepted
203	Non-Authoritative Information
204	No Content
205	Reset Content
206	Partial Content
300	Multiple Choices
301	Moved Permanently
302	Moved Temporarily
303	See Other
304	Not Modified
305	Use Proxy
400	Bad Request
401	Unauthorized
402	Payment Required
403	Forbidden
404	Not Found
405	Method Not Allowed
406	Not Acceptable
407	Proxy Authentication Required
408	Request Time-out
409	Conflict
410	Gone
411	Length Required
412	Precondition Failed

TABLE 2-2. *HTTP Response Codes*

Response Code	Reason
413	Request Entity Too Large
414	Request URI Too Large
415	Unsupported Media Type
500	Internal Server Error
501	Not Implemented
502	Bad Gateway
503	Service Unavailable
504	Gateway Time-out
505	HTTP Version Not Supported

TABLE 2-2. *HTTP Response Codes* (continued)

HTTP 1.1 and Other Enhancements

As mentioned earlier, the first version of HTTP was a simple protocol that allowed its use to explode worldwide. Unfortunately, as you have seen, the simplicity has a downside as well. The major problem HTTP labors under is related to its use of a unique network connection per request. This has several negative impacts, chief among them being significant network and system resource wastage due to the bad ratio of network connections created to actual data served. Additionally, lack of state information creates difficulties for developers wanting to implement sophisticated applications. Another limitation, lack of support for multiple domain names being served from the same IP address, combined with a proliferation of vanity domains, creates additional routing problems on an increasingly overburdened network.

To address many of these issues, enhancements have been introduced. Most of these were initially introduced by vendors or implementers of web client and server software, with Netscape leading much of the charge. To ameliorate the problem of statelessness, Netscape introduced the concept of *cookies*, data created by the server but held by the client and transmitted to the server in subsequent requests. Sophisticated use of cookies significantly enhances developers' abilities to create applications that maintain state information across multiple HTTP requests by encapsulating in a client-held cookie the information necessary to re-create a state.

To reduce network strain and consequently improve performance, several new features have been introduced in new versions of the protocol. The new ability to hold a single connection open, through which multiple HTTP request/response cycles can be made, reduces the significant connection setup/teardown expense on both the network and the server. In addition, the new protocol implements support for *byte-serving*, the request and delivery of a segment of a resource, rather than the entire resource. This is very helpful with display formats such as Portable Document Format (PDF), discussed later in the chapter.

HTTP version 1.1 also introduces the Host: request header. This header is to be sent with all HTTP requests to the server with the actual hostname to which the request is intended. Remember that in version 1.0 of the protocol, the requested hostname, although part of the URL, is not transmitted to the server. If both parties are using browsers and servers that implement support for the Host header, it is possible to serve multiple web sites from a server with a single IP address assigned, rather than have multiple hostnames mapped to multiple IP addresses served by a single server.

The Future of the Protocol

Without question, HTTP will continue to evolve in response to the functional demands of developers and vendors, and to the practical necessity of making efficient use of network and hardware resources. In addition to the evolution of HTTP, a new protocol, the Internet Inter-ORB Protocol (IIOP), is likely to become a major player in the arena of web development. IIOP is a protocol that defines a communication standard to allow requests to be made to CORBA-compliant object request brokers (ORBs). These ORBs can execute various functions and return results back to the calling program. In an IIOP environment, an IIOP client such as Netscape's Communicator can make requests to an ORB, the results of which may be displayed directly or manipulated further by other client-resident code.

Regardless of changes that may be introduced into HTTP, or new protocols that are introduced as complements to HTTP, the open foundation created by HTTP is a solid and stable groundwork on which a new generation of enterprise applications can be developed. To completely appreciate how this new generation of applications may be developed, it is necessary to examine the two primary software components of the web architecture that communicate via HTTP: web servers and web clients. The primary piece of software responsible for implementing the data storage and transmission components of HTTP is the HTTP server itself. The following section examines how web servers operate to fulfill the requests sent to them by web clients.

The Server

As mentioned earlier, the Web is composed of a collection of machines running HTTP servers that service client requests. Although a wide variety of commercial and public domain web server software is available, all the applications share certain common features and functionality. This section describes the generic web server architecture and basic features.

The architecture of the web server is fairly simple. It maintains a listening connection on a TCP port, typically port 80 for unencrypted HTTP requests or port 443 for requests encrypted using Netscape's Secure Sockets Layer (SSL). When a connection is received from a client process, the web server passes this request to another thread to be handled. This multithreaded architecture allows web servers to simultaneously serve requests from multiple users.

NOTE
The Secure Sockets Layer (SSL) is a method of providing a more secure communication channel between the web client and web server by encrypting the contents of the transmission. In its latest versions, it also implements an authentication scheme between client and server.

The thread, which is spawned from the main web server process, then analyzes the request and takes appropriate action based on the content of the request and the server's configuration. The web server first examines the Uniform Resource Identifier (URI) included in the request. The server then maps this URI, which specifies a virtual location into a physical resource reference. This is typically accomplished by a set of mappings between virtual directories and physical disk directories that are specified in the server's configuration files. The process of configuring these mappings using Oracle's web interface to the Oracle Web Application Server is discussed in Chapter 3.

As an example of this mapping behavior, consider accessing an HTML page on our company's site at www.dynamic-info.com. A request received from a browser might be /publications/owshb/, which would be the URI for the home page for this book. When Dynamic Information Systems' web server encounters this page, it maps the virtual directory /publications/owshb to an actual disk directory called /www/publications/owshb. Because the URI ends in a branch—that is, it does not specify a file but simply ends with a slash (/)—the web server looks at its default document configuration parameter, which specifies the document to return if no leaf document is requested by name. On Dynamic Information Systems' web server, this is configured to be index.html.

Thus, after applying these rules, the user request is determined to be for the file located on the server as /www/publication/owshb/index.html. Based on the type of actual resource requested, such as a file or an executable program, the server can take several actions. However, prior to taking action on the resource requests, the next thing that happens is a security check.

Web Server Security

Often, it is desirable to restrict access to certain web-accessible resources to certain parties. An example of this need for security is when a consultancy allows its clients to access prototype applications and work in progress from their location through their firewall. To maintain the confidentiality of this information, the consultancy should do several things, including configuring its web server to restrict access to these resources.

Most web server security is based on categorizing resources into collections of realms. A *realm* is a collection of resources having similar security or access-control requirements. Certain groups can then be granted or denied access to these data realms. A *group* is a collection of users of the server. In addition, access control of a realm can be declared at the physical level, which means permission can be granted or withheld based on the network identity of the machine making the request, rather than on the user of the machine. Chapter 9 discusses the exact manner in which realms and their access controls are configured. For the time being, it can be stated that realms of resources can be defined, and each realm can be protected by group-based and/or physical (IP address) access control.

Now let's return to the server's handling of the incoming HTTP transaction. At this point, the web server compares the requested URI against its lists of protected groups of resources. If the URI is to be protected by IP-based security, the web server checks the IP address of the remote machine against the approved IP-based realms. If the remote address is not appropriately authorized, the server returns an error message, typically response code "403 Forbidden." If the requesting client machine is properly authenticated or if no network address security is applied to the resource, the second layer of access control is examined.

If the requested resource is a member of a realm that enforces group-based access control, the server examines the incoming request headers for an Authorization entry. This header field, if present, should contain one or more tuples of realms, usernames, and passwords associated with the host to which the request was sent. If no such header is present or if a tuple was not included for the realm of which the present resource is a member, the server returns an error message, most commonly "401 Unauthorized." In the response headers, the server includes a WWW-Authenticate header that describes to the web browser how to resubmit the request with the correct credentials. From the end user perspective, this most commonly results in being presented with a dialog box requesting username and password information for the realm. After the user completes the dialog, the original request is re-sent, with the additional username and password information in the Authorization header.

Upon receiving a request with a username and password for the correct realm, the server examines the username and password as being valid and then verifies the user's membership in a group that has been granted access to the realm. If these tests fail, the same "401 Unauthorized" response is returned, although this time the browser typically informs the user that the authorization failed, rather than simply redisplaying the username and password dialog. If these tests are successful, the server can continue with its processing of the request.

Servicing the Request

After the web server has identified the nature of the request and verified that the requesting party is permitted to make such a request, the server must take action to fulfill the request. There are two general things that a web server can do to fulfill a request. The first is to transmit the data contained in a file on the server to the client. The second is to execute a program contained on the server and return the results of the program to the client. The server determines what to do with the request based on the URI requested by the client. The administrator of the web server will have configured certain virtual paths to result in the serving of a file and others to cause a program to be executed. The details of this configuration process in the case of the Spyglass listener, included with Oracle Web Application Server, are described later in this book. Users of other web listeners, such as Netscape or Apache, should consult their documentation for the exact configuration process.

File Serving

File serving is without question the most common web server function. There is no way to know for certain, but as of this writing it is estimated that more than 90 percent of all HTTP requests are handled simply by file serving. Even in many database-powered public web applications, roughly 50 to 60 percent of the requests are serviced by returning files. File serving is also the simplest operation the web server performs. When a web server determines that the requested resource is a file to be returned, the web server simply returns the file to the user agent and records the transaction in the log file. No additional processing is performed.

Although basic file serving is as common as snow in Minnesota, it is not particularly interesting. Building web sites with static pages is certainly easy, as these files are typically either HTML text, which is described more fully later (see "HTML: The Lingua Franca of the Web"), or some type of graphic image. Although these types of files can be combined to create aesthetically pleasing and informative web sites, they lack the ability to alter their behavior in response to either the user or outside events. Web pioneers quickly realized that for more interesting web applications it was necessary to permit the invocation of custom code in response to an HTTP request.

Executable Code Through the Common Gateway Interface

Obviously, more sophisticated applications of web technology require the ability to execute code on the server to generate customized results. Server-executed code is responsible for a great deal of what you see in web pages today. Searches, electronic commerce, and even the simple page counter is created by server-side code.

HTTP was not originally created with support for the execution of user code at the server side. Driven by the need to support code execution, the National Center for Supercomputing Applications (NCSA), busy at work on a web server, took the initiative to define and implement an interface for server code execution. The interface it created is called the Common Gateway Interface (CGI). This support for the execution of custom code was critical to the viability of the HTTP model as an application server. Although scientists at the European Particle Physics laboratory created HTTP, it was the NCSA's creation of CGI and the graphical Mosaic browser that set the stage for the raging success HTTP and the Web would come to enjoy.

CGI is a very simple interface through which a web server executes user code written to conform to the CGI. The interface and its implementation for either the web server developer or the CGI script developer are both quite simple. When the web server receives a request for a resource that it is configured to treat as a CGI script, the following events take place:

1. The web server spawns a new process.

2. The server then sets several environment variables (see Table 2-3).

3. The server invokes the main entry point function of the executable.

4. If called by a POST request, the server passes the additional content to the script by standard input.

5. The invoked executable runs and writes the results to be returned to the user to standard output.

6. The server receives results back from the user code through standard output.

7. The server returns the results back to the browser.

CGI-compliant scripts can be written in virtually any language that can be invoked directly from an operating system's command line. Common languages for CGI script development include Perl, C, Java, command shell languages such as the Korn and Bourne shells, and virtually anything else that can communicate via the stdin and stdout mechanism. In addition, specialized CGI scripts can be created to act as a gateway to another language environment to effectively allow the execution of programs written in other types of languages, even if they do not support standard input and output. It is in this way that PL/SQL programs can be executed as CGI scripts. (However, this is not the only, and not the recommended, way to invoke such scripts.)

For a developer, writing a CGI-compliant script is relatively straightforward. Arguments are received via either standard input (known as stdin) or the *QUERY_STRING* environment variable. The form of these input arguments is described more fully later in this chapter in the discussion of HTML and data entry forms (see "Getting Input: Fill-Out Forms"). The code performs whatever processing is necessary and usually, though not necessarily, returns the results as HTML text via standard output (stdout).

In addition to passing parameters to the script via stdin, the server also sets a number of environment variables for the script to use. These environment variables contain information about the server environment, network connection, and request headers. Because the server defines a fixed set of environment variables prior to invoking the script, server implementation and script development is simplified significantly by not requiring the implementation and invocation, respectively, of callback routines to provide this information. Table 2-3 lists the environment variables and their contents defined by the CGI and initialized by the server prior to user code invocation.

NOTE
For those not familiar with them, environment variables *are variables defined within the operating system or its shell, rather than within an application, that are accessible to any application running within the environment. Typically, environment variables contain data such as the search path for executables, the paths of home directories for applications, or similar information.*

The CGI allows developers to create dynamically generated content with relatively simple scripts. These scripts can perform any number of

AUTH_TYPE	The type of authorization employed.
GATEWAY_INTERFACE	The version of the CGI interface under which the code is being called, typically CGI 1.1.
HTTP_ACCEPT	A comma-delimited list of MIME types for which the browser will accept responses.
HTTP_REFERER	The URL of the page from which this request came. (Like the header field, Referer, this spelling error remains with us.)
HTTP_USER_AGENT	The name, version, and additional information about the client software that made the request. This is usually a browser, although web robots are also user agents.
PATH_INFO	Additional path information listed after the name of the script.
PATH_TRANSLATED	The path of the URI, after converting virtual path names to physical path names.
REMOTE_ADDR	The IP address of the machine that made the request.
REMOTE_HOST	The host name of the machine that made the request.
REMOTE_IDENT	The password submitted by the user.
REMOTE_USER	The username submitted by the user.
SCRIPT_NAME	The name of the executable invoked by the web server.
SERVER_NAME	The host name of the server on which the script is running.
SERVER_PORT	The server port through which the request came.
SERVER_PROTOCOL	The protocol name and version the server is running, usually HTTP 1.0.
SERVER_SOFTWARE	The name and version of the web server that invoked the executable.

TABLE 2-3. *CGI Environment Variables*

functions, including text formatting, directory listing, or database access. However, CGI still requires someone with at least rudimentary development skills to implement. For nondevelopers, static HTML and pictures were still the only option for web development.

Server-Side Includes (SSI)

Largely to create a middle ground, the idea of server-side includes (SSI) was devised. SSI was originally introduced by the NCSA as part of its web server. Some vendors have other names for their SSI mechanisms. Oracle refers to theirs as LiveHTML. Regardless of the name, however, they all serve the same purpose: to allow the delivery of relatively dynamic content via the replacement of embedded tokens in otherwise static HTML files at the time the file is being served.

The goal of SSI is to make it easier for individuals to more easily deliver certain kinds of dynamic content. The bulk of SSI features are rather lightweight, inserting things such as the current date in the document. However, most SSI implementations do allow shell or CGI script execution, so it is an extensible architecture. The benefit of SSI is that individuals who know only HTML can create and modify dynamic pages by embedding various SSI tags in their HTML documents. Although this is not as efficient as executing a script to generate the complete page, it certainly opens new opportunities for customization to less technical users.

As you will see in Chapter 7, Oracle actually expands on this foundation substantially by allowing its LiveHTML cartridge to interact with other cartridges, such as the ODBC access cartridge. By doing this, it is possible to use LiveHTML to embed SQL queries in an HTML document that at run time are replaced by the results of the query. Previously this functionality could only be achieved by developers writing complete scripts.

Server APIs

As with most technologies, there are two divergent paths the web server code execution has taken: one to simplify at the expense of functionality and performance, and another to increase performance and functionality at the expense of simplicity. SSI and LiveHTML aim to deliver simplicity first, functionality and performance second. However, as more people started turning to the Web as an application delivery mechanism, an architecture that delivered more performance and more functionality was necessary.

Because CGI represents a reasonably simple generic interface for executing server-side code, it labors under several shortcomings, primarily related to performance. A major reason for the performance problems in the CGI model is that each invocation of the script is in a new process that requires not only the setup and teardown of the process, but also the setup and teardown of any resources or data structures the script itself may need. Because the performance bottlenecks in CGI become very significant in large-scale application deployment, a solution was needed.

To solve these problems, web server vendors created their own special APIs to improve performance. These APIs serve a similar generic purpose as CGI, namely, allowing the execution of custom processing and the dynamic creation of content. However, they offer much greater efficiency due to their architecture and tighter integration with the web server executable. In addition, most APIs allow user code more access to and control over the transactions that are processed through the web server.

The actual implementation details of the various server APIs vary widely among the different server vendors, although they tend to share some common architectural features. First, they support the invocation of user code in response to various URL requests. Second, when writing to a server API, the custom code runs in a process that persists across multiple requests, rather than the CGI-style "new process for each request" model. Third, they supply callback mechanisms to provide various services to the user code, allowing tighter integration between the developer's code and the web server. Although the callback services provided by each vendor vary widely, nearly all provide the following access points to developer-written code by the server:

- Custom code is called once to initialize its data structures and acquire any resources that would be needed prior to servicing a user request.

- Custom code is called each time a web client request is made for which the server has been configured to pass control to the user code.

- Custom code is called once when the web server is about to shut down to allow it to free any resources and generally clean up after itself.

In addition to these entry points, some web server APIs allow execution of user code for entire classes of requests (or even all requests), typically for pre- or postprocessing of these requests. This type of API functionality is most commonly used to provide security control in the case of preprocessing or more sophisticated auditing or logging features for postprocessing calls.

Overall, the use of web server APIs makes sense for many developers. There are not as many language choices for creating programs as with CGI, as any server API extension is generally implemented as a shared or dynamically linked code library, which usually implies a C compiler or a compiler that can create C-callable code. However, performance improves dramatically in applications such as data-base access because new database connections can be reused rather than re-created for each request. In addition, for some types of applications, this tight integration with the server is necessary to implement the certain functionality.

Nevertheless, as the saying goes, there is no such thing as a free lunch, and server APIs are no exception. Although the tight integration with the server allows user code superior execution speed and more flexibility, the real price paid is in stability. Because user code now runs in an almost interdependent fashion with the web server's kernel, errant or malicious user code executing on the server can cause a complete failure of the web server.

The additional downside is the increase in switching costs to move from one web server vendor to another. As mentioned earlier, each web server has its own API to which user code must be written. Obviously, the major downside to this nonstandardization is the diminished portability of code written to take advantage of the improved performance of the API. Web server vendors are constantly trying to outdo one another in terms of features, performance, and price. Because of this commoditization of the web server, it is a strategic disadvantage to have significant amounts of code that is dependent on a single vendor's web server.

What is needed is a solution that delivers the performance benefits of a server API but with more stability and with preservation of a level of portability among web servers. Oracle's own API-based solution delivers just that combination. When Oracle created its API-based solution, it also created an abstraction layer between the Oracle Web Server API and user code. This abstraction layer is encapsulated by the Web Request Broker (WRB). The WRB allows developers to write code to a single API, which can then be run against any supported web server. With Web Application Server 3.0, Oracle provides WRBs for their bundled Spyglass listener, as well as Netscape, Microsoft, and Apache servers. These four platforms account for the vast majority of workgroup and enterprise web servers running under various flavors of Unix and Windows NT.

There is actually much more to the Web Request Broker than enhanced portability and performance, but these details are not covered here. Chapter 3 introduces the architecture of the WRB and how it fits into the Oracle Web Application Server, while the rest of the book is devoted to using the WRB and its services to create applications.

As you can see, there are a number of different ways in which a web server may respond to the requests put to it by browsers. Although file serving accounts for the greatest volume of web server traffic, the real power of the web server comes from its ability to execute custom code in response to user requests. Due to Oracle's extensible architecture based on CGI, server APIs, and Oracle's Web Request Broker, the web server has today become a popular platform as an application server for a wide variety of applications. The next section describes the user's interface to these application services—the web browser, called the *universal client* by many.

The HTTP Client

HTTP client software, as mentioned earlier, is where much of the power of the Web resides. Minimally, HTTP client software, typically called a browser, provides users a way to navigate through a network of resources stored on disparate computer systems. At its best, the browser can be a universal client to virtually any networked service or application.

Unlike the HTTP model itself, browsers tend to be quite complex pieces of software, commonly several megabytes in size. In some ways this is humorous, given that browsers are often referred to as *thin* clients. These complex programs are themselves virtual operating systems. In the new crop of Network Computers, pioneered by Oracle, the browser is, in fact, the user's only interaction with the computer. This section examines the major components and features of a browser.

Although this book is focused primarily on the server-side development of database-oriented applications, understanding the complete breadth of the target client's functionality is a critical component in delivering the best applications possible. The following section touches on how to take advantage of some of these sophisticated browser features to deliver better applications. For more details about the subject, review some of the books and web sites referenced at the end of this chapter.

HTML: The Lingua Franca of the Web

The primary purpose of a browser is as a display and navigation device. Original browsers could display plain text and images, and render HTML. Hypertext Markup Language (HTML) is the primary display language of the Web. HTML is a fundamentally simple markup language, but has become more complex due to the rapid introduction of new tags by browser vendors. HTML pages contain text interspersed with *tags*, directions to the browser that the user does not see directly but that control the way the content of the page is displayed to the user. Some HTML tags appear alone, and others appear as a pair. For instance, the bold tag pair, <B> and </B>, cause the text between them to appear in boldface. When discussing paired tags, the first tag is known as the *start tag* and the second is known as the *end tag*. One way to think of the start tag is that it turns on or invokes the tag's behavior, and the end tag, if present or applicable, turns off the behavior. Multiple HTML tags can be nested, such as <tagA><tagB>... </tagB></tagA>, or interspersed, such as <tagA><tagB>...</tagA></tagB>.

Start tags can also contain attributes, which are often referred to as parameters or flags. An *attribute* of the tag further defines the effect of the tag or modifies its behavior. For example, the <IMG> tag, which is used to display an image embedded in an HTML page, has a required attribute, SRC, that specifies the URL of the image to be displayed. On the other hand, the <BODY> tag has an optional attribute, BGCOLOR, that specifies what color the background of the page should be. If the BGCOLOR attribute is not specified, the default color is used. These attributes are specified in the start tag as either name/value pairs or, occasionally, just as a named flag.

The following is an example of the use of the <IMG> tag, which specifies the required SRC attribute as well as the optional ALT attribute. The ALT attribute specifies the text that should appear in place of the image if the browser is unable or configured not to load images.

```
<IMG SRC="Images/DynamicLogoSmall.gif" ALT="Dynamic Logo">
```

Although a complete exposition of the entire set of HTML tags is beyond the scope of this book, the following sections introduce many of the basic tag types. Taking full advantage of the potentially rich interface that can be created by HTML requires a thorough understanding of the language and the way in which tags are supported under different browsers.

Page Structure Tags

The structure of the HTML document is described by tags. For instance, the document is supposed to begin with the <HTML> tag and end with the </HTML> tag. Then the head of the document is bounded by <HEAD> and </HEAD> tags, typically followed by the body of the document, with <BODY> and </BODY> tags. The actual content of the page, what is displayed to the user, is placed in the body section of the page.

Not all HTML pages have bodies; some are composed of frames. A *frame* is an independent subdivision of the browser window in which another file, usually an HTML page, can be displayed. An *independent* subdivision means that the content of a frame can be changed without affecting the content of other frames. Frames have many uses in web sites and applications. They can be used to create toolbars similar to those in many standard applications such as Microsoft Word or Excel. They can also be used as convenient navigation aids by placing a list of links to documents in a persistent frame and displaying the documents themselves in a separate frame by targeting the document links to this transient frame. In database-oriented applications, frames can also be used as a way of showing master-detail relationships, in which the detail records are shown in a separate frame from the master record.

Frames themselves are created in a *frameset*, which follows the head section of the page. The following example HTML code is used for Dynamic Information Systems' home page. In this case, a fixed section at the right displays a navigation panel, while the left section is used to display the actual content of the page. Figure 2-2 shows the appearance of the page in a browser.

```
<HEAD>
<TITLE>Welcome To Dynamic Information Systems</TITLE>
</HEAD>
<FRAMESET COLS="175, *">
  <NOFRAMES>
    <a href="main.html">Non-framed home page</a>
  </NOFRAMES>
  <FRAME SRC="buttonbar.html" NAME="listFrame" FRAMEBORDER="NO"
NORESIZE SCROLLING="NO">
  <FRAME SRC="main.html" NAME="contentFrame" FRAMEBORDER="NO" NORESIZE>
</FRAMESET>
```

Basic Text and Layout Formatting Tags

HTML provides a variety of tags for controlling the general appearance of text it renders. There are actually two types of basic text formatting: physical and logical. *Physical formats* are those that instruct the browser to draw text in a certain way (for instance, bold). *Logical formats* are those that declare that a particular section of text is a particular thing (for instance, a heading). In normal usage, there is no difference between the use of the two types of tags. The primary difference is that while the physical format tags apply a specific, definable display attribute to the text,

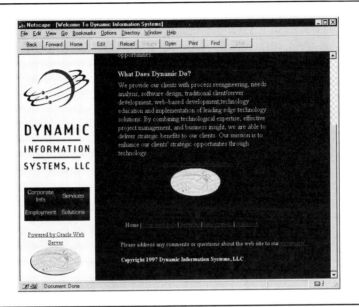

FIGURE 2-2. *An HTML page using frames*

the logical tags affect the display of the text in a browser-dependent manner. This may also be affected by user-specified preferences, although most browsers render the logical tag formats similarly.

NOTE
In principle, logical tags are preferable to physical tags because they describe the nature of the content rather than its appearance. This metacontent could, in turn, be used by parsers, converters, or search engines to more accurately handle the content. In fact, the use of logical tags versus physical tags allows for better rendering by a wider variety of devices, from character-based terminals, to speech synthesizers for the deaf. However, physical format tags tend to be more frequently used by many designers because they allow control over the actual appearance of the text. If the exact output appearance is flexible, it is probably wisest to use logical format tags.

HTML treats all white space as the space character, so the paragraph tag (<P>) is necessary to split text into paragraphs. The <P> tag also renders a blank line between the paragraphs, while its cousin, the break tag (<BR>) simply starts a new line without inserting additional space. A horizontal rule can be used to visually demarcate sections of a page by inserting an <HR> tag.

Some examples of physical format tags are <B>...</B> for bold text, <I>...</I> for italicized text, and <UL>...</UL> for underlined text. Less commonly used is the strikethrough format, indicated by the <S>...</S> tags. In addition, the tags <PRE>...</PRE> are used to indicate that the text being displayed is preformatted, meaning that it should be rendered in a fixed-width font, breaking lines when a carriage return or linefeed is encountered, and rendering all space characters. The <PRE> and </PRE> tags are often used to handle the display of information that comes from a text-based shell script or similar source, where formatting has been applied based on an 80-column display.

Because HTML is specified to use only the lower seven bits for character display (i.e., ASCII values less than 128), displaying extended characters properly requires the escape sequence &#*nnn*; where *nnn* is the base 10 representation of the ASCII value. Any character can be displayed in that way. For instance, to display the letter "A," the escape sequence A can be used. There are five other specialized escape sequences supported in most browsers (although the newest HTML specification defines dozens more). They are

&lt;	Less-than symbol (<)
&gt;	Greater-than symbol (>)
&amp;	Ampersand (&)
&quot;	Quotation mark (officially deprecated, but still common)
	Nonbreaking space (used to keep two words on the same line, as well as to force two or more spaces between words)

In addition to the physical format tags, there are a number of logical format tags. Logical tags, as mentioned, describe the nature of the text rather than directly specifying its appearance. The browser then renders the text in a manner appropriate to its description. Exactly what is appropriate is decided by the browser vendor and may sometimes be altered by user preferences. A common example of a logical format type is the use of the header tags, indicated by the tags <H1>...</H1> through <H6>...</H6>, with <H1> indicating the highest-level heading, and <H6> indicating the lowest level. The typical display of these headers is to start a new line, draw the text in bold and at a size appropriate to the heading level (level 1 being largest), and to add some additional space below the header as if a <P> tag were present.

Other logical format tags include the following: <ADDRESS> or <CITE>, for specifying a section of the page that provides contact information or a citation (typically rendered as italic); <BLOCKQUOTE>, for displaying block quotations (usually rendered as indented text); <CODE>, for displaying code fragments (rendered in a fixed-width font); and <LISTING>, for multiline code listings (similar in function and appearance to the <PRE> tag but usually rendered in a smaller font).

An additional group of tags used to control the layout of the page are tags for displaying lists. HTML supports three primary types of lists: ordered, unordered, and definition. *Ordered lists* display their contents with numbers, while *unordered lists* mark off each item with a bullet. The start tag for the ordered list is <OL> and for the unordered list is <UL>. Either list is composed of list items, each one marked with the <LI> tag. Each list item appears indented on its own line or paragraph preceded by either a number or bullet. As seen below, lists can be nested, to create an outline-like hierarchy, as shown in Figure 2-3.

```
<H2>To do</H3>
<UL>
  <LI>Become Oracle Web Server Guru
    <OL>
      <LI>Order Oracle Web Server
      <LI>Buy <I>Oracle Web Server Handbook</I>
      <LI>Read book
      <LI>Impress friends
    </OL>
  <LI>Middle-east peace
  <LI>Milk
  <LI>Eggs
</UL>
```

Definition lists, enclosed by <DL> and </DL> tags, are useful for displaying glossaries or indices. Instead of one list item, each item is composed of a defined term, preceded by the <DT> tag, and a definition,

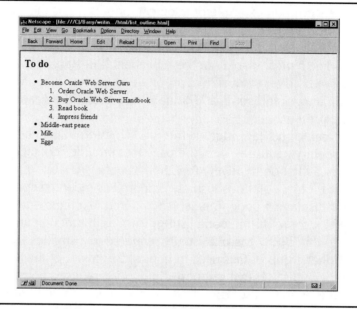

FIGURE 2-3. *An HTML page with a nested outline*

preceded by the <DD> tag. A fourth type of list, *a menu list,* which is enclosed by <MENU> and </MENU> tags, is identical to an unordered list except that there is less space between each list item, for a more compact display.

Putting the "Hyper" into Hypertext: Links and Images

Of course, simple text formatting would hardly set the world on fire, given that we've had this functionality for quite a while. (Even before modern word processors, there was nroff and troff.) What truly makes the Web exciting and drives its popularity is the ability to combine rich text and graphics on the same screen and, most importantly, to allow the seamless navigation from page to page by activating links. The main method of creating links among pages is by the use of <A> (for "anchor") tags.

Anchors have two functions. The primary function is to specify the text (or embedded content) between the <A> and </A> tags as an active object, which when activated (i.e., clicked) will point the browser to a new URL. Anchors of this sort must provide an attribute, HREF (for "hyperreference"), which specifies the URL to jump to when the anchor is activated. The other type of anchor function is a named anchor. Named anchors can be part of an HTTP URL and are used to specify that the browser should scroll the page as necessary to display the area enclosed by the <A> and </A> tags. These are often used to link to specific sections of large documents. For instance, a large HTML file containing a glossary might have all of its entries anchored, so that a referring link could point directly to the entry, rather than just to the glossary.

Embedding images into an HTML page is very straightforward as well. A single tag, <IMG>, specifies that an image should be drawn in the page. The image is specified by the SRC attribute, which accepts a URL as its value. It is displayed inline with the text, so text does not automatically wrap around it. Some browsers support additional attributes that control the manner in which text does wrap around the image and the image's relative position to the text.

Besides simply being used as visual aids, images can be used much like anchors. If an image is enclosed by anchor tags, clicking the image will point the browser at the HREF specified for the anchor. In addition, images can be image maps. An *image map* is the combination of an image and a method of specifying that clicking on certain areas of the image will point the browser at different locations. This is often used to create a graphical navigation panel. Originally, image maps were processed by having the server invoke a CGI program that read the clicked coordinates, compared them to a user-defined file of areas and URLs, and then redirected the browser to the appropriate URL. This was somewhat inefficient, as it required two HTTP transactions to get to the destination. Today, most browsers support client-side image maps that specify the mappings of regions to URLs in the HTML document, allowing the browser to jump directly to the appropriate URL.

Advanced Formatting: Fonts and Tables

Of course, as HTML was used more and more, page designers wanted additional control over the actual physical layout and appearance. This need is especially important for those trying to display structured data, such as database query results. The first significant improvement in this area was HTML tables. Tables in HTML are basically the same as tables in a word processor, composed of cells arranged in rows and columns.

A table is defined by using the <TABLE> tags. Within the table, <TR> (for "table row") tags are used to group rows, while the <TD> (for "table data") tag is used to enclose individual cells in the table. The <TD> supports many attributes, including COLSPAN and ROWSPAN, which indicate the number of columns or rows the cell spans, respectively (the default is one for each). In addition, both horizontal and vertical alignment options can be specified at the cell level with the ALIGN and VALIGN attributes. These attributes and others provide the developer with some very sophisticated capabilities for laying out pages.

Obviously, tables would be extremely useful for database applications that often need to return structured data in a columnar fashion. In addition, they are useful to enforce a more precise layout style for any page. There are few web sites today that do not make extensive use of tables to effectively lay out any page. The next section, "Getting Input: Fill-Out Forms," discusses HTML data-entry forms and how tables play a major part in laying out forms.

The next major advanced formatting tag to be supported by browser vendors is the <FONT> tag. As the name implies, this tag allows control over the actual font used by the browser to render the contained text. The actual display characteristics are defined by the attributes of the <FONT> tag, such as FACE and SIZE. The FACE attribute allows the HTML author to specify, by name, a system font to use. In fact, several choices, delimited by commas, can be specified in descending order of preference. This is commonly used because the Macintosh does not typically have the Arial font installed, and Helvetica is the best substitute. The SIZE attribute does not specify the size of the font in points, as is common in most applications, but rather on a relative scale from 1 to 7, with 3 being the browser's default font size. In addition to specifying the font size explicitly, relative values can be used, such as +1 or –1.

Getting Input: Fill-Out Forms

Until this point, the discussion of HTML has primarily focused on showing the user pages. The user's interaction is basically limited to clicking on text or picture links to move to another location. With more dynamic web sites, however, it is desirable to capture information from the user, either to return a result, collect and act on the information later, or customize the material displayed to the user. For instance, web search engines allow users to enter a description of what they seek, and the search engine returns URLs that may fit the user's search. This is accomplished by HTML forms. Because HTML forms are critical to most database-powered web applications, they are described in some detail.

HTML forms are enclosed by the <FORM> and </FORM> tags. The <FORM> tag has two main attributes, METHOD and ACTION. The

METHOD attribute specifies the type of HTTP method by which to submit the form data, either POST or GET. The difference between the two methods is primarily in the way the web server invokes the server-side code and is described earlier in the chapter in the section "The Protocol Explained." The ACTION attribute specifies the URL against which the HTTP request should be submitted. This URL can specify a CGI script, a WAS cartridge, or a server API program.

Any text, images, or formatting tags can appear between the <FORM> and </FORM> tags. However, the major components of the form are active elements. These include text entry areas, checkboxes, radio buttons, drop-down menus, and multi-element lists, among others. Most of these items are inserted by use of the <INPUT> tag, which accepts a variety of attributes. Almost all of the form input types require a NAME attribute to be useful.

NOTE

With all form data entry elements, the <INPUT> element displays only the data entry element itself and not a label. Use plain or marked-up text or images to provide a label for any fields, buttons, or lists.

When the form data is submitted to the web server, it is sent as a collection of pairs of the form *name=value*, where *name* is the name of the form element as specified by its NAME attribute and *value* has certain characters encoded using various escape characters. Each pair is delimited by the ampersand (&). The encoding process is quite simple, and involves two steps: first, any space characters are replaced by plus signs (+), and most nonalphanumeric characters are encoded in the form %*XX*, where *XX* is the hexadecimal representation of the ISO-8859-1 numerical encoding of the letter. Note that the ISO-8859-1 encoding is usually the same as the ASCII encoding for values less than 128; however, for high-order characters, the encoding value may differ from other extended character sets on certain computers.

The most common form element is a **text** entry field. To create a **text** entry field, insert an <INPUT> tag with the TYPE attribute set to **text**. In addition to the NAME attribute, other optional attributes for the input tag when using text fields are SIZE, MAXLENGTH, and VALUE. The SIZE attribute specifies the width, in characters, of the entry field to be displayed. Because most browsers use a proportional font for their entry fields, this length is an approximate value; typically, a SIZE of 10 will not be wide enough to show 10 capitalized Ws, but will be far wider than 10 capital Is. MAXLENGTH, on the other hand, is an absolute: the user can enter, at most, MAXLENGTH characters into the field. The VALUE attribute is also optional and, if present, specifies the default value of the field. This is useful in a form used for updating a database row, as the current values of the row's columns can be specified with the VALUE attribute.

A related input element, with an identical set of attributes as the **text** element, is the **password** type. Inserted with a tag such as <INPUT TYPE="PASSWORD" NAME="name"...>, it creates an area in which an obscured password can be entered. Rather than echoing the text typed by the user, only asterisks or bullets are displayed, preventing an observer from seeing the text typed.

Because HTTP is a stateless protocol, it is often necessary to find ways to communicate state information between invocation of two server-side programs. For instance, when a form is displayed to update a database row, it is critical to have the primary key of the row passed to the script that will handle the update. However, this should not be a user-editable (or even visible) element. HTML forms support an input type of **hidden**, just for this purpose. A *hidden* element is typically set with a name/value pair that will be sent to the server so the script has all the necessary information to execute. An example of this tag would be

```
<INPUT TYPE="HIDDEN" NAME="row_key" VALUE="365231">
```

HTML <INPUT> tags also support radio buttons and checkboxes. For those who are unclear on the difference, *radio buttons* are used to select exactly one choice among a set of mutually exclusive choices, and *checkboxes* are used to select zero, one, or more choices. To create a set of radio buttons, add a collection of <INPUT> tags with the TYPE attribute set to **radio** and the identical NAME attribute, but unique VALUE attributes. The content of the VALUE attribute of the selected radio button will be sent as the value in the name/value pair for the named variable. To default one of the radio buttons as being selected, use the SELECTED attribute, which is simply a switch and does not take a value. To enforce the "exactly one" nature of radio buttons, be certain to mark one radio button as SELECTED.

Checkboxes are inserted in a very similar manner, except for setting the TYPE attribute to **checkbox**. If multiple checkboxes are on the form, a name/value pair will be sent to the server for every checkbox selected. If several checkboxes that share the same NAME attribute are selected, multiple name/value pairs are submitted to the server, one for each selected checkbox. As with radio buttons, the SELECTED attribute specifies whether or not the checkbox should be checked by default.

Other ways of handling the selection of one or more choices among a list of items are drop-down lists and scrolling lists. In some operating systems, *drop-down lists* are also called *pop-up menus,* but their purpose is the same: they allow the user to select exactly one element from a list of items in a relatively small screen space. *Scrolling lists* serve a similar function but display a scrolling list of elements on the page and can permit the user to select multiple items in the list. Both types of lists are generally referred to as *select lists* in HTML,because they are created by using the <SELECT> and </SELECT> tags. The <SELECT> tag accepts two main attributes: NAME, which specifies the name of the element; and SIZE, which specifies the number of elements to be visible on the page. A SIZE of 1, the default, displays the select list as a drop-down list, while larger values display the list as a scrolling list.

By default, lists allow the selection of only a single element; however, the presence of the MULTIPLE switch attribute permits the user to select multiple elements in a platform-specific way. Under Windows, this is accomplished by either clicking and dragging or holding down the CTRL key while clicking. As with checkboxes, a separate name/value pair will be sent to the server for each list item selected. Some browsers actually permit the MULTIPLE switch to be set for lists with a SIZE of one, and display the list in something resembling a spinner control with which they can select multiple elements. This is a very user-hostile interface element to use for this purpose and should be avoided.

The items in the menu, or list, are specified within the <SELECT> and </SELECT> tags and are identified as options by the <OPTION> tag. The text following the <OPTION> tag is displayed in the list and will be sent to the server as the value in the name/value pair. To return a different value than what is displayed, set the <OPTION> tag's VALUE attribute to the value to be submitted to the server. To default the selection of one or more options in the list, include the <OPTION> tag's SELECTED attribute.

The text entry fields implemented above are good, but what if the application needs to accept multiline user input? In this case, HTML provides a text area, designated by the <TEXTAREA> and </TEXTAREA> tags. This text area can accept multiline input in a space that contains both vertical and horizontal scroll bars. The default content of the text appears between the <TEXTAREA> start and end tags. The name of the form element is specified by the NAME attribute. The height and width of the space are set with the COLS and ROWS attributes, which specify in characters the width and height, respectively, of the entry area. By default, the text in the text area will not wrap. However, Netscape has introduced an attribute, WRAP, that controls this. If the attribute is omitted or set to "off," no wrapping will occur; however, setting it to **virtual** will cause it to wrap on screen but be sent as a contiguous paragraph (no newlines). Setting WRAP to **physical** will wrap the text on screen and insert newlines at line breaks when the form is submitted to the server.

So far you have seen what happens when an HTML form is submitted but not how the form is submitted. There are two input controls that allow the user to submit the form data to the server. The most common is known, not surprisingly, as a *submit button*. Submit buttons are created with the <INPUT> tag of TYPE **submit**. The VALUE attribute, which controls the title displayed in the button, is optional and by default is **submit**. The NAME attribute is also optional, and usually omitted. If a submit button is unnamed, a name/value pair will not be sent to the server for the submit button, which is usually preferred. However, if it is named, a name/value pair is generated. This is useful if two different actions could be taken with the form data: for example, "search this site" and "search the Web."

The second method of submitting form data is by use of an image input. An *image input* is an image the user can click to submit the form. The image used is specified as a URL in the SRC attribute, and the name is specified by the NAME attribute. In addition to causing the form to be submitted, the coordinates at which the user clicked on the image are also submitted, in the format *name.x=x_coordinate?name.y=y_coordinate*. If no name is given to the image, simply x and y are used. This input type is useful for things such as geographic searches.

Another type of button that can be inserted is the reset button. Defined as an <INPUT> element of TYPE **reset**, this button simply resets all form elements to their default values. These are either null or the default specified by the use of the VALUE or SELECTED attribute. Typically, this tag is only useful in a situation where reverting the form element values makes sense, as with a form to update data. It rarely makes much sense on a form for inserting data.

An additional specialized type of form input is a *file upload control*, which allows the user to attach a file to be submitted to the server with additional form content. The control is added using the <INPUT> tag with the TYPE attribute set to **file**. This form tag requires special additional server-side processing to handle and thus is not discussed in detail here. However, for those interested, see RFC 1867 for a description of HTML/HTTP-based file upload.

The following code shows the HTML needed to generate the form displayed in Figure 2-4. This form makes use of almost all manner of input elements, except image inputs.

```
<HTML>
<BODY>
<FORM ACTION="/cgi-bin/rsvp" METHOD="POST">
<INPUT TYPE="HIDDEN" NAME="key_i" VALUE="365231">
<TABLE BORDER=1>
  <TR>
    <TD COLSPAN=2 ALIGN=CENTER><B>Update Your Profile</B></TD>
  </TR>
  <TR>
    <TD ALIGN=RIGHT><B>Name</B></TD>
    <TD><INPUT TYPE="text" NAME="name_i" SIZE=25 MAXLENGTH=40
VALUE="Scott"></TD>
  </TR>
  <TR>
    <TD ALIGN=RIGHT><B>Password</B></TD>
    <TD><INPUT TYPE="password" NAME="pass_i" SIZE=25 MAXLENGTH=40
VALUE="tiger"></TD>
  </TR>
  <TR>
    <TD VALIGN=TOP>
      <B>Favorite Color</B><BR>
      <INPUT TYPE="radio" NAME="color_i"
VALUE="FF0000"><B>Red</B><BR>
      <INPUT TYPE="radio" NAME="color_i"
VALUE="00FF00"><B>Green</B><BR>
      <INPUT TYPE="radio" NAME="color_i" VALUE="0000FF"
CHECKED><B>Blue</B><BR>
    </TD>
    <TD VALIGN=TOP>
      <B>Database Needs</B></BR>
      <INPUT TYPE="checkbox" name="needs_i" VALUE="scale"
CHECKED><B>Scalability</B><BR>
      <INPUT TYPE="checkbox" name="needs_i" VALUE="perf"
CHECKED><B>Performance</B><BR>
      <INPUT TYPE="checkbox" name="needs_i" VALUE="port"
CHECKED><B>Portability</B><BR>
```

```
        <INPUT TYPE="checkbox" name="needs_i" VALUE="web"
CHECKED><B>Web Access</B><BR>
        <INPUT TYPE="checkbox" name="needs_i"
VALUE="simple"><B>Simple</B><BR>
        <INPUT TYPE="checkbox" name="needs_i" VALUE="feat"
CHECKED><B>Features</B><BR>
      </TD>
    </TR>
    <TR>
      <TD VALIGN=TOP ALIGN=CENTER>
        <B>Databases Used</B></BR>
        <SELECT NAME="used_i" SIZE=5 MULTIPLE>
        <OPTION VALUE="db2">DB/2
        <OPTION VALUE="inf">Informix
        <OPTION VALUE="ora" SELECTED>Oracle
        <OPTION VALUE="rdb" SELECTED>Rdb
        <OPTION VALUE="syb">Sybase
        </SELECT>
      </TD>
      <TD VALIGN=TOP ALIGN=CENTER>
        <B>Quote</B><BR>
        <TEXTAREA NAME="quote_i" WRAP=VIRTUAL COLS=40 ROWS=4>The
quick brown fox jumps over the lazy dog 80% (+/-10%) of the
time.</TEXTAREA>
      </TD>
    </TR>
    <TR>
      <TD VALIGN=TOP>
        <B>Favorite RDBMS</B>
        <SELECT NAME="used_i" SIZE=1>
        <OPTION VALUE="db2">DB/2
        <OPTION VALUE="inf">Informix
        <OPTION VALUE="ora" SELECTED>Oracle
        <OPTION VALUE="rdb">Rdb
        <OPTION VALUE="syb">Sybase
        </SELECT>
      </TD>
      <TD ALIGN=CENTER>
        <INPUT TYPE="SUBMIT" VALUE="Send Data">
        <INPUT TYPE="RESET" VALUE="Revert Values">
      </TD>
    </TR>
  </TABLE>
</FORM>
</BODY>
</HTML>
```

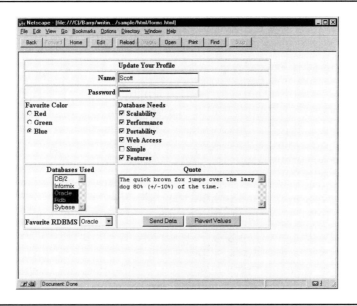

FIGURE 2-4. *An HTML form with many elements*

The following listing shows the actual name/value pairs sent to the server when the form is submitted, using the defaulted values embedded in the form definition. Notice the character escape sequences and the multiple name/value pairs for the field *needs_i*.

```
key_i=365231&name_i=Scott&pass_i=tiger&color_i=0000FF&
needs_i=scale&needs_i=perf&needs_i=port&needs_i=web&
needs_i=feat&used_i=ora&used_i=rdb&
quote_i=The+quick+brown+fox+jumps+over+the+lazy+dog+80%25+%28%2B%2F
-10%25%29+of+the+time.&used_i=ora
```

The combination of the simplicity and expressive power of HTML made it possible for many nontechnical users to stimulate the growth of the Web. Although some web developers refer to *HTML programming,* the term is something of a misnomer. Almost anyone who is capable of using a word processor can pick up the fundamentals of HTML programming in a couple of hours. Taking advantage of more sophisticated features requires some experience, however, and any developer planning to create significant web applications would be well advised to learn the strong points of HTML very well.

Enhanced Display—Beyond HTML

HTML is a reasonably complete markup language, but by design it has two aspects that some developers and designers consider a limitation. First, HTML markup is about content as opposed to presentation. That is, when writing HTML, you typically specify that a piece of text is a certain type of thing. For instance, the HTML expression <H2>Introduction</H2> means that the word "Introduction" is being used as a second-level heading. It is up to the browser to determine how to render this.

Second, HTML is about presenting text information. It originally supported the embedding of graphics, and as mentioned earlier, most browsers supported the use of helper applications for handling content other than text or images. However, the helper applications required additional configuration, thus making them somewhat confusing for novices. Also, they obviously required users to leave their browsers. For the web browser to become a truly universal client, a solution was needed.

To address these two issues, Netscape added the ability for external code to be executed by Navigator to allow other content types to be handled inside the browser and even embedded within HTML pages. This ability to create and use *plug-ins,* as they came to be called, was significant to web designers and developers because it offered a new set of opportunities for displaying information and interfacing with the user. So today, in addition to HTML, several other display formats are common in web applications. None are as commonly used or as simple as HTML, but they offer several options to innovative application developers.

Adobe's Portable Document Format (PDF)

Adobe Systems, the developer of PostScript, also created the Portable Document Format (PDF) and a stand-alone reader called Acrobat. Because PDF, like its cousin PostScript, can be used to precisely lay out the position of objects in any way desired, it was a popular choice for publishing static content that was layout sensitive. Developers could generate PDF files from any application such as Word or Frame Maker using Adobe's Acrobat Exchange. To view these documents, users originally configured the

Acrobat reader as a helper application to view the files. To further support PDF's use in the web environment, Adobe then created a version of Acrobat as a plug-in reader for Netscape Navigator. This allowed the user to view PDF files from within the browser. Next, Adobe added support for embedding hotlinks in PDF files to allow seamless integration into the web-browsing environment.

The byte-serving capability in HTTP version 1.1, discussed earlier, was also a significant boon to PDF use. Because PDF files can be very large, often dozens or even hundreds of pages, while a user may be interested in only a single (or small number) of those pages, the time spent downloading the entire document is largely wasted. The serving of PDF files by byte ranges allows users to fetch only portions of the PDF on appropriately configured servers. In this model, the table of contents or index may be downloaded, and then each page downloaded only as it is requested by the user.

Because of the complete control that developers can achieve with PDF, it is an attractive option for generating reports that have certain appearance requirements or that must also be able to be imaged on a paged device, such as a printer. On the other hand, it is not nearly as simple to code generators of PDF as it is HTML, thus making it less practical for many applications. However, Oracle Reports 2.5.x and higher can generate report output as PDF, including support for drill-down and hyperlinks. Oracle Reports is available as part of Oracle's Developer/2000 product suite. Figure 2-5 shows a sample PDF page.

VRML

A third display language that is becoming more popular is Virtual Reality Modeling Language, or VRML (often pronounced "vermle"). VRML allows the creation of three-dimensional worlds that can be navigated by a browser or helper application. Objects in VRML worlds can be linked to other URLs, as with other web display languages.

For the application developer, VRML's primary appeal rests in the ability to create 3-D representations of data to improve the user experience or to show more information in a single place than would be easily possible in a two-dimensional environment. Significant opportunities exist for using VRML in the creation of web-based decision-support and online analytical processing (OLAP) applications. Figure 2-6 shows an organizational chart

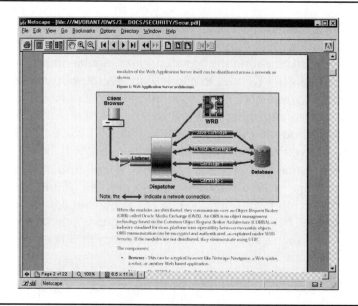

FIGURE 2-5. *A PDF page displayed in a browser*

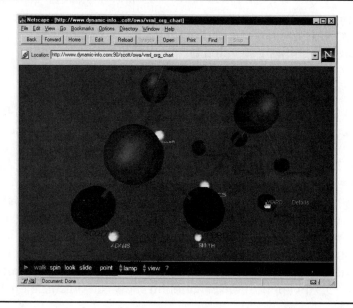

FIGURE 2-6. *A VRML organization chart displayed in a browser*

displayed as a VRML world. The chart is generated dynamically from an Oracle database and was used as a demonstration of Silicon Graphics, Inc.'s VRML and Oracle's web integration for SGI's WebMaster Survival Seminars. The source code for the application is included in Chapter 3. In addition, Oracle provides Oracle Worlds with Web Application Server 3.0, which allows an Oracle7 back-end to manage the data associated with common 3-D worlds expressed in VRML.

MIME Types

Given that modern web browsers are capable of displaying such a wide variety of data formats, how do browsers know which format to use for displaying the results of a request? The process is twofold. First, the server tells the browser in the object header what type of data is being transmitted. Then, based on this information, the browser consults a collection of mapping between types of data and the actions it should take to deal with that data.

The server informs the browser of the type of data with the use of MIME types. The purpose of Multipurpose Internet Mail Exchange (MIME) originally was to accommodate attachments in e-mail. However, it has been applied in other circumstances such as this. MIME types are clearly defined, and your web server must be configured to provide the correct MIME information to the browser.

Server configuration usually involves mapping certain file extensions such as jpeg to a particular MIME type, in this case, image/jpeg. When you programatically generate a response, you must provide the MIME type information, or it will typically default to being either text/html or text/plain. Oracle Web Application Server configuration for MIME types is discussed in Chapter 3, and the VRML example in Chapter 4 illustrates returning dynamic data with a nondefault MIME type.

The browser is configured to respond in certain ways to certain MIME types. In the case of Netscape's Navigator, the configuration is performed under the Helpers tab of the General Preferences dialog. Each MIME type can be associated with a particular action. This may include launching a helper application, invoking a plug-in, or letting the browser handle it internally. Most browsers support several MIME types transparently, while others such as PDF, use a plug-in. Finally, for some MIME types, especially executables, archives, and others, the browser can be instructed to launch another application to handle the data.

Client-Side Executable Code

As has been illustrated, the typical web browser of today packs a great deal of functionality into a simple interface. But all of the content discussed thus far is nonprogrammable. That is, a page can be created in HTML or a world described in VRML. But what about dynamic content and user interaction? Using these technologies, the web browser is only minimally interactive and is not capable of implementing meaningful programmatic functionality.

This section discusses client-side *executable content,* content that actually runs on the client machine. Executable content is what ultimately delivers more client-side functionality and moves the web model beyond the dumb-terminal world. With executable content, a new world of applications open up to deployment via the Web.

There were two driving forces at work in the demand for content that executes at the client side. The first came from creators of primarily static web sites who wanted to enliven their sites to make them more visually appealing. The second came from software developers who viewed client-side execution as a way to extend the web architecture to a true client/server or multitier architecture rather than one that is fundamentally a terminal-based system.

Shockwave

To accommodate the first group, those who wanted to raise the level of sophistication for graphic designs, Macromedia introduced Shockwave. Shockwave is a Netscape plug-in player for dynamic content created in Macromedia's Director product. Although Shockwave can allow for some well-executed interactive designs, it does not aid developers in creating database-driven dynamic content; and since that is the point of this book, further discussion is not provided. If you are interested in more information about Shockwave, see Macromedia's home page at http://www.macromedia.com/.

Java

Unless this book washed up on the deserted island where you have been stranded for the past year or more, you have probably heard of Java and are likely familiar with some of its capabilities. However, because this section is meant to be a comprehensive survey of web-related technology, some discussion is in order.

Java started life inside Sun Microsystems as a project named Oak, in reference to a tree outside the office of one of the project leaders. The stated goal of the Oak project was to create and deliver an application development tool especially suited to lightweight operating environments that allow a networked environment. The target of the Oak project was virtually any stand-alone application running as an embedded system.

That's right: Java started life as a tool to create sophisticated applications in things like thermostats, VCRs, and telephones. Upon a moment's reflection, a robust networkable operating environment allows enormous opportunities for an improved user experience. Imagine a house in which all of the various embedded systems could interoperate (phone, VCR, thermostat, alarm clock, burglar alarm, coffee maker, etc.). With one phone call before leaving the office, a user could turn up the heat in the house and get some coffee brewing so it would be waiting upon arriving home.

Admittedly, this is a little futuristic, even for those who were weaned on *The Jetsons*. Fortuitously for Sun, the rise of the Web was dramatic, and with the lack of client-side executable content, Sun had an outstanding opportunity. It just so happens that many of the features that make a good networked embedded systems environment—robustness, security, processor independence, etc.—also are exceedingly valuable in a thin-client environment such as a web browser.

Given that Sun already had created a great deal of the back-end functionality that was needed, it focused on creating a class library for graphical objects, which came to be known as the Abstract Window Toolkit (AWT). In addition, various classes were created and other class families related to I/O and networking were further fleshed out. Last, Sun worked to get the virtual machine ported to key platforms.

Sun released HotJava, a web browser written in Java for Sun's Solaris operating system, and worked with Netscape to incorporate the Java Virtual Machine (VM) into Netscape's Navigator product. The rest, as they say, is history. To give you an idea of Java's level of mental penetration, Scott McNealy remarked that even before Sun had released the final version of the Java Development Kit, Java had brand recognition five times that of Sun, a multibillion dollar company in business for 14 years.

Having provided the requisite nickel tour of the history of Java, let's examine what Java really is and what impact it can have for web developers. Java has several key design features. In a white paper about the language, Sun defines Java as "a simple, object-oriented, distributed, interpreted, robust, secure, architecture-neutral, portable, high-performance, multithreaded, and dynamic language." In other words, Java is 100 percent of the average programmer's recommended daily allowance of buzzwords. In all fairness, however, the description is quite accurate. To better understand what Java is and why it is having such an impact in the world of information technology, it is worthwhile to examine what each of these attributes really means.

SIMPLE   A goal of Java's design was to create a language that a programmer could learn quickly. To accomplish this, the number of constructs was kept small. In addition, many of the constructs used are very similar to C or C++, allowing a skilled C or C++ programmer to get up to speed quickly in Java development.

Bear in mind that although the Java language is simple, this does not limit its expressiveness or ability to create sophisticated applications. Java's simplicity is an elegant one, like the common brick. However, as simple bricks can be pieced together to form a small house or a palace, so too is the ability of Java to create applications of arbitrary complexity, from single-screen forms to sophisticated business applications.

OBJECT-ORIENTED   Object-oriented languages have a number of benefits for developers. One key idea of object orientation is the bundling of data, and methods that operate on these data, into a class. This is in contrast to a procedural language in which program development is primarily a collection of procedures.

Object-oriented languages have another powerful feature: subclassing. *Subclassing* is the idea that classes are hierarchically organized, and child classes inherit behaviors from their ancestors. This means that if one wants to extend the behavior of a class, a subclass can be created with the new functionality but without one having to rewrite all of the existing functionality. At the same time, the parent class remains unmodified, and any place where it is used remains unaffected.

Java was designed from the start to be object oriented, unlike many languages that have been retrofitted with object extensions. Java's base class libraries are a major asset to the language, as they implement most of the key building blocks for creating sophisticated applications. In addition, object orientation improves reuse opportunities of internally developed or acquired code and allows for easier maintenance.

DISTRIBUTED   Another of Java's key design goals was to support network applications. This is obviously crucial to the creation of new client/server and multitier applications. The base java.net package includes a large number of networking classes, and new Java specifications implement various additional network features such as remote method invocation, to allow transparent execution of code on network nodes other than the one on which the calling machine is running.

INTERPRETED   Java is an interpreted language. That is to say that when a developer compiles a Java class, the output is not machine code, as is the case with a typical compiler, nor are the contents of the class file fed directly to the CPU when the user is executing a Java class, although this is changing somewhat. Java compiles its classes into a byte code that is then executed by the Java Virtual Machine.

In addition to the portability benefits an interpreted language accrues, programs written in interpreted languages have a much shorter write-build-run cycle than noninterpreted languages. This is because the linking process, whereby code in one class or module is able to invoke code in another class or module, occurs at run time as opposed to being fixed at compile time. The downside of an interpreted language is a negative impact on performance. However, later you will see what steps are being taken to minimize this impact (see "High-Performance," below).

ROBUST   Because Java was originally designed for applications that run in various appliances, it had to be designed to write highly reliable code. Embedded-system design is expensive primarily because of the expense of creating highly reliable code using less robust languages. Java is strongly typed, requires explicit declarations, and provides strong support for exception handling. In addition, there are no pointers in Java, which makes invalid or insecure memory access impossible. Finally, Java's automatic allocation and garbage collection of memory removes an entire class of defects that are difficult to detect and debug.

SECURE   Related to the issue of robustness is security. Because Java was designed to be run in a network environment and for important applications, security was a concern from the start. Because of this, Java defines and implements a number of security features that control what running Java code is allowed to do in terms of accessing operating system features, reading and writing files, and network access.

Many developers producing legitimate Java applets to be run inside a browser do find themselves thwarted by Java's security. However, any Java container can implement its own security options inside Java's general model. Expect to see more flexible and configurable security options in future browsers.

ARCHITECTURE-NEUTRAL   Because Java was designed to run on a variety of different devices, it was designed to be architecture-neutral. The only fundamental requirement of the device is that it implement the Java Virtual Machine, the code Sun widely licenses. The boon to developers is that by writing in Java they insulate themselves from the common problem of creating different versions of software for each platform to be supported, or simply not supporting certain platforms. Obviously, architecture neutrality is a major feature for enterprise developers who must deal with a heterogeneous mix of platforms, as well as for people developing for the general audience of the Internet, where every type of machine is a client.

PORTABLE   Architecture neutrality relates to software written using Java. Portability is a trait of the Java environment itself. The Java compiler, javac, for instance, is itself written in Java. Java also defines all data types specifically, allowing for no implementation dependencies. In addition, the Java Virtual Machine is written in ANSI-C with portability to virtually any POSIX-compliant system.

HIGH-PERFORMANCE   This is possibly the one piece of puffery in Sun's description of Java. As mentioned above, all else being equal, code in interpreted languages is inherently slower than identical code compiled into a processor's instruction set. As an example of this, most basic Java implementations run about 20 times slower than C compiled into machine code. However, it is important to note that Java's performance is more than adequate for interactive and networked applications, where there is usually a high latency (relative to processor speed) in either the user or network response. In most productivity applications, the machine spends most of its time sitting idle waiting for input.

In addition, the performance issue will likely diminish or be completely obviated by combined advances in software and hardware technology. On the software front, several solutions are helping to improve Java's performance. At the time of this writing, Asymetrix, Borland, Microsoft, Sun, and others have developed and released just-in-time (JIT) compilers for Java. *JIT compilers* preprocess Java VM instructions into machine native code when they are loaded. Combining this with sophisticated caching techniques allows for near-native performance levels. This is a similar technology to that which allows PowerPC-based Macintosh computers to run software compiled for the Motorola 680X0 instruction set, in some cases even faster than 680X0-based machines themselves. Many OS and hardware vendors, including HP, Apple, and Microsoft, have announced or delivered on plans for implementing JIT compilers for Java on other platforms, and even integrating this Java technology as part of the operating system itself.

On the hardware front, faster processors, particularly RISC-based chips, offer the likelihood of quantum increases in execution speed, sufficient to make interpreted languages more viable for even computationally intensive applications. Another key hardware advance is the creation of Java chips— that is, chips that implement the Java VM instruction set. Sun's picoJava and microJava chips to be used in their Network Computers and other devices are examples of this. For the time being, however, Java alone may not be suitable for applications that demand the highest performance.

MULTITHREADED   Most programs today consist of a single code execution stream running in a single process. Multiple programs on a machine can do different things in parallel, but the individual programs themselves only do one thing at a time. Newer applications are often written with multiple threads, sometimes called *lightweight processes*. Multithreading is at work when Netscape's Navigator is downloading and rendering multiple graphics simultaneously, as well as when web servers handle multiple connections simultaneously. The multithreaded model is especially useful in applications that may spend significant amounts of time waiting for network resources. Running multiple threads means time spent waiting need not be wasted.

As contrasted with most languages, Java is a very easy language in which to develop multithreaded applications. As an example, we once had occasion to create an application that would download an entire web site, graphics and all, to another web server or local directory and realign all the links to point correctly. When we first ran it, we noticed that it spent at least 85 percent of the time downloading from the remote server, as these were mostly foreign sites. By converting the application to a multithreaded model, we could parallelize the process with five to seven simultaneous transfers. The total time to add this support was less than five hours, including creating a status panel that would report status for an arbitrary number of threads.

DYNAMIC Dynamic languages can be defined loosely as those that support interaction with code objects that are undefined or unknown at the time the original code is written. This means support for dynamic linking at run time and run-time type identification, among other features. Java programs, for example, can be written to load a class by its name, determine the superclass of the class, instantiate objects of that class, and operate on these objects, even if the developer didn't know of the class's existence when writing the original program.

As you can see, Java has some design features that make it very well suited to the task of creating programs that are network centric. Its strong support for network operations and architecture neutrality are especially key in this respect. Later in the book, using Java as a server-side environment is discussed, as well as integrating Java applets with the Oracle Web Application Server.

Java's position as the first executable content format, combined with its strong features and capabilities, have made it the dominant format in use today. Although Java has achieved significant market and mind share as the executable content format of choice, there are alternatives to Java that web developers should be aware of.

ActiveX

Microsoft Corporation, a key force behind the growth of the personal computer and an aggressive and dominant player in virtually every product category in which it competes, felt it owed the world a better solution than Java. Or at least it felt it owed it to itself not to have something like Java eat into its perceived dominance in the emerging market of the Web. Strategically, Java had the further impact on Microsoft of possibly rendering operating systems such as Windows completely fungible. The solution Microsoft created is known as ActiveX. "Created" is maybe a misleading word—"restaged" would be a better one. ActiveX is ultimately a rebranding and restaging of Microsoft's OLE Control Extension (OCX) specification.

For those unfamiliar with OCX, it is a component architecture developed by Microsoft to take the Visual Basic Extension (VBX) format to the next level. OCX is also developed for a 32-bit architecture, such as Windows 95 or Windows NT, although it can be used under Windows 3.1 with the Win32 extensions. The OCX architecture is Microsoft's contribution to the world of embeddable objects. There are a number of reasons why readers should be discouraged from using Microsoft's ActiveX technology in developing applications. There are also some reasons to argue in favor of ActiveX technology for certain applications. Surprisingly, some of the reasons for and against using it are the same!

ActiveX objects are compiled into machine code, which, in contrast to Java's byte-code interpreted nature, delivers the fastest possible execution speed. This offers a significant advantage for some applications. This is particularly noticeable with computationally or graphically intensive applications. For instance, you would expect a 3-D equation graphing package to be much more responsive as an ActiveX control than as a Java applet. However, the use of native code means that the control is not platform neutral. As mentioned earlier, a single Java applet can be run on any machine on which the Java Virtual Machine has been implemented. This is nearly every significant platform. In the case of ActiveX, a different ActiveX control must be compiled for each platform, and presently each platform means only one: 32-bit Windows. Although Microsoft promises support for other platforms, it has been slow in releasing that support, and Microsoft in fact subcontracted out the development of Unix and Macintosh support for ActiveX. This may not present a problem for those who expect Microsoft's total dominance of the PC operating system market to continue. However, for those looking at the idea of Network Computers or Java terminals as viable end-user computing platforms, ActiveX may represent a stumbling block.

Another advantage ActiveX controls enjoy over Java is tighter integration with operating system services. This inherently comes along with the OCX architecture, on which ActiveX controls are based. This means that ActiveX controls can read and write files, have more flexibility in accessing network resources, can more easily support printing, and a host of other capabilities compared with more security-bound Java applets.

These limitations are primarily a result of a combination of factors, each of which will probably be addressed in the near future. Browsers and other Java containers will likely incorporate a more sophisticated security architecture that will allow the specification of security constraints on a host-by-host basis. For instance, the browser could be configured to relax security constraints for any applets served by machines on an organization's intranet, while imposing complete constraints on code from untrusted or unknown machines on the Internet.

On the downside, ActiveX controls' easy access to operating system functions opens a gaping security hole that can be exploited by hostile code. It also increases the likelihood of system crashes due to errant code. Currently, there are no announced plans for ActiveX controls to support a stronger security system, and it would likely prove infeasible to implement such support given the architecture itself. A recent article compared the security risks of the two technologies by stating that the security risks with Java were similar to walking across an intersection while the "walk" sign is lit, while the risks with ActiveX were closer to walking across a freeway.

Of course, another downside aspect of ActiveX relates to network object communication and therefore to multitier application partitioning. Java is able to implement networked objects using the Common Object Request Broker Architecture (CORBA). CORBA is the official network object model endorsed by the Object Management Group, a consortium of over 600 technology-driven companies (with one notable exception). This industry support means that in the world of networked objects, Java integration will be straightforward. Believing that 600 out of the 601 largest technology companies couldn't possibly be right, Microsoft chose to implement networked objects using OLE Automation based on an architecture known as the Distributed Component Object Model (DCOM), a less elegant networked object solution. Compared with CORBA, which allows networked objects to reside on virtually any hardware/operating system combination in existence, networked objects using OLE Automation can only be run on—surprise—Microsoft operating systems. This is a fundamental stumbling block to truly integrating ActiveX components in an open-systems-based computing infrastructure. Although Oracle, through its Network Computing Architecture initiatives, and others have taken steps to bridge the gap between CORBA and DCOM, ActiveX integration with industry-standard CORBA would still require at least a gateway.

It is especially important for organizations that have any platform heterogeneity, and those that wish to retain infrastructure flexibility into the future, to recognize that ActiveX runs counter to those objectives. Because the intended audience of this book is enterprise developers whose organizations need scalability and platform independence, further discussion of ActiveX technologies is not provided.

TCL/TK

The Tool Control Language (TCL) has been around for some years now and has become a quite popular scripting language among many Unix developers who use it to create quick graphical interfaces to other system services or to create prototypes of applications that may ultimately be written in another language. In any event, TCL (pronounced "tickle") has proven itself to be a very capable scripting and interface development language for many people.

Tool Control Language, as the name implies, is a language used to control other tools. It is a very simple language; in fact, it is fundamentally just a function caller. Everything in TCL, even loops and other flow-control constructs, is implemented by some other external code, usually written in C, C++, or Java. Given that the language itself is simply a function dispatcher, the real power of TCL is in the functions it can execute. This is where the "TK" in TCL/TK helps. TK is the toolkit that implements a wide number of functions for flow control, interface management, and other tasks such as networking. In addition, it is possible for a developer to extend the TCL environment by creating additional functions in a language such as C.

Sun decided that TCL would also be a good basis for executable content for several reasons. The primary one being that an amateur programmer could likely be more productive using TCL than using Java for simple programming tasks. Because it lacks object orientation, TCL is much more straightforward for a user who is familiar with writing macros or other user-level programming. An additional benefit is that unlike Java or ActiveX, executable content created in TCL does not need to be compiled to be embedded in an HTML page; the TCL source code itself is interpreted at run time. This also acts to reduce the complexity of development for nonprofessional developers. Version 8.0 of TCL does, however, implement a byte-code compiler to increase performance.

To deliver the benefits of TCL/TK in the web environment, Sun created plug-ins for Netscape's Navigator for several platforms: Solaris, Windows 95 and NT, and the Macintosh. As stressed earlier, cross-platform portability is a critical element of any tool used in a web-based environment. In addition, Sun has taken several steps to integrate TCL and Java, paving the way for TCL scripts to glue together Java components, as well as using TCL as a scripting or macro language for Java applications, which suggests some very interesting possibilities.

There are a few other tools for delivering executable content, which are in various stages of development or release. The impact these tools will have on the market is unknown, but it is unlikely that any new languages would overtake either Java or ActiveX as primary client-side scripting languages. However, when evaluating other formats and tools for client-side executable content for use in an enterprise environment, it is wise to examine a variety of characteristics: performance, portability, suitability to the problem domain, support, and available skills.

Client-Side Scripting

Even with the introduction of client-side executable content formats such as Java and ActiveX, web developers were still not satisfied. (People on the bleeding edge are always demanding.) There were two reasons for the dissatisfaction. First, Java applets are embedded in an HTML page and cannot interact with other objects on the page, such as graphics, form elements, etc. Second, despite the early commentary that Java was easy and fun and would let webmasters create sophisticated applications easily, this did not prove to be the case. As mentioned earlier, the reality is that Java is a rich language that requires an understanding of modern programming paradigms to comprehend, and strong rudimentary programming skills to use successfully.

The net result of these two factors is that an individual who was not a skilled programmer was unable to do relatively simple things, such as requiring that an HTML form field not be blank before submitting the form. Even if the webmaster had a CGI form-handling program that allowed the specification of a field as required (in which case the CGI program would return an error message back to the user), this functionality was needed. Increasing web traffic levels meant that smart webmasters wanted to reduce the number of HTTP transactions necessary to do something. Both network and server utilization levels provided a strong argument in favor of it. However, even if network and server resources are infinite in supply and null in cost, the user experience of having validation occur by submitting the request and waiting for a response is less than ideal. Most users of client/server tools are used to field-level validation, or at least near-instant record-level validation. This is not possible in the "dumb client" world of vanilla HTML.

Client-side scripting addresses these problems fairly well. *Client-side scripting languages* can be generically defined as programming languages that are implemented by the browser itself and that are able to, at a minimum, operate on the browser environment and HTML documents. There is nothing to prohibit client-side scripting languages from being made more sophisticated to support interaction with other document types. In fact, the VRML 2.0 Moving Worlds specification makes use of client-side scripting to increase the interactive capability of virtual worlds.

Although the focus of this book is clearly on the development of the server-driven web-based applications, client-side scripting is an important issue for all developers of web applications. Client-side scripting can be used for several things in web-based applications. Client-side data validation is one obvious use alluded to earlier. In addition, client-side scripting can be used to integrate executable content with standard HTML elements, such as forms, to allow the HTML page to serve as an object container, in the way that many client/server tools (including Oracle's Power Objects and Developer/2000 and Microsoft Access) can glue native objects with OCX or VBX objects.

JavaScript

JavaScript was developed by Netscape Communications to address the limitations described above. They made a wise choice to select Java as a "base" language for a number of reasons. ("Base" is in scare quotes because JavaScript bears few similarities to Java beyond its basic syntactic structure.) First, JavaScript has many of the same benefits as Java in terms of simplicity and portability. Second, by using a scripting language derivative of Java, Netscape made it easier for web developers to create client-side solutions while only mentally managing one basic language model. Actually, Java can be used for server-side scripting as well, thus one language can meet virtually all a web developer's needs.

Shortly after the release of JavaScript, developers clamored for an important and overlooked feature in the language: the ability to write scripts that can interact with executable content on the page, such as a Java applet. Netscape addressed this need with a technology known as LiveConnect. LiveConnect allows bi-directional communication between web pages that contain HTML and JavaScript, and Java applets. Java applets can use LiveConnect to access web-page and JavaScript contents, while JavaScript programs can access public methods of Java applets through LiveConnect. This LiveConnect technology, although currently underused, promises some interesting opportunities for developers with its further enhancement in Netscape's new browser, Communicator.

The following listing shows an example of a simple HTML form that uses JavaScript to perform a range check on a field value and report the error to the user if the value entered by the user falls out of bounds. Notice that using JavaScript on an HTML page is a combination of adding JavaScript functions and, typically, using an extended-attribute set of certain tags to control the invocation of the functions. In this example, the text input area has an ONCHANGE attribute that is set to execute a JavaScript function when the user changes the value of the input field.

```
<HTML>
<SCRIPT LANGUAGE="JavaScript">
function rangeCheck(elem, lbound, ubound) {
  if (elem.value > ubound) {
    alert (elem.name + " must be less than or equal to " + ubound);
    elem.focus();
  } else {
    if (elem.value < lbound) {
      alert (elem.name + " must be greater than or equal to " + lbound);
      elem.focus();
    }
  }
}
</SCRIPT>
<BODY>
<FORM ACTION="/scott/owa/formtest2" METHOD="POST">
<B>Value</B>
<INPUT TYPE="text" NAME="val_i" VALUE="9"
ONCHANGE="rangeCheck(this,7,25)">
...
</BODY>
</HTML>
```

VBScript

It should not come as a surprise that Microsoft created its own client-side scripting language for use in Internet Explorer. For individuals familiar with Microsoft's other products, the fact that the script developed is a derivative of Visual Basic is again unsurprising. VBScript delivers fundamentally the same sort of functionality JavaScript combined with LiveConnect implements. Microsoft immediately recognized the need to allow client-side scripts to operate on and communicate with client-side executable objects, so this functionality was present from the start. This was of course made easier by the fact that VBScript is derived from Visual Basic, which contains support for OCX communication.

Developing client-side scripts in JavaScript is a good idea, for two reasons. First, we feel it is a superior scripting language to VBScript, primarily because we feel Java is a better basis point than Basic. Second, Microsoft's Internet Explorer supports the majority of JavaScript, although not consistently, while Netscape's browsers do not support VBScript at all. Thus, browser flexibility is preserved by developing in JavaScript, although a pure Java or pure HTML interface both offer greater portability.

The Future of Client-Side Scripting

New scripting languages may be introduced in the future. One of the specifications Microsoft's ActiveX architecture provides is for the creation and execution of scripting languages with the use of third-party extensions. This is the architecture that allowed Internet Explorer to incorporate support for both JavaScript and VBScript. These extended scripting languages can be used for scripting in Microsoft's server and browser products.

Despite the ability to create new scripting languages, it is unlikely that any new scripting languages will achieve significant usage levels unless a new major browser is introduced. Even if a new browser is introduced, it would almost be a requisite feature that it supports one of the two current languages, most likely JavaScript. A possible exception to this expectation is new client-side scripting languages introduced to support new content types. As mentioned earlier, VRML 2.0 will support a scripting capability.

As you have seen, although servers are the necessary component in the Web, the sophisticated and feature-packed browsers used as web clients are what makes the Web a viable foundation for such a wide variety of applications. By taking advantage of all the browser's different display capabilities and its ability to add client-side processing and interactivity, in addition to employing a database-integrated web server, a complete architecture for sophisticated networked applications can be created.

Conclusion

After reading this chapter, you should have developed sufficient understanding of the architecture and components that compose the foundation of web-based application development. An understanding of these components and their relationships is vital to creating sophisticated web-enabled applications. However, the information here is not sufficient by itself to create truly powerful web-based applications. Sophisticated application designs require leveraging all parts of the architecture and understanding the ins and outs of each component. The resources listed next provide outstanding starting points for further investigation either now or as a reference while developing applications. In the next chapter, you begin server-side web application development with an introduction to the installation and configuration of the Oracle Web Application Server.

For More Information

The number of heterogeneous tools and technologies used in web development presents an educational challenge to developers. The following list provides some suggested resources for more detailed information about many of the subjects that were broadly covered in this chapter.

General Information

A group known as the Internet Literacy Consultants (ILC) maintains the ILC Glossary of Internet Terms, at http://www.matisse.net/files/glossary.html.

The World Wide Web Consortium is the official maintainer of all standards related to the Web; their site is at http://www.w3.org/.

HTTP

The official reference to HTTP is available from the World Wide Web Consortium at http://www.w3.org/Protocols/.

Secure Sockets Layer (SSL)

Netscape Communications, the creator of SSL, maintains the latest SSL information at http://home.netscape.com/assist/security/ssl/index.html.

Common Gateway Interface (CGI)

The NCSA's official guide to the CGI is available at the following site: http://hoohoo.ncsa.uiuc.edu/cgi/overview.html.

Netscape API (NSAPI)

Netscape's guide to NSAPI is available at the following site: http://home.netscape.com/newsref/std/server_api.html.

Internet Information Server API (ISAPI)

Microsoft's reference for the ISAPI is at http://www.microsoft.com/win32dev/apiext/isalegal.htm.

HTML

The official reference on the latest version of HTML is available from the World Wide Web Consortium at http://www.w3.org/pub/WWW/MarkUp/Wilbur/.

A reasonably complete reference to standard HTML and the popular browser extensions, all in one place, can be found at http://www2.wvitcoe.wvnet.edu/~sbolt/html3/.

Another tag reference worth using is at http://www.dummies.com/resources/HTML4DUM/tagindex.htm.

Microsoft provides very good information about its Internet Explorer HTML implementation features at http://www.microsoft.com/workshop/author/default.asp.

Portable Document Format (PDF)

Information about Adobe's Acrobat and PDF can be found at this site: http://www.adobe.com/prodindex/acrobat/details.html.

VRML

The best source of VRML information is at the San Diego Supercomputer Center's VRML Repository located at http://www.sdsc.edu/vrml/.

VRML specifications are available at http://www.sdsc.edu/vrml/spec.html.

Java

The official home of Java is the home page for Sun's JavaSoft business unit at http://www.javasoft.com/.

The Java specification and APIs are available at http://www.javasoft.com:80/products/api-overview.html.

For a comprehensive set of links and descriptions of Java documents, applets, source code, and links, check out Gamelan (pronounced "gamma-lon") at http://java.developer.com/.

If you already know C or C++, the book *Java in a Nutshell,* by David Flanagan (Sebastopol, California: O'Reilly & Associates, 1996), will have you programming in Java quickly.

ActiveX
Microsoft's ActiveX information is available at the following site: http://www.microsoft.com/activex/.

Tool Control Language (TCL)
For TCL information and tools, see the home page of Sun's scripting business unit, SunScript, at http://sunscript.sun.com/.

JavaScript
Netscape's official documentation can be found at http://home.netscape/com/eng/mozilla/3.0/handbook/javascript/index.html.

Microsoft's reference to JScript, its implementation of JavaScript, is at http://www.microsoft.com/jscript/.

David Flanagan also has compiled an outstanding reference on JavaScript, now in its second edition, in *JavaScript, the Definitive Guide* (Sebastopol, California: O'Reilly & Associates, 1997).

VBScript
The official home page of VBScript is available at the following site: http://www.microsoft.com/vbscript/.

CHAPTER 3

WAS Architecture, Installation, and Configuration

y this point you are probably pretty excited to start implementing web applications using the Web Application Server. Obviously, a prerequisite is actually installing the Web Application Server in at least a development environment. This chapter provides an overview of the WAS architecture, as well as guidelines for correctly installing, configuring, troubleshooting, and administering the WAS. Be aware that it is *not* meant to replace the documentation provided by Oracle in these subjects, but rather to augment it by discussing recommended practices and suggesting helpful tips.

Architecture

Before getting into the actual mechanics of the installation process, it is worthwhile to describe the basic architecture of the Web Application Server. By effectively understanding the components that compose the WAS, certain decisions that need to be made during the installation will become more clear. In addition, problems that may be encountered during either installation or ongoing operations should be easier to diagnose when you are armed with the knowledge of the optimal system configuration.

The Web Application Server is composed of a collection of processes that work cooperatively to create a complete application deployment and management platform. The executable components of the Oracle Web Application Server can be broken into three main groups.

The first piece is the HTTP listener, or httpd (for HTTP daemon), which provides an access point through which users request static files or invoke server-side programs. Oracle bundles Spyglass' web listener with the Web Application Server, although other web listeners may be used. These third-party listeners are integrated by using a special Web Request Broker adapter that provides an interface between the listeners' native APIs and the WRB. Currently, Oracle bundles WRB adapters for web listeners from both Netscape and Microsoft. This allows organizations that have already standardized on a certain web listener to take advantage of the value added by Oracle. An Oracle Web Application Server installation includes at least two listeners: one for administering other listeners, the WRB and WRB cartridges; and one or more listeners that actually service requests from users for files or program invocation through the WRB or CGI interfaces.

The functionality created by developers is implemented either as Web Request Broker cartridges or through them. These are executable programs that perform specific services or functions, most typically servicing requests sent to the HTTP listener by a web browser. Some of these cartridges implement interfaces to executing code written in PL/SQL, Java, or Perl. The custom code these cartridges execute are typically referred to as *components*. Other cartridges, and particularly third-party cartridges, may perform specialized processing. For instance, a sales tax cartridge would return the sales tax chargeable on goods or services purchased, by being passed a taxable subtotal and a geographic purchase location. Cartridges and components can communicate among themselves to develop component-based software at the server level.

The glue that binds the HTTP listener to the cartridges is the Web Request Broker. The WRB is the most significant architectural innovation by Oracle in the Web Application Server. It is a CORBA-based request broker that provides an interface through which requests are routed to other executable code. The Web Request Broker enables a web listener to easily balance requests across multiple machines, referred to in this chapter as *nodes*. In addition, the Web Request Broker provides a number of common services to the cartridges and components that are invoked through it, such as transaction management, content services, and Inter-Cartridge Exchange, which allows cartridges to communicate with one another easily. These and other common services are discussed in detail in Chapter 10. A single WRB instance can be used by multiple HTTP listeners.

Each of these groups is composed of one or more processes. They are started and stopped and their status is monitored using a command line tool, owsctl. Under Windows NT installations, these processes are also installed as services, to automate their startup and shutdown behaviors. Table 3-1 enumerates the processes and their functions that will be running on a machine (or machines) on which the WAS has been installed. A "P" indicates a process that must run on the primary server, while an "R" means that the process may run on a remote server as well. This is described in more detail in the "Multiple-Node Installations" section later in the chapter.

In addition to three components mentioned earlier, there is also an Object Request Broker (ORB) that serves as the communications substrate for the listener, the WRB, and the cartridges. With very few exceptions, the

Process Name	Service Name (NT Only)	Runs	Description
oraweb	OracleWWWListener30*name*	P	The web listener process. More than one may be in use on a machine.
mnorbsrv	OraMediaNet_mnorbsrv	P	The main object request broker (ORB) service that manages the mechanics of brokering requests for the WRB.
mnaddsrv	OraMediaNet_mnaddsrv	P	The address server used by the ORB.
mnrpcnmsrv	OraMediaNet_mnrpcnmsrv	P	The RPC name server used by the ORB.
wrbcfg	OraWeb_wrbcfg	P	The WRB configuration provider.
wrblog	OraWeb_wrblog	P	The WRB logging service. Multiple WRB logging services can be run on machines with heavy logging volumes.
wrbasrv wrbahsrv	OraWeb_wrbasrv OraWeb_wrbahsrv	P/R	The WRB authentication services.
wrbroker	OraWeb_wrbroker	P	The Web Request Broker itself.
wrbvpm	OraWeb_wrbvpm	P	The WRB virtual path manager for identifying the cartridge to be invoked form a virtual path in a URL.
wrbfac	OraWeb_wrbfac	P/R	The cartridge factory. This process is responsible for spawning instances of the wrbc process as directed by the WRB.

TABLE 3-1. *Processes (and Windows NT Services) for the WAS*

Process Name	Service Name (NT Only)	Runs	Description
wrbc	N/A	P/R	A web request broker cartridge process. Depending on the installation and activity levels of a server, there may be several, dozens, or hundreds of such processes. Each process controls an instance of some WRB cartridge.

TABLE 3-1. *Processes (and Windows NT Services) for the WAS (continued)*

ORB can be taken for granted as being just another piece of the WRB subsystem. Future versions of WAS, however, will likely further expose the ORB to enhancements and improvements of developers and administrators. The ORB used in version 3.0 of WAS is the MediaNet ORB, developed by Oracle originally for use in the Oracle Video Server. WAS is bundled with version 3.3 of this ORB, which is, with several minor exceptions, 100 percent CORBA 2.0 compliant. Future versions of WAS may offer ORB support from Visigenics.

In addition to these core elements of the OWAS are a collection of development libraries and tools for creating database-integrated and web-delivered applications in a variety of languages, such as Java, PL/SQL, C, and Perl. By supporting a wide variety of different development languages, the Oracle Web Application Server comprises not so much a development tool as it does a development *platform*. Developing applications using the variety of tools available on the OWAS is the primary focus of this book, and begins in the next chapter.

Installation

Before we jump into the development process, however, the Web Application Server has to be installed. Installation of the WAS is a relatively straightforward process, but can be complicated by minor errors along the way. The best way to avoid these errors is by planning the entire installation process in advance. This means that, before installing, you should read through all the installation instructions in the WAS platform-specific documentation, as well as the install.txt and readme files that are included on the distribution media.

Prior Planning Prevents Poor Performance

The next step is planning the type of installation. Oracle Web Application Server has three types of common installations. The first is known as *single*, which is used for systems that will use a single machine to run the HTTP listener, the WRB, and the WRB cartridges. The other two types are used for multiple-node installations. The first of these is a *primary* node installation. In a primary node installation, the machine will be running the WRB processes and usually—but not necessarily—the web listener. The second type of installation for a multiple-node environment is a *remote* node. Remote nodes run only the WRB cartridge factory and some number of wrbc processes to run cartridges. Single-node installations are, as you might imagine, the easiest to install, configure, and otherwise administer, while multiple-node configurations trade simplicity for a significant amount of flexibility and scalability with respect to allocating computing resources across a number of machines.

If you plan to run a distributed installation of WAS, you should either make some further decisions prior to installation or put them off for later resolution. The key decision is to plan which components of the system will be run on which machine. It is possible to run all cartridges on all machines, or only some cartridges on some machines. The factors influencing this decision may include resource availability on various machines, administrative convenience, and other factors. For example, if there are differences in database accessibility or performance on various machines, it makes sense to install cartridges that will use the database on the machines having the best access performance. For a multiple-node installation, it is worth spending some time with a network diagramming tool (or even a drawing tool) to map out which processes will be running on which machines, as well as the network topology of those machines vis-à-vis the rest of the computing infrastructure. This not only will make installation planning more clear, but will give you a necessary road map for your well-organized systems shop.

After planning the high-level architecture of the installation, it is time to get into the details of installing the system on the target system or systems. In the course of the installation, you will be prompted for responses to a number of inquiries. Some of them are standard Oracle installation prompts, such as specifying the ORACLE_HOME directory and the language to be used. Most others, however, are specific to the Web Application Server. Table 3-2 lists the information that you should be prepared to provide to the installer. Note that this list includes all the information requested by the installer under Windows NT examples. For Unix installations, many of the settings are configured in environment variables prior to running the installer. Regardless, make up a worksheet with the values that will be used for this data—an especially useful aid for multiple-node installations, where certain values need to be identical.

Information	Default	Comments
Language	English	This parameter determines the National Language Support setting for the server and will install language-specific text for messages, as appropriate and available. Note that the actual HTML-based configuration pages will remain in English, however.
Company Name	None	If the machine has had previous Oracle installations, the installer will default this to the previously assigned setting.
Oracle Home	Platform-specific	If the machine has had previous Oracle installations, the installer will read the current setting of the ORACLE_HOME environment variable as the default.
Oracle Web Home	%ORACLE_HOME% \ows\3.0	This value will become the setting of the ORAWEB_HOME environment variable.

TABLE 3-2.   *Preinstallation Planning Checklist*

Information	Default	Comments
Site Name	WEBSITE30	A directory with this name will be created in %ORACLE_HOME%\ows, which will contain configuration information and logs for any HTTP listeners, the WRB, and WRB cartridges.
Host Name	The machine name	This item is not needed for a single-machine installation. For a multiple-node installation, it is the machine name of the primary node.
Remote Host List	None	This item needs to be completed for the primary node in a multiple-node installation. It enumerates the machine names of the remote nodes that make up the installation.
UDP Service Port	2649	This specifies the UDP port to be used by the ORB and WRB processes to communicate among multiple nodes. Acceptable values range between 1024 and 65535.
Shared Key	None	This key is entered in hexadecimal format and can be up to 255 bytes long. It is used to encrypt communication between the nodes in a multiple-node implementation. Longer keys provide additional security, with a negligible impact on performance. Leaving this value blank will result in unencrypted communication among the various nodes.
Administrative Listener Port	8888	This is the port on which the administrative listener will run. It is highly recommended that a nondefault value be used for security considerations.

TABLE 3-2. *Preinstallation Planning Checklist (continued)*

Information	Default	Comments
Administrator Name	admin	When connecting to the administrative listener, the browser will prompt for a username and password. This is the username that will be granted access.
Administrator Password	None	This is the password for the administrative user.
Web Listener Name	www	Under Windows NT, the installer can automatically install an HTTP listener to be used for general requests. The name refers to the name under which the listener will be administered.
Web Listener Port	80	The port for the automatically installed general-purpose listener.

TABLE 3-2. *Preinstallation Planning Checklist* (continued)

After preparing an installation planning worksheet, installation can begin in earnest. Because of the operating system–specific nature of the installation process, we will not detail the exact steps here for any platform. However, a few comments can be made. Under Windows NT, logging on as an Administrator is sufficient for performing the entire installation, which is accomplished entirely by the Oracle Installer. The machine should be rebooted after installation to correctly apply the PATH environment variable that the installation modifies.

Generally speaking, under Unix, you face three main sets of tasks: setting up the installation environment by setting environment variables and possibly running one or two shell scripts; running the Oracle Installer; and, finally, running some postinstallation shell scripts. Pay careful attention to which user account should be used for which task. Some actions are to be performed as Oracle, some as root, some as the user that will administer the WAS, and still others as the account under which the WAS will run. Not following these guidelines to the letter can result in problems starting up the system. In some shops, this means having three different people each performing a different part of the installation, unless someone with root installs the system and simply uses **su** to switch accounts. Also note that the administrative listener will, by default, run as whichever user it was that performed the installation.

NOTE
Read the release notes to find out which operating system patches (or Service Packs, to NT folks) need to be applied for the WAS to run. If the patch level on the target system is not up to date, do not even attempt to install until the patches have been applied.

There are two somewhat special types of installations that require some additional effort. The first is an installation in which the WRB services requests from HTTP listeners other than the one bundled by Oracle (for example, Netscape Enterprise Server or Microsoft's Internet Information Server (IIS). WAS includes utilities to register such external listeners. The steps involved in registering these listeners are specific both to the listener type and to the operating system. Fort further information, consult the platform-specific installation guide or access the Register External Listeners link from the Oracle Web Listener administration page. The second type of specialized installation is a distributed or multiple-node installation. We provide additional details about such installations later in the chapter under the heading "Multiple-Node Installations."

Starting and Stopping the WAS

Because the Web Application Server is composed of a number of components, a utility is provided to start up multiple components all at once. This utility, owsctl, has three main functions: start, stop, and status. Each function can be used against a different component of the WAS. For instance, "owsctl start wrb" will start up all the services for the Web Request Broker, including the ORB, the WRB processes, and the WRB cartridge factory. Likewise, "owsctl stop admin" will stop the administrative listener named "admin." On remote nodes, owsctl is used to start the cartridge factory by using "owsctl start cartridge."

It is critical to remember that the WRB must be started before starting any listeners or the cartridge factories on the same node or any remote nodes. Because the listeners and the cartridge factories must connect to the ORB services when they start up, they will hang if the WRB has not fully come up first. Likewise, all listeners and remote cartridge factories must be stopped before shutting down the WRB, or else the dependent processes will hang. If they do hang, either reboot the machine or manually kill the hung processes, depending on your preference and environmental constraints.

NOTE
Be aware that in a multiple-node installation owsctl will need to be run on each node of the installation. Starting the WRB on the primary node does not start the cartridge factories on remote nodes. Also see the documentation or manual pages for owsctl for further details and options.

In the interest of efficiency, we strongly recommend creating shell scripts to automate the startup and shutdown of the WAS, especially in multiple-node installations. Under Unix, it is fairly simple to create a single script that can start up any multiple-node installation by using rlogin to connect to each remote system in turn and to start the appropriate services. Under Windows NT, this may also be accomplished with remote management utilities, although not as easily as under Unix. If rlogin is disabled because of security concerns, telnet can also be used.

A script-based approach to startup and shutdown ensures that a consistent sequence is followed, as well as providing a single administration point if additional nodes are added to the installation or if it is desired that special processes be started on specific nodes. For development installations, it may be worthwhile to implement a "bounce" script that will shut down and restart the WAS in an orderly fashion with a single command, since this sequence must be performed after making configuration changes to the WRB or cartridges. For administrative convenience, it may also be useful to employ more-complex scripts that use rlogin to collect process data from multiple machines and to present it to the administrator in a single output format.

Configuration

After the various components of the Oracle Web Application Server have been installed, and the WRB and administrative listeners started, the next step is configuring and otherwise defining the behavior of the various components of the product. This typically involves two primary steps, both of which can be performed from the administrative listener.

First is setting up some default database accounts, descriptors, and PL/SQL agents, installing the PL/SQL SDK into certain database accounts, and finally installing some demo applications. The accounts and agents are used by the logging service and also provide the ability to browse the database from the administrative listener. To perform these tasks, make sure the WRB and the administrative listener are running and point your browser at the URL http://*host:port*/ows-abin/boot, where *host* is the host name of the machine and *port* is the TCP port on which the administrative listener is running. A page such as that shown in Figure 3-1 will be displayed. Note that you will need to specify the database against which this setup process

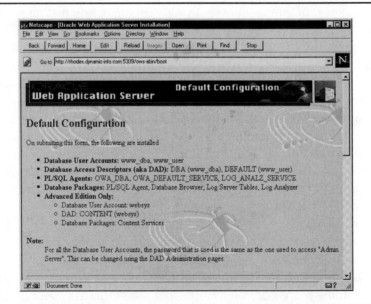

FIGURE 3-1.   *The default configuration page*

will run. If the database is on a different machine than the listener, you will need a SQL*Net connect string as well as the DBA username and password for the database. If the database is local to the listener, only the database SID is necessary. If you do not know what a SID is, you probably just performed a default database install, in which case the SID is most likely ORCL. Note that it may take several minutes for everything to get installed.

The next step is creating (if necessary) and configuring the general purpose HTTP listener(s) appropriately. If using the bundled listener, this is accomplished by going to the listener administration page, shown in Figure 3-2, and using the Create Listener button or the Configure link to configure the listener. If you choose to create a listener, you will need to specify the name of the listener for administrative purposes, the port on which it should listen, the name of the host (for example, www.foobar.com), the root document directory, and, under Unix, the user and group IDs under which the listener should run. The user must be root if using a listening port below 1024. After creating the listener, you can modify it by following the Configure link for the listener. The onscreen help

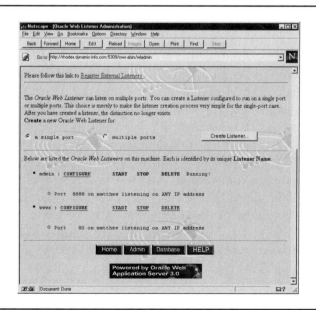

FIGURE 3-2. *The listener administration page*

provided for most of the parameters is more than adequate to describe the configuration options for the listener, so we will not rehash the topic.

This covers the basics. The WRB and HTTP listener(s) should be recycled (shut down and restarted) for configuration changes to be applied. There are, as you might guess, some additional configuration steps that can be performed, such as further configuration of the WRB and of some of the WRB cartridges. Additional configuration information about many of the components can be found in the chapters dealing with the specific cartridge and in Chapter 10, which focuses on the WRB.

CAUTION
One configuration "gotcha" to avoid: When mapping directories and virtual directories for the HTTP listener and the WRB, there is a difference. The HTTP listener expects virtual and file-system directory names to end with a slash (Unix) or a backslash (NT). The WRB expects that they will not end with a slash or a backslash.

Configuration for Multiple Virtual Hosts

It is common, especially for Internet service providers, to have a single machine act as web server for multiple virtual hosts. These may be run either on the same port or on different ports, and they can all share the same IP address. However, the WAS is able to distinguish between requests for each of the virtual hosts by reading a HOST header field from the HTTP request sent by the browser. To configure the listener to use multiple hosts, go to the Addresses and Ports section of the listener configuration page. Specify the names of the different hosts in the Host field and the base directory for each host in the Base Directory field, as shown in Figure 3-3. The appropriate base directory will be prefixed to every URL that arrives, based on the virtual host to which the request was made. Using the settings in Figure 3-3 as an example, if the base directory specified in the Directory Mappings section is /foo/, then the URL http://rhodes.dynamic-info.com/myfile.html will return the file found in /foo/rhodes/myfile.html on the file system.

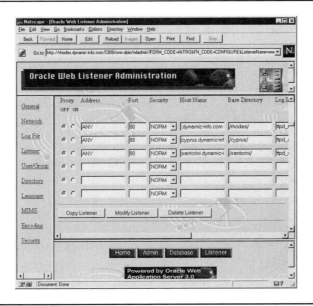

FIGURE 3-3. *Configuration for multiple virtual hosts*

NOTE
*When configuring for multiple hosts, it will
also be necessary to appropriately configure
the virtual directory mappings used by the
Web Request Broker—namely, by adding the
appropriate base directory for the virtual host
to the WRB's mapped virtual directory name.
For instance, in the example above, the virtual
directory mapping for /scott/plsql would need
to be changed to /rhodes/scott/plsql to access
the PL/SQL cartridge using the scott PL/SQL
agent. Of course, if one wanted to use a PL/SQL
agent named rhodes in this case, one could
simply have the WRB virtual directory be
/rhodes/plsql. In this case, the URL sent by the
browser to access the PL/SQL cartridge would
not need to include the PL/SQL agent name.*

Polishing the Installation

At this point, you should have a fully operational installation of the Web Application Server. However, there are still some last bits that should be performed to truly complete the installation of the WAS. These steps are not strictly required, but they add some finishing touches that may be needed for the most effective operation of your environment.

Installing Oracle Enterprise Manager Support

The Web Application Server supports some level of administration via the Oracle Enterprise Manager, version 1.3.5 and above. This requires that the Web Application Server installation be running with version 7.3.3 or higher of the Oracle RDBMS on either the single or the primary node. Also be aware that the administrative listener must be running to use Oracle Web Server Manager from within the Enterprise Manager console. Given that, you may decide not to bother with it. However, if you decide to do so, run the script owsem.sh as the Oracle user, then **su** to root and run the script update_oratab.sh. Both these scripts are found in the install directory inside ORAWEB_HOME.

Customizing the OWA_INIT PL/SQL Package

If you are planning to develop web-accessible PL/SQL components that will be tapped through the PL/SQL cartridge, there are a couple of modifications to the OWA_INIT package that may be necessary.

The first of these modifications is necessary if you plan to use the OWA_COOKIE package to send HTTP cookies to clients for the purpose of creating a stateful application. Cookies can have an expiration date and time associated with them, which is specified in Greenwich Mean Time (GMT). If your system is not set with GMT, but instead with a local time, you will need to modify the OWA_INIT package specification. The specification is found in $ORAWEB_HOME/admin/pubinit.sql. Actually, if you are using Pacific Standard Time, you will not need to modify the file, as that is the default setting. Otherwise, you will need to set the DBMS_SERVER_TIMEZONE package constant to a time zone supported by the SQL *new_time* function, such as CDT, EST, or NST. (A complete list is given in the *SQL Language Reference Manual* under the *new_time* function.) If the system's clock is not set to a supported time zone, you will need to specify the actual number of hours ahead or behind GMT in the constant dbms_server_gmtdiff. This value can be fractional, so as to support local timekeeping, which is a fraction of an hour offset from GMT (handy for those in India, Iran, and parts of Australasia!). The following example shows how to use this feature as necessary. Note the use of fractional offsets.

```
--Configuration for server in Tehran, Iran
dbms_server_gmtdiff = 3.5;
dbms_server_timezone = null;
--Configuration for Minneapolis in Winter
--(maybe better to be in Tehran!)
dbms_server_gmtdiff = null;
dbms_server_timezone = "CST";
```

The other customization is necessary only if you wish to take advantage of the new feature available in WAS version 3.0 that allows the PL/SQL cartridge to use a custom PL/SQL routine for performing authentication. Note that this is different than using the Oracle Basic security scheme, in that Oracle Basic checks for username and password in the Oracle data dictionary, while this feature allows validation of users by executing user-written PL/SQL code. Chapter 9 contains information about using this feature in the section titled "Custom Authentication Using the OWA_SEC Package."

If you modify the OWA_INIT package prior to installing the default DADs and PL/SQL agents, your changes will take effect on installation. Otherwise, you will need to recompile the packages using SQL*Plus or Server Manager into any schemas that had the unmodified packages installed.

Multiple-Node Installations

As stated earlier in this chapter, it is possible to install and configure the Web Application Server components across multiple machines. Doing this enables administrators to improve the performance and possibly also the security of their Web Application Server deployment platform. There are several variations possible in implementing the Web Application Server processes across multiple platforms. The most common installation would be running a single primary node with the core WRB processes as well as the HTTP listener, and then running one or remote nodes (which will actually run the WRB's cartridge factory and the cartridge instances). Figure 3-4 shows where the processes would be running in such a configuration.

An alternate installation would be to create at least three nodes such that one node runs only the HTTP listener, another is the primary WRB node, and one or more systems run as remote nodes. In this case, you would use the installer to install two primary nodes. You would then change the *OMN_ADDR* environment variable on the machine running only the HTTP listener to point to the machine running the WRB (and thus the ORB) processes. As mentioned earlier, you will need to start the WRB node first, followed by the cartridge factory nodes and the listener node. Figure 3-5 illustrates a more sophisticated configuration.

One special type of process distribution may be necessary for some implementations, as illustrated in Figure 3-5, that have two of the remote nodes also running a wrbahsrv process. This relates to authentication services. The Oracle Basic authentication scheme is used to check usernames and passwords against an Oracle database. Because this involves some database accesses to verify the behavior, authentication

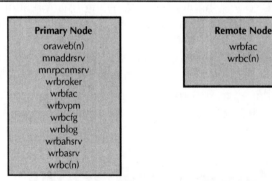

FIGURE 3-4. *Garden-variety multiple-node installation*

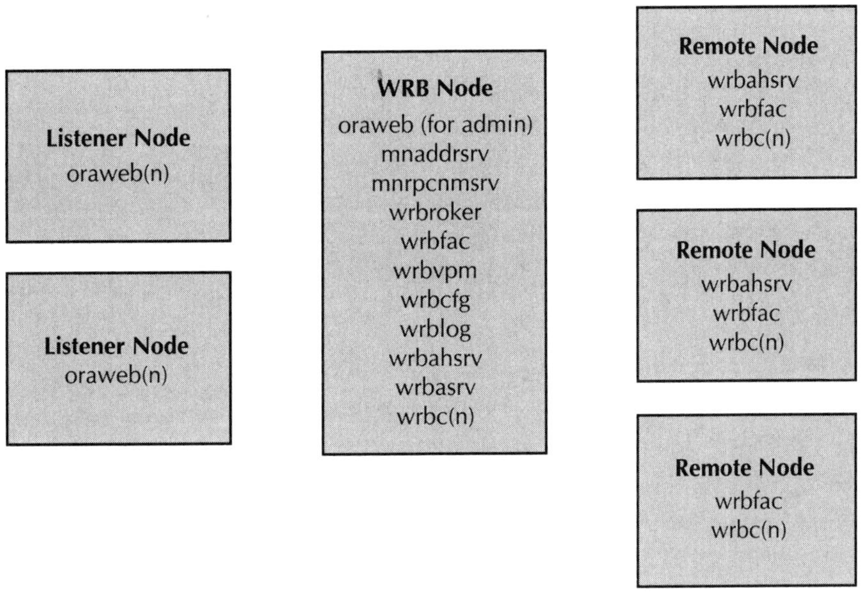

		Remote Node wrbahsrv wrbfac wrbc(n)
Listener Node oraweb(n)	**WRB Node** oraweb (for admin) mnaddrsrv mnrpcnmsrv wrbroker wrbfac wrbvpm wrbcfg wrblog wrbahsrv wrbasrv wrbc(n)	**Remote Node** wrbahsrv wrbfac wrbc(n)
Listener Node oraweb(n)		**Remote Node** wrbfac wrbc(n)

FIGURE 3-5. *Complex multiple-node installation*

in this manner may take an extra fraction of a second. In high-volume operations, contention for accessing the Oracle Basic authentication provider could become a bottleneck. To help with this, just run multiple instances of the authentication process. It does not matter on which machine the additional processes are run. The following command line will get things going:

```
%owsctl start -p wrbahsrv
```

In some larger enterprises, it may be desirable to be running several multiple-node installations of Web Application Server, possibly in a sort of "server farm" environment. If all these installations are on servers that are part of the same network segment, it would be wise to switch the UDP port for each group of nodes. Otherwise, other ORBs will pick up the multicasted UDP signals and waste time filtering them, based on the lists of valid hosts.

NOTE
Because all nodes of a multiple-node installation are governed by the same configuration parameters, make sure that the environment on each is relevantly similar. This would mean things such as using identical aliases to Oracle instances in the TNS (Transparent Network Substrate, Oracle's networking system). If a particular node running the PL/SQL cartridge did not have already defined a certain database alias that is used in a DAD, PL/SQL requests routed to that node would fail. Likewise, if you create Java components that run from the Java package, they, and any supporting .class or .zip files, need to be installed on every node running instances of the Java cartridge.

Troubleshooting

Despite careful planning and a seemingly straightforward installation, you may find that the WAS is simply not working at all. Before getting on the phone to WorldWide Support to claim that you should be assigned a severity 1 TAR, there are a handful of very common problems that should be checked first.

One problem common to Unix installations is simple file permission errors. Often, the HTTP listener cannot access certain needed files—most commonly, log files. Make certain that the account under which the HTTP listener is running has (at minimum) read-write permissions on the log files, the directories containing log files, and the listener's PID file (svXXXX.pid). All of these files are usually placed in subdirectories of the ORAWEB_SITE directory. In addition, it must have read access on any directories and files to be served by the listener, and must have execute permission on any files that are to be executed as CGI programs. Note that the HTTP listener owner does not need execute permission for the WRB or any cartridges, as it does not directly execute them through the operating system.

Another common permission problem is attempting to run the HTTP listener below port 1024 as a user other than root. The solution to this problem is to reconfigure the HTTP listener to either run as root or to listen on a higher-numbered port. Because TCP port 80 is the well-known port for HTTP, it is typically necessary to run listener as root for an organization's main web site. If a higher-numbered port is to be used, it must be specified explicitly in the URL to access the server. This does not, however, mean the listener needs to be started by someone with root permission, for it sets the user ID that it runs when it starts.

A somewhat uncommon cause of the web listener not starting is the presence of an invalid symbolic link in a directory or subdirectory listed in the directory mapping section of the listener configuration section. If your permissions appear to be fine, this is something to check.

A problem that you may encounter when trying to perform the postinstallation configuration tasks (such as creating certain database accounts and installing demos) is not being able to access the Oracle database. This is most typically caused by an error in the TNS configuration. The solution to this problem depends on your organization's Oracle implementation. An Oracle DBA should be able to sort this issue out quite quickly. Nothing special needs to be done to allow the WAS to access the database: if Server Manager can connect from the machine, WAS will also be able to do so.

Although rarely the case on a new install, an occasional cause of the listener's or WRB's failing to function is configuration parameters in the wrb.app or svXXXX.cfg files that are in some way bad. The problem with these errors is that there is no immediately obvious feedback. These errors tend to crop up only after modifying the configuration in some way. The best advice in this case is to use diff or some other comparison tool against the last-known good version of the file and the current file. If reading through the diff output doesn't help you find the error, replace the bad file with the last-known working version and reapply the updates, but try to start the WAS after every couple of changes. This will narrow down the source of the error quite effectively. Obviously, one implication of this advice is that the wrb.app and svXXXX.cfg files should be backed up prior to making anything but the most trivial changes.

A problem that may occur on heavily loaded machines is that the WRB may start before the ORB services have started. This will typically cause owsctl to hang when starting the WRB. The easiest solution is to increase the period that owsctl waits between starting processes. The default time is two seconds; setting it to five or ten seconds is usually sufficient even for busy machines. But if it can be set to 30 or 40 seconds and the WRB still hangs when starting, the ORB is likely not the problem. The wait time used is controlled by the environment variable *OWSCTL_SLEEP*.

The ORB successfully loading can be further verified by using the mnorbls command, which will be located in either $ORACLE_HOME/bin or $ORAWEB_HOME/bin. It should list at least five entries classified as mnorbsrv, and if the WRB does start up, it should have at least another four entries beginning with "wr". If it does not, odds are there is some sort of problem with the ORB executables. If reinstallation does not fix the problem, simply contact WorldWide Support via the SupportLink web site or the telephone. Don't forget that since the ORB was developed for Oracle Video Server, bugs with the ORB will often be categorized under the Video Server listing before they make it to the Web Application Server listings.

Even though the ORB loaded, it may not be sending requests to one or more remote nodes. The most likely reason for this is that the machines have a different UDP address or port specified than the machine running the ORB. All machines in an installation must have the same setting for the OMN_ADDR environment variable. Under Windows NT, this setting can be accessed in the Windows NT registry under HKEY_LOCAL_MACHINE\Software\ORACLE\MediaNet\OMN_ADDR. In Unix implementations, the setting is stored in a file named .omnaddr in the /ows/admin/ows/$ORAWEB_SITE/wrb/config directory. Double-check to make sure the orphaned node is using the same setting as the node running the WRB.

If none of the above tips help, remember to read the platform-specific release notes—most importantly, the section for known problems and limitations. If you still need to contact Oracle's WorldWide Support, please bear in mind that the WAS is a complex piece of software with a large number of constituent pieces. Troubleshooting extremely unique problems may take a fair amount of legwork both from you *and* the support staff. By going through the above steps, you should be able to help the support staff quickly eliminate certain common errors as likely problems and get both of you focused on finding the *real* problem. Of course, when you call, you must have at hand serial numbers, system profiles, variables that you tried to isolate, and the like.

Recovering from a Bad Installation

It happens to everyone sometime . . . the installation that just goes awry. Maybe nothing is working properly, and it appears there is little hope of getting the application to work. Possibly the flaw was something minor, such as running out of disk space at an inopportune moment. Whatever the case, sometimes an installation needs to be rolled back. If possible, it is preferable to use the Oracle Installer to remove the installed components, because it will have mapped which files in which subdirectories made up the installation. However, there may be other files that need to be removed, or the installation may have gone so hopelessly amiss that the Installer cannot even make enough sense of it to perform a proper deinstallation.

Under Unix, tidying up after an uninstall is usually a fairly painless task of simply removing the contents of the /ows directory inside ORACLE_HOME. A "rmdir –r ows" command pretty much restores the system to a preinstall condition, with the exception of some files that should have been removed by the Oracle Installer. If not deinstalled, there is no cause for worry; typically, they can be left alone, as the next install will determine whether they should be overwritten.

For Windows NT installations, however, the process is somewhat more tedious—but let us avoid contemplating the irony of this. During the installation and configuration process, a number of Windows NT registry entries are created, including those used for registering certain components as services as well as setting environment information. The services entries can be found and removed using the Registry Editor application, regedt32, and going to the section HKEY_LOCAL_MACHINE\System\CurrentControlSet. In this section, remove any entries beginning with "OracleWWW," "OraWeb," or "OraMediaNet." Note that remote nodes will most likely only have a single such entry, OraWeb_WRBFAC, so you can be assured the missing services are not the cause of the problems you may have had. Additionally, several entries are made in the registry under HKEY_LOCAL_MACHINE\ Software\ORACLE; these too should be removed. These are ows30, ows30_adpcfg, oraweb_home, oraweb_site, and MediaNet. Again, only *some* of these may be present on remote nodes.

Check the release notes for any additional guidelines governing manual deinstallation. After cleaning up the abortive installation, it may be wise to start over entirely and double-check your installation plan.

Cartridge Installation and Configuration

As mentioned earlier, much of the real power of the Oracle Web Application Server comes from cartridges whose functionality is accessed via the Web Request Broker. Some of these cartridges are provided by Oracle, such as the Java and PL/SQL cartridges, while others may be written by third parties or custom developed.

Configuration of the Oracle-bundled PL/SQL, Java, ODBC, and LiveHTML cartridges is described in the chapter pertaining to the particular cartridge. Most third-party cartridges will have specific installation instructions as well. For details on installing custom-developed cartridges, refer to the "Configuring the WRB to Use the Cartridge" section of Chapter 11.

Ongoing Administration Tasks

Given the fairly clean design of the Web Application Server, ongoing administration of it is quite straightforward—especially if the administrator takes the time to create some shell scripts to automate certain processes. Typically these scripts will assist in managing archiving and otherwise processing log files, monitoring usage levels, and performing other common tasks.

Administrative Road Map

The WAS, as you know by now, is a highly configurable piece of software, and the administrative listener provides access and control to all its settings. Some users find this confusing, because it is not always clear which page to use to modify which type of functionality. To help with this, Figure 3-6 shows the flow of the pages of administrative listener and which pages are used to configure which aspects of the WAS. Be aware that most screens have a toolbar that allows for quick navigation to other sections of the administration pages, although those links have been omitted from the diagram for clarity.

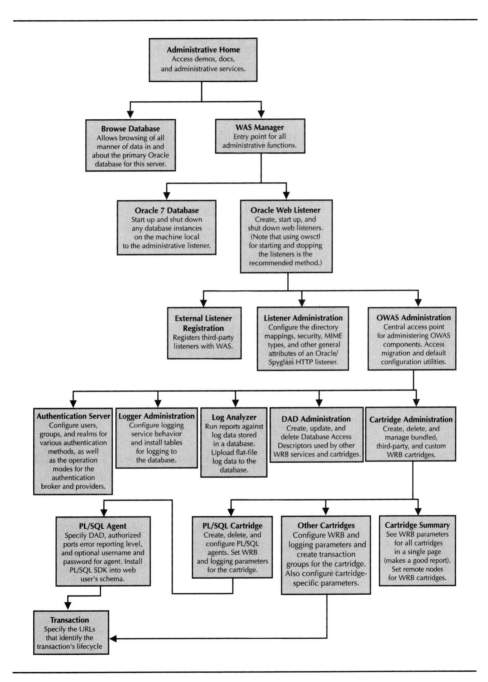

FIGURE 3-6. *Map of administration listener pages*

Performance Considerations

The Web Application Server is a fairly efficient system that operates surprisingly well, even with modest resources. There are a few fairly simple steps that are easily forgotten but that measurably improve system performance.

One of the simplest things to forget is changing the minimum and maximum number of cartridge instances from the default. The default minimum is zero, which means that potentially every request will require the creation of a new wrbc process for the cartridge to handle the request. (In reality, it is usually a few seconds before a wrbc process terminates, during which time it can handle a new request.) Obviously, this would result in less than optimal performance; in fact, it would mean going through basically the same steps as CGI invocation. Thus, the first thing that should be changed is the minimum number of cartridge instances to be running for cartridges to be used. If you never plan to run Perl programs, naturally there is no need to prespawn instances of the Perl cartridge; better, you might simply choose to remove it.

A good rule of thumb for selecting a minimum and maximum number of cartridge instances is to estimate the peak number of concurrent requests that will be handled by a type of cartridge. Set the minimum number of cartridge instances to at least 60 percent of the peak number, and the maximum to 125 percent of the peak value. Of course, this plan must be balanced against memory considerations. If the machine is operating on tight memory constraints, all these active processes may result in excessive memory paging, which will negatively impact performance. Oracle recommends that when all cartridge instances are running, no more than 75 percent of available swap space is being consumed.

Some special considerations should be taken into account for the PL/SQL cartridge. When a PL/SQL cartridge instance begins running, it attempts to connect to every database used by any configured agent. For installations with a large number of defined agents, this can take a significant time hit—especially when the user is staring at his or her browser, waiting for a response. The two ways to address this issue are to increase the minimum number of cartridge instances to 100 percent or more of the estimated peak load, or to partition the agents among multiple unique cartridges. This can be accomplished by manually creating a new cartridge type that is identical to the PLSQL cartridge, but for its name. This cartridge will need to be administered more or less manually, because the special administration pages for the PL/SQL cartridge are hard-coded to reference the cartridge named PL/SQL.

An easy thing to do under Windows NT to improve performance is to make some simple system changes. Under the Performance tab of the System control panel item is a slider for the performance boost given to foreground applications. It should be set to "none" for any NT server that only acts as a server. There is no reason to give any scheduling preference to any desktop applications like the Windows Explorer. By the same token, make sure that there are no "useless" services running on the system. The best way to accomplish this is to install onto a system that has had a fresh operating system installation.

Occasionally, simple disk contention can slow down a web server substantially, especially under load. If possible, keep the log files and the content being served on different physical disks. Because every request will be at least minimally logged, this spreading takes the best advantage of that asynchronous disk access that most hardware provides. On the subject of logging, for production systems, set the threshold severity of errors to log to 1, which will log only serious errors and fatal errors in the WAS program components. See Chapter 10 for additional information about the logging service.

If using the HTTP listener bundled with the WAS, some other things can be done to boost performance. The first is to turn DNS resolution to NEVER, unless it really is needed (which is rarely the case). If reverse DNS lookups are desired for log analysis but not needed for actual run-time services, it would be wise to run a script against the log file that performs the DNS lookups and adds them to the log file. Another performance option is to set the directory rescan interval to a relatively high value. This is the interval at which the HTTP listener will reload the directory listings and "notice" new or changed files (it caches files it has sent once). On most production sites, it is safe to set this value to 3,600 seconds (one hour) or even 86,400 seconds (one day). Obviously, during development of your application, it is best to leave this at zero, so that changes are immediately seen. Both these settings are changed from the listener configuration form. These tips can usually also be applied to other HTTP listeners, although the settings may be differently named.

Related to the issue of directory rescan intervals is the fact that the HTTP listener performs better if there are fewer files in more directories—rather than many files in a single directory. This is a function of the data structures used to keep track of the internal file cache. We typically recommend not more than 100 or so files per directory, just for ease of management and maintenance. But be advised that performance degradation is not visible until substantially more files are present in a directory.

For Unix installations, it is important to tune certain other operating system parameters. Some of these include setting the HTTP listener's processes to have the maximum possible number of file descriptors (usually 1,024), setting the maximum process count for the owner of the WRB and listener processes to the maximum (at least 512), and fine-tuning the TCP/IP parameters for the system.

Beyond these points, the Web Application Server is just another server application—albeit more complex than a mail server but simpler than the Oracle RDBMS. Most typically, the same operating system–specific techniques for tuning any server program for maximum performance will work equally well for getting the most out of the WAS. Happy serving!

Conclusion

At this point, you should have an installed and configured Web Application Server running. Now is the time to start seeing what the WAS is all about: developing and deploying networked applications. The remainder of this book, with the exception of Chapter 9 (on security) and Chapter 12 (which covers Oracle's strategic web direction), is all about application development with the various parts of the WAS.

CHAPTER

4

Web Application Server Development and the PL/SQL SDK

ne of the most significant aspects of the Oracle Web Application Server is the ability it gives developers to create server-side applications using PL/SQL. Given that PL/SQL is an inherently database-aware language, the benefits to developers should be immediately obvious. By developing web applications using PL/SQL, a single language can be used for database access and HTML page generation. This, in turn, can streamline web development in several ways, including requiring fewer source files and reducing integration issues.

Of course, there are many other development languages which the Oracle Web Application Server supports, and these are discussed in varying levels of detail in following chapters. However, this book provides more in-depth discussion of procedural development in PL/SQL and using the Web Application Server SDK's supporting packages for two reasons. First, because it is the technology which is supported in all versions of WebServer and Web Application Server, including version 1.0, which is provided as part of Oracle Universal Server version 7.3. Second, a large number of books have been written about Java and Perl, both of which are supported by Web Application Server 3.0.

Even for those who do not plan to use PL/SQL-stored procedures as the primary means of developing Oracle Web Application Server applications, this chapter is important because it describes the architecture and many data structures and methods which have strong correlates provided for use with other supported languages.

Calling Architecture and the Invocation Process

Before examining how to use PL/SQL and the Oracle Web Application Server SDK to create web applications, it is both necessary and worthwhile to understand how stored procedures are used to generate web pages. The process of invoking stored procedures requires the cooperation of several pieces of the Oracle Web Application Server. Figure 4-1 shows the process by which PL/SQL-stored procedures are invoked to generate web pages. The following narrative may explain it more clearly:

1. The web browser makes a request for a specific URL to the web server.

2. The web server translates the URL request and detects that it is intended to be serviced by the PL/SQL cartridge (based on the directories and paths section of the WRB configuration). The web listener forwards a request to the PL/SQL cartridge using the ORB.

3. The PL/SQL cartridge then also examines the URL to determine which resource (i.e. PL/SQL procedure) is being requested. It also determines the PL/SQL Agent which is to be used for the request. Additionally, it extracts the name/value pairs of parameters passed to it, which are used in the next step.

4. The PL/SQL cartridge next queries the data dictionary of the database specified by the PL/SQL Agent's DAD and determines if a stored procedure or package exists with the name requested and with the same number and names of parameters passed to the WRB originally.

5. If the cartridge finds exactly one appropriate procedure in the schema of interest, it will invoke the stored procedure, passing in parameters as described shortly.

6. As the procedure executes, it writes HTML (or more generally, any valid response) by using the member methods of the HTP package, which are discussed in detail later in this chapter. This data is written into a temporary table in the schema.

7. After the procedure completes execution, the cartridge then calls another PL/SQL-stored procedure which extracts the response data from the schema that was temporarily written in step 6.

8. This response information is passed back to the ORB.

9. In turn, the ORB sends the response back to the HTTP listener, which finally transmits the response to the requesting user agent.

Although much of this process is transparent to the developer, and does not affect the application development, it is important to discuss in more detail how the PL/SQL cartridge determines what stored procedure to call to service a request, and how the passing of parameters to stored procedures is managed. Occasionally, the request failure is caused by a failure to identify a stored procedure to execute, or by an errant parameter passing.

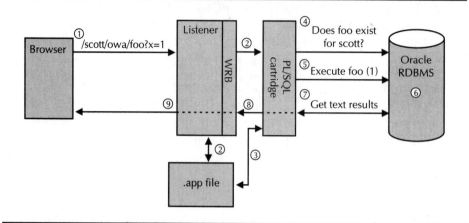

FIGURE 4-1. *Process of invoking a PL/SQL procedure with Web Application Server*

Configuring Directory Mappings for PL/SQL Execution

The second step in the invocation process described previously involves the Web Application Server determining that the URL requested is to be interpreted as requesting the execution of a PL/SQL procedure. As noted, this is accomplished by the WAS consulting its configuration settings. Obviously, for this process to work correctly, the developer or administrator must correctly configure the virtual directory mappings.

There are two ways in which PL/SQL procedures can be invoked via the Web Application Server. The first is by use of the standard CGI calling mechanism. The second is, by way of the PL/SQL cartridge, managed by the Web Request Broker (WRB). Based on the discussions in Chapters 2 and 3, it should be apparent that the WRB is preferable on performance grounds. However, it may be necessary or desirable to invoke the procedures via CGI, possibly to troubleshoot the cartridge or WRB configuration.

NOTE
In both the CGI and WRB calling methods, the virtual path also specifies the PL/SQL Agent to be used.

Regardless of the invocation method to be used, there are some initial steps which must be performed first. These involve the creation and configuration of a Database Access Descriptor (DAD) and a PL/SQL Agent. A DAD defines a database schema which can be used by any WRB cartridge. A PL/SQL Agent specifies a DAD to use for the connection, as well as additional configuration parameters specific to the PL/SQL cartridge.

To create a DAD, access the DAD Administration page from the Web Application Server Administration page. The prompts are reasonably straightforward. You may need a Database Administrator (DBA) if you choose to create a new user to be used for development.

After creating the DAD, you can create a PL/SQL Agent associated with the DAD. PL/SQL Agents are managed as part of the PL/SQL cartridge, and are accessed from its configuration page. Figure 4-2 shows an Agent being configured. If the Agent is using a DAD for a new schema or one which has not had the WAS PL/SQL SDK installed, click the checkbox for installing the packages of the SDK. Note that installing the packages may take several minutes of server processing after submitting the form.

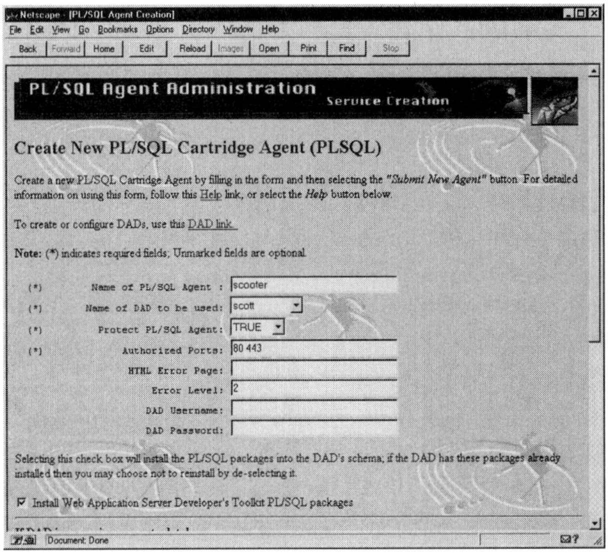

FIGURE 4-2. *Creating and Configuring a PL/SQL Agent*

The configuration parameters of the Agent control much of the run-time behavior when the PL/SQL cartridge is invoked. The Error Level parameter defines the descriptiveness of error messages sent back to the browser if an invocation error occurs. Setting the value to 2 provides maximum reporting, while setting it to 0 simply returns the HTML Error Page that is specified. (Setting it to 1 provides minimal diagnostics.) If the DAD username and password are not specified, the user will be prompted by his or her browser for a valid username password for the database to which the DAD connects. Otherwise, the PL/SQL cartridge will use the username and password specified in the Agent configuration when connecting to the database.

Having created the DAD and the PL/SQL Agent, the Web Application Server can be configured to invoke stored PL/SQL procedures using either the CGI calling mechanism or the PL/SQL cartridge.

NOTE
In versions prior to WAS 3.0, the settings of both the PL/SQL Agent and DAD were rolled into a DCD (Database Connection Descriptor). For purposes of discussing configuration settings for CGI and WRB invocation next, treat references to the PL/SQL Agent and agent_name as DCD and dcd_name, respectively.

Configuration for CGI Invocation

PL/SQL procedures invoked via the CGI mechanism are managed by the Oracle Web Agent CGI script, found in the ORAWEB_HOME/bin/ directory. Because this is simply a standard CGI program (and can in fact be used with almost any CGI-compliant server), the configuration is managed at the web listener level.

To set up a virtual directory, go to the configuration page for the listener and then to the Directory Mapping section, as shown in Figure 4-3. Adding a new virtual path for PL/SQL invocation is as easy as adding another line item to this list. In the default installation, there should be a line item for the virtual directory /ows-bin/. The easiest thing to do is to copy the File System directory for this mapping into a blank line. Then set the Flag to CN, which indicates that URLs should be interpreted nonrecursively and

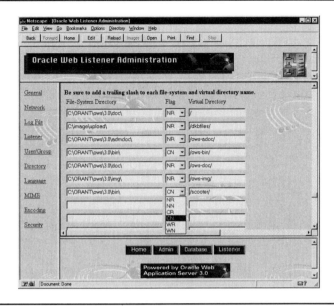

FIGURE 4-3.   *Adding a Virtual Directory Mapping for CGI Invocation*

that the contents of the directory are to be executed via the CGI mechanism, rather than simply read and returned, as would be the case with HTML or image files.

In the virtual directory field of the line item, you should enter **/agent_name/** where agent_name is the name of the PL/SQL Agent to be used. You may prefix any additional virtual parent directories to this string, but you must not suffix the Agent name with any virtual subdirectories. The leading and trailing slashes in the virtual directory name are both significant and required.

To then invoke the CGI script, direct the browser to a URL of the form http://host:port/agent_name/owa/proc. The name of the binary executable for CGI invocation is owa.

Configuration for Cartridge Invocation

As mentioned, cartridge invocation of PL/SQL procedures offers performance improvements compared to CGI. The most immediate being a convenience feature added in version 3.0 of WAS. Upon creation of a

PL/SQL agent, OWAS automatically adds a mapping for the virtual directory /agent_name/plsql to the PL/SQL cartridge. To invoke a PL/SQL procedure using the cartridge simply requires pointing your browser at http://host:port/agent_name/plsql/proc. If it is desirable to add other directory mappings, that can be done from within the WRB parameter configuration page for the PL/SQL cartridge, by updating the Virtual Paths section. As with the CGI configuration, the easiest way to configure is to copy the value of the Physical Path field for this entry into a new, empty line item. Then specify the virtual path to be used. In this case, the virtual path must take the form of /agent_name/anything, where agent_name again is the name of the PL/SQL Agent which specifies the DAD to be used for fulfilling requests, and "anything" refers to any non-null string.

This should not be interpreted to mean, however, that this string can be omitted. It must be present. The PL/SQL cartridge is hard-coded to parse the URL and use the name of the second-rightmost parent directory in the virtual path as the name of the PL/SQL Agent. In addition, please notice that the trailing slash in the virtual path must be omitted, in contrast with the configuration for CGI.

NOTE
Make sure the Agent which will be used is configured to be invoked through the port on which the listener is active. This is accomplished by correctly setting the Authorized Ports field in the Agent configuration screen.

Identifying the Procedure to Invoke and Its Parameters

The PL/SQL cartridge can invoke both stand-alone procedures as well as procedures that are part of a PL/SQL package. Note that it cannot invoke functions because it is not possible to pass a result back to the PL/SQL agent. If the leaf of the URL (that is, the script name) contains a period, such as in epkg.add_emp, the PL/SQL cartridge will first look to see if the package EPKG exists and then to see if it has *add_emp* as a public procedure. A procedure is public if it is defined in the package specification and the package body specification. If it is defined only in the package body, it is private, and can be invoked only by other functions or procedures in the package.

If no period is present in the script name, the cartridge looks for a stored procedure with the appropriate name. In either case, it also gathers the list of parameters provided either at the end of the URL (after the question mark), or, in the case of a POST request, it examines the parameter name/value pairs which make up the request body. It then compares this list of parameters to the parameters of the procedures, or to procedures with the correct name.

One thing to remember about this process is that PL/SQL is polymorphic, meaning several procedures can share the same name, but are differentiated by their parameter lists. This is why the cartridge may find multiple procedures with the same name. The PL/SQL cartridge recognizes and takes advantage of PL/SQL's polymorphic capabilities. Consider a schema which has two procedures with the same name but with different parameters, for example:

```
PROCEDURE add_emp(ename IN VARCHAR2, sal IN NUMBER);
PROCEDURE add_emp(ename IN VARCHAR2, wage IN NUMBER);
```

In this case, if the PL/SQL cartridge is invoked and the add_emp resource is requested, and the parameter names passed in are ename and sal, the first procedure will be invoked. If ename and wage are passed, the second procedure will be invoked. Finally, if the parameters were any other combination, an error would result because the PL/SQL cartridge would not find an appropriate stored procedure to invoke.

Note that if a stored procedure's parameters are declared with defaults, the cartridge can invoke the procedure even if not all parameters are specified. Consider the following procedure declaration which will extract the nth root of a number passed to the procedure and generate an HTML page with the following result:

```
PROCEDURE extract_root(val IN NUMBER, n IN NUMBER:=2);
```

This method will be invoked if val and n are both passed to the cartridge. However, it will also be invoked if only val is passed. In the latter case, the procedure will be invoked with n set to its default value of two, thus returning val's square root. Using defaulted parameters is a great way for developers to use a single processing routine to handle requests from multiple forms, such as a simple version of a search form and a complex version of the form. The only difference in invocation may be that additional options are presented to the user in the complex form that can simply be defaulted in the simple form.

After the PL/SQL cartridge has identified a stored procedure to execute, it manages converting parameters into their correct form. There are two components to this process. First it attempts to cast, or convert, the character string input from the browser's request into the appropriate datatype. Because of this, a procedure can be declared with parameters other than CHAR or VARCHAR2, which makes the declarations more clear and enables the developer to avoid providing code to convert the data.

NOTE

Although this seems like a labor saver at first blush, it is wise to bypass this step by declaring all parameters as type VARCHAR2. The reason for this is that if a parameter passed by the browser is not convertible into the correct datatype, the request will fail and the generic "Request Failed" page will be returned. The developer has no chance to return a meaningful error message to the user, such as "Salary must be a number." This results in a bad application from a user-experience perspective.

Special Cases of Parameter Handling

In addition to basic parameter conversion, the PL/SQL agent also engages in some special processing to accommodate two situations. The first is where multiple name/value pairs are sent by the browser with the same name. That is, when there are multiple data for a single parameter, such as when a list box is able to accept multiple inputs, or similarly, when multiple form elements (most commonly checkboxes) share the same name. When a situation of this nature occurs, the PL/SQL cartridge populates an array (a PL/SQL table, strictly speaking) with one element (row) for each value with the given name association. The PL/SQL table which is populated is of type *owa_util.ident_arr*, a datatype defined in the OWA_UTIL package.

Accommodating this sort of input requires the developer to do two things. First, since a PL/SQL table cannot be defaulted to NULL, there is a potential snag. What if the user doesn't check any checkboxes or select any items from a multiselection list? With no default value, the PL/SQL agent will not be able to find and invoke the procedure correctly. One of two things must be done. The Oracle Web Application Server documentation suggests placing a hidden field on the form that will be submitted with the same name as the multiple selection items. In this case, the HTML fragment might look like this:

```
<input type="hidden" name="vals_in"
value="dummy_value_to_be_ignored">
<input type="checkbox" name="vals_in" value="tr">Trains
<input type="checkbox" name="vals_in" value="bo">Boats
<input type="checkbox" name="vals_in" value="pl">Planes
```

Even if the user checks none of the boxes, vals_in will still be populated with at least the single value, "dummy_value_to_be_ignored". However, always having to insert the placeholder is tedious. Fortunately, there is a more convenient solution. Although a PL/SQL table cannot be defaulted to NULL, it can be defaulted to an empty table. In the OWSH_UTIL package, a collection of utilities provided on the CD-ROM, a package variable, *empty_ident_arr*, is defined which is exactly that—an empty instance of *owa_util.ident_arr*. If the OWSH_UTIL package is installed, any parameter of type *owa_util.ident_arr* can be defaulted to *owsh_util.empty_ident_arr*.

The second issue is extracting the contents of the array. Because PL/SQL versions prior to 2.3 have no method for returning the number of elements in the array, it makes looping through the elements a little tricky. A basic loop must be used, and the table index manually incremented. However, attempting to reference a nonexistent element of a PL/SQL table will result in a no_data_found exception. The key is to isolate the looping construct inside its own block with its own exception handler. The following procedure demonstrates how to put these techniques together to work effectively work with multivalued input through PL/SQL tables:

```
CREATE PROCEDURE multi
        (vals_in INowa_util.ident_arr:=owsh_util.empty_ident_arr)
IS
  counter  INTEGER:=1;  --initialize the counter
BEGIN
  htp.olistOpen;
  --isolate the data extraction loop inside its own block
  BEGIN
    LOOP
      --extract the item from the table element
      htp.listItem(htf.bold(vals_in(counter)));
      counter:=counter+1;
    END LOOP;
    --trap the exception which occurs naturally when there are
    --no more elements in the table
  EXCEPTION
    WHEN no_data_found THEN NULL;
  END;
  htp.olistClose;
  --the loop index in this case will always be one greater than
  --the number of elements in the table.
  --the owa_util.ite procedure is a shorthand for if..then..else
  --If the first parameter is true, then it returns the value of
  --the second parameter otherwise, it returns the third parameter
  htp.header(1,'vals_in contained '||
      (counter-1) || ' item'||
      owa_util.ite((counter-1)=1,'','s') || '.');
END;
```

Of course, if using PL/SQL version 2.3, this can be cleaned up significantly by using the *COUNT* built-in function, written as <table_name>. *COUNT*, which returns the number of elements in a PL/SQL table. Here is the PL/SQL 2.3-savvy version of the multi procedure:

```
PROCEDURE multi
        (vals_in IN owa_util.ident_arr:=owsh_util.empty_ident_arr)
IS
BEGIN
```

```
htp.olistOpen;
FOR counter IN 1..vals_in.count
LOOP
  htp.listItem(htf.bold(vals_in(counter)));
END LOOP;
htp.olistClose;
htp.header(1,'vals_in contained '|| vals_in.count || ' item'||
           owa_util.ite(vals_in.count=1,'','s') || '.');
END;
```

The second special case for which the agent provides nonstandard parameter conversion is the case of images on forms. Image maps can be used either as submit buttons or as stand-alone image form elements which also submit a form when clicked upon. When a user submits a form using an image, the x and y coordinates at which the user clicked are passed with the request as a pair of variables named *image_name.x* and *image_name.y*. The PL/SQL agent stuffs these two values into a point data structure defined in the OWA_IMAGE package. (See the section "The OWA_IMAGE Package" later in this chapter for more information about this data structure and how to use it.)

Now that we have explained the configuration, specification, and administrative components of getting the Oracle Web Application Server to execute PL/SQL procedures and the process the Web Application Server undertakes when executing the procedures, we can discuss how to create these procedures to generate HTML pages and implement the extended functionality that today's web applications demand.

Using the Web Application Server SDK PL/SQL Packages

The Web Application Server PL/SQL SDK includes a number of component libraries (or packages, in PL/SQL parlance), all of which serve various purposes in the creation of database-integrated web applications. This section provides a brief overview of the collection of libraries and what each library does, including some examples of the basic use of key functions in each library. However, the examples provided here are for pedagogical purposes and are fairly simple. Appendix A provides a complete reference to the procedures and functions contained in the packages.

The HTP and HTF Packages

These packages are the primary libraries used for generating the output for dynamic web pages. HTP is the Hypertext Procedure library and HTF is the Hypertext Function library. They contain the routines which handle many of the details of generating HTML output. The members of the HTP package write the generated HTML into an output buffer. After the PL/SQL procedure executes, the Oracle Web Agent (in either its CGI or cartridge incarnation) extracts the spooled output from the buffer and writes it out to the browser's connection.

On the other hand, the HTF functions return a VARCHAR2 result of the appropriate HTML. This allows HTML fragments to be concatenated or otherwise manipulated prior to writing them to the browser. Aside from this, HTP and HTF member methods with the same name have basically identical behaviors.

The following example illustrates the general usage of the routines in the HTP package. It is a simple "Hello World" type of application. A simple procedure such as this is often useful for verifying configuration of a DAD or PL/SQL Agent.

```
CREATE OR REPLACE PROCEDURE hello_world
IS
BEGIN
  htp.htmlOpen;
  htp.headOpen;
  htp.title('Hello World');
  htp.headClose;
  htp.p('The date is: ' || SYSDATE);
  htp.htmlClose;
END;
```

The HTML text produced as a result of this procedure is

```
<html>
<head>
<title>Hello World</title>
</head>
The date is: 01-JAN-96
</html>
```

In addition to these basic HTML tags, the HTP package provides tags for special formatting, such as bold and italic, and tags for generating HTML forms and embedding hypertext links. In fact, the current HTP libraries will always be updated to contain procedures corresponding to virtually every tag which is part of the HTML standard, as well as many browser-extension tags for browsers such as Netscape Navigator and Internet Explorer. Table 4-1 lists the simplified interfaces of some of the more common HTP procedures used in generating HTML output, as well as the HTML output which they generate.

HTP Procedure	HTML Output
htmlOpen	<html>
htmlClose	</html>
bodyOpen	<body>
bodyClose	</body>
print(*string*)	*string*
bold(*string*)	*string*
para	<p>
br	
center(*string*)	<center>*string*</center>
ulistOpen(*clear,wrap,dingbat,source*)	<ul clear="*clear*" wrap="*wrap*" dingbat="*dingbat*" src="*source*">
listItem(*text,clear,dingbat,source*)	<li clear="*clear*" dingbat="*dingbat*" src="*source*">*text*
ulistClose	</ul>
anchor(*url,string*)	<a href="*url*">*string*</a>
heading(*level,string*)	<h*level*>*string*</h*level*>
formOpen(*action,method*)	<form action="*action*" method="*method*">
formText(*name,size,maxlength,value*)	<input type="*text*" name="*name*" size="*size*" maxlength="*maxlength*" value="*value*">
formSelectOpen(*name,prompt,size*)	*prompt*<select name="*name*" prompt="*prompt*" size="*size*">

TABLE 4-1.   *Some Common HTP Routines and the HTML They Produce*

HTP Procedure	HTML Output
formSelectOption(*value,selected*)	<option *selected*>*value*
formSelectClose	</select>
formSubmit(*name,value*)	<input type="submit" name="*name*" value="*value*">
formClose	</form>

TABLE 4-1. *Some Common HTP Routines and the HTML They Produce (continued)*

NOTE
Appendix A has a complete list of the exact interfaces and behaviors of all the HTP and HTF routines, as well as the other packages in the Web Application Server SDK.

As can be seen from browsing the procedure interfaces, the routines allow parameters for virtually all of the known tag attributes. Sometimes the HTML specification (or common browser implementation) specifies an option for a particular tag attribute, but the HTP routine does not have an explicit parameter for specifying it. However, almost every HTP and HTF procedure which generates a tag has as its final parameter a VARCHAR2 value which is plugged into the tag untouched. This is useful for taking advantage of browser-specific tag options, as well as for dealing with new tag options before the updated HTP packages are available.

An example of using this parameter, always named *cattributes* in formal declarations, can be shown in the enhanced version of the select list <OPTION> tag. The basic version of the <OPTION> tag results in the visible label being submitted as the value associated with the select list's named parameter. For example, the following HTML will result in the dept_in parameter being set to "RESEARCH" when the form is submitted:

```
<select name="dept_in">
<option>ACCOUNTING
<option>OPERATIONS
<option selected>RESEARCH
```

```
<option>SALES
</select>
```

However, this is not very convenient if in fact the database column referred to by dept_in is really a number, serving as a foreign key to another table, as is the case with the deptno column in the Oracle demo EMP table. The HTML standard actually supports an additional option for the <OPTION> tag—the value option. If the <OPTION> tag explicitly specifies an alternate value with the value option, then this explicitly declared value will be submitted. In the following case, although the appearance will be the same to the user, the dept_in parameter will be set to "20" upon the form's submission.

```
<select name="dept_in">
<option value="10">ACCOUNTING
<option value="40">OPERATIONS
<option selected value="20">RESEARCH
<option value="30">SALES
</select>
```

Unfortunately, the standard *htp.selectoption* procedure does not provide a special parameter for setting the value option. However, it is very simple to implement this using the cattributes parameter of the *selectoption* procedure. The following snippet shows how this would be done. Notice the use of associative parameter passing with the => notation. This is very convenient when needing to set only the cattributes parameter, when there are a significant number of other parameters which can simply be defaulted.

```
htp.formSelectOpen('dept_in');
htp.formSelectOption('ACCOUNTING',cattributes=>'10');
htp.formSelectOption('OPERATIONS',cattributes=>'40');
htp.formSelectOption('RESEARCH','SELECTED',cattributes=>'20');
htp.formSelectOption('SALES',cattributes=>'30');
htp.formSelectClose;
```

The following is a more complete example of the packages, which makes use of many of the HTP elements to generate a page. Specifically, it includes an HTML form, hyperlinks, and more sophisticated style control. This example is for an in-room checkout application using a network computer in a hotel room.

```
PROCEDURE checkout (room_in IN VARCHAR2)
IS
  v_guest  VARCHAR2(100);
  v_cost   NUMBER(7,2);
BEGIN
htp.htmlOpen;
  htp.headOpen;
  htp.title('Net Checkout');
  htp.headClose;
  htp.bodyOpen;
    SELECT guestname INTO v_guest FROM guest WHERE room=room_in;
    v_cost := hotel.calc_charges(room_in);
      htp.bold('Hello '|| vGuest || ',');
      htp.para;
      htp.p('Thank you for staying at the '||
            'Hotel Sofitel at Redwood Shores.');
      htp.p('The total cost of your stay is ' ||
            htf.bold(v_cost) || '.');
      htp.p('(See an itemization '||
            htf.anchor('itemize?room_in='||room_in, 'here');
htp.para;
      htp.p('If this is in order, you may check out '||
            'now by specifying payment information.');
      htp.formOpen('hotel.billinfo','POST');
      —store the room number in a hidden field, the called
      —procedure will need it to correctly apply the charges
      htp.formHidden('room_in',room_in);
      htp.tableOpen;
      —specify that the contents of the cells in this row should
      —be aligned in the upper-left corner of the cells
      htp.tableRowOpen('left','top');
      htp.tableData(htf.bold('Credit Card Type'));
      htp.tableData(htf.formRadio('cc_type_in','ae','checked') ||
                    htf.bold('American Express') ||
                    htf.br || htf.formRadio('cc_type_in','vi') ||
                    htf.bold('Visa') || htf.br ||
                    htf.formRadio('cc_type_in','mc') ||
                    htf.bold('MasterCard'));
      htp.tableRowClose;
      htp.tableRowOpen;
      htp.tableData(htf.bold('Credit Card Account'));
      htp.tableData(htf.formText('cc_acct_in','18','18'));
      htp.tableRowClose;
      htp.tableRowOpen;
      htp.tableData(htf.bold('Exp. Date (e.g. 09/98)'));
```

```
        htp.tableData(htf.formText('cc_exmon_in','2','2','09')||
                '/' || htf.formText('cc_exyr_in','2','2','98'));
        htp.tableRowClose;
        htp.tableRowOpen;
        —have the next cell span both rows of the table
        htp.tableData( htf.formCheckbox('send_inv_in','T','checked')
                    || htf.bold ('Mail zero-balance invoice.'),
                    ccolspan=>'2');
        htp.tableRowClose;
        htp.tableRowOpen;
        —if the submit button has a name associated with it, an
        —additional name/value pair will be submitted with
        —the form data; setting the name to NULL will simply
        —set the title of the button without causing an additional
        —name value pair to be submitted
        htp.tableData(  htf.formSubmit(NULL,'Settle Account')||
                    htf.bold ('Mail zero-balance invoice.'),
                    ccolspan=>'2');
        htp.tableRowClose;
        htp.tableClose;
    htp.bodyClose;
htp.htmlClose;
END;
```

The HTP and HTF packages are the foundation of a PL/SQL Web Application Server development, because they provide the ability to write data to the browser. By simply combining the standard PL/SQL implementation with these packages, reasonably sophisticated applications can be developed which generate dynamic pages from the database, as well as manipulate the database contents based on user input. However, to move to the next level of sophistication, the other Web Application Server SDK packages must be used.

The OWA_COOKIE Package

The OWA_COOKIE package provides services for reading and writing HTTP cookies. The purpose of HTTP cookies is to allow persistent state information to be carried across multiple, stateless, HTTP transactions. The cookie mechanism was developed originally by Netscape and has now been standardized as part of the official HTTP version 1.1 draft specification, with slight modifications. All major browsers today support the cookie mechanism, and it offers some benefits to HTTP developers.

What is a Cookie?

A brief description of the manner in which cookies work is in order before describing the basic use of this package. A *cookie* is basically a name/value pair which is associated with a specific domain and, optionally, a particular realm within that domain.

If an application developer wants to set a cookie, a special header, Set-Cookie, is returned with the HTTP response to the browser. This header contains three main pieces of information. First, there is the name of the cookie. This should be a unique name which will later be referenced to get at the cookie in other procedures. Second, a value is needed to be associated with the cookie. This is always a text expression. Third, an expiration value should be provided. The expiration value determines how long the browser will keep track of the cookie's name/value pair.

Suppose you have an online commerce application and wish to use cookies to maintain some state information while the user browses through your catalog and places orders. You want to store a cookie named custno which you can use to reference the user's virtual shopping basket, as well as what items the user browses. However, you don't want the browser to store this information indefinitely (maybe for a week only), so if the customer revisits the site in the next seven days, you will retain the contents of her shopping basket, and she could continue shopping as if she never left the site. But if the customer comes back in eight days, she would need to reregister, or some similar action, to continue shopping. Assuming that the customer arrives at our site on June 3, 1997 and is assigned a customer number of 18323, the server would send the following header in its response:

```
Set-Cookie: custno=18323; expires=Sunday, 10-Jun-97 12:00:00 GMT
```

There are two things to note about the expiration. First, the date specification follows the date format used in almost all Internet protocols, specified by RFC 822. However, the time is given in Greenwich Mean Time, which is the only time zone supported for HTTP cookies (even though RFC 822 allows any time zone to be specified). Second, the expiration is optional; however, a missing expiration means "never expire," rather than "expire at the end of this session." That is, if an expiration value is not specified, the cookie will only persist until the user quits the current browser instance.

NOTE
If your application seems to be misbehaving with respect to time-sensitive cookies, make sure you configured the OWA_INIT package for your time zone, as described in Chapter 3.

If it is desirable to destroy the cookie because the transaction that was using the cookie has either completed or been aborted, for example, the expires parameter is used to accomplish this. By sending a Set-Cookie header with the name of the cookie and with the expires parameter set to some arbitrary date in the past, the cookie will be immediately removed from the browser's cookie list. For example, to eliminate the custno cookie, you could send the following Set-Cookie header:

```
Set-Cookie: custno=18323; expires=Sunday, 01-Jan-90 00:00:01 GMT
```

This Set-Cookie header makes use of the three primary components of a cookie. In addition to these main components, there are three other parts of an HTTP cookie: the cookie's security status, and the path and domain to which the cookie applies. The security status of a cookie determines how and when the cookie is transmitted between client and server, such as encrypted versus cleartext. If a cookie is marked as secure, it will only be transmitted over connections running through a Secure Socket Layer (SSL) protocol.

NOTE
The security setting of the cookie has no effect on the manner in which the cookie is stored on the client machine. Because cookies can persist between multiple sessions, the cookies are typically stored locally in a file. The secure flag does not mean this local value is encrypted (although that would be a nice browser feature). Thus, it is unwise to store things like credit card numbers, passwords, or other information in cookies, because it opens data to compromise on the client machine.

To understand the meaning of the path and domain parameters of a cookie, an understanding of the manner in which cookies are communicated by the web browser is necessary. Just as a server can send a Set-Cookie header to indicate to the browser the name/value pair for a cookie, the browser uses its own header, Cookie, to communicate the value of a cookie to the server. For the custno cookie sent above, the Cookie header the client would send to the server in its request header would look like this:

```
Cookie: custno=18323
```

If multiple cookies should be sent, they are sent using a single Cookie header, delimited by semicolons, rather than as multiple headers. For example:

```
Cookie: custno=18323; product=2323; product=2324
```

Notice that this example also shows that a single cookie name can be associated with several values. You will see in a moment how this is accomplished. First, however, you may wonder how the client knows when to send which cookies. For instance, if our user has our custno cookie, the only web application which needs that information is our electronic store. It would be somewhere between useless and highly undesirable to send that cookie in every HTTP request to every server for the next week.

This is where the domain and path parameters play a role. They control which cookies are sent and with which requests. The domain parameter specifies to which domain or subdomain a request must be directed for the cookie to be sent. For instance, the following Set-Cookie header means that the interest cookie will be sent with any request to any host in the dynamic-info.com domain.

```
Set-Cookie: interest=intranet; expires=Sunday, 31-Dec-1999
23:59:59 GMT; domain=.dynamic-info.com
```

The following cookie is used to auto-detect a user when accessing an example web-based PIM application:

```
Set-Cookie: uid=gcase; expires=Sunday, 31-Dec-1999 23:59:59 GMT;
domain=pim.dynamic-info.com
```

In this case, the uid cookie is sent only to requests directed to the host pim.dynamic-info.com, while the interest cookie is sent to any machine in the dynamic-info.com domain, including pim.dynamic-info.com. Thus, if the previous two Set-Cookie headers were sent to the same browser, and that browser now makes a request to a URL residing on pim.dynamic-info.com, the following header would be sent as part of the request:

```
Cookie: interest=intranet; uid=gcase
```

There are two notes about the security features of the domain parameter, the first of which is that a first-level domain cannot be specified. In other words, setting domain=.com will not result in the cookie being sent to every request to any commercial host in the United States, but rather that it is an invalid cookie, and there is no guarantee it will even be sent in requests to the originating domain. The second security feature is that the domain specified must be a domain of which the sending host is a member. For instance, the host www.dynamic-info.com cannot specify a cookie for use by www.oracle.com. Although such restrictions prevent some very neat possibilities of multiple web sites participating in an information-sharing consortium, they serve a significant security purpose.

The path parameter serves a purpose similar to the domain parameter. It allows the developer to specify that a cookie should only be sent in requests for certain URL paths within a particular domain. This is very useful for developers who have cookies which apply only to certain applications. The manner in which it works is very similar to the domain parameter. For instance, the first of the following Set-Cookie headers instructs the browser to send the cookie to any URL within the domain, while the second specifies that the cookie should be sent only with URL requests in the /hr/owa/ virtual path.

```
Set-Cookie: foo=bar; domain=.foobar.com; path=/
Set-Cookie: foo=widget; domain=.foobar.com; path=/hr/owa/
```

These two examples return us to the example shown earlier, where two cookies with same name were returned in a single Cookie header for a request. Notice that the two Set-Cookie headers above specify the same cookie name, and that the second path (/hr/owa/) is a member of the first path (/). This means that a request made to the second path will send both cookies to the server. For example, a request to /hr/owa/give_raise would have the following Cookie header:

```
Cookie: foo=bar; foo=widget
```

Having thoroughly described the actual manner in which cookies work, the OWA_COOKIE package and its usage are very easy to understand. The package defines procedures for four actions: setting cookies, getting cookies by name, enumerating cookies available, and expiring cookies. It also defines a special datatype, cookie, which is a PL/SQL record defined as follows:

```
type cookie is RECORD
(
   name      varchar2(4096),
   vals      vc_arr,
   num_vals  integer
);
```

Note that vc_arr, an array of VARCHAR2(4096) elements, is used to return the values associated with the named cookie. This is necessary because, as outlined earlier, multiple name/value pairs can exist for the cookie, based on the paths specified. When such a situation occurs, the cookie.vals PL/SQL table is populated with one row per value, and cookie.num_vals contains the number of values associated with the name.

Because the set and expire procedures must write in the header portion of the response, they must be called before any procedures from the HTP package begin to write out the body of the response. This also requires that the developer take responsibility for writing out other header fields (minimally, the content type).

The following procedure demonstrates the basic use of the cookie calls. It uses defaulted parameters to simplify the usage. It is actually even a bit of a twist, because one of three possibilities exists: it can be called with no parameters, called to add a name/value pair as a cookie, or called with a cookie name to delete the cookie. It is included on the CD-ROM in the file cooktest.sql. For a detailed description of the procedures, see Appendix A.

```
CREATE OR REPLACE PROCEDURE cooktest(   name IN VARCHAR2:=NULL,
                                        val IN VARCHAR2:=NULL,
                                        exp IN VARCHAR2:=NULL,
                                        del IN VARCHAR2:='no-del')
      IS
        ck_names   owa_cookie.vc_arr;
        ck_values  owa_cookie.vc_arr;
        ck_count   INTEGER;
```

```
  x   INTEGER;
BEGIN
  --We are responsible for manually setting the mime-type
  -- of the page.
  owa_util.mime_header('text/html',FALSE);
  -- Check to see if a cookie is to be added
  IF name IS NOT NULL
  THEN
    owa_cookie.send(name,val,SYSDATE+exp);
  END IF;
  -- Check to see if a cookie is to be deleted
  IF del !='no-del'
  THEN
    owa_cookie.remove(del,'bye-bye');
  END IF;
  -- We are also responsible for manually closing the header
  owa_util.http_header_close;
  owa_cookie.get_all(ck_names,ck_values,ck_count);
  htp.htmlOpen;
    htp.headOpen;
      htp.title('Cookie Sampler (Yum!)');
    htp.headClose;
    htp.bodyOpen(NULL,'bgcolor="#FFFFFF"');
      IF ck_count != 0
      THEN
        htp.header(2,'Cookie list');
        htp.ps('Cookies sent by Browser '||
               'in ''Cookie: '' request header');
        htp.tableOpen;
        htp.tableRowOpen;
        htp.tableHeader('Name');
        htp.tableHeader('Value');
        htp.tableHeader('');
        htp.tableRowClose;
        FOR x IN 1..ck_count
        LOOP
          htp.tableRowOpen;
          htp.tableData(ck_names(x));
          htp.tableData(ck_values(x));
          htp.tableData(htf.anchor(
                        'cooktest?del='||ck_names(x),'DELETE'));
          htp.tableRowClose;
        END LOOP;
        htp.tableClose;
```

```
      END IF;

      htp.hr;
      htp.header(2,'Add a Cookie');
      htp.formOpen('cooktest');
        htp.bold('Cookie Name: ');
        htp.formText('name',40,80,name);
        htp.para;
        htp.bold('Cookie Value: ');
        htp.formText('val',40,80,val);
        htp.para;
        htp.bold('Expires in: ');
        htp.formSelectOpen('exp');
        -- Note the use of the optional "value" parameter
        -- The values themselves are fractions of days
        htp.p('<option value="7"> 1 Week');
        htp.p('<option value="1" selected> 1 Day');
        htp.p('<option value=".04166667"> 1 Hour');
        htp.p('<option value=".010416667"> 15 Minutes');
        htp.p('<option value=".00069444"> 1 Minute');
        htp.formSelectClose;
        htp.formSubmit(NULL,'Add Cookie');
      htp.formClose;
      htp.hr;
    htp.bodyClose;
  htp.htmlClose;
END;
```

Note that when the application is running, it will seem as if the visual display of information lags behind the actual input. This is because what is being sent back in the cookie list are the cookies which the browser sent in its last request. This means that the first time you add a cookie, the cookie list will return empty. This is because the cookie, which was just added, was not sent to the server in the Cookie header field in the request which instructed the server to send the Set-Cookie response header. Similarly, when a cookie is deleted, it will still appear in the cookie list in the response to the deletion request. Figure 4-4 shows this procedure being used.

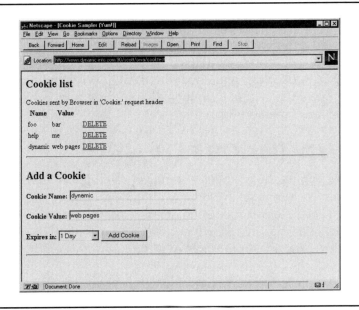

FIGURE 4-4. *Display of cooktest PL/SQL procedure*

NOTE
Many users seem to prefer keeping their browser's cookie notification feature active while browsing the Web. This is fundamentally not a problem; however, if your application is constantly creating, resetting, and deleting cookies, it can make for a very distracting user experience. Although it is tempting to simply ignore these curious or mistrustful users, a better (or at least nicer) strategy may be to only set a single cookie and store the state information in a database table, keyed off of the single cookie's value.

The OWA Package

The OWA package is mentioned here only for completeness. It contains several functions which are used internally to allow the communication between PL/SQL procedures and either the PL/SQL WRB cartridge or the Oracle Web Agent CGI script. Developers should not have occasion to call the OWA package's methods directly.

The OWA_IMAGE Package

The OWA_IMAGE package provides some very simple convenience calls to save developers time when working with images on forms. To explain this process in detail, some explanation of image usage in forms is necessary. Images are defined on forms using the <INPUT> tag with the type parameter set to "image". An example of this tag is as follows:

```
<input type="image" name="var_name" src="/images/button1.jpg">
```

This tag is included as part of a form, and when the user clicks on the image, it causes the form to be submitted to the server. As mentioned earlier, the location of the click will be submitted as two variables. In the case of the tag shown above, the variable *var_name.x* will contain the *x* coordinate of the click, while *var_name.y* contains the *y* coordinate.

Although this is the manner in which the variables are sent to the server by the browser, the PL/SQL agent engages in additional processing before passing the parameters onto the user-written code. Because PL/SQL procedures cannot have periods embedded in them, another way to accommodate the parameter passing is needed. The OWA_IMAGE package defines a datatype called point, which is used to pass these parameters into user code. As mentioned earlier, the PL/SQL agent manages stuffing the *x* and *y* components of the user's click location into the point structure.

The OWA_IMAGE package also contains a couple of convenience calls, get_x and get_y, for extracting the *x* and *y* coordinates. Finally, it defines a *null_point* variable, which developers can use to default parameters of type point. Defaulting these parameters is absolutely necessary if another way to submit the form is available (such as a submit button, or multiple image tags), because no image coordinate information will be sent if the user does not click the image.

The following simple example should make the behavior and functionality of the package more easy to follow. The following HTML code describes a page with a form which, when submitted, triggers the imgtest stored procedure.

```
<html>
<head><title>Form Image Test</title></head>
<body>
<form action="/dcd/owa/imgtest" method=GET>
<input type="image" name="point_in" SRC="/images/bigicon.gif">
</form>
</body>
</html>
```

The imgtest procedure itself is trivial and simply returns the x and y coordinates of the point where the user clicked the image.

```
PROCEDURE imgtest (point_in IN
OWA_IMAGE.POINT:=OWA_IMAGE.NULL_POINT)
IS
BEGIN
  htp.htmlOpen;
    htp.headOpen;
      htp.title('Image Form Submit Example Result');
    htp.headClose;
    htp.bodyOpen(NULL,'bgcolor="#FFFFFF"');
      htp.header(3,'X coordinate = ' || owa_image.get_x(point_in) );
      htp.header(3,'Y coordinate = ' || owa_image.get_y(point_in) );
    htp.bodyClose;
  htp.htmlClose;
END;
```

Although it is technically unnecessary to do so in this case, it is wise to default the point_in parameter generally. This is because an HTML form may have multiple image submit buttons or may allow submissions using either the image or a standard submit button. An example of this would be an application that allows the user to specify attributes of a restaurant (cuisine, price, ambiance) and then submit the form to retrieve all restaurants in the database that match the criteria. However, if there is also an image containing a map of the area and the user submits the form by clicking a location on the image, only those restaurants which meet the original criteria *and* which are within a five-mile radius of the point clicked will be returned. An application such as this would most likely make use of the Oracle Spatial Data option with the Enterprise version of Oracle 7.3 or Oracle8.

Note that images on forms differ from image maps. Image maps are briefly mentioned in Chapter 3, with the discussion of the installation and configuration of the server. The primary difference between the two is that image maps are stand-alone objects and are not associated with a form. The net result is that because they are not part of a form, and therefore lack a variable name, they are not invoked using the *var_name.x* and *var_name.y* variables. Rather, the coordinates are passed directly as part of the URL, with no naming. For instance, clicking at the coordinates 23, 67 on an image map whose HREF is /foo/bar/map would result in a GET request with the following URL, including the query_string component:

```
http://ows.dynamic-info.com/foo/bar/map?23,67
```

However, the PL/SQL agent cannot do anything with this because it does not have any named input arguments with which it can associate formal parameters to a PL/SQL procedure. Sadly, this means that the PL/SQL agent will simply generate an error because it could not find an appropriate stored procedure to invoke. The obvious workaround is to not use standard image maps, but rather to simply use forms with an input object of type image as the only form object. The only drawback to this approach is that it is not possible to have the image map serviced locally by the client-side image map facility supported in most browsers today. Unless the image map must be serviced by a SQL query, it would be more straightforward to simply use the native image map support built into the web listener.

The OWA_PATTERN Package

The purpose of the OWA_PATTERN package is to address the lack of pattern-matching features in PL/SQL. This limitation became particularly noticeable when many users began developing web applications. Pattern-matching capability is useful for data-entry validation tasks. For instance, a field submitted for a phone number can be matched against the generalized pattern of a U.S. 3+7 digit phone number. The OWA_PATTERN package also provides routines for detecting where a match occurs, and also replacing text. The original goal was to provide the bulk of the functionality available within Perl scripts to make it easier (or possible) to port existing scripts written in Perl to the PL/SQL environment.

The OWA_PATTERN package is extremely complex upon first inspection and has some limitations in the way of performance. It is discussed here for completeness and because it is useful for certain tasks. However, given that there now exists a Perl cartridge for the WRB, it is best that Perl be used for tasks which are primarily of a data-munging or text-parsing nature.

The first step to understanding the package is to appreciate that there are three different main procedures—*match, amatch,* and *change*—all of which have several polymorphs. The match procedure has six versions, while amatch and change have four versions each. Unfortunately for neophytes, the three procedures and their variations can result in some confusion. Fortunately, most developers find that they will use only one or two of the variations most consistently, and need not worry about all of the unused variations.

Now, let's look at the datatypes used in the package. The OWA_TEXT package defines a special structure for working around the 32,767 character length limitation of the VARCHAR2 datatype. This type, called multi_line, contains a PL/SQL table of VARCHAR2 elements and bookkeeping information about the number of rows, and whether the last row is completely filled or still has fewer than 32,767 characters. The declarations for the relevant types are as follows:

```
type vc_arr is table of varchar2(32767) index by binary_integer;
type multi_line is record
(
  rows         vc_arr,
  num_rows     integer,
  partial_row boolean
);
```

All of the OWA_PATTERN routines can operate on either multi_line objects or simple VARCHAR2 strings. The calling syntax does not change at all when using them. See the section of Appendix A on OWA_TEXT for a description of how to operate on multi_line objects to populate them and spool their content to HTML pages.

The other data structure to understand is the pattern structure. The match and amatch routines can accept their patterns in either VARCHAR2 format or as this special pattern type. (The change procedure, however, only accepts VARCHAR2 patterns, and it is not clear why.) The purpose of exposing the pattern datatype to the developer is for performance reasons. There is a reasonable amount of overhead associated with parsing the regular expression into the internal format used by the match and amatch routines. If the same expression will be used to check several strings, such as if one had several phone numbers (voice, fax, cellular), a significant savings can be achieved by parsing the expression once and using the preparsed version in each call.

This preparsing is accomplished using the *owa_pattern.getpat* procedure. It accepts a VARCHAR2 expression to be parsed and a pattern variable to hold the result. The issue of parsing regular expressions begs the question of what a regular expression is. Generally, it is an expression composed of characters and metacharacters which allows comparison of a string to a generally defined format. For instance, the SQL *INSTR* function can find an exact string inside another string, as shown here:

```
result := INSTR('webserver handbook','hand');
```

This is useful but very limiting. What if you want to compare a string to see if any substring exists that begins with "web" and ends with "book"? That is to say, you have only general information about the string you wish to find. This is where a regular expression saves the day. A regular expression describes a pattern to be matched, as opposed to a string. For instance, to check for substrings which begin with "web" and end with "book", you would use the regular expression "web.+book".

The ".+" in the middle of the pattern has special meaning. The period is a metacharacter which can match any character except a newline, and the plus sign means "match one or more occurrences of the preceding token." Taken together, the "web.+book" expression says that any occurrence of a string which begins with web, ends with book, and has at least one character between them, but not a newline character, should be matched.

There are a number of metacharacters which are used in regular expressions for the OWA_PATTERN package's routines. Table 4-2 lists these metacharacters and their meanings.

Taken alone, these metacharacters are helpful for building patterns, but for more power and flexibility, quantifiers are necessary. Quantifiers allow a pattern to specify that the pattern should match some number of occurrences of a character or metacharacter. Quantifiers are placed

Metacharacter	Action
^	Matches a newline or the beginning of the target
$	Matches a newline or the end of the target
\n	Matches a newline
.	Matches any character except a newline
\t	Matches a tab
\d	Matches digits (0-9)
\D	Matches nondigits (not 0-9)
\w	Matches alphanumeric word characters (0-9, a-z, A-Z, or _)
\W	Matches nonalphanumeric word characters (not 0-9, a-z, A-Z, or _)
\s	Matches white space characters (space, tab, or newline)
\b	Matches word boundaries (between \w and \W)
\x<HEX>	Matches the value in the current character set of the two hexadecimal digits
\<OCT>	Matches the value in the current character set of the two or three octal digits
\	Used to escape special characters. For instance, \$ will match the dollar sign, as opposed to matching a newline or the end of the target

TABLE 4-2.   *Metacharacters Used in the OWA_PATTERN Package*

immediately following the character or metacharacter to which they apply. Table 4-3 lists the quantifiers available in the OWA_PATTERN procedures.

There are some other characters which have special meaning in the context of the change procedures, but those will be discussed after pattern-matching behaviors have been more thoroughly explained. Let's go through a handful of examples.

To match a date in the format MM/DD/YY or MM-DD-YY, use the pattern "\d\d\W\d\d\W\d\d". This means, "look for two digits, followed by a non-word character, followed by two digits, another non-word character, and two final digits."

Finding phone numbers is always a little tricky, because some people type them with parentheses around the area code, some use dashes, some

Quantifier	Number of Matches
?	0 or 1 occurrence(s)
*	0 or more occurrences (.* matches everything up to a newline)
+	1 or more occurrences
{n}	Exactly *n* occurrences
{n,}	At least *n* occurrences
{n,m}	At least *n*, but no more than *m* occurrences

TABLE 4-3. *Quantifiers Used in the OWA_PATTERN Package*

use spaces, and so forth. Of course, this doesn't even consider the issue of non-U.S. phone numbers, as that would confuse the issue too much. A pattern which does a pretty good job of finding matches for phone numbers is "\d{3}.{0,3}\d{3}.{0,3}\d{4}". As you can see, it is looking for a generic pattern of two groups of three digits followed by a group of four digits.

Those new to patterns may be wondering why the ".{0,3}" quantifier is used, as opposed to ".*", to account for the gaps between the number groups. The reason is that if a pattern-matching engine can match two patterns, one which is shorter and one which is longer, it will always match the longer one. Consider trying to find a phone number in a string such as "Call me at (612) 593-5000 to find out how to fully utilize the Oracle Web Application Server in 1998." If the pattern uses the ".{0,3}" quantifier, the phone number alone will be matched. If the ".*" quantifier is used, the string from "612" through "1998" will be matched.

How about some more patterns? One may wish to check a field for the presence of an Internet e-mail address. Internet e-mail addresses have the format of "username@host.domain". Examples are "webexpert@dynamic-info.com" and "doexx000@mail.genmills.com". To find an e-mail address in a string, the pattern "\w+@.*\.\w+" can be used. This pattern matches the two examples from above, and will match any (we think!) valid SMTP e-mail address. It will fail to find such errant e-mail addresses as bob or foo@bar. Thus, invoking *match* with this pattern against a field which should contain an e-mail address verifies the presence of the address. Using *amatch* will let the developer find the location of the e-mail address in the string.

For those readers who are not experienced grep or Perl users, and even for those of us who are, figuring out the right pattern to use can be tricky sometimes. To speed up the process of trial and error, which some people use, as well as to illustrate the use of the OWA_PATTERN package, the *pat_checker* procedure, shown on the next page, is a handy utility function. It is included on the CD-ROM as patcheck.sql. Called with no parameters, it produces a form which can be filled in as shown in Figure 4-5.

The user can then enter both a pattern and a string of text which the pattern will be compared against. For true propeller heads, a checkbox allows toggling the output of the internal structure of the pattern's data structure. Upon submission, the routine attempts to parse the pattern and returns the searched string with matched patterns colored red and in boldface type. By using this tool, users can get a good handle on how to formulate regular expressions which match as expected. The verbose output is shown in Figure 4-6.

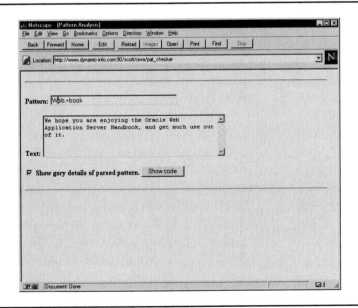

FIGURE 4-5.   *A pattern-checking input form*

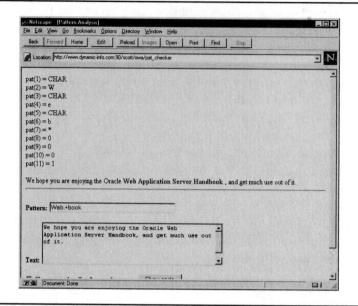

FIGURE 4-6. *The results of the submitted pattern-checking form*

```
CREATE OR REPLACE PROCEDURE pat_checker (pat IN VARCHAR2:=NULL,
                  text IN VARCHAR2:=NULL,
                  show_pat IN VARCHAR2:='N')
IS
  parsed_pat  owa_pattern.pattern;
  i INTEGER;
  rev_text VARCHAR2(32767):= text;
BEGIN
  htp.htmlOpen;
    htp.headOpen;
      htp.title('Pattern Analysis');
    htp.headClose;
    htp.bodyOpen(NULL,'bgcolor="#FFFFFF"');
      IF pat IS NOT NULL
      THEN
        BEGIN
          IF show_pat='Y'
          THEN
            owa_pattern.getpat(pat,parsed_pat);
            i := 1;
            WHILE parsed_pat(i) != 'EOP'
            LOOP
```

```
            htp.print('pat('||i||') = '||parsed_pat(i)||'<br>');
                i := i+1;
              END LOOP;
              htp.para;
            END IF;
            owa_pattern.change(rev_text,pat,
                           '<b><font color="#ff0000"> & </font></b>');
            htp.p(rev_text);
         EXCEPTION
           WHEN OTHERS THEN
              htp.header(2,'An error occured. Check pattern
              format');
              htp.preOpen;
              htp.prints(dbms_utility.format_error_stack);
              htp.preClose;
         END;
      END IF;

      htp.hr;
        htp.formOpen('pat_checker');
          htp.bold('Pattern: ');
          htp.formText('pat',40,80,pat);
          htp.para;
          htp.bold('Text: ');
          htp.formTextAreaOpen2('text',5,50,NULL,'virtual');
          htp.p(text);
          htp.formTextAreaClose;
          htp.para;
          IF show_pat='Y'
          THEN
            htp.formCheckbox('show_pat','Y','CHECKED');
          ELSE
            htp.formCheckbox('show_pat','Y');
          END IF;
          htp.bold('Show gory details of parsed pattern.');
          htp.formSubmit(NULL,'Show code');
        htp.formClose;
      htp.hr;
    htp.bodyClose;
  htp.htmlClose;
END;
```

Now that the idea of formulating patterns to be matched has been exposed, it is possible to move on to the other main features provided by the package, which relate to manipulating the text in the package. There are two main ways in which manipulation can be performed: manually or automatically. Each approach has a certain benefit. Custom-coded manipulation is obviously the most flexible, while the built-in features of the *change* procedure are very easy to implement.

The previously described pat_checker procedure actually introduces the simplest case of changing text, using the ampersand (&). Inside the context of the *owa_pattern.change* procedure, the ampersand will be replaced with the substring matched by the pattern. Thus, in the code above, the to_str instructs the change routine to simply replace the matched pattern with the matched pattern surrounded by some additional formatting tags.

Before discussing the exact manner in which these techniques are implemented, another concept needs to be introduced: backreferences. A *backreference* is the actual content of the text that matches a pattern or subpattern. Subpatterns have not yet been discussed, because they are inapplicable to simple matching and are useful only when changing a string.

A *subpattern* is a member of the pattern to be searched, but it is set off from the rest of the pattern by parentheses. For example, "Hello World" is a pattern, as is (Hello) World, but Hello is a subpattern. Finally, "(Hello) (World)" is a pattern with two subpatterns, "Hello" and "World". Each of these three patterns will match the same thing within a string: "Hello World".

NOTE
For those who wonder how to match the string "(Hello) (World)", it is done by escaping the parentheses so they are interpreted literally, using the backslash (\\) character: "\\(Hello\\) \\(World\\)".

As you can see, subpatterns do not impact the semantics of pattern matching, but they do allow more sophisticated operations on the results. Each subpattern corresponds to a backreference. Backreferences can be used in the to_str parameter to the *owa_pattern.change* procedure. A backreference is written as "\\n", where n is the position of the subpattern relative to other subpatterns within the entire pattern, moving left to right. Thus, in the pattern "(Hello) (World)", "\\1" would refer to "Hello" and "\\2" would refer to "World".

Suppose you need to convert a date from traditional American "MM/DD/YY" format to the more continental "DD/MM/YY" format.

Subpattern replacement with backreferences allows this to be done rather easily, as the following code snippet demonstrates.

```
BEGIN
date_str := '07/27/97';
owa_pattern.change(date_str, '(\d\d)/(\d\d)/(\d\d)','\2/\1/\3');
-- date_str is now equal to '27/07/97'
END;
```

The next level of sophistication in pattern replacement is to use the *owa_pattern.match* procedures. These procedures return an array (PL/SQL table of type owa_text.vc_arr) of the text substrings which match the subpatterns, such that element 1 of the table contains the actual substring matched by the leftmost subpattern, and so on. The following is a simple example demonstrating the use of the match command, simply parsing the date, as shown above, but then using the resulting array to assemble a more complex result:

```
PROCEDURE date_parser (date_in IN VARCHAR2)
IS
components owa_text.vc_arr;
BEGIN
IF (owa_pattern.match(date_in, '(\d\d)/(\d\d)/(\d\d)', components))
THEN
htp.print('The month is '||components(1));
htp.print('The day is '||components(2));
htp.print('The year is '||components(3));
END IF;
END;
```

The routines in this package may initially seem inscrutable, especially for those unfamiliar with regular expressions and pattern matching. However, the reward for learning how to use them to their best effect is reduced programming effort in writing code that must validate or otherwise parse and manipulate user input.

The OWA_UTIL Package

As mentioned earlier, the OWA_UTIL package defines a couple of commonly used datatypes, including ident_arr, which is used to handle multivalued parameters. In addition, the OWA_UTIL package includes three kinds of methods. First are methods for accessing environment information about the request. The second group of methods is provided for manipulating the headers of HTTP responses. Finally, the package includes some convenience methods which are not used frequently in production applications but which are useful in development or for implementing a basic report very quickly. Version 3.0 of the Web Application Server implements some additional functions in the OWA_UTIL package, which are discussed at the end of the section.

The routine *owa_util.get_cgi_env* allows developers to access several CGI environment variables from within their PL/SQL routines. These variables are available regardless of whether the routine itself was invoked through the CGI or cartridge version of the Oracle Web Agent. Table 4-4 is the official list of CGI environment variables. To see exactly which environment variables are available with a particular Web Server version, or to examine the nature of their contents, simply invoke the *owa_util.print_cgi_env* for any PL/SQL Agent. This will return an HTML page listing all currently defined environment variables. The owa_util.print_cgi_env can also be included in a routine to output the exact state of the CGI environment when executing a specific procedure.

SERVER_SOFTWARE	The name and version of the web server which invoked the executable
SERVER_NAME	The hostname of the server on which the script is running
GATEWAY_INTERFACE	The version of the CGI interface under which the code is being called. Typically, this is CGI/1.1
REMOTE_HOST	The hostname of the machine which made the request
REMOTE_ADDR	The IP address of the machine which made the request
AUTH_TYPE	The type of authentication used, if applicable
REMOTE_USER	The username submitted by the user
REMOTE_IDENT	The password submitted by the user
HTTP_ACCEPT	A comma-delimited list of MIME types in which the browser will accept responses

TABLE 4-4. *CGI Environment Variables*

HTTP_USER_AGENT	The name, version and additional information about the client software which made the request. This is usually a browser, although web robots are also user agents
SERVER_PROTOCOL	The protocol name and version which the server is running. Usually HTTP/1.0
SERVER_PORT	The server port through which the request came
SCRIPT_NAME	The name of the script being executed
PATH_INFO	Additional part of the URL after the script name but prior to the query string
PATH_TRANSLATED	The actual path to the script being executed
HTTP_REFERER	The URL of the page from which this request came

TABLE 4-4.   *CGI Environment Variables (continued)*

The environment variables are useful for extracting information about the request, which may then be used to customize the processing or output generated. For example, *HTTP_USER_AGENT* can be used to generate a page with tables, if the browser is known to support them, or simply to use preformatted text tables for less modern browsers. Another nice feature is to use the *HTTP_REFERER* variable (yes, it is spelled incorrectly) to add a "Return to last page" link in every page. The following line illustrates this second case:

```
htp.anchor(owa_util.get_cgi_env('HTTP_REFERER'),'Go whence you
came.');
```

Also useful for many web applications is the ability to generate header fields manually. Oracle WebServer 2.0 added this feature and thus removed a limitation which prevented a variety of functionality from being implemented. By giving the developer complete control over the entire content of the HTTP response, a number of applications open up to the user.

One of the more important functions to call is the *owa_util.mime_header* procedure, which allows the developer to inform the browser how the returned result text of the routine should be interpreted. Some readers may wonder at this point why this routine would be useful. The reason is that it frees the developer from the constraints of HTML. By giving developers the ability to specify that the body of the response should be interpreted as any one of a variety of different MIME types, new application types can be developed.

One example is using the Virtual Reality Modeling Language (VRML), mentioned in Chapter 2, to display results. VRML allows the presentation of arbitrary 3-D worlds, rather than just text. Although many designers use this technology to create virtual malls, homes, and cities, database developers can harness this power as a creative visualization tool or even as an easy way to create 3-D graphs.

In addition to VRML, any type of data which is represented as text can be generated by PL/SQL and written to the web browser. Although HTML and VRML would likely be the most common types of data written by a developer, Adobe's Postscript or Portable Document Format could be used as well, among others. Admittedly, writing code to generate this type of data is much more complex, but it also offers a significant upside in terms of enhanced functionality and superior user presentation.

Whenever a PL/SQL routine explicitly creates any header information, it must close the HTTP header, or else the contents of the header will appear in the user's browser window as if they were part of the body of the response. The headers are closed either by setting the bclose_header parameter of the various procedures to true, which is the default, or by doing so explicitly with the *owa_util.http_header_close* routine. An example of manipulating the headers can be seen in the sample procedure cooktest, outlined previously in the section on the OWA_COOKIE package.

Three other groups of utility functions were added in Oracle Web Application Server version 3.0. First, it includes a convenience call for setting up dynamic SQL cursors and binding variables to cursors in a single step. Also, it includes some convenience calls for table-based output of dynamic SQL. Finally, it implements some routines for generating basic calendar displays as well as provides an easier way to handle date input. The date selection procedure, *owa_util.choose_date*, is demonstrated in the next section's example.

The OWA_OPT_LOCK Package

The OWA_OPT_LOCK package provides services to implement an optimistic locking model in PL/SQL web applications. In database operations, locking is used to prevent two or more users from applying simultaneous updates to an individual record. Without the ability to lock records, the following scenario can be easily imagined:

1. Sue or her agent (application) performs a SELECT against the database and displays it for editing.

2. Immediately after Sue's SELECT, Tom's application also queries the database for the same record and displays the record's data for editing.

3. Sue makes changes to the record, and her application issues an UPDATE against the database to apply her changes.

4. Tom completes his editing, and he too, applies his update to the database, thus overwriting the update that Sue made seconds before.

Neither Tom nor Sue was aware of this just happening. Obviously this is not a desirable state of affairs for a production database application. However, it is a very common problem, typically known as the "lost update" problem, the risk of which must be accommodated. Oracle's RDBMS supports the concept of selecting data "FOR UPDATE," which places a lock on the selected records. Other users connected to the database can query on and view the locked records but cannot make changes to them. This prevents the overwritten updates problem for applications which maintain a persistent database connection, such as SQL*Plus or Oracle Forms.

However, in web applications, there is not a persistent connection between the user and the database. (The WRB does support persistent connections between the Web Application Server and the database.) Thus, Oracle's native locking facilities are not easily amenable to use in a web application. Chapter 10 discusses Oracle's new transaction management facilities and how to use them. These facilities allow for web transactions which are just as robust as any which can be created in a client/server environment.

Although the transaction manager provides a very powerful manner in which to enforce complete transactional integrity, there are two potential reasons one might not want to use these services. First, you may not have the advanced edition of Web Application Server, which is required, and may not wish to acquire it to support relatively simple transactions. The second reason has to do with the typical usage of the application in question.

Suppose the application being developed is used primarily for a single-table query and detail view, but occasional updates are made to the data retrieved. In this case, there are two options. The first is to implement a second screen which users can access specifically to edit the data, and which would be subject to strict transaction control. With the optimistic locking package, you can develop the application such that a single screen can be used for both viewing and editing data. If a user attempts to update a record while an intervening update has been made by another user, such as Tom's update in the previous scenario, the update will be rejected and the user's browser will be updated with the new values of the record, made bySue.

The OWA_OPT_LOCK package implements two general ways to manage optimistic locking. In both cases, information about the original state of the record is obtained from an OWA_OPT_LOCK routine and is stored in the HTML form as hidden fields which are then sent when the form is submitted. The PL/SQL routine managing the update then uses other OWA_OPT_LOCK routines to compare the stored information with the current record information. The information about the current record state can be stored as a simple checksum of the column values, using the *owa_opt_lock.checksum* procedure. Alternatively, the actual contents of the column values themselves can be stored using *owa_opt_lock.store_values* and then compared to the current record state (when an update is submitted) using *owa_opt_lock.verify_values*.

The following example package, found on this CD as the file optlock.sql, demonstrates several features of the SDK. It should be installed into a schema that has access to the demo tables EMP and DEPT. First, it makes extensive use of the HTP and HTF routines to generate frames, forms, and tables. It also uses some date management routines from the OWA_UTIL package. Of course, it primarily shows how to implement optimistic locking using either checksums or hidden values.

This package also makes use of the *owsh_util.get_linked_menu* library routine, which is highly generic and can be used to implement a pop-up menu on an HTML form. It is in many respects an easier-to-use version of *owa_util.listprint*. The menu items are populated from a query and can use the value parameter of the <OPTION> tag. Using this parameter causes the

browser to send the content of *value* rather than the displayed value.
The OWSH_UTIL package can be found on the CD-ROM in the
owshutil.sql file.

```
CREATE OR REPLACE PACKAGE optlock IS
  PROCEDURE main;
  PROCEDURE do_frame (empno_in IN VARCHAR2);
  PROCEDURE do_form_page_cksum (  empno_in IN VARCHAR2,
          err_msg_in IN VARCHAR2:=NULL);
  PROCEDURE do_form_page_hvals (  empno_in IN VARCHAR2,
          err_msg_in IN VARCHAR2:=NULL);
  PROCEDURE do_update_cksum (  ename_in IN VARCHAR2:=NULL,
          job_in IN VARCHAR2:=NULL,
          mgr_in IN VARCHAR2:=NULL,
          hiredate_in IN owa_util.datetype:=owa_util.empty_date,
          sal_in IN VARCHAR2:=NULL,
          comm_in IN VARCHAR2:=NULL,
          deptno_in IN VARCHAR2:=NULL,
          rowid_in IN rowid,
          checksum_in IN NUMBER);
  PROCEDURE do_update_hvals (  ename_in IN VARCHAR2:=NULL,
          job_in IN VARCHAR2:=NULL,
          mgr_in IN VARCHAR2:=NULL,
          hiredate_in IN owa_util.datetype:=owa_util.empty_date,
          sal_in IN VARCHAR2:=NULL,
          comm_in IN VARCHAR2:=NULL,
          deptno_in IN VARCHAR2:=NULL,
          old_emp IN owa_opt_lock.vcArray);
END optlock;
CREATE OR REPLACE PACKAGE BODY optlock IS
  PROCEDURE main
  IS
    CURSOR ecurs IS
      SELECT ename, empno FROM emp ORDER BY ename;
  BEGIN
    htp.htmlOpen;
    htp.headOpen;
    htp.title('OWA_OPT_LOCK Demo');
    htp.headClose;
    htp.bodyOpen;
    htp.header(2,'Please choose an employee record to edit.');
    FOR erec IN ecurs
    LOOP
      htp.anchor('optlock.do_frame?empno_in=' || erec.empno,
          erec.ename);
```

```
      htp.br;
    END LOOP;
    htp.bodyClose;
    htp.htmlClose;
  END;
  PROCEDURE do_frame (empno_in IN VARCHAR2)
  IS
  BEGIN
    htp.htmlOpen;
    htp.headOpen;
    htp.title('OWA_OPT_LOCK Demo');
    htp.headClose;
    htp.framesetOpen(ccols=>'50%,50%');
    htp.frame('optlock.do_form_page_cksum?empno_in=' || empno_in);
    htp.frame('optlock.do_form_page_hvals?empno_in=' || empno_in);
    htp.framesetClose;
    htp.noframesOpen;
    htp.header(2,'Sorry, this demo requires a frames-capable
browser.');
    htp.noframesClose;
    htp.htmlClose;
  END;
  PROCEDURE build_form (  empno_in IN VARCHAR2)
  IS
    erec  emp%rowtype;
  BEGIN
    SELECT * INTO erec FROM emp WHERE empno = empno_in;
    htp.tableOpen;
    htp.tableRowOpen;
    htp.tableData(htf.bold('Name'));
    htp.tableData(htf.formText('ename_in',cvalue=>erec.ename));
    htp.tableRowClose;
    htp.tableRowOpen;
    htp.tableData(htf.bold('Job'));
    htp.tableData(htf.formText('job_in',cvalue=>erec.job));
    htp.tableRowClose;
    htp.tableRowOpen;
    htp.tableData(htf.bold('Manager'));
    htp.tableData(owsh_util.get_linked_menu('mgr_in','emp',
              'ename','empno',
              NULL,'ename',
              erec.mgr));
    htp.tableRowClose;
    htp.tableRowOpen;
    htp.tableData(htf.bold('Hire date'));
```

```
    htp.p('<td>');
    owa_util.choose_date('hiredate_in',NVL(erec.hiredate,SYSDATE));
    htp.p('</td>');
    htp.tableRowClose;
    htp.tableRowOpen;
    htp.tableData(htf.bold('Salary'));
    htp.tableData(htf.formText('sal_in',cvalue=>erec.sal));
    htp.tableRowClose;
    htp.tableRowOpen;
    htp.tableData(htf.bold('Commission'));
    htp.tableData(htf.formText('comm_in',cvalue=>erec.comm));
    htp.tableRowClose;
    htp.tableRowOpen;
    htp.tableData(htf.bold('Department'));
    htp.tableData(owsh_util.get_linked_menu('deptno_in','dept',
             'dname','deptno',
             NULL,'dname',
             erec.deptno));
    htp.tableRowClose;
    htp.tableClose;
    htp.formSubmit(cvalue=>'Update');
END;
PROCEDURE do_form_page_cksum (  empno_in IN VARCHAR2,
        err_msg_in IN VARCHAR2:=NULL)
IS
  v_rowid ROWID;
BEGIN
  IF (err_msg_in IS NOT NULL)
  THEN
    htp.center(htf.header(2,err_msg_in));
  END IF;
  htp.bold('Note: Locking enforced by checksums.');
  SELECT rowid INTO v_rowid FROM emp WHERE empno=empno_in;
  htp.htmlOpen;
  htp.bodyOpen;
  htp.formOpen('optlock.do_update_cksum');
  build_form(empno_in);
  htp.formHidden('checksum_in',
      owa_opt_lock.checksum( USER, 'emp', v_rowid));
  htp.formHidden('rowid_in',v_rowid);
  htp.formClose;
  htp.hr;
  htp.center(htf.anchor('optlock.main','Back to list',
        cattributes=>'target="_top"'));
  htp.bodyClose;
```

```
      htp.htmlClose;
    END;
    PROCEDURE do_form_page_hvals (  empno_in IN VARCHAR2,
            err_msg_in IN VARCHAR2:=NULL)
    IS
      v_rowid ROWID;
    BEGIN
      IF (err_msg_in IS NOT NULL)
      THEN
        htp.center(htf.header(2,err_msg_in));
      END IF;
      htp.bold('Note: Locking enforced by hidden fields.');
      SELECT rowid INTO v_rowid FROM emp WHERE empno=empno_in;
      htp.htmlOpen;
      htp.bodyOpen;
      htp.formOpen('optlock.do_update_hvals');
      build_form(empno_in);
      owa_opt_lock.store_values( USER, 'emp', v_rowid);
      htp.formClose;
      htp.hr;
      htp.center(htf.anchor('optlock.main','Back to list',
            cattributes=>'target="_top"'));
      htp.bodyClose;
      htp.htmlClose;
    END;
    PROCEDURE do_update_cksum (  ename_in IN VARCHAR2:=NULL,
            job_in IN VARCHAR2:=NULL,
            mgr_in IN VARCHAR2:=NULL,
            hiredate_in IN owa_util.datetype:=owa_util.empty_date,
            sal_in IN VARCHAR2:=NULL,
            comm_in IN VARCHAR2:=NULL,
            deptno_in IN VARCHAR2:=NULL,
            rowid_in IN rowid,
            checksum_in IN NUMBER)
    IS
      err_text  VARCHAR2(200);
      v_empno  VARCHAR2(20);
      temp_date DATE;
    BEGIN
      IF (owa_opt_lock.checksum(USER,'emp',rowid_in)=checksum_in)
      THEN
        temp_date := owa_util.todate(hiredate_in);
        UPDATE emp SET ename=ename_in,job=job_in,mgr=mgr_in,
            hiredate=temp_date,
            sal=sal_in, comm=comm_in,deptno=deptno_in
```

```
        WHERE rowid=rowid_in;
     COMMIT;
     err_text:='Update successful.';
   ELSE
     err_text:='An intervening update occured.';
   END IF;
   SELECT empno INTO v_empno FROM emp WHERE rowid=rowid_in;
   do_form_page_cksum(v_empno,err_text);
 END;
 PROCEDURE do_update_hvals (  ename_in IN VARCHAR2:=NULL,
         job_in IN VARCHAR2:=NULL,
         mgr_in IN VARCHAR2:=NULL,
         hiredate_in IN owa_util.datetype:=owa_util.empty_date,
         sal_in IN VARCHAR2:=NULL,
         comm_in IN VARCHAR2:=NULL,
         deptno_in IN VARCHAR2:=NULL,
         old_emp IN owa_opt_lock.vcArray)
 IS
   v_rowid  ROWID;
   err_text  VARCHAR2(200);
   v_empno  VARCHAR2(20);
   temp_date  DATE;
 BEGIN
   v_rowid := owa_opt_lock.get_rowid(old_emp);
   IF (owa_opt_lock.verify_values(old_emp))
   THEN
     temp_date := owa_util.todate(hiredate_in);
     UPDATE emp SET ename=ename_in,job=job_in,mgr=mgr_in,
         hiredate=temp_date,
         sal=sal_in, comm=comm_in,deptno=deptno_in
       WHERE rowid=v_rowid;
     COMMIT;
     err_text:='Update successful.';
   ELSE
     err_text:='An intervening update occured.';
   END IF;
   SELECT empno INTO v_empno FROM emp WHERE rowid=v_rowid;
   do_form_page_hvals(v_empno,err_text);
 END;

END optlock;
```

Figure 4-7 shows the result of using this procedure. A possible enhancement which could be performed to this package is a merge

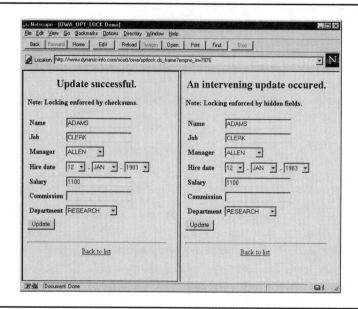

FIGURE 4-7. *Optimistic locking demo in action*

changes feature. In the case of Sue and Tom mentioned previously, if each changed the values of different columns, both sets of changes would be applied. This may or may not be a desirable feature, depending on the circumstances. It is certainly possible, though not trivial to implement, and may make for a superior interface in some cases. Even without such niceties, the OWA_OPT_LOCK allows developers to create robust applications more easily, despite the stateless nature of HTTP.

The OWA_SEC Package

The OWA_SEC package is newly introduced in version 3.0 of Oracle Web Application Server and allows developers to access security-related information such as the username, password, and realm. This can be used to implement different processing based on the username, or to create new types of authorization within PL/SQL. The use of this package is detailed, with an example, in Chapter 9.

The OWA_ICX Package

The OWA_ICX package is newly introduced in version 3.0 of Oracle Web Application Server and provides a PL/SQL interface for accessing other cartridges via Inter-Cartridge Exchange (ICX). As we will discuss further in Chapter 10, ICX is a widely utilized and significant component of the Web Application Server 3.0 architecture.

Generally, the OWA_ICX package allows PL/SQL procedures to call out from the database to other cartridges and services and get results back from them. The use and operation of the package is detailed completely in Chapter 10.

NOTE
The OWA_ICX package allows any PL/SQL procedure to invoke other cartridges, not just procedures which are themselves invoked through the WRB. This means that even database triggers can take advantage of services offered by WRB cartridges.

Debugging PL/SQL Web Applications

Unfortunately, bugs inevitably crop up in the development of software. This section provides information to help developers track down and correct the defects that occur during development.

Errors which occur while attempting to execute a stored procedure, or during execution of the stored procedure, result in the error information being written to an error file with the extension .err and named after the PL/SQL Agent. For instance, a PL/SQL Agent named hr will have errors written to the file hr.err in the log directory within the web server's home directory.

NOTE
Web Application Server 3.0 supports the very nice feature of optionally returning to the browser the same error results which are written to the log file. This avoids the need to examine the log file each time an error is encountered. To enable this option, set the owa_err_level parameter to 2 when configuring the PL/SQL Agent Service. Of course, it would be wise to set it back to 0 or 1 when the system goes into production, so as not to expose any application weaknesses, as well as to avoid confusing users.

This error file information is very helpful when debugging Oracle Web Application Server applications. It provides the complete calling chain of procedures leading up to the error, with line numbers, as well as a complete list of name/value pairs passed as parameters. This information can provide a web developer with almost all the information necessary to identify the source of the fatal error, including the text description of any errors and the line numbers of PL/SQL procedures which triggered the error.

Let's take a moment and review the logged results of a number of different errors and discuss how to investigate and correct the errors. The first is an example of an error log entry for a URL which failed to execute because the stand-alone procedure requested does not exist (the URL was /foobar/owa/notthere):

```
Thu Aug 07 23:47:24 1997
OWS-05101: Agent : execution failed due to Oracle error 6564
ORA-06564: object notthere does not exist
ORA-06512: at "SYS.DBMS_DESCRIBE", line 55
ORA-06512: at line 1
   OWA SERVICE: FOOBAR
   PROCEDURE: notthere
```

This second example is similar but applies to cases when the missing procedure is specified to reside in a package (the URL was /foobar/owa/sample.notthere).

```
Thu Aug 07 14:31:10 1997
OWS-05101: Agent : execution failed due to Oracle error 20001
ORA-20001: ORU-10032: procedure NOTTHERE within package SAMPLE
   does not exist
ORA-06512: at "SYS.DBMS_DESCRIBE", line 145
ORA-06512: at line 1
  OWA SERVICE: FOOBAR
  PROCEDURE: sample.notthere
```

The third example is less common, but should be mentioned for completeness. This error occurs when only the package name is specified in the URL, rather than in the package and corresponding procedure (the URL was /foobar/owa/sample).

```
Thu Aug 07 14:13:30 1997
OWS-05101: Agent : execution failed due to Oracle error 20000
ORA-20000: ORU-10035: cannot describe a package (sample); only a
   procedure within a package
ORA-06512: at "SYS.DBMS_DESCRIBE", line 75
ORA-06512: at line 1
  OWA SERVICE: FOOBAR
  PROCEDURE: sample
```

There are two root causes for these types of errors. First, and very commonly, the procedure name is simply mistyped. Often, the error is a result of failing to specify the member package for the procedure, as in package.procedure. For developers used to working with most development tools, errors of this kind are impossible at run time, because the compiler catches the error during compilation. However, the PL/SQL compiler cannot detect this error, because it results from a typographic error in either an HTML page (if not dynamically generated) or in a PL/SQL string literal, neither of which is examined by the compiler.

The second possibility, although less likely, is that the procedure is correctly named but is not in the schema which the Database Access Descriptor (DAD) is instructed to access. This error occurs in one of three ways: First, a typographic error in the URL may have it accessing a DAD different from the one expected. Second, the DAD or PL/SQL Agent could be incorrectly configured. Third, the procedure may have been inadvertently compiled into the wrong schema. This can easily happen if you have a number of different SQL*Plus sessions active on your desktop, with different users logged in.

Almost invariably, checking these things reveals the source of the error. Let's turn now to a different sort of error. In this case, the *object* (procedure) exists but cannot be executed because of errors in the parameter list. The first type of problem is when the parameters specified in the HTTP request do not match the parameters specified in the interface of the procedure called or invoked. In other words, the parameters do not match in name or in number. The following shows an errant attempt to invoke the *owa_util.showsource* procedure, passing in a parameter named foo with its value set to "bar". This is an error in the name of the parameters.

```
Thu Aug 07 14:19:11 1997
OWS-05111: Agent : no stored procedure matches this call with the
   arguments passed
   OWA SERVICE: FOOBAR
   PROCEDURE: owa_util.showsource
   PARAMETERS:
   ===========
   FOO:
    bar
```

This second example shows the result of attempting to invoke the showsource procedure with no parameters at all.

```
Thu Aug 07 14:30:51 1997
OWS-05101: Agent : execution failed due to Oracle error 6550
ORA-06550: line 1, column 77:
PLS-00306: wrong number or types of arguments in call to 'SHOWSOURCE'
ORA-06550: line 1, column 77:
PL/SQL: Statement ignored
   OWA SERVICE: FOOBAR
   PROCEDURE: owa_util.showsource
```

As before, determining the exact cause of these types of errors is relatively straightforward. The first thing to do is check the parameter names. A typo here cannot be caught by the compiler, just as with the previous example. The second possibility is that the wrong number of parameters are being passed due to an omission in the URL specified. Another possibility is that the developer thought that he or she had defined default parameter values for this procedure but had not.

Similar errors result when the values of the parameters cannot be coerced into the correct types for the stored procedure to accept. This is typically due to errant user input. However, it is unacceptable for the developer not to guard against this error. That is why it was suggested earlier in the chapter to declare all parameters as VARCHAR2, and manage the type conversion internally. This allows a more meaningful error message to be returned to the user.

Consider the following procedure declaration, which expects a single date parameter to be passed to it:

```
PROCEDURE FOO (date_in IN DATE);
```

If this procedure is invoked with the date sent from the browser as a string in the standard Oracle format of "DD-MON-YY", then the value can be correctly cast. However, if the date is sent in an incorrect format, errors will result. The following shows the result of attempting to call the procedure with the date_in parameter set to "07-AUGUST-97", which most users would suspect to be a reasonable date input.

```
Thu Aug 07 23:34:27 1997
OWS-05101: Agent : execution failed due to Oracle error 1858
ORA-01858: a non-numeric character was found where a numeric was expected
ORA-06512: at line 1
  OWA SERVICE: FOOBAR
  PROCEDURE: foo
  PARAMETERS:
  ===========
  DATE_IN:
   07-AUGUST-97
```

Of course, this sort of thing wouldn't even be possible if you were using the date input functions provided in the OWA_UTIL package.

A similar but very uncommon error is OWS-05112, whose description is "Agent: too many procedures matches [*sic*] this call." The only reasonable cause of this error is if two procedures with the same name and the same parameter list exist, save for one difference: one has a parameter(s) defined as a scalar value, while the other declares a parameter of the same name as a PL/SQL table. For example:

```
PROCEDURE bad_proc(id IN VARCHAR2,attr IN VARCHAR2);
PROCEDURE bad_proc(id IN VARCHAR2,attr IN OWA_UTIL.ident_arr);
```

There is never any need to have dual declarations like this. The first procedure can be safely eliminated, so long as the second one can deal with the expected case of a PL/SQL table with a single row. The one drawback this has is that PL/SQL tables cannot be defaulted. Thus, a dummy variable must be used. See our discussion of accepting multivalued input from forms earlier in the chapter, for more details.

Assuming you have worked your way this far and are now at least at the point where the procedure is found and invoked by the Agent correctly, a new set of errors can crop up: those that occur during execution. These errors are just like any other PL/SQL errors; however, that doesn't make them any easier to debug.

In fact, PL/SQL is a somewhat difficult language for which to debug execution errors. This is because it has no run-time debugging facilities. Oracle Procedure Builder, available as part of Developer/2000 as well as separately, does have a PL/SQL debugger, but because it cannot, in its present release, debug PL/SQL version 2 code, it is useless for our purposes. However, the problem is not hopeless. Although it is not always as easy as one would like it to be, the errors can still be tracked down.

The easiest way to find the code causing the problem is to query the USER_SOURCE or ALL_SOURCE tables in the data dictionary. These tables contain the source code for every procedure, function, and package in the schema or database, respectively. The following query, for instance, will show line 72 of the procedure named *badproc*. Remember, the data dictionary stores all object names in uppercase (with a few exceptions), so querying for name="badproc" will return no lines.

```
SELECT text FROM user_source WHERE name='BADPROC' and line=72;
```

This is fine for checking a line occasionally, but it has several drawbacks. First, it means constantly typing the query. Second, one must set the line length and tab stops correctly in SQL*Plus, or the code will often wrap badly. It also only shows one line, which provides very little context. One could eliminate the line query condition, but this is almost always worse if the error is in a large package.

A handy utility you can use is a procedure called *sc*, for *show code*. You can install it into any web schema in which you are developing and then access it from the browser. If called with no parameters, it simply shows a form which lets the user enter a procedure or package name, a line number, and a delta. The *delta* is the number of lines before and after the error line to also display. Figure 4-8 shows the initial screen for the *sc* procedure.

If the *sc* procedure is called with parameters, the source is printed to the HTML page. In addition to printing the requested lines, the error line itself is shown in red, to make it easy to find. At the bottom of the listing, the form is repeated to allow the user to pick another line, delta, or procedure name. Figure 4-9 shows a sample result of calling the sc procedure.

The procedure is included in the file debug.sql on the CD-ROM. It should be installed into the schema which the DAD is configured to access. For convenience, you may want to bookmark the URL to make it easy to access. Be certain to remove the procedure when the site is in production, to prevent individuals from accessing the internal workings of the

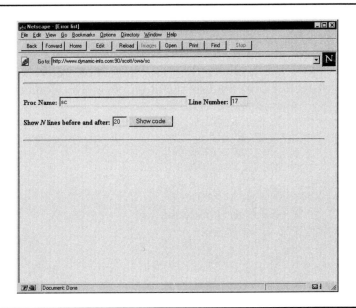

FIGURE 4-8.   *The initial screen of the sc (show code) procedure*

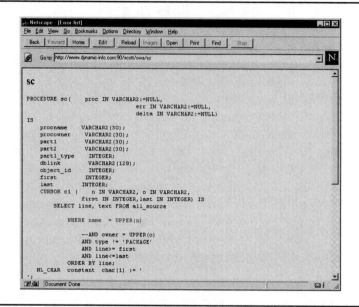

FIGURE 4-9. *The results of invoking the* sc *procedure*

applications. Alternatively, one could alter the code to require a password or to check the IP address of the user agent requesting the source. The source of the procedure follows.

```
CREATE OR REPLACE PROCEDURE sc(  proc IN VARCHAR2:=NULL,
            err IN VARCHAR2:=NULL,
            delta IN VARCHAR2:=NULL)
IS
  procname  VARCHAR2(30);
  procowner  VARCHAR2(30);
  part1    VARCHAR2(30);
  part2    VARCHAR2(30);
  part1_type  INTEGER;
  dblink    VARCHAR2(128);
  object_id  INTEGER;
  first    INTEGER;
  last    INTEGER;
  CURSOR c1 (  n IN VARCHAR2, o IN VARCHAR2,
       first IN INTEGER,last IN INTEGER) IS
    SELECT line, text FROM all_source
     WHERE name  = UPPER(n)
```

```
        - AND owner = UPPER(o)
        AND type != 'PACKAGE BODY'
        AND line>= first
        AND line<=last
      ORDER BY line;
   NL_CHAR  constant  char(1) := '
';
BEGIN
  htp.htmlOpen;
    htp.headOpen;
      htp.title('Error list');
    htp.headClose;
    htp.bodyOpen(NULL,'bgcolor="#FFFFFF"');
      IF proc IS NOT NULL
      THEN
        first:=err-delta;
        last:=err+delta;
        IF (first < 1)
        THEN
          first:=1;
        END IF;
        dbms_utility.name_resolve(  proc, 1, procowner, part1,
                     part2, dblink, part1_type,
                     object_id);

        IF part1_type in (7,8) --if a stand-alone proc or func
        THEN
          procname := part2;
        ELSE
          procname := part1;
        END IF;
        htp.header(2,proc);
        htp.preOpen;
        FOR source_rec in c1 (proc, procowner,first,last)
        LOOP
          -- we convert tabs to four spaces, change the replace
          -- strings of spaces below to alter this
          IF (source_rec.line = err)
          THEN
            htp.print('<font color="#FF0000">');
            htp.prints(translate(
                     REPLACE(source_rec.text,CHR(9),'    '),
                     NL_CHAR,' '));
            htp.print('</font>');
          ELSE
```

```
        htp.prints(translate(
                REPLACE(source_rec.text,CHR(9),'       '),
                NL_CHAR,' '));
      END IF;
    END LOOP;
    htp.preClose;
  END IF;
  htp.hr;
  htp.formOpen('sc');
  htp.bold('Proc Name: ');
  htp.formText('proc',40,80,proc);
  htp.bold('Line Number: ');
  htp.formText('err',4,5,err);
  htp.para;
  htp.bold('Show '||htf.italic('N ') ||
            'lines before and after: ');
  htp.formText('delta',3,3,'20');
  htp.formSubmit(NULL,'Show code');
  htp.formClose;
  htp.hr;
 htp.bodyClose;
 htp.htmlClose;
END;
```

One type of execution error which can be inconvenient to debug is an error which occurs inside the DBMS_SQL package, the package which allows the execution of dynamic SQL statements created at run time. These errors present difficulty because they typically result from a string which is an invalid SQL fragment being passed to be executed as SQL. Because you do not have immediate access to the content of variables while PL/SQL is executing, as you would with a run-time debugger, some inventiveness is necessary to track the error.

One option is to use the DBMS_OUTPUT facilities to write debugging information to a SQL*Plus or Server Manager screen. An option which may work better is to simply include a debug parameter which, when set, causes the SQL string to be output to the HTML page, as opposed to being parsed and executed. This lets the developer immediately see the SQL expression in order to spot any errors, and the code can be pasted from the browser into SQL*Plus and executed. SQL*Plus will then return the exact position of the error in the expression.

The following procedure provides an example. The procedure accepts input from a form which provides a list of employee numbers in emp_list_in and an optional debugging flag in debug_in. The purpose of the procedure is to accept input from this form and build what is effectively an ad hoc query which then returns a list of results to the user. However, if the debug_in flag is set to 'T', the SQL query is displayed instead of executed.

```
CREATE PROCEDURE sql_error (  emp_list_in IN OWA_UTIL.IDENT_ARR,
debug_in IN VARCHAR2 := 'F')
IS
  counter  INTEGER  :=1;
  temp_emp  VARCHAR2(10);
  emp_name  VARCHAR2(200);
  cursor_handle  INTEGER;
  qry_expr  VARCHAR2(2000);
  in_clause  VARCHAR2(1000)  :='';
  dbms_sql_feedback  INTEGER;
BEGIN
  BEGIN
    LOOP
      counter:=counter+1;
      temp_emp := emp_list_in(counter);
      in_clause := in_clause || temp_emp || ',';
    END LOOP;
  EXCEPTION
    WHEN no_data_found THEN NULL;  --i.e., at last element
  END;
  IF (counter = 1)
  THEN
    htp.header(1,'Must specify at least one employee ID');
    RETURN;
  END IF;
  qry_expr := 'SELECT ename FROM emp WHERE empno IN ('
                                    || in_clause || ')';
  IF (debug_in = 'T')
  THEN
    htp.hr;
    htp.p(htf.bold('SQL is: ') || '<br>' || qry_expr);
  ELSE
    cursor_handle := DBMS_SQL.OPEN_CURSOR;
    DBMS_SQL.PARSE(cursor_handle, qry_expr, DBMS_SQL.NATIVE);
    DBMS_SQL.DEFINE_COLUMN(cursor_handle, 1, emp_name,200);
    dbms_sql_feedback:=DBMS_SQL.EXECUTE(cursor_handle);

    WHILE (DBMS_SQL.FETCH_ROWS(cursor_handle)!=0)
    LOOP
      DBMS_SQL.COLUMN_VALUE(cursor_handle, 1, emp_name);
```

```
    htp.p(emp_name);
    htp.para;
  END LOOP;
END IF;
END;
```

When the procedure is executed without the debugging flag set, the following error result is written to the error log file:

```
Wed Feb 05 21:06:24 1997
OWS-05101: Agent : execution failed due to Oracle error 936
ORA-00936: missing expression
ORA-06512: at "SYS.DBMS_SYS_SQL", line 239
ORA-06512: at "SYS.DBMS_SQL", line 25
ORA-06512: at "SCOTT.SQL_ERROR", line 33
ORA-06512: at line 1
  OWA SERVICE: SCOTT
  PROCEDURE: sql_error
  PARAMETERS:
  ===========
  EMP_LIST_IN:
   place_holder
   7369
   7521
   7566
```

As you can see, the log provides sufficient information to know that the SQL statement is causing the error, but it is unknown exactly what error is in the SQL statement itself. Although this is a trivial example, the difficulty is greater with more complex SQL statements. One debugging technique would be to stare at the code until either the source of the error jumps out at you or you go insane, whichever comes first. The debugging code offers a better alternative. If you now call the procedure with the debug parameter set, you can see what SQL statement the code is attempting to execute. An example of the qry_expr is

```
SELECT ename FROM emp WHERE empno IN (7369,7521,7566,)
```

The error should now be immediately apparent: the SQL statement has an IN clause which ends with a trailing comma, and the SQL interpreter expects another term to be included. By simply adding a line to truncate the final comma from in_clause prior to building the query string, you can quickly solve the problem. The following line will do the trick:

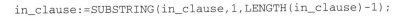
```
in_clause:=SUBSTRING(in_clause,1,LENGTH(in_clause)-1);
```

Obviously, this error is a trivial example. However, the convenient thing about this debugging approach is that for complex query screens, the error may not occur with every different permutation of parameter values. By keeping the toggle feature handy during development, any new SQL error can be quickly diagnosed. It's also very helpful to enable this for the QA staff, as it allows easier and better verification of the query which is supposed to be executed.

NOTE
It may seem tempting to add an exception handler for the entire procedure, such as:

```
EXCEPTION
   WHEN OTHERS THEN
      htp.p('An error occurred, SQL was: ' ||qry_expr);
```

It would be wise to resist this temptation. If you really feel compelled to use an exception handler, try to isolate the exception handler around the call to DBMS_SQL.PARSE. Otherwise, this error handler will mask any errors which are not caused by the dynamic SQL. If you do wrap DBMS_SQL.PARSE to trap this exception, do not forget to close the cursor which the errant query was using.

As was observed earlier in this section, PL/SQL that is executing within the Oracle Server is not easy to debug. However, these tips should make it easier to determine quickly the root cause and source of the error, as well as provide some assistance in writing more defensive code.

Conclusion

In this chapter, you have seen how applications for the Oracle Web Application Server can be developed with PL/SQL, Oracle's procedural extensions to SQL. The Web Application Server SDK provides numerous routines necessary to make PL/SQL web applications which rival those created in virtually any environment. In fact, you have seen that combining the strength of the Web Application Server SDK and PL/SQL's inherently superior integration with the Oracle database makes an unbeatable combination for a wide variety of intranet and Internet applications.

CHAPTER
5

Making the Most
of PL/SQL

hapter 4 introduced the major concepts and libraries associated with PL/SQL web application development. This chapter moves beyond the basic implementation of web applications to introduce some tools and techniques to develop PL/SQL web applications more rapidly and with greater functionality. Some of these techniques make use of the PL/SQL SDK provided with the Oracle Web Application Server (OWAS); however, most make use of some very interesting tools that have been created by others. One is WebAlchemy, a tool for streamlining PL/SQL web development. The second is the Oracle Web Agent Replacement, which incorporates some very useful functionality.

WebAlchemy

Many developers who have worked with GUI tools like Oracle Forms or PowerBuilder complain about the lack of real screen design facilities when they begin web development. Developers with RPG or COBOL experience have much less of a problem with this. Moreover, laying out complex pages in HTML is already tricky, especially with respect to balancing open and closing tags, and it becomes trickier in PL/SQL, where the developer has to develop programs that obey two sets of syntax (PL/SQL and HTML).

Of course there are several tools available for visually building static web pages, such as HoTMetaL or FrontPage. In addition, HTML is not too difficult to write in an editor such as vi. However, the Web Application Server does not provide a way to link these easily created pages to the programmatic control and data access provided by PL/SQL. One sharp Oracle consultant from Australia not only noticed this limitation, he fixed it. Alan Hobbs created WebAlchemy to speed the process of creating PL/SQL procedures that generate HTML output. WebAlchemy can generate almost all the necessary HTP package calls to produce virtually any HTML output. In addition, PL/SQL can be embedded into the HTML in special tags so that the resulting generated PL/SQL source file can often be directly compiled to the database as a completed application module. A beta version of WebAlchemy is included on the CD-ROM. The best place to find future versions of the tool is likely through the Oracle Developer Programme (ODP). We strongly endorse the ODP as a source for tools and information relating to the entire Oracle product line, including the Web Application Server. In addition, the tool may be found at other Oracle web sites as well.

NOTE
Although WebAlchemy was developed by an Oracle employee, it is not a product of Oracle Corporation. Unless and until Oracle brands the WebAlchemy product, please do not attempt to get support for the tool from Oracle Worldwide Support. If you find bugs, Mr. Hobbs invites you to report them to him at ahobbs@lau.oracle.com. However, please do not burden him with support requests.

Using WebAlchemy

The manner in which a developer uses WebAlchemy is fairly straightforward. First, a standard HTML file is produced using either a text or GUI HTML editor. Special comment tags may be inserted into the document, and WebAlchemy will embed these as PL/SQL in the generated file. Next, you open the HTML document in WebAlchemy and generate the PL/SQL needed to produce the page.

To start, create an HTML file using either an editor or a GUI web page design tool such as Adobe's Page Mill or SoftQuad's HoTMetaL. From this document, WebAlchemy can generate the PL/SQL code needed to produce the page using the HTP and HTF routines included in the SDK. For example, consider the following HTML code, which is in a file named test1.html:

```
<HTML>
<HEAD><TITLE>Testing</TITLE></HEAD>
<BODY>
<H1>WebAlchemy Saves Time</H1>
</BODY>
</HTML>
```

The HTML file can then be opened in WebAlchemy. With the file open, simply click the Generate button on the toolbar or choose Generate PL/SQL from the Generate menu. WebAlchemy will then generate the necessary PL/SQL and place it in its own window, which can then be saved to disk or copied to another source file. As shown in Figure 5-1, with the HTML shown above, WebAlchemy will generate the following PL/SQL procedure (excluding the initial comments):

```
CREATE OR REPLACE PROCEDURE test1 AS
BEGIN
  htp.htmlOpen;
  htp.headOpen;
  htp.title( 'Testing');
  htp.headClose;
  htp.bodyOpen;
  htp.header( 1, 'WebAlchemy Saves Time');
  htp.bodyClose;
  htp.htmlClose;
END;
```

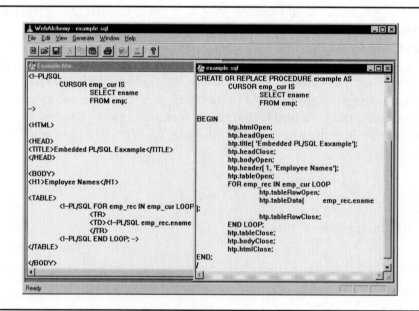

FIGURE 5-1. *WebAlchemy in action: HTML on left; generated PL/SQL on right*

Although this is actually quite impressive to anyone who has slaved through writing thousands of lines of code using the HTP and HTF libraries, the procedure doesn't provide any functionality beyond that of the HTML page. Of course, one could now proceed to modify the procedure to engage in some additional processing. However, if one then made a change to the base HTML file and wanted to regenerate the PL/SQL necessary to produce the page, all the modifications to the original HTML file would need to be applied again. WebAlchemy offers an alternative to this scenario. After creating the base document with all of the appropriate elements, the developer can then embed special HTML comments containing PL/SQL to be inserted into the generated output.

These comments are expressed as follows:

<!--PL/SQL *some_pl_sql_code_here*-->

When such a comment is present, the PL/SQL code placed in the comment will be embedded directly into the generated PL/SQL file, as is. Thus, it is possible for a developer to maintain a single HTML source file that also contains embedded PL/SQL logic in the document. This can be a major labor saver for HTML development. Depending on how well the GUI HTML tool works with adding comments, it may be preferable to simply add PL/SQL tags directly to the HTML file using a text editor rather than using a GUI HTML editor.

NOTE
WebAlchemy's support for HTML is not as lenient as is found in many browsers but is not as strict as a strict HTML syntax checker. Most important, the closing </BODY> tag must be present in the HTML file for WebAlchemy to work properly.

Generation Options

After building an HTML file with embedded PL/SQL commands, completely functional procedures can be generated with WebAlchemy. The tool offers a few options (shown in Figure 5-2) for controlling PL/SQL generation. First, it can generate a separate source file for each procedure or add the procedure to a new or existing package on disk. Second, WebAlchemy can generate calls to HTP and HTF routines using either positional or named parameter passing. Named parameter passing associates the parameter's name and its value with a =>, as in c_attributes=>'color=#FFFFFF'. Positional parameter passing places each parameter into the position where the parameter is listed in its signature.

The third very handy generation option is the Images Directory. If an Images Directory is specified, all references to images shall have a concatenated constant, imagesDir, appended to them. The constant imagesDir will be defined to the entered value in the procedure declarations section. There are some other options as well, which are explained in the WebAlchemy documentation.

Table Output Generation

In most database-driven web applications, tabular output of record lists is necessary. WebAlchemy supports this very well. Because any PL/SQL code can be embedded inside of the PL/SQL comments, you can also embed loops. Thus, the following PL/SQL-commented HTML code will allow

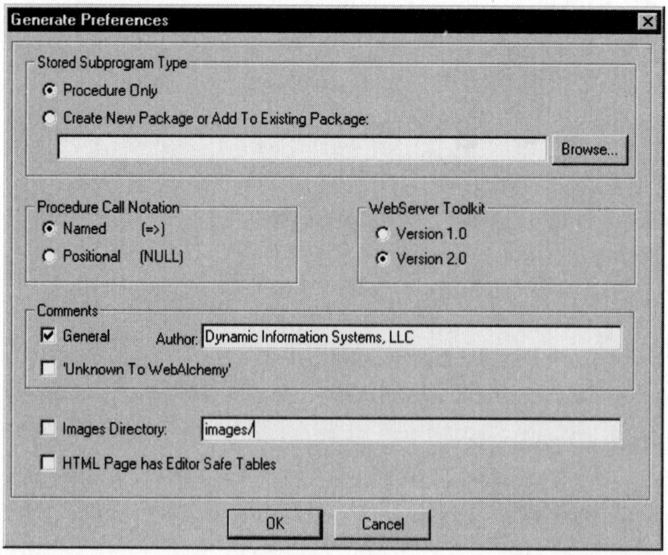

FIGURE 5-2. *WebAlchemy options*

WebAlchemy to generate a table listing all the names in the table of employees. The result of invoking the PL/SQL procedure is shown in Figure 5-3.

```
<!--PL/SQL CURSOR e_curs IS SELECT ename FROM emp;-->
<!--PL/SQL e_rec e_curs%ROWTYPE;-->
<HTML>
<HEAD><TITLE>Employee List</TITLE></HEAD>
<BODY>
<TABLE>
<!--PL/SQL FOR e_rec IN e_curs LOOP-->
<TR>
<TD><!--PL/SQL e_rec.ename--></TD>
</TR>
<!--PL/SQL END LOOP;-->
</TABLE>
</BODY>
</HTML>
```

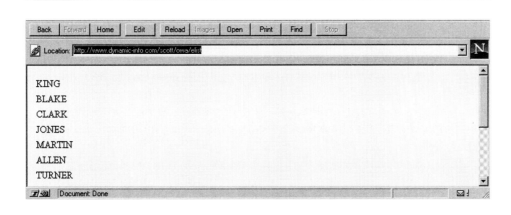

FIGURE 5-3.   *A WebAlchemy-generated page using HTML tables*

NOTE
*Some HTML editors do not accept comments
between the <TABLE> and the first <TR> tag.
WebAlchemy supports an editor-safe table
format. By setting this preference, WebAlchemy
will allow the looping PL/SQL constructs to be
placed outside of the <TABLE> and </TABLE>
tags and will transpose their positions upon
generation. See the WebAlchemy
documentation for more details.*

Conditional Generation

Sometimes it is necessary to generate one of two (or more) different page
formats based on the results of a query or an input parameter. One of
PL/SQL's strengths, in contrast to most HTML template-based web
development tools, is the ability to be completely flexible in the
construction of the page that results from invocation. Although
WebAlchemy provides the ability to work with HTML "templates," the
special PL/SQL comments allow these conditional capabilities to be added
to the base HTML file.

The first step toward accomplishing this is to create an HTML file
containing the HTML necessary to generate any of the pages. For instance,
the screen in Figure 5-4 is used to build an employee information display. It
is composed of three different sections, visibly separated by horizontal
rules. The first will be displayed if the employee has a manager, and it will
display a link that shows the information page associated with the manager.
The second section will be displayed if the employee is the top dog; that is,
if he or she has no superior. Finally, if the procedure is invoked without a
valid employee ID, the third section will be displayed, indicating the error
to the user.

After building this page in the HTML editor, you can now add the
PL/SQL comments to it. Note that the comments being added here must
typically be added with a text editor rather than with a graphical HTML
tool. This is because this example makes use of the PL/SQL tags for
embedding variables populated by a query into a tag. In addition, some of
the comment tags are somewhat unique. Below is the complete HTML file
after embedding the necessary PL/SQL. For readability, PL/SQL comments

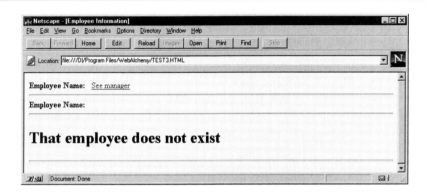

FIGURE 5-4. *Single HTML file for generating three different pages*

are in bold. In addition, notice the underlined section of text about halfway through the file, which is explained a few paragraphs down.

```
<!--PL/SQL CREATE PROCEDURE display_ename (empno_in IN NUMBER) AS -->
<!--PL/SQL v_ename VARCHAR2(50);-->
<!--PL/SQL v_mgr NUMBER;-->
<HTML>
<HEAD><TITLE>Employee Information</TITLE></HEAD>
<BODY>
<!--PL/SQL BEGIN -->
<!--PL/SQL --perform query -->
<!--PL/SQL SELECT ENAME,MGR INTO v_ename,v_mgr
FROM EMP WHERE EMPNO=empno_in; -->
<!--PL/SQL IF v_mgr IS NOT NULL-->
<!--PL/SQL THEN-->
<B>Employee Name: <!--PL/SQL ||v_ename--></B> 
<A HREF="display_ename?empno_in='||v_mgr||'">See manager</A>
<HR>
<!--PL/SQL ELSE-->
<B>Employee Name: <!--PL/SQL ||v_ename--></B>
<HR>
<!--PL/SQL END IF;-->
<!--PL/SQL EXCEPTION-->
<!--PL/SQL WHEN OTHERS THEN-->
<H1>That employee does not exist</H1>
<HR>
<!--PL/SQL END;-->
</BODY>
</HTML>
```

There are a few things to notice about this example. First, we have defined our own procedure name. If the first line in the HTML file is of the form "CREATE PROCEDURE...," WebAlchemy uses the provided procedure name and parameters listed as the method signature during generation. Note that you must include the "IS" or "AS" at the end of the declaration. We have also defined some variables. Any PL/SQL comments appearing before the opening <HTML> tag will be inserted prior to the PL/SQL BEGIN statement in the generated procedure.

The rest of the PL/SQL comments are fairly straightforward. We create a sub-block to allow us to trap the exception of an invalid employee ID being passed to the routine. We then select the data from the database and use an IF..THEN construct to switch between displaying either of the two different screen sections. Finally, we wrap the error message at the bottom in an exception handler.

As for the underlined text in the procedure "'||v_mgr||'," it is used to automatically add the parameter to the generated URL. WebAlchemy will correctly insert this into the procedure. The reason to use this syntax is that WebAlchemy expects a closing quote for the HREF parameter before encountering another opening tag. That is, the following line will produce an error during generation:

```
<A HREF="display_ename?empno_in=<!--PL/SQL v_mgr -->">
```

Because it is preferable to maintain all HTML and PL/SQL in a single source file and to avoid altering the generated PL/SQL source file, we strongly suggest using whatever syntactic tricks are necessary to make WebAlchemy generate exactly what is needed, even if it means embedding calls to htp.print from within a PL/SQL comment. Likewise, during debugging, we recommend changing the code in the embedded comments and regenerating the PL/SQL file rather than changing the generated source file directly. The following is the PL/SQL code generated by WebAlchemy:

```
CREATE PROCEDURE display_ename (empno_in IN NUMBER) AS
    v_ename VARCHAR2(50);
    v_mgr NUMBER;
BEGIN
    htp.htmlOpen;
    htp.headOpen;
    htp.title( 'Employee Information');
    htp.headClose;
    htp.bodyOpen;
```

```
BEGIN
--perform query
  SELECT ENAME,MGR INTO v_ename,v_mgr
    FROM EMP
   WHERE EMPNO=empno_in;
  IF v_mgr IS NOT NULL
  THEN
    htp.bold( 'Employee Name: '||v_ename);
    htp.print( '  ' );
    htp.anchor2( 'display_ename?empno_in='||v_mgr||'', 'See manager');
    htp.hr;
  ELSE
    htp.bold( 'Employee Name: '||v_ename);
    htp.hr;
  END IF;
EXCEPTION
  WHEN OTHERS THEN
    htp.header( 1, 'That employee does not exist');
    htp.hr;
END;
htp.bodyClose;
htp.htmlClose;
END;
```

Figures 5-5, 5-6, and 5-7 show how the procedure can correctly display any of the three different sections, depending on the input.

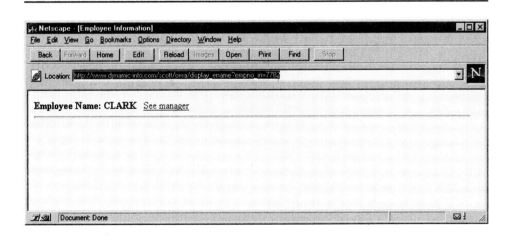

FIGURE 5-5. *Page displaying employee name and link to manager*

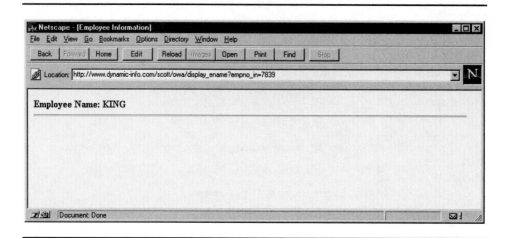

FIGURE 5-6. *Page displaying employee name without manager link*

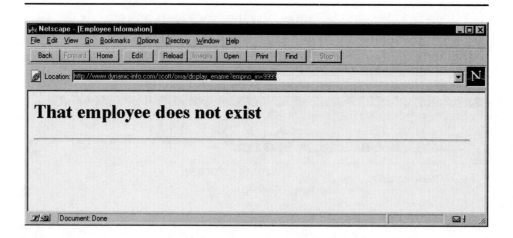

FIGURE 5-7. *Page displaying an error message*

NOTE
The techniques shown above are demonstrated with WebAlchemy beta version 2.1 and may likely continue to work in future releases of the tool. However, because WebAlchemy is a beta product at the time of this writing, individual generation behavior may change as the tool evolves.

As can be seen, WebAlchemy is a major time-saver for web developers using PL/SQL. By generating PL/SQL from HTML files, web developers gain some of the GUI screen layout capabilities that many client/server developers take for granted. Now that you have seen a way to speed PL/SQL-based web development, let's look at using PL/SQL to efficiently implement some specific requirements and features.

Serving Images

Most web applications today are relatively image intensive, compared to the average client/server application. Typically, this is simply a design decision to create visually appealing screens for an application. Often, however, the Web inspires the creation of applications in which images serve an integral purpose. This may be in the form of a product catalog or possibly people's photographs in a human resources database. Whatever the purpose, the issue of managing images in database-driven web applications frequently arises.

NOTE
Although this section focuses on image storage and downloading, the same discussion and techniques apply to any binary file type whether they be JPEG images, WAV sound files, or Excel spreadsheets.

There are two general ways in which to manage images in such applications. The first and most straightforward manner is simply to store the images in operating system files and store only the filename or path information in the database. This model offers the developer an easy method of accessing files and requires no specialized tools for inserting images into the database: simply store the file in the appropriate directory and store the filename in the database. If a file naming convention is enforced, such as by using the product's ID in the root filename, then even the second step is avoided.

However, this is not universally the easiest way to manage images. Often, the driving reason behind storing images in the database is to improve the efficiency of data entry and management. For instance, an Oracle Forms application could be used, in which the user enters detailed product information as well as directly adds images to an area on the form. In this way, all data can be managed from a centralized location.

Once the data is in the database, the web application developer must figure out a way to extract the data and communicate it to the browser for display to the user. There are actually a couple of different ways to accomplish this. One technique makes use of the relatively plain-vanilla implementation of the Web Application Server. The second technique uses a replacement for the standard Oracle Web Agent cartridge, known rather blandly as the Oracle Web Agent Replacement.

Serving Database Images with the Basic Oracle Web Application Server

To serve images stored in a long raw column of the Oracle RDBMS, a PL/SQL utility package called UTL_RAW is used. The UTL_RAW package provides a collection of routines for manipulating data stored in long raw columns. Assuming you have added a column called Picture, which contains the employee's picture, to the EMP table, you could use the following routine to return this picture:

```
CREATE PROCEDURE show_emp_pic (empno_in IN NUMBER)
IS
  v_pict_raw   raw(32760);
BEGIN
  SELECT picture INTO v_pict_raw
    FROM emp
   WHERE empno=empno_in;
```

```
   IF v_pict_raw IS NULL
   THEN
     owa_util.redirect_url('/images/notfound.jpg');
   ELSE
     owa_util.mime_header('image/jpeg');
     htp.prn( utl_raw.cast_to_varchar2( v_pict_raw) );
   END IF;
END;
```

The preceding code makes a couple of assumptions: first, it hard-codes the URL of the image to be displayed if the employee does not have a picture in his or her record; second, it assumes that all pictures are of type JPEG. Within the context of this application, this may be acceptable. However, the table storing the images could be augmented to also store the actual MIME type of the data contained in the picture column. In addition, if this application were being used to download arbitrary files (spreadsheets, pictures, presentations, etc.), then it would be necessary to store the MIME type of the associated data. Otherwise, the browser could not effectively deal with launching the appropriate helper application or saving the file.

Although the "notfound" image could be stored in the database, for instance in a utility image table, we do not recommend it unless it is done for ease of administration. Although the overhead of each piece of the transaction is small, passing the request from the WRB to the PL/SQL agent to the database and back through to the browser does take more time than just letting the HTTP listener stream the file from its file system. The additional overhead increases further if the PL/SQL agent is connecting to the database over the network.

Serving Database Images with the Oracle Web Agent Replacement

Although the preceding technique is quite useful, we tend to endorse another method that makes use of a replacement for the Oracle Web Agent cartridge. It was written by an Oracle sales consultant from Maryland, Tom Kyte (not to be confused with Tom Kite, the pro golfer). The OWA Replacement (OWAR), as it is known, makes serving images stored inside an Oracle database as painless and easy as possible. In addition, the OWAR adds a number of other handy functions, which are discussed later in the chapter.

Of course, the replacement must be installed first. The replacement cartridge source and documentation are included on the CD, along with binaries for SPARC Solaris and Windows NT. In addition, new versions of the cartridge should always be available from the Oracle Government web site at http://govt.us.oracle.com, by following the Downloadable Utilities link. The folks at Oracle Government do a good job of keeping up-to-date web utilities at the source. After obtaining the necessary files, follow along with the installation instructions provided. It requires a slight bit of effort to install the current release with version 3.0 of Oracle Web Application Server. Version 3.0 installation issues are discussed in detail at the end of this chapter.

NOTE
The OWAR actually goes beyond simply providing image-serving capabilities. It also provides the capability to easily upload images to the database from a web browser using the HTML form upload capabilities found in modern browsers such as Netscape Navigator 3.0 and above. This functionality is discussed later in the chapter under "HTML Form File Upload."

There are two specific installation and configuration tasks that must be performed in order to use the OWAR for image serving. First, an image table must be created in the schema owned by the Database Access Descriptor (DAD) used for the request. The default format of this table, as defined in the image.sql file, is as follows:

```
CREATE TABLE image (
    NAME        VARCHAR2(255),
    MIME_TYPE   VARCHAR2(30),
    IMG_SIZE    NUMBER,
    IMAGE       LONG RAW,
    constraint image_pk primary key( name ) )
```

The OWAR can use a table other than one named "IMAGE," but it must be structured in this manner for all the OWAR's functionality to work properly with it. If a table name other than "image" is desired for a particular PL/SQL agent, this can be specified in the cartridge configuration parameters. Create a configuration variable named *plsqlagent*_image_name and set the variable's value to the name of the desired table. Note that *plsqlagent* should be replaced with the name of the PL/SQL agent to which this setting should apply. This allows a developer to specify multiple image tables for multiple Database Connection Descriptors (DCDs). Do not qualify the tablename with a username; the OWAR will do this automatically when it performs the necessary queries.

After the image table has been installed and populated and, if necessary, the configuration parameter specified, accessing the images themselves is very straightforward. It isn't even really a PL/SQL task, since the OWAR does all the real work for the developer. All that is necessary is to reference the image-serving function of the OWAR from an embedded image link or URL. The form of the URI is "/*agent_name*/owai/ *image_name*," where *agent_name* specifies the PL/SQL agent to use and *image_name* is the value of the Name column of the IMAGE table for the row from which the image should be returned.

When such a request is made, the OWAR processes it by selecting the record from the database. It then determines the MIME type of the file based on its reference to the type indicated in the table, as well as the mappings that are defined in the web listener's configuration files. It then sends the file, indicating the MIME type in the header. The USER_PAGES package, which appears later in this chapter in the section "HTML Form File Upload," is an example of embedding a picture using the OWAR.

For developers who support users with slower connections, and especially when the files being stored in the database are things such as spreadsheets or executables, the OWAR can automatically compress the binary object prior to download. To support this functionality, the OWAR is invoked in the same manner as above, but instead of using owai as part of the URI, replace it with owaigz. This invocation method will compress the data on the fly at the server, prior to downloading the object to the browser. Of course, this has the downside of consuming significant server CPU time to perform the compression. However, it should be possible to make reasonable decisions about trading server CPU for improved end-user performance.

VRML

Most of the content displayed from PL/SQL web applications is in the form of text and images, the use of which has been demonstrated up to this point. As mentioned in Chapter 2, however, browsers can display other content very effectively as well. That chapter discussed the Virtual Reality Modeling Language (VRML) as a form in which certain data can be presented usefully.

Oracle provides the Oracle Worlds cartridge for managing database-linked VRML worlds. The cartridge can be installed and configured from the Web Request Broker cartridge configuration screen. The client software is also accessible from the Oracle Worlds configuration screen.

Although the Oracle Worlds cartridge is impressive in its functionality, and we invite the reader to explore it more thoroughly, it is not covered in this book because it is, according to Oracle, a prototype work in progress developed as part of Oracle's research into VRML. In addition, it exclusively supports version 2.0 of the VRML standard, as opposed to version 1.0, which many VRML browsers still use.

It is also possible to generate VRML simply using the PL/SQL cartridge. In fact, the Oracle Worlds cartridge itself is primarily driven by a collection of PL/SQL routines. Because VRML is another text-based display description language, much like HTML, PL/SQL can be used to generate VRML output. In a similar manner, PL/SQL procedures could be written to generate PostScript output; however, this would be significantly more complex.

The following code generates the VRML world shown in Figure 5-8. It displays a three-dimensional organizational chart based on data in the Oracle demo EMP table and maintains the correct hierarchy of subordinates. We developed this for a seminar series presented by Oracle and Silicon Graphics as an example of delivering database content in unique ways via the Web. The organizational chart is unique in a couple of ways. First, each sphere is colored differently, depending on the employee's title. In addition, the size of each sphere varies based on the employee's salary. This is probably not an organizational chart you would want in your office, but it illustrates the use of varying different appearance attributes to convey more information to the user in the same space.

```
PROCEDURE vrml_org_chart IS
    vEmp NUMBER;
    vSal NUMBER;
    vName  VARCHAR2(40);
    vJob  VARCHAR2(40);
    CURSOR minions(bossman NUMBER) IS
      SELECT   empno
        FROM   emp
       WHERE   mgr=bossman;
BEGIN
    owa_util.mime_header('x-world/x-vrml');
    SELECT EMPNO,SAL,ENAME,JOB
      INTO vEmp,vSal,vName,vJob
      FROM emp
     WHERE mgr IS NULL;
    htp.p('#VRML V1.0 ascii');
    htp.p('Separator {');
    htp.p('PerspectiveCamera { position 0 -15 5 orientation '||
          '1 0 0 .79 focalDistance 7.0 heightAngle 1.0}');
    htp.p('Material { ambientColor .2 .2 .2 ');
    htp.p('diffuseColor .8 .8 .8');
    htp.p('specularColor 0 0 0');
    htp.p('emissiveColor 0 0 0');
    htp.p('shininess 0.2');
    htp.p('transparency 0 }');
    htp.p('FontStyle { size .5');
    htp.p('family SERIF');
    htp.p('style NONE }');
    voc_DoSphere(vEmp,1,vSal,vName,vJob);
    htp.p('}');
END;

PROCEDURE voc_doSphere (   emp_in in NUMBER,
                           lvl_in in NUMBER,
                           sal_in in NUMBER,
                           name_in in VARCHAR2,
                           job_in in VARCHAR2 )
IS
    k  NUMBER;
    vEmp  NUMBER;
    vSal  NUMBER;
    vName  VARCHAR2(40);
    vJob  VARCHAR2(40);
```

```
   job_x   VARCHAR2(40);
   delta   NUMBER;
   theta   NUMBER;
   vCount  NUMBER;
   c_alpha  NUMBER;
   c_rad   NUMBER;
   c_ht    NUMBER;
   cx  NUMBER;
   cy  NUMBER;
   cz  NUMBER;
   vRadius  NUMBER;
   CURSOR minions(bossman NUMBER) IS
      SELECT   empno,sal,ename,job
        FROM   emp
       WHERE   mgr=bossman;
begin
  htp.p('WWWAnchor { name "'||owa_util.get_owa_service_path||
        'org.show_emp?empno_in=' || emp_in ||'" description "'||
        name_in||' Details "');
  --do color selection based on job
  htp.p('Separator {');
  job_x:=RTRIM(job_in);
  IF (job_x='CLERK') THEN
    htp.p(' Material { diffuseColor .8 .8 1.0 } ');   --Blue/Grey
  ELSIF (job_x='ANALYST') THEN
    htp.p(' Material { diffuseColor .1526 0 1.0 } ');. --Blue
  ELSIF (job_x='SALESMAN') THEN
    htp.p(' Material { diffuseColor .41132 .05237 1.0 } '); --Prpl
  ELSE  --Manager or president
    htp.p(' Material { diffuseColor 1 .018463 .16225 } ');   --Red
  END IF;
  vRadius:=TRUNC(.5*(sal_in/1000),5);
  htp.p('Sphere { radius '||TO_CHAR(vRadius)||' }');  --draw sphere
  htp.prn('Separator { Translation { translation 0 -'||
          TO_CHAR(vRadius+.5) ||
          ' 0 } AsciiText { string "'||name_in||'"}}');
  htp.p('}}');
  SELECT COUNT (empno) INTO vCount FROM emp WHERE mgr=emp_in;
  IF (vCount != 0)
  THEN
    delta:=(2*3.141595)/vCount;
    theta:=0;
    k:=0;
    IF (vCount=1)
```

```
    THEN
      c_rad:=0;
    ELSE
      c_rad:=  6-lvl_in;
    END IF;
    c_ht:= -5;
    OPEN minions(emp_in);
    LOOP
      FETCH minions INTO vEmp,vSal,vName,vJob;
      EXIT WHEN minions%NOTFOUND;
      theta:=k*delta;
      c_alpha:=theta;
      htp.p(' Separator { ');
      voc_DoLine(c_alpha,c_rad,c_ht,lvl_in);
      htp.p(' } ');
      cx:=TRUNC(c_rad * cos(c_alpha),7);
      cy:=TRUNC(c_rad * sin(c_alpha),7);
      cz:=TRUNC(c_ht,7);
      htp.p(' Separator { ');
      htp.p(' Translation { translation '||TO_CHAR(cx)||' '||
            TO_CHAR(cy)||' '||TO_CHAR(cz)||'}');
      voc_DoSphere(vEmp,lvl_in+1,vSal,vName,vJob);
      htp.p(' } ');
      k:=k+1;
    END LOOP;
    CLOSE minions;
  END IF;
end;
PROCEDURE voc_doLine (c_alpha IN NUMBER
                      c_rad  IN NUMBER,
                      c_ht   IN NUMBER,
                      lvl_in IN NUMBER )
IS
  r_angle  NUMBER;
  c_dist   NUMBER;
  c_beta   NUMBER;
  r_trans_y  NUMBER;
BEGIN
  r_angle:=c_alpha - (3.141595/2.0);
  htp.p('Material { diffuseColor 1 1 '||
        TO_CHAR(TRUNC(1-(1/lvl_in),7) )||' }');
  htp.p('Rotation { rotation 0 0 1 '||
        TO_CHAR(TRUNC(r_angle,7))||' }');

  --We use a lookup table to compute the actual values
```

```
--primarily because PL/SQL does not have an arcsin function
--there are approximations which could be computed, but this
--will have higher performance

--c_dist:=SQRT( (c_rad*c_rad) + (c_ht*c_ht) );
--c_beta:=ARCSIN(c_ht/c_dist);
IF c_rad = 0  --special case
THEN
  c_dist:=5;
  c_beta:=-1.570796;
ELSIF (lvl_in=1) THEN
  c_dist:= TRUNC(SQRT(25+25),7);
  c_beta:= -0.78539;
ELSIF (lvl_in=2) THEN
  c_dist:=TRUNC(SQRT(16+25),7);
  c_beta:=-.89606;
ELSIF (lvl_in=3) THEN
  c_dist:=TRUNC(SQRT(9+25),7);
  c_beta:=-1.03038;
ELSIF (1=0) THEN
  c_dist:=TRUNC(SQRT(6.25+25),7);
  c_beta:=-1.10715;
END IF;
r_angle:=c_beta;
htp.p('Rotation { rotation 1 0 0 '||
      TO_CHAR(TRUNC(r_angle,7))||' }');
r_trans_y:=TRUNC(c_dist/2.0,7);
htp.p(' Translation { translation 0 '||
      TO_CHAR(r_trans_y)|| ' 0 }');
htp.p(' Cylinder { height -'||TO_CHAR(c_dist)||' radius .1}');
END;
```

This is actually a somewhat more complex VRML generation procedure than many simply because of the mathematics involved with the dynamic arrangement of the spheres. Currently, the Oracle World cartridge doesn't support this kind of capability. However, the techniques shown here demonstrate a way to deliver content of a variety of datatypes using the PL/SQL cartridge. The study of 3-D visualization in data analysis techniques continues to find ways to use 3-D viewing as a method to let people visually scan large volumes of data more quickly and discern interesting relationships which may exist in the data.

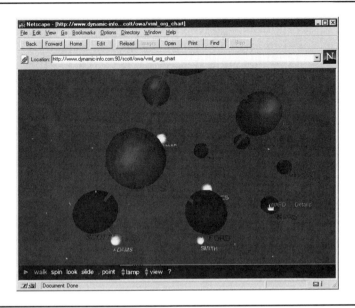

FIGURE 5-8. *VRML organizational chart*

Sophisticated Text Searching with Oracle ConText

The advent of computers has clearly made everyone's life easier. Well, regardless whether the preceding statement is actually true, many people probably feel that computers have exacerbated their information management problems more than solved them (this author included). Most people today are awash in levels of information an order of magnitude higher than in the recent past. Oracle markets an extension to the Oracle RDBMS called ConText, which is a special text-processing and analysis tool. At the time of this writing, ConText is available for Oracle 7 and as a data cartridge for Oracle 8. ConText allows more intelligent queries to be run against databases containing large amounts of text and can process and distill the text based on a variety of attributes.

Web applications offer an enormous opportunity for the development and deployment of sophisticated text management applications such as those that can be created with ConText. This section touches on how to make web applications that are text savvy using Oracle ConText. In fact, with ConText, two levels of sophistication can be employed. The first is enhanced text searching beyond that which is possible with the basic SQL operators such as simple equality or the marginally more flexible LIKE comparison operator. The second level involves making use of ConText's linguistic services.

NOTE
The examples in this section require that the ConText engine be installed, configured, and running in the Oracle environment. Contact your database administrator if you are unsure if it is installed or if you need permission to access its services.

The following is a fairly simple example of the power of ConText. It exploits the advanced text-searching capabilities available in the product using one-step queries. The interface to the package is shown in Figure 5-9. The package could be enhanced by supporting two-step queries with special term highlighting, as well as using ConText's theme and gist functionality, which allows the developer to make use of ConText's ability to summarize and distill the meaningful content of a document. For more information about ConText, consult the ConText Application Developer's Guide, included with the product.

```
CREATE OR REPLACE PACKAGE BODY ConText_demo IS
  PROCEDURE main
  IS
  BEGIN
    htp.htmlOpen;
    htp.headOpen;
    htp.title('Perform Search' );
    htp.headClose;
    htp.bodyOpen;
    htp.formOpen('/scott/plsql/ConText_demo.execute_query',
              'POST');
    htp.tableOpen;
```

```
htp.tableRowOpen;
  htp.tableData('');
  htp.tableData(htf.bold('Term'));
  htp.tableData(htf.bold('Stems'));
  htp.tableData(htf.bold('Fuzzy'));
  htp.tableData(htf.bold('Soundex'));
  htp.tableData(htf.bold('Weight'));
htp.tableRowClose;
htp.tableRowOpen;
  htp.tableData('');
  htp.tableData(htf.formText('term_1'));
  htp.tableData(htf.formCheckbox('attr_1','$'),
               calign=>'CENTER');
  htp.tableData(htf.formCheckbox('attr_1','?'),
               calign=>'CENTER');
  htp.tableData(htf.formCheckbox('attr_1','!'),
               calign=>'CENTER');
  htp.tableData(htf.formText('weight_1',csize=>'2',
               cmaxlength=>'3'),calign=>'CENTER');
htp.tableRowClose;
htp.tableRowOpen;
  htp.p('<TD>');
    htp.formSelectOpen('operator');
    htp.formSelectOption('and',cattributes=>
                                    'SELECTED value="&"');
    htp.formSelectOption('or',cattributes=>'value="|"');
    htp.formSelectOption('accumulate',
                        cattributes=>'value=","');
    htp.formSelectOption('minus',cattributes=>'value="-"');
    htp.formSelectOption('near',cattributes=>'value=";"');
    htp.formSelectClose;
  htp.p('</TD>');
  htp.tableData(htf.formText('term_2'));
  htp.tableData(htf.formCheckbox('attr_2','$'),
                                calign=>'CENTER');
  htp.tableData(htf.formCheckbox('attr_2','?'),
                                calign=>'CENTER');
  htp.tableData(htf.formCheckbox('attr_2','!'),
                                calign=>'CENTER');
  htp.tableData(htf.formText('weight_2',csize=>'2',
                                cmaxlength=>'3'),
               calign=>'CENTER');
htp.tableRowClose;
htp.tableRowOpen;
  htp.tableData(htf.formSubmit,ccolspan=>6,
```

```
                              calign=>'CENTER');
     htp.tableRowClose;
     htp.tableClose;
   htp.formClose;
   htp.bodyClose;
   htp.htmlClose;
END;

PROCEDURE execute_query(term_1 IN VARCHAR2,
                        term_2 IN VARCHAR2,
                        attr_1 IN owa_util.ident_arr:=empty_array,
                        attr_2 IN owa_util.ident_arr:=empty_array,
                        weight_1 IN VARCHAR2, weight_2 IN VARCHAR2,
                        operator IN VARCHAR2)
IS
   t1   VARCHAR2(200);
   t2   VARCHAR2(200);
   qryterm   VARCHAR2(200);
   x   INTEGER;
BEGIN

   htp.htmlOpen;
   htp.headOpen;
   htp.title('Search Results');
   htp.headClose;
   htp.bodyOpen;

   IF term_1 IS NOT NULL
   THEN
     t1 := '{' || term_1 || '}';
     FOR x IN 1..attr_1.COUNT
     LOOP
       t1 := attr_1(x) || t1;
     END LOOP;
     IF weight_1 IS NOT NULL
     THEN
       t1 := '(' || t1 || ')*' || weight_1;
     END IF;

   IF term_2 IS NOT NULL
   THEN
     t2 := '{' || term_2 || '}';
     FOR x IN 1..attr_1.COUNT
     LOOP
       t2 := attr_2(x) || t2;
```

```
    END LOOP;
    IF weight_2 IS NOT NULL
    THEN
      t2 := '(' || t2 || ')*' || weight_2;
    END IF;
    qryterm := '(' || t1 || ')' || operator ||
               '(' || t2 || ')';
  ELSE
    qryterm := t1;
  END IF;

  htp.p(htf.bold('The query was: ') || qryterm );
  htp.tableOpen;
  FOR cur IN ( SELECT docid, doctitle, SCORE(0) scr
          FROM docs
         WHERE CONTAINS(doctext,qryterm,0) > 0
         ORDER BY NVL(SCORE(0),0) )
  LOOP
    htp.tableRowOpen;
    htp.tableData(htf.anchor('ConText_demo.show_doc?docid_in='
                 || cur.docid,cur.doctitle));
    htp.tableData( cur.scr );
    htp.tableRowClose;
  END LOOP;
  htp.tableClose;
  ELSE
    htp.header(1,'You must enter at least the '||
               'first query term.');
  END IF;
  htp.bodyClose;
  htp.htmlClose;
END;

PROCEDURE show_doc(docid_in IN VARCHAR2)
IS
BEGIN
  FOR cur IN (SELECT doctitle,doctext
          FROM docs
         WHERE docid=docid_in)
  LOOP
    htp.htmlOpen;
    htp.headOpen;
    htp.title(cur.doctitle);
    htp.headClose;
    htp.bodyOpen;
```

```
      htp.p(cur.doctext);
      htp.bodyClose;
      htp.htmlClose;
   END LOOP;
END;

END ConText_demo;
```

HTML Form File Upload

As mentioned earlier in the chapter, the Oracle Web Agent Replacement implements a very simple interface for accepting file uploads. Note that the Content Services provided by the Web Request Broker, which are discussed in Chapter 10, allow a C developer to implement similar functionality. However, the mechanism the OWAR implements to allow PL/SQL routines to easily and fully exploit these capabilities is impressive.

Before jumping into the details of the OWAR implementation, let's take a moment to examine the general issue of HTML form-based file uploading.

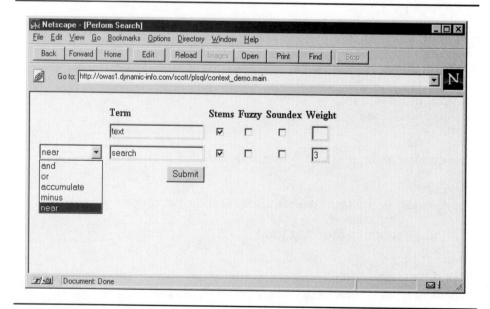

FIGURE 5-9. *Querying a document database with ConText's sophisticated options*

In Navigator version 2.0, Netscape implemented a new value for the TYPE
parameter of the <INPUT> tag: **file**. This option allows the user of the form
to attach a file from a locally accessible volume to the form contents and
upload it to the server, along with any other form data. On the HTML page,
this input element is shown as a text field with a button labeled "Browse..."
next to it (see Figure 5-10). The user can select the image to attach by
clicking the Browse button, which presents the operating-system-specific
get file dialog (or open file dialog). When the user selects a file from the
dialog and accepts it (clicks OK), the fully qualified filename of the file is
displayed in the adjacent text area. When the user submits the form, the
web browser sends a request containing both the encoded form data as
well as the file data itself.

The HTML for building such a form is actually quite straightforward. In
addition to the file input tag for submitting the form, a special content type
must be used for forms that contain file upload information. Normally, the
content type for the form data is not specified and simply defaults to the
MIME type text/x-url-encoded; however, when uploading forms containing
documents, a different MIME type must be specified explicitly. That type is
multipart/form-data and is specified by attaching an ENCTYPE attribute to
the opening <FORM> tag. The following code shows a fragment of HTML
setting up a form that allows users to upload their pictures to the database:

```
<form action="/wa/scott/owaup/emp_info.setempdata"
enctype="multipart/form-data">
<!-- other form data here -->
<b>Your picture</b>:<input type="file" name="img_in">
<p>
<input type=submit>
</form>
```

Before moving on, some configuration steps may be required. To
configure the OWAR for image uploading, there are two main, specific
steps to take. First, make sure the file /owarepl/sql/image.sql is executed
against the database account you will use for image upload. This creates an
image table in the schema owner. This table is necessary regardless of
whether you will be storing the images in the database or in the file system.
Next, if you plan to store images in the file system, which is not done in
this example, you must set a configuration parameter, *plsqlagent*_filedir, to
the path of the directory in which images are to be stored. (As shown
previously, replace *plsqlagent* with the actual name of the agent being

used.) If this parameter is omitted, as it will be for this example, the images will be stored in the table specified by the parameter *plsqlagent*_image_tname.

NOTE
Images can be stored in tables other than the default table named image. However, the column names and types defined in the image table are required.

Having explained the client-side mechanics of setting up an HTML form file upload and the configuration process, let's explore how the OWAR accomplishes the minor miracle of letting a PL/SQL procedure manipulate the uploaded file. The process is remarkably similar to standard invocation of PL/SQL procedures through the PL/SQL cartridge. However, instead of using the standard URI of the form "/scott/owa/pkg.proc" as the action for the form, a URI of the form "/scott/owaup/pkg.proc" is used.

The owaup URI component directs the OWAR to look in the submitted data stream for a file. When it finds a file, it is written to the image table, setting the name to U*xxxxxxx*, where *xxxxxxx* is a zero-padded string of the sequence number obtained from the img_seq sequence. It then invokes the PL/SQL procedure specified in the URL, passing in all parameters as they came from the browser untouched, except for the parameter name associated with the file, whose value is set to the name of the image (U*xxxxxxx*). Thus, the procedure simply is passed the name under which the file is saved in the parameter associated with the file. At this point, the PL/SQL procedure can do whatever it chooses with the information, such as storing the value in a related table.

NOTE
When using the owaup feature to store images in the database, the entire transaction described above is atomic; that is, if the invoked procedure issues a rollback or the procedure fails for some reason, the image will not be stored in the database. However, if the image is being written to the file system, it will remain even if the procedure fails or otherwise rolls back the related database update.

Of course, once the images have been uploaded, the developer can generate pages with those embedded images. The following PL/SQL package illustrates this with a basic application that allows users to create a page of information about themselves, including a photo. Figures 5-10 and 5-11 show an example of the package in action, as it might be used by that unique cultural icon, Fabio.

```
CREATE OR REPLACE PACKAGE BODY user_pages IS

  PROCEDURE main
  IS
  BEGIN

    FOR cur IN (SELECT name,userid FROM pages ORDER BY name)
    LOOP
      htp.anchor('/scott/plsql/user_pages.show_page?uid_in='||
               cur.userid, cur.name);
      htp.br;
    END LOOP;
    htp.anchor('/scott/plsql/user_pages.new_user_form',
              'Add a Page');

  END;
  PROCEDURE new_user_form
  IS
    x INTEGER;
  BEGIN
    htp.htmlOpen;
    htp.headOpen;
    htp.title('New page' );
    htp.headClose;
    htp.bodyOpen;
    --notice the use of /owaup/ as the action associated with
    --the form, as well as adding the enctype attribute
    htp.formOpen('/wa/scott/owaup/user_pages.new_user_upload',
               'POST',
               cattributes=>'enctype="multipart/form-data"');
    htp.tableOpen;
      htp.tableRowOpen;
        htp.tableData(htf.bold('Name:') );
        htp.tableData(htf.formText('name_in') );
      htp.tableRowClose;
      htp.tableRowOpen;
        htp.tableData(htf.bold('Email Address:') );
```

```
      htp.tableData(htf.formText('email_in') );
    htp.tableRowClose;
    htp.tableRowOpen;
      htp.tableData( htf.bold('Meaningful Quotation'),
                      cattributes=>'valign=top');
      htp.tableData(htf.formTextArea('quote_in',7,40));
    htp.tableRowClose;
    htp.tableRowOpen;
      htp.tableData(htf.bold('Your picture:'));
      htp.p('<td><input type="file" name="file_in"></td>');
    htp.tableRowClose;
    htp.tableRowOpen;
      htp.p('<td colspan=2>');
      htp.p('<font size=4><b>Favorite Web Sites</b></font>');
      htp.tableOpen;
        htp.tableRowOpen;
          htp.tableData(htf.bold('Site Name'));
          htp.tableData(htf.bold('Site URL'));
        htp.tableRowClose;
        FOR x IN 1..10
        LOOP
          htp.tableRowOpen;
            htp.tableData(htf.formText('lk_name_in'));
            htp.tableData(htf.formText('lk_url_in'));
          htp.tableRowClose;
        END LOOP;
      htp.tableClose;
      htp.p('</td>');
    htp.tableRowClose;
  htp.tableClose;
  htp.formSubmit;
  htp.formClose;
  htp.bodyClose;
  htp.htmlClose;

END;

PROCEDURE new_user_upload(   file_in IN VARCHAR2,
                             name_in IN VARCHAR2,
                             email_in IN VARCHAR2,
                             quote_in IN VARCHAR2,
                             lk_name_in IN
OWA_UTIL.IDENT_ARR:=empty_ident_arr,
                             lk_url_in IN
OWA_UTIL.IDENT_ARR:=empty_ident_arr)
```

```
IS
  lk_count INTEGER;
  x INTEGER;
  vuid NUMBER(12);
BEGIN
  SELECT seq_uid.nextval INTO vuid FROM dual;
  INSERT INTO pages VALUES (vuid, file_in, name_in,
                              email_in, quote_in);
  lk_count:=lk_name_in.COUNT;
  IF (lk_count > lk_url_in.COUNT)
  THEN
    lk_count:=lk_url_in.COUNT;
  END IF;

  FOR x IN 1..lk_count
  LOOP
    INSERT INTO links VALUES (vuid,lk_name_in(x),lk_url_in(x));
  END LOOP;
  COMMIT;
  show_page (vuid);
END;

PROCEDURE show_page (uid_in IN NUMBER)
IS
BEGIN
  FOR cur IN (SELECT * FROM pages WHERE userid=uid_in)
  LOOP
    htp.htmlOpen;
    htp.headOpen;
    htp.title(cur.name || '''s Page' );
    htp.headClose;
    htp.bodyOpen;
    htp.header(1,'Hi, I''m ' || cur.name );
    --here we embed the image, using the owai call
    htp.img('/wa/scott/owai/'||cur.img_name);
    htp.para;
    htp.bold('My favorite quotation is:');
    htp.blockQuoteOpen;
    htp.p(cur.quote);
    htp.blockQuoteClose;
    htp.bold('My favorite sites are:');
    htp.tableOpen;
    FOR subcur IN (SELECT name,url
                      FROM links
                    WHERE userid=uid_in)
```

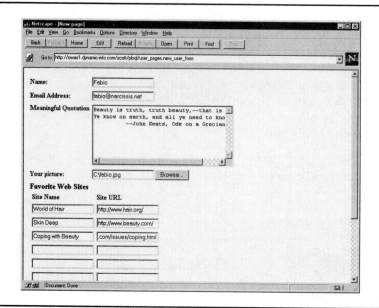

FIGURE 5-10. *Fabio creating his personal page, with an embedded photo*

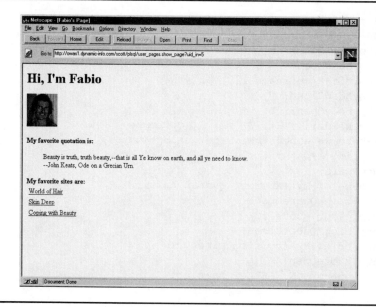

FIGURE 5-11. *Fabio's home page, displaying a picture stored in the database*

```
      LOOP
        htp.tableRowOpen;
        htp.tableData(htf.anchor(subcur.url,subcur.name));
        htp.tableRowClose;
      END LOOP;
      htp.tableClose;
      htp.bodyClose;
      htp.htmlClose;
    END LOOP;
  END;

END user_pages;
```

How to Execute a Procedure as the Default Document

This chapter has hopefully shown how developers can take their PL/SQL web development to the next level. We would like to close by solving a problem many developers encounter. Without a doubt, the most common question we have received from people who actually know the Oracle Web Application Server pretty well is "how can one have the root page of the site execute a procedure?" For instance, if the user browses to http://www.dynamic-info.com/, how can the response be generated by a PL/SQL (or any) procedure? The answer, which for some people is easily worth the price of the book, is very, very simple. It's really only three steps. This example uses Windows NT, but it's almost identical for any Unix platform as well.

1. Change the web listener's initial file to something like index.cmd, instead of index.html. On a Unix system, you might want to make it index.ksh, index.csh, or whatever extension is preferred for writing a trivially small script.

2. Change the Directories section of the listener configuration so that the root directory—the one whose virtual path is simply a slash (/)—is a CGI-style directory, most likely type CN. These first two steps will instruct the listener to run the program named index.cmd in the file system directory specified for the root virtual directory.

3. Create the index.cmd script itself. All that actually needs to be done is to echo a single header field to the browser: Location. For Windows NT, the entire script is the following two lines:

```
@echo off
echo Location: http://www.dynamic-info.com/scott/plsql/foo.bar
```

Of course, Location can be set to any URL that should be invoked. When a browser requests the root document from the site, the script will be run. This will send back the Location header, which in turn will redirect the browser to whatever wild and wonderful procedure should be executed. Simple.

As an exercise for readers who like things a little more complicated, it is possible to invoke the CGI version of the Oracle Web Agent (owa) from within the initial script. To do so, you must first reset three CGI variables: *SCRIPT_NAME*, *PATH_TRANSLATED*, and *PATH_INFO*. *SCRIPT_NAME* must be set to /*agent_name*/owa; *PATH_TRANSLATED* must be set to *ORAWEB_HOME*/bin/*proc_name*; and *PATH_INFO* must be set to /*proc_name*. After setting these variables, the owa CGI executable can be invoked. (Make sure the path is either fully specified or the working directory is changed first.) This is more complex but does have a benefit in that it doesn't generate an additional HTTP request/response transaction because of the redirection.

Conclusion

In this chapter, you have seen how to implement some extremely sophisticated functionality that can be incorporated into a variety of web applications. Much of this functionality has been implemented by making use of a variety of third-party tools or by incorporating other technologies such as VRML or ConText into an application. This underscores the point that the Web Application Server is not simply a development tool but rather an application platform. Because of the standards-based open architecture of the Web as well as Oracle's development of OWAS to integrate with other Oracle tools, there is virtually no limit to the types of applications that can be developed using the OWAS.

PostScript: Final Notes About Installing and Configuring the Oracle Web Agent Replacement

This chapter has shown some of the things OWAR can accomplish. OWAR can also be used for a number of other tasks, such as executing PL/SQL procedures as pre- or postprocessing tasks, providing detailed timing information, and adding database-based authentication functionality for versions of the Oracle WebServer prior to 3.0.

The OWAR is available in both source code and binary forms. Binaries are provided for Windows NT and SPARC Solaris. The installation instructions provided with the tool should be sufficient for installation with version 2.x of the Oracle WebServer. For Web Application Server version 3.0, the issues are documented, but a little assistance may be in order.

TIP

A very quick and easy way to make use of the OWAR without having to create numerous virtual path mappings to the cartridge is to define a single virtual path that can be appended to every URI. For instance, defining a single virtual path of /owar will cause the WRB to hand any request whose URI begins with /owar to the OWAR cartridge. Thus, /owar/scott/owai/imgname, /owar/scott/owaup/pkg.proc, and /owar/scott/owaigz/imgname would all be handled by the OWAR.

The major consideration is that the OWAR expects an owa.cfg file to be present and available to describe the names and connection information for various PL/SQL agents that have been created. These owa.cfg files are present in version 2.x of the WebServer, but are replaced by information stored in the wrb.app file in version 3.0 of the Web Application Server.

Thus, to successfully use the OWAR with version 3.0, this file must be provided by the developer. If upgrading from a version 2.x installation, simply copy the owa.cfg file and direct the OWAR as to its location. However, if the version 3.0 installation is clean, the developer must manually create the owa.cfg file. To ease this process, we created the following, quite trivial utility (included on the CD), which can generate the necessary file. It requires the table DCD_LIST, defined after the package.

```
CREATE OR REPLACE PACKAGE BODY cfg_maker AS
   PROCEDURE main
   IS
   BEGIN
     list_dcds;
   END;

   PROCEDURE list_dcds
   IS
     x   INTEGER;
   BEGIN
     htp.htmlOpen;
     htp.headOpen;
     htp.title( 'Database Connection Descriptor Creation');
     htp.headClose;
     htp.bodyOpen( cattributes => ' text="#000088"' ||
                 'link="#BB0000" vlink="#BB0000"' );
     SELECT COUNT(*) INTO x FROM dcd_list;
     IF x!=0
     THEN
       FOR cur IN (SELECT dcd_name FROM dcd_list ORDER BY dcd_name)
       LOOP
         htp.bold(cur.dcd_name);
         htp.anchor('cfg_maker.delete_dcd?dcd_name_in='||
                   cur.dcd_name,'DELETE');
         htp.br;
       END LOOP;
     END IF;
     htp.anchor('cfg_maker.add_dcd',htf.bold('Create new DCD'));
     htp.para;
     htp.anchor('cfg_maker.gen_cfg',htf.bold('Generate the owa.cfg file'));
     htp.bodyClose;
     htp.htmlClose;
   END;

   PROCEDURE add_dcd
   IS
   BEGIN
```

```
htp.htmlOpen;
htp.headOpen;
htp.title( 'Database Connection Descriptor Creation');
htp.headClose;
htp.bodyOpen( cattributes => ' text="#000088"'||
               'link="#BB0000" vlink="#BB0000"' );
htp.br( cclear => 'right');
htp.header( 2, htf.fontOpen( ccolor => '#BB0000') ||
 htf.em( 'Create New DCD (Database Connection Descriptor') ||
 htf.fontClose);
htp.print( 'From this screen, you can create a new '||
             'Database Connection Descriptor. Create a '||
             'new DCD by filling in the fields below, '||
             'selecting to create a new PL/SQL Agent '||
             'Database User, install the WebServer '||
             'Developer''s Toolkit, and then selecting the ' );
htp.em( '"Submit New Service"');
htp.print( 'button.  ' );
htp.para;
htp.formOpen( curl => 'cfg_maker.insert_dcd',
               cmethod => 'POST');
htp.preOpen;
htp.print('(*) indicates required fields.');
htp.print('(+) indicates that one of these two '||
           'fields is required. ');
htp.print('(-) indicates the field can be automatically '||
           'filled upon submission.');
htp.preClose;
htp.bold('(*) DCD name:' );
htp.formText( cname => 'dcd_name_in', csize => '30',
               cvalue => '');
htp.br;
htp.bold( '(*) PL/SQL Agent Database User:  ' );
htp.formText( cname => 'owa_user_in', csize => '30',
               cvalue => '');
htp.br;
htp.bold( 'Identified by: ' );
htp.formPassword( cname => 'owa_pass_in', csize => '25',
                   cvalue => '');
htp.br;
htp.bold( '(*) ORACLE_HOME:               ' );
htp.formText( cname => 'owa_home_in', csize => '30',
               cvalue => '');
htp.br;
htp.bold( '(+) ORACLE_SID:                ' );
```

```
  htp.formText( cname => 'owa_sid_in', csize => '30',
            cvalue => '');
  htp.br;
  htp.bold( '(+) SQL*Net V2 Service:            ' );
  htp.formText( cname => 'owa_connstr_in', csize => '30',
            cvalue => '');
  htp.br;
  htp.bold( '(*) Authorized Ports (separate by spaces):' );
  htp.formText( cname => 'owa_valport_in', csize => '30',
            cvalue => '');
  htp.br;
  htp.bold( 'Log File Directory: ' );
  htp.formText( cname => 'owa_logdir_in', csize => '28',
            cvalue => '');
  htp.br;
  htp.bold( 'HTML Error Page:' );
  htp.formText( cname => 'owa_errpage_in', csize => '28',
            cvalue => '');
  htp.br;
  htp.bold( '(-) NLS Language:' );
  htp.formText( cname => 'owa_nlslang_in', csize => '30',
            cvalue => '');
  htp.br;
  htp.hr;
  htp.formSubmit;
  htp.formClose;
  htp.hr;
  htp.bodyClose;
  htp.htmlClose;
END;
PROCEDURE delete_dcd(dcd_name_in IN VARCHAR2)
IS
BEGIN
  DELETE FROM dcd_list WHERE dcd_name=dcd_name_in;
  COMMIT;
  list_dcds;
END;
PROCEDURE insert_dcd(dcd_name_in IN VARCHAR2:=NULL,
                     owa_user_in IN VARCHAR2:=NULL,
                     owa_pass_in IN VARCHAR2:=NULL,
                     owa_home_in IN VARCHAR2:=NULL,
                     owa_sid_in IN VARCHAR2:=NULL,
                     owa_connstr_in IN VARCHAR2:=NULL,
                     owa_valport_in IN VARCHAR2:=NULL,
                     owa_logdir_in IN VARCHAR2:=NULL,
```

```
                        owa_errpage_in IN VARCHAR2:=NULL,
                        owa_nlslang_in IN VARCHAR2:=NULL)
IS
BEGIN
  INSERT INTO dcd_list
  VALUES (dcd_name_in,owa_user_in,owa_pass_in,owa_home_in,
          owa_sid_in,owa_connstr_in,owa_valport_in,
          owa_logdir_in,owa_errpage_in,owa_nlslang_in);
  COMMIT;
  htp.header(1,'DCD '||dcd_name_in||' added.');
  list_dcds;
END;


PROCEDURE attrout (attr_in IN VARCHAR2, val_in IN VARCHAR2)
IS
BEGIN
  IF val_in IS NOT NULL
  THEN
    htp.p('(');
    htp.p(attr_in||'='||val_in);
    htp.p(')');
  END IF;
END;


PROCEDURE gen_cfg
IS
  CURSOR dcd_cur IS SELECT * FROM dcd_list;
  cur dcd_cur%ROWTYPE;
BEGIN
  owa_util.mime_header('text/plain');
  FOR cur IN dcd_cur
  LOOP
    htp.p('#');
    htp.p('');
    htp.p('(');
    htp.p('owa_service='||cur.dcd_name);
    attrout('owa_user',cur.owa_user);
    attrout('owa_password',cur.owa_pass);
    attrout('oracle_home',cur.owa_home);
    attrout('oracle_sid',cur.owa_sid);
    attrout('owa_connect_string',cur.owa_connstr);
    attrout('owa_valid_ports',cur.owa_valport);
    attrout('owa_log_dir',cur.owa_logdir);
    attrout('owa_error_page',cur.owa_errpage);
    attrout('owa_nls_lang',cur.owa_nlslang);
```

```
      END LOOP;
      htp.p(')');
      htp.p('');
      htp.p('');
    END;
END cfg_maker;
CREATE TABLE dcd_list (
  dcd_name   VARCHAR2(30),
  owa_user   VARCHAR2(30),
  owa_pass   VARCHAR2(30),
  owa_home   VARCHAR2(30),
  owa_sid    VARCHAR2(30),
  owa_connstr  VARCHAR2(30),
  owa_valport  VARCHAR2(30),
  owa_logdir   VARCHAR2(200),
  owa_errpage  VARCHAR2(200),
  owa_nlslang  VARCHAR2(30)
)
```

CHAPTER

6

Java Development for the Web Application Server

he Oracle Web Application Server (WAS) is more than a development tool: it is a development architecture. As we mentioned when introducing the architecture of the WAS, it allows the creation of cartridges which interface directly with the WRB, as well as components, which are accessed through a "gateway" cartridge. We have previously shown how to create components for the PL/SQL cartridge: PL/SQL programs which generate responses of HTML (or other MIME types) to HTTP requests received by the WAS. In this chapter, we demonstrate how to create Java components.

NOTE
This chapter assumes the reader is familiar with writing programs in Java and understands the general language structure and how to use the Java compiler. There are many books of varying quality available. If the reader is already familiar with C or C++, O'Reilly's Java in a Nutshell *is an excellent little book which provides all the basics a C programmer needs to make the move to Java. It's also a great Java class reference.*

Architecture, Invocation, and Configuration

To aid understanding of the Web Application Server, a brief examination of the architecture of the Java Cartridge is in order. The cartridge, like all other cartridges, interfaces with the Web Request Broker (WRB). Requests pass through the web listener to the WRB, based on the specified directory mappings. In turn, if the virtual path is identified by the WRB as one which should be handled by the Java cartridge, the WRB passes control to the cartridge.

The Java cartridge's main activities are to provide some processing and services before, during, and after the developer's component executes, as well as to maintain a Java Virtual Machine instance. The services the cartridge provides vary between versions 2.x and 3.0 of the WebServer and are discussed in more detail later in the chapter. For present purposes, it is sufficient to say that the main thing the cartridge does is run the Java class named in the final leaf of the requested URL by loading it and invoking its main() method. The URL http://www.oraweb.com/java/MyClass, for example, would cause the cartridge to load the class named MyClass and attempt to invoke it's main() method, assuming that the class is available and the cartridge and WRB are correctly configured.

This brings us to our next point: configuring the Java cartridge is quite straightforward. As with the other Web Request Broker components, any necessary virtual paths through which Java components are to be accessed must be added to the Applications and Directories section of the WRB configuration page and their App. Field set to "JAVA" to make use of the Java cartridge. An easier alternative is to add the mappings to the Java cartridge's WRB parameter configuration page. The physical path field in either section is ignored by the cartridge, but one may wish to set it to some meaningful value indicating where the source or class files are being stored. At this point, Java components can be invoked through the WRB.

The Java cartridge itself also has a few configuration parameters that are set up via the Java cartridge configuration page. This page is accessed from the Web Request Broker configuration page by following the link to modify the Java cartridge's parameters. The cartridge accepts the following parameters with the following meanings:

CLASSPATH	This is the list of directories and .zip files in which the Java Virtual Machine associated with the Java cartridge will be able to access classes. This must always include the path to the base classes.zip file provided with the Java installation, and will typically also include a path to the oracle.zip file which contains Oracle-provided classes for database access, HTML generation, and other services. It must also include any directories and .zip files in which user-written classes which are to be available for invocation reside.
LD_LIBRARY_PATH	This is the list of directories in which the system should look for needed shared libraries. This must include the $ORAWEB_HOME/bin directory, as well as any directories which hold shared libraries used by Java native methods.
MaxRequests	This is the maximum number of requests which the cartridge can service.

JAVA_COMPILER	Optional. If present, it specifies the shared library which contains the Just-In-Time compiler to be used by the Java VM. See the section "Performance Improvements," near the end of the chapter.
JavaCacheTimeout	Optional. See the section "Notes on Development and Debugging Java Components," for the exact usage. Note that this parameter should never be set in a production environment.

Now that the Java cartridge is configured and the Java compiler and libraries are available, we're ready to start developing components in Java.

NOTE
The LD_LIBRARY_PATH configuration setting is very important. If it is incorrectly configured, it can cause significant problems, even core dumps on Unix. Be especially sensitive to this variable setting when upgrading Oracle versions 7.x to 7.3 or 8.x, as the Oracle Call Interface libraries used by the Java cartridge must correctly match for the database version installed.

Developing Components for the Java Cartridge

Components targeted for the Java cartridge are, of course, written in Java, and make use of a collection of classes which Oracle has provided with WebServer. These libraries are slightly different between version 2.x and 3.x of the WebServer. In this chapter, we attempt to make mention of both versions, although version 3.0 is the primary focus.

All Java components are themselves public Java classes, whose compiled .class file is available in the appropriate directory so that it can be accessed via the cartridge. The Java cartridge finds and loads the .class file, which is of the same name as the leaf URL, and invokes its main procedure passing in the arguments in the args array of String elements.

NOTE
The cartridge itself has a running instance of the Java Virtual Machine, which caches class definitions. This means that when a class is recompiled and its new .class file replaces an old one, if the component is invoked again, it will make use of the cached version of the code. To make sure the code is reloaded, the Java cartridge must be restarted, usually meaning the listener and the WRB must be restarted. This can make debugging somewhat difficult. See the section "Notes on Development and Debugging Java Components," later in the chapter, for some tips in getting around this feature.

Generating HTML

The most basic thing a Java component can do is to simply generate static HTML and return the result to the client browser. This can be accomplished through a couple of different means. The following three examples are all of the "Hello World!" variety, but there are a number of features about them which should be distinguished. This first example shows a request being generated.

```java
import oracle.html.*;

class HelloWorld{
  public static void main(String args[]) {

    // Create an HtmlHead object to represent the
    // <HEAD>..</HEAD> tags
    // Pass in a title for the page.

    HtmlHead hd = new HtmlHead ( "Hello World" );

    // Create an HtmlBody object to contain the
    // main content of the page

    HtmlBody bd = new HtmlBody ();
```

```
    // Create an HtmlPage object composed of a head and body

    HtmlPage pg = new HtmlPage ( hd, bd );

    // Add the string "Hello World" to the body

    bd.addItem( new SimpleItem( "Hello World" ) );

    // Print the HTTP header information

    pg.printHeader();

    // Print the contents of the page object

    pg.print();
  }
}
```

The result of this procedure is the following HTML, which, when rendered by a browser, simply displays the string "Hello World" in a window named Hello World.

```
<HTML>
<!--  Generated by Oracle.html  -->
<HEAD>
<TITLE>Hello World</TITLE>
</HEAD>
<BODY>
Hello World
</BODY>
</HTML>
```

As you can see, HTML output is generated by instantiating, manipulating, and combining Java objects which are then actually converted to HTML at the time the HtmlPage object's print() method is invoked. Prior to that, no HTML is generated. This actually results in a very flexible architecture for generating an HTML response because portions of the page can be created and manipulated in any order, without impacting their output order. In addition, the classes hide some of the tedium and complexity of exact HTML syntax.

Of course, in exchange for the flexibility and power, some convenience and simplicity are traded. In many server scripting languages, developers may want to simply stream text to the browser, in a manner similar to Perl or with a string of htp.p calls within a PL/SQL component. Of course, this is still possible in Java components. For those among us who feel that something more direct is in order, the following example accomplishes the same end result as the code above, but with many less keystrokes:

```
// The simplest server-side Java component
// target: Oracle Web Server Java Cartridge version 2.x
class HelloWorld2{
  public static void main(String args[]) {
    System.out.println("Content-type:  text/html\n");
    System.out.println("<html><head>Hello World</head>);
    System.out.println("<body>Hello World</body></html>");
  }
}
```

The preceding example is specifically aimed at WebServer version 2.x, although it will compile and run against version 3.0 as well. In version 3.0, direct access to the HTML response is best accomplished with the HtmlStream object. This is because the System.out.println calls are not thread-safe, and this may cause problems. In versions prior to 3.0, there is no choice but to use the System.out object. The following example shows the use of the HtmlStream object:

```
import oracle.java.*;
class HelloWorld3{
  public static void main(String args[]) {

    // Get the unique HtmlStream for this request.
    // Note that theStream() is a static method.

    HtmlStream stream = HtmlStream.theStream();
    stream.println( "Content-type:  text/html\n" );
    stream.println( "Hello World" );
  }
}
```

Although some may prefer directly interfacing to the output stream, in this chapter we focus on making the most of the convenience classes which Oracle provides in the ORACLE.HTML package. The collection is quite comprehensive in its support for numerous HTML tags, including several Netscape-specific features. In addition, the abstraction of HTML into classes allows development effort to focus on the actual logic, rather than the details of the HTML standard. Of course, it also means that changes in the standard for HTML would likely require changes only to the class responsible for the HTML tag or item, rather than changes to the code which is using the HTML item. In addition, one would use the HtmlStream directly to return non-HTML data, as in the case of an application server which is part of a three-tier application, or to display a VRML world.

Within the oracle.html package, the basic unit of HTML is an HTML item, which is any object implementing the IHtmlItem interface. An HTML item can be a simple object (that is, text), or it can be a compound item, such as a table, form, or entire page. It can also be a special item, such as a form field, a cell in a table, or an image.

Basic Text, Formatting, and Images

From the Hello World programs above, a brief view of generating HTML elements can be gained. Generating basic HTML pages is quite straightforward. The following example program creates a wide variety of different HTML objects which are converted to HTML by the HtmlPage.print() method and sent back to the browser. The result is shown in Figure 6-1. Examine the inline comments to see exactly how different

FIGURE 6-1. *Screen shot of class BasicHTML output*

HTML elements are used. Appendix B lists all of the defined classes and their methods.

```
import oracle.html.*;
class BasicHTML{
  public static void main(String args[]) {
    HtmlHead hd = new HtmlHead ( "Basic Text Display" );
    HtmlBody bd = new HtmlBody ();
    // Create an HtmlPage object composed of a head and body
    HtmlPage pg = new HtmlPage ( hd, bd );
    // Set up the background and foreground (text) color for
    // the page. Notice that we can set up colors a number
    // of different ways, some include:
    // Creating a new Color object with the Red, Green and Blue
    // components of the color specified as numbers (0-255)
    pg.setBackgroundColor( new Color (255,255,255) );
    // Using a string which describes the color
    pg.setForegroundColor( "#000000" );
    // Using a constant from oracle.html.Color
    pg.setActivatedLinkColor ( Color.white );
    // Next, we create a CompoundItem to hold a banner, which
    // will contain a number of constituent elements.
    // We will populate the banner later.
    CompoundItem banner = new CompoundItem();
    // Add the banner to the body of the page
    bd.addItem( banner );
    // The SimpleItem class defines a some constants for
    // the paragraph "<p>" tag, the line break "<br>" tag,
    // and the horizontal rule "<hr>" tag.
    bd.addItem( SimpleItem.Paragraph );
    // Add some simple formatted text items to the page,
    // using the setXXX() methods inherited from the
    // oracle.html.Item abstract class
    bd.addItem( new SimpleItem( "Big " ).setFontSize( 7 ) );
    bd.addItem( new SimpleItem( "Bold " ).setBold() );
    bd.addItem( new SimpleItem( "Italic " ).setItal() );
    bd.addItem( SimpleItem.Paragraph );
    bd.addItem( SimpleItem.Paragraph );
    // The following line shows how modifiers can be strung
    // together to set the text with more complex format control
    // [Line broken up for publication]
    bd.addItem( new SimpleItem( "Big, bold &amp; italic" )
            .setBold().setItal().setFontSize( 7 ) );
    bd.addItem( SimpleItem.Paragraph );
    bd.addItem( new SimpleItem( "This example demonstrates:" ) );
```

```
// Create an unordered list with a number of items.
UnOrderedList ul = new UnOrderedList();
// Note the convenience call. Methods which implement the
// addItem() method can accept either a string or an HtmlItem.
// If addItem() is called with a String, it simply converts
// it to a SimpleItem and adds it normally.
ul.addItem(new SimpleItem( "Basic text formats" ) );
ul.addItem( "Setting up a page" );
ul.addItem(new SimpleItem( "Creating hypertext links" ) );
ul.addItem( "Embedding graphics" );
ul.addItem(new SimpleItem( "Basic lists" ) );
bd.addItem( ul );
bd.addItem( SimpleItem.Paragraph );
// Add a link to go to the Oracle home page
bd.addItem( "Go to the " );
bd.addItem( new Link ( "http://www.oracle.com/",
                              "Oracle home page" ) );
// Fill in the banner now. Even though the banner has been
// added to the page already, we can still change it because
// no HTML output has been generated yet. Since we still
// have an object reference, we can do anything with it
// we wish.
// First, add a simple horizontal rule tag. Another constant
// provided by the SimpleItem class
banner.addItem( SimpleItem.HorizontalRule );
// The Image class can be instantiated three ways, in the
// following we specify the image, the alternate text
// (if images are not displayed), the alignment options, and
// whether this is an image map, which it is not.
// Note the second parameter "\"Dynamic Logo\"" we need to
// explicitly place the quotation marks here because of a
// bug in the oracle.html.Image class.
// Note that we also apply the setCenter() method the
// image object, which it inherits from the base
// oracle.html.Item class.
// Note #2: The oracle.html package with Version 3.0 of Web
// Application Server includes a more robust Image class
// which allows more control over various options such as
// BORDER, HSPACE, VSPACE, etc.
Image img = new Image(
   "http://www.dynamic-info.com/Images/DynamicLogoSmall.gif",
              "\"Dynamic Logo\"", IVAlign.NONE, false );
img.setCenter();
// Now, create a link from the image
Link homeLink = new Link("http://www.dynamic-info.com/",img);
banner.addItem( homeLink );
```

```
    // The following item shows how to directly embed HTML into
    // an object. In this case, it is useful, because we wish to
    // add some options to the <HR> tag, and oracle.html doesn't
    // provide a class for doing so in Web Server version 2.x
    banner.addItem( "<hr width=\"50%\" size=\"5\">"  );
    // The following will work well, however, in version 3.0
    /*
    banner.addItem(new HorizontalRule("CENTER", false, 5,"50%" );
    */
    // Print the HTTP header information
    pg.printHeader();
    // Print the contents of the page object
    pg.print();
  }
}
```

Tables

Most HTML pages, especially those displaying query results or any sort of list, make use of HTML tables extensively to provide superior control of formatting. In fact, the ORACLE.HTML package provides a number of classes which are used to generate tables. The easiest to use is without question the DynamicTable class. This class implements a table which can have an arbitrary number of rows added to it. This is accomplished by creating TableRow objects, populating them with TableDataCell or TableHeaderCell objects, and adding the TableRow objects to the DynamicTable object. The following snippet demonstrates this technique:

```
import oracle.html.*;
public class TableSample {
  public static void main (String args[]) throws HtmlException {
    HtmlHead hd = new HtmlHead("A Square Table");
    HtmlBody bd = new HtmlBody();
    HtmlPage pg = new HtmlPage(hd, bd);
  // Create the DynamicTable for a two-column table
  DynamicTable tab = new DynamicTable(2);
  // Create the row of column headings
  TableRow row = new TableRow();
  row.addCell(new TableHeaderCell(
                      new SimpleItem( "i" ).setItal() ) );
  CompoundItem label = new CompoundItem();
  label.addItem( new SimpleItem("i").setItal() );
  label.addItem( new SimpleItem("2").setSuper() );
  row.addCell( new TableHeaderCell( label ) );
  tab.addRow(row);
```

```
// Create rows for each of 100 numbers and their squares
for (int i = 1; i <= 100; i++) {
  row = new TableRow();
  row.addCell( new TableDataCell( new SimpleItem( i ) ) );
  row.addCell( new TableDataCell( new SimpleItem( i*i ) ) );
  tab.addRow(row);
}
// Add the table to the page and output
pg.addItem(tab);
pg.printHeader();
pg.print();
}
}
```

Forms

Almost any dynamic, database-driven web application needs to make use of HTML forms to capture user input for database storage or query conditions. As with other HTML objects, oracle.html provides classes for encapsulating HTML forms and their elements in Java objects. The following snippet generates a simple form using several of these objects. Additional classes are available for checkboxes, image buttons, and file upload items. Figure 6-2 shows the HTML result displayed from the class.

```
import oracle.html.*;
public class FormSample {
  public static void main (String args[]) throws HtmlException {
    HtmlHead hd = new HtmlHead("Get InFORMed");
    HtmlBody bd = new HtmlBody();
    HtmlPage pg = new HtmlPage(hd, bd);
  // Create the form object, specify its submit action and method
  Form frm = new Form( "POST",
                       "http://host.com/java/handleForm/" );
  // Create and add a section to enter a name
  form.addItem ( new SimpleItem ( "Name " ).setBold() );
  form.addItem (new TextField ("name", 40, 40, "Your name here" );
  form.addItem ( SimpleItem.Paragraph );
  form.addItem ( new SimpleItem ( "I love Paris " ).setBold() );
  // Create up a drop-down or popup menu with some options
  Select choices = new Select ( "lovesparis" )
  choices.addOption( new Option( "in the Springtime",
                                 "spring", true ) );
  choices.addOption( new Option( "in the Fall", "fall", false ) );
  choices.addOption(new Option("in the Winter, when it Drizzles",
```

```
                                        "winter", false ) );
choices.addOption(new Option("in the Summer, when it Sizzles",
                              "summer", false ) );
choices.addOption( new Option( "every moment of the year",
                                "always", false ) );
form.addItem ( choices );
form.addItem ( SimpleItem.Paragraph );
form.addItem ( new SimpleItem (
                    "I like Java because" ).setBold() );
form.addItem ( new SimpleItem ( "<BR>" ));
// Create a TextArea and add it to the form
TextArea ta = new TextArea( "javacomment",40,5 );
ta.setDefaultContent( "The usual reasons" );
form.addItem ( ta );
form.addItem ( SimpleItem.Paragraph );
// Add a submit button with "Send Answers" as the button title
form.addItem ( new Submit( null, "Send answers" ) );
pg.addItem(form);
pg.printHeader();
pg.print();
  }
}
```

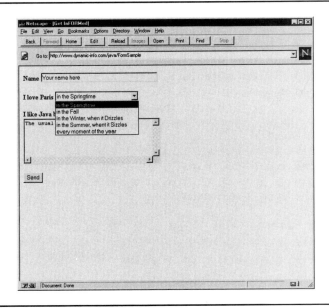

FIGURE 6-2. *Output of FormSample class*

Frames

Many HTML applications make extensive use of frames. Oracle provides the oracle.html.Frame and oracle.html.Frameset classes to generate the HTML necessary to use frames. Frame pages are created in a manner similar to standard pages, but instead of having a page composed of a header and a body (HtmlHead and HtmlBody objects), the page is composed of a header and a frameset (HtmlHead and Frameset objects). Each Frameset object is, in turn, composed of Frame objects. The following example demonstrates a frame-based page:

```java
// A server-side Java Component demonstrating frames
// target: Oracle Web Server Java Cartridge version 2.x, 3.0
import oracle.html.*;
class FrameTest{
  public static void main(String args[]) {
    //set up the basic page, head and frameset
    HtmlHead hd = new HtmlHead();
    Frameset theFrameset = new Frameset();
    HtmlPage pg = new HtmlPage( hd, theFrameset );
    // Set the page title
    hd.setTitle("Looking for Something?");
    // Set up the frame structure and the HTML which will appear
    // if the user's browser is not frame-capable
    theFrameset.setRows( "50%,50%" );
    theFrameset.setAltHtml(new SimpleItem("No Frames, too bad."));
    // Set up the URLs to which each frame points
    theFrameset.addFrame( new Frame(
            "http://www.altavista.digital.com/", "alta_vista" ) );
    theFrameset.addFrame( new Frame(
                      "http://www.yahoo.com/", "yahoo" ) );
    // Output the HTTP header information
    pg.printHeader();
    // This next line is to work around a bug which is in
    // versions 2.0-3.0b3, namely, that the HtmlPage.print()
    // method does not actually output the HTML associated
    // with the page's HtmlHead item.
    pg.getHead().print();
    // Output the HTML associated with the page
    pg.print();
  }
}
```

The Frameset class does not fully implement the browser frames standard. According to the standard, a frameset can actually contain embedded framesets. The Frameset class only allows Frame objects to be added to it; there is no addFrameset() method. However, there is a workaround for this. A Frameset object can be constructed with a passed Container of what it assumes are Frames. By placing Frameset objects in the Container object, multiple framesets can be nested. The following code listing demonstrates the technique:

```java
// A server-side Java Component which allows embedded framesets
// target: Oracle Web Server Java Cartridge version 2.x, 3.0
import oracle.html.*;
class AdvFrames{
  public static void main(String args[]) {
    //set up the basic page, head and frameset
    HtmlHead hd = new HtmlHead();
    // Put logo in every frame
    Frame theFrame = new Frame (
"http://www.dynamic-info.com/Images/DynamicLogoSmall.gif");
    // Create & populate a frameset for the upper half of the page
    Frameset upperFrameset = new Frameset( "*,*,*" , "" );
    upperFrameset.addFrame(theFrame);
    upperFrameset.addFrame(theFrame);
    upperFrameset.addFrame(theFrame);
    // Create & populate a frameset for the lower half of the page
    Frameset lowerFrameset = new Frameset( "" , "*,*,*" );
    lowerFrameset.addFrame(theFrame);
    lowerFrameset.addFrame(theFrame);
    lowerFrameset.addFrame(theFrame);
    // Put the two frames inside of a container
    Container frames = new Container();
    frames.addItem(upperFrameset);
    frames.addItem(lowerFrameset);
    CompoundItem bummerText = new CompoundItem().addItem(
                    new SimpleItem("No Frames, too bad."));
    // Set up the top-level frameset, passing in
    // the Container for the frames
    Frameset mainFrameset = new Frameset(
                    "*,*", "", bummerText, frames);
    HtmlPage pg = new HtmlPage( hd, mainFrameset );
    // Set the page title
```

```
      hd.setTitle( "I've been framed!" );
      // Output the HTTP header information
      pg.printHeader();
      // Force Head output
      pg.getHead().print();
      // Output the HTML associated with the page
      pg.print();
   }
}
```

A Note About Coding Styles

If you look at the code examples which Oracle provides with the Web
Application Server, you will see expressions such as the following:

```
Form frm = new Form("GET", "table");
   frm
      .addItem(new SimpleItem("Please let us know more about
                                yourself").setBold())
      .addItem(SimpleItem.Paragraph)
      .addItem(new SimpleItem("Name: ").setBold().setItal())
      .addItem(new TextField("name", 32, 16, ""))
      .addItem(SimpleItem.LineBreak)
      .addItem(new SimpleItem("Age:   ").setCode().setEmphasis())
      .addItem(new PasswordField("age", 32, 16, ""))
      .addItem(SimpleItem.Paragraph);
```

This is different from the syntax we tend to follow in this book but is
perfectly valid. The HTML Item objects are very similar to Java's AWT
Containers, in the respect that AWT containers (which extend AWT
Component) implement the add() method such that it adds an object to the
container, but then returns the container itself as the result. This lets the
developer string multiple add calls together in a single line of code. The
Oracle HTML library is the same, in that classes which implement
oracle.html.IHtmlItem implement an addItem method which returns the
object to which the code just added an item. Personally, we feel that it is
much easier for the reader to write the code such that each addItem call
stands alone. However, this is just an opinion, and reasonable people may
differ in this respect.

Parameter Extraction and Manipulation

Of course, most applications will need to be more sophisticated than simply writing out some simple HTML text and will need to vary their behavior based on user input submitted in the request. This could be as simple as selecting a specific record based on a user-specified query criteria or something more complex, such as if the user specifies the values of the columns for a record insert or update.

When developing with PL/SQL, this problem was basically avoided by virtue of the direct mapping between the PL/SQL procedure signature (the parameter names and types to be passed) and the URL and parameters which were to be passed from the browser. When using PL/SQL, the developer expends little or no effort in mapping between the parameters passed by the browser and the parameters which much be acted on by the business logic. This is not the case in most web server development, and in Java it's not always as easy as with PL/SQL.

In fact, there is a difference in parameter handling for Java code written for version 2.x of the WebServer and that written for version 3.0 of the Web Application Server. This difference is somewhat significant, and we are happy to report that the implementation for parameter handling in version 3.0 is greatly superior to that provided in version 2.x. Because this book is geared to people using both versions of WebServer, and to make those using version 3.0 understand just how easy they have it, we will run through both methods of parameter extraction and handling.

In versions 2.0 and 2.1 of the WebServer, all parameters come to the class' main procedure in the args array. The WRB does manage the transparency of invocation via either POST or GET, which is an improvement over the typical process of performing parameter handling for CGI. In fact, the args array is already formatted into a standard form. Specifically, the Java cartridge, prior to invoking the class' main procedure, does the following:

- Replaces all escaped characters with their correct equivalents (for example, "Vernon%20Keenan" becomes "Vernon Keenan").

■ Places parameters into a standard name=value format, even if
only a name is specified. For example, if the URL contained
"foo=1&bar&x=2," then the args array would contain
{"foo=1", "bar=", "x=2"}.

In version 3.0 of Web Application Server, parameters are much
more accessible, thanks to the services provided by the class called
oracle.owas.wrb.services.http.HTTP (that's a mouthful!). Its functionality
is as big as its fully qualified name. In addition to managing the conversion
of escape characters, it provides several routines such as
getURLParameter(paramName), which returns the value of a parameter
based on a key name (but only the first one if multiple name/value pairs
are submitted). It can also return all the parameters in either a hashtable
or a pair of vectors using the getURLParameters(hashtable) or
getURLParameters(namevector,valuevector) method. To deal effectively with
a multivalued parameter, the vector pair is the best way to access all the
values of the parameter. These methods operate on the HTTP object retrieved
by the static method HTTP.getRequest(). An example of their usage is

```
HTTP rq = HTTP.getRequest();
String empName = rq.getURLParameter( "empname" );
```

Accessing and Controlling HTTP Header Information

Often, it is necessary to set the content of various HTTP headers explicitly
or directly. This may be to set refresh intervals, the content-type of the
response, and various other information. In addition, it may be necessary to
access header information sent by the HTTP client with the request, for
instance to examine the username or browser which is being used to make
the request.

In WebServer version 2.x, getting direct access to request headers is not
possible. However, some data from the headers, those items related to the
browser, are available indirectly by examining certain environment variables
through the System.getProperty() method. Supported properties are
userAgent.browser, userAgent.majorVersion, userAgent.minorVersion, and
userAgent.buildVersion. These properties are also available in version 3.0.

Also in version 3.0, this capability is enhanced by the HTTP class
introduced in the previous section. Most importantly, it provides the

getHeaders() method, which returns the names of all available headers and values as a hashtable, and the getHeader(headername), which returns the header data for a named header. It also provides a number of convenience calls, such as getAcceptLanguage() and getPreferredAcceptCharset(), for easy access to this header information. The following example simply lists the headers and their contents to an HTML body object:

```
HTTP rq = HTTP.getRequest();
Hashtable heads = rq.getHeaders( "empname" );
Enumeration enum = heads.keys();
while ( enum.hasMoreElements() ) {
  String headNm = (String) enum.nextElement();
  bd.addItem( headNm + " = =");
  bd.addItem( heads.get( headNm ) );
  bd.addItem( SimpleItem.Paragraph );
}
```

NOTE
The HTTP class also provides getCGIEnvironments() and getCGIEnvironment(varname) methods to access CGI environment variables in a manner identical to the similarly named getHeaders() and getHeader() methods.

All versions of the Web Application Server support the complete control of HTTP response header generation. See the second two Hello World programs earlier in the chapter: they both write directly to the output stream. To customize the headers, simply output any custom headers directly to either System.out or the HtmlStream, but do not call HtmlPage.printHeader(), which is only to be called if default headers are acceptable. After explicitly generating and sending the headers (with a terminating double-newline), it is safe to call HtmlPage.print() to send the HTML to the browser.

Database Access

Of course, we are using the Oracle Web Application Server, and thus most users will probably want to use their server-side Java components to query or update an Oracle database. Not surprisingly, the Oracle Web Application Server comes with classes to streamline these functions. In fact, there are actually a couple of ways in which WebServer Java components can access Oracle data.

One way is using the Java Database Connectivity (JDBC) package designed by Sun. In fact, by the time this is in print, Oracle may have released their own production-grade JDBC drivers especially for the Oracle database.

The second way, and more our focus in this case, is by creating wrapper classes in Java which provide an interface to PL/SQL procedures. This allows developers to code database manipulation code in PL/SQL and then access it from within Java programs in a semi-transparent fashion. These wrapper classes are created by the pl2java utility which Oracle provides with the Web Application Server. In fact, this offers a couple of benefits for developers. First, it allows the developer to create Java-based access to existing PL/SQL code, isolating data manipulation or business logic to a single location. Second, it provides an easy way to offload certain processing to the database engine. For instance, a PL/SQL procedure could be created which performs a number of queries, manipulates those queries, and returns a single result. This will often result in overall higher run-time performance.

Generating Wrappers with pl2java

The pl2java command is available in the bin directory inside the ORAWEB_HOME directory. It is actually just a command-line wrapper which invokes the pl2java class within the Java environment. That's right, pl2java is itself a Java program. Nonetheless, it is invoked like any other application—from the command line. Before doing this however, a special PL/SQL package must be installed by the SYS database user. To install the package, have a database administrator run the dbpkins.sql script (found in the ORAWEB_HOME/java/sql directory) to install it into the SYS schema. A corresponding script, dbpkdins.sql, is available to remove the package. This package allows the pl2java utility to extract the information about the PL/SQL packages and procedures, which is necessary to generate the wrapper classes.

If the necessary PL/SQL packages have been installed on the system, pl2java can be invoked from the command line in the following manner:

```
> pl2java [options] username/password[@connect-string] packagename...
```

The pl2java utility will then create a wrapper class for each package enumerated at the end of the command line. The class will contain a wrapper method for each procedure or function in the PL/SQL package which can be created. Some PL/SQL datatypes are not supported, and wrapper methods will not be generated for those procedures which make use of those datatypes in the method signature. See the next section for a more detailed description of supported datatypes.

The username, password, and connect-string parameters have the usual meaning, but must connect as the owner of the PL/SQL package for which the wrapper classes are to be generated; access via a synonym is not sufficient. The utility can also create wrappers for PL/SQL procedures and functions which are not encapsulated in a single package if no package names are listed and the -class option is used. The options supplied at the command line have the following meanings:

- *-package packagename*   Specifies a Java package of which the generated class should be a member. Do not confuse with the *packagename* parameter which specifies for which PL/SQL package to generate a class.

- *-class classname*   Has two meanings: If no *packagename* is specified at the command line, a Java class of named *classname* will be generated containing all of the unpackaged PL/SQL-stored procedures and functions in the user's schema. If a *packagename* is specified at the command line, the wrapper class for the first *packagename* on the command line will be named *classname*.

- *-d directory*   Specifies the directory into which classes should be generated. The default is the current working directory.

NOTE
Although the connect string is optional, you must have configured your environment with the correct SID to which to connect. If you are uncertain that your environment has been configured with a valid Oracle SID, it is best to explicitly set the connect string.

The resulting Java source file generated will provide a collection of methods with names identical to those names defined in the PL/SQL package. The following listings demonstrate the transformation. The first shows a PL/SQL package declaration, and the second shows the resulting Java source file created by pl2java. The next section describes the new object types that show up in the Java method signatures.

```
CREATE OR REPLACE PACKAGE EmpReport IS
    TYPE str_table IS TABLE OF VARCHAR2(30) INDEX BY BINARY_INTEGER;
    TYPE num_table IS TABLE OF NUMBER(10) INDEX BY BINARY_INTEGER;
    TYPE date_table IS TABLE OF DATE INDEX BY BINARY_INTEGER;
    FUNCTION count_employees RETURN NUMBER;
    PROCEDURE list_employees (emp_name OUT str_table,
                              emp_no OUT num_table,
                              emp_hire OUT date_table,
                              emp_mgr OUT num_table);
    FUNCTION get_emp_name (emp_no IN NUMBER) RETURN VARCHAR2;
END EmpReport;
```

```
import oracle.rdbms.*;
import oracle.plsql.*;
public class EmpReport {
  private Session _dbSession;
  private static final String _pkgName = "EmpReport";
  public EmpReport(Session dbSession) { _dbSession = dbSession; }
  private Statement _count_employees0_stmt;
  public PDouble count_employees() throws ServerException {
    //...
  }
  private Statement _get_emp_name0_stmt;
  public int get_emp_name_0_return_length = 255;
  public PStringBuffer get_emp_name(PDouble emp_no)
                    throws ServerException {
//...
  }
  private Statement _list_employees0_stmt;
  public void list_employees(PStringBuffer[] emp_name,
        PDouble[] emp_no,
        PDate[] emp_hire,
        PDouble[] emp_mgr) throws ServerException {
    //...
  }
}
```

Make sure that the wrapper classes are available to the Java Virtual Machine via the CLASSPATH for the Java cartridge, as well as to the Java compiler (such as javac). When you create classes that use the wrappers, you will be unable to compile or run them without the wrapper classes being accessible.

Understanding the Datatypes

Communicating data between Oracle and Java requires passing data from methods of the wrapper class to the calling class. The wrapper class manages the actual process of querying the database, extracting the data, and placing that data into Java objects. This process can initially confuse many new component developers. Although both Java and Oracle support the same types of data, such as strings, dates, and numbers, there are different classes used for objects which will interact with the Oracle system than for those which are used solely within Java.

These differences in datatype are due to a fundamental difference between Java and Oracle basic types. SQL, and therefore Oracle, supports the concept of null values. Although Java supports a concept of null, this is different from a null value. In Java, assigning a variable a null value means that no object is associated with that variable. On the other hand, a null column value in Oracle certainly doesn't mean that there is not a column for the row! Rather it just indicates that no actual data is stored in the column.

To implement support for the SQL null concept, Oracle provides the ORACLE.PLSQL package. This package provides, among other things, a base class called PValue, which implements isNull(), setNull(), and setNotNull() methods. These methods are used to access the SQL-oriented "nullness" of the object. From this base class, several classes are derived for mapping additional PL/SQL datatypes to Java objects. For instance, a SQL DATE maps to a PDate object. Of course, you will typically need to convert these data items into Java types to perform any additional handling or output. Each of the PValue descendants implements its own method for returning their data in a standard Java base type or java.lang object. Table 6-1 shows the mapping among PL/SQL data type, the special wrapper class used by Java to access the Oracle data, the native Java type or class which will be most commonly used to operate on the data, and the conversion method in the wrapper class to convert the data to the standard Java type.

Although pl2java can handle most PL/SQL datatypes using the PValue descendants, there are some which it cannot encapsulate. Therefore, PL/SQL procedures or functions accepting parameters or returning results with these datatypes cannot be wrapped as Java methods. Some of these are most easily mapped onto other PValue descendants, while others

PL/SQL Datatype	Wrapper	Java Types	Conversion Method
BINARY_INTEGER NATURAL	PInteger	int	intValue()
BOOLEAN	PBoolean	boolean	booleanValue()
CHAR CHARACTER LONG STRING VARCHAR VARCHAR2	PStringBuffer	String StringBuffer char[]	stringValue(), toString() stringBufferValue() charValue()
DATE	PDate	date	dateValue()
NUMBER DEC, DECIMAL DOUBLE PRECISION FLOAT INT, INTEGER NUMERIC REAL SMALLINT	PDouble	int	intValue()
LONG RAW RAW	PByteArray	byte[]	byteArrayValue() getByteArray(byte[])
PL/SQL tables	Represent as an array of PValue descendants (e.g. PDouble[])		

TABLE 6-1. *Data Types and Classes Used for Oracle Database Access in Java*

simply are not amenable to passing back in a native format. Table 6-2 lists those datatypes, as well as a substitution strategy for getting the needed data back to the Java component.

Be aware that the default data size for a PL/SQL function which returns a variable length result, such as VARCHAR2, LONG, RAW, or LONG RAW, is 255 bytes. If it is necessary to get more than 255 bytes back, either pass the data back through a PL/SQL OUT parameter or modify the generated Java source file for the wrapper. For every function which returns a variable-length result, a public class variable will be defined with the name *functionname_overloadnumber_return_length*, where *overloadnumber* distinguishes among a named method which is polymorphic (i.e., has several unique method signatures). The variable should be assigned the desired default length of the return result. You can find the overload number for a specific method signature by using the standard DBMS_DESCRIBE PL/SQL package. A more direct route might be scanning the source file for the method signature you want to affect, as the public class variable is defined right above the method signature. For methods which have no overloads (i.e., only a single method signature for a function name), overloadnumber will be zero (0).

Unwrappable PL/SQL Datatype	Substitution Strategy
POSITIVE	Use BINARY_INTEGER instead
PL/SQL tables of BINARY_INTEGER or NATURAL	Use PL/SQL table of NUMBER
PL/SQL table of LONG	Either fetch each long as a scalar or use a table of VARCHAR2
PL/SQL table of BOOLEAN	Use a PL/SQL table of NUMBER, using zero for false and one for true
ROWID	Convert to text and use VARCHAR2 or CHAR
MSLABEL	Convert to text and use VARCHAR2 or CHAR
PL/SQL records	Break up and return as individual values
PL/SQL tables of records	Break up and return as individual tables

TABLE 6-2.   *Datatypes Which Cannot be Mapped Directly to Java by pl2java*

NOTE
If the PL/SQL package you are attempting to wrap is an existing package which is likely in use by others, do not change the unwrappable procedures themselves. Create a second PL/SQL procedure which handles the data conversion. This protects the other code using the package from errors.

Using Wrappers Inside Java Components

Now that the wrappers have been created with pl2java, the next step is to make use of them inside a Java class to access the database and return results to the user. This is accomplished by using a number of classes from the ORACLE.RDBMS and ORACLE.PLSQL packages. Invoking the PL/SQL procedure through the wrapper requires five main steps:

1. A *session*, a connection to the database, must be created using the oracle.rdbms.Session class. This session is established by constructing a Session object and passing in the appropriate username, password, and connect-string information for the database which contains the PL/SQL packages the wrapper classes target. Prior to this, the static Session method setProperty() should be called to set the correct value for ORACLE_HOME. This value may be hard-coded or obtained at run time via the System.getProperty() Java method.

2. The variables which will be parameters to or results from the PL/SQL wrapper classes must be declared and populated with objects of the appropriate types.

3. The wrapper class for the PL/SQL package must be instantiated, passing the Session object from the first step to the constructor.

4. The wrapper class' methods are invoked, passing in the parameters declared and populated in the second step. The results of these methods are then cast into the correct Java types and further processed or inserted into the HTML page.

5. Finally, the logoff() method for the Session object must be invoked. This terminates the database connection. This should happen when

the Java Virtual Machine performs garbage collection and
eliminates the unreferenced Session object, but it is wise to free the
resources explicitly as a practical matter.

The following listings are used to produce the page in Figure 6-3. These
listings demonstrate the general technique of invoking PL/SQL procedures
from within Java classes. The first listing is for a PL/SQL package,
EmpReport, which is converted to EmpReport.class by the pl2java utility.

```
CREATE OR REPLACE PACKAGE AS EmpReport AS
  FUNCTION count_employees RETURN NUMBER
  IS
    v_result  NUMBER;
  BEGIN
    SELECT COUNT(empno) INTO v_result FROM emp;
    RETURN v_result;
  END;
 PROCEDURE list_employees (emp_name OUT str_table,
                           emp_no OUT num_table,
                           emp_hire OUT date_table,
                           emp_mgr OUT num_table)
  IS
    CURSOR foo_cur IS SELECT ename, empno, hiredate, mgr FROM emp;
    i  INTEGER :=1;
  BEGIN
    i:=1;
    FOR tcurs IN foo_cur
    LOOP
      emp_name(i):=tcurs.ename;
      emp_no(i):=tcurs.empno;
      emp_hire(i):=tcurs.hiredate;
      emp_mgr(i):=tcurs.mgr;
      i:= i+1;
    END LOOP;
  END;
  FUNCTION get_emp_name (emp_no IN NUMBER) RETURN VARCHAR2
  IS
    v_result VARCHAR2(200);
  BEGIN
    SELECT ename INTO v_result FROM emp WHERE empno=emp_no;
    RETURN (v_result);
  END;
END EmpReport;
```

The second listing is for EmployeeList.java, which then connects to the database, invokes various PL/SQL procedures through the EmpReport wrapper class, and returns the HTML page.

```java
import oracle.rdbms.*;
import oracle.plsql.*;
import oracle.html.*;
public class EmployeeList {
  public static void main (String args[]) throws HtmlException {
    HtmlHead hd = new HtmlHead("Employee Listing");
    HtmlBody bd = new HtmlBody();
    HtmlPage pg = new HtmlPage(hd, bd);
  // We output the header now, because we may unexpectedly
  // terminate page generation later, and generating the header
  // saves us multiple calls later.
  pg.printHeader();
    Session session;
  // create a database session and logon
  try {
    session = new Session( "scott/tiger" );
  } catch (ServerException e) {
    bd.addItem(new SimpleItem("Logon fails: " + e.getSqlerrm()));
    pg.print();
    return;
  }
  // create a new instance of EmpReport package
  EmpReport empRept = new EmpReport(session);
  // Create objects to encapsulate PL/SQL values that are
  // used as parameters
  PDouble        pEmployeeCount;
  PStringBuffer  pEmployeeName[];
  PDouble        pEmployeeNumber[];
  PDate          pEmployeeHired[];
  PDouble        pEmployeeManager[];
    // call EmpReport package to count the number of employees
  try {
    pEmployeeCount = empRept.count_employees();
  } catch (ServerException e) {
    bd.addItem("Failure at emp_count: " + e.getSqlerrm());
    pg.print();
    return;
  }
  // Convert the PDouble value to a Java int
  int employeeCount = (int)pEmployeeCount.doubleValue();
  if (employeeCount == 0) {
```

```
    bd.addItem("No employees in database.");
    pg.print();
    return;
}
// Allocate arrays for employee data
pEmployeeName      = new PStringBuffer[employeeCount];
pEmployeeNumber    = new PDouble[employeeCount];
pEmployeeHired     = new PDate[employeeCount];
pEmployeeManager   = new PDouble[employeeCount];
// Allocate the actual objects into which employee data will
// be populated
for(int i = 0; i < employeeCount; i++) {
    // Max length of employee name is 30 characters
    pEmployeeName[i]   = new PStringBuffer(30);
    pEmployeeNumber[i] = new PDouble();
    pEmployeeHired[i] = new PDate();
    pEmployeeManager[i] = new PDouble();
}
//  Invoke list_employees to retrieve employee data
try {
    empRept.list_employees( pEmployeeName, pEmployeeNumber,
                            pEmployeeHired, pEmployeeManager );
} catch (ServerException e) {
    bd.addItem("Failure at list_employees: " + e.getSqlerrm());
    hp.print();
    return;
}
// Generate the table containing the information
DynamicTable tab = new DynamicTable(4);
TableRow row = new TableRow();
row.addCell(new TableHeaderCell("Employee Name"));
row.addCell(new TableHeaderCell("Hire Date"));
row.addCell(new TableHeaderCell("Employee Number"));
row.addCell(new TableHeaderCell("Manager"));
tab.addRow(row);
for (int i = 0; i < employeeCount; i++) {
    row = new TableRow();
    row.addCell( new TableDataCell(
                    pEmployeeName[i].toString() ) );
    row.addCell( new TableDataCell(
                    pEmployeeHired[i].dateValue().toString() ) );
    row.addCell( new TableDataCell(
                    pEmployeeNumber[i].toString()));
    // Make sure MGR isn't null, it will be for the big boss
    if (pEmployeeManager[i].isNull()) {
```

```
      row.addCell(new TableDataCell(""));
    } else {
      try {
        // Get the Manager's name by get_emp_name
        row.addCell( new TableDataCell(
                        empRept.get_emp_name(
                        pEmployeeManager[i]).toString() ) );
      } catch (ServerException e){
        row.addCell( "Failure at get_emp_name: "+e.getSqlerrm() );
        pg.print();
        return;
      }
    }
    tab.addRow(row);
  }
  // Add the table to the page and output
  pg.addItem(tab);
  pg.print();
  // logoff from database
  try {
    session.logoff();
  } catch (ServerException e){
    // We don't actually need to do anything with this exception.
    ;
  }
  }
}
```

Dynamic SQL Without JDBC

Some people suggest that JDBC should be employed for database access
because it allows the dynamic generation and execution of SQL queries,
which is not possible with pl2java-created wrapper classes. Of course,
pl2java is only able to wrap procedures, and although PL/SQL procedures
are able to accept a variable number of parameters, they are not able to
return a variable number of results. There are actually a couple of solutions
to the problem of Dynamic SQL without resorting to JDBC.

First, it is possible to place all the burden on a PL/SQL procedure.
Consider a PL/SQL procedure which accepts a SQL expression and returns
a simple text object which is an HTML table of the results. This procedure
would internally use the DBMS_SQL package to dynamically execute the
query and retrieve the results and use the HTF package to generate the

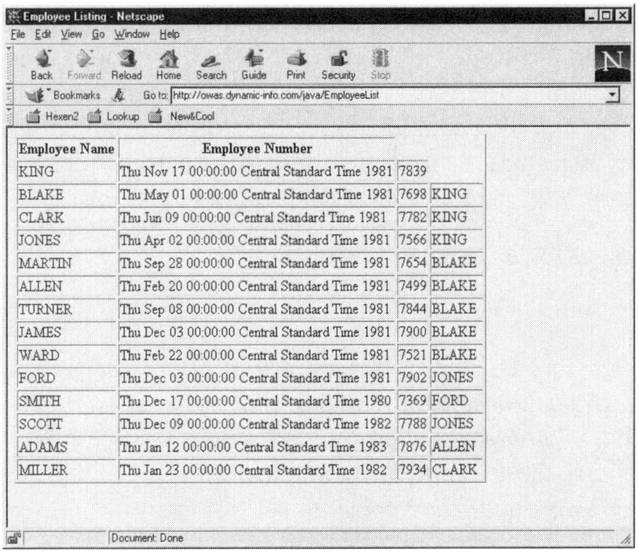

FIGURE 6-3.   *Results of EmployeeList.main()*

HTML string, which would be returned to the Java component. (This would be similar to using the ODBC cartridge in tableprint mode.)

The more flexible, and arguably better, way to accomplish this is to simply create a Java wrapper for the DBMS_SQL package which would then allow the Java component to execute queries directly and retrieve their results just as would be possible from within PL/SQL. It is easy to forget that Java wrappers can be created for any package, even those which are developed by Oracle as PL/SQL packages. From a general perspective, this means that the techniques shown here for Dynamic SQL can also be put to use with the DBMS_JOB package for automating database tasks, the DBMS_LOCK package for managing custom resource locks, and with other features as well.

As with any access to PL/SQL from Java, the first step is to actually create the package wrappers using pl2java. The key issue is that to create the wrappers, pl2java must be run with the username and password of the owner of the package, not simply a user who has access to the package from a synonym. In the case of DBMS_SQL and other Oracle-supplied packages, the package is owned by the SYS schema, also known as the user internal. This means that creating the wrapper classes requires having the password to this highly privileged user. Most likely, you will need to get your database administrator (DBA) to run pl2java for you, as most good DBAs will not hand out this password to anyone. (Exercise for the reader: the password is usually available in clear text on the machine. Do you know where?) Assuming the internal user's password is "manager," the following command line will create the wrapper class for DBMS_SQL:

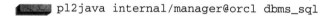

```
pl2java internal/manager@orcl dbms_sql
```

NOTE
You can reassure your DBA that programs accessing the database via the wrapper class will not have internal privileges but only the privileges associated with the user for whom the session was established at run time.

Having properly created the Java class wrapper for the DBMS_SQL package, the following code demonstrates how to use it. Of course, the example assumes a basic understanding of the DBMS_SQL PL/SQL package and its usage, but it should be easy to follow along.

```
import oracle.html.*;
import oracle.plsql.*;
import oracle.rdbms.*;
import java.util.*;
import java.io.*;
import java.lang.*;
// This sample demonstrates access to Dynamic SQL from within
// Java without the need to use JDBC.
public class dsqldemo {
  public static void main(String args[])
   {
     // Initial Page Setup
     HtmlHead hd = new HtmlHead("Java Dynamic SQL Example");
     HtmlBody bd = new HtmlBody();
     bd.setBackgroundColor( Color.white );
     HtmlPage hp = new HtmlPage(hd, bd);
     bd.addItem( new SimpleItem(
                    "Tables and Dynamic SQL" ).setHeading(2) );
     // Set the properties for the connection
     Session.setProperty("ORACLE_HOME",
```

```
                        System.getProperty("ORACLE_HOME");
// Create the session and attempt to connect
// Note that we declare dbsession outside of the try..catch
// block so it is accessible. If it were defined
// inside the try block, it would only be accessible in
// that block.
Session dbsession;
try {
  dbsession = new Session ( "scott/tiger" );
  bd.addItem(new SimpleItem( "Logon Successful" ).setBold() );
} catch (ServerException e) {
  bd.addItem( "An error occurred at logon." );
  bd.addItem(new SimpleItem( e.getSqlerrm() ).setBold() );
  bd.addItem(new SimpleItem( e.getSqlcode() ).setBold() );
  return;
}
// Create the Dynamic SQL object with the database session
dbms_sql dsql = new dbms_sql( dbsession );
// sql_curs is the reference value which is used to maintain
// access to the cursor
PDouble  sql_curs;
// Attempt to open the cursor
try {
  sql_curs = dsql.open_cursor();
} catch (ServerException e) {
  bd.addItem( "An error occurred at dbms_sql.open_cursor." );
  bd.addItem(new SimpleItem( e.getSqlerrm() ).setBold() );
  bd.addItem(new SimpleItem( e.getSqlcode() ).setBold() );
  pg.print();
  return;
}
// Instantiate the objects which will be used to communicate
// with the DBMS_SQL package through the wrapper
// Although in this case, we use a fixed text string, it could
// of course be any text string, likely created from parameters
// supplied by the user
PStringBuffer qryStr = new PStringBuffer(
          "SELECT ename,empno FROM emp ORDER BY sal DESC");
PStringBuffer p_ename = new PStringBuffer(30);
PStringBuffer p_empno = new PStringBuffer(30);
PDouble exec_type = new PDouble (0);
// We use the stmt variable to keep track of where in the
// process we are, so that if an error occurs, we know
// which DBMS_SQL call failed.
```

```
String stmt = null;
try {
  // From here, it is the same as Dynamic SQL
  // from within PL/SQL.
  // First, we parse the statement
  stmt = "dbms_sql.parse";
  dsql.parse( sql_curs, qryStr, exec_type);
  // Next we define the column mappings.
  // Note that we need to instantiate PDoubles to pass as
  // parameters. It would be nice if we could simply pass
  // an Int, but that is not an option.
  stmt = "dbms_sql.define_column";
  dsql.define_column( sql_curs,
                  new PDouble(1), p_ename, new PDouble(30) );
  dsql.define_column( sql_curs,
                  new PDouble(2), p_empno, new PDouble(30) );
  // Execute the SQL query
  stmt = "dbms_sql.execute";
  dsql.execute( sql_curs );
  // Create a Dynamic table to hold the results, and set up
  // the column headers.
  DynamicTable tab = new DynamicTable(2);
  TableRow hdrRow = new TableRow(2);
  hdrRow.addCell( new TableDataCell (
                  new SimpleItem("ENAME").setBold() ) );
  hdrRow.addCell( new TableDataCell (
                  new SimpleItem("EMPNO").setBold() ) );
  tab.addRow(hdrRow);
  // Now we fetch the rows, one by one, extract the
  // column values for each row, and add the row to
  // the dynamic table.
  // The while loop exits when dbms_sql.fetch_rows()
  // returns zero, indicating that no more records
  // are available.
  stmt = "dbms_sql.fetch_rows";
  PDouble fetch_result;
  while ( dsql.fetch_rows( sql_curs ).intValue() != 0 ) {
    stmt = "dbms_sql.column_value";
    dsql.column_value( sql_curs, new PDouble(1), p_ename );
    dsql.column_value( sql_curs, new PDouble(2), p_empno );
    TableRow dataRow = new TableRow(2);
    dataRow.addCell( p_ename.toString() );
    dataRow.addCell( p_empno.toString() );
    tab.addRow(dataRow);
  }
```

```
      // Add the table to the body
      bd.addItem(tab);
    } catch (ServerException e) {
      bd.addItem( "An error occurred at " + stmt );
      bd.addItem(new SimpleItem( e.getSqlerrm() ).setBold() );
      bd.addItem(new SimpleItem( e.getSqlcode() ).setBold() );
      try { dsql.close_cursor( sql_curs ); }
      catch (ServerException e1) { return; };
      pg.print();
      return;
    }
    stmt = "dbms_sql.close_cursor";
    try { dsql.close_cursor( sql_curs ); }
    catch (ServerException e) { return; };
    try {
      dbsession.logoff();
      bd.addItem(new SimpleItem( "Logoff Successful" ).setBold());
    } catch (ServerException e) {
      bd.addItem(new SimpleItem( "An error occurred at logoff" ).setBold() );
      bd.addItem(new SimpleItem( e.getSqlerrm() ).setBold() );
      bd.addItem(new SimpleItem( e.getSqlcode() ).setBold() );
      pg.print();
      return;
    }
    // print out the header information
    pg.printHeader();
    // print out the content of this page
    pg.print();
  }
}
```

Extended Java Cartridge Usage

So far, we've covered most of the fundamentals of the Java cartridge, as
well as some advanced techniques. However, the Java cartridge has even
more extensive capabilities than we have had space to explore in detail.
Here are some additional features of the Java cartridge which we will touch
on briefly but that we suggest the reader explore further.

Security Considerations

There is a potentially enormous security hole which the Java cartridge
introduces. Although the default configuration with which Oracle Web

Application Server preconfigures itself shows virtual directories mapping onto file system directories which contain Java class files and shows that these virtual directories should map onto the Java cartridge, the file system directory makes no difference to the class file access. Rather, class access is governed by the Java Virtual Machine's access to the class based on the CLASS_PATH. Thus any class which is available to the Virtual Machine via the CLASS_PATH and has a method with the signature main(String args[]) can be invoked through any virtual directory mapped to that Java cartridge which owns that VM.

To defend against this, the best course of action is to create a secured instance of the Java cartridge. This can be done either to the default cartridge or by creating a new Java cartridge instance. The default is named JAVA, so let's name the secure cartridge SJAVA. Simply add an SJAVA item to the Applications and Objects section of the WRB configuration area, using the same Object Path and Entry Point information as for the Java cartridge. In addition, you will need to modify the appropriate application configuration file to add a section for the SJAVA configuration parameters. This is most easily done by copying and pasting the [JAVA] section in the configuration file and changing [JAVA] to [SJAVA]. The following is an abridged version of a configuration file which had these changes applied:

```
[Apps]
;
; APP       Object Path                         Entry Point   Min    Max
; ===       ===========                         ===========   ===    ===
JAVA        %ORAWEB_HOME%/lib/libjava.so        ojsdinit      0      100
SJAVA       %ORAWEB_HOME%/lib/libjava.so        ojsdinit      0      100

; ...

[JAVA]
CLASSPATH          = %ORAWEB_HOME%/java/harmless.zip:...
LD_LIBRARY_PATH    = %ORAWEB_HOME%/lib:%ORAWEB_HOME%/java/lib
JAVA_HOME          = %ORAWEB_HOME%/java

[SJAVA]
CLASSPATH          =
%ORAWEB_HOME%/java/danger.zip:%ORAWEB_HOME%/java/harmless.zip:...
LD_LIBRARY_PATH    = %ORAWEB_HOME%/lib:%ORAWEB_HOME%/java/lib
JAVA_HOME          = %ORAWEB_HOME%/java
```

With these changes in place, simply create certain virtual directories which are secured and map on the SJAVA cartridge instance and other unsecured virtual directories which make use of the standard JAVA cartridge instance. With the preceding example, virtual paths using the SJAVA instance can access classes in either harmless.zip or danger.zip. However, access through the virtual paths mapped to the JAVA instance can only invoke classes in harmless.zip.

In general the best strategy is to narrowly define the CLASS_PATH to not include any classes which are not necessary for the web application. Of course, classes which do not have a main method are safe from access through the WRB, so there is no need to worry about a malicious user accessing the wrapper class for DBMS_SQL, which we implemented earlier.

Performance Improvements

Because Java is an interpreted language, executed by a virtual machine rather than an actual chip, it does labor under some performance constraints. This is usually not a problem for server-side applications because they require very little processing power compared to processor-intensive GUI applications which perform similar functions. However, if it is necessary to get the last drop of performance out of the Java component, a couple of options exist.

First, certain methods (even main) could be implemented as native methods written in C and compiled into platform-specific object code. This would certainly offer a performance improvement, but requires additional overhead and eliminates one of the best advantages of writing code in Java. In addition, it would not be possible to make use of all the convenience classes provided in ORACLE.HTML from a native method. With all this, it would be easier to simply write a WRB cartridge in C.

The second and much easier method is to use a Just-In-Time compiler. A Just-In-Time (JIT) compiler is a compiler which converts the Java byte codes into actual machine byte codes immediately before they are needed. Some JIT Compilers can then cache these compiled native byte codes until they are needed again. This results in a performance improvement over basic byte code execution by the Virtual Machine, but is not usually as fast as actually using native methods. On the other hand, implementing a JIT is almost trivial, given the plug-in support the Java VM provides for JIT compilers. To use a JIT Compiler, simply add another configuration parameter, java_compiler, to the Java cartridge configuration form and set its value to the name of the shared object library or dynamically linked library which implements the JIT Compiler. (For instance, Sun's library is libsunwjit.so.) Note that the library must be available in a directory whose path is specified in the ld_library_path configuration parameter.

Implementing Business-Aware HTML Items

One way to take advantage of the object-oriented architecture of Java is to create subclasses of the oracle.html.Item or oracle.html.CompoundItem which, in addition to returning an HTML result, also implement business logic. Consider, for example, a class HTMLStockInfo which accepts a ticker symbol with its constructor and whose toHtml() method extracts data from the database, populates an HTML table with the data, and returns the HTML for the completed table. With that functionality in place, the main procedure need only make a call such as the following to include a complete stock information table in the page:

```
pg.addItem( new HTMLStockInfo( "ORCL" ) );
```

Separating Business Logic from Display

Another technique for isolating the need for code changes to discrete pieces of business logic is to instantiate the HtmlPage class passing a file to the constructor. The file should be a standard HTML file. This file can contain any text. In addition, the HtmlPage provides a special feature. If the HTML file contains any tags of the form <WRB_INC NAME="name" VALUE="defaultValue">, then these tags can be replaced at run time with any HtmlItem subclass by invoking the HtmlPage.setItemAt(name, HtmlItem) method.

The upshot of this functionality is that a skilled developer can create Java classes which can read HTML files and replace certain <WRB_INC> tags with values extracted from the database. Then the supported <WRB_INC> tags and their meanings can be documented and provided to a more graphic-oriented developer who is then responsible for maintaining the purely cosmetic aspects of the page. This both eases initial development

and reduces the likelihood of maintenance requiring changes to the main
Java code.

The following two listings demonstrate this process. The first listing is for
an HTML file which contains a <WRB_INC> tag, and the second is for the
Java class which uses it as a base document into which a table is inserted.
The table contains a listing of all parameters passed to the procedure in the
args[] array, as well as all defined environment variables.

```html
<!-- sample.html -->
<HTML>
<HEAD>
<TITLE>You Gotta Keep em' Separated</TITLE>
</HEAD>
<BODY BGCOLOR="#FFFFFF">
<P>
<HR>
<H2>This page demonstrates a technique for separating display
behavior from business logic and processing.</H2>
<HR>
<P>
Through the use of <B>HtmlFile</B> and the special tag
<B>&ltWRB_INC&gt</B> you can wrap your legacy Html file
as Java IHtmlItem.
<P>
As an example, the following table is generated by oracle.html,
and inserted using the following tag:
<P>
<PRE>
&ltWRB_INC NAME="table1" VALUE="LISTING_VALUE"&gt
</PRE>
<P>
<WRB_INC NAME="table1" VALUE="LISTING_TABLE">
</BODY>
</HTML>
```

```java
// FileDemo.java
import java.util.*;
import oracle.html.*;
import java.io.File;

public class FileDemo {
  public static void main(String args[]) {
```

```
    // Generate a table with all parameters to the args[] array,
    // followed by all defined environment variables
    DynamicTable tab = new DynamicTable(2);
    int argct = args.length;
    for (int i = 0; i < args.length; i++) {
      TableRow row = new TableRow();
      row.addCell(new TableDataCell(
                      "args[" + String.valueOf(i) + "]"));
      row.addCell(new TableDataCell(args[i]));
      tab.addRow(row);
    }
    Properties allProps = System.getProperties();
    int propct = allProps.size();
    // Use a little shorthand for working with enumerations,
    // not very clear upon first read, but a somewhat
    // common Java idiom
    for (Enumeration propEnum = allProps.keys();
                    propEnum.hasMoreElements(); )
    {
      String tempKey = propEnum.nextElement().toString();
      TableRow row = new TableRow();
      row.addCell(new TableDataCell(tempKey));
      row.addCell(new TableDataCell(
                      allProps.getProperty(tempKey)));
      tab.addRow(row);
    }
    // Get the file pathname from a relative path
    File f = new File(System.getProperty("ORACLE_HOME") +
                    "\\ows20\\sample\\java\\sample.html");
    TableRow row = new TableRow();
    row.addCell(new TableDataCell( "This file" ));
    row.addCell(new TableDataCell( f.toString ));
    tab.addRow(row);
    // Create a new HTML page passing a file as a constructor
    HtmlPage pg = new HtmlPage(f);
    // Replaces the <WRB_INC NAME="table1"> tag with the HTML
    // content generated by tab.toHtml()
    pg.setItemAt( "table1", tab );
    pg.printHeader();
    pg.print();
  }
}
```

Accessing WRB Services and Native Methods

The most significant general enhancement in Web Application Server version 3.0 is a completely reworked and enhanced Web Request Broker mechanism which provides a variety of services to the various cartridges which are invoked through it. The components written for the Java cartridge do not have direct access to all of these services, but they do have direct access to the Logger service through the oracle.owas.wrb.services. logger.OutputLogStream class.

The OutputLogStream class streamlines the writing of messages to the centralized logging system. These messages can be used to provide information to the administrator of the production web environment, as well as for debugging. Basically, the class is an output stream which encapsulates native method calls to the WRB Logger service. The following snippet demonstrates the use of the Logger service. However, it doesn't demonstrate good error messages. Developers should try to provide sufficient information in production-grade error messages to allow an administrator to solve the problem.

```
// Instantiate the OutputLogStream class
OutputLogStream log = OutputLogStream("MyComponentName");

// Output an error message
log.println(OutputLogStream.SEVERITY_FATAL,
            "Unrecoverable error.");
```

Although Oracle does not provide wrappers for other WRB classes in version 3.0, more probably will be forthcoming in version 3.1 and beyond. In the meantime, if a WRB service is absolutely necessary, a developer could create Java classes which encapsulate native method calls to other WRB services. There are various Java books and documents on this subject generally, but the key thing to note is that the WRB context identifier which is needed for all WRB calls can be obtained from the static method oracle.owas.wrb.WRB.getWRBContext(), which returns a 64-bit Java long. This long can then be passed to the native methods and cast to a void* in the C implementation of the native method calls to WRB services. Note that whatever shared libraries are used to implement these methods, they must be available in some directory specified in the ld_library_path Java cartridge configuration.

Notes on Development and Debugging Java Components

Like much server-side development, debugging Java components is not entirely easy. This is because it is difficult, if not impossible, to invoke the entire component in a debuggable environment. If a test harness is created to invoke the cartridge separately from the Web Request Broker, a large number of lines of code must be commented out or have replacement stubs used for them (for instance, any HtmlStream or HTTP object access, as well as any WRB services). Because of this, the typical development cycle for a component works like this: the developer edits code, compiles it, invokes it from the browser, identifies a bug, finds and corrects it, and the cycle begins again. Usually messages are logged either directly to the HTML page or to the Logger service (in version 3.0) to alert the developer to the state of variables or the execution path being taken, as there is no debugger access. To say the least, this is somewhat tedious.

To make things even more troublesome, the Java cartridge has a persistent Virtual Machine which caches the class code across invocations. This means that when the newly compiled class is made available to the cartridge, it will almost always still invoke its cached version of the code, the one with the defect—more fun. There are a couple of workarounds for this. First, a unique name can be assigned to each iteration of the class (MyBuggyClass1, MyBuggyClass2, etc.), but this causes problems because the name needs to be changed for whatever link or form is being used to invoke the class. Second, the WRB can be shut down and restarted. On a fast machine, this is not too big a problem, but it is just another step in the process.

In version 3.0, a configuration parameter for the Java cartridge is available which instructs the cartridge to reload the class from disk for each invocation. Add the JavaCacheTimeout to the list of cartridge parameters with a value of zero (0). This should instruct the Java cartridge to reload the class from its .class file any time it is invoked. Note that using this parameter will obviously reduce performance slightly and may result in some instability (this is the old Heisenberg uncertainty principle as applied to software*), so the configuration parameter should be removed for any WRB running in a production environment.

Another debugging approach is to run the Java component in a stand-alone mode, executing the cartridge's main procedure from the command line and providing all parameters directly. With some additional code tweaking, all output results can be directed to standard output, which can be piped to a file and then viewed in a browser. This is not necessarily easy, but the Java debugger can be more easily used in this mode.

Of course, all of this leads to the major point that the best way to eliminate defects is not through the edit-compile-debug cycle of system-level testing but rather by a combination of unit testing and actually reading the code! Capers Jones, one of the great minds in the world of software development found that system-level testing finds anywhere between 20 and 60 percent of the defects in the software. This means that testing typically misses more defects than it identifies. Of course, even complex web projects are still reasonably simple compared to enterprise-wide client/server or mainframe-hosted OLTP projects. (Anybody heard of a $50 million intranet project? They happen in the client/server and mainframe worlds with some regularity.) Regardless, the fact remains: system testing is not enough.

In fact, unit testing coupled with actually reading the code is a much better tack in any project. Unit testing itself can identify between 10 and 50 percent of the defects in a program. Code walkthroughs, where two developers examine and discuss the code in the interest of finding defects, can identify between 30 and 70 percent of the errors in a program. Somewhat more formal are code reviews or code readings, where two or more developers take the time to read through the source code written by a third developer. The reviews have been shown to find twice as many defects per hour of effort as testing. The most formal and regimented

---

* For those who are wondering, the Heisenberg uncertainty principle postulates that in the world of quantum mechanics, we can never perfectly measure the natural behavior or attributes of something (in his case, particles) because by our very presence as an observer, we alter the natural system which we are trying to measure. Of course, every software developer knows this is true in our domain: how many times have you encountered a crashing bug which does not cause a crash if run inside a truss or debugger?

process, a code inspection, combines both the advance reading of the code with a discussion and has been shown to identify between 60 and 90 percent of a program's defects. Wow! Maybe the inconvenience of the edit-compile-debug cycle will encourage developers to use more efficacious quality assurance techniques. As the developer's refrain goes, "That's not a bug, it's a feature."

Conclusion

Although PL/SQL is the "official" procedural language used by most Oracle tools and the RDBMS, Java is becoming the language of choice in the emerging field of network computing. Because of its increasing use in this arena, competence in Java is becoming more common, and in fact, the language may become the "COBOL of the 90s" in terms of the amount of development performed with the language. Fortunately, Oracle Web Application Server can make effective use of Java as a tool for creating custom components to deliver application services to users or other components. By coupling the strengths of the Web Application Server (scalability, portability, ICX bus, CORBA compliance) with those of Java (portability, object orientation, wide availability of libraries), organizations can efficiently create and deploy powerful applications across their enterprise. It is expected that versions 3.1 and higher of the Web Application Server will further enhance and extend support for Java in many ways, including the support for CORBA-based interaction between server components and applets, so this aspect of the Web Application Server should only increase in sophistication.

CHAPTER

7

Using the
LiveHTML Cartridge

hroughout the past few chapters we have discussed methods to dynamically generate web pages that are able to respond to user input and incorporate data stored in an Oracle database. The methods we have discussed—PL/SQL and Java—allow very sophisticated functionality to be implemented. However, they are more complex than is suitable for use by even quite technically savvy end users.

For some types of applications, it would be desirable to allow the creation of dynamic web pages by people without programming skills. This would open the opportunity to create web pages with dynamically generated content to any users who can produce HTML. The easiest way to allow this is to create a set of relatively simple tags that can be incorporated into HTML but that are interpreted by the server when the page is served. This capability is known commonly as *server-side includes.*

Server-side includes, or SSI, facilities were originally built into NCSA's Web Server, just as the NCSA initially devised the CGI standard. In versions 2.0 and later, Oracle Web Application Server implements the basic SSI facilities outlined by NCSA, and in versions 3.0 and later, it builds on those to implement an extremely powerful and sophisticated SSI mechanism. Oracle refers to its SSI implementation as LiveHTML.

In this chapter we will begin by describing LiveHTML as implemented prior to version 3.0, and then move on to discuss the extended functionality implemented by taking advantage of the new features as well as LiveHTML's ability to integrate with other cartridges through Oracle's Inter-Cartridge Exchange (ICX).

Configuring and Using the LiveHTML Cartridge

As with all cartridges we have discussed, the LiveHTML cartridge has its own configuration settings. As usual, the configuration of the cartridge involves both defining what user requests will be passed to the cartridge and determining the manner in which it will interpret requests.

Configuration of the WRB to pass requests to the LiveHTML cartridge is accomplished in a manner similar to that of all other cartridges. In the Applications and Directories section of the WRB configuration page, an additional line item must be added for any virtual paths that are to be processed by the LiveHTML cartridge. In a different fashion from the Oracle

Web Agent cartridge, but identical to that of the Java cartridge, the Physical Directory field for the virtual path specifies the actual file system directory where the LiveHTML files reside. Setting the application field to "SSI" indicates that requests for the virtual path are to be passed to the LiveHTML cartridge.

The LiveHTML cartridge itself also accepts several configuration parameters that define how it handles requests passed to it. These are accessed by following the "Modify" link in the Cartridge configuration section of the WRB Configuration page. The default values of the four parameters are usually acceptable, although it may be desirable to change them for certain implementations.

The first parameter, EnableLiveHTML, is by default set to TRUE, meaning that the cartridge will parse appropriate files and perform any necessary execution of LiveHTML commands and finally substitute their output. Setting this parameter to FALSE would have all requests returned directly to the browser unparsed, as if the file had been accessed directly through the web listener.

The second parameter, ParseHTMLExtn, specifies whether files with the extension .html should be parsed. The default value of TRUE causes such files to be parsed. Setting this parameter to FALSE causes such files to be returned to the browser unparsed. The primary purpose of this parameter is performance-oriented. By not parsing plain HTML files lacking any LiveHTML tags, the cartridge consumes fewer system resources when servicing requests for simple HTML files.

The third parameter, EnableExecTag, which is by default set to TRUE, determines how embedded exec commands should be handled. As is described later, the exec command is capable of executing a CGI or shell script from within a LiveHTML file. This may have security implications, especially because the WRB often runs as a highly privileged user. Its default value of TRUE means that the cartridge will execute the scripts passed to the exec command. Setting the parameter to FALSE disables this feature.

The fourth and final (under versions through 2.1) parameter, ExtensionList, is used to specify which files will be parsed by the LiveHTML interpreter. Any files ending in any of the extensions listed will be parsed, while others will be returned unparsed. The list is space-delimited, and the extensions do not include the period character. The default setting is "html shtml lhtml".

Version 3.0 includes a fifth parameter, EnableICX, that has the same effect on the request command that EnableExec has on the exec command. The default value of TRUE indicates that requested commands will be interpreted, while setting the parameter to FALSE will disable these commands. Because security permissions can be effectively enforced with ICX-based requests rather than simple exec calls, it would be wise to disable the exec feature but to leave the request command enabled.

NOTE
In version 3.0, the configuration screen has been reworked significantly, allowing selection of these configuration options using radio buttons. The actual parameter names, however, are the same.

There are two new parameters in WAS version 3.0 that cannot be accessed through the configuration page and require the administrator to manually add them to the wrb.app file. The first is AppMimeTypes, which can contain a list, not of MIME types, as you might expect, but of file extensions. If this parameter is set, WAS will dispatch any request for a file ending in a specified extension to the LiveHTML cartridge. For example, setting AppMimeTypes to "shtml" will result in any request for a file with an .shtml extension being sent to the LiveHTML cartridge for processing. The second manually configurable new parameter is DefaultTarget, which specifies the default filename to use for a request if no file is specified in the URL. If left blank, the default value of index.html is used.

Of course, changing any of the configuration parameters for either the WRB or the cartridge itself requires that the configuration information be reloaded. Use the owsctl utility to stop and start the WRB and any web listeners to force a configuration data reload.

LiveHTML Syntax

LiveHTML commands are embedded into otherwise garden-variety HTML pages. By convention, these enhanced pages are identified by the extension .shtml, although the cartridge can be configured to preprocess files with the .html extension. These commands are executed and replaced with the results of the command, if applicable.

The commands are embedded inside HTML comments. HTML comments are opened by the string "<!--" and terminated by "-->". By embedding the command inside a comment, the commands will not be displayed on the user's browser if the file is inadvertently downloaded through an access path that does not invoke the LiveHTML interpreter.

To distinguish LiveHTML commands from genuine comments, or comments that contain information interpreted elsewhere (such as browser scripts), all LiveHTML commands are preceded by a hash symbol (#) immediately following the comment opening string, for example, "<!--#exec...-->". Most LiveHTML commands accept parameters, typically as pairs of names and values, separated by an equal sign (=), identical to the way tag parameters are handled in plain HTML. The generic syntax for a LiveHTML command is

<!--#*command param1*="*value1*" *param2*="*value2*"...*paramN*="*valueN*"-->

An example of a complete specification of a LiveHTML command, config, is

```
<!--#config errmsg="Oh no! An error occurred."-->
```

As can be seen, LiveHTML syntax is very straightforward and can be understood and implemented by anyone capable of writing HTML. This opens up the ability to create rudimentary dynamic content to a much wider audience.

Also working to maintain its simplicity, LiveHTML is actually composed of a fairly small number of commands, although many of them accept a number of different parameters. The following commands are those implemented by the LiveHTML cartridge in both Oracle WebServer 2.0 and Oracle Web Application Server 3.0.

Note that LiveHTML commands cannot be nested. As an example, the following command will result in an error:

```
<!--#exec cgi="/cgi/counter?<!--#echo var="DOCUMENT_URL"-->"-->
```

LiveHTML Commands

The config Command

The config command allows various execution options to be configured. These will determine how certain other LiveHTML commands will behave.

Because LiveHTML files are interpreted linearly, from beginning to end, these configuration options must be set prior to executing the command that they are to affect.

NOTE
The config command can be called multiple times in the same LiveHTML file, each time setting the same option to a different value.

errmsg

Allows the developer to specify the text message that will be substituted into the HTML in place of a LiveHTML command if an error occurs while executing the command. This can be any text, including HTML. It is recommended that you alter this from the default, possibly providing a link to notify an individual. For example:

```
<!--#config errmsg="An error occurred, please notify the
    <a href="mailto:mgr@oraweb.com?subject=LiveHTML+Error">
    webmaster
    </a>"
-->
```

NOTE
A little-known feature of the mailto: anchor is the ability to also pass a subject along with the message. This saves the end user time and also makes it easy for a mail-sorting program to prioritize incoming e-mail to the often-deluged webmaster account.

cmdecho

Specifies whether the results of non-CGI scripts executed by the exec command have their results, through stdout, inserted into the HTML document. The two possible values of this parameter are ON and OFF. The default is OFF and means that the output will not be inserted into the returned document. See the example in the exec section.

cmdprefix and cmdpostfix

Specifies strings that will be prepended or appended, respectively, to each line of command output from stdout when using the exec command to execute a shell script. This is useful for adding additional HTML tags to each line to control formatting. Uses may include breaking up output into separate lines or placing the items in an ordered list. See the section "The exec Command" for an example of this option's use.

sizefmt

Specifies the manner in which the size of file returned by the fsize command will be formatted. There are only two possible values for this parameter. First is "bytes", which displays the exact number of bytes in the file and is the default value. For more readability, it may be wise to use "abbrev", which will result in output of file sizes in kilobytes or megabytes, depending on which is appropriate.

timefmt

Specifies how the results of the echo command for either DATE_LOCAL or DATE_GMT or for the output of the flastmod command (see the section later in this chapter) will be formatted. The options are listed in in Table 7-1. Formatting is controlled by a string identical to the format parameter to the Unix *stftime* routine. The strftime command allows an enormous number of different flags, which appear below. In addition to these tokens, any plain text can be embedded in the format string, which allows the format string to embed an "at" or "on" to produce a formatted time such as "1/1/98 at 12:31 P.M."

Some examples include

```
<!--#config timefmt="%A, %B %d, %Y, at %I:%M %p"-->
```

This string produces output such as "Tuesday, August 13, 1996, at 03:42 PM".

```
<!--#config timefmt="%T on %d-%b-%Y"-->
```

This string produces output such as "15:42:17 on 13-Aug-1996".

The include Command

This command specifies that a file should be read and embedded in the current document in the position where this tag appears. This file can be a

Token	Behavior
%%	Inserts a literal "%"
%a	Locale's abbreviated weekday name
%A	Locale's full weekday name
%b	Locale's abbreviated month name
%B	Locale's full month name
%c	Locale's appropriate date and time representation
%C	Locale's date and time representation as produced by date(1)
%C	Century number (the year divided by 100 and truncated to an integer as a decimal number [1,99]); single digits are preceded by 0
%d	Day of month [1,31]; single digits are preceded by 0
%D	Date as %m/%d/%y
%e	Day of month [1,31]; single digits are preceded by a space
%h	Locale's abbreviated month name
%H	Hour (24-hour clock) [0,23]; single digits are preceded by 0
%I	Hour (12-hour clock) [1,12]; single digits are preceded by 0
%j	Day number of year [1,366]; single digits are preceded by 0
%k	Hour (24-hour clock) [0,23]; single digits are preceded by a blank
%l	Hour (12-hour clock) [1,12]; single digits are preceded by a blank
%m	Month number [1,12]; single digits are preceded by 0
%M	Minute [00,59]; leading zero is permitted but not required
%n	Inserts a newline
%p	Locale's equivalent of either a.m. or p.m.
%r	Appropriate time representation in 12-hour clock format with %p
%R	Time as %H:%M
%S	Seconds [00,61]
%t	Inserts a tab
%T	Time as %H:%M:%S
%u	Weekday as a decimal number [1,7], with 1 representing Sunday
%U	Week number of year as a decimal number [00,53], with Sunday as the first day of week 1

TABLE 7-1. *Options for Configuring timefmt*

Token	Behavior
%V	Week number of year as a decimal number [01,53], with Monday as the first day of the week. If the week containing 1 January has four or more days in the new year, then it is considered week 1; otherwise, it is week 53 of the previous year, and the next week is week 1.
%w	Weekday as a decimal number [0,6], with 0 representing Sunday
%W	Week number of year as a decimal number [00,53], with Monday as the first day of week 1
%x	Locale's appropriate date representation
%X	Locale's appropriate time representation
%y	Year within century [00,99]
%Y	Year, including the century (for example, 1993)
%Z	Time zone name or abbreviation, or no bytes if no time zone information exists

TABLE 7-1.   *Options for Configuring timefmt* (continued)

standard HTML file, another LiveHTML file, or any ASCII text file. If the file is a LiveHTML file, based on the extension, virtual path, and other configuration settings, the LiveHTML cartridge will interpret and process LiveHTML commands in the included file.

This capability is very useful for web site management, because the include command can be used to embed common or boilerplate elements very easily, such as a page header or footer. If all files make use of the LiveHTML preprocessor, extensive cosmetic updates can be made to the site simply by changing the included boilerplate files.

There are two possible, but mutually exclusive, parameters that the include command accepts. Both specify where the file to be included can be found. First is the "file" parameter, which specifies the file location relative to the current working directory as a physical path. The current working directory is the directory in which the currently interpreted LiveHTML file resides.

The second choice is the "virtual" parameter, which accepts a string containing a virtual pathname. The LiveHTML cartridge consults the virtual directory mapping information configured for the WebServer.

Note, however, that CGI scripts cannot be executed through the include command, even if the virtual directory has been configured as a CGI directory.

For example, suppose that the file currently being interpreted was accessed by the user as "/docs/info/example.shtml" and that inside the physical directory to which "/docs/info/" maps refers there is another directory named "/includes". Assuming that the virtual mapping to /docs/info/ is configured as recursive and non-CGI, both the following commands will include the same file.

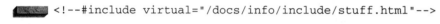

```
<!--#include virtual="/docs/info/include/stuff.html"-->

<!--#include file="include/stuff.html"-->
```

Note that the use of absolute pathnames or references to parent directories as values of the file parameter are forbidden, and will not include a file. Thus, the only documents that can be included are those that reside in a subdirectory of the current directory or those that could be otherwise directly accessed from a remote browser.

NOTE
The LiveHTML interpreter will go into an infinite loop if the include command recursively includes a file. The only way to stop it is to kill the runaway process. Of course, it will stop naturally when the host runs out of either virtual memory or disk space. An example of such a problem would be a file accessed through the virtual path of "/docs/bad.html" that contains the following line:

```
<!--#include virtual="/docs/bad.html"-->
```

The echo Command

This command replaces an environment variable in the document being processed. It accepts a single required parameter, "var". The value of var specifies what environment variable should be inserted; this includes any CGI environment variable, as well as six special LiveHTML environment variables. The six LiveHTML variables and their meanings are shown in Table 7-2. Supported CGI variables are shown in Table 7-3.

NOTE
Although the LiveHTML interpreter will interpret LiveHTML tags in included files, the environment variables set, which is used by the echo command, is set by the interpreter only for the outermost file (the file the browser originally requested). For example, using include to insert the following file will result in the actual file path and modification date being displayed for the file that included the file, rather than the included file itself.

```
<!--#config timefmt="%A, %B %d, %Y, at %I:%M %p"-->
<b>This file was last modified on: <!--echo var="LAST_MODIFIED"--></b>
```

Environment Variable	Meaning of Value
DOCUMENT_NAME	The name of the current file being processed.
DOCUMENT_URL	The virtual path to the current file.
QUERY_STRING_UNESCAPED	The query string, if present, that was sent with the GET request for the file. The query string will have had HTTP escape sequences replaced with the correct characters, and will have characters special to the shell escaped with a period ("."). *Note:* This differs from the implementation I have. In this case, QUERY_STRING is available.
DATE_LOCAL	The current date and time relative to the current location. It will be output in the format specified by the last config timefmt command.
DATE_GMT	Same as DATE_LOCAL, except using Greenwich Mean Time.
LAST_MODIFIED	The last modification date of the file being processed. It will be output in the format specified by the last config timefmt command.

TABLE 7-2.   *LiveHTML Environment Variables*

Environment Variable	Meaning of Value
SERVER_SOFTWARE	The name and version of the web server that invoked the executable.
SERVER_NAME	The host name of the server on which the script is running.
GATEWAY_INTERFACE	The version of the CGI interface under which the code is being called. Typically, this is CGI/1.1.
REMOTE_HOST	The host name of the machine that made the request.
REMOTE_ADDR	The IP address of the machine that made the request.
AUTH_TYPE	The type of authentication used, if applicable.
REMOTE_USER	The username submitted by the user.
REMOTE_IDENT	The password submitted by the user.
HTTP_ACCEPT	A comma-delimited list of MIME types in which the browser will accept responses.
HTTP_USER_AGENT	The name and version of, and additional information about, the client software that made the request. This is usually a browser, although web robots are also user agents.
SERVER_PROTOCOL	The protocol name and version that the server is running. Usually, HTTP/1.0.
SERVER_PORT	The server port through which the request came.
SCRIPT_NAME	The name of the script being executed.
PATH_INFO	Additional part of the URL after the script name but prior to the query string.
PATH_TRANSLATED	The actual path to the script being executed.
HTTP_REFERER	The URL of the page from which this request came.
QUERY_STRING	The query string, if present, that was sent with the GET request for the file.

TABLE 7-3. *CGI Environment Variables*

The exec Command

In version 2.1 and prior, exec is the most powerful LiveHTML command available. It allows the execution of scripts or other executables from within a LiveHTML page. Note that because of the power exec enables, the administrator can control whether the command is available. The command takes one of two mutually exclusive parameters that control how the script is executed as well as how the output, if any, from the script is processed.

If the "cgi" parameter is used, the script to be executed is specified by its virtual path. The LiveHTML interpreter consults the virtual paths specified for the web listener through which it was invoked. The script to be executed can also have parameters passed to it via a query screen, as with any GET request. The following example will execute and embed the results of a PL/SQL procedure *list_people* that is part of a package named DIRECTORY, while passing the parameter "dept" with a value of 20. This could be used, for instance, to list the names and phone numbers of sales contacts on a department home page.

```
<!--#exec cgi="/samp/owa/directory.list_people?dept=20"-->
```

In addition to CGI-based scripts, the exec command allows developers to embed calls to other scripts or to any command that can be run from the system's shell prompt. The script is specified by its fully qualified pathname. The command is executed as if it were typed at the command line, and thus any necessary switches or parameters can be set in this manner. Various settings specified by the config command control whether the results of the script (through stdout) are embedded in the document and, if so, how they are formatted.

The following example executes the finger command against a network service provider. The response to the finger is a listing of current network status. The result is embedded in the document, with "<BR>" tags inserted after each line in stdout, to allow the correct display on the user's web browser. (The <BR> tag, for those who need to be refreshed, indicates to the browser to insert a line break.)

```
<!--#config cmdecho=ON--><!-- must set to ON to return result -->
<!--#config cmdpostfix="<br>"-->
<!--#exec cmd="/bin/finger support@myisp.net"-->
```

The flastmod Command

This command inserts the last modification date of the file specified. The date is output in the format specified by the last config command that specified a timefmt, or the default time format if one is not specified. It accepts either of the same two mutually exclusive parameters as the include command. Either "file" may be specified, which is a file path relative to the current working directory; or "virtual" may be used, which allows the specification of the file using the virtual directory mappings configured for the web listener.

The fsize Command

This command inserts the size of the file specified. The size is output in the format specified by the last config sizefmt command. It take the same two mutually exclusive parameters as the include or flastmod commands.

The request Command

In version 3.0 of Web Application Server and later, Oracle has significantly enhanced support for LiveHTML by taking advantage of the ICX communication bus and allowing LiveHTML documents to invoke other cartridge services through ICX. This opens an enormous opportunity for HTML authors to create solutions that are also able to incorporate more complex data retrieval or processing, while remaining relatively easy to implement.

The LiveHTML interpreter implements ICX support with a single new command: request. The request command instructs the LiveHTML cartridge to invoke an available WRB-compliant cartridge, perform some operation, and place the results of the operation in the document being processed.

NOTE
The results of the cartridge invocation must be of the MIME type text/html.

The request command accepts a single parameter, URL. URL is a fully qualified URL, just as if it were entered in a browser's "Location" box. As mentioned in Chapter 2, complete, or fully qualified, URLs to HTTP-based services have the following form:

http://{*username:password@*}*host*{*:port*}/*path*{*?query_string*}

This is the exact format in which the request command accepts values for the URL parameter. The WRB handles routing the request to the correct cartridge by examining the virtual directory configuration. A simple example of a request command is

```
<!--#request url="http://www.oraweb.com/demo/hello?foo=bar"-->
```

NOTE

If a username and password are required to access the service directly (that is, from a browser), they must be specified in the URL passed to the request command. The LiveHTML cartridge will not proxy the authorization request back to the browser.

Initially, it may seem that the request command functions in a manner basically similar to that of the exec command with the CGI parameter used, except for having to specify the full URL request. However, it is far more powerful than it seems. It gains additional power inherently by using ICX, so that, unlike the exec command, URLs in the request command are served by the WRB, which allows them to execute across different machines, use pooled resources, and take advantage of other WRB features.

Beyond merely getting the additional performance and management benefits of the WRB ICX interface, however, the request command also performs some additional preprocessing of the URL parameter before invoking it through ICX. This additional processing makes the request command much more flexible and useful than exec.

The first preprocessing step performed is variable substitution. In the example above, the path, parameter, and value passed to the cartridge in the query string are all hard-coded literals. Variable substitution allows the request URL to reference parameters passed to the LiveHTML file being currently processed. For example, consider a LiveHTML page invoked with the following URL:

```
http://www.oraweb.com/live/test.shtml?name=king&title=president
```

When using the exec command, the passed arguments of name and title cannot be accessed, and consequently cannot be directly passed onto the

CGI script. With the request tag, however, any token beginning with the dollar sign ($) will be substituted with the value of the parameter passed when requesting the LiveHTML document. For example, consider the following request command:

```
<!--#request URL="http://www.oraweb.com/test/owa/emp.add?
      name=$name&title=$title"-->
```

Prior to passing the URL request to the WRB, the request command replaces $name and $title with the values passed into the page, so the request made via ICX is for this URL:

```
http://www.oraweb.com/test/owa/emp.add?name=king&title=president
```

NOTE
The variable substitution can occur anywhere in the URL parameter, not just in the query string. This allows, for instance, the username and password, the database connection descriptor, and even the host to be specified in arguments in the LiveHTML document request.

In addition to variable substitution, the request command performs another type of preprocessing. For any string within single quotes (''), the request command will properly escape any necessary characters. This is primarily a convenience feature, to save the LiveHTML author the trouble of manually escaping spaces and other characters. As an example of both types of preprocessing at work, consider a LiveHTML document with the following line:

```
<!--#request url="http://www.oraweb.com/test/sql?qry='select *
      from foo where bar=$where'"-->
```

When a browser requests the document with a URL such as the following,

```
http://www.oraweb.com/live/test2.shtml?where=123
```

two steps will take place prior to passing the request to ICX. First, the string "$where" is substituted with the value of "123" from the query string.

Second, the HTTP special characters in the substring "select…123" (which was "select…$where"), such as spaces and the equal sign, are properly escaped, producing the final URL to be passed to the ICX engine of

```
http://www.oraweb.com/test/sql?qry=select+*+from+foo+where+bar%3D123
```

There is a restriction on the automatic escaping of characters: single-quoted strings may only be used when specifying the value of the parameter being passed with the cartridge request. For example, both of the following are in error.

```
<!--#request url="http://'www.oraweb.com'/test3/sql?foo=bar"-->
<!--#request url="http://www.oraweb.com/test3/sql?'my param'=bar"-->
```

The restriction is rather obvious when one considers that host names and parameter names must both conform to naming conventions that do not support escaped characters. Thus, this restriction does not in any way present a limitation of functionality, but rather acts to enforce DNS and HTTP standards.

NOTE
If it is necessary to use either the single quote or the dollar sign literally, they should be escaped by preceding them with the back slash ("\"). To include a literal back slash, include two of them; "\\" is processed into "\".

Debugging LiveHTML

LiveHTML is a fairly simple language for embedding tags, and offers the advantage that not too many errors can occur with its execution. Most errors will tend to be the result of an error made in invoking another cartridge service or script when using the request or exec commands.

CAUTION
In the first production releases of Web Application Server 3.0, the LiveHTML cartridge will fail if it processes a request tag that returns more than 10K of data.

Tutorial: Improving Web Sites and Easing Administration with LiveHTML

As is evident, LiveHTML equips nonprogrammers with the ability to add dynamic content to their web pages. In addition, by using the request tag, they can easily access custom-developed (or "shrink-wrapped") services to their pages. By doing this, moderately generic code can be used to empower less technical users to become more "self-service" in their web site development. The following tutorial demonstrates this type of synergy in using LiveHTML.

Consider a large organization that has many departments. This organization has extremely cutting-edge employees, and every department wants its own web site featured on the company intranet. Almost all of them want some fairly common features: to provide certain files for download that describe the department's role, list any active projects, and offer other information. Also, most want a directory of the employees' names, titles, telephone extensions, and e-mail addresses within the department.

However—and no surprise here—none of the departments wants to dedicate any more time than is necessary to keep the site up to date. But they *do* want to be able to control the complete look and feel of the site (since most of the departments have a good deal of self-esteem invested in their own group identity). Without LiveHTML, fulfilling all of these needs is a virtually impossible task. With LiveHTML, however, it is all in a day's work. Let's walk through how to meet all the objectives.

Objective One: Ease of Maintenance

Most web sites have a reasonably consistent graphic look and "feel" across pages. There are common header and footer elements, as well as button bars and other tools for ease of navigation. With typical plain HTML documents, it is a significant inconvenience for a user to update these common elements across dozens or hundreds of pages (say, because the department's name changes). LiveHTML provides a way to easily address these issues.

The following three code listings show three files. The first two, header.shtml and footer.shtml, are considered "boilerplate"; that is, they contain content or page elements that are to appear on every page in the web site. The third page, an example home page, uses the LiveHTML include command to include these files in the page prior to returning them to the browser. The net result: a consistent look for all the web pages without the webmaster's having to duplicate these elements for every single web page.

```
<body bgcolor="#FFFFFF">
<image src="/corp/image/logo.jpg">
<image src="/acctg/image/logo.jpg">
```

Listing 7-1: /acctg/templates/header.shtml

```
<hr>
<address>
For comments about these web pages, please email the
<a href="mailto:fred@company.com">Accounting Web Master</a>
</address>
</body>
```

Listing 7-2: /acctg/templates/footer.shtml

```
<html>
<head>
<title>Accounting a-go-go</title>
</head>
<!--#include virtual="/acctg/templates/header.shtml"-->
<H1>Welcome to the Accounting Home Page</H1>
Here in Accounting, we do all kinds of fascinating, yet somehow
underappreciated things like: paying bills, auditing accounts,
rejecting expense reports, [blah, blah, blah]
<!--#include virtual="/acctg/templates/footer.shtml"-->
</html>
```

Listing 7-3: /acctg/index.html

Of course, the real benefit occurs when the user decides to change some common element of the page. For instance, to add an "Ask Accounting" feature to every page in the site, the user need only modify the footer.shtml file, as shown in the fourth listing:

```
<hr>
<form action="mailto:fred@company.com?subject=question" method="POST">
<table>
<tr><td colspan=2>
<b>Question for Accounting? Ask it here!</b>
<td></tr>
<td><textarea name="Q">Type your question here.</textarea></td>
<td><input type="submit" value="Submit"></td></tr>
</table>
</form>
<address>
For comments about these web pages, please email the
<a href="mailto:fred@company.com">Accounting Web Master</a>
</address>
</body>
```

Listing 7-4 /acctg/templates/footer.shtml (revised)

Obviously, this is *much* better than having to change every page in the entire web site. Don't forget that the files to be embedded can be arbitrarily small or large. This could mean using an include file just to specify the background color or image to be used on the web site, or using include files to build a complex, but standard, layout around each page's content.

Objective Two: Document Information (flastmod, fsize)

One problem from which many web sites suffer is a lack of currency, both real and perceived. Documents are put on the site once, only to be updated infrequently, if ever. Additionally, frequent visitors to the site often have no way of knowing if any particular document has been updated. One technique many organizations use is to place a modification date next to the link. By doing this, a user can identify the age of files that are accessible, as well as see the age of the document being currently viewed.

```
<html>
<head><title>File Archive</title></head>
<!--#include virtual="/acctg/templates/header.shtml"-->
<h1>Welcome to the Accounting File Archive</h1>
<table>
<tr>
```

```
<td><b>Description</b></td>
<td><b>Last Changed</b></td>
<td><b>File Size</b></td></tr>
<tr>
<td><a href="/acctg/doc/info.html"><b>Department Info<b></a></td>
<td><!--flastmod virtual="/acctg/doc/info.html"--></td>
<td><!--fsize virtual="/acctg/doc/info.html"--></td>
</tr>
<!-- Additional rows of files here -->
</table>
<!--#include virtual="/acctg/templates/footer.shtml"-->
</html>
```

NOTE
The flastmod and fsize commands cannot make use of a partially qualified path when using their virtual parameter. Most web browsers are able to construct a fully qualified path from a path fragment, either from the URL of the current file, or from the <BASE> tag in the <HEAD>…</HEAD> section of the HTML document. For instance, if the anchor tag specifies an href of "info.html" within a page whose URL is "http://www.abc.com/acctg/doc/files.html", the browser will actually know to request the full path, "/acctg/doc/files.html", from the host at www.abc.com/. The LiveHTML interpreter cannot make this inference. Thus, you must get used to specifying the virtual paths in full.

Objective Three: Department Directory (Request with ODBC)

Another feature of a departmental web site that many users would find useful is the listing of various employee-contact information for members of the department. This is especially helpful if the directory is combined with employees' roles and responsibilities. This allows users to quickly see whom they may need to contact within a department about a given question or issue (particularly important, since many companies now use interminable telephone trees).

Obviously, one way to accomplish this would be to maintain a static page of all individuals in the department. On the other hand, this seems undesirable, as it requires significant manual labor to constantly update the page when employees come to the department or move to new areas of the company or are promoted. A better solution would be to allow access to a database of such information, thus allowing the page to be constantly updated automatically.

Although a database seems an easy way to handle the situation, choosing the manner in which database access is made presents two options. First, a programmer could implement a PL/SQL procedure that, when passed the name of the department, displays a list of employees and their phone numbers. This package could then be accessed either directly or through a LiveHTML request command.

The drawback of this approach is that the output is hard-coded by the original programmer. This means that every department will have the same listing, with the same format and same rows displayed, and with the same (limited) control over actual data displayed, in terms of restricting the rows or columns to be displayed. This may be undesirable for a department that wishes possibly to segment its listings, or to further subdivide or order them based on roles.

Fortunately, the ODBC cartridge makes it quite straightforward to empower end users with this kind of flexibility. By configuring the ODBC cartridge to access a database containing employee information by department, department-level webmasters with some SQL background can easily construct a database query displaying any information they choose, in the format that suits their needs and tastes.

As discussed in Chapter 8, the ODBC cartridge allows three different invocation options: execute, tableprint, and stringprint. The execute function is used for insertions, updates, and deletions, so it is not useful in this case. In fact, it may be wise to restrict the privileges on the table to prevent such operations on it via the web user.

The tableprint function displays results using an unadorned HTML table. This is fine for a quick listing, but still doesn't give the department-level webmasters significant control over the appearance of output. The stringprint feature, however, gives complete flexibility in the manner in which the document is displayed.

The stringprint function generates the resulting HTML to be displayed by the browser, based on substituting database query results into a string, once per row returned. Although this is not as flexible as manually creating a script with PL/SQL or Java, it is clearly capable of addressing at least 90 percent of the potential user population. In fact, it probably offers more flexibility than most users will even desire.

There are basically three steps to using the ODBC cartridge in a LiveHTML request. First, the data source from which data will be queried and displayed must be identified. Second, the query used to return the correct columns from the relevant rows must be formulated. Third, if using the stringprint function, the output string must be defined. Each of these steps is quite straightforward, assuming the data exists. (We assume in this tutorial that the ODBC data sources have already been configured.)

The data source can typically be obtained from the administrator of the Oracle Web Server, who would have configured the ODBC cartridge and defined the accessible data sources. He or she should also be able to provide the user with the username and password with which to connect to the database.

Conclusion

In this chapter, the reader has seen the functionality in Oracle's implementation of server-side includes. This capability allows an easy way for end users to maintain more complex web sites, by using features such as file inclusion. It also allows programmers and less technical web developers to work in concert to develop highly dynamic web sites or applications, in which the interface is partially unlinked from the procedural code. This makes life easier for both the HTML artist and the application code developer. Although LiveHTML is not as flexible an environment for application development as a full procedural language (such as PL/SQL or Java), it does offer many features that provide the right level of functionality with the minimum complexity.

CHAPTER

8

The ODBC Cartridge

he Oracle Web Application Server is probably of greatest interest to organizations which need to access data residing within Oracle's relational database system. However, although Oracle does own the lion's share of the database market, with upwards of 50 percent of relational data being stored in Oracle databases, it is occasionally necessary to access data from other databases, such as DB/2, Informix, or Sybase. This chapter focuses on how to use the Oracle Web Application Server to access data stored in non-Oracle databases.

Accessing Non-Oracle Data with Oracle Web Application Server

If you are using the Oracle Web Application Server, there are three tools available to access non-Oracle data. The first is through Oracle's database gateway technology and its assortment of Transparent or Procedural Gateways for over 30 databases. The second is by using the Java Database Connectivity (JDBC) classes, which are similar to ODBC and allow Java classes to access data from a wide variety of sources. The third, and our current area of interest, is through the use of the ODBC cartridge which is included with the Oracle Web Application Server in versions 3.0 and later. A nonproduct option would be for developers to write their own WRB cartridges, which makes use of a database vendor's APIs to directly access those foreign databases. This cartridge could be accessed either directly by web browsers or through the WRB's Inter-Cartridge Exchange facilities.

Before moving forward to discuss how to make use of the ODBC cartridge, however, we want to discuss the architectural differences and implications for choosing between the Gateway- and ODBC-based approaches. Chapter 12 discusses the JDBC architecture, how it works, and what tools Oracle provides for using it.

Oracle Transparent Gateways

Oracle's Transparent Gateways are available for a very wide variety of third-party database products, ranging from semi-proprietary databases to the SQL/400 engine found on the AS/400 platform and more mainstream RDBMS software from Sybase and Informix.

NOTE
The Gateway Toolkit is also available, which allows a gateway to be implemented for any database for which a Windows NT ODBC driver is available.

The key feature of data access using Transparent Gateways is that it is, surprise, transparent. What this means, specifically, is that accessing data through these gateways is identical to accessing Oracle data. The remote databases are accessed using SQL*Net the same way in which Oracle databases themselves are accessed. This means that any SQL*Net-compatible tool, from the Web Application Server to Designer/2000, can be used to get at the data in these remote data sources. The database gateway is, by all appearances, an Oracle database.

A second significant implication is that because these databases are accessed via SQL*Net, it is possible to have database queries which span across both Oracle and non-Oracle data, even engaging in relational joins across the databases. In addition, PL/SQL procedures can reference this remote data by using the DBlink facility. This means that PL/SQL procedures invoked via the Oracle Web Agent can be written to operate on data not just from Oracle but from almost any vendor. Even the oracle.session class in the Java toolkit supplied with the Web Application Server can support connections to these databases through the gateway.

Obviously, Transparent Gateway technology has a great deal of power, and strong arguments exist for using it when creating universal front-ends to corporate data. This is especially true if it is necessary to build content from heterogeneous data sources. Given that Oracle's web toolset is the most comprehensive of any available, using it to access even non-Oracle data makes sense.

A second type of gateway technology which Oracle provides is the Procedural Gateway. Procedural gateways are targeted at accessing transactional services on corporate mainframes in a fairly transparent fashion. While a Transparent Gateway is designed to allow Oracle developers to treat heterogeneous database tables as being Oracle tables, the Procedural Gateways allow developers to access remote mainframe transaction procedures as if they were Oracle-stored procedures.

ODBC

The third alternative for accessing non-Oracle data when using the Oracle Web Application Server is to employ the ODBC cartridge. This cartridge implements an ODBC client which can be accessed either directly from a web browser or from other cartridges via Inter-Cartridge Exchange (ICX). Before jumping into the use of the cartridge, a quick discussion of ODBC itself is in order.

Using ODBC for heterogeneous data access has some differences compared to using Transparent Gateway technology. One immediate benefit is that it is included with Web Application Server version 3.0 and beyond, without requiring any additional licensing costs. Another benefit for some is that it can be accessed without the use of PL/SQL. The flip side of this is that it does not offer the same level of flexibility with respect to data manipulation as can be achieved with gateway technology, which may render it impractical for some applications.

Probably the best use of the ODBC cartridge for many organizations is as a method to allow moderately knowledgeable users of SQL and HTML to build simple database-enabled applications. In this chapter, we will discuss this application, as well as the potentially more advanced uses of the cartridge with Java or PL/SQL. Of course, before anything can be done with the cartridge, it must first be configured correctly.

ODBC Cartridge Configuration

Configuring the ODBC cartridge is fairly trivial, as the ODBC cartridge itself has no configuration options. Simply specify an application directory mapping inside the WRB configuration for the ODBC cartridge, and the ODBC cartridge can be invoked. However, there are several other components of the ODBC environment which must also be configured for the cartridge to work correctly, most notably the drivers to various data sources.

The ODBC cartridge presently supports access to four databases via ODBC: Informix, Sybase, Microsoft SQL Server, and the Oracle RDBMS. It provides the necessary drivers and utilities needed to access data in any of these databases. However, it is necessary to define how these supported data sources are to be accessed by the ODBC driver manager. This is accomplished by editing the .odbc.ini file, which resides in the home directory of the account running the Web Request Broker.

NOTE
These instructions are intended for users of WebServer on various flavors of Unix. Users of the Oracle Web Application Server under Windows NT can ignore the next few paragraphs. For users of Windows NT, the correct and very easy way to edit ODBC data sources is using the ODBC control panel. Refer to the online help for the exact manner in which to configure the various data sources available.

Configuring the .odbc.ini File

The .odbc.ini file contains two required sections, one labeled "ODBC Data Sources," which contains a list of names of data sources which will be defined elsewhere in the file. The second required section is labeled "ODBC" and contains some generic ODBC driver configuration information. In addition to these required sections, the file also contains one section for each Data Source Name specified in the first section, which describes how to access the data source. The contents of these sections vary for each brand of database. The following example .odbc.ini file shows several of the main components which control the configuration of ODBC and the accessible data sources.

```
[ODBC Data Sources]
o7 = Oracle7
s10 = Sybase10
i7 = Informix7
m65 = Microsoft SQL Server 6.5
[o7]
Driver=/orahome/ows/3_0/cartx/wodbc/util/drivers/vsorac.so.1
Server=dev1
  [s10]
Driver=/orahome/ows/3_0/cartx/wodbc/util/drivers/vssyb.so.1
Server=SYBASE10
Database=devsyb1
[i7]
Driver=/orahome/ows/3_0/cartx/wodbc/util/drivers/vsifmx7.so.1
Server=devifmx1
  [m65]
```

```
Driver=/orahome/ows/3_0/cartx/wodbc/util/drivers/vsorac.so.1
Description=Visigenic Microsoft SQL Server Driver
Database=devms1
Network=nettcplib
Address=tester,1433
[ODBC]
InstallDir=/orahome/ows/3_0/cartx/wodbc/util
Trace=0
TraceFile=/orahome/ows/3_0/cartx/wodbc/log/odbc.trc
```

Specifying Available ODBC Data Sources

The ODBC Data Sources section is populated by adding any number of entries in the following format:

> *data_source_name=source_description*

where *data_source_name* is the name by which you will refer to the data source both later in this file, as well as when accessing the data via the ODBC cartridge. The *source_description* section may provide a text description of the data source or the driver being used. However, *source_description* is optional.

Configuring ODBC Data Sources

For each entry created in the ODBC Data Sources section, it is necessary to add another entry named for each data source's name and containing information the database-specific ODBC driver needs to access the database. Because this information is database specific, each vendor requires it in a slightly different format.

CONFIGURING AN ORACLE7 ODBC DATA SOURCE   To
configure a data source for an Oracle7 database, add an entry in the .odbc.ini file *after* the ODBC Data Sources section in the following format:

> [*data_source_name*]
> Driver=*driver_path*
> Server=*connect_string*

The section heading, *data_source_name,* must match a data source specified in the first section of the file. The first item, *driver_path,* describes where the shared library which implements the database-specific ODBC driver resides. The actual database to access is specified by *connect_string*, which is a standard SQL*Net version 2 TNS service name. This is the same name used when configuring a DAD or when connecting to the database with SQL*Plus. These names are specified in the tnsnames.ora file inside the $ORACLE_HOME/network/admin/ directory. Ask your database administrator (DBA) or refer to Oracle's documentation on how to create new service names in the tnsnames.ora file.

CONFIGURING A SYBASE SYSTEM 10 ODBC DATA SOURCE   To configure a data source for a Sybase database, add an entry in the .odbc.ini file *after* the ODBC Data Sources section in the following format:

[*data_source_name*]
Driver=*driver_path*
Server=*server_name*
Database=*db_name*

As before, the section heading, *data_source_name*, must match a data source specified in the first section of the file. The first item, *driver_path*, points to the shared library which implements the Sybase-specific ODBC driver. Unlike the Oracle configuration, two pieces of information specify which database to access. The *first, server_name*, names the Sybase engine to which the connection should be made, and *the second, db_name*, specifies the database running on that engine.

Before accessing the Sybase database through ODBC, it is also necessary to perform some other configuration tasks, specifically modifying the Sybase interfaces file, which is similar in purpose to Oracle's tnsnames file. A utility, SYBINIT, is included with Oracle Web Application Server to streamline this process. Before running SYBINIT, two environment variables must be set. If you are using the C shell, set them as follows:

```
% setenv ORAWEB_CARTX=$ORAWEB_HOME/cartx
% setenv SYBASE=$ORAWEB_CARTX/wodbc/1.0/vissyb10
```

Then, to run SYBINIT, simply type the following:

```
% cd $SYBASE/install
% ./sybinit
```

The SYBINIT utility is menu driven and will guide you through the process of editing the interfaces file. For additional information on the SYBINIT utility, see the documentation that came with the Oracle Web Application Server or refer to a Sybase DBA.

CONFIGURING AN INFORMIX DATA SOURCE   To configure a data source for an Informix database, add an entry in the .odbc.ini file *after* the ODBC Data Sources section in the following format:

> [*data_source_name*]
> Driver=*driver_path*
> Database=*db_name*

As before, the section heading, *data_source_name,* must match a data source specified in the first section of the file. The first item, *driver_path,* points to the shared library which implements the Informix ODBC driver. The second, *db_name,* specifies the database which is to be accessed and may include an Informix server qualifier.

There are additional configuration tasks which must be performed to access an Informix database. These tasks vary slightly by platform and the connectivity type employed. See the documentation which came with your version of the Oracle Web Server for information on these additional tasks.

CONFIGURING A MICROSOFT SQL SERVER DATA SOURCE
To configure a data source for a Microsoft SQL Server database, add an entry in the .odbc.ini file *after* the ODBC Data Sources section in the following format:

> [*data_source_name*]
> Driver=*driver_path*
> Description=*description*
> Database=*db_name*
> Network=*network_lib*
> Address=*network_address*[,*port*]

As always, the section heading, *data_source_name,* must match a data source specified in the first section of the file. The first item, *driver_path,* points to the shared library which implements the SQL Server ODBC driver. The second, *description,* describes the database driver used to connect to the data source. In this case, simply use "Visigneic Microsoft SQL Server Driver." The third, *db_name,* specifies the database which is to be accessed. Next, the Microsoft SQL Server Net_Library shared library is specified by the *network_lib* parameter. Under Unix, this is typically "netlibtcp." Finally, *address* and *port* specify the machine and port at which to access the database. The address can be specified either as a DNS-resolvable host name or in w.x.y.z notation. The port is optional and will default to 1433. If the SQL Server database is listening on a port other than 1433, specify it explicitly.

Because all address information is specified in the .odbc.ini. file, no additional configuration tasks are necessary to access a SQL Server database.

Configuring ODBC Options
The last part of the .odbc.ini file are the settings for three ODBC options. The section is entered as follows:

```
[ODBC]
InstallDir=odbc_root
Trace=on_off
TraceFile=trace_file_name
```

The defaults included in the file should be sufficient. The *odbc_root* specifies the root directory where ODBC is installed. Set *on_off* to 1 to enable tracing and 0 to disable it. If tracing is enabled, trace information is written to *trace_file_name.* Note that enabling tracing of ODBC calls reduces performance of the cartridge, as all calls are logged to a file. Tracing should always be disabled in a production environment and used only for debugging purposes.

ODBC Cartridge Invocation
Now that the cartridge and data sources are configured, it is time to start using the cartridge. The ODBC Cartridge can be invoked via three different entry points. Each entry point performs a similar task, namely executing a SQL statement, but they each differ in how the results are returned. The three entry points, or *modes,* as we shall also refer to them are *Execute,*

TablePrint, and *StringPrint.* All three of these entry points execute a SQL statement through an ODBC driver and then return results as text output.

NOTE
The ODBC cartridge's only means of returning results is through text which is typically inserted into HTML output. There is no "out of band" communication separate from the result text, such as an error indicator variable or coded function return value.

Access to the ODBC cartridge is made by invoking a URL of this form:

http://*hostname:port*/odbc/*request_mode*   \
            [?*param1=value1...paramN=valueN*]

where *hostname* and *port* identify the web listener through which the request is directed; odbc specifies that the request should be fulfilled by the ODBC cartridge (based on the mapping configured for the WRB); and *request_mode* is one of *execute, stringprint, or tableprint.* Additional parameters to these entry points are passed in via the usual method. In this case, a GET-style request is illustrated, although a POST-style request could be used. In the case of a POST request, the name/value pairs of parameters are passed in through the request body.

Execute Mode

The ODBC cartridge's *execute* entry point, or mode, causes a passed SQL statement to be executed but only returns a result indicating the success or failure of the operation. The *execute* mode is typically used to perform either Data Manipulation Language (DML) operations—those operations which alter the data in the database, such as INSERT, UPDATE, and DELETE—or to execute Data Definition Language (DDL) operations—those that alter the structure of the database, such as CREATE TABLE, ALTER INDEX, and DROP VIEW. Of course, a SELECT statement could be issued, although typically this would be useless, as the primary purpose of a SELECT tends to be querying data to display.

The *execute* entry point is accessed with five mandatory parameters specified. These parameters and their meanings are discussed in the following sections.

database

The *database* parameter specifies the brand of database being accessed. The following table shows valid options for this parameter.

Parameter Value	RDBMS
ORACLE7	Oracle7 Server
SYBASE10	Sybase SQL Server Release 10
INFORMIX7	INFORMIX-OnLine Dynamic Server or INFORMIX-SE
MSSQL6	Microsoft SQL Server 6.0

dsn

The *dsn* parameter specifies the Data Source Name (DSN) to be accessed. Only DSNs which are listed in the .odbc.ini file are acceptable values for this parameter. See the configuration section earlier in the chapter to see how to configure a new DSN.

Omitting this parameter will result in the OWB-01003 error "Unable to find dsn (data source name) in the URL". Passing a dsn name which is not in the .odbc.ini. file will result in the OWB-01001 error "Logon failed".

username

The *username* parameter, not surprisingly, specifies the database username with which to log on to the database specified by the *dsn* parameter.

Omitting this parameter will result in the OWB-01005 error "Unable to find username in the URL". Passing a username which is not valid for the database specified by the dsn will result in the OWB-01001 error "Logon failed".

password

This parameter specifies the password associated with the database user given for *username*.

Omitting this parameter will result in the OWB-01006 error "Unable to find password in the URL". Passing an incorrect password will, as expected, result in the OWB-01001 error "Logon failed".

sql

The *sql* parameter contains the ODBC-standard SQL string to be executed. This parameter is the real meat of the ODBC cartridge. The cartridge passes whatever SQL statement is specified to the database via ODBC for execution. This parameter may also contain substitution variables, also referred to as *input parameters*. Input parameters are sections of the SQL string which are to be populated with values of other parameters passed to the cartridge.

Input parameters are specified by preceding the name in the SQL expression with a colon (:). These variables are then substituted with the values of parameters bearing the same name which are passed to the cartridge. For instance, consider a call such that the SQL parameter contains the expression "WHERE ename=:emp_name" and an additional parameter named "emp_name" is passed to the cartridge with the value of KING.

```
.../odbc/execute?database=ORACLE7&dsn=o7book&          \
                username=scott&password=tiger&          \
                sql=DELETE+FROM+emp+WHERE+ename=          \
                :emp_name&emp_name=KING
```

Upon invoking the cartridge with this URL, the resulting SQL which will be sent to the database would be "WHERE ename='KING'". As another example, the following HTML code is for a page with a form, the submission of which will delete employees whose salary is above a user-specified level by invoking the ODBC cartridge. Notice the use of hidden variables to hard-code the database and user to access.

```
<html>
<form action="POST" method="http://www.oraweb.com/odbc/execute">
<input type="hidden" name="database" value="ORACLE7">
<input type="hidden" name="dsn" value="o7book">
<input type="hidden" name="username" value="scott">
<input type="hidden" name="password" value="tiger">
<input type="hidden" name="sql"
```

```
        value="delete from emp where sal>:max_sal">
<b>Delete employees with salaries greater than:</b>
<input type="text" name="max_sal" value="500">
<br>
<input type="submit">
</form>
</html>
```

NOTE
If an input parameter is referenced in the SQL parameter but was not passed to the cartridge with a name/value pair, the cartridge will generate error OWB-01010: "Unable to find variable in the URL". If you encounter this error, double-check to make sure that you have included all parameters as well as spelled them identically both in the name/value pair and in the SQL statement.

The ODBC cartridge by default ignores datatypes when it substitutes passed values for input parameters. That is, based on the format of the parameter (for example, "emp_name=KING" or "max_sal=500"), the cartridge will simply pass the characters (in this case, "KING" or "500") on to the ODBC driver, relying on the database to perform implicit conversions. An *implicit conversion* occurs when the database can transparently convert a character string such as "07/27/97", for example, into the correct representation for the column or variable to which it is to be applied. In the case of the string "07/27/97", this would mean converting it to the internal representation of the date (27 July 1997) if it were being applied to a datetime column.

If the underlying database is unable to handle implicit conversions, it is necessary to instruct the cartridge to perform these conversions explicitly prior to passing the data on to the ODBC driver. This is accomplished by adding a suffix to the names of input parameter name/value pairs. The suffix instructs the ODBC cartridge how to convert the variables before passing them to the driver. Note that the suffix is added only to the parameter names in the name/value pairs; it is *not* added to the parameter name when it appears in the SQL parameter. For example, consider the sample request used here:

```
.../odbc/execute?database=ORACLE7&dsn=o7book&              \
                username=scott&password=tiger&             \
                sql=DELETE+FROM+emp+WHERE+ename=           \
                :emp_name&emp_name=KING
```

To explicitly instruct the ODBC cartridge to convert the *emp_name* parameter to the CHAR datatype before passing it to the driver, you would add the _char suffix to the second occurrence of emp_name in the name/value pair. The correct use would be

```
.../odbc/execute?database=ORACLE7&dsn=o7book&              \
                username=scott&password=tiger&             \
                sql=DELETE+FROM+emp+WHERE+ename=           \
                :emp_name&emp_name_char=KING
```

Table 8-1 shows the appropriate suffixes for the different native datatypes found in Oracle 7. Tables 8-2 through 8-4 do the same for Informix Online and SE, Sybase SQL Server Release 10, and Microsoft SQL Server 6.5, respectively.

Tableprint Mode

The *tableprint* mode, or entry point, differs from the *execute* mode in that it is used for issuing SELECT statements and producing HTML output of the

Native Datatype	SQL Datatype	Suffix
CHAR	CHAR	_CHAR
DATE	TIMESTAMP	_DTME
FLOAT	FLOAT	_FLOT
LONG	LONGVARCHAR	_LCHR
LONG RAW	LONGVARBINARY	_LBIN
NUMBER	FLOAT	_FLOT
NUMBER(38)	INTEGER	INTG
NUMBER(P,S)DECIMAL	_DECL	
RAW	BINARY	_BINY
VARCHAR2	VARCHAR	_VCHR

TABLE 8-1. *Oracle7 Datatypes and Suffixes*

Native Datatype	SQL Datatype	Suffix
BYTE	LONGVARBINARY	_LBIN
CHAR	CHAR	_CHAR
DATE	DATE	_DATE
DATETIME	TIMESTAMP	_DTME
DECIMAL, FIXED	DECIMAL	_DECL
DECIMAL, FLOATING POINT	DOUBLEPRECISION	_DUBL
FLOAT	DOUBLEPRECISION	_DUBL
INTEGER	INTEGER	_INTG
INTERVAL	CHAR	_CHAR
MONEY	DECIMAL	_DECL
SERIAL	INTEGER	_INTG
SMALLFLOAT	FLOAT	_REAL
SMALLINT	SMALLINT	_SINT
TEXT	LONGVARCHAR	_LCHR
VARCHAR	VARCHAR	_VCHR

TABLE 8-2. *Informix Online and SE Datatypes and Suffixes*

query results formatted as HTML tables. This makes the *tableprint* mode ideal for generating query output which simply needs to be displayed to the user in a readable format but without significant regard for appearance.

The *tableprint* mode requires all of the same parameters, with the same meanings as in the *execute* mode. Additionally, it accepts two optional parameters, which are described next.

maxrows
The *maxrows* parameter specifies the maximum number of rows to display. If omitted, the default is 25.

minrows
The *minrows* parameter specifies the minimum number of rows to display. If omitted, the default is zero. We must confess, the actual purpose of this parameter eludes us.

Native Datatype	SQL Datatype	Suffix
BINARY	BINARY	_BINY
BIT	BIT	_BBIT
CHAR	CHAR	_CHAR
DATETIME	TIMESTAMP	_DTME
DECIMAL	DECIMAL	_DECL
FLOAT	FLOAT	_FLOT
IMAGE	LONGVARBINARY	_LBIN
INT	INTEGER	_INTG
MONEY	DECIMAL	_DECL
NCHAR	CHAR	_CHAR
NUMERIC	NUMERIC	_NUMR
NVARCHAR	VARCHAR	_VCHR
REAL	REAL	_REAL
SMALLDATETIME	TIMESTAMP	_DTME
SMALLINT	SMALLINT	_SINT
SMALLMONEY	DECIMAL	_DECL
SYSNAME	VARCHAR	_VCHR
TEXT	LONGVARCHAR	_LCHR
TIMESTAMP	VARBINARY	_VBIN
TINYINT	TINYINT	_TINT
VARBINARY	VARBINARY	_VBIN
VARCHAR	VARCHAR	_VCHR

TABLE 8-3. *Sybase SQL Server Release 10 Datatypes and Suffixes*

An example of invoking the ODBC cartridge with the *tableprint* entry point follows:

```
.../odbc/tableprint?database=ORACLE7&dsn=o7book&      \
                username=scott&password=tiger&        \
                sql=SELECT+ename+FROM+emp
```

Native Datatype	SQL Datatype	Suffix
BINARY	BINARY	_BINY
BIT	BIT	_BBIT
CHAR	CHAR	_CHAR
DATETIME	TIMESTAMP	_DTME
DECIMAL	DECIMAL	_DECL
IMAGE	LONGVARBINARY	_LBIN
INT	INTEGER	_INTG
MONEY	DECIMAL	_DECL
NUMERIC	NUMERIC	_NUMR
REAL	REAL	_REAL
SMALLDATETIME	TIMESTAMP	_DTME
SMALLINT	SMALLINT	_SINT
SMALLMONEY	DECIMAL	_DECL
SYSNAME	VARCHAR	_VCHR
TEXT	LONGVARCHAR	_LCHR
TIMESTAMP	VARBINARY	_VBIN
TINYINT	TINYINT	_TINT
VARBINARY	VARBINARY	_VBIN
VARCHAR	VARCHAR	_VCHR

TABLE 8-4. *Microsoft SQL Server 6.5 Datatypes and Suffixes*

Stringprint Mode

Although the *tableprint* entry point provides at least some formatting of its output, it is rather limited. The *stringprint* entry point, on the other hand, provides a great deal of flexibility in specifying the nature of the output. Like, *tableprint*, the *stringprint* entry point requires all of the same parameters as the *execute* entry point. In addition, it accepts the following two other parameters.

maxrows

As with *tableprint*, this specifies the maximum number of rows to display. If omitted, the default is 25.

outputstring

This parameter specifies a printf output style to display each row of the results. Use the syntax %*n* to indicate where column data is to be inserted, where *n* is the column number to be inserted. In a query such as SELECT empno, ename FROM…, %1 would be replaced with the value of *empno*, and %2 would be replaced with the value of *ename*.

Because any string can be specified for the *outputstring* parameter, the developer gains significant flexibility. For example, the following URL will produce a list of departments and locations:

```
.../odbc/stringprint?database=ORACLE7&dsn=o7book&          \
                   username=scott&password=tiger&          \
                   sql=SELECT+dname,loc+FROM+dept&         \
                   outputstring=The+%1+department+is+      \
                   located+in+%2.<br>
```

The *stringprint* entry point can also be used to control formatting inside of tables, although it must then be invoked from within another cartridge, such as LiveHTML, because the table will need to be bounded by <TABLE> and </TABLE> tags.

ODBC Cartridge Usage with LiveHTML

The ODBC cartridge is, unlike most other cartridges bundled with Oracle Web Application Server, a utility cartridge intended primarily to service requests from other cartridges and components. In this section we describe integrating the ODBC cartridge into solutions written using LiveHTML. Some surprisingly sophisticated output control can be obtained by using the LiveHTML #request command to invoke the ODBC cartridge's services.

```
<!--list.html -->
<html>
<head>
<title>Employee List</title>
```

```
</head>
<body>
<b>Follow the link for an employee for more information</b>
<br>
<table>
<!--#request url="http://oweb:88/odbc/stringprint?              \
            database=ORACLE7&dsn=dev3&username=scott&           \
            password=tiger&sql='SELECT ename,empno               \
            FROM emp'&format='<tr><td>                           \
            <a href="detail.html?empno=%2">%1</a.>               \
            </td></tr>'"-->
</table>
</body>
</html>
```

The next file is used to display the details about the employee. For
clarity, only a few fields are displayed from the employee record. Notice
the self-join in the SQL statement.

```
<!--details.html-->
<html>
<head>
<title>Employee Details</title>
</head>
<body>
<!--#request url="http://oweb:88/odbc/stringprint?                    \
            database=ORACLE7&dsn=dev3&username=scott&                 \
            password=tiger&sql='SELECT a.ename,a.sal,                 \
            b.ename FROM emp a,emp b WHERE                            \
            a.empno=$empno andb.empno=a.mgr'&outputstring= \
            '<h2>%1</h2><table><tr><td><b>Salary</b>                  \
            </td><td>%2</td></tr><tr><td><b>Manager</b>               \
            </td><td>%3</td></tr></table>'" -->                       \
</body>
</html>
```

It would be possible to make further use of the ODBC and LiveHTML
synergies to implement record insertion functionality using a form which
defines form inputs named empno_in, ename_in, and sal_in and having the
form invoke a LiveHTML document which contains the following request:

```
<!--#request url="http://oweb:88/odbc/execute?database=ORACLE7       \
            &dsn=dev3&username=scott&password=tiger&                  \
            sql='INSERT INTO emp VALUES(empno=:empno,ename=           \
```

```
:ename,sal=:sal)'&empno='$empno_in'&            \
ename='$ename'&sal_in='$sal_in'" -->
```

Combining LiveHTML and ODBC allows those not familiar with procedural or object-oriented languages such as PL/SQL or Java to create more sophisticated web applications than previously possible. For many, this combination may be the extent of their data access and manipulation needs. Of course, the ODBC cartridge can also be invoked from other cartridges, such as a C cartridge, which might prefer to simply call the ODBC cartridge to insert a record into a transaction database.

A Note About Security and the ODBC Cartridge

Because the ODBC cartridge allows invocation of arbitrary SQL queries directly from the browser, the public availability and knowledge of the cartridge can pose a potential security risk. Consider someone typing the following URL into their browser:

```
www.yourcompany.com/odbc/execute?                \
database=ORACLE7&dsn=oe&username=scott&           \
password=tiger&sql=delete+from+customer
```

Scary. As we mention in Chapter 9, which focuses on security, it is wise simply to delete the directory mappings for any cartridge which is not to be used. However, if the ODBC cartridge is being used, there are still a couple of steps which can be taken to protect the integrity of the data. This discussion applies to any cartridge which should not generally be invoked directly by a browser.

Because the cartridge should typically never need to be invoked directly from the browser, a first step toward security may be anonymity. Change the default WRB Application directory mapping for the ODBC cartridge from /odbc/ to something more obscure. This, of course, doesn't prevent access but certainly reduces the risk from random hacking or error.

A better step is to actually restrict access to the cartridge with either IP address or password protection, using the web listener's security mappings. If IP-based mappings are used, the process is somewhat simplified because all requests will be coming from a definable subnet, and no additional effort is required on the part of the developers. The most extreme level of such IP restriction would be to restrict access to localhost, namely allowing ODBC to be invoked only from the same machine as is running the WRB. Note that this may cause problems if the system is configured in a multinode fashion: cartridges executing on other nodes would be unable to access the ODBC cartridge.

If, however, it is desirable to restrict cartridge access to only approved developers, password security is ideal. Consider, for instance, that it is necessary to give a broad class of users access to LiveHTML functionality, but access to the direct database operations is to be restricted only to certain, more sophisticated, users. In this case, the ODBC application's mapped directory can have password control added from the web listener's configuration. The developers need only add the appropriate username and password information to the #request commands within their LiveHTML files, as shown here:

```
<!--#request url="sql:maniac@www.company.com/odbc/execute?..."-->
```

The OCI Cartridge

In addition to the ODBC cartridge, Oracle provides a cartridge with an external interface identical to that of the ODBC cartridge in the OCI cartridge. Although the interface is the same, the internal operation of the OCI cartridge is quite different. Instead of using database-independent ODBC calls to access databases, the OCI cartridge makes use of the Oracle Call Interface (OCI), which is the primary method of accessing Oracle databases through C code. The exact mechanics of the implementation are not important for users of the cartridge; however, the use of the OCI has significant performance implications. Because database queries do not incur the overhead associated with ODBC's abstraction layer, database accesses are performed much faster.

To use the OCI cartridge, the same *execute, tableprint,* and *stringprint* calls can be invoked to achieve behavior identical to that in the ODBC cartridge. However, instead of passing in the *database* and *dsn* parameters to the commands, the *connect* parameter is passed with a SQL*Net connect string. Of course, the *username* and *password* parameters must be included, as with the ODBC cartridge. Developers can find the OCI cartridge on their installation CD (if available for their platform) in the /platform/CoolStuff/ directory. Also included in this directory (as available) is the Rdb cartridge, which when used against an Rdb database in which the Rdb Web Agent has been installed, allows the developer to access Rdb databases in much the same way as the OCI cartridge allows access to Oracle.

Conclusion

The ODBC cartridge is an outstanding example of a utility cartridge which can provide services to other cartridges and components. It can be used both by sophisticated users to access data from within LiveHTML, as well as by developers to access data in non-Oracle databases. As more utility cartridges such as this are created, the promise of component-based software development at the server side comes closer to being realized.

CHAPTER
9

Oracle Web
Application
Server Security

he security and integrity of data resources are always critical concerns to organizations. These security concerns are always particularly acute when new technologies are introduced. In the case of the Web, these fears were further accentuated by the fact that early web servers received a great deal of press about significant security holes. These defects were largely due to the nature of these early servers: most were developed by students without the rigorous quality assurance process that would have been enforced in a commercial software development shop.

The Oracle Web Application Server and most web server software available today do a more than adequate job of providing facilities for implementing security features. By understanding the security features available, users can learn how to apply them separately or in combination to address the security needs of their organizations.

This chapter has two primary goals. First, it details all of the possible ways in which security features can be implemented using the Oracle Web Application Server, including user-based, IP-based, database-driven, and custom authentication, as well as the Secure Sockets Layer (SSL). Second, it provides some process suggestions for implementing appropriate levels of security in the Oracle Web Application Server. After reading this chapter, you should be able to implement web server security to create a security solution that meets the objectives of almost any organization.

User-Based Authentication

The first general type of security the Oracle Web Application Server offers is the ability to require users to authenticate themselves by providing a username and password that the web server can check against a preconfigured list of users, their groups, and realms of resources to which these groups have access.

This process requires user participation in the validation process. The chain of events that takes place with username/password authentication is as follows:

1. A request for a URL is sent by the browser to the server.

2. Based on settings in the configuration files, the server determines that the URL requested is part of a realm of resources that are to be protected.

3. The server reads the username and password from the relevant request headers. If they are present, it compares them to username/password pairs that are members of a group with access permissions for the realm.

4. If the username and password are present in the configuration file, the request is served as usual.

   If no username and password headers are provided or if the username and password are invalid for the realm, the server returns a "401 Unauthorized" response code.

5. If the request is served, the browser then presents the user with a dialog box requesting username and password information.

6. The user can complete the dialog and accept it. If the dialog is accepted, the request is resubmitted to the server with the provided username/password information, and the process begins again.

Indeed, most users familiar with the Web have seen this authentication behavior already. With some minor variations in configuration methods among various web servers, it is the most common method used to secure web-accessible resources. This chapter focuses on the configuration process for the Spyglass listener, which Oracle bundles with the Oracle Web Application Server. If you are using a different server, such as Apache or Netscape, please consult the server documentation for configuration information, because although most of the same access controls will be available, the method of configuring them will vary.

Configuring Username and Password Security

Configuring username and password security in the Oracle Web Application Server is fairly straightforward. There are two types of name-based security: Basic and Digest. The manner in which they are configured is identical, and the appearance to the user is the same regardless of which type is used. The key difference is the manner in which passwords are transmitted across the network. *Basic* authentication methods transmit both the username and password with every request, whereas *Digest* authentication only requires that a checksum of the password be transmitted. The use of the checksum allows the request to prove that the requester knows the password without actually sending the password.

The username/password security model makes use of the concept of users, groups, and realms. *Users* are members of groups, and *groups* are privileged to access various *realms*. One or more resources on the Oracle Web Application Server (specified by their virtual paths) can be specified as being in a realm of protection. Figure 9-1 shows the relationships among the various entities.

Configuring a security scheme such as this is fairly simple. First, go to the listener configuration page and follow the link to Security. This page will allow you to configure security protocol information managed by the web listener. The Web Request Broker provides similar services. These

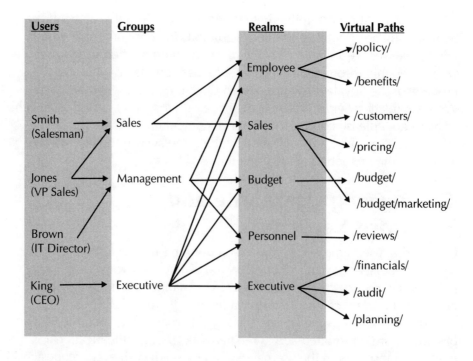

FIGURE 9-1.   *Relationships among security entities*

settings can be applied from the WRB configuration pages or the individual cartridge configuration pages.

Second, define a collection of usernames and passwords for which access is to be controlled. These are the usernames and passwords the web user will enter in the browser's built-in "challenge" dialog.

Third, define a group (or groups) to which the users will belong. Specify the users that are members of this group by entering their names in a space-delimited list in the User(s) field next to the Group Name field.

Next, name a realm for which security will be controlled. The realm name should be reasonably descriptive, especially if it is expected that multiple realms will be defined. Next to the Realms field, enter a space-delimited list of groups that will be permitted access to this realm. Figure 9-2 shows an example configuration of users, groups, and realms.

Once an authentication model has been set up, it must be applied to one or more virtual paths. The security models defined here apply only to

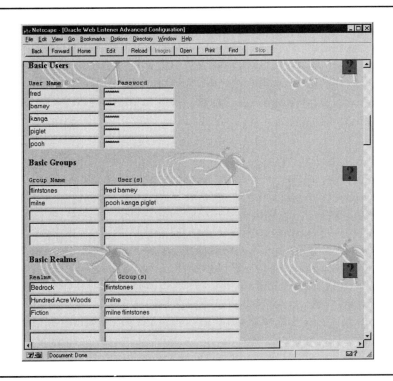

FIGURE 9-2. *Configuring users, groups, and realms*

virtual paths specified in the URL, not directly to actual file system paths on the web server. These virtual paths may ultimately refer to files or to services that will be invoked by the Web Request Broker. For the listener, path permissions are defined in the Protection section of the web listener security configuration page; for the Web Request Broker, they are defined in the Virtual Path Protection section of a cartridge's configuration page.

There are three different ways in which objects in the virtual path can be secured. Securable entities are referred to here as files and directories, but they can of course be virtual paths that map to a cartridge or function rather than a real directory or file. First, an individual file can be secured by specifying the virtual path to the file. In the following example, the single file, diary.html, is secured in the secrets directory.

```
/secrets/diary.html
```

Second, an entire virtual directory can be secured by simply not specifying a file in the virtual path. Here, the entire top_secret directory is secured:

```
/secrets/top_secret/
```

Finally, a wildcard (*) can be used to secure files with certain names in the virtual directory. In the following example, a wildcard is used to secure all the really secret documents whose names begin with "eyes_only."

```
/secrets/top_secret/eyes_only*
```

Typically, the second type (securing the entire directory) is used, although each specification may be useful in different situations.

To permit access to a resource by users in the Basic authentication group defined in the preceding examples, enter the virtual path in Virtual Path field. Next, choose Basic from the Basic/Digest pop-up menu and specify the name of the realm to which the user group was granted access. Leave the remaining fields blank for the time being. Their use will be discussed in a moment.

Remember, these are virtual directories being specified, so this authentication method can be used to secure PL/SQL agent execution as well. For instance, if an agent named "foobar" has been configured, one could specify the virtual resource to be protected as /foobar/ or /foobar/owa. This chapter also covers special options for securing access to the database (see "Database-Controlled Authentication," later in this chapter). Figures 9-3 and 9-4 show the differences in specifying secured virtual paths for both the web listener and a WRB cartridge.

After all necessary fields have been completed, click the Modify Listener button, which appears under most field groups on the page. This will submit the changes to the administrative server, which will then update the appropriate configuration file with the new information. The completed page should display the information just entered, except that all the user passwords will be blank. Don't worry about this; they are in the database, and it is not necessary to enter the missing passwords the next time the form is submitted. However, if it is necessary to change a user's password, it can simply be entered in the password field.

Next, the listener needs to be restarted to make use of the security scheme as configured. Do this by following the Listener Home link at the bottom of the page. From here, the listener can be stopped and restarted. When securing a WRB cartridge, the WRB itself must be restarted, which requires using the owsctl utility. Be certain to first shut down any listeners that would be attached to the WRB before shutting down the WRB itself.

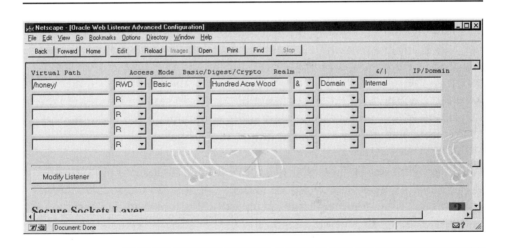

FIGURE 9-3. *Protecting virtual paths for the web listener*

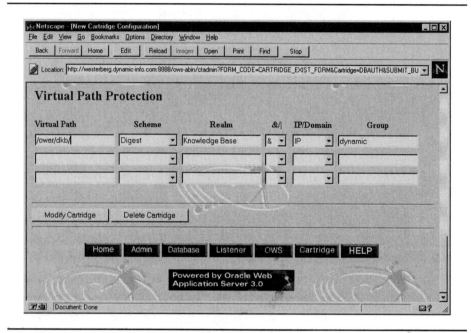

FIGURE 9-4. *Protecting virtual paths for WRB cartridges*

Note that if there is an error in the configuration, such as when specifying a nonexistent group as part of a realm, or a nonexistent realm as part of a Protection, the listener will not restart. If necessary, correct the errors on the security configuration page, submit the changes, and attempt to restart the listener. Of course, if a telnet or rlogin session is active to the server, the owsctl utility can be used at the command line, which may be faster than cycling the web listener from the web-based administration pages.

Speaking of saving time, you may have noticed that since the Oracle Web Application Server configuration page only allows the specification of six users at a time, adding a large number of users may rapidly become cumbersome. If you're using version 2.1 or earlier of the Oracle WebServer, there is a fairly easy solution: direct modification of the listener configuration file.

In the admin directory inside the Web Server directory, there are configuration files named sv*AAAA*.cfg, where *AAAA* is the name of a configured listener. Open up the file with a text editor. It appears remarkably similar to an .INI file in Microsoft Windows. Scroll to the section with the [Security] header, near the end of the file. Assuming the server was configured like the examples shown previously, it should have several lines, like this:

```
Basic {
(Users)
clinton: damato
(Groups)
us: clinton
(Realms)
NATO: us
}
```

At this point, the basic structure of the file should be apparent. Specifically, in the (Users) section, users and passwords are listed in the format "user:<space>password." To add more users to the group, just add more username/password pairs. For adding a large number of users, this is much faster than repeatedly submitting the security form. As mentioned, this can only be done with Oracle WebServer 2.1 and earlier versions. Oracle Web Application Server 3.0 actually changes a vast number of implementation details of the security system. The format of the previous example is not used, nor are passwords stored in clear text. They are encrypted in a manner similar to how Oracle passwords are stored in the database.

Digest Authentication

Digest-based security is also supported in the Oracle Web Application Server. From an administrative perspective, configuring Digest authentication is identical to the steps involved in setting up Basic authentication except that Digest is selected from the Basic/Digest pop-up menu in the protection section.

Assuming the browsers that will be accessing the site are capable of using Digest authentication (most current browsers can), it is generally the preferable choice. Unlike Basic authentication, which involves sending the password in an effectively clear-text string (actually, it is encoded in Base64 format), Digest authentication sends the username as clear text and the password as an MD5 checksum, based on the password the user enters into the challenge dialog. Unlike Base64, which is easily decoded, the MD5 checksum cannot be decoded to reveal the password submitted.

Domain- and IP-Based Authentication

Basic and Digest authentication methods require a user to provide credentials that allow the web server to identify the user as approved. The other generic type of security is based on authenticating the machine from which the request is made. This is akin to checking a Caller ID box attached to a phone rather than asking who is calling. The benefits and drawbacks are parallel as well.

Consider a product specialist at a company in a highly competitive, fast-moving industry. He is supposed to provide important prospective customers with information about products or versions under development in order to presell the company on the technology or persuade them to delay making a purchasing decision in favor of a competitor. Of course, this information is oftentimes reasonably well guarded and, all things being equal, should be kept from competitors. One day someone calls, identifies herself as Jane Doe, a purchasing manager at BigCo, and wants information about the product. Unknowingly, this product specialist provides all the information to the marketing manager of his biggest competitor. Oops—Caller ID might have helped.

A similar goal is at work with domain- and IP-address-driven authentication schemes. These methods verify where the request originated from and restrict resources based on the network location of the requester. They can be used separately from, or in conjunction with, username/password-controlled access.

Of course, domain-based verification is not particularly helpful for selectively restricting access. The problem exists mainly because not every machine is identified by name in a reversible DNS (Domain Name System) server. Even if machines are identified, the DNS server often resides inside the company's firewall and cannot be accessed from the outside. Thus, a restriction pair such as "+* -.worstcompetitor.com" is pretty useless for restricting access. In addition, an unauthorized user could easily access the site through a private ISP (Internet service provider) such as America Online or UUNet.

IP-based verification also is not very useful for selective exclusion because it may be impossible to identify all the addresses or subnets that need to be blocked. However, both of these systems are very useful for allowing access to a defined group of users, either inside or outside an organization. Such techniques are useful for securing special project-oriented web sites in which several people from multiple organizations may collaborate.

Database-Controlled Authentication

In a well-run Oracle operation, the concepts of user grants and roles are used heavily to enforce security restrictions. A *grant* is a privilege a database user can be given. Such privileges include connecting to the database, querying a table, and creating another user account. Individual database users can be granted a wide variety of permissions, both at the system level and at the object level. For instance, a user can be permitted to query a specific table, such as item_price, but not permitted to update, insert, or delete rows in the table.

Roles are collections of grants. Think of a role as a generic description of a user class such as, for example, manager. The manager role can be granted all sorts of different permissions at the system and object levels. Then, when our trusty Oracle user Scott becomes a manager, all those permissions can be given to him by a single line:

```
SQL>GRANT manager TO scott;
```

Grants and roles are a major boon to application developers and administrators of the production database alike. These capabilities free the application developer from having to implement sophisticated access control privileges in the application, and the administrator can easily change and control user permissions as their needs or job roles change. Without grants, access control must be implemented by any application connecting to the database, and security would be instantly defeated by any malicious user with access to a command-line tool such as SQL*Plus. Without roles, DBAs would have the much more cumbersome task of issuing hundreds or thousands of distinct grants for any sort of human resource change.

However, until version 3.0 of the Oracle Web Application Server, such features were lost in web application development. Because versions 1.0 and 2.0 of Database Connection Descriptor had a hard-coded user associated with them, all requests were processed through this user. The net result was that applications implemented using the WebServer SDK were unable to take advantage of already-defined grants, and developers were forced to implement their own security system as part of the application. Moreover, different usernames and passwords had to be assigned and maintained for both the database and the WebServer (assuming users were accessing the database through other means, such as a client/server application).

To address these limitations, Oracle implemented a new security model in version 3.0 of the Oracle Web Application Server. This model is generically referred to as *database authentication* because it relies on the database to perform user authentication. This means that users created in the Oracle database can use their assigned usernames and passwords to connect to it.

In addition to using their standard username/password pairs, users are also effectively logged on to the database as themselves when accessing the system through the Oracle Web Application Server. That is, all of their permissions, grants, and roles are enforced during PL/SQL execution. The benefits here should be immediately obvious. (In fact, how to implement this capability was a question many developers at large Oracle shops used to ask frequently.) Until Web Application Server 3.0, something other than the PL/SQL Web Agent was used to implement the feature (usually a C program using the Oracle Call Interface).

Thankfully, version 3.0 of the Oracle Web Application Server makes this previously burdensome or problematic functionality very easy to implement. Now, when configuring a Database Access Descriptor (DAD) and its associated PL/SQL agent via the HTML-based administration utility, you can simply leave the username and password blank.

Custom Authentication Using the OWA_SEC Package

In addition to implementing security through the built-in services, it may often be desirable to implement a customized security model. The

OWA_SEC package, implemented in versions 3.0 and above of the Oracle Web Application Server, is a PL/SQL package that allows developers to implement their own security procedures and take special action, depending on the user accessing the system. By using the functions in the OWA_SEC package, developers can write customized PL/SQL to authenticate users.

Three custom authentication modes exist. The mode in use by the PL/SQL cartridge is set by a call to the OWA_SEC package using one of three constants to specify the mode. The default setting is no custom authentication and is specified by the OWA_SEC.NO_CHECK constant. The second mode is package specific, in which each package can be protected by a unique function. This mode is set with the OWA_SEC.PER_PACKAGE. The third mode is specified by the global constant OWA_SEC.GLOBAL, and a single function is used to globally authenticate any request to the PL/SQL cartridge.

To specify the manner of custom authentication to be applied, other than OWA_SEC.NO_CHECK, the OWA_INIT package must be modified. This involves altering the /admin/privinit.sql file to call the *owa_sec.set_authorization* routine with the correct setting. In addition, if the mode is set to OWA_SEC.GLOBAL, the default implementation of the *owa_init.authorize* function should be altered to implement the appropriate authorization controls. The other choice is to set the authorization mode to OWA_SEC.PER_PACKAGE, in which case each package invoked will first have its *authorize* function executed. If the call is to an unpackaged procedure, the stored function *authorize* shall be invoked to provide authentication. The signature of each *authorize* function discussed here is the same:

```
FUNCTION authorize RETURN BOOLEAN
```

The *authorize* function typically controls user access based on the username, password, IP address, or DNS name associated with the request. These attributes can be accessed using the OWA_SEC wrapper functions: *get_user_id*, *get_password*, *get_client_ip*, and *get_client_hostname*. In addition, *authorize* will use the *owa_sec.set_protection_realm* procedure to define the name of the realm with which the access is controlled by the procedure. As mentioned earlier, browsers remember the usernames and passwords associated with realms until they are exited, so users are not prompted for their passwords every time a procedure from the realm is accessed.

A fairly sophisticated version of a global control routine is shown in the following listing. It allows the assignment of temporary user accounts to an otherwise intranet-only set of applications. A temporary account is created with a username and an expiration. This first time it is accessed, the password submitted with the username is used as the password for the account, and future access is permitted only from the same IP address as the first access.

```
CREATE OR REPLACE PACKAGE BODY owa_init IS
        -- define the procedure that will handle
        -- authentication requests for the DAD
        FUNCTION authorize RETURN BOOLEAN
        IS
            c_ip        owa_util.ip_address;
            c_psswd     VARCHAR2(50);
            c_uname     VARCHAR2(50);
            t_ipa       NUMBER;
            s_ipa       NUMBER:
            s_exp       DATE;
            s_psswd     VARCHAR2(50);
        BEGIN
            -- set the name of the realm, this is arbitrary,
            -- but the browser will display it in its challenge
            -- dialog, so use something sensible
            owa_sec.set_protection_realm('Private');
            c_ip := owa_sec.get_client_ip;
            -- any request that is from the subnet 127.0.0.* is
            -- automatically accepted. If wanting to grant access to
            -- a class B address, only c_ip(1) and c_ip(2) need
            -- be checked.
            IF ((c_ip(1) = 127) AND (c_ip(2) = 0) AND (c_ip(3)= 0))
            THEN
                RETURN TRUE;
            ELSE
                c_uname := owa_sec.get_user_id;
                c_psswd := owa_sec.get_password;
                BEGIN
                    SELECT password,ipaddress,expiry
                        INTO s_psswd, s_ipa, s_exp
                        FROM tempaccess
                       WHERE username = c_uname;
                EXCEPTION
```

```
                     -- fail if username not found;
                  WHEN OTHERS THEN
                         RETURN FALSE;
            END;
            -- convert ip address into a numerical format
            t_ipa = (c_ip(1) * 16777216)+
                    (c_ip(3) * 65536) +
                    (c_ip(3) * 256) +
                    c_ip(4);
            -- see if the account has expired
            IF (s_exp < SYSDATE)
            THEN
                DELETE FROM tempaccess
                 WHERE username = c_uname;
                RETURN FALSE;
            ELSE
                -- check if user has already logged in, if not,
                -- the password sent with the current request
                -- becomes the user's password
                IF s_psswd IS NULL
                THEN
                    UPDATE tempaccess
                       SET password=c_psswd, ipaddress=s_ipa
                     WHERE username = c_uname;
                    RETURN TRUE;
                ELSE
                    -- finally, check if password and ip address
                    -- match, if they don't delete the account,
                    -- as it has been compromised
                    IF ((s_ipa = t_ipa) AND (s_psswd = c_psswd))
                    THEN
                         RETURN TRUE;
                    ELSE
                        DELETE FROM tempaccess
                         WHERE username = c_uname;
                        RETURN FALSE;
                    END IF;
                END IF;
            END IF;
        END IF;
    END;
BEGIN
    -- package initialization sets the authentication
    -- mode to global, so owa_init.authorize will be
    -- executed for every request coming through
```

```
    -- the DAD that accesses this package
    owa_sec.set_authorization(OWA_SEC.GLOBAL);
END;
```

The complete flexibility and control provided by using PL/SQL-defined authorization controls should be evident. Rather than storing username and password information in the configuration files, this information can more easily be maintained in an Oracle database table and can be used in other procedures to more easily implement user settings or provide user-specific filters on certain data.

Tutorial: Setting Up the Secure Sockets Layer (SSL)

Any comprehensive security strategy must address the following issues: authorization, authentication, and encryption. *Authorization* is the practice of validating a user by username and password. *Authentication* is any process used to verify communication is taking place between appropriate machines. In the Oracle Web Application Server, both of these steps are referred to as authentication. *Encryption* is used to protect the contents of a communication session from being disclosed to an untrusted third party.

You have seen how authorization schemes can be implemented using Basic and Digest schemes and how IP- and domain-based methods provide some level of authentication control from the server's perspective. However, for many types of transactions, especially those involving sensitive financial or personal information, users would like the additional confidence of encryption. In some respects this is humorous, given how cavalier people are with such information in a nonelectronic setting.

The Oracle Web Application Server supports encryption between browser and server using the Secure Sockets Layer (SSL), a public-key cryptosystem developed by Netscape Communications. In addition to providing encryption services, many browsers compare the DNS name of the server being accessed to the DNS name for which the key is registered, alerting the user to any discrepancy. This provides a rudimentary level of assurance as to the authenticity of the server being accessed.

Configuring your Oracle Web Application Server to use SSL is a multipart process. First, a request for a key must be generated and submitted to a certifying authority, such as VeriSign. After the certifying authority approves the request, it sends back a public key. When the key has been received, the Oracle Web Application Server can be configured to use the key.

Enrolling with VeriSign

The first step in getting a Digital ID for a web server is to enroll with VeriSign, the primary certifying authority. To begin the enrollment process, visit the VeriSign web site at digitalid.verisign.com. From there, follow the link to get a Digital ID for a web server, then the link to run SSL, and then select Oracle from the list of vendors. You will be presented with a very brief and generic overview of the key request process. At the bottom of the page, follow the Begin link to move on with the process.

The next form is an automated request letter generation form. Fill out all the fields (server name, business location, technical and billing contacts, and billing information). If your company has a D-U-N-S number from Dun & Bradstreet, this will typically help expedite VeriSign's due diligence process in verifying your company's right to use the distinguished name.

By pressing the Continue button, the VeriSign server will generate an authorization letter. This letter must also have information added to it regarding the authorized company representative making the request. (It would be worthwhile to print a copy of this letter for future reference.) Clicking the Agree button will take you to a page outlining how to generate the key request for each different server.

Generating a Key Request

To generate a request, use the genreq utility. Execute it at the command line. Enter **G** at the first prompt to begin the request generation process. It will prompt you through the following steps:

1. You will be prompted for a password used to generate the private key. It must be at least eight characters long. After entering the password, you will be prompted to verify the password. Although the Oracle documentation claims the password will never be used again after the confirmation prompt, we still suggest remembering the password and possibly keeping it documented in a secure location, such as a safety deposit box, along with the rest of the paperwork and files generated in this process.

2. You will then be prompted for the public exponent to use. The default is Fermat 4, or 65537. The only other valid exponent at this time is 3. We suggest using Fermat 4.

3. Next, genreq will prompt you for a modulus size, in bits. All else held equal, a larger modulus will result in a more secure key pair. The default, and largest, size for servers outside the United States is 512 bits. Of course, this is because cryptographic technology is officially considered a munition for export purposes. However, thanks to the Second Amendment, here in the U.S. we can use any modulus size up to 1,024 bits. The default is 768 bits. We suggest choosing a random number somewhere near the upper end of this range (between 950 and 1,020 bits).

4. You will then be prompted to choose a method of generating a random seed that will in turn be used to generate the key pair. There are three options:

- If you enter **F**, you will be prompted to enter a full pathname to a file on the local file system. Any file that is larger than 256 bytes can be used. Ideally, the file should not contain proprietary information, nor should its contents be easily guessed.

- If you enter **K**, you will be prompted to type random keys on the keyboard. The genreq utility uses the time between the keystrokes to create the seed. Do not allow more than a two-second gap between keystrokes. The program requests several hundred random keystrokes. (It would be handy if there were a toddler or small child available for this task!) The computer will beep and inform you when sufficient keys have been entered.

- If you enter **B**, you will be prompted both for a filename as well as keystrokes. Obviously, this dual option is the most secure and is thus recommended.

5. Now genreq will prompt you for filenames to use to save the three files it generates. All files will be initially written in the current working directory, although they can be moved anywhere after genreq completes.

■ First, genreq prompts you for a filename that will contain the Oracle Web Application Server's distinguished name. Any filename with a .der extension can be used. This example uses the name distname.der.

■ Second, you will be prompted for the name of a file in which to store the Oracle Web Application Server's private key. Again, this can be any file with a .der extension. This example uses the name privkey.der.

■ Finally, you must enter the name of a file into which the certificate request will be written. This will be sent to VeriSign in the next step of the request process. Any filename with a .pkc extension can be used. This example uses the name request.pkc.

6. You will then be prompted for the following information about your organization and the server. Be certain it exactly matches the information you submitted in the VeriSign enrollment.

■ **Common Name**   The fully qualified DNS name of the machine on which the Digital ID will be used, for example, www.dynamic-info.com.

■ **Email Address**   The technical contact's e-mail address.

■ **Organization**   Your company's legal name.

■ **Organizational Unit**   Either a department or division, or for companies doing business as another company, this can be used for the D/B/A company name. The utility requires some input here, so type a space if it is not applicable.

■ **Locality**   The city, principality, or country where your organization is located. This is not where the Oracle Web Application Server will physically reside.

■ **State or Province**   The location of the company, not the Oracle Web Application Server. (Abbreviations are not accepted by VeriSign, so spell out the name.)

■ **Country**   The two-character ISO country code for the country in which the business operates. For the United States this is US, for Canada it is CA, and for Japan it is JP. A list of other codes can be found at the following web address:

www.oraweb.com/book/misc/country_codes.html

7. The genreq utility will then process the information. When all files have been written, it will respond with "Done" and return you to the main menu. Type **Q** to quit genreq.

Requesting the Key

After you have enrolled with VeriSign and generated the key request, the next step is to send the request to VeriSign. Use your e-mail program to send a message to oracle-request-id@verisign.com. Note that your message must be sent to this address, as each web server generates different certificate requests, and the VeriSign processor is configured differently for each server. In the e-mail message, send the complete contents of the certificate request file created by genreq. In our example, it is in a file named request.pkc.

At this point, VeriSign will begin processing your request. You may be required to complete or submit additional documentation or proof of right to use the distinguished name. If you are at a new or small company, or are outside the United States, including this documentation immediately will expedite the process. The proof must be submitted in English (translated by an official authority) and should be one of the following types of documents:

- Business license

- Partnership papers

- Articles of incorporation or organization

- For universities, a notarized letter from the office of the dean

- For government entities, a notarized letter from a properly authorized person

- An official trademark registration

Be certain to include the UIN (Universal Internet Number), which VeriSign will send in response to the certificate request. This information, along with payment information, can be faxed to VeriSign in California, at (415) 961-7300, or sent via postal mail to the following address:

VeriSign, Inc.
2593 Coast Road
Mountain View, CA 94043

VeriSign will contact you directly if there is any additional information or documentation necessary to complete your request. Otherwise, you should receive a Digital ID from VeriSign in three to five days, although it can take as long as 14 days.

Installing the Key and Configuring the Oracle Web Application Server

In a few days, VeriSign will send the requester a key file via e-mail to the address specified in the request. This response should be saved using the e-mail reader into a file with a .der extension. This example uses cert.der. After saving the file, use a text editor to strip all information above the BEGIN CERTIFICATE and below the END CERTIFICATE line. Leave both the BEGIN CERTIFICATE and END CERTIFICATE lines intact.

You may wish to set up a directory containing all of the SSL files you will use, such as ssl, inside the Oracle Web Application Server home directory. Also, place two subdirectories inside the main directory, one named ca and one named crl. This will make sense in a minute. Next, move the cert.der file (the one you just saved) into the ssl directory. Also, move the first two files you created in step 5 of the request generation task (called distname.der and privkey.der in step 5) into the ssl directory.

Next, use a web browser to go to the WebServer Administration page. Follow the links to the listener configuration page for the listener that is to be SSL-enabled. Then go to the security configuration page. At the bottom is a section for configuring SSL. Complete the following fields in that section:

- **Certificate File** This should specify the path to the cert.der file.

- **Distinguished Name File** This should specify the path to the file created by genreq (distname.der in our example).

- **Key File** This is the path to the private-key file created by genreq (privkey.der in our example).

■ **Certifying Authority Directory** This should provide the path to the ca subdirectory inside the ssl directory created earlier.

■ **Certificate Revocation List Directory** This should provide the path to the crl subdirectory inside the ssl directory created earlier.

Submit the form, and the Oracle Web Application Server will perform all necessary tasks to use the key pair. The final step is to configure the listener to use SSL. Again, go to the listener configuration form for the listener in question. In the addresses and ports section, enable SSL for the address/port pair by choosing it from the Security pop-up menu. The well-known port for SSL-secured HTTP is 443, although any port can be used.

Note that in order to access port 443 directly, you should use HTTPS instead of HTTP as the prefix for the URL. For instance, if the URL http://www.dynamic-info.com/ specifies a connection to a machine on port 80, then https://www.dynamic-info.com/ will connect to the same machine, but on port 443. As with HTTP, a port other than the well-known port may be specified by postfixing the machine name with :*port*. For example, accessing the URL https://www.dynamic-info.com:90/ will use SSL services but will connect to port 90 instead of port 443.

Fortunately, SSL certificates only need to be set up once. It is a somewhat tedious process, but as soon as your organization has set up one certificate, certificates for other servers in your domain can be obtained much more easily and less expensively as well. For now, however, your Web Application Server should be sufficiently secure for electronic commerce and transmission of other sensitive information.

Security Recommendations

Good security is not just implemented by Oracle Web Application Server software. Strong security comes from the combination of properly configured hardware and software combined with a security policy that is appropriately developed and adhered to. Implementing such a policy is critical. This section is not meant to serve as an example of a comprehensive security policy. Instead, it provides a list of certain tips for enhancing the security of an Oracle Web Application Server installation, as well as traps to avoid. Different applications and operating environments demand or constrain many security choices. Some suggestions specific to the Oracle Web Application Server are provided. They should be taken in concert with an organization's existing security regime.

- Don't use the default port for the Administrative listener. It is surprising how many Oracle-driven web servers allow access to administrative features just by fetching hostname:9999 or hostname:8888. And if a weak password is used, it can be an invitation to disaster caused by either a malicious hacker or a curious user.

- Don't use the default username restriction to the administrative server. Edit the configuration file to enforce an IP restriction permitting access to a single IP address.

- Avoid installing any of the bundled demo applications and remove the virtual path mappings for all of the demo applications.

- Shut down the Administrative listener when it is not needed. This not only completely prevents web access to administrative functions, but also reduces the number of running services, which frees up system resources. The listener can be started from the command line with the **owsctl** command when it needs to be used by the administrator.

- On a machine susceptible to malicious attacks, it would be wise to consider shutting down all other unnecessary services on the machine and to be extremely vigilant with, or eliminate altogether, access control to such services as telnet and rlogin.

- If it is necessary to deliver data from a production database via an Internet-accessible web server, it is wise to run a database server outside the firewall. The contents of that database should be replicated (through snapshots or other propagation methods) from the production database inside the firewall. Ideally, the propagation should be driven from inside, with the update connection initiated from inside the firewall.

    If the delivery of real-time data from a production system is required, or if data must be inserted or updated in real time from web requests, it will be necessary to prick a small hole in the firewall. Make certain that the firewall solution supports SQL*Net. It would also be wise to use an encrypted SQL*Net connection, possibly using hardware or stack-level encryption. The SQL*Net Advanced Networking option can provide some assistance in this area as well.

■ Make use of Oracle's security model to adequately secure the user that the Database Access Descriptor (DAD) is configured to use. The best way to manage this is to configure used resources as follows: First, create all objects in one user schema. Let's call this user "developer." Then create a second user (for instance, "www_user"), which is the user specified in the DAD. When connected to the database as developer, grant www_user the minimally sufficient privileges on all objects necessary to run the application. Finally, create synonyms to allow www_user to access the necessary developer objects without specifying the developer schema.

Be especially sensitive to the permissions granted on objects if fully ad hoc queries are implemented by passing untouched user input to the DBMS_SQL package for dynamic SQL execution. For example, having a user enter **DELETE FROM customer** would be disastrous.

■ Fortunately, unlike some SQL execution methods, the DBMS_SQL package prevents a significant security breach by executing only a single command per EXECUTE call. For instance, consider a procedure containing the following code:

```
qry_expr:='SELECT name,phone FROM customer WHERE zip=' ||zip_in;
DBMS_SQL.EXECUTE(qry_expr);
```

If a malicious user attempts to compromise the system by entering **12345; DELETE FROM customer** as the value submitted to zip_in, an error will occur and the deletion will not. SQL commands passed to DBMS_SQL cannot contain the semicolon to delimit commands. Be aware that some other tools on the market are not as secure in the way they handle dynamic SQL execution.

■ In order to restrict access to ad hoc queries, it is wise to prevent access to the *owa_util.show_source* and *owa_util.table_print* procedures. Both of these procedures can easily be called directly by an individual that understands Oracle and the Web Application Server SDK. Although neither routine is capable of destroying data itself, each allows a prying user access to data that should be controlled and also allows users to find and possibly exploit security holes in user-written PL/SQL code.

The best way to handle this is to use the package_protect PL/SQL cartridge configuration setting to prevent access to the packages in the Web Application Server SDK directly from a browser or via Inter-Cartridge Exchange (ICX). When protected, these procedures can only be invoked by other PL/SQL procedures.

Conclusion

This chapter has described the myriad of security features and options in the Oracle Web Application Server. Some are very easy to configure; some are more complex. Each serves a specific function in a comprehensive security policy. By using different methods, alone or in combination, as well as following our additional security recommendations, the Oracle Web Application Server and its applications need not represent a security risk to any organization.

In addition to the security approaches and solutions described in this chapter, there are other methods that can be employed to provide additional layers of security. The Oracle Security Server supports the issuing and verification of SSL client certificates, which can be accessed from cartridges written using the Web Request Broker's API. See the documentation for the Oracle Security Server for additional information about client certificate generation.

Without question, the most important suggestion for maintaining security is to thoroughly read the documentation and release notes in each version of the Oracle Web Application Server to be aware of any new features that can be used to better protect your system.

CHAPTER
10

Web Request Broker
Architecture and Services

e introduced the Web Request Broker (WRB) earlier in the book while talking about configuring the web server and application cartridges. In this chapter, we go into detail about the architecture, function, and purpose of the WRB, as well as examine the services that it provides to application developers to make their lives easier while allowing them to create more robust and feature-rich web applications. After reading this chapter, a developer should be able to make use of all the services of the WRB using each of the primary development languages supported by the Oracle Web Application Server: C, Java, LiveHTML, and PL/SQL.

Architecture

As mentioned in Chapter 3, the Web Request Broker stands as an enormous architectural innovation in the Web Application Server. It provides a foundation for developing large-scale application development and deployment environments that can span multiple systems for performance, scalability, and fault-tolerance.

Although it is possible to make use of the services of the Web Request Broker without having a full understanding of it, such an understanding invariably proves helpful both in configuration and development as well as in debugging and performance tuning. The Web Request Broker is typically used to refer to the collection of components necessary to manage the invocation of cartridges and components, typically as a result of requests sent to a web listener by a browser. In fact, the WRB itself is only one part of the collection of processes and services that are necessary to manage the cartridge process. The Web Request Broker works with an object request broker (ORB), which is compliant with the Common Object Request Broker Architecture (CORBA). The WRB system receives requests (dispatched from the web listener) for object services (such as to invoke a PL/SQL procedure or a LiveHTML page) and forwards these requests to the appropriate cartridges, instances of which the system has started as necessary.

Components and Processes

The collected WRB system is made up of ten main processes. Three are directly related to the ORB services provided by Oracle Media Net: mnorbsrv, mnaddsrv, and mnrpcmnsrv. These are, respectively, the ORB service itself, the ORB's address server, and the RPC (Remote Procedure

Call) name server. These services are started prior to the other WRB services, as the WRB and its services are themselves accessed via the ORB.

The next processes to be started are the WRB configuration provider and the Logger service, wrbcfg and wrblog. These are followed by the two processes that manage the WRB authentication broker and provider services, wrbasrv and wrbahsrv. At this point, the Web Request Broker process itself, wrbroker, is started. The virtual path manager, wrbvpm, is then started to manage mapping virtual paths to certain cartridge services, as specified in the configuration files. Finally, the WRB's cartridge factory, wrbfac, is started. The cartridge factory itself is responsible for creating cartridge instances, which are all processes named wrbc.

When running the Web Application Server, the flow of control is basically that as illustrated by the diagram in Figure 10-1. When a request first comes to the WAS, the listener determines if the request is to be handled by a cartridge and, if so, what type. The listener then dispatches the request to the ORB. If the ORB is aware of an available cartridge instance, it directly forwards the request to that instance. On the other hand, if no available cartridge instances of the needed type are started or available, it alerts the listener to this fact. The listener, in turn, instructs the WRB to start a new cartridge instance, in which case the cartridge instance is created by the WRB cartridge factory and the instance is registered with the ORB. The request can then be dispatched to this newly created instance.

The cartridge instance itself is a combination of the WRB application engine, which knows how to invoke the cartridge written by the developer, as well as the cartridge code itself. The WRB application engine (a wrbc process) first invokes the cartridge's authorization function and, if the authorization is successful, invokes the cartridge's execution function. The execution function is typically the "workhorse" function that performs any processing necessary and sends any results back to the listener. The engine, in turn, returns these results to the listener through the ORB, at which point they are finally sent back to the user's browser.

It is possible to run all these processes on a single machine, or to distribute them across a variety of devices, referred to as *nodes*. If the system is configured to support multiple nodes, then one node is designated to be the *primary node*. This is the node with which the HTTP listener communicates. The listener may either be on the primary node or be from a different machine. The primary node has running instances of all the ORB and WRB processes enumerated earlier. Other nodes are referred to as

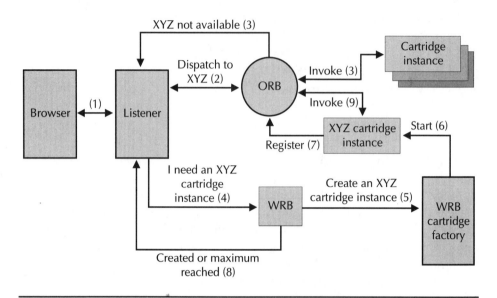

FIGURE 10-1. *Cartridge invocation with the Web Request Broker*

remote nodes. These nodes are slaves to the directives of the primary node, and only the WRB cartridge factory and cartridge instances themselves run on remote nodes. Optionally, authentication services can be balanced across servers as well.

An important implication of each cartridge instance running as a separate process is that it is not possible for an errant cartridge to crash the web listener itself. Only the cartridge's process will die, and although the request being serviced will fail, a new cartridge instance of that type will be started, as needed, to service other requests. This fault tolerance with respect to user-written or third-party code is a major advantage of the Web Application Server architecture.

NOTE
Distribution of cartridge processes across multiple nodes is only possible with the Advanced Edition of Oracle Web Application Server version 3.0.

Writing cartridges for the Web Request Broker is not fundamentally complex. Cartridges developed for the WRB are at this time written in C and must only implement a small handful of entry-point functions to support invocation through the WRB. In addition, these cartridges will typically make use of a variety of services provided by the WRB. The same is also true of components written for use with other cartridges we have examined earlier. For instance, user-written code in PL/SQL, Java, or LiveHTML can make use of many of the WRB services. These services, the functionality they provide, and the method of invoking them from various components and cartridges are the primary focus of this chapter.

Cartridge Architecture

The next chapter thoroughly describes the construction of cartridges for use with the Oracle Web Application Server. However, to provide some context for the remaining discussion in this chapter, a brief overview of the implementation of a cartridge is in order. As mentioned earlier, cartridges presently must be written in C, although other languages should be supported in future releases of the product. A cartridge must implement a main entry-point function, which is the entry point specified in the cartridge configuration page and saved in the wrb.app file. This entry point is used to pass function pointers to the WRB execution engine. These are pointers to the functions that implement support for various phases of the cartridge's lifecycle—minimally, this are initialization, execution, and shutdown. In addition, support may be implemented both for calls that provide authorization services and for those that return version information.

When writing a cartridge, developers use the base WRB API (Application Program Interface) to handle most of the work of extracting request parameters and headers and sending responses to the client. This frees the developer to focus on implementing a solution, rather than the tedious, but often error-prone, busywork of string parsing. In addition, it provides functions for accessing the configuration data from the WRB's configuration files, as well as manipulating WRB parameter blocks used by many API functions for passing data (a collection of name/value pairs).

The parameter block management functions include *WRB_createPBlock*, which creates a new parameter block; *WRB_copyPBlock*, which duplicates an existing block; and *WRB_destroyPBlock*, which frees the memory associated with the block. Elements are inserted into the blocks with *WRB_addPBBElem* and deleted with *WRB_delPBElem*. The API provides several ways to access the contents of the blocks. For example, *WRB_findPBElem* lets the developer access an element by name, while *WRB_findPBElemVal* returns the value associated with the passed name. One can call *WRB_numPBElem* to get the count of the parameter block elements, and then access each element by its index, by using *WRB_walkPBlock*. A parameter block can also be accessed as an enumeration, by using *WRB_firstPBElem* and *WRB_nextPBElem*; the latter of which returns a null when all elements have been traversed.

For accessing information associated with a request, the API provides *WRB_getParsedContent*, which populates a parameter block with name/ value pairs from the request. *WRB_getCookies* and *WRB_recvHeaders* provide a similar function but return name/value pairs of cookie data or request headers, respectively. If accepting a form upload containing multipart data (such as a file upload), *WRB_getMultipartData* can be used to have the WRB extract the name/value pairs into a parameter block and return a pointer to (and size of) the arbitrarily formatted data attached to the request—usually, the uploaded file. If the developer simply must access the request content directly, *WRB_read* can be used for this purpose.

In addition to getting information about the request, the developer can access the current environment variables with *WRB_getEnvironment* and can get information about the listener, such as virtual directory mappings or supported MIME types, using *WRB_getListenerInfo*. Information from the WRB configuration files is fairly easy to access using one of three routines. The first, *WRB_getAppConfigVal*, returns the value associated with a given name in the current cartridge's section of the WRB configuration file. *WRB_getAppConfigSection* returns a parameter block containing all the name/value pairs from the application's configuration section. If the developer needs to read from several configuration sections, the *WRB_getMultAppConfigSection* function is used, which returns a block containing the names of all cartridges beginning with the specified string, each of which is linked to a parameter block of all the cartridge's configuration name/value pairs.

As the developer is processing the input and preparing the results to be sent back to the user, she would use routines such as *WRB_printf* and *WRB_write* to write formatted or unformatted output to the buffer that will be sent to the client. Before writing anything to the request body, however, any headers must be sent first. To set any headers for the response, the developer can create a parameter block composed of header names and values, and then call the *WRB_sendHeader* function. A convenience call for setting up cookies is provided in *WRB_setCookies*, which properly formats the name, value, domain, and expiration date before adding it to the header.

The WRB API provides several routines for special security management. The function *WRB_setAuthServer* is used to specify protection scheme and realm combinations, and is typically called in the cartridge's Authorization or Init functions. *WRB_setAuthDigest* and *WRB_setAuthBasic* are used for defining new authentication realms on the fly. Cartridges are also able to access a DER-encoded client-side Secure Sockets Layer certificate using the *WRB_getClientCert* function. The header and environment settings are always available to cartridge authors for defining customized authentication methods.

In the next chapter, the WRB API will be demonstrated in detail. However, the overview provided here should allow readers to think about the way different WRB API calls can be used in conjunction with the services described next when creating a cartridge. The entire set of WRB API functions, as well as those for the C APIs of all WRB services, is listed in a handy format in Appendix C.

Services

Although the primary function of the Web Request Broker is to invoke cartridges to service requests from web browsers, it also provides numerous services to these cartridges. In addition to the WRB's fault tolerance with respect to user-written cartridges, it is these services that distinguishes the WRB from basic API systems such as those found in Netscape Enterprise Server, Microsoft Internet Information Server, and the Apache server.

The Web Request Broker provides five main services, each discussed in this chapter. The transaction service allows fully controlled database transactions to span several HTTP requests. Inter-Cartridge Exchange allows code in one cartridge to request services from other cartridges. The Logger service provides a common interface for cartridges to write log data that can be better managed by the web server administrator. Session management services allow developers to (almost transparently) maintain state information across HTTP requests without manually managing cookies or writing state information to a database. Finally, Content services provide developers with a repository system for storing arbitrary files or data objects.

Most of these services must be enabled for the cartridge that will be accessing them. This is accomplished by selecting the appropriate service in the Services list of the New or Update Cartridge Configuration page, as shown in Figure 10-2. Alternately, one can enter the name of the service to be used by a cartridge in the Applications and Services section of the WRB Administration page.

Transaction Management

One of the most significant features introduced in version 3.0 of Oracle Web Application Server is database transaction management. This service overcomes the limitation in current web-based applications caused by its statelessness: the difficulty in implementing robust transactional capabilities.

NOTE
This service is available only with the Advanced Edition of Oracle Web Application Server version 3.0.

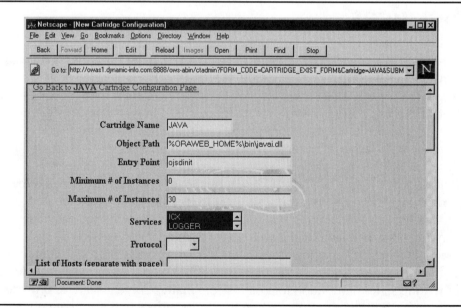

FIGURE 10-2. *Enabling WRB services for a cartridge*

Purpose

As we have mentioned elsewhere in this book, HTTP is a stateless protocol, and as such causes some difficulties in designing and implementing certain types of web applications. Most notably, these include many business applications in which the page to be displayed or the action to be taken by the server depends on previous actions of the user. Another issue is one in which the action that the application takes depends on the actions of other users or processes of the application.

Earlier, we described the use of the HTTP Cookie mechanism to maintain state information about the current user's session. In Chapter 4, we described how to create and manipulate cookies directly in PL/SQL. Later in this chapter, we describe some session management capabilities that the WRB provides for use by cartridges and Java components. Cookie-based state management is very effective for allowing developers to create state-dependent applications, such as displaying certain information (depending on preferences the user has submitted) or returning the user to a correct catalog page after viewing his virtual shopping basket.

However, cookies do not solve one of the fundamental problems of developing fully functional, enterprise-grade applications for HTTP. This problem is the difficulty in implementing transaction control. Readers familiar with database applications should have a keen understanding both of transactions and of the key purpose they serve in applications. For those unfamiliar with the need or the problem, it can be described briefly.

Transaction management can be broken down into four components, which some commentators refer to as ACID properties. ACID stands for the four features that robust transaction systems must support: atomicity, consistency, isolation, and durability. A transaction is a unit of work against a database (or other transaction-capable resource) that supports those four properties. To better appreciate the implications of transaction management, understanding what each of the four ACID properties entails is necessary.

The property of *atomicity* states that transactions have an all-or-nothing character. That is, a transaction may be a collection of several steps (for instance: three database updates, two deletes, and an insert), all of which are applied or unapplied to the database *as a group*. A transaction management system cannot allow just one (or two, or three) of the component changes to be applied to the database without applying *all* the component changes.

The *consistency* property simply states that a transaction applied to an internally consistent database will leave the database internally consistent. This mostly means that integrity constraints imposed by the database (typically declarative) are enforced for the entire transaction. If any component of the transaction would violate the consistency property, the atomicity property requires that the entire transaction be aborted.

An extremely critical feature of the transaction control is the *isolation* property, which requires that the transaction's behavior is in no way affected by the presence or activity within other transactions taking place against the database. Specifically, this means that the transaction only "sees" the database as if it were the only transaction in process and that its results are identical to what they would be if it were running alone.

There are two major implications of isolation. First, the need for isolation basically requires that the database must support the concept of locking changeable resources that are in use by a transaction. This lock is necessary to prevent other transactions from attempting to change the resources. If two transactions attempted to change the same resource, the results of the transaction running might not be identical to those of running the transaction alone. The second implication is that changes applied to a database within a transaction are invisible to other transactions until they are applied, or committed to the database. For instance, if Transaction A is has added a record to the EMP table but has not yet committed its changes, the new record will not be visible to Transaction B if it queries the EMP table.

The final property, *durability,* states that once a transaction is applied to a database, any effects of the transaction persist through a failure of the database. This requires that all changes specified by a transaction are written to nonvolatile memory (that is, to disk), and that the database management system (software and hardware combined) supports recovery even in the event of memory or disk failure.

As might be imagined, implementing complete and robust transaction control is no mean feat. In fact, the complexity of implementing robust support for all ACID properties, while still maintaining high performance, is much of what keeps companies like Oracle in the black (aside from their superlative web tools). At the same time, all these attributes are vitally important for every mission-critical application of any level of complexity.

Prior to the transaction management capabilities provided in Oracle Web Application Server 3.0, applications developed for the Web typically supported all the ACID properties for any database access or updates triggered by a single HTTP request—but *not* for a collection of updates or accesses spanning several HTTP requests. This was an obvious limitation to using the standard HTTP interface in business applications.

Architecture

The transaction manager implements the XA interface for distributed transaction processing. The XA interface was defined by the X/Open Company, Ltd., an organization responsible for defining standards related to open systems architectures.

NOTE

In 1996, X/Open and the Open Software Foundation (OSF), a similar standards organization, consolidated into The Open Group, which oversees and directs the activities of the OSF and X/Open. Its web site can be found at http://www.opengroup.org/.

Lifecycle of a Transaction

A transaction is a collection of one or more updates or accesses to a database. A transaction has a beginning, a middle, and one of two possible ends—either committing, which permanently applies all changes made during the transaction to the database, or rolling back, which cancels the transaction without committing. In many database management systems or 4GL development tools, transactions are started implicitly. For instance, the first DML (Data Manipulation Language) operation that is made against a database may initiate a transaction. All following DML operations are grouped into that transaction until either a COMMIT or a ROLLBACK statement is issued to the database.

With the WRB transaction services, transactions are started explicitly by accessing a particular URL. Other URLs are "members" of transaction, meaning that the WRB transaction service will allow the cartridge instance to join the transaction currently in progress. Finally, a transaction ends when either the commit URL or the rollback URL is accessed.

Service Usage

Transaction management can be implemented and controlled in two ways. The first is through configuration of the WRB to provide transaction control to specific URLs that access, for instance, PL/SQL components. The second is by directly invoking the transaction management functions.

TRANSACTIONS WITH THE PL/SQL CARTRIDGE   As mentioned earlier, a transaction can be said to have a lifecycle. Thus, when creating a PL/SQL package that will be under transaction control, it should contain exactly one procedure to initiate the transaction, and exactly one procedure each to commit and roll back the transaction. It can also contain any number of procedures that are members of the transaction, that is, procedures that will execute within the transaction initiated by invoking these starting procedures. The following package, TEST_TRANS, is an extremely minimal example of a package that can be used to implement transaction control. It contains four procedures—*beg, com, rb,* and *add_form*—which allow the user to begin, commit, roll back, and add data within a transaction, respectively. The procedure expects a table, tttab, containing a single VARCHAR2 column, foo. The configuration examples below are based on this procedure. Note that the procedure itself makes no transaction control calls whatsoever, and thus the developer can remain blissfully ignorant of the transaction control, which will be managed entirely by the WRB transaction services.

```
CREATE OR REPLACE PACKAGE BODY test_trans IS

    PROCEDURE beg
    IS
    BEGIN
      htp.header(1,'Transaction started');
      add_form;
    END;

    PROCEDURE com
    IS
    BEGIN
      htp.header(1,'Transaction committed');
```

```
    htp.anchor('test_trans.beg', 'Start new Transaction');
END;

PROCEDURE rb
IS
BEGIN
  htp.header(1,'Transaction rolled back');
  htp.anchor('test_trans.beg', 'Start new Transaction');

END;

PROCEDURE add_form (foo_in IN VARCHAR2:=NULL)
IS
BEGIN
  IF foo_in IS NOT NULL
  THEN
    INSERT INTO tttab VALUES (foo_in);
  END IF;
  FOR cur IN (SELECT foo FROM tttab)
  LOOP
    htp.p(cur.foo ||'<BR>');
  END LOOP;
  htp.para;
  htp.formOpen('test_trans.add_form','GET');
  htp.bold('Add an item:');
  htp.formText('foo_in',15,15);
  htp.formSubmit;
  htp.formClose;
  htp.para;
  htp.anchor('test_trans.com', 'Commit Changes');
  htp.para;
  htp.anchor('test_trans.rb', 'Rollback Changes');
END;

END test_trans;
```

After creating this procedure in the database, we can now transaction-enable it. This process is used to associate certain procedures with different parts of the lifecycle of the transaction. WRB transactions for PL/SQL procedures are created by associating them with specific PL/SQL agents. This is accomplished by going to the Cartridge Administration page, following the link to the PL/SQL cartridge, and choosing the link of a PL/SQL agent. At the bottom of the PL/SQL Agent configuration page is a section for transactions, which lists any existing transactions and allows the creation of new transactions. Creating a WRB-managed transaction requires setting values for the fields shown in Figure 10-3.

The meanings of the fields are reasonably straightforward. Each transaction is given a name, which should be unique across the WRB instance. The Begin Transaction URI contains the Uniform Resource Identifier, which represents the start of the transaction. The URI of a resource is the URL of the resource with the protocol and host specification removed. Thus, if the URL of the beginning of the transaction is http://owas1/scott/plsql/test_trans.beg, the URI will be /scott/plsql/ test_trans.beg. Notice that the leading forward slash (/) is part of the URI specification.

The Commit Transaction URI and Rollback Transaction URI fields should be entered similarly to the Begin Transaction URI field. The Transaction Timeout is the number of seconds that can elapse between calls to member transaction functions before the transaction is automatically rolled back by the WRB. The Transactional Boundaries field defines the set of URIs that are members of the transaction—that is,

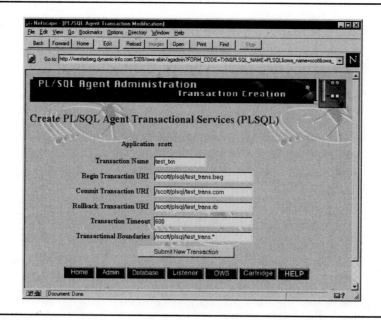

FIGURE 10-3. *PL/SQL agent transaction setup*

those URLs whose database changes will be associated as part of an atomic transaction.

NOTE

To have the WRB manage these transactions, the transaction service must be specified for the PL/SQL cartridge. This can be set either from the Cartridge Configuration Update form (Figure 10-3) or from the WRB Administration form, in the Applications and Services section.

Now that everything is configured, when a browser requests the begin transaction URI, a transaction will be initiated. This will cause several cookies to be sent along with the response, which will allow the transaction management services to associate future browser requests with the transaction in progress. Specifically, the cookies set are OWS_VERSION, OWS_TXNAME, OWS_XID, OWS_KEY, and OWSRMID0. The browser then sends these cookies when it makes requests for the *test_trans.add_form*, *test_trans.rb*, or *test_trans.com* procedures, and the WRB transaction services correctly group these requests as part of a transaction. The user can repeatedly call the *add_form* procedure during the transaction. Following the link to the *rb* procedure will cause all changes to the database to be rolled back, while following the link to the com procedure will cause all changes to reapplied.

NOTE

If a user directly requests a procedure that is within the boundaries of a WRB transaction, but does not first access the Begin Transaction procedure, the database update will be applied immediately and cannot be rolled back. To prevent this, procedures that are members of a transaction may wish to test for the presence of one or more of the cookies that the transaction manager will set, and then simply redirect the browser to the Begin Transaction URL if they are not present.

TRANSACTION CONTROL FOR C CARTRIDGES Cartridges
written for use by the WRB API have direct access to the WRB's transaction
management services through the WRB's transaction API. To use the API,
the developer must write her code to do a couple of things. First, database
access is controlled using a DAD, the name of which is passed to the
transaction API through the *tx_reg* function. The database is then opened
using the *tx_open* call. Next, all database access code must be written,
either by using the OCI (Oracle Call Interface) directly, or by using Pro*C,
which translates embedded SQL commands into OCI calls. However, the
OCI calls are not to be used for transaction management; instead, only
the *tx_begin, tx_commit,* or *tx_rollback* functions of the WRB transaction
facilities can be used.

The Web Request Broker manages the transaction between HTTP
requests. The WRB recognizes an HTTP request as being a member, either
by use of a cookie or by a specially encoded URL. These special identifiers
are set using *tx_annotate_path* or *tx_annotate_url* functions. The function
tx_set_transaction_timeout allows the developer to specify a timeout
period, after which the transaction is automatically rolled back. If the
transaction is completed normally, the *tx_close* function can be used to
close the database resource manager opened with *tx_open*.

The Oracle Web Application Server installation includes a basic sample
that illustrates the use of the transaction management facilities as part of a
full cartridge implementation. Because it can be difficult to immediately see
the salient aspects of the code that have relevance transactions, we are not
providing such an extended example. Instead, the following code is an
extremely abridged version of a cartridge, showing only the init and exec
functions, and making only the calls relevant to the WRB transaction
management API.

```
WRBReturnCode txn_init( WRBCtx, ctx )
dvoid    *WRBCtx;
dvoid    **ctx;
{
  if (tx_reg("SCOTT") != TX_OK)
    return (WRB_ABORT);
  if (tx_open() != TX_OK)
    return (WRB_ABORT);
  return (WRB_DONE);
}
```

```
WRBReturnCode txn_exec( WRBCtx, ctx )
dvoid    *WRBCtx;
dvoid    *ctx;
{
  TXINFO    *info;
  info = ( TXINFO *) malloc( sizeof( TXINFO ) );
  uri = WRBGetURI (WRBCtx);
  if (strstr(uri, "begintxn"))
  {
    if ((!tx_info(info)) &&
             (info->transaction_state == TX_INACTIVE ))
    {
      if (tx_begin() == TX_OK)
        WRB_printf(WRBCtx,
               (text *)"Success: Started Transaction\n");
      else {
        WRB_printf(WRBCtx,
               (text *)"Error: failed to being transaction\n");
        free(info);
        return WRB_ABORT;
      }
    } else
      WRB_printf(WRBCtx,
               (text *)"Error: other transaction in progress\n");
  }
  else if (strstr(uri, "com"))
    {
    if ((!tx_info(info)) &&
             (info->transaction_state == TX_ACTIVE ))
    {
      if (tx_commit() != TX_OK)
      {
        WRB_printf(WRBCtx, (text *)"Error: commit failed\n");
        return WRB_ABORT;
      }
    } else
      WRB_printf(WRBCtx,(text *)"Error: no transaction active\n");
  }
  else if (strstr(uri, "rb"))
  {
    if ((!tx_info(info)) &&
             (info->transaction_state == TX_ACTIVE ))
    {
      if (tx_rollback() != TX_OK) {
        WRB_printf(WRBCtx, (text *)"Error: rollback failed\n");
```

```
        return WRB_ABORT;
    }
  } else
    WRB_printf(WRBCtx,(text *)"Error: no transaction active\n");
  }
  else if (strstr (uri, "quit"))  //optional call
  {
    WRB_printf(WRBCtx,
              (text *)"Success: Cartridge instance exiting.\n");
    tx_close();
    return WRB_ABORT;
  }
  else if (strstr (uri, "dosomething"))
  {
    if ((!tx_info(info)) &&
        (info->transaction_state == TX_INACTIVE ))
    {
      WRB_printf(WRBCtx,(text *)"Not in transactional context\n");
    }
    else
    {
      // In a real application, OCI or Pro*C calls would be
      // used to manipulate the database
    }
  }
  //Any other URLs to this cartridge get caught here
  else if ((!tx_info(info)) &&
          (info->transaction_state == TX_ACTIVE ))
      WRB_printf(WRBCtx, (text *)"Inside Transaction Now\n");
  else
      WRB_printf(WRBCtx, (text *)"Outside Transaction Now\n");
  tx_annotate_path((text *) "/txndemo/");
  free(info);
  return (WRB_DONE);
}
```

Because a DAD is used with the transaction management API, developers would typically want to use the WRB API's *WRB_getAppConfigSection* or *WRB_getAppConfigValue* to access the name of the DAD to use from a user-defined configuration setting. Another option would be to interpret information provided in the URL to indicate the DAD to use. This would allow different cartridge instances to make use of different DADs, in a manner similar to the use of the PL/SQL cartridge.

TRANSACTIONS FOR JAVA COMPONENTS   Currently, the WRB does not provide transaction services to components written for the Java cartridge. In addition, database access via PL/SQL wrappers created with pl2java are not able to have transaction control applied to them. However, by enabling the WRB session support for the Java cartridge and using a JDBC database access method, it is possible for a developer to implement similar functionality. Generally, this is achieved by doing the following:

- Enabling session management for the Java cartridge.

- Storing the JDBC session object in a static class property.

- Using the JDBC session during calls to the cartridge.

- Providing special URL codes to allow access to JDBC calls that either commit or roll back the in-progress transaction.

- Most importantly, incorporating a timestamp property, which is set each time the component is invoked. If the time between invocations of the component is greater than a constant value (which should be the same as the timeout property for the session manager), the component should automatically roll back the current transaction.

- In addition, if the component receives a request to begin a transaction while it still has an in-progress transaction, the in-progress transaction must be rolled back prior to beginning the new transaction.

Oracle may implement configuration-based transaction control for Java components at some time in the future, although it has not announced to do so. In the meantime, the above steps allow the developer to address the fundamental requirement of transaction control within Java applications. An alternative to these might be to write Java native methods for both making OCI calls as well as making transaction manager calls from within the Java component.

InterCartridge Exchange

Although we have mostly discussed using WRB cartridges to service requests from web browsers, we mentioned in Chapter 8 that the ODBC cartridge primarily services requests generated by other cartridges or cartridge components. The method used to invoke such components is the Inter-Cartridge Exchange (ICX). This capability is an extremely important feature of version 3.0 of the Oracle Web Application Server.

ICX is a procedure call method modeled on HTTP. It provides a straightforward interface through which cartridges and their components can invoke procedures or request services either from other cartridges or from an arbitrary HTTP URL. If ICX is used to invoke a URL that resides within the same ORB system as the cartridge making the request, then ICX can directly invoke the Dispatcher. Otherwise, ICX acts as an HTTP client and makes the request through the network, in a manner almost identical to that of a browser.

Invocation from PL/SQL

As mentioned in Chapter 4, PL/SQL routines can call other cartridge services using a special package. Any PL/SQL procedure can take advantage of this functionality, whether the calling PL/SQL procedure is invoked via the Web Request Broker, or from SQL*Plus, or as a trigger, and so on. This is accomplished via the use of the PL/SQL package UTL_HTTP, which should be installed automatically with version 7.3.3 or higher of the Oracle RDBMS.

NOTE
The UTL_HTTP package is only available in version 7.3.3 and higher of the Oracle RDBMS. Simply compiling the UTLSQURL.sql file against an earlier RDBMS version will not be successful. If you carry a current support agreement with Oracle for the RDBMS, an upgrade to 7.3.3 can be obtained by contacting Oracle WorldWide Support.

MAKING A REQUEST   There are only two calls that a developer may use to access ICX services from within her PL/SQL routines. These calls in turn call wrappers to the native functions described in the section on accessing ICX from C cartridges using the ICX API.

The first call that can be used is *utl_http.request*. This procedure takes a single parameter, the URL from which data is to be retrieved. It returns, as its result, a VARCHAR2 containing the first 2,000 characters of content from the URL. For ICX calls that are expected to return a relatively small bit of information, this procedure works very well.

```
PROCEDURE test_icx
IS
BEGIN
  htp.htmlOpen;
  htp.bodyOpen;
  -- generate some of the page here
  htp.bold('Our stock performance:');
  htp.br;
  -- access external service for stock quote
  resp := utl_http.request('http://owas1.dynamic-info.com/scott'||
          '/plsql/stock.get_quote_insert?symbol_in=ORCL');
  -- simply embed the response in the output stream
  htp.p(resp);
  -- generate the rest of the page here
  htp.bodyClose;
  htp.htmlClose;
END;
```

Of course, results of more than 2,000 characters will often need to be retrieved and processed. The package includes the routine *request_pieces*, which can retrieve an entire request of virtually any size into a PL/SQL table of 2,000-character chunks. This enables a PL/SQL application handle responses of an arbitrary size.

CAUTION
Be aware that PL/SQL ICX requests are serviced through the database, rather than through the WRB. Thus, if there are difficulties in accessing a particular URL via the ICX facilities, it is irrelevant to verify the accessibility of the site from the web server itself. Test access to the URL from a browser installed on the same machine as the database, and one running with the same user privileges and environment settings and variables as the instance. ICX should effectively handle any URL that can be accessed in this manner.

PROCESSING THE RESULTS As we have seen, getting the HTML response back from the UTL_HTTP package is quite straightforward. However, now a slightly trickier problem arises: what can be done with the results? Because many requests that may be made via the UTL_HTTP will return either plain text or HTML text, the content is often not immediately useful (at least, not easily useful) to a program. Often it will contain a great number of HTML tags or much extraneous material. This is not as easy to deal with as getting back results from a simple function or via OUT or IN OUT parameters. In a few pages, we shall discuss an easy way to pass data via ICX using a standard URL-encoded format, as is used when sending form data from a browser to a web server.

On the CD, we include a PL/SQL package, owsh_param_util, which accepts a string of text in the format "name1=value1&name2=value2&..." and in return passes back a parameter block structure containing two PL/SQL tables, one of names, the other of values. The main routine is *xurl_to_pblock*, which is shown here. The package contains the supporting routines used by this function.

```
FUNCTION xurl_to_pblock (v_xurl_string_in IN VARCHAR2)
        RETURN pblock
IS
  v_xurl        VARCHAR2(2000);
  v_value_pairs_tab  parsed_strings_tabtype;
  v_value_pairs_tab_count  NUMBER;
  v_params_tab       parsed_strings_tabtype;
  v_params_tab_count  NUMBER;
  v_pairs_hold_tab  parsed_strings_tabtype;
  v_names_arr       name_arr;
  v_values_arr      value_arr;
  v_pblock_out      pblock;
BEGIN
  /* replace '+'s with spaces */
  v_xurl := TRANSLATE(v_xurl_string_in, '+', ' ');
  /* parse input string on '&' into value pairs */
  v_value_pairs_tab := param_util.STRING_TOKENIZER(v_xurl, '&');
  v_value_pairs_tab_count := v_value_pairs_tab.COUNT;
  /* put value pairs into one long array */
  FOR counter1 IN 0..(v_value_pairs_tab_count -1) LOOP
    v_pairs_hold_tab := param_util.STRING_TOKENIZER(
                            v_value_pairs_tab(counter1), '=');
    v_params_tab(counter1*2) := v_pairs_hold_tab(0);
    v_params_tab(counter1*2 + 1) := v_pairs_hold_tab(1);
```

```
      END LOOP;
      v_params_tab_count := v_params_tab.COUNT;
      /* take value pairs array and put each
          element into its respective category array */
      FOR counter2 IN 0..(v_value_pairs_tab_count -1) LOOP
        v_names_arr(counter2) := v_params_tab(2*counter2);
        v_values_arr(counter2) := v_params_tab(2*counter2 + 1);
      END LOOP;
      --replace '%xx' hex areas with proper ascii characters
      FOR counter3 IN 0..(v_value_pairs_tab_count -1) LOOP
        v_names_arr(counter3) := HEXSTRINGTOASCII(
                                         v_names_arr(counter3));
        v_values_arr(counter3) := HEXSTRINGTOASCII(
                                         v_values_arr(counter3));
      END LOOP;
      /* assign values to pblock */
      v_pblock_out.num_pairs := v_value_pairs_tab_count;
      v_pblock_out.v_names := v_names_arr;
      v_pblock_out.v_values := v_values_arr;
      RETURN v_pblock_out;
    EXCEPTION
      WHEN OTHERS THEN
        htp.p(SQLCODE || '     ' || SQLERRM);
      END;
```

Using ICX with C Cartridges

To invoke another cartridge from within a C cartridge, the WRB's Intercartridge Exchange API is used. This API is made up of routines named WRB_ICX*x*, where *x* stands for the routine suffix. To use the ICX services from C, the developer first calls *WRB_ICXcreateRequest*, passing in a URL; this returns a handle to the ICX structure, which is then passed to the other routines. Next, the developer may set certain attributes of the request, assuming it is not a simple GET-type request. To set the username and password for the request, *WRB_ICXsetAuthInfo* is used. To set header information, a WRB parameter block is created and passed to *WRB_ICXsetHeader*, which can also incorporate the data from the original request to the cartridge (that is, headers from the browser that invoked the developer's cartridge). *WRB_ICXsetMethod* is used to specify whether the request is of a type other than GET, such as POST or DELETE. Finally, *WRB_ICXsetContent* is used to set the actual content of the request by passing in a WRB parameter block.

After configuring the request as necessary, the request can then be submitted to the ICX services for retrieval and processing. This is done by invoking the *WRB_ICXmakeRequest* function. This function actually makes the request through either HTTP or the WRB dispatcher, depending on the location of the request. It may return the entire request content, or a limited amount, depending on the passed chunkSize value. If the function returns with WRB_MOREDATA, then the *WRB_ICXfetchMoreData* function can be used to retrieve the entire request. Also, after the request has been made, the API functions *WRB_ICXgetParsedHeader*, *WRB_ICXgetHeaderVal*, and *WRB_ICXgetInfo* can be invoked to access all headers; a single header by name; or the response code, HTTP version, response reason, or realm of the request—all respectively.

To control the use of proxies while using ICX, the *WRB_ICXsetProxy* and *WRB_ICXsetNoProxy* methods can be used. The *WRB_ICXsetProxy* function is used to specify the address of the proxy to use for HTTP requests, while the *WRB_ICXsetNoProxy* function is used to enumerate the hosts for which the proxy services should not be used (typically those hosts that are locally accessible). The same can be accomplished by setting the *http_proxy* and *no_proxy* environment variables. This is both easier for the developer to implement, and typically easier for the end user to configure.

The following listing shows the most rudimentary example of making an ICX call from a C cartridge. It simply makes a request and passes the information returned straight back to the browser, without any processing.

```
void embed_quote (void) {
    HANDLE    retval;
    ub4       rval;
    ub4       ckSz = 0;
    ub4       len;
    char      *response;

       /* Create the request.
        Note that the GET method is used by default, unless
        a call to WRB_ICXSetMethod is made. Thus, we embed
        the parameters in the URL itself.
       */

       /* N.B. URL wrapped for publication*/
       if (!(request = WRB_ICXcreateRequest(WRBCtx,
         (text *) "http://owas1.dynamic-info.com/scott
```

```
    /plsql/stock.get_quote_insert?symbol_in=ORCL")))
  {
    return WRB_ERROR;
  }
  /* execute the request and send the result directly to the
     browser. This is reasonable because the response is
     especially formatted for embedding in an HTML page.
  */
  retval = WRB_ICXmakeRequest(WRBCtx, request, (void **)&response,
                              &len, ckSz ,TRUE);
  /* There's really not much to do with the error, since we
     are only passing the information directly to the browser.
  */
  if (rval == WRB_FAIL) { return WRB_ERROR; }
  else                  { return WRB_DONE;  }
}
```

Obviously, this routine is doing very little, given that *WRB_ICXmakeRequest* is being directed simply to stream the results back to the browser. A more significant use of the ICX facility would be to capture the data and process it in some way. This is typically done by using some routines to break the results into easily manageable chunks of data, so that the data of interest can be more easily accessed.

Using ICX with Java

Oracle Web Application Server does not support ICX calls from components written for the Java cartridge. However, because of Java's network-aware capabilities, it is possible to obtain the same services from the java.net.URL class included with the Java Developer's Kit (JDK). The class implements a method, getContent(), which can be used for easily fetching some types of content from a URL. Fetching a plain-text document from the web in Java takes only three lines of code. In the following class, however, we implement a specialized ICX class that is able to request a plain-text document from any URL, fetch that document, and then split it into a collection of name-value pairs. This follows the behavior implemented in the PL/SQL package above, and makes it extremely easy to access cartridges that conform to these ICX conventions.

```
import java.io.*
import java.net.*
import java.util.*
```

```java
public class FakeICX {

  Hashtable values = null;

  public String FakeICX (String theURL)
     throws MalformedURLException, IOException
  {
    URL url = new URL (theURL);
    String theStr = url.getContent();
    populateHashtable(theStr);
  }

  private final void populateHashtable(String expr)
  {
    if (expr == null) return null;

    int idx = -1,
      cnt = 1;
    //count the number of name/value paris in the string
    while ((idx = expr.indexOf('&', idx+1)) != -1)   cnt ++;
    values = new Hashtable(cnt);
    for (idx=0, cnt=0; cnt<pairs.length; cnt++) {
      int eq  = expr.indexOf('=', idx);
      int end = expr.indexOf('&', idx);

      if (end == -1)  end = query.length();
      //-- test if no equality sign present
      if (eq == -1  ||  eq >= end) {
        value1 = FakeICX.URLDecode(expr.substring(idx,end));
        value2 = "";
      } else {
        value1 = FakeICX.URLDecode(expr.substring(idx,eq));
        value2 = FakeICX.URLDecode(expr.substring(eq+1,end));
      }
      if(values.get(value1) == null) {
        v_temp.addElement(value2);
        values.put(value1, v_temp);
      } else {
        v_temp = (Vector) values.get(value1);
        v_temp.addElement(value2);
      }
      idx = end + 1;
    }
  }
```

```
public final static String URLDecode(String str)
{
  if (str == null)  return  null;
  char[] res  = new char[str.length()];
  int    didx = 0;
  //sidx index for in string; didx index for out string
  for (int sidx=0; sidx<str.length(); sidx++)  {
    char ch = str.charAt(sidx);
    if (ch == '+')
      res[didx++] = ' ';
    else if (ch == '%') {
      try {
        res[didx++] =
          (char) Integer.parseInt(str.substring(
                                    sidx+1,sidx+3), 16);
        sidx += 2;
      } catch (NumberFormatException e) {
        //skip the errant code
        sidx += 2;
      }
    } else {
      res[didx++] = ch;
    }
  return String.valueOf(res, 0, didx);;
}

public String getAsString(String key) {
  Vector v_temp = null;
  String s_return;
  try {
    v_temp = (Vector) values.get(key);
    s_return = (String) v_temp.elementAt(0);
  } catch (Exception e) {
    s_return = "##";
  }
  return s_return;
}

public Vector getAsVector(String key) {
  Vector v_return = null;
  String s_return;
  try {
    v_return = (Vector) values.get(key);
  } catch (Exception e) {
```

```
      v_return = null;
      v_return = new Vector();
      v_return.addElement( "##" );
    }
    return v_return;
  }
}
```

Version 1.0.2 of the JDK, which is the version used by the Oracle Web Application Server, only supports automatic translation of certain MIME types, and the sole text type it supports is text/plain. If access to other types of text (or other) data is necessary, the URL can be used to open a URLConnection, from which the input and output streams can be obtained and manipulated. If only the input stream is needed, the URL class' openStream() method is sufficient. The above class could be significantly enhanced by implementing multiple methods that would better mirror the WRB's native ICX API. Doing so would enhance its flexibility at accommodating other data types, as well as creating more consistency between the C and Java access methods. This could be accomplished in a fairly straightforward manner by simply wrapping many of the URLConnection methods. For example, use setRequestProperty() to emulate *WRB_ICXsetHeader* and use the getOutputStream() method to send the content that would be specified in *WRB_ICXsetContent*.

Using ICX from LiveHTML

The LiveHTML cartridge is able to use ICX to embed content from other services into the page being processed. To accomplish this, the REQUEST tag is used, specifying the URL to which the request is directed. Parameters passed to the LiveHTML page can, in turn, be passed onto the called procedure. This process is fully described in Chapter 7.

Writing Cartridges and Components for Ease of Access by ICX

If a cartridge or component is being designed for use as a utility to be called by other cartridges or components, there are some design issues to consider when creating the utility. As mentioned earlier, the most difficult part of making an ICX call is accessing the desired information from the returned result data. To address this inconvenience, it is wise to provide entry points to the cartridge that return the raw responses with as little formatting as possible.

   This is actually quite straightforward and requires very little extra effort. The key is to factor out a cartridge's or component's functionality such that there is one routine responsible for the logical purpose, plus one or more that formats the results. For instance, consider a PL/SQL component that implements a stock-quoting functionality, by querying a table populated by a daemon that accessed a live stock-feed from a stock exchange. This component would definitely implement a procedure that would output an HTML page of various stock information, formatted in a table, possibly with a link to a graph, and so on. However, such a component would be very inconvenient to call via ICX, because there would be all manner of extraneous formatting information to strip away to get at the desired information: the stock's data.

   To allow the component to better support invocation via ICX, we should break into two parts the functionality of the procedure described above. If the single procedure above were named *get_quote*, and if it accepted a ticker symbol and an optional date (to get historical information), we would create two procedures: *get_quote* and *get_quote_logic*. Both would accept the same sets of parameters, but *get_quote_logic* would populate a collection of OUT parameters, which would contain the key data, such as the high and low price and trading volume for the day. The *get_quote* procedure would call the *get_quote_logic* procedure to gather the results, and would then format them into an HTML page.

   Now, if we want to make the component's services, easily callable by ICX, we can easily create a new PL/SQL procedure, say *get_quote_icx*, which invokes *get_quote_logic*, but instead of placing the results into some complex HTML format, simply returns them in a format that is easily machine decodable. The exact format to be used is open to debate; still, given that the response must be in a character stream, we feel that the URL encoding that is standard in HTTP provides a good format—one that is well-known, easily parsed, and capable of representing any text. As a convention, we encourage developers to use this method of returning ICX. The following (abridged) package demonstrates this sort of factoring of functionality. The procedure *param_util.url_encode* is included in the PARAM_UTIL package found on the CD packaged with this book. Its purpose is to encode escaped characters correctly for use by the extraction routines shown earlier in Java and PL/SQL. Java actually includes the necessary encoding functionality in the URLEncoder.encode static method, available in the java.net package.

```
CREATE OR REPLACE PACKAGE stock IS
   PROCEDURE get_quote (symbol_in IN VARCHAR2,
                        date_in IN DATE:=NULL);
   PROCEDURE get_quote_logic (symbol_in IN VARCHAR2,
                   date_in IN DATE:=NULL, status_out OUT VARCHAR2,
                   high_out OUT NUMBER, low_out OUT NUMBER,
                   close_out OUT NUMBER, volume_out OUT NUMBER);
   PROCEDURE get_quote_icx (symbol_in IN VARCHAR2,
                        date_in IN DATE:=NULL);
END;

CREATE OR REPLACE PACKAGE BODY stock IS

   PROCEDURE get_quote (symbol_in IN VARCHAR2,
                        date_in IN DATE:=NULL)
   IS
   --initialize variables
   BEGIN
     get_quote_logic (symbol_in, date_in, status, high,
                      low, close, volume);
     IF (status == 'OK')
     THEN
     --format results into attractive HTML format;
     ELSE
       htp.header(1,status);
     END IF;
   END;

   PROCEDURE get_quote_logic (symbol_in IN VARCHAR2,
                   date_in IN DATE:=NULL, status_out OUT VARCHAR2,
                   high_out OUT NUMBER, low_out OUT NUMBER,
                   close_out OUT NUMBER, volume_out OUT NUMBER)
   IS
   BEGIN
     status_out:='OK';
     SELECT high, low, close, volume
       INTO high_out, low_out, close_out, volume_out
       FROM stock_tab
      WHERE symbol = symbol_in
        AND date_stamp = date_in;
   EXCEPTION
     WHEN OTHERS THEN
```

```
            status_out := 'ERROR: Unknown error.';
    END;

    PROCEDURE get_quote_icx (symbol_in IN VARCHAR2,
                             date_in IN DATE:=NULL)
    IS
    --initialize variables
    BEGIN
      --set text type to plain for easier access
      --from java components.
      owa_util.mime_header ('text/plain',TRUE);
      get_quote_logic (symbol_in, date_in, status, high,
                       low, close, volume);
      IF (status == 'OK')
      THEN
        -- Send back results in encoded plain text
        htp.p( 'status=' || owsh_util.url_encode(status) ||
            '&high=' || owsh_util.url_encode(high) ||
            '&low=' || owsh_util.url_encode(low) ||
            '&close=' || owsh_util.url_encode(close) ||
            '&volume=' || owsh_util.url_encode(volume) );
      ELSE
        htp.p( 'status=' || owsh_util.url_encode(status) );
      END IF;
    END;

END;
```

Another option that developers may choose is simply to return the information in a special format, suitable for embedding within an HTML page. This would mean not including opening or closing <HTML>, <HEAD>, or <BODY> tags, as well as formatting it in (ideally) a compact and generally attractive format. The C example earlier makes use of such a procedure, named *get_quote_insert*. This procedure might likely format the information into a compact table format, possibly including a source attribution and a link to the home page of the site providing the stock quoting service. This sort of ICX-friendly formatting function would make it very easy for a service to generate pages that collect information from a variety of different organizations. As an example, a LiveHTML-based home page of a company could embed a request of this sort in the page to access a stock quote service and then embed the current price quotation of its stock. The company embedding the quote adds useful information to its home page with very little effort, while the company providing the

embedded quote may embed some small amount of free advertising, or
generate click-through traffic to its own site.

Logging

All web servers generate log files that record requests made to the web
server. These logs minimally contain the time of the request, the source IP
address of the request, the URI requested, the response code, and the size
of the response block. This information is valuable for both public and
intranet servers for monitoring usage levels as well as gauging interest in
certain resources. This information may then be used to properly tune the
server, to identify a time when adding machines may be necessary, and
even to justify the expansion of web-based services.

Oracle Web Application Server 3.0 provides some very sophisticated
logging services that are of use both to application developers and to
webmasters. The real power of the logging services is that it provides a
centralized location for collecting and examining alert, warning, and error
messages from all components of a Web Application Server system. The
web listener itself logs all activity through the logging subsystem. The
logging services are quite interesting because they allow web listener
activity to be logged in one of two places. First, logs can be written to
operating system files, in which case the logging services manage archiving
these logs at definable intervals.

Alternately, the logging service provides the ability to log this activity to
a database. This allows some quite sophisticated log management and
analysis functionality to be available directly from the Web Application
Server administration pages. Figure 10-4 shows an example of defining a
customizable report that can be run against the logs in the database.

NOTE
Logging all activity to the database, especially if logging items of any severity level, can have a significant impact on the database and can even effect the performance of the web site. If this functionality is to be used, especially on a more active site, we suggest that the logging be done to an Oracle instance running local to the WRB. Further, this instance should be tuned for a large number of updates, especially setting high values for sequence_cache_hash_buckets *and* sequence_cache_entries, *at least 89 and 100, respectively. Additionally, unless the logging data is absolutely critical, do not run the instance in ARCHIVELOG mode. It is unlikely that it will be worthwhile to perform a full recovery of the database if it only contains logging information. For analysis purposes, it likely is worthwhile to simply replicate all data from the log tables to a separate database periodically and then to truncate the live log table. (Be sure to truncate, not delete, to avoid writing rollback information for transaction.)*

The Logger service actually support three types of logs. The first is the Common or Extended Log Format (CLF/XLF) log, which contains

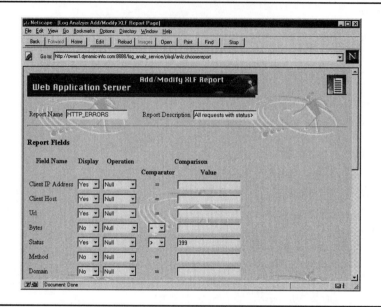

FIGURE 10-4. *Configuring a custom report of the log files*

information logged by the web listener. The second is the system messages log, which contains information logged by the WRB and its cartridges and components, as well as cartridges or components written by third-party developers. The third log contains client-defined name/value pairs for use with logging performance statistics, debugging information, or other data. As shown in Figure 10-5, the Logger service configuration page allows the location of the different log types to be specified (whether database or files) and also allows filtering of the information logged, based on severity or a component mask.

Developers write log data from their cartridges by using the Logger's API. These messages can be written either to the database or to special log files whose names and locations are defined programmatically by the cartridge; they can also be written to a location defined by the user. The user can specify the log location as Logger defaults and can define cartridge-specific locations. Typically, it is the preferred behavior simply to use the user-defined locations, which require no special effort by the developer (he or she simply indicates that the default location is to be used when opening the log).

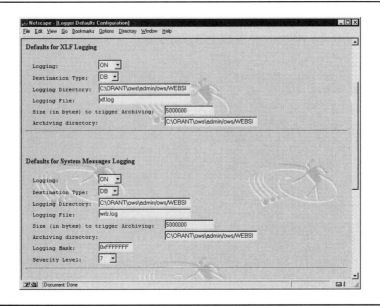

FIGURE 10-5. *Configuring the Logger service defaults*

The Oracle Web Application Server documentation provides some conventions that we recommend following with respect to which severity levels to use for what kind of logging messages. These are shown in Table 10-1. In addition, it suggests formatting error messages in a style consistent with that which the core OWAS components use. This is the standard Oracle error format of "APP-00000: Description," with the APP section being a unique three-character application code, and the 00000 indicating a specific error number. If writing information that is not an error but consists simply of debugging data, it is recommended to prefix the message with 11 spaces, so that all the messages will align (whether they are errors or simple messages).

Accessing from C Cartridges
Accessing the Logger service from C is extremely simple. The API has only four calls: *WRB_LOGopen*, *WRB_LOGwriteMessage*, *WRB_LOGwriteAttribute*, and *WRB_LOGclose*. You can probably guess as to each one's purpose. When calling *WRB_LOGopen*, the developer specifies whether he or she will be writing attribute or message information and the source to which it should be written, either explicitly specifying database or file system storage, or simply using the defaults.

Error Type	Severity Level	Recommended Usage
Fatal errors	0	Indicates a core failure occurred.
Soft errors	1–3	Use 1 for a file or resource access failure.
Warning	4–6	Use 4 for a configuration error.
Tracings	7–10	Use 7 to indicate entry into the initialization, termination, or reloading states. Use 8 to indicate entry into the authentication or execution states.
Debugging	11–15	Use 11 for printing debugging variables.

TABLE 10-1. *Conventional Use of Logging Severity*

WRB_LOGopen then returns a handle to the log that was opened. This handle is then passed first to the *WRB_LOGwrite* routines to write data to the log, and then to *WRB_LOGclose* to close it when finished. The developer could have multiple log handles and could write general information to one log and highly detailed information to another. In this case, the general information would typically be written to the default location, while detailed information might be written to a special location. The following sample writes to two logs, the messages log and the client-defined attributes log.

```
WRBReturnCode
Log_Exec(dvoid *WRBCtx, dvoid *appCtx)
{
    WAPIReturnCode   retval;
    ub4     msgLog,attrLog;

    retval = WRB_LOGopen(WRBCtx,&msgLog,WRBLogSysMsg,
                    WRBLogDestDefault,null);
    retval = WRB_LOGopen(WRBCtx,&attrLog,WRBLogClientDefAttrib,
                                WRBLogDestDefault,null);

    retval = WRB_LOGwriteMessage(WRBCtx,msgLog,(text *)"LOGD",
                    (text *) "LOG-00000: Nothing to report");
    retval = WRB_LOGwriteMessage(WRBCtx,attrLog,(text *)"LOGD",
                    (text *) "pi", (text *) "3.14159" );
```

```
    retval = WRB_LOGclose(WRBCtx,msgLog);
    retval = WRB_LOGclose(WRBCtx,attrLog);
    return (WRB_DONE);
}
```

Accessing from Java

Logging is the only WRB service for which a direct interface from Java is
provided by Oracle. The is accomplished with the OutputLogStream class.
By instantiating this class and using its print or println methods, Java
components can write anything necessary to the Logger service. The
following listing shows the basic use of this class in a Java component.

```
class LogDemo{
  public static void main(String args[]) {
  // log to the default location, with the component name "LogDemo"
  OutputLogStream log = new OutputLogStream("LogDemo");
  try {
    // write out useful debugging information
    // notice the 11 spaces before the message
    for(int i=0; i<=10; i++) {
      log.println(15, "            Loop iteration");
    }
  } catch (Exception e) {
    log.println(1,"LOG-00001: Unexpected error occurred. "+e.getMessage());
  }
}
```

Session Management Services

We touched briefly on the issue of session management early in this
chapter when discussing the transaction management services the WRB
provides. We also referred, in this and other chapters, to the practice of
using HTTP cookies to manage state information for a single user as he
travels through a web site or application. One drawback of using cookies
for state management is that this places an additional burden on the
developer that would not be present in an application not based on HTTP.

The WRB's session management services make use of cookies, but they
mask from the developer the details of implementing cookie management.
Rather, the developer is allowed to work with data structure native to the
language being used, with the WRB working to synchronize the various

components. Figure 10-6 shows the only step necessary to session-enable a cartridge, namely selecting the Enabled option for the Client Sessions option in the cartridge configuration page.

Session Management for C Cartridges

Managing session information for a C cartridge is reasonably straightforward. Each of the public WRB-callable functions that are to be implemented by a cartridge are passed to an application context. This context can be a pointer to any data structure that the developer may wish to maintain. The application developer allocates resources for the application context in its initialization code, and then can access or modify the contents during the main invocation routines.

```
WRBReturnCode
Session_Init(dvoid *WRBCtx, dvoid **appCtx)
{
  mySessionData *ctx;
  ctx = (mySessionData *)malloc(sizeof(mySessionData));
  *appCtx = ctx;
  return (WRB_DONE);
}


WRBReturnCode
Session_Exec(dvoid *WRBCtx, dvoid *appCtx)
{
  mySessionData *ctx = (mySessionData *)appCtx;
  // do something with the context data, either
  // reading or writing to it.
  return (WRB_DONE);
}


WRBReturnCode
Session_Shutdown(dvoid *WRBCtx, dvoid *appCtx)
{
  mySessionData *ctx = (mySessionData *)appCtx;
  // the cartridge must free its own context structure
  // note that if the context structure contains pointers to
  // additional memory structures, these must be freed explicitly.
  free(ctx);
  return (WRB_DONE);
}
```

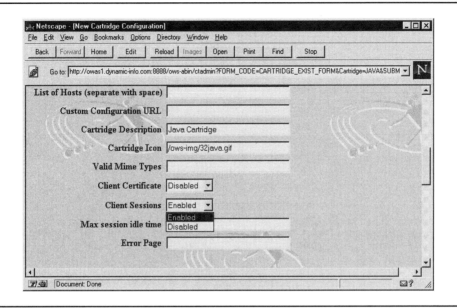

FIGURE 10-6.   *Adding statefulness in one click*

Session Management for Java Components

Maintaining persistent data across multiple invocations of a Java component is quite simple. The best way to do so is to simply declare as static class properties any information that is to be maintained across the session. If session management is enabled for the cartridge, the WRB will use the same instance of the Java virtual machine each time the same browser makes a request of the component within its timeout period. Because the same Virtual Machine (VM) instance is used for each invocation, the static properties of the entry-point class are guaranteed to be preserved across invocations for a given session.

The following example class is more fleshed out than the C cartridge discussed above, as it actually makes some use of its stored data. Unlike the C cartridge, however, the Java component does not have the responsibility of managing an application context specifically. Rather, the static properties are simply preserved across invocations of the Java cartridge instance.

```
public class StateDemo
{
  // The value stored in any static property
  // persist across invocations.

  private static String last_words = "Brand New Instance";

  public static void main (String args[])
  {
    HTTP request = HTTP.getRequest();
    HtmlStream out = HtmlStream.theStream();
    out.println("Content-type: text/html\n");
    out.println("<html><head><title>State</title></head><body>");
    out.println("<H1>Previous comment: " + last_words + "</H1>");
    out.println("<form action=\"StateDemo\" method=GET>");
    out.println("<B>Enter some text</B>");
    out.println("<input type=text name=comment>");
    out.println("<input type=submit></form></body></html>");
    last_words = request.getURLParameter("comment");
    if (last_words == null) {
      last_words = "<<null>>";
    }
  }
}
```

A comment about Java session management is in order. Because session management is an attribute applied to the entire cartridge, the features will be used when invoking both Java components that do not require the session management services *and* those that do. The solution to this problem is to create multiple instances of the Java cartridge, with respect to securing certain classes, as discussed in the Java cartridge chapter. By doing this, one cartridge instance can make use of session management for components that require it, while other cartridges not requiring state information do not incur the session management overhead.

Session Management for PL/SQL

PL/SQL does not make direct use of the WRB's session management facilities. There are, however, a couple of workarounds. The recommended approach is to make use of cookies, using the OWA_COOKIE package. We illustrated this approach in detail in Chapter 4. Another option is to make use of the transaction services and to write data into temporary tables that could be queried but that would be visible only to the user of the current transaction.

Content Services

An additional service the Oracle Web Application Server provides is an API for storing in content repositories a variety of binary objects, such as images, spreadsheets, word processor files, or other arbitrary objects. This allows developers to implement applications that require sophisticated document management capabilities using the Oracle Web Application Server. Such applications include litigation support, workflow, or pure document repositories.

The Content service stores and retrieves documents from either an Oracle database or the file system. In both cases, it maintains a variety of data about the document in the Content services repository. This repository is fairly simple, being composed of four tables. Such data includes fields for authorship, for creation and modification dates, and for content types, as well as support for user-defined attributes to be included as name-value pairs. Storing these attributes enhances the ability of the developer to quickly access documents based on virtually any criteria.

Content services are presently only available to C cartridges, although any cartridge that can access the database could query the content repository. Oracle provides two cartridges in the standard release that make use of the Content services. The first is an application that allows the storage of binary objects, either sent via HTML form upload capabilities or accessed from another URL using ICX. In addition, it demonstrates the use of user-defined attributes and the general mechanics of a functional document management application. It is one of the more complex example applications provided with the OWAS, but for those attempting to develop systems using Content services, a thorough understanding of it will prove invaluable.

The second cartridge application is the MyWRBApp example, which uses the Content services repository as a simple database for storing records of information about the user. Given the preferred choice of a robust SQL database, we would not recommend this technique in a production application. However, it quickly illustrates the basics of storing and retrieving data from the Content repository.

NOTE
This service is available only with the Advanced Edition of Oracle Web Application Server version 3.0.

The actual API itself is not large. To begin accessing the Content services, a call to *WRB_CNTopenRepository* must be made, passing in the username, the password, and the connect string for the schema owning the repository. This returns a handle to the repository that was opened. Note that multiple repositories, owned by multiple schemas, can be manipulated by a single cartridge just by calling *WRB_CNTopenRepository* multiple times and maintaining the separate handles. To create, read, or write a document to or from the repository, the *WRB_CNTopenDocument* function is called with the name and with the correct create, read, or write flags. It then returns a document handle that can be used with other document manipulation routines.

The document's attributes can then be set or read with the *WRB_CNTsetAttributes* or *WRB_CNTgetAttributes* functions, respectively. Both of these routines use a WRB parameter block to pass the attribute names and values. Not surprisingly, *WRB_CNTreadDocument* and *WRB_CNTwriteDocument* are used to read or write the open document. If writing to a document, the *WRB_CNTflushDocument* function saves changes to an open document. When finished manipulating the document, call *WRB_CNTcloseDocument* to close the document. Any changes made will be automatically applied, so it is not necessary to first call *WRB_CNTflushDocument*. To delete a document, call *WRB_CNTdestroyDocument*, passing in only the name of the document to be deleted.

Although the API does provide a routine, called *WRB_CNTlistDocuments*, to retrieve a list of all documents in the repository, there are no routines provided by the API to search the repository. Thus, if the cartridge must support searching the repository, the method that must be employed is to use direct queries against the repository tables. As we mentioned earlier, the schema is only four tables, and so can be queried quite simply. Figure 10-7 illustrates the repository schema. Columns in bold indicate the primary keys of the tables. In addition, a PL/SQL package, OWS_CS, provides a number of calls for accessing basic information and illustrates the sorts of data stored in the repository.

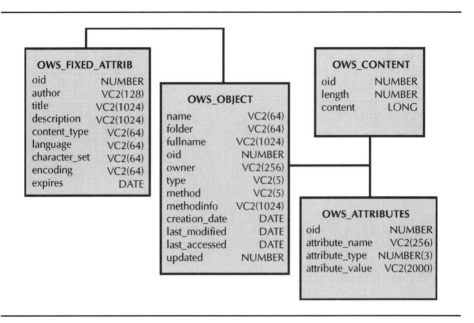

FIGURE 10-7. *Content repository schema*

NOTE
Although it is possible to insert data and update it in the repository table directly, we don't recommend doing this—except possibly for attributes data. Because the internal workings of the Content services API are not publicly documented, they may change, and thus user-written code for directly manipulating the repository will likely fail.

Conclusion

In this chapter, the reader has been exposed to the sophisticated set of services provided by the Web Request Broker. Beyond the benefits the WRB architecture and related services provide in terms of scalability and operational stability, it is these services that make the Oracle Web Application Server such an attractive platform for developing sophisticated web applications. In the next chapter, we show how to harness these services and the WRB API to create a WRB cartridge in the C language.

CHAPTER
11

Developing WRB
Cartridges in C

n the previous chapter, we examined the architecture of the Web Request Broker and the services it can provide to WRB cartridges and components executed by those cartridges. In this chapter we describe the actual mechanics of implementing a WRB cartridge in C. Choosing to develop cartridges using C, rather than writing components using languages such as Java or PL/SQL, presents the developer with several trade-offs.

On the downside, C is not as forgiving a language as PL/SQL or Java. Also, writing a cartridge is somewhat more complex than is simply writing a PL/SQL procedure or Java component—both because of the additional effort involved in using a 3GL versus a 4GL, and because additional functions must be implemented for a cartridge (as opposed to a component). Components do not have the responsibility of managing all their interactions with the WRB, while a cartridge must explicitly manage these interactions. Perhaps the most significant issue, however, is the loss of portability of components across operating systems, as compared to a cartridge's requiring unique binary executables for each platform. Because PL/SQL, Java, and Perl are all supported nearly transparently across platforms, no additional effort is needed to move an application from Windows NT to a more robust Unix operating system running on more powerful hardware.

In exchange for this effort, though, developers *do* gain some benefits. First among these is performance. Because cartridges written in C are compiled into machine code, rather than being interpreted or compiled into a p-code, they offer significant performance advantages over components written in Java, PL/SQL, and Perl.

A second benefit the developer gains is access and flexibility. Cartridges written in C have access to the complete WRB API, something not always available to components. Because components themselves are executed via cartridges, the calling cartridge may provide callback mechanisms to access WRB services, although strictly speaking they need not. For example, no components written in Java, PL/SQL, or Perl can access the Content Services API, while WRB Transaction Services are available only to PL/SQL components. In addition to the WRB API, C cartridges can access any operating system or shared library functionality that is desired. Because of portability concerns, such access is not typically available to components.

A final benefit involves code migration. Cartridges written in C can call functions written in virtually any language, so long as the language can be compiled to a shared library, or to a DLL under Windows NT. Because of this, C cartridges are outstanding for creating wrappers to existing code written in C or many other languages. This may offer a much safer path to making the functionality of certain existing applications available via the Web. Because the cartridge developer can call routines that have already been written to implement the necessary transaction processing or business rules, the development effort is reduced substantially.

Basic Operation of a Cartridge

Before diving into the mechanics of implementing a cartridge, a brief architectural discussion is in order. In previous chapters we have discussed the architecture of the Web Request Broker, although this has been done primarily from either a high-level perspective or a WRB-centric perspective. The cartridge-centric view of the world is a little different.

As discussed before, a WRB cartridge instance is really two things: the WRB cartridge wrapper and the cartridge code. The cartridge wrapper implements the nuts and bolts of the interface between the WRB and the developer code. When a cartridge instance is to be spawned, a wrbc process is started, loads the shared library or dynamic link library (DLL) associated with a named cartridge type, and begins working.

The first thing the cartridge wrapper does is invoke the cartridge's primary entry point (specified in the cartridge's configuration settings) and request from the cartridge a list of function pointers. It accepts the same list of function pointers, regardless of the cartridge. The cartridge wrapper does not map specific URL requests to unique cartridge functions; that is the cartridge's responsibility. Rather, it needs pointers to at least one and at most six specific functions (seven functions, under version 2.0). It will then invoke the functions for which it gets pointers at various points during the cartridge instance's lifecycle.

The first function is the Init function, which is invoked exactly once in a cartridge's lifecycle. The Init function is responsible for allocating any persistent data structures and performing any setup necessary before a cartridge is to be invoked to service a client request. This function returns an *application context* to the cartridge wrapper, in the form of a pointer to a data structure. This context is untouched by the cartridge wrapper and the WRB, except to pass it as a parameter to most other callbacks.

The second function is the Authorize function, which allows the cartridge to perform customized authorization of a caller before processing a request. This is an optional function and, if it is not implemented, access control to the cartridge can still be provided via the standard WRB security management features. Even when it is implemented, if the cartridge's Init function uses the WRB API function *WRB_setAuthServer* to specify an access restriction, the Authorize function will not be called, and the WRB and web listener will manage all access control. Otherwise, the Authorize function will be invoked once per request made by a caller.

The third function is the Exec function, which is where the rubber meets the road. All the real functionality of the cartridge is accessed by the Exec function. This function will be called once per request that was successfully authorized, either by the Authorize function or by the WRB. This function typically calls other functions within the cartridge's shared library that do the real work associated with the request.

The fourth function, Shutdown, is used to implement code that cleans up any data structures or resource allocations that may have been made by the Init function or by various invocations of the Exec function. This is the last function called by the cartridge wrapper before the cartridge instance is terminated. Regardless of the result returned by the Shutdown function, the cartridge instance will be terminated. That is to say, there is no way for the cartridge instance to request to stay alive.

The previous four functions represent the core of the functionality of the cartridge. Two informational utility functions that cartridges should implement are Version and Version_Free. If Version is implemented in a cartridge, it must also implement Version_Free. Version may be called at any time during a cartridge's lifecycle by Web Application Server utilities. When Version is called, it should return a string containing version information. After Version is called, the utility will call Version_Free to allow the cartridge to release the memory allocated by the Version function.

A function that was optional for cartridges under WebServer 2.0 was the Reload function. In version 3.0 of Web Application Server, this function is no longer called. Its purpose was to support the reloading of configuration data while the cartridge instance was running. This would be triggered by a configuration data reload of the web listener or WRB. Armed with this general understanding of how a cartridge works, you can now begin to build cartridges in C. The next section will introduce the mechanics of implementing a cartridge.

Developing Cartridges in C Using the WRB API

Developing cartridges for the WRB using C is not a difficult process, and this section steps through the implementation of a very simple cartridge. The cartridge extends the functionality found in the HelloWorld cartridge that ships with Web Application Server. It can be found in the $ORAWEB_HOME/sample/wrbsdk/helloworld directory. It is a complete cartridge, with the exception of leaving the Version and Version_Free functions unimplemented. It does very little, however, so we will augment it to illustrate some common functions. The cartridge is suitable for showing several types of functionality: performing authorization, maintaining state information, reading parameters, invoking different behavior depending on the URL requested, and writing HTML to the client.

Coding the Cartridge

The first thing to do is copy the helloworld directory to a new directory, and possibly rename the helloworld.c file to say, getset.c. Depending on the platform and tools with which you are developing, you may need to create a project or alter the make file. On Unix or if using a traditional make tool, simply replace occurrences of "helloworld" in the make file with "getset". If using Visual C/C++ on Windows NT, the best approach is to create a new Dynamic-Link Library project *without* the MFC classes. When developing cartridges, the MFC or other GUI-oriented libraries will not typically be useful. Add the getset.c to the project, and ensure that the oratypes.h and wrb.h headers and the wrb.lib are in the project's INCLUDE and LIBPATH paths, respectively.

Defining the Cartridge's Public Access Methods

Now the cartridge writing can begin in earnest. The functionality to be added to the original HelloWorld cartridge is the ability to display a simple message when the cartridge's gettext method is invoked, and to support changing the displayed message from the settext method. Each of these methods, or *verbs*, will accept one parameter. The settext method will accept the text of the message to be displayed in subsequent gettext calls, and the gettext method will accept a formatting command. Assuming that we configure the cartridge to be invoked with the virtual path /getset, these

methods will be accessed by URLs of the form http://hostname/getset/
settext?message=value and http://hostname/getset/gettext?format=value.

It is handy to define constants to use for the named method a cartridge
supports, so that if the name needs to be changed later, it can be done
more easily. The first thing to do, then, is to define the following constants
in getset.c, which will be used elsewhere in the cartridge.

```
#define SETTEXT_VERB   "settext"
#define MESSAGE_PARAM "message"
#define GETTEXT_VERB   "gettext"
#define FORMAT_PARAM  "format"
```

Defining the Persistent Context Data Structure

As mentioned earlier, cartridges are able to create an application context
in their Init function that the WRB maintains for the cartridge between
invocations. The application context is a cartridge-specific block of data
that can maintain the current state of the component, as well as handles to
any files or resources that the cartridge may want to keep open between
invocations. You can think of this context as the "global variables" shared
between the various functions of your component, although it is a
somewhat imperfect analogy.

Because the cartridge we are developing has minimal information that
needs to be preserved between calls, the application context is very simple,
as seen in the myappctx data structure it uses. It simply contains an array of
characters to hold the current message.

```
#define MESSAGE_LEN    256
typedef struct myappctx {
    char currentMessage[MESSAGE_LEN];
} myappctx;
```

Writing the Main Entrypoint Function

As described earlier, the first thing the cartridge wrapper does is call the
method defined in the cartridge's configuration section as the entrypoint.
This function is responsible for returning a number of function pointers to
the cartridge wrapper that the wrapper will then call as the Init, Authorize,
Exec, Shutdown, Version, and Version_Free functions. Although these
functions have yet to be written, we can still implement the entrypoint
function, because we already know what the names and interfaces to the

functions are. The following code shows the implementation of the entrypoint.

```
WRBReturnCode getset_Entry(WRBCallbacks *WRBCalls)
{
    WRBCalls->init_WRBCallback = getset_Init;
    WRBCalls->authorize_WRBCallback = getset_Authorize;
    WRBCalls->exec_WRBCallback = getset_Exec;
    WRBCalls->shut_WRBCallback = getset_Shutdown;
    return (WRB_DONE);
}
```

Writing the Init Function

The next logical function to implement is the Init function, which will be the first function to be called after the cartridge entrypoint. The Init function is responsible for allocating the memory for the application context and populating it with any default values. Note that the application context itself is opaque to the WRB, just as the WRB context is opaque to the cartridge. In this case, the task is fairly straightforward, as seen in the implementation.

```
static WRBReturnCode getset_Init(void *WRBCtx, void **appCtx)
{
    myappctx *ctx = (myappctx *)malloc(sizeof(myappctx));
    strcpy(ctx->currentMessage, "Default Message.");
    *appCtx = ctx;
    return (WRB_DONE);
}
```

The Shutdown Function

Before jumping into the Authorize or Exec functions, which implement the unique functionality of the cartridge, we can implement the Shutdown function. This function will be called when the cartridge is about to be terminated. It provides the cartridge an opportunity to release any memory or resources held by it. In this case, the function is very simple.

```
static WRBReturnCode getset_Shutdown(void *WRBCtx, void *appCtx)
{
    myappctx *ctx = (myappctx *)appCtx;
    free(ctx);
    return (WRB_DONE);
}
```

The Authorize Function

We will leave the Authorize function as implemented in helloworld.c basically untouched, other than to alter the name. Notice that the routine makes use of the *WRBGetUserID* and *WRBGetPassword* functions, which are part of the WRB API implemented in version 2.0 of Oracle WebServer, although they are still supported in the version 3.0 API. If the username and password are either missing or not correct, it instructs the browser to provide Basic authentication information for the realm Hello World.

```
static WRBReturnCode
getset_Authorize(void *WRBCtx, void *appCtx, boolean *bAuthorized)
{
    myappctx *ctx = (myappctx *)appCtx;
    char *userID, *password;

    userID   = WRBGetUserID(WRBCtx);
    password = WRBGetPassword(WRBCtx);

    if ((((userID != (char*)NULL) && !strcmp(userID, "guest") &&
        (password != (char*)NULL) && !strcmp(password, "welcome"))))
     *bAuthorized = TRUE;
        return (WRB_DONE);
    else
    {
     *bAuthorized = FALSE;
        WRB_setAuthBasic(WRBCtx, (text *) "Hello World");
        return (WRB_DONE);
    }
}
```

The Exec Function

A cartridge's Exec function is invoked via the WRB with every request that the cartridge is to service. The Exec function will typically examine the request and invoke one or more functions, depending on the request made by the client. Effectively, the Exec function acts as a dispatcher within the cartridge. Because this cartridge implements two exposed functions, *settext* and *gettext*, the Exec function itself needs to provide dispatching for each. The following implementation illustrates the use of cascading if...else constructs to accomplish this. For a slightly different approach to the dispatch functions, examine the source of the WRB Content Services example cartridge, which ships with Web Application Server.

If no leaf was provided that matches one of the two exposed functions, a cartridge should do one of two things. One option would be to display a default page, consisting perhaps of the home page of the cartridge or possibly an information page on the cartridge developers, or even a page offering help on the correct use of the cartridge. Another option is to treat such a request as the starting point of the use of the cartridge. In a cartridge that provides catalog services, a request with no leaf could possibly return the first page of the product hierarchy or a search page. To keep this introduction brief, we do the somewhat user-unfriendly thing of returning an HTTP error message indicating that the user made a bad request.

```
static WRBReturnCode getset_Exec(void *WRBCtx, void *appCtx)
{
    myappctx *ctx = (myappctx *)appCtx;

  /* Get the leaf portion of the request */
    text    *uri = WRB_getRequestInfo(WRBCtx, WRBR_URI);

    if (!strncmp((char*)uri, SETTEXT_VERB,
                          strlen(SETTEXT_VERB)))
  {
        return (setText(ctx, WRBCtx));
    }
    else if (!strncmp((char*)uri, GETTEXT_VERB,
                             strlen(GETTEXT_VERB)))
  {
        return(getText(ctx, WRBCtx));
    }

    /* bad URL--send HTTP error using version 2.0 API function */
  /* HTTP Error 400 means "bad request"                      */
    WRBReturnHTTPError(WRBCtx, (WRBErrorCode)400, NULL, TRUE);
    return(WRB_DONE);
}
```

Of course, the Exec function is not actually doing much work; it simply invokes one of two functions to perform any real activities. Both of them must extract a parameter sent in the request, and then either set the value of the message to be displayed or display the previously set message. Extracting parameters is accomplished by using the *WRB_getParsedContent* API call, which populates a parameter block with all the submitted name/value pairs. The *WRB_findPBElemVal* function can then be used to access the value of a parameter given the name. Of course, the *WRB_destroyPBlock* function must be called to release the memory associated with the parameter block. The following two listings show the implementation of the C *setText* and *getText* functions.

```
static WRBReturnCode setText(myappctx *ctx, void *WRBCtx)
{
    WRBpBlock hPBlock;
    char wbuf[1024];
    char *msg;

    /* get form data */
    WRB_getParsedContent(WRBCtx, &hPBlock);

    msg = WRB_findPBElemVal(WRBCtx, hPBlock,
                                    (text *)MESSAGE_PARAM, -1);
    strcpy(ctx->currentMessage, msg);

    /* generate a response */
    sprintf(wbuf, "Your message [%s] was saved.", msg);
    writeReply(WRBCtx, wbuf);

    /* free parameter block */
    WRB_destroyPBlock(WRBCtx, hPBlock);

    return (WRB_DONE);
}

static WRBReturnCode getText(myappctx *ctx, void *WRBCtx)
{
    WRBpBlock hPBlock;
    char wbuf[1024];
    char *fmt;

    /* get form data */
    WRB_getParsedContent(WRBCtx, &hPBlock);

    fmt = WRB_findPBElemVal(WRBCtx, hPBlock,
                                    (text *)FORMAT_PARAM, -1);
    /* generate a response */
    sprintf(wbuf, "<%s>%s</%s>", fmt, ctx->currentMessage, fmt);
    writeReply(WRBCtx, wbuf);

    /* free the parameter block*/
    WRB_destroyPBlock(WRBCtx, hPBlock);
```

```
      return (WRB_DONE);
}
```

Both the *getText* and *setText* functions call the *writeReply* function. This function provides a simple wrapper for sending a response back to the user. Notice that it only makes use of the *WRB_printf* API call to write data directly to the response stream. This is definitely the most straightforward way to write out a simple response, but may become cumbersome when dealing with more sophisticated pages.

```
static void writeReply (void *WRBCtx, char *message)
{
    /* write response page */
    WRB_printf(WRBCtx, (text *)"Content-type: text/html\n\n");
    WRB_printf(WRBCtx,
             (text *)"<HEAD><TITLE>GETSET Test</TITLE></HEAD>\n");
    WRB_printf(WRBCtx, (text *)"<BODY BGCOLOR=\"#FFFFFF\">\n");
    WRB_printf(WRBCtx, (text *) message);
    WRB_printf(WRBCtx, (text *)"</BODY>\n");
}
```

If you have followed along with the bouncing ball, you should now have a source file, getset.c, which can be compiled into a DLL (.dll) or a shared object (commonly .so or .sl), depending on your platform. Take the steps appropriate to your development tools to build and link the library, correcting any errors in the make or source file as necessary. The shared library that has been created is your cartridge. The next step is to configure the Web Request Broker to use it.

Configuring the WRB to Use the Cartridge

Making the cartridge available to the WRB is fairly straightforward. Create a directory named getset under the $ORACLE_HOME/ows/cartx. Add a directory named bin to the getset directory. (In a few pages we discuss this further.) Place the shared object or DLL in the bin directory. This is not absolutely necessary, but it is a poor practice to simply have cartridges strewn about the file system in a disorganized fashion.

Next use a web browser to access the Cartridge Administration page. Follow the Add New Cartridge link. This page allows a cartridge to be installed from a configuration file. We have not created a configuration file yet, so instead follow the link to Add New Cartridge with Manual

Configuration. Figure 11-1 shows the manual cartridge configuration form with all necessary fields completed to register the cartridge.

Many of the fields on the form that have been left blank are associated with various WRB services and were described in Chapter 10. The Cartridge Name field is the name, six or fewer characters long, that the WRB knows the cartridge as. The Cartridge Description field is a more verbose or meaningful name for the cartridge that is used on some configuration pages. The Object Path field identifies the fully qualified pathname of the shared object or DLL, while the Entry Point field is the name of the cartridge's entrypoint function.

Other fields can be used to specify a customized error page or add support for other services. Since the GETSET cartridge does not make use of any additional WRB services, most of the fields can safely be ignored. The only additional step is to specify at least one virtual path associated with the cartridge. As shown in Figure 11-2, we have used /getset as the virtual path. Note that the path must not include a trailing slash. The physical path is set to the cartridge's bin directory. The physical path is the working directory for the cartridge when invoked via the WRB. Because we do not

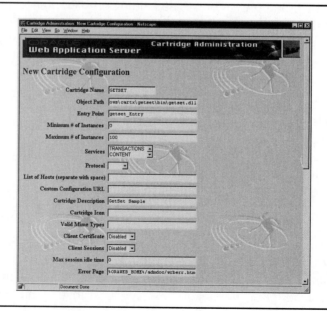

FIGURE 11-1. *Configuring the GETSET cartridge for the WRB*

make use of a working directory, where it points is not important for this cartridge.

At this point, the cartridge should be "good to go," as they say in Wisconsin. The only thing left to do is to shut down and restart the WRB and web listener so that the WRB will reload its configuration data for the new cartridge. Be certain to follow the correct order; the WRB should be the last thing shut down and the first thing started. If everything has gone well up to this point, the cartridge can now be invoked from a web browser.

Testing the Cartridge

The most important step in the development process is always making sure that the installed system is operating correctly. Given the relative simplicity of the cartridge, it is highly unlikely that any functional errors could have cropped up, so the most likely problems found (if any) would be related to configuration. The best way to test the cartridge is to create a small HTML page that can invoke the cartridge. The HTML for such a page would look something like the following listing, but with hostname and port changed to match the host running your cartridge.

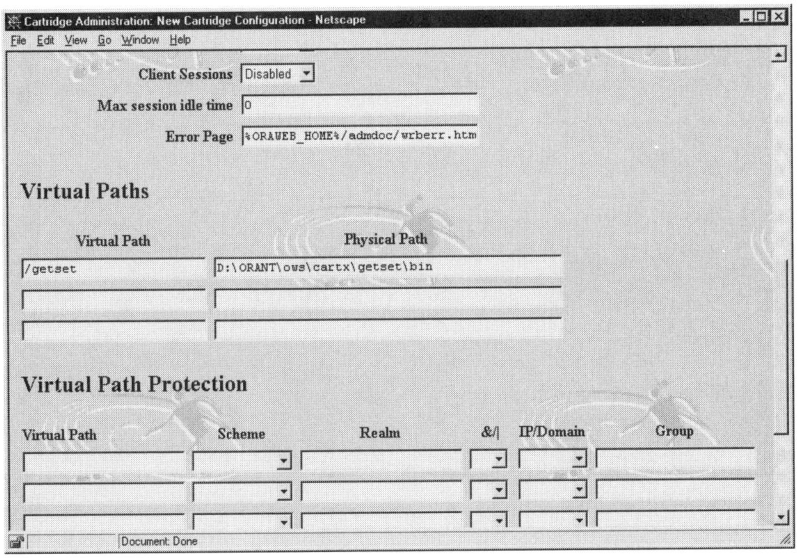

FIGURE 11-2. *Associating a virtual path with a cartridge*

```
<HTML>
<HEAD><TITLE>GETSET Cartridge Test Page</TITLE></HEAD>
<BODY>
<FORM METHOD="GET" ACTION="http://hostname:port/getset/settext">
<INPUT TYPE="text" NAME="message">
<INPUT TYPE="submit" value="Set Text">
</FORM>
<HR>
<FORM METHOD="GET" ACTION="http://hostname:port/getset/gettext">
<SELECT NAME="format">
<OPTION SELECTED VALUE="B">Bold
<OPTION VALUE="I">Italic
<OPTION VALUE="U">Underline
<OPTION VALUE="H1">Header 1
<OPTION VALUE="H2">Header 2
</SELECT>
<INPUT TYPE="submit" value="Get Text">
</FORM>
</BODY>
</HTML>
```

As seen in Figure 11-3, the page contains two forms, one to invoke the *settext* function and the other to execute *gettext*. Figures 11-4 and 11-5 show the result of executing the cartridge's various functions.

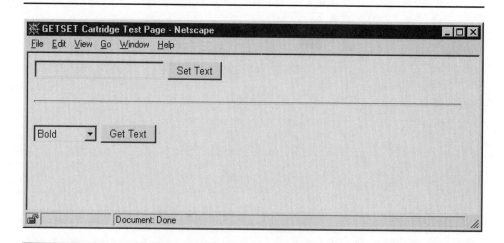

FIGURE 11-3. *The GETSET cartridge testing form*

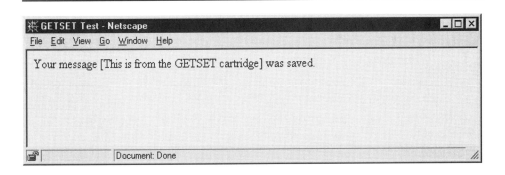

FIGURE 11-4. *The result of the* settext *cartridge function*

Expanding on the Foundation

As it stands, the GETSET cartridge does not do very much—it only demonstrates his section discusses how to implement some of those features in the cartridge. The focus here is on the core WRB API. Chapter 10 discussed making use of the WRB's services from within C cartridges.

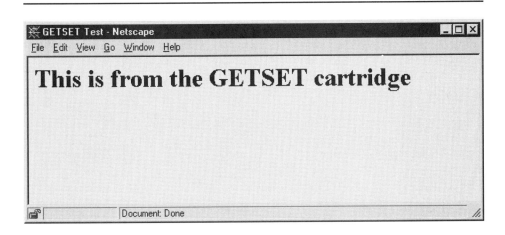

FIGURE 11-5. *The result of the* gettext *cartridge function*

Streamlining Installation and Configuration

As mentioned earlier, it is possible to create an .app file for a cartridge, to relieve the user from having to manually (and possibly incorrectly) enter all of the cartridge's configuration data. This is a significant time-saver for the individual installing the cartridge, as well as a boon for the developer, for fewer problem reports will come out of incorrect installation or configuration.

The cartridge configuration file is structured in basically the same format as the WRB.app file, which is in the format used by Windows-style .ini files. Such files are divided into *subjects*, which are tagged in square brackets. Within each subject are multiple name/value pairs, where the name and value are each on a line, separated by an equal sign. The best way to create an .app file for a new cartridge is to start with the mycart.sample file, which can be found in the OWAS distribution inside $ORAWEB_HOME/doc.

The .app file can specify several classes of information about the cartridge's configuration. First, and most importantly, it can specify the WRB parameters for the cartridge, such as the location of the cartridge's shared library file. Second, it can contain a section titled "[cartparams]," which specifies cartridge-specific name/value pairs to be read via the *WRB_GetAppConfig()* function. It can specify virtual paths that should map to the cartridge in an appsmap section, as well as additional virtual directories that the web listener should manage, listed in a dirmap section. Finally, it can be used to define transactions for the cartridge. The following listing shows a simple .app file for our GETSET cartridge. Tables 11-1, 11-2, 11-3, and 11-4 define the various attributes that can be defined in each section of the .app file.

```
[cartridge GETSET]
OBJPATH = %ORACLE_HOME%\ows\cartx\getset\bin\getset.dll
ENTRYPOINT = getset_Entry
MIN = 0
MAX = 100
VERSION = 1.0.0.0.1
OWS_VERSION = 3.0.0.0.0
ADMIN_DESC = $CARTRIDGE$ Cartridge
ADMIN_ICON = /getset-stuff/getset.gif

[appsmap /getset]
```

```
PPATH = %ORACLE_HOME%\ows\cartx\getset\bin

[cartparams]
default_msg = No message yet

[dirmap /getset-stuff]
PPATH = %ORACLE_HOME%\ows\cartx\getset\stuff
TYPE = NR
```

OBJPATH	The fully qualified pathname to the DLL or shared library containing the cartridge code. This value is required.
ENTRYPOINT	The name of your cartridge's entrypoint procedure. This value is required.
MIN	The minimum number of cartridge instances to be running simultaneously.
MAX	The maximum number of cartridge instances to be running simultaneously.
VERSION	The version number of the cartridge.
OWS_VERSION	The minimal version of the Oracle WebServer or Web Application Server with which the cartridge is compatible.
ADMIN_DESC	The name of the cartridge when shown in the Cartridge Administration page.
ADMIN_ICON	A URL that points to an image to be shown with the cartridge on the Cartridge Administration page. It will be scaled to 32 pixels by 32 pixels regardless of its actual size.
ADMIN_URL	A URL that points to an HTML file or CGI script that should be accessed for managing configuration settings.
ADMIN_ERR	A URL that points to an HTML page to return if an error occurs during cartridge execution that causes the cartridge to terminate prematurely.
MIMETYPES	Specifies the extensions that the listener should route to the cartridge. See the online help for cartridge configuration for a detailed explanation of its meaning.
PROTOCOL	Specifies under which protocol the cartridge should run. Valid choices are ORB, INMEMORY, and LIGHTWEIGHT. Typically left unspecified for the administrator to decide.

TABLE 11-1.   *Cartridge Parameters Used in the [cartridge cartname] Section*

HOSTS	Specifies a comma-delimited set of hosts that should run this cartridge. Typically left unspecified for the administrator to decide.
SERVICE	Specifies a comma-delimited set of WRB services of which the cartridge makes use. Possible values are any combination of TRANSACTION, CONTENT, ICX, or LOGGER.
GETCLIENTCERT	Either DISABLED or ENABLED, to specify whether a client certificate should be obtained from browsers making requests to the cartridge. The default is to be DISABLED.
SESSION	Either DISABLED or ENABLED, to specify whether the cartridge should make use of the WRB's session-management capabilities, as described in Chapter 10.
SESSIONIDLE	Specifies a value in seconds for which a session may be idle before it is dropped by the WRB.
LOGSYS	Either ON or OFF, to specify whether message-logging services will be used.
LOGATTRIB	Either ON or OFF, to specify whether cartridge-defined attribute-logging services will be used.
LOGMASK	A 32-bit mask value, specified in hexadecimal, that will be associated with log messages written by this cartridge. See the section "Logging" in Chapter 10 for information on using masks when generating log reports.
LOGLEVEL	A value between 0 and 15, indicating the minimum severity of messages that will be written to log for this cartridge.
LOGDEST_TYPE	Either DB or FS, indicating the default destination for log messages written by this cartridge. The default destination can be overridden by the cartridge at run time.
LOGDEST_DIR	A pathname to a directory in which log files for this cartridge should be written. The directory should not include a trailing slash.
LOGDEST_FNAME	The simple name (not a full path) of the file into which log messages should be written by the cartridge.

TABLE 11-1. *Cartridge Parameters Used in the [cartridge cartname] Section* (continued)

PPATH	The physical path to use as the working directory when the cartridge is accessed through the virtual path specified in the section header. This is required.
PROTSTRING	A protection string of the form "*Scheme*(*realm*) [{&,}] {IP,Domain}(*group*)" such as "Basic(myRealm) & IP(localIPs)".

TABLE 11-2.   *Application Mapping Parameters Used in One or More [appsmap /virtual-path] Sections*

PTYPE	Any combination of R, W, and D to specify the types of access permitted on the files, where R, W, and D indicate Read, Write, and Delete, respectively. Note that this is required if a PROTSTRING is specified for the directory.
TYPE	Specifies how the directory map should be used. One of NR, NN, CR, CN, WR, or WN, where the first letter specifies if the contents of the directory should be treated as Normal files, CGI programs, or WinCGI programs; and the second character specifies whether the directory should be accessible recursively or nonrecursively. The NR type is most common for directories containing standard HTML and images.

TABLE 11-3.   *Web Listener Directory Mapping Parameters Used in One or More [dirmap /virtual-path] Sections*

BEGIN	A URL that marks the beginning of a transaction. This is required.
COMMIT	A URL that indicates that the in-progress transaction should be committed. This is required.
ROLLBACK	A URL that indicates that the in-progress transaction should be rolled back. This is required.
BELONGTO	Multiple BELONGTO name/value pairs may be specified indicating all the URLs that are part of the transaction. At least one BELONGTO entry is required.
TIMEOUT	The period, in seconds, for which the transaction will live if no activity takes place. After the timeout period elapses, the transaction will be rolled back.
REGISTER	Specifies a resource manager (a DAD) to register for the transaction.

TABLE 11-4. *Transaction Parameters Used in One or More [carttrx trxnName] Sections*

After creating the cartridge's .app file, there are two ways in which the cartridge can be installed. On option is to specify the cartridge's .app file in the Add New Cartridge page under Cartridge Administration, as shown in Figure 11-6. The other choice is to use the wrcfreg command-line utility. The syntax for using wrcfreg can be found in $ORAWEB_HOME/ doc/wrcfreg.man.

Saving Time with the Cartridge Wizard

As can be seen, much of the code that makes up a cartridge is primarily focused on generic interactions with the WRB, such as function dispatching and parameter extraction. In fact, the actual functionality of the GETSET cartridge described earlier is only a few lines of code in the *getText* and *setText* functions. To relieve cartridge developers from some of this tedium, John Ogilvie, a consultant with Oracle Services, created a Cartridge Wizard, which is distributed by the Oracle Developer Programme.

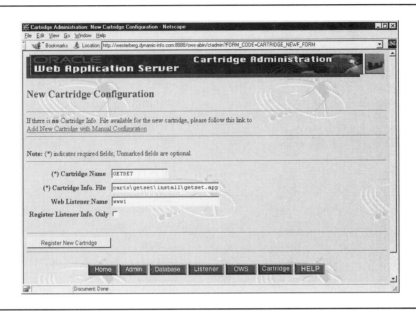

FIGURE 11-6. *Installing a cartridge with an .app file*

The Cartridge Wizard is made up of two components: a Java component that is to be run via the Web Application Server's Java cartridge, and a Java applet that provides the wizard interface. After collecting the information from the user, the applet sends a single request to the server component, which then returns an HTML page with links to generated source and make files, as well as an HTML page for testing the functions. Installation instructions are provided in the Cartridge Wizard distribution.

The Cartridge Wizard applet steps the developer through a series of screens that define what WRB Services the cartridge uses, what the application context should be, and what configuration data should be read from the WRB .app file. The developer can then describe the functions that the cartridge will expose, as well as the parameters it will accept. Figures 11-7, 11-8, and 11-9 show the Cartridge Wizard being used to develop the SonOfGetSet cartridge.

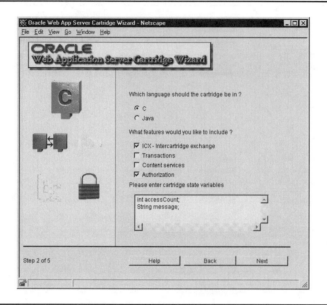

FIGURE 11-7. *Defining basic cartridge information*

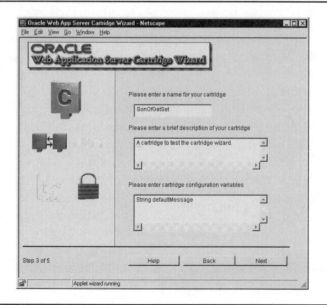

FIGURE 11-8. *Specifying the configuration parameters to read*

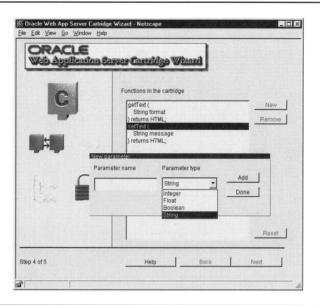

FIGURE 11-9. *Defining the exposed cartridge functions*

After stepping through the five screens of the Cartridge Wizard, it is possible to generate the cartridge. This sends a request to the server-side Java component, which then generates a source file for the cartridge as well as a make file and an HTML testing page, and returns to the browser an HTML page containing links to the various components as well as source files containing sample code for accessing certain WRB services. Figure 11-10 shows the result of a successful generation.

If the default generation behavior of the Cartridge Wizard does not meet all your needs, the source code to the server-side Java component is provided in the distribution. In addition, because the Cartridge Wizard uses a source file template (the default is simple.c.tem) for generation, it is very easy both to change things such as standard headers and to add common utility functions to the template.

In the currently available release, the Cartridge Wizard has a couple of minor shortcomings. First, it makes use primarily of the version 2.0 WRB API rather than the version 3.0 API. Second, it occasionally generates code that may not compile with only slight modifications. Most unfortunate is that the server component does not easily run without modification under

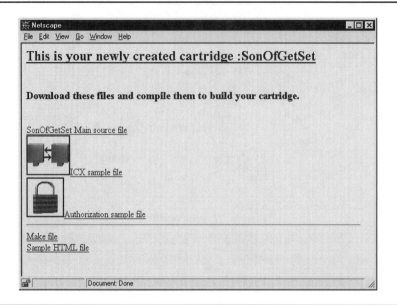

FIGURE 11-10. *Cartridge Wizard results*

Windows NT. This can be readily remedied, however, by altering the *CONFIG_FILE* static variable in cartwiz.java. With luck, these will be addressed in a future release.

Migrating CGI Programs to Cartridges

Many organizations may have already implemented web-based applications using CGI programs written in C. Of course, these can be used unchanged with the Web Application Server, but there are several benefits to converting CGI programs into cartridges. Additionally, the effort involved in such a migration is minimal in comparison.

The major benefits that developers reap when implementing web applications as cartridges rather than CGI programs are three: better performance; easier application development and deployment; and the support of all the WRB services, such as transaction support, automatic session management, and integrated logging services. Although some of this functionality could be implemented manually by the developer of a

CGI program, such code is decidedly nontrivial to write, and would represent a major, if not insurmountable, challenge to most developers.

In exchange for these benefits, there are really only a few steps that a developer must take to convert an application currently implemented in CGI into a WRB cartridge. The process is further simplified to the extent that the CGI program has been developed in a fairly modular manner. The best way to begin is either with a basic cartridge template or by using the Cartridge Wizard to build the cartridge framework. Obviously, using the Cartridge Wizard will provide a bigger head start.

Next, it is time to examine the CGI code related to initialization and cleanup. Initialization code that really only needs to occur once, such as code to connect to a database or to open a file, should be moved into the cartridge's Init function, and its corresponding cleanup code (closing the database connection or file) should be moved into the Shutdown function. Code that performs some sort of setup that will be unique to each invocation should be moved either into the beginning of the Exec function, or at the beginning of one of the functions called by the Exec function dispatcher.

If you have used the Cartridge Wizard to create the framework, code has already been generated to extract parameters from the request. If using another template, you will need to write code to do this, using the *WRB_getParsedContent* API function. In either case, you will need to alter your code, if necessary, to accept the parameters in this new fashion. Note that, unlike in a CGI, it will not be necessary to decode the parameter values, as the WRB will have already performed the replacement on escaped character sequences. In addition, you will need to place your main processing code into either the Exec function or a function called by the Exec function's dispatcher.

Finally, the code that writes responses back to the browser will need to be changed. CGIs write their responses to standard output, while cartridges must send responses through the WRBs API calls. If your CGI code only uses printf statements to write content, the task is very easy, as all of the *printf* calls can simply be changed to *WRB_printf* calls, using your editor's global replace utility.

At this point, the only step left is to compile the cartridge. Unlike a CGI, which is a stand-alone executable, a cartridge must be compiled into a shared library. If you used the Cartridge Wizard, it will have created a make file automatically; otherwise, you can alter one provided with the sample cartridges in the Web Application Server distribution. From here, you should be able to install and run the cartridge as described previously.

If you have several CGI programs that are actually part of one application, you may wish to consolidate them into a single cartridge so that they can share common initialization and cleanup code, as well as take advantage of the WRB session management services to more easily provide stateful behavior.

Closing Thoughts on Cartridges

In this chapter you have learned the basic mechanics of creating a cartridge and interacting with the major calls in the WRB core API. Combined with the information in Chapter 10 on using the WRB's services from C, you can begin writing cartridges of virtually any complexity. If you plan to write cartridges that access the Oracle RDBMS, you should consider reading the *Oracle Developer's Guide,* by David McClanahan, part of the Oracle Press series. It provides a comprehensive examination of accessing Oracle from C programs. Before you get started, however, here are some additional tips that may ease your cartridge development experiences.

Planning for Portability

As mentioned earlier, cartridges written in C are inherently less portable than components written in Java or PL/SQL. However, there are some steps that a developer may take to improve this situation. The WRB and WRB service APIs themselves, along with most Oracle APIs (such as the OCI), are portable across Windows NT and most flavors of Unix. To ensure the portability of your cartridge as a whole, try to use only the standard ANSI libraries, or libraries that are themselves cross-platform. If this is possible, porting your cartridge to a new platform should be as simple as copying the source files, applying some slight alterations to the make file, and running the compiler and linker.

Implementing Detailed Logging

Cartridges are difficult to debug, since they are executed indirectly by the WRB. Fortunately, the WRB provides some reasonably sophisticated logging services to cartridges. By using the WRB Logger service, you can fairly easily write tracing and debugging messages, the logging of which can be disabled or enabled at run time.

Windows NT: Threads Versus Processes

If developing a cartridge for use under Windows NT, it is possible to implement a cartridge using either threads or processes. A thread is sometimes known as a lightweight process, because it incurs less overhead in terms of memory usage and the speed with which context switches can occur. However, there are two major implications of using the thread-based cartridge model. The first impacts system stability: an error or crash in a thread (which is servicing one request) can in fact bring down its entire process (including other threads servicing other requests). The second consideration of the thread model relates to development, for designing a thread-safe cartridge under Windows NT requires some additional effort.

The most significant issue is avoiding the use of global variables in a thread-based cartridge. The reason for this is that global variables are shared by all threads in a process. If global variables are absolutely(!) necessary, implement appropriate synchronization. Note that if you're developing a cartridge using the Pro*C libraries from Oracle, you must use a local SQL context (sqlca) rather than the default behavior of storing the sqlca in a global variable. This is accomplished by defining SQLCA_NONE in your source file prior to including the sqlca.h header.

In addition, robust error handling and exception handling are obviously even more important in thread-based cartridges, because an error can cause multiple client requests to fail. A useful, but not entirely portable, way to improve error handling is to make use of the try-except and try-finally exception-handling structures provided in the Microsoft C compiler.

Conclusion

In this chapter we have seen how to use C to implement WRB cartridges. Of all possible application development options for the Web Application Server, it is such cartridges that offer the most performance and flexibility for web developers. Although creating these cartridges is not a trivial exercise, the services provided by the WRB API certainly reduce the effort needed by developers to use C as a web development language. Armed with this final development option, no web development challenge should be insurmountable either in terms of performance or functionality.

CHAPTER
12

Oracle Web
Technologies

hrough the previous 11 chapters, you will have developed a solid understanding of the Oracle Web Application Server and learned how to create dynamic applications using a variety of different development languages. In this chapter we introduce a number of other areas in which Oracle is developing new web-oriented products, as well as refining web-enabling products that presently exist. Most of the tools are based on the Web Application Server, or work in conjunction with applications developed for it.

Oracle and the Network Computing Architecture

The foundation of Oracle's web initiatives are driven by the Network Computing Architecture introduced by Oracle in the recent past. The NCA is a standards-driven approach to the development and deployment of scalable and robust "network-centric" applications that are able to interoperate effectively in a distributed environment.

Although Oracle coined the term Network Computing Architecture, there is nothing inherent in the architecture that is tied to Oracle technology. Rather, it is a reasonably abstract model of multitier. component-based software in which components across tiers rely on standard network communication standards to interoperate. The major standards at work are HTTP and CORBA. The software components themselves are deployed, executed, and otherwise administered by various server applications. In this context, a web browser is a server, providing a context for executing a Java applet (this is similar to the X Window meaning of "server").

Oracle is structuring all its web-oriented development to be compliant with the computing model defined by NCA, and this is a real benefit for developers who use Oracle product. By having a unifying architecture in place, it allows developers to use the Web as an environment in which applications using a wide variety of tools can be brought together.

Oracle's Java Initiatives

Java is clearly poised to become a progressively more mainstream language over the next several years, especially given its outstanding suitability to developing network savvy and applications that are lightweight and can be deployed via the network onto virtually any platform. The growth of Sun Microsystems' Java has hardly been lost on Oracle, and in fact Oracle has made some significant developments in the use of Java as a programming language.

We have already seen the support for Java within Web Application Server, but there are many other areas in which Oracle has been developing Java support in its product line. These changes range from "middleware," to client tools, to changes to the RDBMS itself. Some of them are still in development, but several useful tools are available today.

JDBC

JDBC, the Java Database Connectivity API, provides a standard API through which Java applets or programs can access relational databases. It is similar in some respects to ODBC, the database access API that has been a standard under Windows for several years. By providing a standard API that acts as an abstraction layer, it is possible to create Java programs or applets that are able to be almost trivially switched between database engines, so long as they provide JDBC support. For instance, an applet could be developed running against Personal Oracle Lite, and then deployed against the enterprise version of the Oracle RDBMS.

Oracle has been quite responsive in addressing the need for JDBC drivers. The JDBC standard actually defines four types of drivers, described in Table 12-1.

Developing with JDBC is actually quite straightforward. The following code listing shows the fundamentals of a program that uses JDBC to access an Oracle database. The major steps are loading the driver class using the class name, establishing a connection from the driver manager, and then creating and executing the SQL statement. Results are returned from the query in a ResultSet object, which is accessed in a manner similar to an enumeration for doing row fetches, and similar to a vector for extracting column values for the current row.

```
import jdbc.sql.*;
import java.io.*;
import java.util.*;

public class jdbctest
{
    static final String drvrNm =
                    "oracle.jdbc.dnlddriver.OracleDriver";
```

```
// Build the connect string
static final String driver = "jdbc:oracle:dnldthin";
static final String username = "scott";
static final String password = "tiger";
static final String hostname = "prince.dynamic-info.com";
static final String port = "1526";
static final String sid = "purple";
static final String cnctStr = driver + ":" + username + "/" +
                              password + "@" + hostname + ":" +
                              port + ":" + sid;

static final String query = "SELECT empno,ename,sal " +
                            "  FROM emp " +
                            "ORDER BY empno";

static Connection conn;      //the database connection

public static final void main(String args[]) {
    try {
        //  Load the JDBC driver using the forName
        //  interface. This allows the driver to
        //    be specified as a string in a properties
        // list or a parameter.
        Class.forName (drvrNm);

        //  Obtain a connection to a database
        conn = DriverManager.getConnection (cnctStr);

        //  Create a statement object
        Statement stmt = conn.createStatement ();

        //  Execute the query into a result set
        ResultSet rset = stmt.executeQuery (query);

        //  Loop through the result set in an manner
        //  similar to an enumeration and print the
        //  contents of the columns.
        while (rset.next ()){
            System.out.println ( rset.getString (1) + "   " +
                                 rset.getString (2) + "   " +
                                 rset.getString (3) );
        }

        System.out.println("Done");
```

```
    } catch (Exception e) {
        //  Provide debugging information
        System.out.println(e.toString());
        e.printStackTrace(System.out);
    }
  }
}
```

Developers at Oracle have actually implemented both Type 2 and Type 4 JDBC drivers for both Oracle7 and Oracle8. The Type 2 driver makes use of OCI libraries available on the client machine, while the Type 4 driver can connect directly to an Oracle database from any pure-Java environment.

Since both drivers were developed by Oracle, they are able to take better advantage of Oracle-specific features such as support for new

JDBC Driver Type	Description
Type 1	A Java wrapper for ODBC, such that all JDBC calls invoke native ODBC calls, which in turn access a database-specific ODBC driver. This requires the presence of some type of native code libraries on the client system.
Type 2	A Java wrapper for a database-specific call interface, such as the Oracle Call Interface. Like Type 1 drivers, Type 2 drivers require the presence of installed native libraries on the client machine.
Type 3	A 100-percent-pure-Java client implementation that communicates through a proxy on a server. This proxy then uses either ODBC or a native call interface to access a database and to return results back to the client. The client component of a Type 3 driver is 100 percent Java and can be downloaded at run time.
Type 4	A 100-percent-pure-Java implementation of the database's native connectivity protocol. In the case of Oracle, this is SQL*Net. The use of Type 4 drivers allows a Java applet or application to connect directly to a database, the same as a traditional client/server application.

TABLE 12-1. *Defined Types of JDBC Drivers*

Oracle8 datatypes like BLOBs, CLOBs, and BFILEs. In addition, they implement several optimizations such as rows prefetching, batched updates, and control over data streaming. Further, because the Type 4 driver provides what is effectively a Java implementation of the standard SQL*Net driver, and is able to connect directly to an Oracle database, it will almost universally provide better performance than a Type 3 driver in a pure-Java environment.

J/SQL

While JDBC provides a complete standardized API for accessing a database using dynamic SQL, Oracle has also created and released J/SQL, a precompiler-based tool for using embedded SQL inside Java programs. Developers familiar with other Oracle precompilers such as Pro*C or Pro*COBOL will see some similarities between the two products. However, J/SQL has a very Java-like feel to its precompiler syntax.

J/SQL, like Oracle's other precompiler products, processes a source file prior to being compiled by the main compiler—javac, in the case of Java. Developers writing code to use J/SQL include various embedded static SQL commands in their source file that are then converted by the J/SQL precompiler into JDBC calls. When we say static SQL commands, this means that the result domain (that is, the tables to be queried and the columns from those tables) as well as the structure of any WHERE, ORDER BY, or other ancillary clauses are fixed at design time, rather than generated dynamically at run time. Such static SQL statement can still be parameterized, so that a variable can be substituted as a literal value in a query condition.

This is identical to the manner in which SQL access is performed using Pro*C or PL/SQL. Of course, in C the OCI can be used to execute dynamic SQL statements; PL/SQL supports dynamic SQL via the DBMS_SQL package, and Java supports it via JDBC. You may be wondering what possible benefit there is to using J/SQL rather than simply using JDBC, given that dynamic SQL offers the developer much more power and flexibility than static SQL.

There are actually two major reasons. The first is that it generally is much easier to implement SQL calls using embedded SQL rather than JDBC calls. The second is compile-time validation of the SQL itself, which saves significant time in the debugging cycle. Because dynamic SQL is not

known until run time, JDBC calls cannot be checked for validity, that is, if
they reference tables or columns that do not exist, or if a SQL statement is
simply wrong. J/SQL *does* perform this validation during compilation,
however—meaning that no SQL syntax or referencing errors will make it
into the application. If you are truly intent on avoiding the semantic checks,
however, they can be disabled during precompilation.

As we mentioned, embedded SQL is easier to work with than JDBC for
most SQL statements. One of the major reasons for this is that it
automatically deals with issues like binding program variables to SQL
parameters. This is especially useful for programs that do a significant
number of inserts or updates to a database, rather than queries alone. The
following listing shows the use of J/SQL for performing basically the same
operation as in the JDBC listing earlier. Notice that it is roughly half the
number of lines of the previous example.

```java
import oracle.jsql.*;
import java.sql.*;

SQL.cursor (EmpCursor (Double EMPNO, String ENAME, Double SAL));

class jsqltest
{
  public static void main (String args[])
    throws SQLException
  {
    try {
        Class.forName("oracle.jdbc.OracleDriver");
    } catch (ClassNotFoundException e) {
        System.out.println("Could not load the driver");
    }

    JSQLContext ctx =
              new JSQLContext ("jdbc:oracle:", "scott", "tiger");
    EmpCursor c =
              SQL.exec ((EmpCursor) select empno, ename, sal
                                    from emp);

    while (c.next()) {
      System.out.println( c.EMPNO() +"  "+c.ENAME()+" "+ c.SAL());
    }
  }
}
```

When this file is sent to the J/SQL precompiler, it creates private classes for the declared cursors, with methods named for each of the columns in the cursor, which return the value of the column in the current row. It is these methods that are actually being called in the output line near the end of the listing. It then inserts all the necessary code to prepare and execute the statements using JDBC. As we noted earlier, embedded SQL is very convenient for dealing with inserts and updates because it automatically manages the binding of variables to elements of the SQL statement. The following listing shows a J/SQL program that inserts a row into the DEPT table using column values passed in at the command line.

```
import oracle.jsql.*;
import java.sql.*;

class adddept
{
  public static void main (String args[])
    throws SQLException
  {
    try {
        Class.forName("oracle.jdbc.OracleDriver");
    } catch (ClassNotFoundException e) {
        System.out.println("Could not load the driver");
    }

    JSQLContext ctx =
              new JSQLContext ("jdbc:oracle:", "scott", "tiger");

    int p_deptno = Integer.parseInt(args[0]);
    String p_dname = args[1];
    String p_loc = args[2]

    SQL.exec (insert into dept values(:p_deptno,:p_dname,:p_loc));

  }
}
```

Java Stored Procedures

A major advancement being undertaken by Oracle in its Java support is the plan for version 8.1 of the RDBMS to support database-stored procedures and triggers written in Java, in addition to continued support for PL/SQL.

This is a very promising move for developers, as it offers the ability to create truly three-tier applications with a single language. Such applications offer developers enormous flexibility with respect to relatively easy application partitioning across clients, application servers, and the RDBMS.

JBuilder

Not all of Oracle's Java development initiatives have been focused on SQL and database activities. Oracle is working in concert with Borland to deliver an enhanced version of JBuilder, Borland's Java development integrated development environment (IDE). The enhanced product is expected to extend JBuilder's existing support for developing database-savvy Java applets and applications, as well as providing enhanced support for building distributed application with CORBA support, perhaps with a GUI-based editor for creating binds to CORBA-accessible services. Even without Oracle's enhancements, though, JBuilder is a pretty slick product for creating Java GUIs.

Web Features in Other Oracle Products

Although Java is a major technology for network computing, nearly all of Oracle's products are undergoing transformations to better implement web technologies. In this section we provide a sketch of the web-oriented enhancements to some of these products.

Developer/2000

Oracle's Developer/2000 is the firm's enterprise client/server development environment. It is composed of several components, including Oracle Forms and Oracle Reports. In recent releases of the tool, Oracle has added significant levels of web functionality that allow the deployment of complete web applications using Developer/2000.

First, Oracle Forms was web-enabled by creating a display engine for the Forms run time as a Java applet. This allows complete Oracle Forms applications to be run from inside a browser (or using Sun Microsystems' AppletViewer). These applications are nearly identical in appearance and function to the same application deployed via a Windows or Motif version of runform, the Oracle Forms run-time engine, as can be seen in Figures 12-1 and 12-2.

The Java applet running the Oracle Forms display engine communicates with a Forms server. The applet is responsible only for managing screen display, while all of the application logic is executed on the Forms server. This means that all database interactions, as well as any processing logic encapsulated in Forms triggers, do not run inside of Java. In effect, the applet is much like an X Window workstation, in which the workstation only manages screen updates and captures user input, while an application server processes the user input and directs the workstation to update its screen. This innovation was possible because of the unique design or Oracle Forms in which the application was designed with a loose coupling between the display behavior and the application logic. This loose coupling was initially implemented to ease support for portability across multiple platforms such as Motif, Windows, and Macintosh. The selection of such a model turned out to be very fortuitous in this case.

The second major Developer/2000 enhancement is the creation of a web-accessible Oracle Reports server. The web-accessible component is based on the Oracle Reports Multitier Server. The Reports MTS (not to be confused with the Oracle RDBMS MTS, or Multi-Threaded Server) can process multiple generation jobs asynchronously, either from the command line as part of a batch process, or via CGI-style or WRB cartridge invocation. This server is able to accept a request to run a report and return it back to a web browser in either HTML or PDF format.

The Reports server is very flexible, both in terms of managing its processing behavior as well as actually running reports. Reports can be run with parameters submitted at run time, and they can use different database logons to run the same report as different users. In addition, the generated reports can include charts and graphs from Oracle Graphics and can also support drill-down reporting through hyperlinks. Most impressive, however, is the visual fidelity to the originally designed report. Figure 12-3 shows a simple report displayed within the runform application, while Figures 12-4 and 12-5 show the same report returned by the MTS in both HTML and PDF formats.

There are several ways in which organizations can gain benefit from these enhancements to Developer/2000. The most immediate benefit many organizations will realize is the easy delivery of reports via the Web that

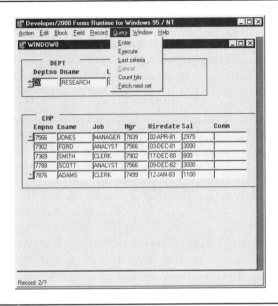

FIGURE 12-1.   *A form running using runform for Windows*

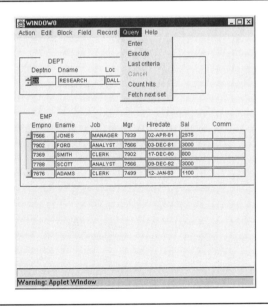

FIGURE 12-2.   *The same form running in Java*

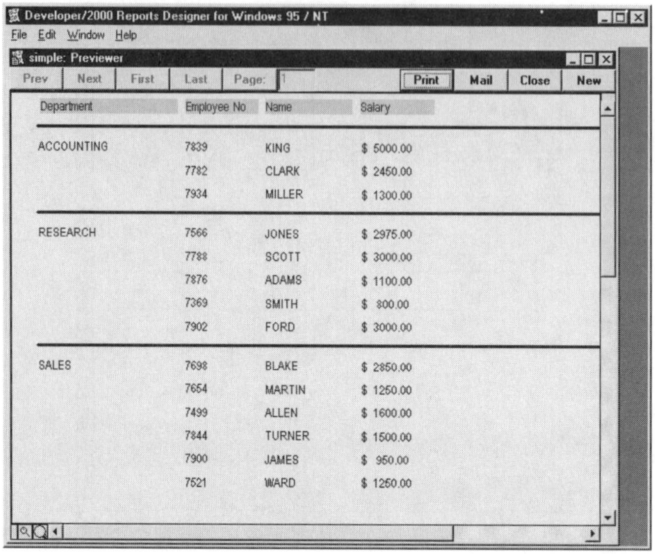

FIGURE 12-3. *An Oracle report previewed in Oracle Reports' run time*

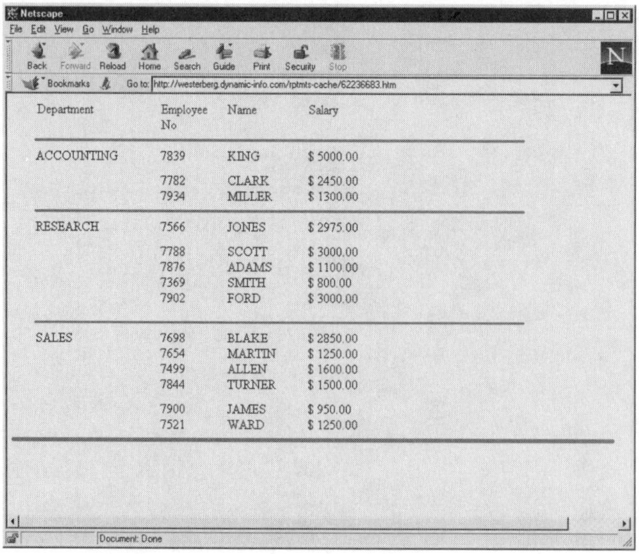

FIGURE 12-4. *The same report generated into HTML*

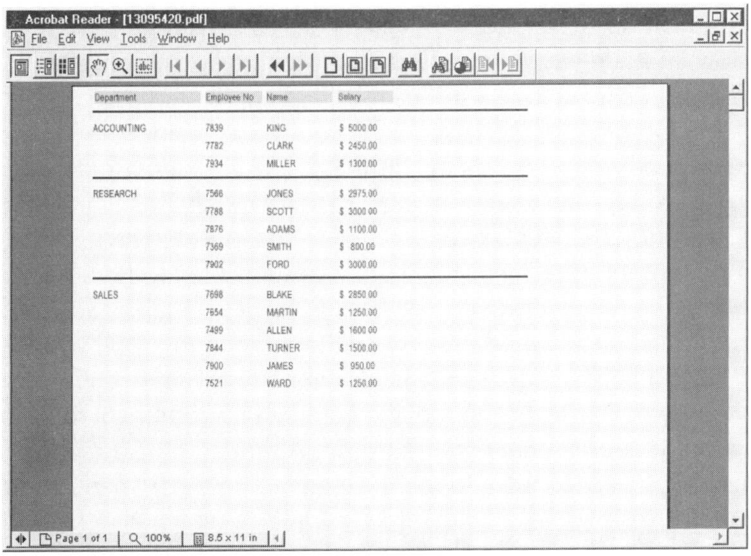

FIGURE 12-5. *The same report, now generated into PDF*

are suitable for printing, in terms of header and footer control, page breaks, and other common features. Even if only used for HTML reporting, Oracle Reports offers a significantly faster path to developing inquiry-based web pages than manual coding of either PL/SQL or Java.

Web-deployed Oracle Forms are most valuable to organizations that already have an existing base of applications developed in Oracle Forms. Assuming that the Forms modules were designed in a sufficiently platform-neutral manner, they can be easily delivered via an intranet, and, with a little more effort, via the Internet. Any additional effort for Internet deployment is primarily a factor of setting up the Forms server outside the firewall, but letting it access an Oracle database inside the firewall. However, the memory footprint required by the server-side process for each user—as well as the number of classes to be downloaded to the client—may make Forms-based application impractical for public web applications that will have high public-user volumes in which each user is only using the application for a few moments.

The portability boundary is largely the same as for designing Oracle Forms applications to be run across other platforms. Obviously, things such as OCX or VBX controls are not supported, and user exits also have some unique implications. User exits are extensions to Developer/2000 applications that are written in a language such as C and compiled into native code and executed by various run-time applications such as Forms, Reports, and Graphics. When user exits are invoked using the Forms Server, they are run on the server. This means that if a user exit performs some type of GUI processing, such as displaying a dialog box, the display will pop up on the server, not the client. The final major unsupported area is that the multiple-document interface (MDI) behavior supported in Forms does not translate into the Java world very well. Thus, to be available, any toolbars or consoles must be assigned to Forms rather than to the MDI window. Additionally, the When-Mouse-Enter, When-Mouse-Leave, and When-Mouse-Move triggers are not executed when running a form in Java, as each would require a network roundtrip. Although not supported in Developer/2000 version 1.5, Bubble Help (aka ToolTips), menu shortcuts, and combo boxes will be available in version 2.0, which is in beta at the time of this writing.

Designer/2000

Oracle's Designer/2000 is the company's process and application modeling and design tool. It provides a flexible CASE environment that supports the application development process at any or all stages of development: business process modeling, system design, and on through application generation. The flexibility that Designer/2000 provides with respect to generation is especially interesting for web development. In addition to generating traditional client/server applications using Developer/2000 or Visual Basic, it is able to generate complete web applications for use with the PL/SQL cartridge.

Developers who are used to manual development using either straight code editors or GUI development tools may find the high-level modeling approach used with Designer/2000 somewhat disconcerting. However, it does offer some significant benefits in terms of allowing developers to focus on the model of the application being implemented, rather than the actual nuts and bolts of the application. In addition, because applications are developed at the model level rather than the language level, it is possible to create multiple versions of the same application—one using Oracle Forms and another using generated HTML, for instance.

Many developers do not like code generators, because they typically produce applications that are aesthetically challenged. Although there is no argument that the default web applications generated from a Designer/2000 model are bland, the appearance and functionality of the generated applications can be defined almost completely with generation preferences set at global, page, and even individual field levels. These preferences are then stored in the repository along with the application model, and will be applied with any future generation of the application. In fact, there are more than 130 top-level preferences that can be customized, including document templates, color schemes, font selections, table usage, and others. Figure 12-6 shows you the number and variety of such options.

In addition to tools and servers, Oracle has garnered a substantial share of the business applications market. Given the foundation on which the members of the Oracle Applications suite are built—namely the Oracle RDBMS, Designer/2000, and Developer/2000—it should come as no surprise that significant web-accessible functionality has been added to the

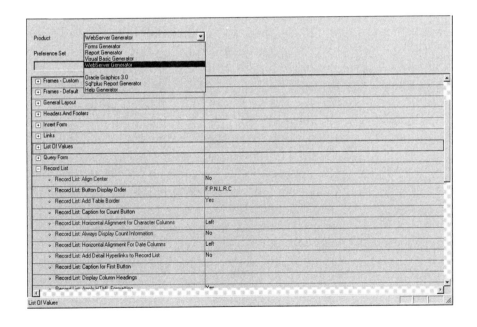

FIGURE 12-6.   *Options for Designer/2000 web application generation*

Applications suite. In addition to the web-enabling of its traditionally back-office-oriented applications, Oracle has created a more consumer-oriented electronic commerce application server that is usable independent of the back-office application suite.

Self-Service Oracle Applications for the Web

For organizations that are using the Oracle Applications suite for areas such as Order Entry, Purchasing, or HR, Oracle's applications group has created a collection of self-service applications, to allow customers or employees access self-service functionality from various applications. Using WebCustomer, organizations can provide a user friendly web shopping interface to allow customers to place orders via the Web that flow directly into the order process built in Oracle Order Entry, via the standard OrderImport process.

Unlike electronic commerce applications developed as more or less stand-alone systems, such as OpenMarket, the benefit of WebCustomer is that the orders entered by customers can flow directly into the order process implemented in Oracle applications. In addition, there is a single point of administration, as WebCustomer can gather customer-specific pricing, availability, and shipping rules from those configured in the standard Order Entry system.

A similar application is implemented for internal requisitions and purchasing within WebEmployee, in which a user can shop through a catalog of items available for purchase. After building their requisition, it can be submitted. WebEmployee then manages such workflow issues as routing the requisition for approval if it is over certain predefined amounts. WebEmployee also provides an interface for posting internal job openings and performing other common HR tasks.

WebSupplier is Oracle's self-service application geared toward a company's vendors. It allows vendors to access information about the receipt of deliveries they have sent to the company, as well as payment status and other information. WebSupplier makes a company easier to work with from a supplier's perspective while reducing the costs associated with fielding calls from vendors about payment status and other issues.

It is also possible for these self-service applications to be customized in various ways. Oracle provides a repository-based system for developing inquiry applications for producing customized drill-down web pages that report on data from any of the applications in the suite. In addition, customized functions can also be installed into the applications in a bolt-on fashion, similar to the standard character-based or client/server applications. Aside from these areas, however, customizing the self-service applications is a decidedly nontrivial process, requiring a solid understanding of both web development and the Oracle Applications suite.

Web-Enabled Oracle Applications

The other area in which Oracle's applications group has enhanced its Applications suite is in the implementation of web-enabled Oracle applications. This web-enabled version is basically the standard Smart Client implementation deployed via the web-enabled version of Oracle Forms, running the various forms in a Java applet.

This is a major boon to many firms that previously faced two options: use the character-mode version of Oracle Applications on relatively low-cost, low-administration terminals on Network Computers (NCs), or install the Smart Client (GUI) version of the Applications on fairly expensive Windows PCs. By using the web-enabled Applications, organizations can use NCs as low-cost terminal devices while still getting the usability benefits of a GUI implementation.

Internet Commerce Server

While WebCustomer provides users of the Oracle Applications suite with a web-accessible front-end to Order Entry, Oracle also has developed a second electronic commerce application for a broader market. Internet Commerce Server is an application for providing electronic storefront services with basically turnkey support for most features needed for consumer sales on the Internet.

Two major differences between WebCustomer and Internet Commerce Server should be observed. The first is technical: WebCustomer is implemented in PL/SQL, while Internet Commerce Server was developed in Java. The second difference is even more crucial: Internet Commerce Server is strongly suited to consumer sales, while WebCustomer is geared more strongly toward business-to-business sales.

Oracle has made enhancements to many other products as well. Oracle's OLAP product, Express, offers some sophisticated web support through a WRB cartridge that can deliver multidimensional query applications via the Web. Discover/2000, a query tool oriented toward end users, can output its results as collections of HTML pages, and a cartridge version would not be out of reach in the future. Overall, the prospects are very bright that Oracle developers will be looking to port existing or new applications to the Web.

Conclusion

Oracle has provided developers with a wide array of tools with which to implement web-accessible applications. I hope that this chapter and the entire book have given you some ideas about applications that you can deploy via the Web, as well as armed you with the knowledge to develop them to suit your needs.

Of course, the Web Application Server is Oracle's focal point and foundation of many of its network computing developments, and it will continue to be enhanced to support this role. Look for administration utilities to be improved, to make the implementation and management of highly distributed installations easier. Also expect the number and depth of WRB services to be expanded, as well as more support implemented for languages (besides C) in accessing these services. This book will be updated to show how to exploit all these new features as they become available.

APPENDIX

A

HTP and HTF Packages

he purpose of the HTP and HTF packages is to generate HTML. Optimal use of these packages may require looking into the details of HTML.

NOTE
All routines listed from package HTP have counterparts in the package HTF. The routines are identical except that HTP routines write their output directly to the buffer to be returned to the web browser, while HTF routines are all functions that return a VARCHAR2.

Functions and Procedures

htp.address (cvalue, cnowrap, cclear, cattributes)

PURPOSE   Used to insert text into the HTML document, bounded by <ADDRESS> and </ADDRESS> tags.

PARAMETERS

Name		Type	Default	Usage
cvalue	→	VARCHAR2		String to appear between <ADDRESS> and </ADDRESS> tags.
cnowrap	→	VARCHAR2	NULL	If nonnull, the **nowrap** attribute is added to the opening <ADDRESS> tag.
cclear	→	VARCHAR2	NULL	Value of the **clear** attribute.
cattributes	→	VARCHAR2	NULL	Contents inserted directly into the opening <ADDRESS> tag.

GENERATES

```
<ADDRESS CLEAR="cclear" NOWRAP cattributes>cvalue</ADDRESS>
```

htp.anchor2 (curl, ctext, cname, ctarget, cattributes)

PURPOSE Used to insert a hypertext anchor into the HTML document, using the <A> and </A> tags.

PARAMETERS

Name		Type	Default	Usage
curl	→	VARCHAR2		URL to which this anchor points.
ctext	→	VARCHAR2	NULL	String to appear between <A> and </A> tags.
cname	→	VARCHAR2	NULL	Name of the anchor, to be referenced from other URLs.
ctarget	→	VARCHAR2	NULL	Name of the window or frame to which this link is directed. Special values include _top, _parent, and _blank, whose meanings should be clear. Frames are named by using the name parameter of the <FRAME> tag.
cattributes	→	VARCHAR2	NULL	Contents inserted directly into the opening <A> tag. This may include the **rev** and **rel** attributes. See htp.linkRel and htp.linkRev for a description of these attributes.

GENERATES

```
<A HREF="curl" NAME="cname" TARGET="ctarget" cattributes>ctext</A>
```

NOTE
This procedure has a bug with respect to the complete use of the anchor tag. Anchors may be used that do not specify a URL, but rather only a name, which are then used as targets by URLs. This package, however, requires a nonnull URL, and thus cannot generate the needed tag usage. We recommend using the htp.p routine to write the tag out directly, such as this:

```
htp.p('<A NAME="section1">Section 1: The PL/SQL SDK</A>');
```

There is also another function, htp.anchor, which is identical to htp.anchor2, except that it does not accept the *ctarget* parameter.

htp.appletOpen (ccode, cheight, cwidth, cattributes)

PURPOSE Used to begin invocation of a Java applet. Can also specify parameters to the Java applet using the htp.param procedure. If the CLASSPATH environment variable is not set in the browser, the cattributes parameter may need to be used to set the CODEBASE attribute.

PARAMETERS

Name		Type	Default	Usage
ccode	→	VARCHAR2		Value of the **code** attribute, which specifies name of applet class.
cheight	→	NUMBER	NULL	Value of the **height** attribute.
cwidth	→	NUMBER	NULL	Value of the **width** attribute.
cattributes	→	VARCHAR2	NULL	Contents inserted directly into the opening <APPLETOPEN> tag.

GENERATES

```
<APPLET CODE=ccode HEIGHT=cheight WIDTH=cwidth>
```

htp.appletClose

PURPOSE Used to close the applet-embedding directive opened with the <APPLET> tag.

PARAMETERS None.

GENERATES

```
</APPLET>
```

htp.area (ccoords, cshape, chref, cnoref, ctarget, cattributes)

PURPOSE Used to define a client-side image map. The <AREA> HTML tag defines areas within the image and destinations of the areas.

PARAMETERS

Name		Type	Default	Usage
ccoord	→	VARCHAR2		Value of the **coords** attribute.
cshape	→	VARCHAR2	NULL	Value of the **shape** attribute.
chref	→	VARCHAR2	NULL	Value of the **href** attribute.
cnoref	→	VARCHAR2	NULL	If nonnull, the **nohref** attribute is added to the tag.
ctarget	→	VARCHAR2	NULL	Value of the **target** attribute.
cattribute	→	VARCHAR2	NULL	Contents inserted directly into the opening <AREA> tag.

GENERATES

```
<AREA COORDS="ccoords" SHAPE="cshape" HREF="chref"
NOHREF TARGET="ctarget" catributes>
```

htp.base (ctarget, cattributes)

PURPOSE   Generates the <BASE> tag, which specifies the default target window or frame into which URLs should be loaded when following anchors. We discourage the use of this routine because it does not allow the developer to override the **href** attribute of the <BASE> tag, as it inserts the URL of the currently generated document for the **href** attribute. The **href** attribute is a URL from which relative URLs should be completed. If not specified, the effective base for relative URL addressing is the current document's URL. For example, regardless of the location of the document, the link in the following HTML snippet will be directed to http://www.oraweb.com/a/b/c/foo.html and opened in a new window.

```
<HEAD>
<BASE HREF="http://www.oraweb.com/a/b/" target="_blank">
</HEAD>
<A HREF="c/foo.html">
```

PARAMETERS

Name		Type	Default	Usage
ctarget	→	VARCHAR2	NULL	Value of the **target** attribute, which establishes a window name to which all links in this document are targeted.
cattribute	→	VARCHAR2	NULL	Contents inserted directly into the <BASE> tag.

GENERATES

```
<BASE HREF="<current URL>" TARGET="ctarget" cattributes>
```

htp.basefont (nsize)

PURPOSE   Used to specify the base font size for a web page.

PARAMETERS

Name		Type	Default	Usage
nsize	→	VARCHAR2		Value of the **size** attribute.

GENERATES

```
<BASEFONT SIZE="nsize"
```

htp.bgsound (csrc, cloop, cattributes)

PURPOSE   Used to include audio for a web page.

PARAMETERS

Name		Type	Default	Usage
csrc	→	VARCHAR2		Value of the **src** attribute.
cloop	→	VARCHAR2	NULL	Value of the **loop** attribute.
cattribute	→	VARCHAR2	NULL	Contents inserted directly into the opening <BGSOUND> tag.

GENERATES

```
<BGSOUND SRC="csrc" LOOP="cloop" attributes>
```

htp.big (ctext, cattributes)

PURPOSE   Used to direct browser to render the text in a bigger font.

PARAMETERS

Name		Type	Default	Usage
ctext	→	VARCHAR2		String to appear between <BIG> and </BIG> tags.
cattributes	→	VARCHAR2	NULL	Contents inserted directly into the opening <BIG> tag.

GENERATES

```
<BIG cattributes>ctext</BIG>
```

htp.blockquoteOpen (cnowrap, cclear, cattributes)

PURPOSE   Used to mark a section of quoted text.

PARAMETERS

Name		Type	Default	Usage
cnowrap	→	VARCHAR2	NULL	If nonnull, the **nowrap** attribute is added to the tag.
cclear	→	VARCHAR2	NULL	Value of the **clear** attribute.
cattributes	→	VARCHAR2	NULL	Contents inserted directly into the <BLOCKQUOTE> tag.

GENERATES

```
<BLOCKQUOTE CLEAR="cclear" NOWRAP cattributes>
```

htp.blockquoteClose

PURPOSE   Used to mark the end of a section of quoted text.

PARAMETERS   None.

GENERATES

```
</BLOCKQUOTE>
```

htp.bodyOpen

PURPOSE   Used to mark the beginning of the body section of an HTML document. If creating a page composed of frames, do not use a body. Use the <NOFRAMES>…</NOFRAMES> block to display the content shown in frame-challenged browsers.

PARAMETERS

Name		Type	Default	Usage
cbackground	→	VARCHAR2	NULL	Value of the **background** attribute, which specifies a graphic file to use for the background of the document.
cattributes	→	VARCHAR2	NULL	Contents inserted directly into the opening <A> tag.

GENERATES

 `<BODY background="cbackground" cattributes>`

htp.bodyClose

PURPOSE   Used to mark the end of the body section of an HTML document.

PARAMETERS   None.

GENERATES

 `</BODY>`

htp.bold (ctext, cattributes)

PURPOSE   Used to direct browser to display the text in boldface.

PARAMETERS

Name		Type	Default	Usage
ctext	→	VARCHAR2	NULL	String to appear between <B> and </B> tags.
cattributes	→	VARCHAR2	NULL	Contents inserted directly into the opening <B> tag.

GENERATES

```
<B cattributes>ctext</B>
```

htp.br

PURPOSE   Generates the </MENU> tag, which ends a list that presents one line per item. The items in the list appear more compact than an unordered list. The htp.listItem defines the list items in a menu list.

PARAMETERS

Name		Type	Default	Usage
cclear	→	VARCHAR2	NULL	Value of the **clear** attribute.
cattributes	→	VARCHAR2	NULL	Contents inserted directly into the opening tag.

GENERATES

```
<BR CLEAR="cclear" cattributes>
```

htp.center (ctext)

PURPOSE   Used to center a section of text within a web page.

PARAMETERS

Name		Type	Default	Usage
ctext	→	VARCHAR2	NULL	String to appear between <CENTER> and </CENTER> tags.

GENERATES

```
<CENTER>ctext</CENTER>
```

htp.centerOpen

PURPOSE   Used to mark the section of text to center.

PARAMETERS   None.

GENERATES

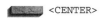 `<CENTER>`

htp.centerClose

PURPOSE   Used to mark the end of a section of text to center.

PARAMETERS   None.

GENERATES

 `</CENTER>`

htp.cite (ctext, cattributes)

PURPOSE   Indicates that the text is a citation and should be rendered appropriately.

PARAMETERS

Name		Type	Default	Usage
ctext	→	VARCHAR2		String to appear between <CITE> and </CITE> tags.
cattributes	→	VARCHAR2	NULL	Contents inserted directly into the opening <CITE> tag.

GENERATES

`<CITE cattributes>ctext</CITE>`

htp.code (ctext, cattributes)

PURPOSE   Indicates that the text is a source code listing and should be rendered appropriately, typically in a monospace font.

PARAMETERS

Name		Type	Default	Usage
ctext	→	VARCHAR2		String to appear between <CODE> and </CODE> tags.

Name	Type	Default	Usage
cattributes →	VARCHAR2	NULL	Contents inserted directly into the opening <CODE> tag.

GENERATES

```
<CODE cattributes>ctext</CODE>
```

htp.comment (ctext)

PURPOSE   Used to embed a comment in a generated page. The text inside the comment will not be visible to the user.

PARAMETERS

Name	Type	Default	Usage
ctext →	VARCHAR2		String to appear between <!— and —> comment boundaries.

GENERATES

```
<!--ctext -->
```

htp.dfn (ctext)

PURPOSE   Indicates that the text is a definition and should be rendered appropriately, most typically in italics.

PARAMETERS

Name	Type	Default	Usage
ctext →	VARCHAR2		String to appear between <DFN> and </DFN> tags.

GENERATES

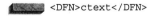

```
<DFN>ctext</DFN>
```

htp.dirlistOpen

PURPOSE   Used to generate tags that indicate the start of a directory list section. A directory list presents a list of items that contain up to 20 characters. Items in this list are typically arranged in columns, usually 24 characters wide. The, <LI> tag generated by htp.listItem must appear directly after this tag is used to define the items in the list.

PARAMETERS   None.

GENERATES

```
<DIR>
```

htp.dirlistClose

PURPOSE   Used to generate tags that close a directory list section.

PARAMETERS   None.

GENERATES

```
</DIR>
```

htp.div (calign, cattributes)

PURPOSE   Used to create document divisions that apply the **align** (and potentially other) attributes to enclosed paragraphs, blockquotes, and so on. To close a document division, it is necessary to call htp.p('</DIV>').

PARAMETERS

Name		Type	Default	Usage
calign	→	VARCHAR2	NULL	Value of the **align** attribute.
cattributes	→	VARCHAR2	NULL	Contents inserted directly into the opening <DIV> tag.

GENERATES

```
<DIV ALIGN="calign" cattributes>
```

htp.dlistOpen (cclear, cattributes)

PURPOSE   Used to create a definition list. A definition list looks like a glossary and contains both terms and definitions. Terms are inserted using htp.dlistTerm, and definitions are inserted using htp.dlistDef.

PARAMETERS

Name		Type	Default	Usage
cclear	→	VARCHAR2	NULL	Value of the **clear** attribute.
cattributes	→	VARCHAR2	NULL	Contents inserted directly into the opening <DL> tag. A common use would be to specify COMPACT, which renders the definition list in a more compact format.

GENERATES

```
<DL CLEAR="cclear" cattributes>
```

htp.dlistClose

PURPOSE   Used to close a definition list.

PARAMETERS   None.

GENERATES

```
</DL>
```

htp.dlistDef (ctext, cclear, cattributes)

PURPOSE   Used to insert definitions of terms. Used in the context of the definition list <DL>, where terms are tagged with <DT> and definitions are tagged with <DD>. Note that the use of a <DD> tag without a corresponding <DT> tag is deprecated in HTML version 3.0.

PARAMETERS

Name		Type	Default	Usage
ctext	→	VARCHAR2		String to appear between <DD> and </DD> tags.
cclear	→	VARCHAR2	NULL	Value of the **clear** attribute.
cattributes	→	VARCHAR2	NULL	Contents inserted directly into the opening <DD> tag.

GENERATES

```
<DD CLEAR="cclear" cattributes>ctext</DD>
```

htp.dlistTerm (ctext, cclear, cattributes)

PURPOSE   Used to define a term in a definition list <DL>.

PARAMETERS

Name		Type	Default	Usage
ctext	→	VARCHAR2		String to appear between <DT> and </DT> tags.
cclear	→	VARCHAR2	NULL	Value of the **clear** attribute.
cattributes	→	VARCHAR2	NULL	Contents inserted directly into the opening <DT> tag.

GENERATES

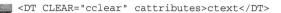

```
<DT CLEAR="cclear" cattributes>ctext</DT>
```

htp.em (ctext, cattributes)

PURPOSE   Used to define text to be emphasized.

PARAMETERS

Name		Type	Default	Usage
ctext	→	VARCHAR2		String to appear between <EM> and </EM> tags.
cattributes	→	VARCHAR2	NULL	Contents inserted directly into the opening <EM> tag.

GENERATES

 `<EM cattributes>ctext</EM>`

htp.emphasis (ctext, cattributes)

PURPOSE   Used to define text to be emphasized.

PARAMETERS

Name		Type	Default	Usage
ctext	→	VARCHAR2		String to appear between <EM> and </EM> tags.
cattributes	→	VARCHAR2	NULL	Contents inserted directly into the opening <EM> tag.

GENERATES

 `<EM cattributes>ctext</EM>`

htp.fontOpen (ccolor, cface, csize, cattributes)

PURPOSE   Used to mark the beginning of a section of text with the specified font characteristics.

PARAMETERS

Name		Type	Default	Usage
ccolor	→	VARCHAR2	NULL	Value of the **color** attribute, specified in the format #RRGGBB where each letter pair is a hexadecimal value between 00 and FF. #000000 is black, while #FFFFFF is white. Alternately, a named color can be used. Standard named colors supported by the HTML 3.2 standard are aqua, black, blue, fuchsia, gray, green, lime, maroon, navy, olive, purple, red, silver, teal, white, and yellow.
cface	→	VARCHAR2	NULL	Value of the **face** attribute. This can be a comma-delimited list of fonts. The first available font in the list will be used.
csize	→	VARCHAR2	NULL	Value of the **size** attribute.
cattributes	→	VARCHAR2	NULL	Contents inserted directly into the opening <FONT> tag.

GENERATES

`<FONT COLOR="ccolor" FACE="cface" SIZE="csize" cattributes>`

htp.fontClose

PURPOSE Used to mark the end of a section of text with font characteristics defined by the balancing <FONT> tag.

PARAMETERS None.

GENERATES

`</FONT>`

htp.formCheckbox (cname, cvalue, cchecked, cattributes)

PURPOSE Used to insert a checkbox element in a form. A checkbox element is a button that the user can toggle on or off.

PARAMETERS

Name		Type	Default	Usage
cname	→	VARCHAR2		Value of the **name** attribute.
cvalue	→	VARCHAR2	ON	Value of the **value** attribute. If the checkbox is checked, on form submission, a name/value pair will be sent to the server where the name is cname and the value is cvalue. If the checkbox is unchecked, no name/value pair will be sent.
cchecked	→	VARCHAR2	NULL	If nonnull, the checked attribute is added to the tag. This indicates that the box should appear checked by default.
cattributes	→	VARCHAR2	NULL	Contents inserted directly into the <INPUT> tag.

GENERATES

`<INPUT TYPE="checkbox" NAME="cname" VALUE="cvalue" CHECKED cattributes>`

htp.formOpen (curl, cmethod, ctarget, cenctype, cattributes)

PURPOSE   Used to create a form section in an HTML document.

PARAMETERS

Name		Type	Default	Usage
curl	→	VARCHAR2		The URL of the WRB cartridge or CGI script to which the contents of the form is sent. This parameter is required.
cmethod	→	VARCHAR2	POST	Value of the **method** attribute. The value can be "GET" or "POST."
ctarget	→	VARCHAR2		Value of the **target** attribute.
cenctype	→	VARCHAR2	NULL	Value of the **enctype** attribute.
cattributes	→	VARCHAR2	NULL	Contents inserted directly into the opening <> tag.

GENERATES

```
<FORM ACTION="curl" METHOD="cmethod" TARGET="ctarget"
ENCTYPE="cenctype" cattributes>
```

htp.formClose

PURPOSE   Used to indicate the end of a form section in an HTML document.

PARAMETERS   None.

GENERATES

```
</FORM>
```

htp.formHidden (cname, cvalue, cattributes)

PURPOSE   Used to insert a hidden form element. This element is not seen by the user and is used to send additional values to the server when the form is submitted.

PARAMETERS

Name		Type	Default	Usage
cname	→	VARCHAR2		Value of the **name** attribute.
cvalue	→	VARCHAR2	ON	Value of the **value** attribute.
cattributes	→	VARCHAR2	NULL	Contents inserted directly into the <INPUT> tag.

GENERATES

```
<INPUT TYPE="hidden" NAME="cname" VALUE="cvalue" cattributes>
```

htp.formImage (cname, csrc, calign, cattributes)

PURPOSE   Used to create an image field on which the user can click and cause the form to be submitted immediately. The coordinates of the selected point are measured in pixels, and are returned (along with other components of the form) in two name/value pairs. The x-coordinate is submitted under the name of the field with ".x" appended, and the y-coordintate with the ".y" appended. Any VALUE attribute is ignored. Also see the OWA_IMAGE package, most particularly the owa_image.point datatype, which is used by the PL/SQL cartridge to handle the passing of an image coordinate.

PARAMETERS

Name		Type	Default	Usage
cname	→	VARCHAR2		Value of the **name** attribute.
csrc	→	VARCHAR2		Value of the **src** attribute, which specifies the URL of the image to be displayed.
calign	→	VARCHAR2	NULL	Value of the **align** attribute.
cattributes	→	VARCHAR2	NULL	Contents inserted directly into the <INPUT> tag.

GENERATES

```
<INPUT TYPE="image" NAME="cname" SRC=csrc" ALIGN="calign"
cattributes>
```

htp.formPassword (cname, csize, cmaxlength, cvalue, cattributes)

PURPOSE   Used to create a single-line text entry field. When the user enters text in the field, each character is represented by one asterisk (*). This is usually used for entering passwords.

PARAMETERS

Name		Type	Default	Usage
cname	→	VARCHAR2		Value of the **name** attribute.
cmaxlength	→	VARCHAR2	NULL	Value of the **maxlength** attribute.
cvalue	→	VARCHAR2	NULL	Value of the **value** attribute.
csize	→	VARCHAR2		Value of the **size** attribute.
cattributes	→	VARCHAR2	NULL	Contents inserted directly into the <INPUT> tag.

GENERATES

```
<INPUT TYPE="password" NAME="cname" SIZE="csize"
MAXLENGTH="cmaxlength" VALUE="cvalue">
```

htp.formRadio (cname, cvalue, cchecked, cattributes)

PURPOSE   Used to create a radio button on the HTML form. Sets of radio buttons are created by adding to a form multiple radio buttons that share the same **name** attribute. The **value** attribute of the selected radio button will be sent to the server when the form is submitted.

PARAMETERS

Name		Type	Default	Usage
cname	→	VARCHAR2		Value of the **name** attribute.
cvalue	→	VARCHAR2		Value of the **value** attribute.
cchecked	→	VARCHAR2	NULL	If nonnull, the **checked** attribute is added to the tag.
cattributes	→	VARCHAR2	NULL	Contents inserted directly into the <INPUT> tag.

GENERATES

```
<INPUT TYPE="radio" NAME="cname" VALUE="cvalue" CHECKED cattributes>
```

htp.formReset (cvalue, cattributes)

PURPOSE   Used to create a button that, when clicked, resets all the form fields to their initial values.

PARAMETERS

Name		Type	Default	Usage
cvalue	→	VARCHAR2	RESET	Value of the **value** attribute.
cattributes	→	VARCHAR2	NULL	Contents inserted directly into the opening <> tag.

GENERATES

```
<INPUT TYPE="reset" VALUE="cvalue" cattributes>
```

htp.formSelectOpen (cname, cprompt, nsize, cattributes)

PURPOSE   Used to create a select form element. A select form element is a list box, from which the user can select one or more values. The values are inserted using htp.formSelectOption.

PARAMETERS

Name		Type	Default	Usage
cname	→	VARCHAR2		Value of the **name** attribute.
cprompt	→	VARCHAR2	NULL	The string preceding the list box.
nsize	→	VARCHAR2	NULL	Value of the **size** attribute. If not specified or not set to 1, the list will appear as a pop-up or drop-down menu, otherwise it will appear as a scrolling list box.
cattributes	→	VARCHAR2	NULL	Contents inserted directly into the <SELECT> tag. Most commonly, this will be left blank or set to MULTIPLE, if a multiple choice selection can be made. Note that if the **size** attribute is 1, MULTIPLE will be ignored.

GENERATES

 `<OPTION SELECTED cattributes>cvalue`

htp.formSelectClose

PURPOSE   Used to mark the end of a Select form element.

PARAMETERS   None.

GENERATES

 `<OPTION SELECTED cattributes>cvalue`

htp.formSubmit (cname, cvalue, cattributes)

PURPOSE   Used to create a button that, when clicked, submits the form's contents to the server.

PARAMETERS

Name		Type	Default	Usage
cname	→	VARCHAR2	NULL	Value of the **name** attribute. If nonnull, an additional name/value pair will be submitted for the button. This is useful if there are multiple submit actions (e.g., UPDATE or DELETE).
cvalue	→	VARCHAR2	SUBMIT	Value of the **value** attribute. This is the value sent in the name/value pair if the **name** attribute is present. Regardless, it is the label displayed on the button.
cattributes	→	VARCHAR2	NULL	Contents inserted directly into the <INPUT> tag.

GENERATES

`<INPUT TYPE="submit" NAME="cname" VALUE="cvalue" cattributes>`

htp.formText (cname, csize, cmaxlength, cvalue, cattributes)

PURPOSE   Used to create a field for a single line of text.

PARAMETERS

Name		Type	Default	Usage
cname	→	VARCHAR2		Value of the **name** attribute.
csize	→	VARCHAR2	NULL	Value of the **size** attribute.
cmaxlength	→	VARCHAR2	NULL	Value of the **maxlength** attribute.
cvalue	→	VARCHAR2	NULL	Value of the **value** attribute.
cattributes	→	VARCHAR2	NULL	Contents inserted directly into the \<INPUT> tag.

GENERATES

```
<INPUT TYPE="text" NAME="cname" SIZE="csize" MAXLENGTH="cmaxlength"
VALUE="cvalue" cattributes>
```

htp.formTextarea (cname, nrows, ncolumns, calign, cattributes)

PURPOSE   Used to create a text field that has no predefined text in the text area. This field is used to enable the user to enter several lines of text.

PARAMETERS

Name		Type	Default	Usage
cname	→	VARCHAR2		Value of the **name** attribute.
nrows	→	INTEGER		Value of the **rows** attribute.
ncolumns	→	INTEGER		Value of the **columns** attribute.
calign	→	VARCHAR2	NULL	Value of the **align** attribute.
cattributes	→	VARCHAR2	NULL	Contents inserted directly into the opening \<TEXTAREA> tag.

GENERATES

```
<TEXTAREA NAME="cname" ROWS="nrows" COLS="ncolumns" ALIGN="calign"
cattributes></TEXTAREA>
```

htp.formTextarea2 (cname, nrows, ncolumns, calign, cwrap, cattributes)

PURPOSE   This is similar to htp.formTextarea, although Textarea2 has the cwrap parameter, which specifies a wrap style.

PARAMETERS

Name		Type	Default	Usage
cname	→	VARCHAR2		Value of the **name** attribute.
nrows	→	INTEGER		Value of the **rows** attribute.
ncolumns	→	INTEGER		Value of the **columns** attribute.
calign	→	VARCHAR2	NULL	Value of the **align** attribute.
cwrap	→	VARCHAR2	NULL	Value of the **wrap** attribute. This can be one of: OFF, indicating no wrapping (the default); SOFT, which will wrap text on screen but will not add the hard line breaks when submitting the form; or HARD, which will wrap on screen *and* add the line breaks when submitting the form.
cattributes	→	VARCHAR2	NULL	Contents inserted directly into the opening <TEXTAREA> tag.

GENERATES

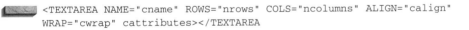

```
<TEXTAREA NAME="cname" ROWS="nrows" COLS="ncolumns" ALIGN="calign"
WRAP="cwrap" cattributes></TEXTAREA
```

htp.formTextareaOpen (cname, nrows, ncolumns, calign, cattributes)

PURPOSE   Used to create a text area form element.

PARAMETERS

Name		Type	Default	Usage
cname	→	VARCHAR2		Value of the **name** attribute.
nrows	→	INTEGER		Value of the **rows** attribute.
ncolumns	→	INTEGER		Value of the **columns** attribute.

Name		Type	Default	Usage
calign	→	VARCHAR2	NULL	Value of the **align** attribute.
cwrap	→	VARCHAR2	NULL	Value of the **wrap** attribute. This can be one of: OFF, indicating no wrapping (the default); SOFT, which will wrap text on screen but will not add the hard line breaks when submitting the form; or HARD, which will wrap on screen *and* add the line breaks when submitting the form.
cattributes	→	VARCHAR2	NULL	Contents inserted directly into the opening <TEXTAREA> tag.

GENERATES

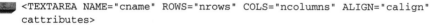

```
<TEXTAREA NAME="cname" ROWS="nrows" COLS="ncolumns" ALIGN="calign"
cattributes>
```

htp.formTextareaOpen2 (cname, nrows, ncolumns, calign, cwrap, cattributes)

PURPOSE   Has the cwrap parameter, which specifies a wrap style.

PARAMETERS

Name		Type	Default	Usage
cname	→	VARCHAR2		Value of the **name** attribute.
nrows	→	INTEGER		Value of the **rows** attribute.
ncolumns	→	INTEGER		Value of the **columns** attribute.
calign	→	VARCHAR2	NULL	Value of the **align** attribute.
cwrap	→	VARCHAR2	NULL	Value of the **wrap** attribute.
cattributes	→	VARCHAR2	NULL	Contents inserted directly into the opening <TEXTAREA> tag.

GENERATES

```
<TEXTAREA NAME="cname" ROWS="nrows" COLS="ncolumns" ALIGN="calign"
WRAP="cwrap" cattributes>
```

htp.formTextareaClose

PURPOSE   Used to mark the end of a text area form element.

PARAMETERS   None.

GENERATES

```
</TEXTAREA>
```

htp.frame

PURPOSE   Used to define the characteristics of a frame created by <FRAMESET> tag.

PARAMETERS

Name		Type	Default	Usage
csrc	→	VARCHAR2		URL to display in the frame.
cname	→	VARCHAR2	NULL	Value of the **name** attribute.
cmarginwidth	→	VARCHAR2	NULL	Value of the **marginwidth** attribute.
cmarginheight	→	VARCHAR2	NULL	Value of the **marginheight** attribute.
cscrolling	→	VARCHAR2	NULL	Value of the **scrolling** attribute.
noresize	→	VARCHAR2	NULL	If nonnull, the **noresize** attribute is added to the tag.
cattributes	→	VARCHAR2	NULL	Contents inserted directly into the opening <FRAME> tag.

GENERATES

```
<FRAME SRC="csrc" NAME="cname" MARGINWIDTH="cmarginwidth"
MARGINHEIGHT="cmarginheight">
```

htp.framesetOpen (crows, ccols, cattributes)

PURPOSE   Used to define a frameset section.

PARAMETERS

Name		Type	Default	Usage
crows	→	VARCHAR2	NULL	Value of the **rows** attribute.
ccols	→	VARCHAR2	NULL	Value of the **cols** attribute.
cattributes	→	VARCHAR2	NULL	Contents inserted directly into the opening <FRAMESET> tag.

GENERATES

```
<FRAMESET ROWS="nrows" COLS="ccols">
```

htp.framesetClose

PURPOSE   Used to mark the end of a frameset section.

PARAMETERS   None.

GENERATES

```
</FRAMESET>
```

htp.headOpen

PURPOSE   Used to mark the HTML head section.

PARAMETERS   None.

GENERATES

```
<HEAD>
```

htp.headClose

PURPOSE   Used to mark the close of the HTML head section.

PARAMETERS   None.

GENERATES

```
</HEAD>
```

htp.header

PURPOSE   Used to generate opening heading tags and corresponding closing tags.

PARAMETERS

Name		Type	Default	Usage
nsize	→	INTEGER		Value of the **size** attribute.
cheader	→	VARCHAR2	NULL	Text to display in the heading.
calign	→	VARCHAR2	NULL	Value of the **align** attribute.
cnowrap	→	VARCHAR2	NULL	Value of the **nowrap** attribute.
cclear	→	VARCHAR2	NULL	Value of the **clear** attribute.
cattributes	→	VARCHAR2	NULL	Contents inserted directly into the opening <H*n*> tag.

GENERATES

```
<Hnsize ALIGN="calign" NOWRAP CLEAR="cclear" cattributes>cheader</Hnsize>
```

htp.hr (cclear, csrc, cattributes)

PURPOSE   Generates the <HR> tag, which generates a line in the HTML document.

PARAMETERS

Name		Type	Default	Usage
cclear	→	VARCHAR2	NULL	Value of the **clear** attribute.
csrc	→	VARCHAR2	NULL	Value of the **src** attribute, which specifies a custom image as the source of the line.
cattributes	→	VARCHAR2	NULL	Contents inserted directly into the opening tag.

GENERATES

```
HR CLEAR="cclear" SRC="csrc" cattributes>
```

htp.htmlOpen

PURPOSE   Generates tags that mark the beginning of an HTML document.

PARAMETERS   None.

GENERATES

`<HTML>`

htp.htmlClose

PURPOSE   Generates tags that mark the end of an HTML document.

PARAMETERS   None.

GENERATES

`</HTML>`

htp.img2 (curl, calign, calt, cismap, cattributes)

PURPOSE   Used to direct browser to load an image onto the HTML page, which can use a client-side image map specified in the cusemap parameter. See the htp.map function.

PARAMETERS

Name		Type	Default	Usage
curl	→	VARCHAR2	NULL	Value of the **src** attribute.
calign	→	VARCHAR2	NULL	Value of the **align** attribute.
calt	→	VARCHAR2	NULL	Value of the **alt** attribute, which specifies alternative text to display if the browser does not support images.
cismap	→	VARCHAR2	NULL	Value of the **usemap** attribute, which specifies the name of the client-side image map to use.
cusemap	→	VARCHAR2	NULL	If nonnull, the **ismap** attribute is added to the tag. The attribute indicates that the image is an image map.
cattributes	→	VARCHAR2	NULL	Contents inserted directly into the <IMG> tag.

GENERATES

```
<IMG SRC="curl" ALIGN="calign" ALT="calt" ISMAP USEMAP="cusemap"
cattributes>
```

htp.img (curl, calign, calt, cismap, cattributes)

PURPOSE   Used to direct browser to load an image onto the HTML page.

PARAMETERS

Name		Type	Default	Usage
curl	→	VARCHAR2	NULL	Value of the **src** attribute.
calign	→	VARCHAR2	NULL	Value of the **align** attribute.
calt	→	VARCHAR2	NULL	Value of the **alt** attribute, which specifies alternative text to display if the browser does not support images.
cismap	→	VARCHAR2	NULL	If nonnull, the **ismap** attribute is added to the tag. The attribute indicates that the image is an image map.
cattributes	→	VARCHAR2	NULL	Contents inserted directly into the <IMG> tag.

GENERATES

```
<IMG SRC="curl" ALIGN="calign" ALT="calt" ISMAP cattributes>
```

htp.isindex (cprompt, curl)

PURPOSE   Used to create a single entry field with a prompting text, such as "enter value", and then sends that value to the URL on the page or program.

PARAMETERS

Name		Type	Default	Usage
cprompt	→	VARCHAR2	NULL	Value of the **prompt** attribute.
curl	→	VARCHAR2	NULL	Value of the **src** attribute.

GENERATES

```
<ISINDEX PROMPT="cprompt" HREF="curl">
```

htp.italic (ctext, cattributes)

PURPOSE   Used to direct the browser to render the section in italics.

PARAMETERS

Name		Type	Default	Usage
ctext	→	VARCHAR2		The text to be rendered in italics.
cattributes	→	VARCHAR2	NULL	Contents inserted directly into the opening <I> tag.

GENERATES

```
<I cattributes>ctext</I>
```

htp.kbd

PURPOSE   This subprogram does the same thing as htp.keyboard.

PARAMETERS

Name		Type	Default	Usage
ctext	→	VARCHAR2		The text to be rendered in monospace.
cattributes	→	VARCHAR2	NULL	Contents inserted directly into the opening <KBD> tag.

GENERATES

```
<KBD cattributes>ctext</KBD>
```

htp.keyboard (ctext, cattributes)

PURPOSE   Used to direct the browser to render the text in monospace.

PARAMETERS

Name		Type	Default	Usage
ctext	→	VARCHAR2		The text to be rendered in monospace.
cattributes	→	VARCHAR2	NULL	Contents inserted directly into the opening <KBD> tag.

GENERATES

 `<KBD cattributes>ctext</KBD>`

htp.line (cclear, csrc, cattributes)

PURPOSE   Generates the <HR> tag, which generates a line in the HTML document.

PARAMETERS

Name		Type	Default	Usage
cclear	→	VARCHAR2	NULL	Value of the **clear** attribute.
csrc	→	VARCHAR2	NULL	Value of the **src** attribute, which specifies a custom image as the source of the line.
cattributes	→	VARCHAR2	NULL	Contents inserted directly into the opening <HR> tag. Most commonly, the **width** or **align** attributes are specified. The **width** attribute can be specified either in absolute units or as a percentage of the current page or frame width.

GENERATES

 `HR CLEAR="cclear" SRC="csrc" cattributes>`

htp.linkRel (crel, curl, ctitle)

PURPOSE   Generates the <LINK> tag with the **rel** attribute, which specifies that the document referenced by the **href** document has the relationship with the current document described by the **rev** attribute. This is only used when the **href** attribute is present. This tag indicates a relationship between documents, but does not create a link. To create a link, use htp.anchor or htp.anchor2. Defined relationship links could be used by future browsers to build intelligent custom toolbars for a document, in which case the title **attribute** would specify the button label. They could also be used by search engines and other systems that make use of content.

PARAMETERS

Name		Type	Default	Usage
crel	→	VARCHAR2		Value of the **rel** attribute.
curl	→	VARCHAR2		Value of the **href** attribute.
ctitle	→	VARCHAR2	NULL	Value of the **title** attribute.

GENERATES

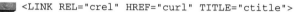
```
<LINK REL="crel" HREF="curl" TITLE="ctitle">
```

htp.linkRev (crev, curl, ctitle)

PURPOSE   Generates the <LINK> tag with the **rev** attribute, which specifies that the current document has the relationship with the document referenced by the **href** document specified by the **rev** attribute. This is only used when the **href** attribute is present. This tag indicates a relationship between documents, but does not create a link. It generates the <LINK> tag with the REV attribute, which gives the relationship described by the hypertext link from the target to the anchor. This is the opposite of htp.linkRel. This tag also indicates a relationship between documents, without creating a link.To create a link, use htp.anchor or htp.anchor2.

PARAMETERS

Name		Type	Default	Usage
crel	→	VARCHAR2		Value of the **rel** attribute.
curl	→	VARCHAR2		Value of the **href** attribute.
ctitle	→	VARCHAR2	NULL	Value of the **title** attribute.

GENERATES

```
<LINK REV="crev" HREF="curl" TITLE="ctitle">
```

htp.listHeader (ctext, cattributes)

PURPOSE   Generates the <LH> and </LH> tags, which print an HTML tag at the beginning of the list. Note that most browsers do not support this tag. However, if and when it becomes widely supported, the <LH> tag should appear after the opening <DL>, <OL>, or <UL> tag and before the first <LI> or <DT> tag within the list.

PARAMETERS

Name		Type	Default	Usage
ctext	→	VARCHAR2		The text to be placed between \<LH\> and \</LH\>.
cattributes	→	VARCHAR2	NULL	Contents inserted directly into the opening \<LH\> tag.

GENERATES

 `<LH cattributes>ctext</LH>`

htp.listingOpen

PURPOSE   Generates the tags that mark the beginning of a section of fixed-width text in the body of an HTML page.

PARAMETERS   None.

GENERATES

 `<LISTING>`

htp.listingClose

PURPOSE   Generates the tags that mark the end of a section of fixed-width text in the body of an HTML page.

PARAMETERS   None.

GENERATES

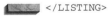 `</LISTING>`

htp.listItem (ctext, cclear, cdingbat, csrc, cattributes)

PURPOSE   Generates the \<LI\> tag, which indicates a list item.

PARAMETERS

Name		Type	Default	Usage
ctext	→	VARCHAR2	NULL	The text for the list item.
cclear	→	VARCHAR2	NULL	Value of the **clear** attribute.
cdingbat	→	VARCHAR2	NULL	Value of the **dingbat** attribute.
csrc	→	VARCHAR2	NULL	Value of the **src** attribute.
cattributes	→	VARCHAR2	NULL	Contents inserted directly into the opening <LI> tag.

GENERATES

```
<LI CLEAR="ccl;ear" DINGBAT="cdingbat" SRC="csrc" cattributes>ctext
```

htp.mailto (caddress, ctext, cname, cattributes)

PURPOSE   Generates the <A> tag with the HREF set to "mailto" prepended to the mail address argument.

PARAMETERS

Name		Type	Default	Usage
caddress	→	VARCHAR2		E-mail address of recipient.
ctext	→	VARCHAR2		The clickable portion of the link. Usually the name of the recipient.
cname	→	VARCHAR2		Value for the **name** attribute.
cattributes	→	VARCHAR2	NULL	Contents inserted directly into the opening <A> tag.

GENERATES

```
<A HREF="mailto:caddress" cattributes>ctext</A>
```

htp.mapOpen (cname, cattributes)

PURPOSE   Generates the <MAP> tag, which marks the beginning of a client-side image map. See the htp.area procedure for specifying regions within the map.

PARAMETERS

Name		Type	Default	Usage
cname	→	VARCHAR2		Value of the **name** attribute.
cattributes	→	VARCHAR2	NULL	Contents inserted directly into the opening <MAP> tag.

GENERATES

```
<MAP NAME="cname" cattributes>
```

htp.mapClose

PURPOSE   Generates the </MAP> tag, which marks the end of a client-side image map.

PARAMETERS   None.

GENERATES

```
</MAP>
```

htp.menulistOpen

PURPOSE   Generates the <MENU> tag, which creates a list that presents one line per item. The items in the list appear more compact than an unordered list. The htp.listItem defines the list items in a menu list.

PARAMETERS   None.

GENERATES

```
<MENU>
```

htp.menulistClose

PURPOSE   Generates the </MENU> tag, which ends a menu list.

PARAMETERS   None.

GENERATES

 `</MENU>`

htp.meta (chttp_equiv, cname, ccontent)

PURPOSE   Generates the <META> tag, which enables you to imbed meta-information about the document and also specify values for HTTP headers. For example, you can specify the expiration date, keyword, and author name.

PARAMETERS

Name		Type	Default	Usage
chttp_equiv	→	VARCHAR2		Value of the **http_equiv** attribute.
cname	→	VARCHAR2		Value of the **name** attribute.
ccontent	→	VARCHAR2		Value of the **content** attribute.

GENERATES

 `<META HTTP-EQUIV="chttp_equiv" NAME ="cname" CONTENT="ccontent">`

htp.nl

PURPOSE   Generates the <BR> tag, which begins a new line of text.

PARAMETERS

Name		Type	Default	Usage
cclear	→	VARCHAR2	NULL	Value of the **clear** attribute.
cattributes	→	VARCHAR2	NULL	Contents inserted directly into the opening tag.

GENERATES

 `<BR CLEAR="cclear" cattributes>`

htp.nobr

PURPOSE   Generates the <NOBR> and </NOBR> tags, which turn off line-breaking in a section of text.

PARAMETERS

Name		Type	Default	Usage
ctext	→	VARCHAR2		The text that is to be rendered on one line.

GENERATES

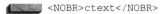

```
<NOBR>ctext</NOBR>
```

htp.noframesOpen

PURPOSE   Generates the <NOFRAMES> tag , which marks the beginning of a no-frames section.

PARAMETERS   None.

GENERATES

```
<NOFRAMES>
```

htp.noframesClose

PURPOSE   Generates the </NOFRAMES> tag , which marks the end of a no-frames section.

PARAMETERS   None.

GENERATES

```
</NOFRAMES>
```

htp.olistOpen (cclear,cwrap, cattributes)

PURPOSE   Generates the <OL> tag, which defines the beginning of an ordered list. An ordered list presents a list of numbered items. The numbered items are added using htp.list.Item.

PARAMETERS

Name		Type	Default	Usage
cclear	→	VARCHAR2	NULL	Value of the **clear** attribute.
cwrap	→	VARCHAR2	NULL	Value of the **wrap** attribute.
cattributes	→	VARCHAR2	NULL	Contents inserted directly into the opening <OL> tag.

GENERATES

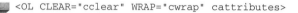

```
<OL CLEAR="cclear" WRAP="cwrap" cattributes>
```

htp.olistClose

PURPOSE Generates the </OL> tag, which defines the end of an ordered list. An ordered list presents a list of numbered items. The numbered items are added using htp.list.Item.

PARAMETERS None.

GENERATES

```
</OL>
```

htp.para

PURPOSE Generates the <P> tag, which indicates that the text after the tag is to be formatted as a paragraph. Use htp.paragraph for setting attributes of the <P> tag.

PARAMETERS None.

GENERATES

```
<P>
```

htp.paragraph (calign, cnowrap, cclear, cattributes)

PURPOSE Generates the <P> tag, which indicates that the text after the tag is to be formatted as a paragraph. The htp.paragraph procedure enables you to add attributes to the tag.

PARAMETERS

Name		Type	Default	Usage
calign	$\rightarrow$	VARCHAR2	NULL	Value of the **align** attribute.
cnowrap	$\rightarrow$	VARCHAR2	NULL	If nonnull, the **nowrap** attribute is added to the tag.
cclear	$\rightarrow$	VARCHAR2	NULL	Value of the **clear** attribute.
cattributes	$\rightarrow$	VARCHAR2	NULL	Contents inserted directly into the opening <P> tag.

GENERATES

```
<P ALIGN="calign" NOWRAP CLEAR="cclear" cattributes>
```

htp.param

PURPOSE Generates <PARAM> tag, which specifies parameters for Java applets. The values can reference HTML variables. To invoke a Java applet from a page, use htp.appletopen to begin the invocation, use one htp.param for each desired name/value pair, and use htp.appletclose to end the applet invocation.

PARAMETERS

Name		Type	Default	Usage
cname	$\rightarrow$	VARCHAR2		Value of the **name** attribute.
cvalue	$\rightarrow$	INTEGER		Value of the **value** attribute.

GENERATES

```
<PARAM NAME="cname" VALUE="cvalue">
```

htp.plaintext (ctext, cattributes)

PURPOSE Generates tags that direct the browser to render the text they surround in fixed-width type.

PARAMETERS

Name		Type	Default	Usage
ctext	→	VARCHAR2		The text to be rendered in fixed-width font.
cattributes	→	VARCHAR2	NULL	Contents inserted directly into the opening <PLAINTEXT> tag.

GENERATES

```
<PLAINTEXT cattributes>ctext</PLAINTEXT>
```

htp.preOpen (cclear, cwidth, cattributes)

PURPOSE   Generates the <PRE> tag, which marks the beginning of preformatted text in the body of the HTML page.

PARAMETERS

Name		Type	Default	Usage
cclear	→	VARCHAR2	NULL	Value of the **clear** attribute.
cwidth	→	VARCHAR2	NULL	Value of the **width** attribute.
cattributes	→	VARCHAR2	NULL	Contents inserted directly into the opening <PRE> tag.

GENERATES

```
<PRE CLEAR="cclear" WIDTH="cwidth" cattributes>
```

htp.preClose

PURPOSE   Generates the </PRE> tag, which marks the end of preformatted text in the body of the HTML page.

PARAMETERS   None.

GENERATES

```
</PRE>
```

htp.print (cbuf | dbuf | nbuf)

PURPOSE   This procedure generates the specified parameter as a string terminated with a newline character. Notice that it is overloaded and accepts a single parameter that is a DATE, a VARCHAR2, or a NUMBER.

PARAMETERS

Name		Type	Default	Usage
cbuf or dbuf or nbuf	→	VARCHAR2 or DATE or NUMBER		The item to convert to a string (if necessary) and output.

GENERATES   Generates the string representation of the parameter terminated by a newline character.

htp.prints(ctext), htp.ps(ctext)

PURPOSE   Generates a string and replace all occurrences of the following characters with the corresponding escape sequence. Note that although htp.prints is not overloaded like htp.p, PL/SQL will perform automatic conversions of most datatypes into VARCHAR2.

Replaces this character	With this escape sequence
<	<
>	>
"	"
&	&
%	%25 (%is a wildcard in SQL)

PARAMETERS

Name		Type	Default	Usage
ctext	→	VARCHAR2		The string on which to perform escape substitutions and output.

GENERATES   htp.prints generates an HTML-escaped string.

htp.prn (cbuf | dbuf | nbuf)

PURPOSE   This procedure generates the specified parameter as a string, but, unlike htp.print, it is not terminated with a newline character. This is useful if making multiple calls to build a single line of preformatted text. Notice that it is overloaded and accepts a single parameter, which is a DATE, a VARCHAR2, or a NUMBER.

PARAMETERS

Name		Type	Default	Usage
cbuf or dbuf or nbuf	→	VARCHAR2 or DATE or NUMBER		The item to convert to a string (if necessary) and output.

GENERATES   Generates the string representation of the parameter.

htp.s (ctext, cattributes)

PURPOSE   Generates the <S> and </S> tags, which direct the browser to render the text they surround in strikethrough type.

PARAMETERS

Name		Type	Default	Usage
ctext	→	VARCHAR2		The text to render in strikethrough type.
cattributes	→	VARCHAR2	NULL	Contents inserted directly into the opening <S> TAG.

GENERATES

```
<S cattributes>ctext</S>
```

htp.sample

PURPOSE   Generates the <SAMP> and </SAMP> tags, which direct the browser to render the text they surround in monospace font.

PARAMETERS

Name		Type	Default	Usage
ctext	→	VARCHAR2		The text to render in monospace font.
cattributes	→	VARCHAR2	NULL	Contents inserted directly into the opening <SAMP> tag.

GENERATES

```
<SAMP cattributes>ctext</SAMP>
```

htp.script (cscript, clanguage)

PURPOSE   Generates the tags that contain a script written in languages such as JavaScript and VBscript.

PARAMETERS

Name		Type	Default	Usage
cscript	→	VARCHAR2		Text that makes up the script itself, not the name of a file containing the script.
clanguage	→	VARCHAR2	NULL	Language in which script is written. If this parameter is omitted, the user's browser determines the scripting language.

GENERATES

```
<SCRIPT LANGUGE=clanguage>cscript</SCRIPT>
```

htp.small (ctext, cattributes)

PURPOSE   Inserts tags that direct browser to render the text they surround using small font.

PARAMETERS

Name		Type	Default	Usage
ctext	→	VARCHAR2		The text to render in a small font.
cattributes	→	VARCHAR2	NULL	Contents inserted directly into the opening <SMALL> tag.

GENERATES

```
<SMALL cattributes>ctext</SMALL>
```

htp.strike (ctext, cattributes)

PURPOSE   Used to direct browser to render the text in strikethrough type.

PARAMETERS

Name		Type	Default	Usage
ctext	→	VARCHAR2		The text to render in a strikethrough type.
cattributes	→	VARCHAR2	NULL	Contents inserted directly into the opening <STRIKE> tag.

GENERATES

```
<STRIKE cattributes>ctext</STRIKE>
```

htp.strong (ctext, cattributes)

PURPOSE   Used to direct browser to render the text in bold.

PARAMETERS

Name		Type	Default	Usage
ctext	→	VARCHAR2		The text to render in a bold font.
cattributes	→	VARCHAR2	NULL	Contents inserted directly into the opening <STRONG> tag.

GENERATES

```
<STRONG cattributes>ctext</STRONG>
```

htp.style (cstyle)

PURPOSE   Used to generate tags, which include a style sheet in your web page. Style sheets are a feature of HTML 3.2. More information about style sheets is available at http://www.w3.org. This feature is generally not compatible with browsers that support only HTML versions 2.0 or earlier. Such browsers will ignore this tag.

PARAMETERS

Name		Type	Default	Usage
cstyle	→	VARCHAR2		The style information to include.

GENERATES

 `<STYLE>cstyle</STYLE>`

htp.sub (ctext, calign, cattributes)

PURPOSE   Used to direct the browser to render the text as subscript.

PARAMETERS

Name		Type	Default	Usage
ctext	→	VARCHAR2		The text to render in subscript.
calign	→	VARCHAR2	NULL	Value for the **align** attribute.
cattributes	→	VARCHAR2	NULL	Contents inserted directly into the opening <SUB> tag.

GENERATES

 `<SUB ALIGN="calign" cattributes>ctext</SUB>`

htp.sup (ctext,calign, cattributes)

PURPOSE   Used to direct the browser to render the text as superscript.

PARAMETERS

Name		Type	Default	Usage
ctext	→	VARCHAR2		The text to render in superscript.
calign	→	VARCHAR2	NULL	Value for the **align** attribute.
cattributes	→	VARCHAR2	NULL	Contents inserted directly into the opening <SUP> tag.

GENERATES

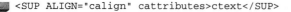

```
<SUP ALIGN="calign" cattributes>ctext</SUP>
```

htp.tableCaption (ccaption, calign, cattributes)

PURPOSE   Used to place a caption in an HTML table.

PARAMETERS

Name		Type	Default	Usage
ccaption	→	VARCHAR2		The text for the caption.
calign	→	VARCHAR2	NULL	Value for the **align** attribute.
cattributes	→	VARCHAR2	NULL	Contents inserted directly into the opening <SUB> TAG.

GENERATES

```
<CAPTION ALIGN="calign" cattributes>ccaption</CAPTION>
```

htp.tableData (cvalue, calign, cdp, cnowrap, crowspan, ccolspan, cattributes)

PURPOSE   Used to insert data into a cell of an HTML table.

PARAMETERS

Name		Type	Default	Usage
cvalue	→	VARCHAR2	NULL	The text to render in subscript.
calign	→	VARCHAR2	NULL	Value for the **align** attribute.
cdp	→	VARCHAR2	NULL	Value for the **dp** attribute.
cnowrap	→	VARCHAR2	NULL	If nonnull, the **nowrap** attribute is added to the tag.
crowspan	→	VARCHAR2	NULL	Value for the **rowspan** attribute.
ccolspan	→	VARCHAR2	NULL	Value for the **colspan** attribute.
cattributes	→	VARCHAR2	NULL	Contents inserted directly into the opening <TD> tag.

GENERATES

```
<TD ALIGN="calign" DP="cdp" ROWSPAN="crowspan" COLSPAN="ccolspan" NOWRAP
cattributes>
```

htp.tableHeader (cvalue, calign, cdp, cnowrap, crowspan, ccolspan, cattributes)

PURPOSE   Used to insert a header cell in an HTML table. <TH>s are simailar to <TD>s except that the text in rows are usually rendered in bold type.

PARAMETERS

Name		Type	Default	Usage
cvalue	→	VARCHAR2	NULL	The text to render in subscript.
calign	→	VARCHAR2	NULL	Value for the **align** attribute.
cdp	→	VARCHAR2	NULL	Value for the **dp** attribute.
cnowrap	→	VARCHAR2	NULL	If nonnull, the **nowrap** attribute is added to the tag.
crowspan	→	VARCHAR2	NULL	Value for the **rowspan** attribute.
ccolspan	→	VARCHAR2	NULL	Value for the **colspan** attribute.
cattributes	→	VARCHAR2	NULL	Contents inserted directly into the opening <TD> tag.

GENERATES

```
<TH ALIGN="calign" DP="cdp" ROWSPAN="crowspan" COLSPAN="ccolspan" NOWRAP
cattributes>
```

htp.tableOpen

PURPOSE   Defines the beginning of an HTML table.

PARAMETERS

Name		Type	Default	Usage
cborder	→	VARCHAR2	NULL	Value for the **border** attribute.
calign	→	VARCHAR2	NULL	Value for the **align** attribute.
cnowrap	→	VARCHAR2	NULL	If nonnull, the nowrap attribute is added to the tag.
cclear	→	VARCHAR2	NULL	Value for the **clear** attribute.
cattributes	→	VARCHAR2	NULL	Contents inserted directly into the opening <TABLE> tag.

GENERATES

 `<TABLE "cborder" NOWRAP ALIGN="calign" CLEAR="cclear" cattributes>`

htp.tableClose

PURPOSE   Defines the end of an HTML table.

PARAMETERS   None.

GENERATES

 `</TABLE>`

htp.tableRowOpen (calign, cvalign, cdp, cnowrap, cattributes)

PURPOSE   Used to insert a new row in an HTML table.

PARAMETERS

Name		Type	Default	Usage
calign	→	VARCHAR2	NULL	Value for the **align** attribute.
cvalign	→	VARCHAR2	NULL	Value for the **valign** attribute.
cdp	→	VARCHAR2	NULL	Value for the **dp** attribute.
cnowrap	→	VARCHAR2	NULL	If nonnull, the **nowrap** attribute is added to the tag.
cattributes	→	VARCHAR2	NULL	Contents inserted directly into the opening <TR> tag.

GENERATES

`<TR ALIGN="calign" VALIGN="cvalign" DP="cdp" NOWRAP cattributes>`

htp.tableRowClose

PURPOSE   Used to close a row in an HTML table.

PARAMETERS   None.

GENERATES

 `</TR>`

htp.teletype (ctext, cattributes)

PURPOSE   Used to direct the browser to render the text in a fixed width typewriter font—for example, the Courier font.

PARAMETERS

Name		Type	Default	Usage
ctext	$\rightarrow$	VARCHAR2		The text to render in a fixed-width typewriter font.
cattributes	$\rightarrow$	VARCHAR2	NULL	Contents inserted directly into the opening <TT> tag.

GENERATES

 `<TT cattributes>ctext</TT>`

htp.title

PURPOSE   Used to specify the title of the document, which will be displayed in the title bar of the browser window. The title should be specified between calls to the htp.headOpen and htp.headClose.

PARAMETERS

Name		Type	Default	Usage
ctitle	$\rightarrow$	VARCHAR2		The text to display in the title bar of the browser window.

GENERATES

 `<TITLE>ctitle</TITLE>`

htp.ulistOpen (cclear, calign, cdingbat, csrc, cattributes)

PURPOSE   Used to define an unordered list. An unordered list presents listed items marked off by bullets. Items are added with htp.listItem.

PARAMETERS

Name		Type	Default	Usage
cclear	→	VARCHAR2	NULL	Value for the **clear** attribute.
calign	→	VARCHAR2	NULL	Value for the **wrap** attribute.
cdingbat	→	VARCHAR2	NULL	Value for the **dingbat** attribute.
csrc	→	VARCHAR2	NULL	Value for the **src** attribute.
cattributes	→	VARCHAR2	NULL	Contents inserted directly into the <UL> tag.

GENERATES

```
<UL CLEAR="cclear" WRAP="cwrap" DINGBAT="cdingbat" SRC="csrc" cattributes>
```

htp.ulistClose

PURPOSE   Used to define the end of an unordered list.

PARAMETERS   None.

GENERATES

```
</UL>
```

htp.underline (ctext, cattributes)

PURPOSE   Used to direct the browser to render the text with an underline.

PARAMETERS

Name		Type	Default	Usage
ctext	→	VARCHAR2		The text to render with an underline.
cattributes	→	VARCHAR2	NULL	Contents inserted directly into the opening <U> tag.

GENERATES

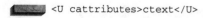

```
<U cattributes>ctext</U>
```

htp.variable (ctext, cattributes)

PURPOSE   Used to indicate that the text is a variable. Such text is typically rendered in italics by browsers.

PARAMETERS

Name		Type	Default	Usage
ctext	→	VARCHAR2		The text to render in italics
cattributes	→	VARCHAR2	NULL	Contents inserted directly into the opening <VAR> tag.

GENERATES

 <VAR cattributes>ctext</VAR>

htp.wbr

PURPOSE   Used to insert a soft line break within a section of NOBR text.

PARAMETERS   None.

GENERATES

 <WBR>

OWA_COOKIE Package

 NOTE
This section describes the functions, procedures, and datatypes in the OWA_COOKIE package in the PL/SQL Web Toolkit. Parameters that have default values are optional.

Datatypes and Constants

OWA_COOKIE.COOKIE

PURPOSE   Because cookies sent via HTTP can have multiple values associated with the same cookie name, a data structure is needed to hold these multiple values.

PARAMETERS

Name		Type	Default	Usage
name	→	VARCHAR2		Name of cookie.
vals	→	VC_ARR		A table of VARCHAR2(4096) that holds all values associated with a cookie.
num_vals	→	INTEGER		Number of elements in the vals vc_arr array.

Functions and Procedures

owa_cookie.get (name in VARCHAR2) return cookie

PURPOSE   Returns the values associated with the specified cookie. The values are returned in a owa_cookie.cookie datatype.

PARAMETERS

Name		Type	Default	Usage
name	→	VARCHAR2		Name of cookie.

GENERATES   owa_cookie.get generates an owa_cookie.cookie datatype.

owa_cookie.get_all procedure (name, vals, num_vals)

PURPOSE   Returns all cookie names and their values from the client's browser. The values appear in the order in which they were sent from the browser.

PARAMETERS

Name		Type	Default	Usage
name	→	VARCHAR2		Name of cookie.
vals	→	VC_ARR		Values associated with cookie.
num_vals	→	INTEGER		Number of cookie/value pairs.

owa_cookie.remove procedure (name, value, path)

PURPOSE   Forces a cookie to expire immediately by setting the "expires" field of a Set-Cookie line in the HTTP header to "01-Jan-1990". This procedure must be called within the context of an HTTP header.

PARAMETERS

Name		Type	Default	Usage
name	→	VARCHAR2		Name of cookie.
value	→	VARCHAR2		Value associated with cookie.
num_vals	→	INTEGER	Null	Currently unused.

GENERATES

```
Set-Cookie:  <name>=<value> expires=01-JAN-1990
```

owa_cookie.send procedure (name, value, expires, path, domain, secure)

PURPOSE   Generates a Set-Cookie line, which transmits a cookie to the client. This procedure must occur in the context of an HTTP header.

PARAMETERS

Name		Type	Default	Usage
name	→	VARCHAR2		Name of cookie.
value	→	VARCHAR2		Value associated with cookie.
expires	→	DATE	NULL	Date at which cookie will expire.
path		VARCHAR2	NULL	Value for the path field.
domain		VARCHAR2	NULL	Value for the domain field.
secure		VARCHAR2	NULL	If nonnull, the "secure" field is added to the line.

GENERATES

```
Set-Cookie: <name>=<value> expires=<expires> path=<path> domain=<domain> secure
```

OWA_IMAGE Package

NOTE
This section describes the functions, procedures, and datatypes in the OWA_IMAGE package in the PL/SQL Web Toolkit. Parameters that have default values are optional.

Datatypes and Constants

OWA_IMAGE.NULL_POINT package variable

DESCRIPTION   Package variable that can be used to default parameters to routines expecting an owa_image.point as input.

PURPOSE   This package variable of type point is used to default point parameters. Both the X and the Y fields of this variable are NULL.

OWA_IMAGE.POINT

DESCRIPTION   Datatype defined as TABLE OF VARCHAR2(32767) INDEX BY BINARY_INTEGER

PURPOSE   This datatype is a PL/SQL table used to accept calls from a web browser when submitting a form by clicking on an image. This datatype provides the *x* and *y* coordinates of a user's click on an image map.

Functions and Procedures

owa_image.get_x function

PURPOSE   Returns the *x* coordinate of the point where the user clicked on an image map.

RETURNS   The *y* coordinate as an integer.

owa_image.get_y function

PURPOSE   Returns the *y* coordinate of the point where the user clicked on an image map.

RETURNS   The *y* coordinate as an integer.

OWA_OPT_LOCK Package

NOTE
This section describes the functions, procedures, and datatypes in the OWA_OPT_LOCK package in the PL/SQL Web Toolkit. Parameters that have default values are optional.

Datatypes and Constants

owa_opt_lock.vcArray datatype

DESCRIPTION   Datatype defined as TABLE OF VARCHAR2(2000) INDEX BY BINARY_INTEGER

PURPOSE   This datatype is a PL/SQL table used to accept calls from a web browser that is using the owa_opt_lock.store_values and owa_opt_lock.verify_values routines to detect intervening updates.

Functions and Procedures

owa_opt_lock.checksum (p_buff, p_owner, p_tname, p_rowid) return number

PURPOSE   Returns a checksum value for a specified string, or for a row in a table. For a row in a table, the function calculates the checksum value based on the values of the columns in the row. This function comes in two versions:
    The first version returns a checksum based on the specified string. This is a "pure" 32-bit checksum executed by the database and based on the Internet 1 protocol.

The second version returns a checksum based on the values of a row in a table. This is an "impure" 32-bit checksum based on the Internet 1 protocol.

PARAMETERS

Name		Type	Default	Usage
p_buff	→	VARCHAR2		The string for which you want to calculate the checksum.
p_owner	→	VARCHAR2		The owner of the table.
p_tname	→			The table name.
p_rowid	→			The row in p_tname for which you want to calculate the checksum value. You can use the *owa_opt_lock.get_rowid* function to convert vcArray values to proper rowids.

RETURNS   A checksum value.

owa_opt_lock.get_rowid (p_old_values) return rowid;

PURPOSE   Returns the ROWID datatype from the specified owa_opt_lock.vcArray datatype.

PARAMETERS

Name		Type	Default	Usage
P_old_values	→			Usually passed in from an HTML form.

RETURNS   A ROWID.

owa_opt_lock.store_values(p_owner, p_tname, p_rowid);

PURPOSE   This procedure stores the column values of the row that you want to update later. The values are stored in hidden HTML form elements. Before updating the row, compare these values to the current row values to ensure that the values in the row have not been changed. If the values have been changed, warn the users and let them decide if the update should still take place.

PARAMETERS

Name		Type	Default	Usage
p_owner	→	VARCHAR2		The owner of the table.
p_tname	→	VARCHAR2		The name of the table.
p_rowid	→	ROWID		The row for which values are stored.

GENERATES   owa_opt_lock.store_values generates a series of hidden form elements, each named "old_*p_tname*," where p_tname is the name of table passed into this routine. Three elements are added, to hold the name of the table owner, the name of the table, and the rowid. In addition, one element is added for each column in the table, which holds the current value of the column for the specified row.

The PL/SQL routine that will be invoked when the form contains these embedded elements must accept a parameter named "old_*p_tname*" of type owa_opt_lock.vcArray. This parameter can then be passed to owa_opt_lock.verify_values, to determine if an intervening update has occurred.

owa_opt_lock.verify_values(p_old_values in vcArray) return boolean;

PURPOSE   Verifies whether the values in the speciifed row have been updated since the last query. This function is used with the owa_opt_lock.store_values procedure.

PARAMETERS

Name		Type	Default	Usage
p_old_values	→			A PL/SQL table containing the following information: p_old_values(1) specifies the owner of the table, p_old_values(2) specifies the table, p_old_values(3) specifies the rowid of the row being verified. The remaining indices contain values for the columns in the table.

GENERATES   owa_opt_lock.verify_values generates TRUE if no other update has been performed, otherwise FALSE.

OWA_PATTERN Package

NOTE
This section describes the functions, procedures, and datatypes in the OWA_PATTERN package in the PL/SQL Web Toolkit. Parameters that have default values are optional. See Chapter 4 for an in-depth discussion of using this package.

Datatypes and Constants

owa_pattern.pattern datatype

DESCRIPTION   Datatype defined as TABLE OF VARCHAR2(4) INDEX BY BINARY_INTEGER

PURPOSE   This datatype is used to store regular expressions in a parsed format. The advantage is that a pattern can be used as both an input and an output parameter. Thus, the same regular expression can be passed to OWA_PATTERN function calls, and it must be parsed only once.

Functions and Procedures

owa_pattern.amatch(line, from_loc, pat, flags) return integer;
owa_pattern.amatch(line, from_loc, pat, flags) return integer;
owa_pattern.amatch(line, from_loc, pat, backrefs, flags) return integer;
owa_pattern.amatch(line, from_loc, pat, backrefs, flags) return integer;

PURPOSE   Enables one to specify whether a pattern occurs in a particular location in a string. There are four versions of this function. The first and second versions do not save the matched tokens (these are saved in the backrefs parameters in the third and fourth versions). The pat parameter, which can be a VARCHAR2 or a pattern datatype, is the difference between the first two versions. The difference between the third and fourth versions is also the pat parameter.

If multiple overlapping strings can match the regular expression, this function takes the longest match.

PARAMETERS

Name		Type	Default	Usage
line	→	VARCHAR2		The text to be searched.
from_loc	→	INTEGER		The location (in number of characters) in the line where the search is to begin.
pat	→ or ↔	VARCHAR2 or owa_pattern.pattern		The string to match. It can contain regular expressions. This can be either a VARCHAR2 or a pattern. If it is a pattern, the output value of this parameter is the pattern matched.
backrefs	←	owa_text.vc_arr		The text that is matched. Each token that is matched is placed in a cell in the owa_text.vc_arr datatype PL/SQL table.
flags	→	VARCHAR2	NULL	Whether or not the search is case-sensitive. If Value of this parameter is "I", the search is case-sensitive, otherwise the search is case-sensitive.

RETURNS   The index of the character after the end of the match, counting from the beginning of the line. If there is no match, the function returns 0.

owa_pattern.change(line, from_str, to_str, flags);

PURPOSE   This function or procedure performs a search and replace on a string or multi_line datatype. If multiple overlapping strings can match the regular expression, this function takes the longest match.

PARAMETERS

Name		Type	Default	Usage
line	↔	VARCHAR2		The text to be searched. The output value of this parameter is the altered string.
mline	↔	owa_text.multi_line		The text to be searched. This is an owa_text.multi_line datatype. The output value of this parameter is the altered string.
from_str	→	VARCHAR2		The regular expression to replace.

Name		Type	Default	Usage
to_str	→	VARCHAR2		The substitution pattern.
flags	→	VARCHAR2	NULL	Whether or not the search is case-sensitive and whether or not changes are to be made globally. If "i" is specified, the search is case-insensitive. If "g" is specified, changes are made to all matches. Otherwise, the function stops after the first match and substitution is made.

RETURNS   The function returns the number of substitutions made.

owa_pattern.getpat(arg in VARCHAR2, pat in out pattern);

PURPOSE   Converts a VARCHAR2 string into an owa_pattern.pattern datatype.

PARAMETERS

Name		Type	Default	Usage
arg	→			The string to convert.
pat	↔			The owa_ pattern.pattern datatype initialized with arg.

owa_pattern.match(line, pat, flags) return boolean;
owa_pattern.match(line, pat, backrefs, flags) return boolean;
owa_pattern.match(mline, pat, rlist, flags) return boolean;

PURPOSE   This function determines whether a string contains the specified pattern. The pattern can contain regular expressions. If multiple overlapping strings can match the regular expression, this function takes the longest match.

PARAMETERS

Name		Type	Default	Usage
line	→	VARCHAR2		The text to be searched.
mline	→	owa_text.multi_line		The text to be searched. This is an owa_text.multi_line datatype.

Name	Type		Default	Usage
pat	→ or ↔	VARCHAR2		The pattern to match. This can be either a VARCHAR2 or an owa_pattern.pattern datatype. If it is a pattern, the output value of this parameter is the pattern matched.
backrefs	←	owa_text.vc_arr		The text that is matched. Each token that is matched is placed in a cell in the owa_text.vc_arr datatype PL/SQL table.
rlist	←	VARCHAR2		Output parameter containing a list of matches.
flags	→	VARCHAR2	NULL	Whether or not the search is case-sensitive and whether or not changes are to be made globally. If "i" is specified, the search is case-insensitive. If "g" is specified, changes are made to all matches. Otherwise, the function stops after the first match and substitution is made.

GENERATES   owa_pattern.match generates TRUE if a match was found, otherwise FALSE.

OWA_SEC Package

NOTE
This section describes the functions, procedures, and datatypes in the OWA_SEC package in the PL/SQL Web Toolkit. Parameters that have default values are optional. See Chapter 9 for additional details about this package.

Functions and Procedures

owa_sec.get_client_hostname return **VARCHAR2;**

PURPOSE   Returns the hostname of the client.

PARAMETERS   None.

RETURNS   Hostname.

owa_sec.get_client_ip return owa_util.ip_address;

PURPOSE   Returns the IP address of the client.

PARAMETERS   None.

RETURNS   The IP address. The owa_util.ip_address datatype is a PL/SQL table where the first four elements contain the four octets of the IP address. For example, if the IP address is 206.6.56.125 and the variable ipaddr is of the owa_util.ip_address datatype, the variable would contain the following values:

```
ipaddr(1) = 206
ipaddr(2) = 6
ipaddr(3) = 56
ipaddr(4) = 125
```

owa_sec.get_password return VARCHAR2;

PURPOSE   Returns the password that user used to log in.

PARAMETERS   None.

GENERATES   Generates the password that the user entered at the browser's username/password dialog box.

owa_sec.get_user_id return VARCHAR2;

PURPOSE   Returns the username that the user used to log in.

PARAMETERS   None.

RETURNS   The username that the user entered at the browser's username/password dialog box.

owa_sec.set_authorization(scheme in integer);

PURPOSE   Sets the authorization scheme for a PL/SQL Agent. Setting the scheme parameter to GLOBAL or PER_PACKAGE enables you to perform or define your own authentication routine. This procedure is called in the initialization portion of the OWA_INIT package.

PARAMETERS   A single parameter *scheme*, which is one of the following:

- ■ OWA_SEC.NO_CHECK   Specifies that the PL/SQL application is not to do any custom authentication. This is the default.

- ■ OWA_SEC.GLOBAL   Specifies that the *owa_init.authorize* function is to be used to authorize the user. Function must be defined in the OWA_INIT package.

- ■ OWA_SEC.PER_PACKAGE   Specifies that the *package.authorize* function or the anonymous *authorize* function is to be used to authorize the user. This function must be defined. If the request is for a procedure defined in a package, the *package.authorize* function is called. If the request is for a procedure that is *not* in a package, the anonymous *authorize* function is called.

owa_sec.set_protection_realm(realm in VARCHAR2);

PURPOSE   Sets the realm of the page that is returned to the user. To succeed, the user needs to enter a username and login that already exist in the realm of the authorization.

PARAMETERS   Following is the parameter for owa_sec.set_protection_realm:

- ■ **realm**   The realm in which the page should belong. This string is displayed to the user.

OWA_TEXT Package

NOTE
This section describes the functions, procedures, and datatypes in the OWA_TEXT package in the PL/SQL Web Toolkit. Parameters that have default values are optional.

Datatypes and Constants

OWA_TEXT.MULTI_LINE

DESCRIPTION   A PL/SQL record with the following fields:

Name	Type	Usage
rows	vc_arr	Contains text.
num_rows	INTEGER	Number of rows with text.
partial_row	BOOLEAN	TRUE if last row is only partially used.

PURPOSE   Used to hold larger amounts of text for processing by various routines, such as OWA_PATTERN.

OWA_TEXT.ROW_LIST

DESCRIPTION   A PL/SQL record with the following fields:

Name	Type	Usage
rows	int_arr	Contains line numbers of relevant rows.
num_rows	INTEGER	The number of rows.

PURPOSE   Used to return results from certain routines in the OWA_PATTERN package.

OWA_TEXT.VC_ARR

DESCRIPTION   Datatype defined as TABLE OF VARCHAR2(32767) INDEX BY BINARY_INTEGER.

PURPOSE   Used in the owa_text.multi_line datatype.

Functions and Procedures

owa_text.add2multi(stream, mline, continue)

PURPOSE   Adds content to an existing owa_text.multi_line datatype.

PARAMETERS

Name		Type	Default	Usage
stream	→	VARCHAR2		The text to add.
mline	↔	MULTI_LINE		An existing owa_text.multi_line object. The output of this parameter includes the contents of the stream.

Name	Type	Default	Usage
continue →	ï		If TRUE, the procedure appends the stream within the previous final row (assuming it is less than 32K). If FALSE, the procedure places the stream in a new row.

RETURNS   The mline parameter is updated.

owa_text.new_row_list;

PURPOSE   This function or procedure creates a new owa_text.row_list datatype. The function version takes no parameters and returns a new empty row_list. The procedure version creates the row_list datatype as an output parameter.

PARAMETERS

Name	Type	Default	Usage
rlist →			Output parameter containing the new row_list datatype.

RETURNS   The function version returns the new row_list datatype.

owa_text.print_multi(mline in multi_line);

PURPOSE   Procedure uses htp.print to print the "rows" field of the owa_text.multi_line datatype.

PARAMETERS

Name	Type	Default	Usage
mline →			The multi_line datatype to print out.

GENERATES   Generates the contents of the multi_line.

owa_text.print_row_list(rlist in row_list);

PURPOSE   Procedure uses htp.print to print the "rows" field of the owa_text.row_list datatype.

PARAMETERS

Name	Type	Default	Usage
rlist	→		The row_list datatype to print out.

GENERATES   Generates the contents of the row_list.

owa_text.stream2multi(stream, mline);

PURPOSE   Used to convert a string to a multi_line datatype.

PARAMETERS

Name	Type	Default	Usage
stream	→ VARCHAR2		The string to convert.
mline	→		The stream in owa_text.multi_line datatype format.

OWA_UTIL Package

NOTE
This section describes the functions, procedures, and datatypes in the OWA_UTIL package in the PL/SQL Web Toolkit. Parameters that have default values are optional.

Datatypes and Constants

OWA_UTIL.DATETYPE

DESCRIPTION   Datatype defined as TABLE OF VARCHAR2 (10) INDEX BY BINARY_INTEGER.

PURPOSE   This datatype is used to accept date input from an HTML form containing a set of drop-down menus generated by the owa_util.choose_date procedure that are used to select the month, day, and year. The *owa_util.todate* function converts an item of this type to the type DATE, which is understood and properly handled as data by both SQL and PL/SQL.

OWA_UTIL.IDENT_ARR

DESCRIPTION   Datatype defined as TABLE OF VARCHAR2(30) INDEX BY BINARY_INTEGER.

PURPOSE   This is a datatype used to accept all the values from a collection of name-value pairs sent by a browser that share the same name. See Chapter 4 for a discussion of the use of this datatype.

OWA_UTIL.IP_ADDRESS

DESCRIPTION   Datatype defined as TABLE OF INTEGER INDEX BY BINARY_INTEGER.

PURPOSE   Datatype used by the *owa_sec.get_client_ip* function to return an IP address as an array of four octets. See the OWA_SEC package for more information.

Functions and Procedures

owa_util.bind_variables(theQuery, bv1Name, bv1Value, bv2Name, bv2Value, bv3Name, bv3Value, …, bv25Name, bv25Value);

PURPOSE   Prepares an SQL query by binding variables to it, and stores the output in an opened cursor. This function is normally used as a parameter to a procedure, to which can be sent a dynamically generated query. Up to 25 bind variables can be specified.

PARAMETERS

Name		Type	Default	Usage
theQuery	→	VARCHAR2	NULL	The SQL query statement. This must be a SELECT statement.
bv1Name	→	VARCHAR2	NULL	The name of the variable.
bv1Value	→	VARCHAR2	NULL	Value of the variable.

RETURNS   An integer, identifying the opened cursor.

owa_util.calendarprint(p_query, p_mf_only);
owa_util.calendarprint(p_cursor, p_mf_only);

PURPOSE   Procedure creates a calendar in HTML. Each date in the calendar
can contain any number of hypertext links. To achieve this effect, design the
query as follows:

- The first column should be a DATE. This is used to correlate the
  information produced by the query with the calendar output automatically
  generated by the procedure. The query output must be sorted on this
  column using ORDER BY.

- The second column contains the text, if any, that should be printed for that date.

- The third column contains the destination for automatically generated
  links. Each item in the second column becomes a hypertext link to the
  destination given in this column. If this column is omitted, the items in the
  second column are simple text, not links.

- This procedure has two versions. Version 1 uses a hard-coded query stored
  in a VARCHAR2 string. Version2 uses a dynamic query prepared with the
  owa_util.bind_variables function.

PARAMETERS, VERSION I

Name		Type	Default	Usage
p_query	→	VARCHAR2		A PL/SQL query. (See preceding description of what query should return.)
p_mf_only	→	VARCHAR2	NULL	If "N" (the default), the generated calendar includes Sunday through Saturday. Otherwise, it includes Monday through Friday only.

PARAMETERS, VERSION 2

Name		Type	Default	Usage
p_cursor	→	INTEGER		A PL/SQL cursor containing the same format as p_query.
p_mf_only	→	VARCHAR2	NULL	If "N" (the default), the generated calendar includes Sunday through Saturday. Otherwise, it includes Monday through Friday only.

GENERATES   owa_util.calendarprint generates as many one-month calendars as are necessary to display all the dates. Figure A-1 shows the results of the following procedures.

```
CREATE OR REPLACE PROCEDURE caltest
IS
  qry  VARCHAR2(4096);
BEGIN
  qry := 'SELECT HIREDATE, ENAME,NULL FROM EMP';
  owa_util.calendarprint(qry);
END;
```

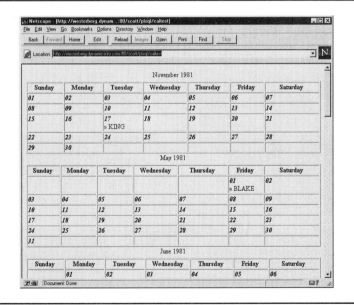

FIGURE A-1.   *Output of the calendarprint routine*

owa_util.cellsprint(p_theQuery, p_max_rows, p_format_numbers);
owa_util.cellsprint(p_theCursor, p_max_rows, p_format_numbers);
owa_util.cellsprint(p_theQuery, p_max_rows, p_format_numbers,
p_skip_rec,p_more_data);
owa_util.cellsprint(p_theCursor, p_max_rows, p_format_numbers,
p_skip_rec,p_more_data);

PURPOSE   Generates an HTML table from the output of an SQL query. SQL atomic data items are mapped to HTML cells and SQL rows to HTML rows. Code must be written to begin and end the HTML table.

There are four versions to this procedure. The first and second versions display rows (up to the specified maximum) returned by the query or cursor. The third and fourth versions allow exclusion of the specified number of rows from the HTML table. The third and fourth versions can also be used to scroll through result sets by saving the last row seen in a hidden form element.

PARAMETERS, VERSION I

Name		Type	Default	Usage
p_theQuery	→	VARCHAR2		The SQL select statement.
p_max_rows	→	NUMBER		Maximum number of rows to print.
p_format_numbers	→	VARCHAR2	NULL	If nonnull, number fields are right-justified and rounded to two decimal places.

PARAMETERS, VERSION 2

Name		Type	Default	Usage
p_theCursor	→	INTEGER		A cursor ID. Can be the return value from the *owa_util.bind_variables* function.
p_max_rows	→	NUMBER	100	Maximum number of rows to print.
p_format_numbers	→	VARCHAR2	NULL	If nonnull, number fields are right-justified and rounded to two decimal places.

PARAMETERS, VERSION 3

Name		Type	Default	Usage
p_theQuery	→	VARCHAR2		The SQL select statement.
p_max_rows	→	NUMBER	100	Maximum number of rows to print.
p_format_numbers	→	VARCHAR2	NULL	If nonnull, number fields are right-justified and rounded to two decimal places.
p_skip_rec		NUMBER	0	Number of rows to exclude from the HTML table.
p_more_data	←	BOOLEAN		TRUE if there are more rows in the query or cursor, otherwise FALSE.

PARAMETERS, VERSION 4

Name		Type	Default	Usage
p_theCursor	→	INTEGER		A cursor ID. Can be the return value from the *owa_util.bind_variables* function.
p_max_rows	→	NUMBER	100	Maximum number of rows to print.
p_format_numbers	→	VARCHAR2	NULL	If nonnull, number fields are right-justified and rounded to two decimal places.
p_skip_rec		NUMBER	0	Number of rows to exclude from the HTML table.
p_more_data	←	BOOLEAN		TRUE if there are more rows in the query or cursor, otherwise FALSE.

GENERATES

```
<tr><td>QueryResultItem</td><td>QueryResultItem</td></tr>
<tr><td>QueryResultItem</td><td>QueryResultItem</td></tr>
```

owa_util.choose_date(p_name, p_date);

PURPOSE   Generates three HTML form elements that allow user to select the day, month, and year. The parameter in the procedure that receives the data from these elements should be owa_util.dateType datatype. The *owa_util.todate* function can also be used to convert the owa_util.dateType datatype to the standard Oracle DATE datatype.

PARAMETERS

Name		Type	Default	Usage
p_name	→	VARCHAR2		The name of the form elements.
p_date	→	DATE	SYSDATE	The initial date that is selected when the HTML page is displayed.

GENERATES   owa_util.choose_date generates a collection of three pop-up menus for choosing a date, such as shown in Figure A-2.

owa_util.get_cgi_env(param_name in VARCHAR2) return VARCHAR2;

PURPOSE   Returns the value of the specified CGI environment variable. Although the WRB is not operated through CGI, many WRB cartridges, including the PL/SQL cartridge, can make use of CGI environment variables.

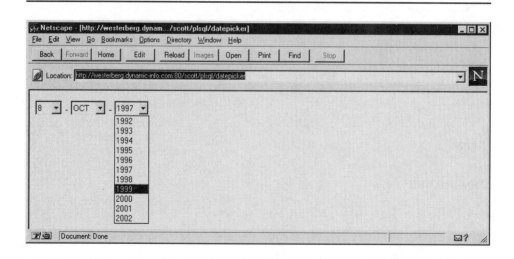

FIGURE A-2.   *The date selection controls generated by owa_util.choose_date*

PARAMETERS

Name	Type	Default	Usage
param_name →	VARCHAR2		The name of the CGI environment variable. It is case-sensitive.

RETURNS   The value of the specified CGI environment variable. If the variable is not defined, the function returns NULL.

owa_util.get_owa_service_path return **VARCHAR2;**

PURPOSE   Returns the full virtual path of the PL/SQL Agent that is handling the request.

PARAMETERS   None.

RETURNS   A virtual path of the PL/SQL Agent that is handling the request.

owa_util.get_procedure return **VARCHAR2;**

PURPOSE   Returns the name of the procedure that is being invoked by the PL/SQL Agent.

PARAMETERS   None.

RETURNS   The name of a procedure, including the package name, if the procedure is defined in a package.

owa_util.http_header_close;

PURPOSE   Generates a newline character to close the HTTP header. Use this procedure if the header has not been explicitly closed, by using the bclose_header parameter, in calls such as owa_util.mime_header procedure, owa_util.redirect_url procedure, or owa_util.status_line procedure. The HTTP header must be closed before any htp.print or htp.prn calls.

PARAMETERS   None.

GENERATES   owa_util.http_header_close; generates a newline character, which closes the HTTP header.

owa_util.listprint(p_theQuery, p_cname, p_nsize, p_multiple);
owa_util.listprint(p_theCursor, p_cname, p_nsize, p_multiple);

PURPOSE   Procedure generates an HTML selection list form element from the output of an SQL query. The columns in the output of the query are handled in the following way:

■ The first column specifies values that are to sent back as the value in the name/value pairs when the form is submitted. These values are used for the VALUE attribute of the OPTION tag.

■ The second column specifies the values that the user sees in the list.

■ The third column specifies whether the row is marked as SELECTED in the OPTION tag. If value is nonnull, the row is selected.

PARAMETERS, VERSION 1

Name		Type	Default	Usage
p_theQuery	→	VARCHAR2		SQL query.
p_cname	→	VARCHAR2		Name of the HTML form element.
p_nsize	→	NUMBER		The size of the form element. This controls the number of items the user can see without scrolling.
p_multiple	→	BOOLEAN	FALSE	Indicates whether multiple selection is permitted.

PARAMETERS, VERSION 2

Name		Type	Default	Usage
p_theCursor	→	VARCHAR2		Cursor ID. Can be the return value from the *owa_util.bind_variables* function.
p_cname	→	VARCHAR2		Name of the HTML form element.
p_nsize	→	NUMBER		The size of the form element. This controls the number of items the user can see without scrolling.
p_multiple	→	BOOLEAN	FALSE	Indicates whether multiple selection is permitted.

GENERATES

```
<SELECT NAME="p_cname" SIZE="p_nsize">
<OPTION SELECTED value="value_from_column1">value_from_column2
<OPTION SELECTED value="value_from_column1"> value_from_column2
[...repeats as necessary]
</SELECT>
```

owa_util.mime_header(ccontent_type, bclose_header);

PURPOSE   Changes the deafult MIME header returned by the PL/SQL Agent. This procedure must come before any htp.print or htp.prn calls, to direct the PL/SQL Agent not to use the default.

PARAMETERS

Name		Type	Default	Usage
ccontent_type	→	VARCHAR2	TEXT/HTML	The MIME type to generate.
bclose_header	→	BOOLEAN	TRUE	Indicates whether to close the HTTP header. If TRUE, two newlines are sent, which closes the HTTP header. If not TRUE, one newline is sent and the HTTP header is still open.

GENERATES

```
Content-type: <ccontent_type>\n\n
```

owa_util.print_cgi_env;

PURPOSE   Generates all the CGI environment variables and their values made available by the Pl/SQL Agent to the PL/SQL procedure.

PARAMETERS   None.

GENERATES   owa_util.print_cgi_env; generates a list in the following format:

```
cgi_env_var_name = value\n
```

owa_util.redirect_url(curl, bclose_header)

PURPOSE Procedure specifies that the Web Application Server is to visit the specified URL. The URL may specify either a web page to return or a program to execute. This procedure must come before any htp.print or htp.prn calls, to tell the PL/SQL Agent to do the redirect.

PARAMETERS

Name		Type	Default	Usage
curl	→	VARCHAR2		The URL to visit.
bclose_header	→	BOOLEAN	TRUE	Indicates whether to close the HTTP header. If TRUE, two newlines are sent, which closes the HTTP header. If not TRUE, one newline is sent and the HTTP header is still open.

GENERATES

```
Location: <curl>\n\n
```

owa_util.showpage;

PURPOSE Used to print out the HTML output of a procedure in SQL*Plus, SQL*DBA, or Oracle Server Manager. The procedure must use the HTP packages to generate the HTML page, and must also be issued after the procedure has been called and before any other HTP subprograms are directly or indirectly called. This method is useful for generating pages filled with static data as well as for testing.

This procedure uses DBMS_OUTPUT and is limited to 255 characters per line and an overall buffer size of 1,000,000 bytes.

PARAMETERS None.

GENERATES Generates the output of any calls to the HTP package is displayed in SQL*Plus, SQL*DBA, or Oracle Server Manager. For example:

```
SQL> set serveroutput on
SQL> spool gretzky.html
SQL> execute hockey.pass('Gretzky')
SQL> execute owa_util.showpage
[ page output displayed here]
SQL> exit
```

owa_util.showsource (cname in **VARCHAR2**);

PURPOSE   Prints the source of the specified procedure, function, or package. If specifying a procedure or function that belongs to a package, the entire package is displayed.

PARAMETERS

Name		Type	Default	Usage
cname	→	VARCHAR2		The name of the procedure or function.

GENERATES   Generates the source code of the specified function, procedure, or package.

owa_util.signature;
owa_util.signature (cname in **VARCHAR2**);

PURPOSE   Generates an HTML line followed by a signature line on the HTML document. If a parameter is specified, the procedure also generates a hypertext link to view the PL/SQL source for that procedure. The link calls the owa_util.showsource procedure.

PARAMETERS

Name		Type	Default	Usage
cname	→	VARCHAR2		The name of the procedure or function whose source needs to be shown.

GENERATES   Without a parameter, owa_util.signature generates a simple tagline, such as:

```
<B>
This page was produced by the PL/SQL Agent on May 1, 1998 09:30
</B>
```

With a parameter, the procedure generates a signature line and includes a link to the owa_util.showsource procedure:

```
<B>
This page was produced by the PL/SQL Agent on May 1, 1998 09:30
</B>
<A HREF="showsource">View PL/SQL Source</A>
```

owa_util.status_line(nstatus, creason, bclose_header)

PURPOSE   Procedure sends a standard HTTP status code to the client. This procedure must come before any htp.print or htp.prn calls so that the status code is returned as part of the header, rather than as content data.

PARAMETERS

Name		Type	Default	Usage
nstatus	→	INTEGER		The status code.
creason	→	VARCHAR2	NULL	The string for the status code.
bclose_header	→	BOOLEAN	TRUE	Indicates whether to close the HTTP header. If TRUE, two newlines are sent, which closes the HTTP header. If not TRUE, one newline is sent and the HTTP header is still open.

GENERATES

```
Status: <nstatus> <creason>\n\n
```

owa_util.tablePrint (ctable, cattributes, ntable_type, ccolumns, cclauses, ccol_aliases, nrow_min, nrow_max) return boolean;

PURPOSE   This function generates either preformatted or HTML tables (depending on the capabilities of the user's browser) from database tables. Note that the RAW columns are supported, but LONG RAW columns are not. References to LONG RAW columns will print the result "Not Printable". In this function, cattributes is the second, rather than the last, parameter.

PARAMETERS

Name		Type	Default	Usage
ctable	→	VARCHAR2		The database table.
cattributes	→	VARCHAR2	NULL	Other attributes to be included as-is in the tag.

Name	Type	Default	Usage
ntable_type →	INTEGER	HTML_TABLE	Indicates how to generate the table. Specify "HTML_TABLE" to generate the table using <TABLE> tags or "PRE_TABLE" to generate the table using the <PRE> tags.
ccolumns →	VARCHAR2	'*'	A comma-delimited list of columns from ctable to be included in the generated table.
cclauses →	VARCHAR2	NULL	WHERE or ORDER BY clauses, which allow specification of which rows should be retrieved from the database and how to order them.
ccol_aliases →	VARCHAR2	NULL	A comma-delimited list of headings for the generated table.
nrow_min →	NUMBER	0	The first row (of rows retrieved) to be displayed.
nrow_max →	NUMBER	NULL	The last row (of rows retrieved) to be displayed.

GENERATES owa_util.tablePrint generates a preformatted or HTML table.

RETURNS TRUE if there are more rows beyond the nrow_max requested, otherwise FALSE. This allows the developer to support paging through a table many rows at a time.

owa_util.todate(p_dateArray) return date;

PURPOSE Converts the owa_util.dateType datatype to the standard Oracle database DATE type.

PARAMETERS

Name	Type	Default	Usage
p_dateArray →			Value to convert.

RETURNS The date represented by the date array.

owa_util.who_called_me(owner, name, lineno, caller_t);

PURPOSE Procedure returns information (in the form of output parameters) about the PL/SQL code unit that invoked it.

PARAMETERS

Name	Type	Default	Usage
owner	← VARCHAR2		The owner of the program unit.
name	← VARCHAR2		The name of the program unit. This is the name of the package (if the calling unit is wrapped in a package) and the name of the procedure or function (if the calling program unit is a stand-alone procedure or function). If the calling program unit is part of an anonymous block, this is null.
lineno	← NUMBER		The line number within the program unit where the call was made.
caller_t	← VARCHAR2		Type of program that made the call. The possibilities are package body, anonymous block.procedure, and function. Procedure and function are used only for stand-alone procedures and functions.

GENERATES

```
Status: <nstatus> <creason>\n\n
```

APPENDIX

B

Java Reference

his appendix describes the classes which Oracle provides with the Oracle Web Application Server to interface with the OWAS Java cartridge. The classes are grouped within packages and subpackages. Rather than provide a detailed description of each method, a paragraph introducing the class describes the purpose of the class and the usage of any nonobvious methods. Following this description is an enumeration of all class and instance variables and methods, including any parameters and their data types.

Package oracle.html

The oracle.html package provides a number of classes for creating and manipulating the components that compose an HTML page.

oracle.html.Anchor

This class is used to specify an interdocument point of reference at which a hyperlink may point.

```
public class Anchor extends Item {
        // Public Constructors
        public Anchor(String name, String text)
        // Public Instance Methods
        public Anchor addItem(IHtmlItem item)
        public String name()
        public Anchor setName(String name)
        public String toHTML() // overrides Item.toHTML
        public synchronized String toString() // overrides Item.toString
        // Protected Instance Methods
        protected String startTag() // overrides Item.startTag
        protected String endTag() // overrides Item.endTag
}
```

oracle.html.Applet

This class encapsulates the HTML tags necessary to embed a Java applet on an HTML page. The addParam() method is used to embed any applet-specific parameters.

```
public class Applet extends Item implements IVAlign, IHAlign {
        // Public Constructors
        public Applet(String code, int width, int height)
        // Public Instance Methods
```

```
        public Applet addParam(String name, String value)
        public Applet setAlign(String align)
        public Applet setAltHtml(Item item)
        public Applet setAltHtml(Container cItems)
        public Applet setAltText(String text)
        public Applet setCode(String code)
        public Applet setCodebase(String codebase)
        public Applet setHeight(int height)
        public Applet setHSpace(int hspace)
        public Applet setName(String name)
        public Applet setVSpace(int vspace)
        public Applet setWidth(int width)
        public String toHTML() // overrides Item.toHTML
        public synchronized String toString() // overrides Item.toString
        // Protected Instance Methods
        protected String startTag() // overrides Item.startTag
        protected String endTag() // overrides Item.endTag
    }
```

oracle.html.BlockQuote

This class extends CompoundItem, and thus the addItem() method is available to add the text that is to appear as a block quote in the HTML page.

```
    public class BlockQuote extends CompoundItem {
        // Public Constructors
        public BlockQuote ()
        // Protected Instance Methods
        protected String startTag() // overrides Item.startTag
        protected String endTag() // overrides Item.endTag
    }
```

oracle.html.CheckBox

Encapsulates a checkbox object for use in an HTML form.

```
    public class CheckBox extends Item {
        // Public Constructors
        public Checkbox(String name, String value)
        public Checkbox(String name, String value, boolean state)
        // Public Instance Methods
        protected String startTag() // overrides Item.startTag
        public String toHTML() // overrides Item.toHTML
    }
```

oracle.html.Color

Encapsulates a color datum for use of various HTML objects.

```
public class Color extends Object {
    // Public final static variables
    public final static Color aqua
    public final static Color black
    public final static Color blue
    public final static Color cyan
    public final static Color darkGray
    public final static Color fuchsia
    public final static Color gray
    public final static Color green
    public final static Color lightGray
    public final static Color lime
    public final static Color magenta
    public final static Color maroon
    public final static Color navy
    public final static Color olive
    public final static Color orange
    public final static Color pink
    public final static Color red
    public final static Color silver
    public final static Color teal
    public final static Color yellow
    // Public Constructors
    public Color(String rgb)
    public Color(String r, String g, String b)
    public Color(int r, int g, int b)
    public Color(java.awt.Color color)
    // Public Instance Methods
    public String toString() // overrides Object.toString
}
```

oracle.html.Comment

This class is used to embed a comment in an HTML page being built by the application.

```
public class Comment extends IHtmlItemImpl {
    // Public Constructors
    public Comment (String content)
```

```
// Public Instance Methods
public String toHTML() // overrides IHtmlItemImpl.toHTML
public synchronized String toString() // overrides Object.toString
// Protected Instance Methods
protected String startTag()
protected String endTag()
}
```

oracle.html.CompoundItem

The CompoundItem class is a base class used to implement an HTML item that itself is composed of a collection of items. It is basically identical to Container, except that CompoundItem derives from Item, while Container derives from IHtmlItemImpl. The class includes methods to add elements to an object and access the elements that compose the object.

```
public class CompoundItem extends Item {
        // Public final static variables
        public final static int INITIAL_CAPACITY
        // Public Constructors
        public CompoundItem()
        public CompoundItem(int initCapacity)
        // Public Instance Methods
        public synchronized CompoundItem addItem(IHtmlItem item)
        public synchronized CompoundItem addItem(String string)
        public synchronized IHtmlItem itemAt(int index)
        public synchronized Enumeration items()
        public synchronized CompoundItem setItemAt(IHtmlItem item, int index)
        public int size()
        public String toHTML() // overrides Item.toHTML
        public synchronized String toString() // overrides Item.toString
}
```

oracle.html.Container

The CompoundItem class is a base class used to implement an HTML item that is a container for other items. It is basically identical to CompoundItem, except that CompoundItem derives from Item, while Container derives from IHtmlItemImpl. The class includes methods to add elements to the container and access the elements that are contained.

```
public class Container extends IHtmlItemImpl {
    // Public Constructors
    public Container()
    public Container (int initCapacity)
    // Public Instance Methods
    public synchronized Container addItem(IHtmlItem item)
    public synchronized Container addItem(String string)
    public synchronized IHtmlItem itemAt(int index)
    public synchronized Enumeration items()
    public synchronized Container setItemAt(IHtmlItem item, int index)
    public int size()
    public String toHTML() // overrides IHtmlItemImpl.toHTML
    public synchronized String toString() // overrides Object.toString
}
```

oracle.html.DefinitionList

A subclass of List that implements support for an HTML definition list.

```
public class DefinitionList extends List {
    // Public Constructors
    public DefinitionList ()
    public DefinitionList (boolean compact)
    // Public Instance Methods
    public DefinitionList addItem(IHtmlItem defterm, IHtmlItem defn)
    public DefinitionList addItem(Container defterms, IHtmlItem defn)
    public String toHTML() // overrides List.toHTML
    // Protected Instance Methods
    protected String startTag() // overrides List.startTag
    protected String endTag()// overrides List.endTag
}
```

oracle.html.DirectoryList

A subclass of List that implements support for an HTML directory list.

```
public class DirectoryList extends List {
    // Public Constructors
    public DirectoryList ()
    public DirectoryList (boolean compact)
    // Protected Instance Methods
    protected String startTag() // overrides List.startTag
    protected String endTag()// overrides List.endTag
}
```

oracle.html.DynamicTable

A DynamicTable is used to build an HTML table for a page. It is very good for displaying rows of tabular data from a query. It can be instantiated, and then have rows added to it dynamically, such as in a loop through a result set.

```
public class DynamicTable extends Table {
        // Public Constructors
        public DynamicTable (int cols)
        // Public Instance Methods
        public int getNumRows()
        public DynamicTable addRow()
        public DynamicTable addRow(int numRows)
        public DynamicTable addRow(TableRow row)
        public DynamicTable setCellAt(int col_num, int row_num, SimpleItem item)
        public synchronized String toHTML() // overrides Item.toHTML
        public synchronized String toString() // overrides Item.toString
}
```

oracle.html.Embed

This class encapsulates the HTML tags necessary to embed content on an HTML page. The addParam() method is used to embed any parameters specific to the content.

```
public class Embed extends IHtmlItemImpl {
        // Public Constructors
        public Embed(String src, int width, int height)
        // Public Instance Methods
        public Embed addParam(String name, String value)
        public Embed setHeight(int height)
        public Embed setSrc (String src)
        public Embed setWidth(int width)
        public String toHTML() // overrides IHtmlItemImpl.toHTML
        public synchronized String toString() // overrides Object.toString
}
```

oracle.html.Form

This class is used to create an HTML form for use on an HTML page. After creating the form, various objects are added to it with addItem(). The *method* parameter may be GET or POST, and the action specifies the URL to which the form submission should be directed.

```
public class Form extends CompoundItem {
        // Public Constructors
        public Form(String method, String action, String target, String enctype)
        public Form(String method, String action, String target)
        public Form(String method, String action)
        // Public Instance Methods
        public synchronized String toString() // overrides CompoundItem.toString
        // Protected Instance Methods
        protected String startTag() // overrides Item.startTag
        protected String endTag()// overrides Item.endTag
}
```

oracle.html.Frame

This class encapsulates the HTML tags to describe a frame on an HTML page, which is placed on the page with the Frameset object.

```
public class Frame extends Item {
        // Public Constructors
        public Frame (String src, String name, int marginWidth, int
                        marginHeight, String
                        scrolling, boolean noresize)
        public Frame (String src)
        public Frame (String src, String name)
        // Public Instance Methods
        public Frame setSrc(String src)
        public String endTag() // overrides Item.endTag
        public Frame setMarginHeight(int marginHeight)
        public Frame setMarginWidth(int marginWidth)
        public Frame setName(String name)
        public Frame setNoResize(boolean noresize)
        public Frame setScrolling(String scrolling)
        public String startTag() // overrides Item.startTag
        public String toHTML() // overrides Item.toHTML
}
```

oracle.html.Frameset

This class encapsulates the HTML tags necessary to define the set of frames that compose a page. Note that if the constructor with no parameters is used, either setCols() or setRows() must be called.

```
public class Frameset extends Item {
        // Public Constructors
        public Frameset(String rows, String cols, CompoundItem
                        altHtml, Container frames)
        public Frameset(String rows, String cols)
        public Frameset()
        // Public Instance Methods
        public Frameset addFrame(Frame frame)
        public String endTag() // overrides Item.endTag
        public Frameset setAltHtml(CompoundItem altHtml)
        public Frameset setAltHtml(SimpleItem altHtml)
        public Frameset setCols(String cols)
        public Frameset setRows(String rows)
        public String startTag() // overrides Item.startTag
        public String toHTML() // overrides Item.toHTML
}
```

oracle.html.Hidden

Encapsulates a hidden object for use in an HTML form, most typically to pass
values between server process invocations.

```
public class Hidden extends Item {
        // Public Constructors
        public Hidden(String name, String value)
        // Public Instance Methods
        protected String startTag() // overrides Item.startTag
        public String toHTML() // overrides Item.toHTML
}
```

oracle.html.HtmlBody

A class for building the body of an HTML page. Typically an HtmlBody object is
created, and added to an HtmlPage object. In turn, other objects from the
oracle.html package are added to the HtmlBody object.

```
public class HtmlBody extends Container {
        // Public Constructors
        public HtmlBody(String bimg, String bcolor, String fcolor, String flinkcolor,
                        String uflinkcolor, String alinkcolor)
        public HtmlBody()
        // Public Instance Methods
        public HtmlBody addItem(Container containerItem)
```

```
        public HtmlBody setBackgroundImage(String img)
        public HtmlBody setActivatedLinkColor(Color color)
        public HtmlBody setActivatedLinkColor(String color)
        public HtmlBody setBackgroundColor(Color color)
        public HtmlBody setBackgroundColor(String color)
        public HtmlBody setFollowedLinkColor(Color color)
        public HtmlBody setFollowedLinkColor(String color)
        public HtmlBody setForegroundColor(Color color)
        public HtmlBody setForegroundColor(String color)
        public HtmlBody setUnfollowedLinkColor(Color color)
        public HtmlBody setUnfollowedLinkColor(String color)
        public String toHTML() // overrides Container.toHTML
        public String toString() // overrides Container.toString
        // Protected Instance Methods
        protected String startTag()
        protected String endTag()
    }
```

oracle.html.HtmlException

A standard exception generated by errors when using classes from the oracle.html package.

```
    public class HtmlException extends Exception {
        // Public Constructors
        public HtmlException ()
        public HtmlException (String s)
    }
```

oracle.html.HtmlFile

Implements an interface for loading an HTML file from a local file with support for replacing tags with generated HTML. This allows the logic to be developed separately from the presentation appearance of a page. Use the setItemAt method to replace tags of the form <WRB_INC NAME="x" VALUE="y">. In this case, the *VALUE* attribute indicates the default HTML with which to replace the tag, if no explicit call to setItemAt() is made by the program.

```
    public class HtmlFile extends IHtmlItemImpl {
        // Public Constructors
        public HtmlFile (File file, int numkeys)
        public HtmlFile (File file)
        public HtmlFile (String filename)
```

```
        // Public Instance Methods
        public HtmlFile setItemAt (String tag, IHtmlImpl item)
        public String toHTML() // overrides IHtmlItemImpl.toHTML
        public String toString() // overrides Object.toString
}
```

oracle.html.HtmlHead

Defines the attributes of a page's <HEAD> section.

```
    public class HtmlHead extends IHtmlItemImpl {
        // Public Constructors
        public HtmlHead(String title, String base, String baseTarget, boolean index)
        public HtmlHead(String title)
        public HtmlHead()
        // Public Instance Methods
        public HtmlHead addLink(IHtmlItem hi)
        public HtmlHead addLink(HeadLink link)
        public HtmlHead addStyle(Style s)
        public HtmlHead addMetaInfo(MetaInfo mi)
        public HtmlHead setBase(String base)
        public HtmlHead setBase(URL base)
        public HtmlHead setBaseTarget(String baseTarget)
        public HtmlHead setTitle(String title)
        public synchronized String toHTML() // overrides IHtmlItemImpl.toHTML
        public synchronized String toString() // overrides Object.toString
        // Protected Instance Methods
        protected String startTag()
        protected String endTag()
}
```

oracle.html.HtmlPage

Implements an HTML page. This class supports three main types of constructors. It can create a page based on an existing file (such as HtmlFile), a page composed of multiple frames, or a standard page with a body. To send the page to the browser, invoke the HtmlPage object's printHeader() and inherited print() methods.

```
    public class HtmlPage extends Container {
        // Public final static variables
        public final static int NORMAL_DOC
        public final static int FRAME_DOC
        public final static int FILE_DOC
        // Public Constructors
```

```
        public HtmlPage(int type, HtmlHead head, HtmlBody body,
                 Frameset frameset, File file)
        public HtmlPage(HtmlHead head, HtmlBody body)
        public HtmlPage(HtmlHead head, Frameset frameset)
        public HtmlPage(File file)
        public HtmlPage(String title)
        public HtmlPage ()
        // Public Instance Methods
        public HtmlPage addItem(IHtmlItem item)
        public HtmlBody getBody()
        public HtmlHead getHead()
        public void printHeader()
        public void printHeader(OutputStream out)
        public HtmlPage setActivatedLinkColor(Color color)
        public HtmlPage setActivatedLinkColor(String color)
        public HtmlPage setBackgroundColor(Color color)
        public HtmlPage setBackgroundColor(String color)
        public HtmlPage setBackgroundImage(String img)
        public HtmlPage setBody(HtmlBody body)
        public HtmlPage setFollowedLinkColor(Color color)
        public HtmlPage setFollowedLinkColor(String color)
        public HtmlPage setForegroundColor(Color color)
        public HtmlPage setForegroundColor(String color)
        public HtmlPage setHead(HtmlHead head)
        public HtmlPage setItemAt(String tag, IHtmlItem item)
        public HtmlPage setUnfollowedLinkColor(Color color)
        public HtmlPage setUnfollowedLinkColor(String color)
        public HtmlPage setTitle(String title)
        protected String startTag() // overrides Item.startTag
        public String toHTML() // overrides Container.toHTML
        public String toString() // overrides Container.toString
        // Protected Instance Methods
        protected String startTag()
        protected String endTag()
    }
```

oracle.html.HtmlRuntimeException

```
    public class HtmlRuntimeException extends RuntimeException {
        // Public Constructors
        public HtmlRuntimeException ()
        public HtmlRuntimeException (String s)
    }
```

oracle.html.HtmlStream

This class implements an output stream that is used to write data back to the user agent making the request. It is not typically necessary to access this class directly, but rather it is typical to use the printHeader() and print() methods of the HtmlPage object. If direct output to the stream is necessary, the theStream() static method returns the HtmlStream object for the current request.

```
public class HtmlStream extends Object {
        // Public Class Methods
        public static HtmlStream theStream()
        // Public Instance Methods
        public synchronized void print(String str, boolean bUnicode)
        public synchronized void print(String str)
        public synchronized void print(Object obj)
        public synchronized void print(IHtmlItem item)
        public synchronized void println()
        public synchronized void println(String str, boolean bUnicode)
        public synchronized void println(String str)
        public synchronized void setUnicodeOutput(boolean bUnicode)
        public boolean unicodeOutput()
        public synchronized void write(int b) throws IOException
        public synchronized void write(byte b[], int offset, int length)
                                        throws IOException
        public synchronized void write(byte b[]) throws IOException
}
```

oracle.html.IHAlign

An interface to implement common constant expressions for various horizontal alignment attributes.

```
public interface IHAlign extends Object {
        // Public final static variables
        public final static int CENTER
        public final static int LEFT
        public final static int MAX
        public final static int MIN
        public final static int NONE
        public final static int RIGHT
        public final static String Str[]
}
```

oracle.html.IHtmlItem

A generic interface that many classes in oracle.html package implement.

```
public interface IHtmlItem extends Object {
        // Public final static variables
        // Abstract Public Instance Methods
        public abstract String toHTML()
        public abstract void print()
        public abstract void print(OutputStream out)
}
```

oracle.html.IHtmlItemImpl

A generic implementation of the IHtmlItem interface that saves some effort in implementing the IHtmlItem interface.

```
public interface IHtmlItem extends Object {
        // Public final static variables
        // Abstract Public Instance Methods
        public abstract String toHTML()
        public abstract void print()
        public abstract void print(OutputStream out)
}
```

oracle.html.ITableFrame

An interface to define a collection of constants associated with a table's frame attributes.

```
public interface ITableFrame extends Object {
        // Public final static variables
        public final static int ABOVE
        public final static int BELOW
        public final static int BORDER
        public final static int BOX
        public final static int HSIDES
        public final static int LHS
        public final static int RHS
        public final static String Str[]
        public final static int VOLD
        public final static int VSIDES
}
```

oracle.html.ITableRules

An interface that defines constants associated with a table's layout rules.

```
public interface ITableRules extends Object {
        // Public final static variables
        public final static int ALL
        public final static int BASIC
        public final static int COLS
        public final static int NONE
        public final static int ROWS
        public final static String Str[]
}
```

oracle.html.ITarget

An interface to define some of the common constant expressions associated with a form or link's TARGET attribute.

```
public interface ITarget extends Object {
        // Public final static variables
        public final static int BLANK
        public final static int PARENT
        public final static int SELF
        public final static String Str[]
        public final static int TOP
}
```

oracle.html.IVAlign

An interface to implement common constant expressions for various vertical alignment attributes.

```
public interface IVAlign extends Object {
        // Public final static variables
        public final static int BASELINE
        public final static int BOTTOM
        public final static int MAX
        public final static int MIDDLE
        public final static int MIN
        public final static int NONE
        public final static String Str[]
        public final static int TOP
}
```

oracle.html.Image

This class encapsulates the HTML tags necessary to embed an image on an HTML page.

```
public class Image extends Item implements IVAlign, IHAlign {
        // Public Constructors
        public Image(String imgURI, String altTxt, int halign, int valign,
                        int width, int height, int border, int hspace, int vspace,
                        boolean ismap, String usemap)
        public Image(String imgURI, String altTxt, int valign, boolean
                        ismap, String usemap)
        public Image(String imgURI)
        public Image(String imgURI, int valign, boolean ismap,
                        String usemap)
        // Public Instance Methods
        public String startTag() // overrides Item.startTag
        public String toHTML() // overrides Item.toHTML
        public String toString() // overrides Item.toString
}
```

oracle.html.ImageMap

An object used to define an image map. The active areas of the image map are then defined by creating ImageMapArea objects and adding them to the image map via the addItem() method. The image map is associated with an image by passing the name given to the image map to the *usemap* parameter of the Image object constructor.

```
public class ImageMap extends Container {
        // Public Constructors
        public ImageMap(String name)
        // Public Instance Methods
        public String toHTML() // overrides Container.toHTML
        public String toString() // overrides Container.toString
        // Protected Instance Methods
        protected String startTag()
        protected String endTag()
}
```

oracle.html.ImageMapArea

Objects of this type are created and added to ImageMap objects to describe the regions within the image map. The *shape* parameter to the constructor can be one of RECT, POLY, CIRCLE, or DEFAULT. The meaning of the *coordinates* parameter varies, based on the type of shape being created.

```
public class ImageMapArea extends IHtmlItemImpl {
    // Public Constructors
    public ImageMapArea(String shape, String coords, String href, String altTxt)
    public ImageMapArea(String shape, String coords, String href)
    // Public Instance Methods
    public String toHTML() // overrides IHtmlItemImpl.toHTML
    public synchronized String toString() // overrides Object.toString
}
```

oracle.html.Item

Item is an abstract class that implements the basic markup functionality required of most HTML items.

```
public class Item extends IHtmlItemImpl {
    // Public Final Static Properties
    public final static int ATTR_ALGN_CENTER
    public final static int ATTR_BIG
    public final static int ATTR_BOLD
    public final static int ATTR_CITATION
    public final static int ATTR_CODE
    public final static int ATTR_DEFINITION
    public final static int ATTR_EMPHASIS
    public final static int ATTR_FONT_BOLD
    public final static int ATTR_FONT_ITALIC
    public final static int ATTR_FONT_STRIKE
    public final static int ATTR_FONT_TELETYPE
    public final static int ATTR_FONT_UNDERLINE
    public final static int ATTR_FONT_BIG
    public final static int ATTR_FONT_SMALL
    public final static int ATTR_FONT_SUB
    public final static int ATTR_FONT_SUPER
    public final static int ATTR_ITALIC
    public final static int ATTR_KEYBOARD
    public final static int ATTR_PHRASE_CITATION
    public final static int ATTR_PHRASE_CODE
```

```
public final static int ATTR_PHRASE_DEFINITION
public final static int ATTR_PHRASE_EMPHASIS
public final static int ATTR_PHRASE_KEYBOARD
public final static int ATTR_PHRASE_SAMPLE
public final static int ATTR_PHRASE_STRONG
public final static int ATTR_PHRASE_VARIABLE
public final static int ATTR_SAMPLE
public final static int ATTR_SMALL
public final static int ATTR_STRIKE
public final static int ATTR_STRONG
public final static int ATTR_SUB
public final static int ATTR_SUPER
public final static int ATTR_TELETYPE
public final static int ATTR_UNDERLINE
public final static int ATTR_VARIABLE
// Public Constructors
public Item(boolean citation, boolean code, boolean emphasis,
          boolean keyboard,
          boolean sample, boolean strongEmphasis, boolean
          variable, boolean
          italic, boolean bold, boolean teletype, int heading)
public Item()
// Public Instance Methods
public Item clearAttr(int attr)
public Item setAttr(int attr)
public Item setAttr(int attr, boolean val)
public Item setBold()
public Item setBold(boolean val)
public Item setCenter()
public Item setCenter(boolean val)
public Item setCite()
public Item setCite(boolean val)
public Item setCode()
public Item setCode(boolean val)
public Item setDefinition()
public Item setDefinition(boolean val)
public Item setEmphasis()
public Item setEmphasis(boolean val)
public Item setFontBig()
public Item setFontBig(boolean val)
public Item setFontColor(Color color)
public Item setFontSize(int size)
```

```
        public Item setFontSmall()
        public Item setFontSmall(boolean val)
        public Item setFontSubscript()
        public Item setFontSubscript(boolean val)
        public Item setFontSuperscript()
        public Item setFontSuperscript(boolean val)
        public Item setHeading(int i)
        public Item setItal()
        public Item setItal(boolean val)
        public Item setKeyboard()
        public Item setKeyboard(boolean val)
        public Item setSample()
        public Item setSample(boolean val)
        public Item setStrike()
        public Item setStrike(boolean val)
        public Item setStrongEmphasis()
        public Item setStrongEmphasis(boolean val)
        public Item setStyleElement(StyleElement elem)
        public Item setTeletype()
        public Item setTeletype(boolean val)
        public Item setUnderline()
        public Item setUnderline(boolean val)
        public Item setVariable()
        public Item setVariable(boolean val)
        protected StyleElement styleElement()
        protected String styleEndTag()
        protected String styleStartTag()
        protected String styleTag()
        public String toHTML() // overrides IHtmlItemImpl.toHTML
        public String toString() // overrides Object.toString
        //Protected Instance Methods
        protected String startTag()
        protected String endTag()
    }
```

oracle.html.Link

This class encapsulates the HTML tags necessary to link to another document within an HTML document.

```
    public class Link extends Item {
        // Public Constructors
        public Link(String url, IHtmlItem item, String target)
```

```
            public Link(String url, IHtmlItem item)
            public Link(String url, String text)
            public Link(Anchor anchor, IHtmlItem item)
            // Public Instance Methods
            public Link addItem(IHtmlItem item)
            public synchronized String toHTML() // overrides Item.toHTML
            //Protected Instance Methods
            protected String endTag() // overrides Item.endTag
            protected String startTag() // overrides Item.startTag
    }
```

oracle.html.List

This object is the base object for more specialized lists such as DefinitionList,
MenuList, and OrderedList. It is rarely useful to apply this base List object directly.

```
    public class List extends Item {
            //Public final static variables
            public final static int DEFINITION
            public final static int DIRECTORY
            public final static int MENU
            public final static int ORDERED
            public final static int UNORDERED
            //Protected instance variables
            protected CompoundItem list_
            protected boolean compact_
            // Public Constructors
            public List(int type, boolean compact)
            // Protected Constructors
            protected List(boolean compact)
            protected List()
            // Public Instance Methods
            public synchronized List addItem(IHtmlItem item)
            public synchronized List addItem(String string)
            public synchronized IHtmlItem itemAt(int index)
            public synchronized List setItemAt(IHtmlItem item, int index)
            public int size()
            public String toHTML() // overrides Item.toHTML
            public String toString() // overrides Item.toString
            // Protected Instance Methods
            protected String endTag() // overrides Item.endTag
            protected boolean getCompact()
            protected CompoundItem getList()
            protected String startTag() // overrides Item.startTag
    }
```

oracle.html.MenuList

A subclass of List that implements support for an HTML menu list.

```
public class MenuList extends List {
        // Public Constructors
        public MenuList(boolean compact)
        public MenuList()
        // Protected Instance Methods
        protected String startTag() // overrides List.startTag
        protected String endTag()// overrides List.endTag
}
```

oracle.html.MetaInfo

A class used to embed <META> tags into an HTML page.

```
public class MetaInfo extends IHtmlItemImpl {
        // Public Constructors
        public MetaInfo(String equiv, String name, String content, String url)
        public MetaInfo(String equiv, String content)
        // Public Instance Methods
        public String toHTML() // overrides IHtmlItemImpl.toHTML
        public String toString() // overrides Object.toString
}
```

oracle.html.Option

Encapsulates a choice for use in a select list.

```
public class Option extends Item {
        // Public Constructors
        public Option(String txt, String val, boolean state)
        public Option(String txt)
        // Public Instance Methods
        protected String startTag() // overrides Item.startTag
        public String toHTML() // overrides Item.toHTML
}
```

oracle.html.OrderedList

A subclass of List that implements support for an HTML ordered list. Ordered list items are preceded by numbers. By specifying a *start* other than 1 in the constructor, the list can start with a different base numbering.

```
public class OrderedList extends List {
     // Public Constructors
     public OrderedList(String type, int start, boolean compact)
     public OrderedList()
     // Protected Instance Methods
     protected String endTag()// overrides List.endTag
     protected String startTag() // overrides List.startTag
}
```

oracle.html.PasswordField

Used to insert a password field (which doesn't echo what the user types) into an HTML form.

```
public class PasswordField extends FormElement {
     // Public Constructors
     public PasswordField(String name, int maxlength, int size, String value)
     public PasswordField(String name)
}
```

oracle.html.Preformat

Indicates that the text that is added to this object should be surrounded by <PRE> and </PRE> tags.

```
public class Preformat extends CompoundItem {
     // Public Constructors
     public Preformat(int width)
     public Preformat()
     // Protected Instance Methods
     protected String endTag() // overrides Item.endTag
     protected String startTag() // overrides Item.startTag
}
```

oracle.html.Radio

Encapsulates a radio button for use in an HTML form.

```
public class Radio extends Item {
     // Public Constructors
     public Radio(String name, String value, boolean state)
     public Radio(String name, String value)
     // Public Instance Methods
```

```
        public String startTag() // overrides Item.startTag
        public String toHTML() // overrides Item.toHTML
}
```

oracle.html.Reset

Encapsulates a reset button for use in an HTML form.

```
    public class Reset extends Item {
        // Public Constructors
        public Reset(String value)
        public Reset()
        // Public Instance Methods
        public String toHTML() // overrides Item.toHTML
        // Protected Instance Methods
        protected String startTag() // overrides Item.startTag
}
```

oracle.html.Select

Encapsulates a selection control for use in an HTML form. This can be either a pop-up menu (if the constructor's *size* parameter is set to 1) or a list box (if *size* is greater than 1).

```
    public class Select extends Item {
        // Public Constructors
        public Select(String name, int size, boolean multiple)
        public Select(String name)
        // Public Instance Methods
        public Select addOption(Option op)
        public int NumOptions() //deprecated, use size()
        public int size()
        public String toHTML() // overrides Item.toHTML
        public String toString() // overrides Item.toString
        // Protected Instance Methods
        protected String endTag() // overrides Item.endTag
        protected String startTag() // overrides Item.startTag
}
```

oracle.html.SimpleItem

Used for passing an object that implements the HtmlItem interface but that would otherwise be plain text. Constructors are provided to convert most native Java types into a text-based representation. The constants Paragraph, LineBreak, and HorizontalRule are provided for convenience, and can be added directly to any Container or CompoundItem.

```
public class SimpleItem extends Item {
        // Public final static variables
        public final static SimpleItem Paragraph
        public final static SimpleItem LineBreak
        public final static SimpleItem HorizontalRule
        // Public Constructors
        public SimpleItem()
        public SimpleItem(String s)
        public SimpleItem(int i)
        public SimpleItem(long l)
        public SimpleItem(float f)
        public SimpleItem(double d)
        public SimpleItem(boolean b)
        public SimpleItem(char c)
        public SimpleItem(char data[])
        public SimpleItem(Object o)
        // Public Instance Methods
        public Select addOption(Option op)
        public int NumOptions()  //deprecated, use size()
        public int size()
        public String toHTML() // overrides Item.toHTML
        public String toString() // overrides Item.toString
        // Protected Instance Methods
        protected String styleTag() // overrides Item.styleTag
}
```

oracle.html.Submit

Encapsulates a reset button for use in an HTML form. Multiple submit buttons with the same name but different values can be used to perform different actions, based on the button's title. For example, one button could delete a record, while another could update it.

```
public class Submit extends Item {
        // Public Constructors
        public Submit(String name, String value)
        public Submit()
        // Public Instance Methods
        public String toHTML() // overrides Item.toHTML
```

```
        // Protected Instance Methods
        protected String startTag() // overrides Item.startTag
}
```

oracle.html.Table

An abstract class used to implement a table. See its descendants for usage.

```
    public class Table extends Item implements IHAlign, ITableFrame, ITableRules {
        // Public Constructors
        public Table(String caption, String width, int border, int cellspacing, int
                cellpadding)
        public Table()
        // Protected Constructors
        protected Table(String caption, int border, int cellspacing, int
                    cellpadding, String width, int halign, int frame,
                    int rules)
        // Public Instance Method
        public String backgroundImage()
        public String backgroundColor()
        public int border()
        public String borderColor()
        public String caption()
        public String captionAlign()
        public int cellPadding()
        public int cellspacing()
        public String endTag() // overrides Item.endTag
        public int frame()
        public int hAlign()
        public int rules()
        public Table setBackgroundColor(String color)
        public Table setBackgroundColor(Color color)
        public Table setBackgroundImage(String url)
        public Table setBorder(int border)
        public Table setBorderColor(String color)
        public Table setBorderColor(Color color)
        public Table setCaption(String caption)
        public Table setCaption(String caption, String align)
        public Table setCellSpacing(int cellspacing)
        public Table setCellPadding(int cellpadding)
        public Table setFrame(int frame)
        public Table setIHAlign(int ha)
        public Table setRules(int rules)
```

```
        public Table setWidth(String width)
        public String startTag() // overrides Item.startTag
        public String width()
}
```

oracle.html.TableCell

An abstract class for implementing the core behavior of a table cell.

```
    public class TableCell extends Item implements IHAlign, IVAlign {
        // Public Constructors
        public TableCell()
        // Public Instance Method
        public String backgroundColor()
        public String borderColor()
        public String endTag() // overrides Item.endTag
        public int halign()
        public Table setBackgroundColor(String color)
        public Table setBackgroundColor(Color color)
        public Table setBorderColor(String color)
        public Table setBorderColor(Color color)
        public Table setHAlign(int halign)
        public Table setVAlign(int valign)
        public String startTag() // overrides Item.startTag
        public int valign()
}
```

oracle.html.TableDataCell

A concrete class for implementing a basic table cell. Note that for simple cells (that is, those that do not require any additional attributes for the <TD> tag), it is easiest to simply call TableRow's addCell() or setCellAt() methods with a String or SimpleItem object, rather than manually creating the TableDataCell object. However, TableDataCell provides a variety of calls necessary for more sophisticated formatting.

```
    public class TableDataCell extends TableCell {
        // Public Constructors
        public TableDataCell(int valign, int halign, int height, int width,
                             int rowspan, int colspan, boolean nowrap,
                             IHtmlItem content)
        public TableDataCell(int valign, int halign, int rowspan,
```

```
                          int colspan, boolean nowrap,
                          IHtmlItem content)
    public TableDataCell(IHtmlItem content)
    public TableDataCell()
    public TableDataCell(String content)
    // Public Instance Methods
    public TableDataCell addItem(IHtmlItem newItem)
    public TableDataCell addItem(String str)
    public int colSpan()
    public int height()
    public boolean noWrap()
    public int rowSpan()
    public TableDataCell setColSpan(int colSpan)
    public TableDataCell setHeight(int height)
    public TableDataCell setNoWrap(boolean noWrap)
    public TableDataCell setRowSpan(int rowSpan)
    public TableDataCell setWidth(int width)
    public int width()
    public String toHTML() //Overrides Item.toHTML
    public synchronized String toString() //Overrides Item.toString
    // Protected Instance Methods
    protected String startTag() //Overrides Item.startTag
    protected String endTag() //Overrides Item.endTag
}
```

oracle.html.TableHeaderCell

Implements a table header cell, which is basically identical to a table data cell other than typically being rendered by browsers in bold.

```
public class TableHeaderCell extends TableDataCell {
    // Public Constructors
    public TableHeaderCell (int valign, int halign, int rowspan,
                          int colspan, boolean nowrap,
                          IHtmlItem content)
    public TableDataCell(IHtmlItem content)
    public TableDataCell(String content)
    // Protected Instance Methods
    protected String startTag() //Overrides TableDataCell.startTag
    protected String endTag() //Overrides TableDataCell.endTag
}
```

oracle.html.TableRow

TableRow objects are used as containers for TableCell objects and, in turn, are added to Table objects.

```
public class TableRow extends Item {
        // Public Constructors
        public TableRow()
        public TableRow(int initCapacity)
        public TableRow(int initCapacity, int halign, int valign)
        // Public Instance Methods
        public synchronized TableRow addCell(TableCell cell)
        public synchronized TableRow addCell(String str)
        public int cells()
        public synchronized TableCell cellAt(int index)
        public TableRow setIHAlign(int halign)
        public TableRow setIVAlign(int valign)
        public synchronized TableRow setCellAt(int index, SimpleItem item)
        public synchronized String toHTML() //Overrides Item.toHTML
        public TableRow setBackgroundColor(String color)
        public TableRow setBackgroundColor(Color color)
        public TableRow setBorderColor(String color)
        public TableRow setBorderColor(Color color)
        public synchronized String toString() //Overrides Item.toString
}
```

oracle.html.TableRowCell

This class is typically instantiated automatically when adding items to TableRow, and is not typically called directly.

```
public class TableRowCell extends TableCell {
        // Public Constructors
        public TableRowCell(int valign, int halign)
        public TableRowCell()
        // Public Instance Methods
        public String toHTML() //Overrides Item.toHTML
        public String toString() //Overrides Item.toString
        // Protected Instance Methods
        protected String startTag() //Overrides Item.startTag
}
```

oracle.html.TextArea

This class is used to create and insert a text area into an HTML form. A text area is a input field that accepts multiple lines of input, in contrast to the single-line support of TextField.

```
public class TextArea extends Item {
    // Public Constructors
    public TextArea(String name, int cols, int rows, String val)
    public TextArea(String name, int cols, int rows)
    // Public Instance Methods
    public TextArea setCols(int cols)
    public TextArea setRows(int rows)
    public TextArea setDefaultContent(String val)
    public String toHTML() // overrides Item.toHTML
    // Protected Instance Methods
    protected String endTag() // overrides Item.endTag
    protected String startTag() // overrides Item.startTag
}
```

oracle.html.TextField

Used for creating a single-line text entry field for use in an HTML form.

```
public class TextField extends FormElement {
    // Public Constructors
    public TextField(String name, int maxlength, int size, String value)
    public TextField(String name)
}
```

oracle.html.UnOrderedList

A subclass of List that implements support for an HTML unordered list. Unordered list items are preceded with bullets, rather than numbers.

```
public class UnOrderedList extends List {
    // Public Constructors
    public UnOrderedList(String type, boolean compact)
    public UnOrderedList()
    // Protected Instance Methods
    protected String endTag() // overrides List.endTag
    protected String startTag() // overrides List.startTag
}
```

oracle.html.XObject

The XObject class implements an OBJECT element of an HTML page as specified in version 3.2 of the HTML standard.

```
public class XObject extends Item, implement IVAlign, IHAlign {
    // Public Constructors
    public XObject(String classID, String codeBase, String codeType,
            String data, boolean declare, String align, int border, int
            width, int height, int vspace, int hspace, String name,
            String standby, boolean shapes, String useMap)
    public XObject(String classID, String codeBase, String codeType,
            String data, boolean declare)
    // Public Instance Methods
    public XObject addParam(String name, String value)
    public XObject setAlign(String align)
    public XObject setBorder(int border)
    public XObject setClassID(String classID)
    public XObject setCodeBase(String codeBase)
    public XObject setCodeType(String codeType)
    public XObject setData(String data)
    public XObject setDeclare(boolean declare)
    public XObject setHeight(int height)
    public XObject setHSpace(int hspace)
    public XObject setName(String name)
    public XObject setShapes(boolean shapes)
    public XObject setStandby(String standby)
    public XObject setUseMap(String useMap)
    public XObject setVSpace(int vspace)
    public XObject setWidth(int width)
    public String toHTML() // overrides Item.toHTML
    public synchronized String toString() // overrides Item.toString
    // Protected Instance Methods
    protected String startTag() // overrides Item.startTag
    protected String endTag() // overrides Item.endTag
}
```

Package oracle.lang

This package provides the NLS class that, among other things, implements utility functions for mapping between Unicode and NLS character sets.

oracle.lang.CharacterSetException

```
public class CharacterSetException extends NLSRuntimeException {
    // Public Constructors
    public CharacterSetException(String s)
}
```

oracle.lang.NLS

This class provides support for Oracle's National Language Support services from within Java. In the current implementation, however, only the 7-bit ASCII character set is supported.

```
public class NLS extends Object {
    // Public static final variables
    public final static int ASCII
    // No constructors
    // Public Class Methods
    public static int NLSBufferSize(char str[], int charSet)
    public static int length(byte str[], int length, int charSet)
    public static int Unicode2NLS(char src[], byte dst[], int srcBegin,
                                  int srcEnd, int dstBegin, int charSet)
    public static int NLS2Unicode(byte src[],char dst[], int srcBegin,
                                  int srcEnd, int dstBegin, int charSet)
    public static int currentCharSet()
    public static synchronized void setCurrentCharSet(int charSet)
}
```

oracle.lang.NLSRuntimeException

```
public class NLSRuntimeException extends RuntimeException {
    // Public Constructors
    public NLSRuntimeException(String s)
}
```

Package oracle.owas.wrb

This package and its subpackages support access to various parts of the WRB services that would not otherwise be accessible from within Java.

oracle.owas.wrb.WRB

The setClientContext() method sets the client context. The client context will be saved until the Java interpreter cartridge shuts down or is reset by a new context. The getWRBContext() method can be used by classes that use native methods to access the WRB API.

```
public class WRB extends Object {
        // Public Class Methods
        public static Object getClientContext()
        public static long getWRBContext() throws WRBNotRunningException
        public static void setClientContext(Object context)
}
```

Package oracle.owas.wrb.nls

This package provides classes for supporting Oracle's National Language Support system, and for converting between NLS and Unicode, ISO or IANA standard names and encodings.

oracle.owas.wrb.nls.CharacterSet

CharacterSet is an abstract class that can be used to implement specific support for character sets. Developers will rarely have a need to create concrete classes that inherit from CharacterSet, but will instead access CharacterSet subclasses from the CharacterSetManager static methods.

```
public class CharacterSet extends Object {
        // Public static final variables
        public final static String DEFAULT_NLS_LANG
        // Public Constructors
        public CharacterSet()
        // Public Abstract Instance Methods
        public abstract int bytesToChars(byte src[], char dst[],
                                int srcBegin, int length,
                                int dstBegin)
        public abstract int charsToBytes(char src[], byte dst[],
                                int srcBegin, int length, int
                                dstBegin)
        public abstract String getName()
```

```
// Public Instance Methods
public int bytesToBytes(byte src[], byte dst[], int srcBegin,
                        int length, CharacterSet srcCharSet, int dstBegin)
public String bytesToString(byte bytes[])
public boolean equals(CharacterSet charSet)
public abstract int getMaxBytesPerChar()
public int minByteSize(int charCount)
public int minByteSize(char chars[], int begin, int length)
public int minByteSize(char chars[])
public abstract int minCharSize(int byteCount)
public int minCharSize(byte bytes[], int begin, int length)
public int minCharSize(byte bytes[])
public int minByteSize(int byteCount, CharacterSet srcCharSet)
public int minByteSize(byte bytes[], CharacterSet srcCharSet)
public int minByteSize(byte bytes[], int begin, int length,
                       CharacterSet srcCharSet)
public byte[] stringToBytes(String string)
}
```

oracle.owas.wrb.nls.CharacterSetException

```
public class CharacterSetException extends NLSRuntimeException {
    // Public Constructors
    public CharacterSetException(String s)
}
```

oracle.owas.wrb.nls.CharacterSetManager

This class manages various character sets used by Oracle.

```
public class CharacterSetManager extends Object {
    // Public static final variables
    public final static int ORACLE_CHARSET
    public final static int IANA_CHARSET
    // Public Class Methods
    public static CharacterSet getCharacterSet()

    public static CharacterSet getCharacterSet(String name)
    public static CharacterSet getCharacterSet(int type, String name)
}
```

oracle.owas.wrb.nls.NLS_LANG

This class provides support for managing Oracle NLS language information. The static methods convert between ISO or IANA standard names and Oracle NLS names. The instance methods set the NLS attributes for the object. The default NLS language is AMERICAN_AMERICA.US7ASCII.

```
public class NLS_LANG extends Object {
        // Public static final variables
        public final static String DEFAULT_NLS_LANG
        // Public Constructors
        public NLS_LANG()
        public NLS_LANG(String NLS_LANG)
        public NLS_LANG(String acceptLanguage, String NLS_LANG)
        // Public Class Methods
        public static NLS_LANG getCurrent()
        public static String getIANACharacterSet(String charSet)
        public static String getISOLanguage(String language)
        public static String getISOTerritory(String territory)
        public static String getOracleLanguage(String language)
        public static String getOracleTerritory(String territory)
        public static String getOracleCharacterSet(String name)
        // Public Instance Methods
        public void setAcceptLanguage(String acceptLanguage, String NLS_LANG)
        public String getContentLanguage()
        public synchronized void setValue(String NLS_LANG)
        public String getValue()
        public String getLanguage()
        public String getTerritory()
        public String getCharacterSet()
        public String getISOLanguage()
        public String getIANACharacterSet()
        public String getISOTerritory()
        public void setCharacterSet(String characterSet)
        public void setLanguage(String language)
        public void setTerritory(String territory)
        public String toString() // overrides Object.toString
}
```

oracle.owas.wrb.nls.NLSRuntimeException

```
public class NLSRuntimeException extends RuntimeException {
        // Public Constructors
```

```
            public NLSRuntimeException(String s)
      }
```

Package oracle.owas.wrb.services.http

This package only contains a single class—HTTP—for use by developers.

oracle.owas.wrb.services.http.HTTP

This class manages information associated with the current HTTP request that is being serviced by the WRB Java cartridge. Note that objects of this class are not created by the user, but rather the single HTTP object for the request is accessed with the getRequest() method.

```
      public class HTTP extends Object {
            // Public Class Methods
            public static HTTP getRequest()
            // Public Instance Methods
            public String getAcceptCharset(String preferredCharset)
            public Enumeration getAcceptCharsets()
            public Enumeration getAcceptLanguages()
            public String getAcceptLanguage(String preferredLang)
            public String getCGIEnvironment(String name)
            public Hashtable getCGIEnvironments()
            public String getHeader(String name)
            public Hashtable getHeaders()
            public String getPreferredAcceptCharset()
            public String getPreferredAcceptLanguage()
            public CharacterSet getURLCharacterSet()
            public void getURLParameters(Hashtable table)
            public Hashtable getURLParameters()
            public void getURLParameters(Vector names, Vector values)
            public String getURLParameter(String name)
            public synchronized void setURLCharacterSet(String charSet)
            public synchronized void setURLCharacterSet(String
                                          charSetParamName, String
                                          defaultCharSet)
            public synchronized void setURLCharacterSet(CharacterSet charSet)
      }
```

Package oracle.owas.wrb.services.logger

This package provides a single class that is used by developers, OutputLogStream. This class offers access to the WRB logging service.

oracle.owas.wrb.services.logger.OutputLogStream

This class provides a Java wrapper to the WRB's logging service.

```
public class OutputLogStream extends PrintStream {
    // Public final static variables
    public final static int DEST_DEFAULT
    public final static int DEST_DATABASE
    public final static int DEST_FILESYSTEM
    public final static int SEVERITY_FATAL
    public final static int SEVERITY_ERROR
    public final static int SEVERITY_WARNING
    public final static int SEVERITY_INIT_TERM_RELOAD
    public final static int SEVERITY_AUTH_EXEC
    public final static int SEVERITY_DEBUG
    // Public Constructors
    public OutputLogStream() throws IOException
    public OutputLogStream(String component) throws IOException
    public OutputLogStream(String component, int destination, File file) throws
                    IOException
    public OutputLogStream(String component, int destination, File file,
                    CharacterSet charSet) throws IOException
    public PBoolean()
    public PBoolean(boolean value)
    // Public Instance Methods
    public synchronized void print(String s) // overrides PrintStream.print
    public void println(int severity) // overrides PrintStream.println
    public synchronized void println(int severity, Object obj)
    public synchronized void println(int severity, String s)
    public synchronized void println(int severity, char s[])
    public synchronized void println(int severity, char c)
    public synchronized void println(int severity, int i)
    public synchronized void println(int severity, long l)
    public synchronized void println(int severity, float f)
    public synchronized void println(int severity, double d)
    public synchronized void println(int severity, boolean b)
    public synchronized void setSeverity(int severity)
    public synchronized int getSeverity()
}
```

Package oracle.plsql

The oracle.plsql package provides a collection of classes that are used to interoperate with the Oracle database. These classes are primarily used when working with the wrapper classes generated by the pl2java utility.

oracle.plsql.NonUniformSizeException

This exception is generated because the values in a PL/SQL array have sizes that are not uniform.

```
public class NonUniformSizeException extends PLSQLRuntimeException {
    // Public Constructors
    public NonUniformSizeException(String s)
}
```

oracle.plsql.NullValueException

This exception is generated if attempting to get an item that is null. Use the isNull() method of PValue subclasses to check if the value is null prior to attempting access.

```
public class NullValueException extends PLSQLRuntimeException {
    // Public Constructors
    public NullValueException(String s)
}
```

oracle.plsql.PBoolean

This class implements a wrapper for an Oracle BOOLEAN value.

```
public class PBoolean extends PValue {
    // Public Constructors
    public PBoolean()
    public PBoolean(boolean value)
    // Public Instance Methods
    public boolean booleanValue() throws NullValueException
    public void copy(PBoolean value)
    public void setValue(boolean value)
    public String toString() // overrides PValue.toString
}
```

oracle.plsql.PByteArray

This class implements a wrapper for RAW or LONG RAW columns using a Java array of bytes.

```
public class PByteArray extends PValue {
    // Public Constructors
    public PByteArray(int length)
    public PByteArray(int length, byte value[])
    public PByteArray(byte value[])
    // Public Instance Methods
    public byte[] byteArrayValue() throws NullValueException
    public synchronized Object clone() // overrides PValue.clone
    public void copy(PByteArray value)
    public void getByteArray(byte buffer[]) throws NullValueException
    public int length()
    public void setValue(byte value[])
    public String toString() // overrides PValue.toString
    public void useBuffer(boolean use)
}
```

oracle.plsql.PDate

This class implements a wrapper for an Oracle DATE value. Note that in Java 1.0, date support is limited in terms of the class's functionality as well as the supported date ranges.

```
public class PDate extends PValue {
    // Public Constructors
    public PDate(Date value)
    public PDate()
    // Public Instance Methods
    public void copy(PDate value)
    public Date dateValue() throws NullValueException
    public void getDate(Date date) throws NullValueException
    public void setValue(Date date)
    public synchronized Object clone() // overrides PValue.clone
    public String toString() // overrides PValue.toString
}
```

oracle.plsql.PDouble

This class implements a wrapper for an Oracle NUMBER value. If the number is an integer, PInteger may also be used.

```
public class PDouble extends PValue {
      // Public Constructors
      public PDouble(double value)
      public PDouble(int value)
      public PDouble()
      // Public Instance Methods
      public void copy(PDouble value)
      public double doubleValue() throws NullValueException
      public int intValue() throws NullValueException
      public void setValue(double value)
      public void setValue(int value)
      public String toString() // overrides PValue.toString
}
```

oracle.plsql.PInteger

This class implements an integer wrapper for an Oracle NUMBER value.

```
public class PInteger extends PValue {
      // Public Constructors
      public PInteger(int value)
      public PInteger()
      // Public Instance Methods
      public void copy(PInteger value)
      public int intValue() throws NullValueException
      public void setValue(int value)
      public String toString() // overrides PValue.toString
}
```

oracle.plsql.PLSQLRuntimeException

```
public class PLSQLRuntimeException extends RuntimeException {
      // Public Constructors
      public PLSQLRuntimeException(String s)
}
```

oracle.plsql.PStringBuffer

This class implements a wrapper for an Oracle CHAR, VARCHAR2, or LONG value. This class has similar functionality to java.lang.StringBuffer. This class also automatically converts strings into the NLS character set that is specified in oracle.lang.NLS.

```
public class PStringBuffer extends PValue {
    // Public Constructors
    public PStringBuffer(int capacity)
    public PStringBuffer(int length, String str)
    public PStringBuffer(String str)
    public PStringBuffer(int length, StringBuffer str)
    // Public Instance Methods
    public int capacity()
    public synchronized Object clone() // overrides PValue.clone
    public void copy(PStringBuffer value)
    public _CharacterSet getOutputCharacterSet()
    public byte[] getByteArray() throws NullValueException
    public void getStringBuffer(StringBuffer str) throws NullValueException
    public int getValue(byte dst[], int dstBegin) // overrides PValue.getValue
    public int length()
    public void setOutputCharacterSet(_CharacterSet characterSet)
    public void setValue(String value)
    public void setValue(StringBuffer value)
    public StringBuffer stringBufferValue() throws NullValueException
    public String stringValue() throws NullValueException
    public byte[] toByteArray() throws NullValueException
    public char[] toCharArray() throws NullValueException
    public String toString() // overrides PValue.toString
    public void useBuffer(boolean use)
}
```

oracle.plsql.PValue

This is the base class of all Java wrappers for SQL or PL/SQL types. Its primary function is to provide support for objects whose value may be null.

```
public class PValue extends Object implements Cloneable {
    // Public Instance Methods
    public Object clone() // overrides Object.clone
    public void copy(PValue value)
```

```
        public boolean isNull()
        public void setNull()
        public String toString() // overrides Object.toString
}
```

oracle.plsql.VariableException

```
public class VariableException extends Exception {
        // Public Constructors
        public VariableException(String s)
}
```

Package oracle.rdbms

The primary class in the oracle.rdbms package is Session, which implements a connection to an Oracle database. This Session object is used by Java wrappers for PL/SQL packages created with pl2java.

oracle.rdbms.ServerException

This exception is triggered by errors either during connection to the RDBMS or during execution of a stored procedure or other database operation. It provides the getSqlcode() and getSqlerrm() methods to access the error number as well as the text description of the error.

```
public class ServerException extends Exception {
        // Public Constructors
        public ServerException (int sqlcode, String sqlerrm)
        // Public Instance Methods
        public int getSqlcode()
        public String getSqlerrm()
}
```

oracle.rdbms.Session

The Session class provides the mechanism through which database connections are made for use with the Java wrapper classes generated by pl2java. The setProperty() method provides a mechanism for setting environment variables such as ORACLE_HOME, while the setSessionProperty() sets session properties, such as NLS languages and formats.

```
public class Session extends Object {
    // Public Constructors
    public Session()
    public Session(Properties props)
    public Session(String username, String password, String connectStr)
            throws ServerException
    public Session(String username, String password, String connectStr,
            Properties props) throws ServerException
    public Session(String usernamePassword) throws ServerException
    public Session(String usernamePassword, Properties props) throws
            ServerException
    //Public Instance Methods
    public void logon(String username, String password, String connectStr)
            throws ServerException
    public void autoCommit(boolean autoCommit) throws ServerException
    public int charToByteSize(int charCount)
    public void commit() throws ServerException
    public int getMaxChars() throws ServerException
    public int getMaxChars(int maxChars) throws ServerException
    public int getMaxRows(int rowSize) throws ServerException
    public int getMaxRows(int rowSize, int maxRows)
            throws ServerException
    public static String getProperty(String name)
    public String getSessionInfo()
    public String getSessionProperty(String name)
            throws ServerException
    public boolean isConnected() throws ServerException
    public void logoff() throws ServerException
    public void logon(String usernamePassword)
            throws ServerException
    public void rollback() throws ServerException
    public static void setProperty(String name, String value)
    public void setSessionProperty(String name, String value) throws
            ServerException
    public void setProperties(boolean check)
    // Protected Instance Methods
    protected void finalize() throws Throwable // overrides Object.finalize
}
```

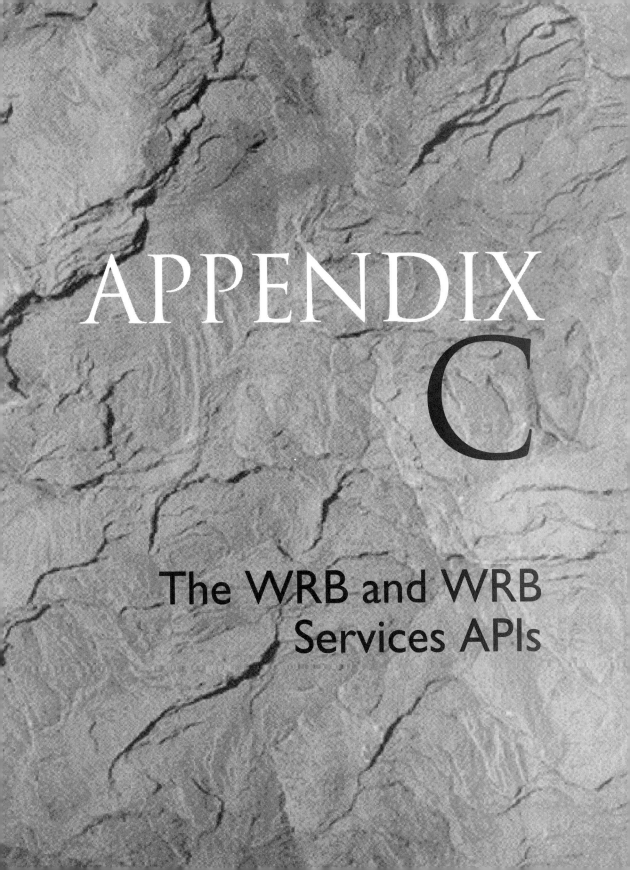

APPENDIX
C

The WRB and WRB Services APIs

his appendix describes the data structures and methods used by the various components of the WRB. See Chapters 10 and 11 for more detailed tutorial information about how to create a cartridge and how to use the various WRB service APIs.

WRB Engine API

Datatypes

WRBpBlockElem, the Web Request Broker Parameter Block

The WRBpBlockElem structure is a key datatype used by many of the WRB API functions. Its primary purpose is to encapsulate a collection of name-value pairs such as form element names and values, or HTTP request header names and values. The subsection "Working with Parameter Blocks" below details the utility functions that are available for working with arrays of WRBpBlockElem.

DEFINITION

```
typedef struct _WRBPBElem
{
  text *szParamName;
  sb4 nParamName;
  text *szParamValue;
  sb4 nParamValue;
  ub2 nParamType;
  dvoid *pNVdata;
} WRBpBlockElem;
```

ELEMENTS

Element	Type	Description
szParamName	text *	The name component of the name-value pair.
nParamName	sb4	The size, in bytes, of the szParamName element. If -1, szParamName will be interpreted as a standard C (i.e., null-terminated) string.
szParamValue	text *	The value component of the name-value pair.
nParamValue	sb4	The size, in bytes, of the szParamValue element. If -1, szParamValue will be interpreted as a standard C (i.e., null-terminated) string.

Element	Type	Description
nParamType	ub2	Specifies the datatype as which the content of szParamValue should be interpreted. See Table C-1 for a list of values and their meanings.
pNVdata	dvoid *	Used by certain WRB API calls such as WRB_getMultAppConfigSection() to associate other arbitrary data with a name-value pair.

WRBErrorCode

The WRBErrorCode type is mapped to the sb4 datatype. The codes used as WRBErrorCode are simply integers representing a subset of the standard HTTP errors that are cast to the WRBErrorCode type. The table under "Meanings" below shows the error codes supported as return values and their meanings.

DEFINITION

 `typedef sb4 WRBErrorCode;`

MEANINGS

WRBErrorCode Value	Meaning
200	OK
201	Created
202	Accepted
203	Non-Authoritative Information
204	No Content
300	Multiple Choices
301	Moved Permanently
302	Moved Temporarily
303	See Other
304	Not Modified
400	Bad Request
401	Unauthorized
402	Payment Required
403	Forbidden
404	Not Found
500	Internal Server Error
501	Not Implemented
502	Bad Gateway
503	Service Unavailable

Parameter Type (nParamType)	Interpret szParamValue as:
WRBPT_DONTCARE	Unspecified
WRBPT_NUMBER	Number
WRBPT_STRING	Character string
WRBPT_DATE	Calendar date in SQL date type format
WRBPT_RAW	Raw binary data

TABLE C-1. *Possible Values of WRBpBlockElem.nParamType*

WRBReturnCode

The WRBReturnCode type is an enumeration used to specify return values passed back by a cartridge to the WRB. In addition, several WRB API functions return a WRBReturnCode rather than a WAPIReturnCode. The meanings of the various result codes are listed in the table under "Meanings" below.

DEFINITION

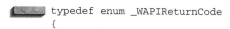

```
typedef enum _WRBReturnCode
{
  WRB_DONE,
  WRB_ERROR,
  WRB_ABORT
} WRBReturnCode;
```

MEANINGS

Value	Meaning
WRB_DONE	Routine completed normally.
{WRB_ERROR	An error occurred during execution.
WRB_ABORT	A serious error occurred during execution and the calling wrbc process should terminate immediately.

WAPIReturnCode

The WAPIReturnCode type is an enumeration used to specify return values from many of the core WRB API functions. The meanings of the various result codes are listed in the table under "Meanings" below.

DEFINITION

```
typedef enum _WAPIReturnCode
{
```

```
    WRB_SUCCESS = 0,
    WRB_FAIL = -1,
    WRB_NOTLOADED = -2,
    WRB_LOWMEM = -3,
    WRB_TOOLATE = -100,
    WRB_AUTHNEEDED = -101,
    WRB_MOREDATA = -102,
    WRB_OUTSIDE = -200,
    WRB_PROTOCOL_ERROR = -201,
    WRB_MIXED = -202,
    WRB_HAZARD = -203,
    WRB_COMMITTED = -204,
    WRB_ROLLBACK = -205
} WAPIReturnCode;
```

MEANINGS

Value	Meaning
WRB_SUCCESS	Normal, successful execution.
WRB_FAIL	An error occurred.
WRB_NOTLOADED	Returned if a call is made to a service that is not loaded.
WRB_LOWMEM	Indicates that a call to malloc() failed.
WRB_TOOLATE	Returned if cartridge attempts to write HTTP header after writing other data to the stream.
WRB_MOREDATA	Not an error, but returned by ICX_MakeRequest if not all data was returned in first request.
WRB_OUTSIDE	Resource Manager in a local transaction.
WRB_PROTOCOL_ERROR	Made call in improper context.
WRB_MIXED	Returns if a transaction using two-phase commit was partially committed or rolled back.
WRB_HAZARD	Returns if a transaction using two-phase commit may be partially committed or rolled back. This may require action by a DBA to force the transaction.
WRB_COMMITED	Transaction committed normally.
WRB_ROLLBACK	Transaction rolled back normally.

The WRBEntry Structure

The WRBGetParsedContent() and WRBGetNamedEntry() functions use the WRBEntry type to store name-value pairs extracted from the query string or POST data that accompanies an HTTP request.

```
typedef struct _WRBEntry {
   char *name;
   char *value;
} WRBEntry;
```

Working with Parameter Blocks

> **NOTE**
> *Several routines return pointers to a*
> *WRBpBlockElem. In these cases, the returned value*
> *points to the WRBpBlock structure, not to a copy of*
> *the element. Thus, the pointer will be valid only*
> *until the element or WRBpBlock itself is deleted.*
> *One should not attempt to free the storage referred*
> *to by the pointer.*

WRB_addPBElem()

PURPOSE AND USAGE   WRB_addPBElem() adds an element to a specified
parameter block. You must first have created the parameter block with
WRB_createPBlock().

SYNTAX

WAPIReturnCode WRB_addPBElem (dvoid *WRBCtx, WRBpBlock hPBlock,
                     text *szParamName, sb4 nParamName,
                     dvoid *vParamValue, sb4 nParamValue,
                     ub2 nParamType);

PARAMETERS

Parameter	Type	Description
WRBCtx	dvoid *	The pointer to the opaque WRB context object that the WRB application engine passed to your cartridge function.
hPBlock	WRBpBlock	The parameter block.
szParamName	text *	The name of the element to be added.
nParamName	sb4	The size in bytes of the name of the element to be added. If you set this parameter to -1, the function uses the strlen() library function to determine the length of the element name.

Parameter	Type	Description
vParamValue	dvoid *	The value of the element to be added.
nParamValue	sb4	The size in bytes of the name of the element to be added. If you set this parameter to -1, the function uses the strlen() library function to determine the length of the element value.
nParamType	ub2	The parameter type. See Table C-1, earlier in this appendix, for possible values.

RETURN VALUES   WRB_addPBElem() returns a value of type WAPIReturnCode.

WRB_copyPBlock()

PURPOSE AND USAGE   WRB_copyPBlock() creates a copy of the specified parameter block.

SYNTAX

WRBpBlock WRB_copyPBlock(dvoid *WRBCtx, WRBpBlock hPBlock);

PARAMETERS

Parameter	Type	Description
WRBCtx	void *	The pointer to the opaque WRB context object that the WRB application engine passed to your cartridge function
hPBlock	WRBpBlock	The parameter block you want to copy

RETURN VALUES   WRB_copyPBlock() returns a value of type WRBpBlock that identifies a copy of the specified parameter block. WRB_copyPBlock() returns NULL on failure.

WRB_createPBlock()

PURPOSE AND USAGE   WRB_createPBlock() allocates a parameter block.

SYNTAX

WRBpBlock WRB_createPBlock (dvoid *WRBCtx);

PARAMETERS

Parameter	Type	Description
WRBCtx	void *	The pointer to the opaque WRB context object that the WRB application engine passed to your cartridge function

RETURN VALUES   WRB_createPBlock() returns a variable of type WRBpBlock that identifies the newly created parameter block. WRB_createPBlock() returns NULL on failure.

WRB_delPBElem()

PURPOSE AND USAGE   WRB_delPBElem() deletes an element from a parameter block, given the element's name.

SYNTAX

```
WAPIReturnCode WRB_delPBElem (dvoid *WRBCtx,WRBpBlock hPBlock,
                            text *szName, sb4 nNamel);
```

PARAMETERS

Parameter	Type	Description
WRBCtx	void *	The pointer to the opaque WRB context object that the WRB application engine passed to your cartridge function.
hPBlock	WRBpBlock	The parameter block.
szName	text *	The name of the element to be deleted from the parameter block.
nName1	sb4	The length in bytes of the element name. If this parameter is set to -1, the function uses strlen() function to determine the length of the element name.

RETURN VALUES   WRB_delPBElem() returns a value of type WAPIReturnCode.

WRB_destroyPBlock()

PURPOSE AND USAGE   WRB_destroyPBlock() destroys a specified parameter block and frees the associated resources. Unless noted elsewhere, this routine must be called for any parameter block that you have finished using.

SYNTAX

WAPIReturnCode WRB_destroyPBlock (dvoid *WRBCtx,
                                  WRBpBlock hPBlock);

PARAMETERS

Parameter	Type	Description
WRBCtx	void *	The pointer to the opaque WRB context object that the WRB application engine passed to your cartridge function
hPBlock	WRBpBlock	The parameter block to be destroyed

RETURN VALUES WRB_destroyPBlock() returns a value of type WAPIReturnCode.

WRB_findPBElem()

PURPOSE AND USAGE WRB_findPBElem() finds an element in a parameter block, given a name, and returns a pointer to it.

SYNTAX

WRBpBlockElem * WRB_findPBElem(dvoid *WRBCtx, WRBpBlock hPBlock,
                                text *szName, sb4 nNamel);

PARAMETERS

Parameter	Type	Description
WRBCtx	void *	The pointer to the opaque WRB context object that the WRB application engine passed to your cartridge function.
hPBlock	WRBpBlock	The parameter block to be searched.
szName	text *	The element name for which to search.
nNamel	sb4	The length in bytes of the element name. If you set this parameter to -1, the function uses the strlen() library function to determine the length of the element name.

RETURN VALUES WRB_findPBElem() returns a pointer to the parameter block element identified by szName. WRB_findPBElem() returns NULL on failure.

WRB_findPBElemVal()

PURPOSE AND USAGE   WRB_findPBElemVal() finds and returns the value of a named element in a parameter block. Unlike WRB_findPBElem, this routine simply returns a pointer to the text value associated with the name.

SYNTAX

```
text * WRB_findPBElemVal( dvoid *WRBCtx, WRBpBlock hPBlock,
                text *szName, sb4 nNamel);
```

PARAMETERS

Parameter	Type	Description
WRBCtx	void *	The pointer to the opaque WRB context object that the WRB application engine passed to your cartridge function.
hPBlock	WRBpBlock	The parameter block to be searched.
szName	text *	The element name for which to search.
nNamel	sb4	The length in bytes of the element name. If you set this parameter to -1, the function uses the strlen() library function to determine the length of the element name.

RETURN VALUES   WRB_findPBElemVal() returns a pointer to text string containing the value of the parameter block element identified by szName. WRB_findPBElemVal() returns NULL on failure.

WRB_firstPBElem()

PURPOSE AND USAGE   WRB_firstPBElem() returns a pointer to the first element in a parameter block. In conjunction with WRB_nextPBElem(), this routine provides classic enumeration-style access to a WRBpBlock. Note that this method of access is more efficient than the array-style access provided by WRB_walkPBlock().

SYNTAX

```
WRBpBlockElem * WRB_firstPBElem( dvoid *WRBCtx, WRBpBlock hPBlock,
                dvoid ** pos);
```

PARAMETERS

Parameter	Type	Description
WRBCtx	void *	The pointer to the opaque WRB context object that the WRB application engine passed to your cartridge function
hPBlock	WRBpBlock	The parameter block to be searched
pos	dvoid **	A pointer to the location in which the function places an opaque pointer representing the next available parameter block element

RETURN VALUES   WRB_firstBElem() returns a pointer to the first element in a parameter block element. WRB_firstPBElem() returns NULL on failure.

WRB_nextPBElem()

PURPOSE AND USAGE   WRB_nextPBElem() returns a pointer to the next available element in a parameter block. WRB_nextPBElem() is used with WRB_firstPBElem() to iterate through a parameter block. You must call WRB_firstPBElem() to initialize the pos parameter before calling WRB_nextPBElem().

SYNTAX

```
WRBpBlockElem * WRB_firstPBElem( dvoid *WRBCtx, WRBpBlock hPBlock,
                                 dvoid ** pos);
```

PARAMETERS

Parameter	Type	Description
WRBCtx	void *	The pointer to the opaque WRB context object that the WRB application engine passed to your cartridge function.
{hPBlock	WRBpBlock	The parameter block to be searched.
pos	dvoid *	An opaque pointer representing the next available parameter block element. You must first initialize this value by calling WRB_firstPBElem().

RETURN VALUES   WRB_nextBElem() returns a pointer to the next available element in a parameter block element. WRB_nextPBElem() returns NULL on failure.

WRB_numPBElem()

PURPOSE AND USAGE WRB_numPBElem() returns the number of elements in a parameter block. Typically used in conjunction with WRB_walkPBlock().

SYNTAX

sb4 WRB_numPBElem (dvoid *WRBCtx, WRBpBlock hPBlock);

PARAMETERS

Parameter	Type	Description
WRBCtx	void *	The pointer to the opaque WRB context object that the WRB application engine passed to your cartridge function
hPBlock	WRBpBlock	The parameter block

RETURN VALUES WRB_numPBElem() returns the number of elements in a specified parameter block.

WRB_walkPBlock()

PURPOSE AND USAGE WRB_walkPBlock() returns a pointer to the element at a specified position in a parameter block. You can use WRB_numPBElem() and WRB_walkPBlock() to iterate through the elements of a parameter block in a for loop, or if array-style read access to the block is necessary.

SYNTAX

WRBpBlockElem * WRB_walkPBlock (dvoid *WRBCtx, WRBpBlock hPBlock, sb4 nPosition);

PARAMETERS

Parameter	Type	Description
WRBCtx	dvoid *	The pointer to the opaque WRB context object that the WRB application engine passed to your cartridge function
hPBlock	WRBpBlock	The parameter block
nPosition	sb4	The position of the element in the parameter block

RETURN VALUES   WRB_walkPBlock() returns a pointer to the element at a specified position in a parameter block. WRB_walkPBlock() returns NULL on failure.

Configuration Functions

WRB_getAppConfigSection()

PURPOSE AND USAGE   WRB_getAppConfigSection() passes back a parameter block containing the name-value pairs defined in a specified section of the WRB configuration. You can use WRB_getAppConfigSection() to retrieve configuration data for your own cartridge or other cartridges. You must call WRB_destroyPBlock() on the parameter block when you are finished with it.

SYNTAX

```
WAPIReturnCode WRB_getAppConfigSection( dvoid *WRBCtx,
                                        text *szSectionName,
                                        WRBpBlock *hSection);
```

PARAMETERS

Parameter	Type	Description
WRBCtx	void *	The pointer to the opaque WRB context object that the WRB application engine passed to your cartridge function
szSectionName	text *	The name of the cartridge configuration section you want to retrieve
hSection	WRBpBlock *	A pointer to the location where the function places the parameter block containing the name/value pairs retrieved from the specified section

RETURN VALUES   WRB_getAppConfigSection() returns a value of type WAPIReturnCode.

WRB_getAppConfigVal()

PURPOSE AND USAGE   WRB_getAppConfigVal() returns the value of a named parameter defined in the specified section of the WRB configuration data.

You can use WRB_getAppConfigVal() to retrieve the value of a configuration parameter when you know the parameter's name.

SYNTAX

text * WRB_getAppConfigVal(dvoid *WRBCtx, text *szSectionName,
                            text *szName);

PARAMETERS

Parameter	Type	Description
WRBCtx	void *	The pointer to the opaque WRB context object that the WRB application engine passed to your cartridge function
szSectionName	text *	The name of the WRB configuration section to search
szName	text *	The name of the configuration parameter for which you want the value

RETURN VALUES   WRB_getAppConfigVal() returns a pointer to a text string containing the value of the specified parameter defined in the specified section of the WRB configuration data.

WRB_getCartridgeName()

PURPOSE AND USAGE   WRB_getCartridgeName() returns the name by which the calling cartridge is identified in the WRB configuration.

SYNTAX

text * WRB_getCartridgeName(dvoid *WRBCtx);

PARAMETERS

Parameter	Type	Description
WRBCtx	void *	The pointer to the opaque WRB context object that the WRB application engine passed to your cartridge function

RETURN VALUES   WRB_getCartridgeName() returns a pointer to a text string containing the name by which the calling cartridge is identified in the WRB configuration data.

WRB_getCookies()

PURPOSE AND USAGE   WRB_getCookies() passes back a parameter block containing the cookies associated with the current request. You can use WRB_getCookies() to get the cookies associated with the current request in the form of a parameter block. You need only declare a variable of type WRBpBlock and pass its address as hPBlock. You must call WRB_destroyPBlock() to free the parameter block when you are done using it.

SYNTAX

WAPIReturnCode WRB_getCookies(dvoid *WRBCtx, WRBpBlock *hPBlock);

PARAMETERS

Parameter	Type	Description
WRBCtx	void *	The pointer to the opaque WRB context object that the WRB application engine passed to your cartridge function
hPBlock	WRBpBlock *	The location in which the function stores a parameter block containing the request cookies

RETURN VALUES   WRB_getCookies() returns a value of type WAPIReturnCode.

WRB_getMultAppConfigSection()

PURPOSE AND USAGE   WRB_getMultAppConfigSection() passes back a parameter block containing the name/value pairs defined in all WRB configuration data sections that have names starting with a specified string. You can use WRB_getMultAppConfigSection() to retrieve configuration data for several similarly named cartridges at once. The parameter block passed back has an element for each section in the WRB configuration data. Each section's parameter block element in turn uses its pNBdata member to point to a parameter block containing the name-value pairs defined by that configuration section.

   You must call WRB_destroyPBlock() on the parameter block, as well as the child paramter blocks, when you are finished with it.

SYNTAX

WAPIReturnCode WRB_getMultAppConfigSection(dvoid *WRBCtx,
                                            text *szSectionPrefix,
                                            WRBpBlock *hSection);

PARAMETERS

Parameter	Type	Description
WRBCtx	void *	The pointer to the opaque WRB context object that the WRB application engine passed to your cartridge function.
szSectionPrefix	text *	The prefix string identifying the cartridge configuration sections you want to retrieve. The function retrieves all sections with names that start with this string. If you pass "" (the empty string) for this parameter, the function retrieves the configuration data for all cartridges.
hSection	WRBpBlock *	A pointer to the location where the function places the parameter block containing the name/value pairs retrieved from the specified section.

RETURN VALUES   WRB_getMultAppConfigSection() returns a value of type WAPIReturnCode.

WRB_getORACLE_ HOME()

PURPOSE AND USAGE   WRB_getORACLE_ HOME() returns the value of the ORACLE_ HOME environment variable defined in the environment of the calling cartridge.

SYNTAX

```
text * WRB_getORACLE_ HOME( dvoid *WRBCtx);
```

PARAMETERS

Parameter	Type	Description
WRBCtx	void *	The pointer to the opaque WRB context object that the WRB application engine passed to your cartridge function

RETURN VALUES   WRB_getORACLE_ HOME() returns the value of the ORACLE_ HOME environment variable, or NULL if ORACLE_ HOME is not set.

Run-Time Environment Functions

WRB_getEnvironment()

PURPOSE AND USAGE   WRB_getEnvironment() retrieves the environment variables currently defined in the environment inherited by the calling cartridge and passes back this information in the form of a parameter block it creates. Note that all environment variables available to CGI programs are provided to cartridges by the WRB. The memory used by the parameter block must be freed with WRB_destroyPBlock().

SYNTAX

```
WAPIReturnCode WRB_getEnvironment( dvoid *WRBCtx,
                                    WRBpBlock *hEnvironment);
```

PARAMETERS

Parameter	Type	Description
WRBCtx	void *	The pointer to the opaque WRB context object that the WRB application engine passed to your cartridge function
hEnvironment	WRBpBlock *	A pointer to the location in which the function places the parameter block containing the cartridge environment variables

RETURN VALUES   WRB_getEnvironment() returns a value of type WAPIReturnCode.

WRB_getListenerInfo()

PURPOSE AND USAGE   WRB_getListenerInfo() returns a parameter block containing information about the web listener that forwarded the current request, such as the listener's virtual directory mappings. You can use WRB_getListenerInfo() to get information about the configuration of the web listener that forwarded the current request. See the table under "Listener Information Types" below for data available.

SYNTAX

WRBpBlock WRB_getListenerInfo(dvoid *WRBCtx, ub2 nInfoType);

PARAMETERS

Parameter	Type	Description
WRBCtx	void *	The pointer to the opaque WRB context object that the WRB application engine passed to your cartridge function.
nInfoType	ub2	Specifies the type of information being requested. This must be one of the values listed in Listener Information Types.

LISTENER INFORMATION TYPES

Listener Information Type (nInfoType)	Behavior
WRBL_ DIRMAPS	Requests the listener's virtual-to-physical directory mappings
WRBL_ MIMETYPES	Requests a list of the MIME types the listener supports

RETURN VALUES   WRB_getListenerInfo() returns a parameter block containing the requested information about the web listener that forwarded the current request, or NULL on failure.

Request Parsing Functions

WRB_getParsedContent()

PURPOSE AND USAGE   WRB_getParsedContent() retrieves the current HTTP request's query string if the request method is GET, or its POST data if the request method is POST. WRB_getParsedContent() parses this data and passes it back in a parameter block. Each element in the parameter block contains the name and value of a POST data or query string entry, such as passed by an HTML form. The parameter block must be freed by the cartridge.

SYNTAX

WAPIReturnCode WRB_getParsedContent(dvoid *WRBCtx,
                                     WRBpBlock *hQueryString);

PARAMETERS

Parameter	Type	Description
WRBCtx	void *	The pointer to the opaque WRB context object that the WRB application engine passed to your cartridge function
hQueryString	WRBpBlock *	A pointer to the location in which the function places the parameter block containing the query string or POST data

RETURN VALUES   WRB_getParsedContent() returns a value of type WAPIReturnCode.

WRB_getRequestInfo()

PURPOSE AND USAGE   WRB_getRequestInfo() returns a specific piece of information about an incoming request. Table C-2 enumerates the defined constants that can be passed to WRB_getRequestInfo and the value that will be returned for each information type.

Request Information Type (nInfoType)	Returns
WRBR_ URI	Request URI
WRBR_ URL	Request URL
WRBR_ LISTENERTYPE	The type of listener, such as Oracle WebServer
WRBR_ VIRTUALPATH	Request Virtual path (a substring of the request URI)
WRBR_ PHYSICALPATH	Physical path, if any, to which the virtual path is mapped
WRBR_ QUERYSTRING	Query String of the request
WRBR_ LANGUAGE	Comma-separated list of languages the requestor can accept
WRBR_ ENCODING	Comma-separated list of encodings the requestor can accept
WRBR_ REQMIMETYPE	MIME type of the request
WRBR_ USER	The username provided by the requestor in response to an authentication challenge
WRBR_ PASSWORD	The password provided by the requestor in response to an authentication challenge
WRBR_ IP	The requestor's IP address in dotted quad notation

TABLE C-2.   *Types of Available Request Information*

SYNTAX

text * WRB_getRequestInfo(dvoid *WRBCtx, ub2 nInfoType);

PARAMETERS

Parameter	Type	Description
WRBCtx	void *	The pointer to the opaque WRB context object that the WRB application engine passed to your cartridge function.
nInfoType	ub2	Specifies the type of information being requested. This must be one of the values listed in Request.

RETURN VALUES   WRB_getRequestInfo() returns a pointer to the requested information in the form of a character string. WRB_getRequestInfo() returns NULL on failure.

WRB_read()

PURPOSE AND USAGE   WRB_read() reads the specified number of bytes from the request POST data. You can call WRB_read() from your Exec function to get the POST data associated with the current request. If the POST data is in the form of name/value pairs, it is more convenient to call WRB_getParsedContent(). WRB_read(), however, is useful if raw POST data must be read.

SYNTAX

sb4 WRB_read(dvoid *WRBCtx, text *sBuffer, sb4 nBufferSize);

PARAMETERS

Parameter	Type	Description
WRBCtx	dvoid *	The pointer to the opaque WRB context object that the WRB application engine passed to your cartridge function.
sBuffer	text *	A pointer to the buffer into which the function is to read the POST data. You must provide the storage for this buffer.
nBufferSize	sb4	The size of the buffer in bytes.

RETURN VALUES   WRB_read() returns the number of bytes read, or -1 when an error occurs.

WRB_recvHeaders()

PURPOSE AND USAGE WRB_recvHeaders() creates and passes back a parameter block containing the HTTP headers associated with the current request. The parameter block must be freed by the cartridge.

SYNTAX

```
WAPIReturnCode WRB_recvHeaders( dvoid *WRBCtx,
                                WRBpBlock *hPBlock);
```

PARAMETERS

Parameter	Type	Description
WRBCtx	dvoid *	The pointer to the opaque WRB context object that the WRB application engine passed to your cartridge function
hPBlock	WRBpBlock *	The location in which the function stores a parameter block containing the request headers

RETURN VALUES WRB_recvHeaders() returns a value of type WAPIReturnCode.

Response Generation Functions

WRB_annotateURL()

PURPOSE AND USAGE WRB_annotateURL() is a convenience call that appends the specified query string data to the specified URL and writes the result to the requestor.

SYNTAX

```
sb4 WRB_annotateURL( dvoid *WRBCtx, text *url,
                     WRBpBlock hArguments);
```

PARAMETERS

Parameter	Type	Description
WRBCtx	void *	The pointer to the opaque WRB context object that the WRB application engine passed to your cartridge function

Parameter	Type	Description
url	text *	The text of the base URL without the query string, including "http://", the host name, port (if necessary), and the URI
hArguments	WRBpBlock	A parameter block containing the name-value pairs to be appended to the URL as the query string

RETURN VALUES   WRB_annotateURL() returns the number of bytes written to the requestor, or -1 if an error occurs.

WRB_printf()

PURPOSE AND USAGE   WRB_printf() constructs a text buffer according to the specified format string and writes it to the requestor. In addition to two required parameters, WRB_printf() accepts a variable number of arguments in the manner of the C standard I/ O library function printf(3).

SYNTAX

sb4 WRB_printf(dvoid *WRBCtx, text *formatStr, ...);

PARAMETERS

Parameter	Type	Description
WRBCtx	dvoid *	The pointer to the opaque WRB context object that the WRB application engine passed to your cartridge function
formatStr	text *	A pointer to a text string that specifies the format of the output buffer

RETURN VALUES   WRB_printf() returns the number of bytes written, or -1 if an error occurs.

WRB_sendHeader()

PURPOSE AND USAGE   WRB_sendHeader() sends to the requestor the response headers for the current request. To use, you must create a parameter block and add elements to it for each header, such that the name is the header type and the value is the header content. You must not call WRB_sendHeader() after calling WRBClientWrite().

SYNTAX

WAPIReturnCode WRB_sendHeader(dvoid *WRBCtx, WRBpBlock hPBlock);

PARAMETERS

Parameter	Type	Description
WRBCtx	dvoid *	The pointer to the opaque WRB context object that the WRB application engine passed to your cartridge function
hPBlock	WRBpBlock	The parameter block containing the header data to be set in response to the current request

RETURN VALUES   WRB_sendHeader() returns a value of type WAPIReturnCode. If you call WRB_sendHeader() after calling WRBClientWrite(), WRB_sendHeader() fails and returns WRB_TOOLATE.

WRB_setCookies()

PURPOSE AND USAGE   WRB_setCookies() adds a cookie to the response header for the current request. It can be called repeatedly to set multiple cookies.

SYNTAX

WAPIReturnCode WRB_setCookies(dvoid *WRBCtx, text *name,
                               text *value, text *domain,
                               text *path, text *expire,
                               boolean secure);

PARAMETERS

Parameter	Type	Description
WRBCtx	dvoid *	The pointer to the opaque WRB context object that the WRB application engine passed to your cartridge function.
name	text *	The cookie name.
value	text *	The cookie value.
domain	text *	The DNS domain to which you want the requestor to send the cookie on future request. This is often the domain where your cartridge is running.
path	text *	The URI path for which you want the requestor to send the cookie. This is often a URI that refers to your cartridge.

Parameter	Type	Description
expire	text *	The cookie expiration date. This must be in the standard date format and specified for GMT.
secure	boolean	If set to TRUE, this parameter specifies that the function should use SSL to send cookies.

RETURN VALUES   WRB_setCookies() returns a value of type WAPIReturnCode.

WRB_write()

PURPOSE AND USAGE   WRB_write() writes the specified number of bytes from the specified buffer to the requestor.

SYNTAX

sb4 WRB_write(dvoid *WRBCtx, text *sBuffer, sb4 nBufferSize);

PARAMETERS

Parameter	Type	Description
WRBCtx	dvoid *	The pointer to the opaque WRB context object that the WRB application engine passed to your cartridge function
{sBuffer	text *	A pointer to the buffer containing the data to be written
nBufferSize	sb4	The size of the buffer in bytes

RETURN VALUES   WRB_write() returns the number of bytes written, or -1 when an error occurs.

Authorization Functions

WRB_setAuthBasic()

PURPOSE AND USAGE   You can call WRB_setAuthBasic() in your Authorize function to create a basic authentication realm that your cartridge can use to authenticate requestors. If a cartridge uses WRB_setAuthBasic() to create a realm, its Authorize function is responsible for authentication for the cartridge. Use WRB_setAuthServer() in the cartridge's Init function to specify that the authentication server perform authentication for your cartridge.

SYNTAX

WAPIReturnCode WRB_setAuthBasic(dvoid *WRBCtx, text *szRealm);

PARAMETERS

Parameter	Type	Description
WRBCtx	dvoid *	The pointer to the opaque WRB context object that the WRB application engine passed to your cartridge function
szRealm	text *	The name of the realm to be created

RETURN VALUES   WRB_setAuthBasic() returns a value of type WAPIReturnCode.

WRB_setAuthDigest()

PURPOSE AND USAGE   You can call WRB_setAuthDigest() in your Authorize function to create a digest authentication realm that your cartridge can use to authenticate requestors. If a cartridge uses WRB_ setAuthDigest() to create a realm, its Authorize function is responsible for authentication for the cartridge. Use WRB_setAuthServer() in the cartridge's Init function to specify that the authentication server perform authentication for your cartridge.

SYNTAX

WAPIReturnCode WRB_setAuthDigest(dvoid *WRBCtx, text *szRealm,
                                  text *szOpaque, text *szNonce,
                                  text *szStale);

PARAMETERS

Parameter	Type	Description
WRBCtx	dvoid *	The pointer to the opaque WRB context object that the WRB application engine passed to your cartridge function
szRealm	text *	The realm name
szOpaque	text *	The semantics of this parameter are defined in the internet RFC on digest encodings.
szNonce	text *	The semantics of this parameter are defined in the internet RFC on digest encodings.
szStale	text *	The semantics of this parameter are defined in the internet RFC on digest encodings.

WRB_setAuthServer()

PURPOSE AND USAGE   WRB_setAuthServer() specifies authentication and/or restriction schemes for the authentication server to use in authenticating requestors issuing requests to the calling cartridge. You can call WRB_setAuthServer() in your Init or Authorize function to specify a combination of existing authentication and/or restriction schemes for the authentication server to use in authenticating requestors issuing requests to your cartridge. The schemes are specified in the szProtectString parameter as follows:

scheme (*realm*) [*op scheme* (*realm*) [*op scheme* (*realm*) ...]]

Where *op* is one of "& " (the "and" operator) or "| " (the "or" operator). No operator grouping is permitted, and the operators are evaluated from left to right as in C.

The *scheme* can be one of Basic, Digest, Basic_Oracle, IP, or Domain. The *realm* must be defined in the WRB configuration data either as an authentication realm (for authentication schemes) or as a group name (for IP- or Domain-based restrictions).

SYNTAX

WAPIReturnCode WRB_setAuthServer(dvoid *WRBCtx,
                                                        text *szProtectStr);

PARAMETERS

Parameter	Type	Description
WRBCtx	dvoid *	The pointer to the opaque WRB context object that the WRB application engine passed to your cartridge function
szProtectString	text *	A text string that specifies the authentication or restriction schemes that the authentication server should use in authenticating requestors

RETURN VALUES   WRB_setAuthServer() returns a value of type WAPIReturnCode.

Content Service API

Functions

WRB_CNTopenRepository()

PURPOSE AND USAGE   WRB_CNTopenRepository() establishes a connection to a content repository, such as a database, and returns a pointer to the repository that you can pass to subsequent Content Service API functions.

SYNTAX

```
dvoid * WRB_CNTopenRepository (void *WRBCtx, text *user,
                              text *passwd, text *connectstr);
```

PARAMETERS

Parameter	Type	Description
WRBCtx	void *	The pointer to the opaque WRB context object that the WRB application engine passed to your cartridge function.
user	text *	The user name, such as a database user ID, to be used in connecting to the repository.
passwd	text *	The password of the specified user.
connectstr	text *	The connect string, such as a SQL* Net V2 connect string, to be used to connect to a remote repository. For local databases, installed in the same ORACLE_ HOME directory as the WRB Dispatcher, you may pass NULL for this parameter.

RETURN VALUES   WRB_CNTopenRepository() returns a pointer to the specified repository, or NULL on failure.

WRB_CNTcloseRepository()

PURPOSE AND USAGE   WRB_CNTcloseRepository() closes the connection to the specified repository after it is finished being used.

SYNTAX

WAPIReturnCode WRB_CNTcloseRepository (void *WRBCtx,
dvoid * hRepository);

PARAMETERS

Parameter	Type	Description
WRBCtx	void *	The pointer to the opaque WRB context object that the WRB application engine passed to your cartridge function
hRepository	dvoid *	The pointer to the repository to close

RETURN VALUES   WRB_CNTcloseRepository() returns a value of type WAPIReturnCode.

WRB_CNTopenDocument()

PURPOSE AND USAGE   WRB_CNTopenDocument() finds (or creates, if necessary) a specified document in a content repository and returns a pointer to it that you can use with other Content Service API functions. Note that the flags available for *mode* can be or'd to conjoin modes (e.g., "WRBCS_OPEN | WRBCS_READ").

SYNTAX

dvoid * WRB_CNTopenDocument (void *WRBCtx, dvoid * hRepository,
text *szDocName, ub2 mode);

MODE FLAGS

Mode Flag	Meaning
WRBCS_ CREATE	Create the document if it does not exist
WRBCS_ OPEN	Open the document
WRBCS_ READ	Open the document for reading
WRBCS_ WRITE	Open the document for writing

PARAMETERS

Parameter	Type	Description
WRBCtx	void *	The pointer to the opaque WRB context object that the WRB application engine passed to your cartridge function.
hRepository	dvoid *	A pointer to the repository that contains the document.
szDocName	text *	A pointer to the document name.
mode	ub2	The flags encoded in this field specify whether to open the document for reading and/or writing, and whether to create the document if it does not exist.

RETURN VALUES   WRB_CNTopenDocument() returns a pointer to the specified document, or NULL on failure.

WRB_CNTcloseDocument()

PURPOSE AND USAGE   WRB_CNTcloseDocument() applies any changes and closes the specified document in a content repository.

SYNTAX

```
WAPIReturnCode WRB_CNTcloseDocument (void *WRBCtx,
                                       dvoid * hDocument);
```

PARAMETERS

Parameter	Type	Description
WRBCtx	void *	The pointer to the opaque WRB context object that the WRB application engine passed to your cartridge function
hDocument	dvoid *	A pointer to the document to be closed

RETURN VALUES   WRB_CNTcloseDocument() returns a value of type WAPIReturnCode.

WRB_CNTdestroyDocument()

PURPOSE AND USAGE   WRB_CNTdestroyDocument() deletes a specified document from a content repository.

SYNTAX

```
WAPIReturnCode WRB_CNTdestroyDocument (void *WRBCtx,
                                       dvoid * hRepository,
                                       text *szDocName);
```

PARAMETERS

Parameter	Type	Description
WRBCtx	void *	The pointer to the opaque WRB context object that the WRB application engine passed to your cartridge function.
hRepository	dvoid *	A pointer to the repository from which the specified document is to be deleted. This should be the pointer returned by WRB_CNTopenRepository().
szDocName	text *	A pointer to the name of the document to be deleted.

RETURN VALUES   WRB_CNTdestroyDocument() returns a value of type WAPIReturnCode.

WRB_CNTgetAttributes()

PURPOSE AND USAGE   WRB_CNTgetAttributes() passes back a pointer to a WRBpBlock containing the attributes for the specified document in a content repository. The attributes referred to in table under "Return Values" below are defined in the WRBpBlock.

SYNTAX

```
WAPIReturnCode WRB_CNTgetAttributes (void *WRBCtx,
                                     dvoid * hDocument,
                                     dvoid * hAttributes);
```

PARAMETERS

Parameter	Type	Description
WRBCtx	void *	The pointer to the opaque WRB context object that the WRB application engine passed to your cartridge function.
hDocument	dvoid *	A pointer to a document. This should be the pointer returned by WRB_CNTopenDocument().
hAttributes	dvoid *	A pointer to a parameter block. You must call WRB_createPBlock() beforehand to allocate the parameter block.

RETURN VALUES   WRB_CNTgetAttributes() returns a value of type WAPIReturnCode.

Attribute Name	Attribute Type	Description
author	WRBPT_ STRING	The name of the document author.
method	WRBPT_ STRING	Specifies whether the document is stored in a database or a file system.
content_type	WRBPT_ STRING	The MIME type and subtype of the document.
methodinfo	WRBPT_ STRING	Specifies the file system path of a document stored in a file system. This attribute is NULL for documents stored in databases.
creation_date	WRBPT_ DATE	The date the document was created.
name	WRBPT_ STRING	The document name.
description	WRBPT_ STRING	A text string describing the document. This string must be no longer than 2,000 bytes.
encoding	WRBPT_ STRING	The encoding applied to the document, if any, such as compress or gzip.
owner	WRBPT_ STRING	The user ID of the document owner.
expires	WRBPT_ DATE	The date after which you may delete the document.
path	WRBPT_ STRING	The full path of the document in the content repository, which is the concatenation of the folder and name attributes.
folder	WRBPT_ STRING	The content repository folder that contains the document.
title	WRBPT_ STRING	The HTML title of the document, if any.

Attribute Name	Attribute Type	Description
language	WRBPT_ STRING	The language in which the document is written.
type	WRBPT_ TYPE	Specifies whether the document is in text or binary format.
last_modified	WRBPT_ DATE	The date and time when the document was last modified.

WRB_CNTsetAttributes()

PURPOSE AND USAGE   WRB_CNTsetAttributes() sets the document attributes for a specified document in a content repository. Before calling WRB_CNTsetAttributes() on a document, you must first call WRB_CNTopenDocument() to open the document. See the table under the preceding "Return Values" heading for descriptions of the possible attributes.

SYNTAX

```
WAPIReturnCode WRB_CNTsetAttributes (void *WRBCtx,
                                     dvoid * hDocument,
                                     dvoid * hAttributes);
```

PARAMETERS

Parameter	Type	Description
WRBCtx	void *	The pointer to the opaque WRB context object that the WRB application engine passed to your cartridge function.
hDocument	dvoid *	A pointer to a document. This should be the pointer returned by WRB_CNTopenDocument().
hAttributes	dvoid *	A pointer to a parameter block containing the document attributes to be set. You must call WRB_createPBlock() beforehand to allocate the parameter block.

RETURN VALUES   WRB_CNTsetAttributes() returns a value of type WAPIReturnCode.

WRB_CNTreadDocument()

PURPOSE AND USAGE   WRB_CNTreadDocument() reads a specified number of bytes from the current position in a document in a content repository into a buffer provided by the caller. Before calling WRB_CNTreadDocument() on a document, you must first call WRB_CNTopenDocument() to open the document.

SYNTAX

sb4 WRB_CNTreadDocument (void *WRBCtx, dvoid * hDocument,
ub1 *buffer, sb4 buffersz);

PARAMETERS

Parameter	Type	Description
WRBCtx	void *	The pointer to the opaque WRB context object that the WRB application engine passed to your cartridge function.
hDocument	dvoid *	A pointer to the document from which to read. This should be the pointer returned by WRB_CNTopenDocument().
buffer	ub1*	A pointer to the buffer in which to store the data that is read. You must provide the storage for this buffer.
buffersz	sb4	The size of the buffer.

RETURN VALUES   WRB_CNTreadDocument() returns the number of bytes successfully read from the specified document.

WRB_CNTwriteDocument()

PURPOSE AND USAGE   WRB_CNTwriteDocument() writes the contents of the specified buffer to the current position in a document. When you call WRB_CNTwriteDocument() to modify a document, you modify your own private copy of the document. These changes will not be applied to the original document, until calling WRB_CNTflushDocument() or WRB_CNTcloseDocument().

Before calling WRB_CNTwriteDocument() on a document, you must first call WRB_CNTopenDocument() to open the document.

SYNTAX

sb4 WRB_CNTwriteDocument (void *WRBCtx, dvoid * hDocument,
ub1 *buffer, sb4 buffersz);

PARAMETERS

Parameter	Type	Description
WRBCtx	void *	The pointer to the opaque WRB context object that the WRB application engine passed to your cartridge function.
hDocument	dvoid *	A pointer to a document. This should be the pointer returned by WRB_CNTopenDocument().
buffer	ub1*	A pointer to the buffer containing the data to be written.
buffersz	sb4	The number of bytes to be written.

RETURN VALUES   WRB_CNTwriteDocument() returns the number of bytes successfully written to the specified document.

WRB_CNTflushDocument()

PURPOSE AND USAGE   WRB_CNTflushDocument() updates the original document stored in a repository to reflect buffered changes to the document. When you call WRB_CNTwriteDocument(), you modify your own private copy of a document in a content repository. To apply those changes to the original document, you must call WRB_CNTflushDocument(). If you are finished with the document, you may just call WRB_CNTcloseDocument(), which flushes the document before closing it.

SYNTAX

WAPIReturnCode WRB_CNTflushDocument (void *WRBCtx,
dvoid * hDocument);

PARAMETERS

Parameter	Type	Description
WRBCtx	void *	The pointer to the opaque WRB context object that the WRB application engine passed to your cartridge function.
hDocument	dvoid *	A pointer to the document to be synchronized. This should be the pointer returned by WRB_CNTopenDocument().

RETURN VALUES   WRB_CNTflushDocument() returns a value of type
WAPIReturnCode.

Inter-Cartridge Exchange API

Datatypes

WRBInfoType
The WRBInfoType is used to specify which information to retrieve when using
WRB_ICXgetInfo().

DEFINITION

```
typedef enum _WRBInfoType
{
  STATUSCODE,
  HTTPVERSION,
  REASONPHRASE,
  REALM
} WRBInfoType;
```

WRBMethod
The WRBMethhod type is an enumeration used to specify the HTTP method to use
when making a request via ICX. See WRB_ICXsetMethod().

DEFINITION

```
typedef enum _WRBMethod
{
  OPTIONS,
  GET,
  HEAD,
  POST,
  PUT,
  DELETE,
  TRACE
} WRBMethod;
```

Functions

WRB_ICXcreateRequest()

PURPOSE AND USAGE   WRB_ICXcreateRequest() allocates and returns a handle to a request object used by other routines in the API. To actually issue a request, you must call WRB_ICXmakeRequest() with the returned request object. To terminate the request, or when the request is complete, you must call WRB_ICXdestroyRequest() to free resources allocated for the request.

SYNTAX

dvoid * WRB_ICXcreateRequest(void *WRBCtx, text *url);

PARAMETERS

Parameter	Type	Description
WRBCtx	void *	The pointer to the opaque WRB context object that the WRB application engine passed to your cartridge function
url	text *	A pointer to the request URL

RETURN VALUES   WRB_ICXcreateRequest() returns a handle to the newly created request object, or NULL on failure.

WRB_ICXdestroyRequest()

PURPOSE AND USAGE   WRB_ICXdestroyRequest() frees resources allocated for the request. You must call WRB_ICXdestroyRequest() on a request when the request is completed.

SYNTAX

WAPIReturnCode WRB_ICXdestroyRequest(void *WRBCtx,
                                      dvoid * hRequest);

PARAMETERS

Parameter	Type	Description
WRBCtx	void *	The pointer to the opaque WRB context object that the WRB application engine passed to your cartridge function.
hRequest	dvoid *	Identifies the request to be destroyed. This should be the handle returned by WRB_ICXcreateRequest().

RETURN VALUES   WRB_ICXdestroyRequest() returns a value of type WAPIReturnCode.

WRB_ICXfetchMoreData()

PURPOSE AND USAGE   WRB_ICXfetchMoreData() retrieves the requested number of bytes, or the number of bytes available, when a previous call to WRB_ICXmakeRequest() has returned WRB_MOREDATA.

SYNTAX

```
WRBAPIReturnCode WRB_ICXfetchMoreData( dvoid *WRBCtx,
                                       dvoid *hRequest,
                                       dvoid ** response,
                                       ub4 *responseLength,
                                       ub4 chunkSize);
```

PARAMETERS

Parameter	Type	Description
WRBCtx	void *	The pointer to the opaque WRB context object that the WRB application engine passed to your cartridge function.
hRequest	dvoid *	Identifies the request to be issued.
response	void **	A pointer to the location in which the function is to store a pointer to the response data.
responseLength	ub4 *	A pointer to the location in which the function is to store the length in bytes of the reponse data.
chunkSize	ub4	If this parameter is nonzero, the size of the request response in bytes will be limited to this value. In this case, you must call WRB_ICXfetchMoreData() repeatedly until you have received the entire response. If this parameter is zero, no data is passed back.

RETURN VALUES   WRB_ICXfetchMoreData() returns a value of type WAPIReturnCode.

WRB_ICXgetHeaderVal()

PURPOSE AND USAGE   WRB_ICXgetHeaderVal() returns the pointer to the value of a specified HTTP header from the response to a request issued by WRB_ICXmakeRequest().

SYNTAX

        text * WRB_ICXgetHeaderVal(void *WRBCtx, dvoid * hRequest,
                                text *name);

PARAMETERS

Parameter	Type	Description
WRBCtx	void *	The pointer to the opaque WRB context object that the WRB application engine passed to your cartridge function
hRequest	dvoid *	Identifies the request for which the header value is to be extracted from the response
name	text *	A pointer to the name of the header for which you want the value

RETURN VALUES   WRB_ICXgetHeaderVal() returns the value of the specified header, or NULL on failure.

WRB_ICXgetInfo()

PURPOSE AND USAGE   WRB_ICXgetInfo() returns a string containing information about a specified request. The infoType parameter specifies the kind of information to be returned. Must be called after a request completes.

SYNTAX

        text * WRB_ICXgetInfo(void *WRBCtx, dvoid * hRequest,
                        WRBInfoType infoType);

PARAMETERS

Parameter	Type	Description
WRBCtx	void *	The pointer to the opaque WRB context object that the WRB application engine passed to your cartridge function.
hRequest	dvoid *	Identifies the request about which you want information.
infoType	WRBInfoType	A code that identifies the type of information you want. See The WRBInfoType Enumerated Type, at the beginning of the "Datatypes" section above, for more information.

RETURN VALUES   WRB_ICXgetInfo() returns a pointer to the requested information as a character string, or NULL on failure.

WRB_ICXgetParsedHeader()

PURPOSE AND USAGE   WRB_ICXgetParsedHeader() passes back the header values of the response to an ICX request issued by WRB_ICXmakeRequest().

SYNTAX

```
WAPIReturnCode WRB_ICXgetParsedHeader( void *WRBCtx,
                                       dvoid * hRequest,
                                       WRBpBlock *hPblock);
```

PARAMETERS

Parameter	Type	Description
WRBCtx	void *	The pointer to the opaque WRB context object that the WRB application engine passed to your cartridge function
hRequest	dvoid *	Identifies the request
hPblock	WRBpBlock *	A pointer to the location in which the function is to store the parameter block containing the parsed header data

RETURN VALUES   WRB_ICXgetParsedHeader() returns a value of type WAPIReturnCode.

WRB_ICXmakeRequest()

PURPOSE AND USAGE   WRB_ICXmakeRequest() actually issues the specified request. After you have called WRB_ICXcreateRequest() to create a request, and called other Intercartridge Exchange API functions such as WRB_ICXsetHeader() and WRB_ICXsetContent() to prepare the request, you can call WRB_ICXmakeRequest() to issue the request.

SYNTAX

```
WAPIReturnCode WRB_ICXmakeRequest( void *WRBCtx, dvoid * hRequest,
                                   void ** response,
                                   ub4 *responseLength,
                                   ub4 chunkSize,
                                   ub1 sendToBrowser);
```

PARAMETERS

Parameter	Type	Description
WRBCtx	void *	The pointer to the opaque WRB context object that the WRB application engine passed to your cartridge function.
hRequest	dvoid *	Identifies the request to be issued.
response	void **	A pointer to the location in which the function is to store a pointer to the response data.
responseLength	ub4 *	A pointer to the location in which the function is to store the length in bytes of the reponse data.
chunkSize	ub4	If this parameter is nonzero, the size of the request response in bytes will be limited to this value. In this case, you must call WRB_ICXfetchMoreData() repeatedly until you have received the entire response.
sendToBrowser	ub1	If this parameter is nonzero, the response from the request will be sent directly to the originating browser; in this case, the response parameter will contain NULL on return.

RETURN VALUES   WRB_ICXmakeRequest() returns a value of type WAPIReturnCode.

WRB_ICXsetAuthInfo()

PURPOSE AND USAGE   WRB_ICXsetAuthInfo() sets the authentication header data to accompany the specified request.

SYNTAX

> WAPIReturnCode WRB_ICXsetAuthInfo(void *WRBCtx, dvoid * hRequest,
> text *username, text *password);

PARAMETERS

Parameter	Type	Description
WRBCtx	void *	The pointer to the opaque WRB context object that the WRB application engine passed to your cartridge function.
hRequest	dvoid *	Identifies the request for which authentication is to be established. This should be a handle returned by WRB_ICXcreateRequest().
username	text *	A pointer to a username for request authentication. The username must be defined in the specified realm.
password	text *	A pointer to the password for the username.

RETURN VALUES   WRB_ICXsetAuthMethod() returns a value of type WAPIReturnCode.

WRB_ICXsetContent()

PURPOSE AND USAGE   WRB_ICXsetContent() sets a request's content, in the form of the name/value pairs in a WRBpBlock.

SYNTAX

> WAPIReturnCode WRB_ICXsetContent(void *WRBCtx, dvoid * hRequest,
> WRBpBlock hPBlock);

PARAMETERS

Parameter	Type	Description
WRBCtx	void *	The pointer to the opaque WRB context object that the WRB application engine passed to your cartridge function.
hRequest	dvoid *	Identifies the request for which content is to be specfied. This should be a handle returned by WRB_ICXcreateRequest().
hPBlock	WRBpBlock	The parameter block containing the content.

RETURN VALUES   WRB_ICXsetContent() returns a value of type WAPIReturnCode.

WRB_ICXsetHeader()

PURPOSE AND USAGE   WRB_ICXsetHeader() sets HTTP header data contained in a WRBpBlock for a specified request.

SYNTAX

```
WAPIReturnCode WRB_ICXsetHeader( void *WRBCtx, dvoid * hRequest,
                        WRBpBlock hPBlock,
                        boolean useOldHdr);
```

PARAMETERS

Parameter	Type	Description
WRBCtx	void *	The pointer to the opaque WRB context object that the WRB application engine passed to your cartridge function.
hRequest	dvoid *	Identifies the request for which headers are to be set. This should be the handle returned by WRB_ICXcreateRequest().
hPBlock	WRBpBlock	The parameter block containing the header information.
useOldHdr	boolean	When set to TRUE, the ICX request will incorporate header data from the original request in addition to the data defined by the parameter block. When set to FALSE, only header data from the parameter block is used.

RETURN VALUES   WRB_ICXsetHeader() returns a value of type WAPIReturnCode.

WRB_ICXsetMethod()

PURPOSE AND USAGE   WRB_ICXsetMethod() sets the request method, such as GET or POST, for a specified request. If not called, the GET method is used by default.

SYNTAX

> WAPIReturnCode WRB_ICXsetMethod(void *WRBCtx, dvoid * hRequest,
>   WRBMethod method);

PARAMETERS

Parameter	Type	Description
WRBCtx	void *	The pointer to the opaque WRB context object that the WRB application engine passed to your cartridge function.
hRequest	dvoid *	Identifies the request for which the method is to be set. This should be the handle returned by WRB_ICXcreateRequest().
method	WRBMethod	Specifies the request method.

RETURN VALUES   WRB_ICXsetMethod() returns a value of type WAPIReturnCode.

WRB_ICXsetNoProxy()

PURPOSE AND USAGE   WRB_ICXsetNoProxy() specifies the DNS domains for which the proxy server specified by WRB_ICXsetProxy() should not be used, in the form of a string containing a comma-separated list of domains.

SYNTAX

> WAPIReturnCode WRB_ICXsetNoProxy(void *WRBCtx, text *noProxy);

PARAMETERS

Parameter	Type	Description
WRBCtx	void *	The pointer to the opaque WRB context object that the WRB application engine passed to your cartridge function
noProxy	text *	A pointer to a comma-separated list of DNS domains to which requests should be sent directly, without proxy server intervention

RETURN VALUES   WRB_ICXsetNoProxy() returns a value of type WAPIReturnCode.

WRB_ICXsetProxy()

PURPOSE AND USAGE   WRB_ICXsetProxy() specifies a proxy server to use in making future ICX requests that are to be routed outside a firewall.

SYNTAX

WAPIReturnCode WRB_ICXsetProxy(void *WRBCtx, text *proxyAddress);

PARAMETERS

Parameter	Type	Description
WRBCtx	void *	The pointer to the opaque WRB context object that the WRB application engine passed to your cartridge function
proxyAddress	text *	The proxy address in character-string form

RETURN VALUES   WRB_ICXsetProxy() returns a value of type WAPIReturnCode.

Transaction Management API

Note that when using the Transaction Management API to provide transaction control, it is imperative that a cartridge *not* use the database's native API to perform commit and rollback functions. Only the Transaction Service API should be used for such functions.

Datatypes

The TXINFO Structure

The TXINFO structure encodes information about a transaction. WRB_TXNtransactionInfo() returns a pointer to this structure.

DEFINITION

```
struct tx_info_t
{
  XID                    xid;
  COMMIT_RETURN          when_return;
  TRANSACTION_CONTROL    transaction_control;
  TRANSACTION_TIMEOUT    transaction_timeout;
  TRANSACTION_STATE      transaction_state;
};
```

ELEMENTS

Element	Type	Description
xid	XID	An internal transaction data structure.
commit_return	long	Unused by WRB Transaction Service.
transaction_control	long	Unused by WRB Transaction Service.
transaction_timeout	long	The number of seconds a transaction may remain idle before being marked for rollback.
transaction_state	long	May be one of TX_ACTIVE, TX_INACTIVE, or TX_TIMEOUT_ROLLBACK_ONLY. Only transactions with the state TX_ACTIVE may be committed.

Functions

WRB_TXNannotatePath()

PURPOSE AND USAGE   WRB_TXNannotatePath() appends the current transaction context to the specified cartridge virtual path and writes the result to the requestor. WRB_TXNannotatePath() uses the HTTP cookie mechanism to identify member transactions. Note that this routine must be called once for each virtual path that is able to join the transaction.

SYNTAX

sb4 WRB_TXNannotatePath(dvoid *WRBCtx, text *szPath);

PARAMETERS

Parameter	Type	Description
WRBCtx	void *	The pointer to the opaque WRB context object that the WRB application engine passed to your cartridge function.
szPath	text *	The text of the cartridge virtual path. This can include a terminating wildcard; for example, "/cart/*" would indicate that access to any URL that begins with /cart/ should also send the transaction ID.

RETURN VALUES WRB_annotatePath() returns the number of bytes written to the requestor, or -1 when an error occurs.

WRB_TXNannotateURL()

PURPOSE AND USAGE WRB_TXNannotateURL() appends the current transaction context and the specified query string data to the specified URL and writes the result to the requestor. For browsers or clients that do not (or will not) support cookies, this routine must be used in place of WRB_TXNannotatePath(). This includes Java applets that may be accessing the cartridge's services, as the java.net library does not support cookies. Note that you must use an annotated URL for every link on the page being generated that is to rejoin the transaction. This includes standards links, as well as the ACTION attribute of a <FORM> tag.

SYNTAX

sb4 WRB_TXNannotateURL(dvoid *WRBCtx, text *url,
                        WRBpBlock hArguments);

PARAMETERS

Parameter	Type	Description
WRBCtx	void *	The pointer to the opaque WRB context object that the WRB application engine passed to your cartridge function
url	text *	The text of the base URL without the query string, including "http://", the host name, port (if necessary), and the URI
hArguments	WRBpBlock	A parameter block containing the name/value pairs to be appended to the URL as the query string

RETURN VALUES   WRB_annotateURL() returns the number of bytes written to the requestor, or -1 when an error occurs.

WRB_TXNbeginTransaction()

PURPOSE AND USAGE   WRB_TXNbeginTransaction() marks the beginning of a resource manager transaction and allocates a transaction context. After you call WRB_TXNbeginTransaction(), you must call WRB_TXNregisterRM() to establish the resource manager to use in the transaction.

SYNTAX

    WAPIReturnCode WRB_TXNbeginTransaction (void *WRBCtx);

PARAMETERS

Parameter	Type	Description
WRBCtx	void *	The pointer to the opaque WRB context object that the WRB application engine passed to your cartridge function

RETURN VALUES   WRB_TXNbeginTransaction() returns a value of type WAPIReturnCode.

WRB_TXNcloseRM()

PURPOSE AND USAGE   WRB_TXNcloseRM() disconnects from the specified resource manager. You should call WRB_TXNcloseRM() to disconnect from the resource manager when your transactions with the resource manager are complete.

SYNTAX

    WAPIReturnCode WRB_TXNcloseRM (void *WRBCtx, dvoid * hResource);

PARAMETERS

Parameter	Type	Description
WRBCtx	void *	The pointer to the opaque WRB context object that the WRB application engine passed to your cartridge function
hResource	dvoid *	A pointer to the resource manager from which to disconnect

RETURN VALUES   WRB_TXNcloseRM() returns a value of type WAPIReturnCode.

WRB_TXNcommitTransaction()

PURPOSE AND USAGE   WRB_TXNcommitTransaction() commits the current transaction and deletes the current transaction context.

SYNTAX

WAPIReturnCode WRB_TXNcommitTransaction (void *WRBCtx);

PARAMETERS

Parameter	Type	Description
WRBCtx	void *	The pointer to the opaque WRB context object that the WRB application engine passed to your cartridge function

RETURN VALUES   WRB_TXNcommitTransaction() returns a value of type WAPIReturnCode.

WRB_TXNinTransaction()

PURPOSE AND USAGE   WRB_TXNinTransaction() returns a Boolean value indicating whether there is a transaction in progress. Used in a cartridge's Exec function to determine whether to continue an existing transaction or begin a new transaction.

SYNTAX

Boolean WRB_TXNinTransaction (dvoid *WRBCtx);

PARAMETERS

Parameter	Type	Description
WRBCtx	void *	The pointer to the opaque WRB context object that the WRB application engine passed to your cartridge function

RETURN VALUES   WRB_TXNinTransaction() returns TRUE if there is a transaction in progess, FALSE otherwise.

WRB_TXNopenRM()

PURPOSE AND USAGE   WRB_TXNopenRM() connects to a resource manager using the specified login data. In Web Application Server version 3.0, the resource manager must be an Oracle database.

SYNTAX

> dvoid * WRB_TXNopenRM (void *WRBCtx, text *user, text *passwd,
>   text *connectstr);

PARAMETERS

Parameter	Type	Description
WRBCtx	void *	The pointer to the opaque WRB context object that the WRB application engine passed to your cartridge function.
user	text *	The user name, such as a database user ID, to be used in connecting to the repository.
passwd	text *	The password of the specified user.
connectstr	text *	The connect string, such as a SQL* Net V2 connect string, to be used in identifying a remote resource manager. For local databases, installed in the same ORACLE_ HOME directory as the WRB Dispatcher, you may pass NULL for this parameter.

RETURN VALUES   WRB_TXNopenRM() returns a pointer to the specified resource manager, or NULL on failure.

WRB_TXNregisterRM()

PURPOSE AND USAGE   WRB_TXNregisterRM() establishes the resource manager that the current transaction is to use. Prior to calling WRB_TXNregisterRM(), you must have called WRB_TXNopenRM() to get a pointer to the resource manager, as well as WRB_TXNbeginTransaction() to establish an active transaction.

SYNTAX

> WAPIReturnCode WRB_TXNregisterRM (void *WRBCtx,
>   dvoid * hResource);

PARAMETERS

Parameter	Type	Description
WRBCtx	void *	The pointer to the opaque WRB context object that the WRB application engine passed to your cartridge function.
hResource	dvoid *	A pointer to the resource manager to be used in the current transaction. This should be the pointer returned by WRB_TXNopenRM().

RETURN VALUES   WRB_TXNregisterRM() returns a value of type WAPIReturnCode.

WRB_TXNresourceInfo()

PURPOSE AND USAGE   WRB_TXNresourceInfo() returns a pointer to the resource manager for the specified resource. This pointer is used in calls to the database access API used in the cartridge.

SYNTAX

dvoid * WRB_TXNresourceInfo (void *WRBCtx, dvoid * hResource,
                    ub2 nResMgrType);

PARAMETERS

Parameter	Type	Description
WRBCtx	void *	The pointer to the opaque WRB context object that the WRB application engine passed to your cartridge function.
hResourceManager	dvoid *	A pointer to the resource manager. This should be the value returned by WRB_TXNopenRM().
nResMgrType	ub2	The resource manager type. See the following for the possible value.

RESOURCE MANAGER TYPE

Resource Manager Type	Description
WRBTS_ LDADEF	Use this value for OCI database access.

RETURN VALUES   WRB_TXNresourceInfo() returns a pointer to the resource manager for the specified resource. WRB_TXNresourceInfo() returns NULL on failure.

WRB_TXNrollbackTransaction()

PURPOSE AND USAGE   WRB_TXNrollbackTransaction() rolls back, or abandons, the current transaction and destroys the current transaction context.

SYNTAX

   WAPIReturnCode WRB_TXNrollbackTransaction (void *WRBCtx);

PARAMETERS

Parameter	Type	Description
WRBCtx	void *	The pointer to the opaque WRB context object that the WRB application engine passed to your cartridge function

RETURN VALUES   WRB_TXNrollbackTransaction() returns a value of type WAPIReturnCode.

WRB_TXNsetTimeout()

PURPOSE AND USAGE   WRB_TXNsetTimeout() sets the timeout period for future transactions initiated by the calling cartridge. This function must be called prior to invoking WRB_TXNopenRM().

SYNTAX

   WAPIReturnCode WRB_TXNsetTimeout (void *WRBCtx, sb4 timeout);

PARAMETERS

Parameter	Type	Description
WRBCtx	void *	The pointer to the opaque WRB context object that the WRB application engine passed to your cartridge function
timeout	sb4	The timeout period in seconds

RETURN VALUES   WRB_TXNsetTimeout() returns a value of type WAPIReturnCode.

WRB_TXNtransactionInfo()

PURPOSE AND USAGE   WRB_TXNtransactionInfo() returns a pointer to the TXINFO structure for the current transaction.

SYNTAX

TXINFO * WRB_TXNtransactionInfo (void *WRBCtx);

PARAMETERS

Parameter	Type	Description
WRBCtx	void *	The pointer to the opaque WRB context object that the WRB application engine passed to your cartridge function

RETURN VALUES   WRB_TXNtransactionInfo() returns a pointer to a TXINFO structure that encodes information about the current transaction. WRB_TXNtransactionInfo() returns NULL on failure.

WRB_TXNtxnEnabled()

PURPOSE AND USAGE   WRB_TXNtxnEnabled() returns a Boolean value indicating whether the Transaction Service is currently enabled.

SYNTAX

Boolean WRB_TXNtxnEnabled(dvoid *WRBCtx);

PARAMETERS

Parameter	Type	Description
WRBCtx	void *	The pointer to the opaque WRB context object that the WRB application engine passed to your cartridge function

RETURN VALUES   WRB_TXNtxnEnabled() returns TRUE if the Transaction Service is enabled, FALSE otherwise.

Logger Service API

The Logger service is used to write information to one or more Web Application Server logs. Functions are available to write both name-value pairs as well as the more common error reports. See Chapter 10 for a discussion of the technical and conventional usage of these functions.

Datatypes

WRBLogDestType

This is an enumeration used with WRB_LOGOpen() to specify the destination of messages written to the log. See the table under "Meanings" below, for meanings of each item.

DEFINITION

```
typedef enum _WRBLogDestType
{
  WRBLogDestDefault = 0,
  WRBLogDestDb = 1,
  WRBLogDestFs = 2
} WRBLogDestType;
```

MEANINGS

Value	Meaning
WRBLogDestDefault	Use the default logging destination.
WRBLogDestDb	Log information to the database.
WRBLogDestFs	Log information to a standard file.

WRBLogSeverity

This is an enumeration used with WRB_WriteMessage() to indicate the severity of the error.

DEFINITION

```
typedef enum _WRBLogSeverity
{
  WRBLogSevFatal = 0,
  WRBLogSevErr = 1,
  WRBLogSevWarn = 4,
  WRBLogSevTraItr = 7,
```

```
  WRBLogSevAe = 8,
  WRBLogSevDebug = 11
} WRBLogSeverity;
```

WRBLogType

This is an enumeration used with WRB_LOGOpen() to specify the type of log to
open. See the table under "Meanings" below, for meanings of each item.

DEFINITION

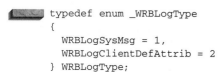

```
typedef enum _WRBLogType
{
  WRBLogSysMsg = 1,
  WRBLogClientDefAttrib = 2
} WRBLogType;
```

MEANINGS

Value	Meaning
WRBLogSysMsg	Use the log for standard messages.
WRBLogClientDefAttrib	Use the log for cartridge-defined name/value pairs.

Functions

WRB_LOGClose()

PURPOSE AND USAGE   WRB_LOGClose() closes the file or database
connection specified by logHdl.

SYNTAX

WAPIReturnCode WRB_LOGClose(void *WRBCtx, ub4 logHdl);

PARAMETERS

Parameter	Type	Description
WRBCtx	void *	The pointer to the opaque WRB context object that the WRB application engine passed to your cartridge function
logHdl	ub4	A handle to a log created by WRB_LOGOpen()

RETURN VALUES   WRB_LOGClose() returns WAPIReturnCode.

WRB_LOGOpen()

PURPOSE AND USAGE   WRB_LOGOpen() opens a file or database connection.

SYNTAX

```
WAPIReturnCode WRB_LOGOpen( void *WRBCtx, ub4 *logHdl,
                WRBLogType type, WRBLogDestType dest,
                char *filename );
```

PARAMETERS

Parameter	Type	Description
WRBCtx	void *	The pointer to the opaque WRB context object that the WRB application engine passed to your cartridge function
logHdl	ub4 *	Returns a handle to the log
type	WRBLogType	A value identifying the log entry as a message or a client attribute
dest	WRBLogDestType	A value identifying whether to log in a file or database
filename	char *	The name of the file, if logging in a file, or a dummy name (which is ignored), if logging to a database

RETURN VALUES   WRB_LOGOpen() returns a value of type WAPIReturnCode.

WRB_LOGWriteAttribute()

PURPOSE AND USAGE   WRB_LOGWriteAttribute() writes a cartridge-defined attribute and value to the log specified by logHdl. This provide a flexible way of writing tracing information to the log that is easily searchable by log parsers.

SYNTAX

```
WAPIReturnCode WRB_LOGWriteAttribute( void *WRBCtx,
                ub4 logHdl,
                char *component, int id,
                char *name, char *value);
```

PARAMETERS

Parameter	Type	Description
WRBCtx	void *	The pointer to the opaque WRB context object that the WRB application engine passed to your cartridge function
logHdl	ub4	A handle to a log created by WRB_LOGOpen()
component	char *	Text description to identify the type of cartridge, such as "java"
id	int	The particular instance of the cartridge
name	char *	Text identifying a particular attribute you wish to log
value	char *	Additional text to qualify the attribute you have named

RETURN VALUES   WRB_LOGWriteAttribute() returns WAPIReturnCode.

WRB_LOGWriteMessage()

PURPOSE AND USAGE   WRB_LOGWriteMessage() writes a message to the log specified by logHdl. You call WRB_LOGWriteMessage() from your cartridge to write a system message to the storage specified by logHdl. See Chapter 10 for a discussion of the recommended conventional use of the *severity* and *msg* parameters.

SYNTAX

```
WAPIReturnCode WRB_LOGWriteMessage( void *WRBCtx,
                ub4 logHdl,
                char *component, int id,
                char *msg, int severity);
```

PARAMETERS

Parameter	Type	Description
WRBCtx	void *	The pointer to the opaque WRB context object that the WRB application engine passed to your cartridge function
logHdl	ub4	A handle to a log created by WRB_LOGOpen()
component	char *	Text description to identify the type of cartridge, such as "java"
id	int	The particular instance of the cartridge
msg	char *	Text you wish to log
severity	int	A number you wish to associate with the message

RETURN VALUES   WRB_LOGWriteMessage() returns WAPIReturnCode.

INDEX

A

ACID properties of WRB transaction
management
  atomicity, 357-358
  consistency, 357-358
  durability, 357-358
  isolation, 357-358
ACM SIGCHI (Association for Computing
  Machinery's special interest group in
  Computer-Human Interaction), 14
ActiveX, 76-78, 86
Adobe
  Page Mill, 187
  Portable Document Format, 13
Anchors, 56-57
APIs (Application Program Interfaces)
  Internet Information Server (ISAPI),
    85
  Java Database Connectivity (JDBC),
    423-426
  Netscape (NSAPI), 85
  ODBC, 423
  server APIs, 47-50

Web Request Broker (WRB) API,
  and cartridges in C, 397-407
Application
  architects, and web-based benefits,
    9-14
    cross-platform and thin-client
      support, 9
    dynamic user interface
      generation, 9
    lightweight interfaces among
      applications, 10
    new application design
      challenges and
      opportunities, 14
    query, reporting, and
      transaction-intensive
      applications, 11-13
    remote user support, 10
  distribution efficiency, 6
  mapping, parameters for, 411
  OWAS writing services for, 5
Application context, and Init function, 395
Architecture
  cartridge operation, and, 395-396
  Java cartridge, basic functioning of,
    230-232

623

P

T

License Terms
for Oracle Software

Global License Terms

Enabling the Information Age™

العربية/المملكة العربية السعودية

تنبيه: بمجرد فتح هذا الملف أو استعمال البرامج الموجودة داخله، فإن الشروط التالية سوف تخضع للتطبيق تلقائيا. وإذا وجدت أن البرامج أو هذه الشروط غير مقبولة لـك، أعد البرامج خلال ثلاثـون (٣٠) يوما إلى الشركة التي استلمت البرامج منها لاسترداد نقودك.

إن شركة أوراكل السعودية (أوراكل) تمنحك (بصفتك العميل) ترخيصا لاستعمال البرامج المرفقة والوثائق (البرامج) المشار إليها أدناه.

الترخيص: للعميل الحق في إستعمال البرامج ضمن حدود المنطقة في إطار بيئة التشغيل المعرفة من قبل أوراكل. أما (أ) إلى المدى المحدد في وثيقة الطلبية أو شهادة إستخدام الـبرامج التي يحصل العميل عليهـا من أوراكل أو موزعيها أو (ب) إذا ـ يحدد هذا المدى فستستخدم لمستعمل واحد على جهاز كمبيوتر واحد. ويجوز للعميل أن يستخدم البرامج حصريا لعملياته الداخلية في معالجة البيانات ويجوز للعميل أن يستنسـخ نسخة واحدة من كل برنامج مرخص على سبيل الاحتياط. ويمكن تضمين ما يفيد حقوق عمل نسخ إضافية في وثيقة الطلبية أو شهادة إستخدام البرامج. لن يتم عمل أية نسخ أخرى إلا بموافقة أوراكل الخطية المسبقة. يلتزم العميل بعدم (أ) إزالة أي تعريف للمنتج أو ملصقات حقوق الطبع أو أية ملاحظات أخرى أو قيود ملكية على البرامج أو (ب) إستعمال البرامج لأغراض المشاركة التجارية أو الإيجار أو لاستعمالات مكتب خدمات أو (ج) نقل ملكية أو بيع أو التنازل أو خلاف ذلك إحالة البرامج إلى أي طرف آخر بدون موافقة أوراكل الخطية المسبقة أو (د) التسبب أو السماح بعمليات الهندسة الإرتجاعيـة أو العكسيـة أو حل البرامج أو (هـ) الكشف عن نتائج أية اختبارات لأي برنامج لأي طرف آخر بدون الموافقة الخطية المسبقة لشركة أوراكل. تخضع كافة عمليات نقل البرامج لأنظمة ورسوم النقل المعتمدة مـن قبل أوراكل. ويحـق للعميل أن يستعمل من البرامج الموجودة في هذا الملف بعض البرامج المحددة في وثيقة الطلبية أو شهادة إستخدام البرامج.

حقوق الطبع/ ملكية البرامج: تعتبر هذه البرامج ملكية عالمة لشركة أوراكل لذا فهي محمية بقانون حقوق الطبع وحقوق الملكية الفكرية الأخرى. يكتسب العميل فقط حق إستعمال البرامج ولا يعطيه ذلك أية حقوق، صريحة كانت أو ضمنية، في البرامج أو البيانات التي تشكل البرامج بخلاف ما هو محدد في هذا الترخيص. وتحتفظ أوراكل أو حامل ترخيصها في كافة الأوقات بكل الحقوق والملكية والمصالح، بما في ذلك حقوق الملكية الفكرية في البرامج والبيانات.

ضمانات محدودة/العلاجات الحصرية: تضمن أوراكل لمدة تسعين (٩٠) يوماً من تاريخ التسليم إلى العميل (أ) خلو البيانات الموجودة من عيوب المواد والمصنعية تحت الإستخدام الإعتيادي، و (ب) تأديـة البرامج غير المعدلة بصورة جوهرية للوظائف الموصوفة في الوثائق المزودة من قبل أوراكل عند تشغيل هذه البرامج على الكمبيوتر ونظام التشغيل المخصصين. بالمقابل، لا تضمن أوراكل أن البرامج سوف تفي بمتطلبات العميل أو أن البرامج سوف تعمل في التوليفات أو التشكيلات التي قد تختارها العميل أو تشغيل البرامج لن يتعطل أو يعمل بدون أخطاء أو أن كافة أخطاء البرامج سوف يتـم إصلاحها. إن هذه الضمانات هـي ضمانات حصرية وتحل محل كل الضمانات والشروط الأخرى، سواء كانت صريحة أو ضمنية، بموجب القانون أو خلافه، بما في ذلك الضمانات الضمنية لقابليتها التسويقية أو لياقتها لغرض محدد. وإذا أبلغ العميل عن أي خطأ في برنامج ما خلال فترة التسعين (٩٠) يوم، فسوف تقوم أوراكل حسب خيارها، إما بإصلاح الخطأ أو إعطاء العميل طريقة معقولة لحصر الخطأ أو إعادة رسوم الترخيص مقابل تسلمها للبرامج مـن العميل. أما فيما يخص أي بيانات معيبة، فإن أوراكل تلتزم باستبدالها بدون مقابل إذا أعيد ذلك إلى أوراكل خلال فترة التسعين (٩٠) يوم. إن العلاجات أعلاه تشكل العلاجات الحصرية والوحيدة التـي يحصل عليها العميل لخرق الضمان. وبموجب هذا الضمان المحدود، فإن العميل يحصل على حقوق قانونية محددة.

تحديد المسئولية: لن تكون أوراكل مسئولة عن أية أضرار غير مباشرة أو عرضية أو خاصة أو إستتباعية أو أية أضرار عن خسارة الإنتاج أو الإيرادات أو البيانات أو إستعمالات البيانات التي يتكبدهـا العميل أو أى طرف آخر سواء في إجراء تعاقدي أو شخصي، حتى وإن بلغ أوراكل أو أي شخص آخر باحتمالية هذه الأضرار. إن مسئولية أوراكل عن الأضرار لن تزيد بأي حال من الأحـوال عـن الرسوم التـي يدفعهـا العميل نظير هذا الترخيص.

المنطقة: تعني المنطقة المملكة العربية السعودية ما ـ يحدد خلاف ذلك في وثيقة الطلبية أو شهادة إستخدام البرامج.

على العميل أن يتقيد تماما بكافة قوانين وأنظمة الولايات المتحدة الأمريكية والمملكة العربية السعودية (قوانين التصدير) بما يكفل له أن البرامج وأية منتجات مباشرة فـا (١) لا يتم تصديرهـا بطريقـة مباشـرة أو غـير مباشرة بصورة تشكل إنتهاكا لقوانين التصدير أو (٢) لا تستعمل في غرض محظور بموجب قوانين التصدير، بما يشمل ولا يقتصر على إنتشار الأسلحة الذرية أو الكيماوية أو الجرثومية. تخضع هـذه الإتفاقية وكافة الإجراءات المتعلقة بها لقوانين المملكة العربية السعودية. ويجوز لشركة أوراكل أن تتحرى وتدقق في إستعمالات العميل للبرامج. إن هذا الترخيص ينسخ كافة شروط شراء أية طلبية شراء للعميل أو أية طلبية أخرى للعميل.

تعريفات شهادة إستخدام البرامج:

الوسائل المعاصرة/الدخوليات المعاصرة: أقصى عدد من وسائل الإدخال التي ستدخل على البرامج في أية نقطة زمنية. وفي حالة إستعمال تجمع من البرامج أو الأجهزة (على سبيل المثال شاشة تـي يـه) فـإن هـذا العدد يجب أن يحتسب في طرف مقدمة التجمع.

العميل: جهاز كمبيوتر واحد (١) يستخدم من قبل شخص واحد في ذات الوقت (و ٢) يطبق برامج أوراكل في ذاكرة عملية أو يخزن البرامج على جهاز تخزين محلي.

المستعمل: فرد مصرح له من قبل العميل باستخدام البرامج، بصرف النظر عما إذا كان هذا المستعمل يستخدم هذه البرامج بصورة فعالة في أي زمن محدد.

صندوق البريد: النقطة التي يرسل منها أو يستقبل فيها البريد الإلكتروني. ويتم تأسيس صندوق البريد بمجرد فتح حساب أو إنشاء تطبيق للعميل في مكتب أوراكل.

中文／中国

ORACLE 公司程序使用许可条款

注意： 如果您打开这个软件包或使用包内的软件，下列条款将适用于您. 如果本软件或下列条款令您无法接受， 敬请于三十日内将本软件退回于所出售之公司，以得到退款.

ORACLE公司或其分支机构(简称"ORACLE")基于下述条件授予您(简称"用户")使用本软件及相关资料(简称"程序")之许可证.

许可证： 用户有权在ORACLE认可的操作环境下使用本程序. 该环境包括: (A) 已在 ORACLE或其分销商发给用户的订购文件或程序使用证中特别指定；或 (B) 如果不存在前述指定，则适用于单机之单个用户. 用户只能为自己的内部数据处理系统而使用该程序. 对每个获得使用许可的程序，用户可以复制一个备份；如需更多复制件，则应在订购文件或程序使用证中载明. 未获 ORACLE 事先书面许可，不能制作第二份以上复制品. 用户不得: (A)去掉程序上的产品识别标识、版权告示或 其它告示及 专用权限制说明等; (B)为商业性计时使用、租赁或服务机构而使用本程序; (C)未经 ORACLE 事先书面许可将程序转让、出售、分配或以其它方式转移给第三人; (D)放任或允许对本程序的转换加工、拆装或 反编译; 或 (E)未经ORACLE事先书面批准将程序的对比测验结果披露于第三人. 所有的程序转让都必须遵循ORACLE 的转让政策和费用. 用户只被授权在订购文件或程序使用证中表明的条件下使用包内的程序.

程序的著作权／所有权： 本程序是ORACLE拥有产权之产品，受著作权法及其它知识产权法的保护. 用户只获得了使用本程序之权利，而没用对程序或包含程序之媒体通过明示或默示方式获得超出上述许可证表明权利之外的任何其它权利. ORACLE或其许可人将永远保有对程序和媒体的各种权利、所有权和利益，包括知识产权.

有限保证／单一补偿： 从程序送至用户之日起 90 天内，ORACLE保证: (A)所提供之媒体在正常使用状态下没有材料和工艺方面的缺陷，和 (B) 未经改动的程序在指定的计算机和操作系统内，将完全按照ORACLE说明文件中描述的功能执行.

ORACLE将不保证： 本程序将完全满足客户的各种要求. 本程序将在客户选择使用的组合系统内顺利运行，程序的运行将不出现中断、错误或者所有程序错误都被纠正. 这些保证是唯一的、排他的，将取代所有其他明示或默示

保证，包括销售商的默示保证或适于特定目的之保证．如果用户在90天内指出了程序中的错误，ORACLE将根据实际情况或者帮助用户纠正错误，或者向用户提供一个可以克服错误的合理程序，或者允许用户退货，由公司退款．如果用户在90天内将有问题的软件媒体退还，ORACLE将负责免费更换．上述措施是ORACLE不能履行前述保证义务时的唯一的和排他的补偿方式．这个有限保证赋予用户某些特定法律权利，用户可能享有其他权利，但将因国家而异．

责任限制：ORACLE将不对用户或任何第三人所遭受的任何间接的、突发的、特别的或持续的损害，或者因利润、收入、数据或数据使用损失所引起之损害负责，无论该损害属于违反合同性质还是侵权性质，即使事先向ORACLE咨询过发生该种损害之可能性亦不例外．ORACLE对所有损害之赔偿责任将不超过用户所支付之使用许可费．

权利限制：用户应全面遵守美国和其他国家的所有法律、法规 (简称"出口法")，确保本程序及其直接产品：(1)在出口过程中不直接或间接违反出口法；或(2)不被用于任何出口法所禁止之目的，包括但不限于原子、化学或生物武器等扩散．本许可证及其相关活动将适用美国加利福尼亚州法例．ORACLE有权检查、监督用户对程序的使用．用户订购单或其它用户订购文件中列明的各种条款将全部被本许可证取代．

程序使用证之定义：

并行设备 / 并行访问：在特定时刻运行该程序的输入设备的最大数目．如果使用复合软件或者硬件 (例如TP监视器)，该输入设备的最大数目必须在其终端前测定．

客户机：一台计算机：(1)在特定时刻只被一人使用；和 (2)在本地存储系统中运行ORACLE公司的软件或在本地存储器中储存该软件．

使用人：由用户授权使用程序的人，无论该人在特定时间是否积极使用该程序．

邮件信箱：收发电子邮件的节点，该信箱通过使用人在ORACLE中心网络的开户或开户申请所创建．

中文／台灣

Oracle程式授權條款

注意：如果你打開這個包裝或使用包裝內的軟體，以下條款
將予適用。如果軟體或這些條款不能為您所接受，
請於30日內將本軟體退還本公司，您將獲得退款。

Oracle公司或其子公司（"Oracle"）授權您（"顧客"）使
用包裝內軟體及文件（"程式"）之權利，詳述如下。

授權：顧客擁有在由Oracle如下所認定的操作環境中使用程
式的權利，(a)於訂貨文件或由Oracle或其經銷商給予顧客
的「程式使用證」之記載範圍內，或(b)如果未記載，其使用
範圍以在單一電腦上為單一使用者所使用為限。顧客僅能為
其自身內部資料進行操作而使用本程式。顧客可以就每一個
經授權之程式做一份拷貝為備份，或按訂貨文件或程式使用
證之記載而為另外的拷貝。若無Oracle事先書面同意，顧客
不得為其他拷貝。顧客並不得：(a)自程式除去任何產品之辨
認型號、著作權之通知、其他通知、或與使用權利有關之限
制；(b)將程式按時間分配由多人為商業性使用、出租，或做
為服務站使用；(c)無Oracle事先書面同意，而將程式轉讓
或出賣給任何他人；(d)致使或允許程式的反工程、分解或解
碼；或(e)在未得Oracle事先書面核准而洩露任何程式的任
何基準測試結果給第三人。所有程式的轉讓應依Oracle的轉
讓政策及其所訂費用辦理，顧客僅有依訂貨文件或程式使用
證之記載使用本包裝內軟體之權利。

程式著作權／所有權：程式係Oracle之專屬產品且為著作
權及其他智慧財產權法律所保護。顧客僅取得使用程式的權
利，且除了記載於本授權之權利外，無論明示或暗示，並不
取得程式中或含程式的媒介中之任何其他權利。Oracle或其
授權人在任何時間均保留所有權利及利益，包括程式中或其
媒介中的智慧財產權。

限制保證／惟一救濟：Oracle保證自交付顧客日起算90日
內：(a)在正常使用下，內含的媒介在材質及手工並無瑕疵；
且(b)如使用在指定的電腦及操作系統時，未修改的程式將執
行由Oracle提供之文件中所記載的功能。Oracle並不保證
：程式將符合顧客的要求，程式會與顧客所選擇使用之其他
程式合併執行，程式的執行是不中斷的或無錯誤的，或所有
程式錯誤將被更正。本授權所載保證是排他的且取代所有
無論明示的或暗示的其他保證，包括一定商品品質之暗示保
證或為適合特定目的之暗示保證。若顧客在90日內通知程式
中的錯誤，Oracle將依其選擇，改正錯誤，提供顧客一個合
理的程序以克服錯誤，或於顧客退還程式給Oracle後由其返
還授權費用。如顧客於90日內歸還Oracle之任何有瑕疵之

媒介，Ｏｒａｃｌｅ將免費更換。上述保證係惟一且排他的救濟。
本限制保證將給與您特別的法律權利，但您可能隨各州規定
而有其他的權利。

責任限制：Ｏｒａｃｌｅ對顧客或任何第三人所生任何間接的、
零星的、特別的或衍生的損害，或因利潤、收入、資料或資
料使用損失所生之損害，無論係以契約訴訟或侵權訴訟方式
為之，即使Ｏｒａｃｌｅ已經被告知此種損害的可能性，
Ｏｒａｃｌｅ在本條款下之損害責任不得超過顧客為本授權所付
的費用。

權利限制：送往美國國防部的程式係受限制的權利並適用下
列規定，權利限制標示：政府使用、重製或公開係受目前技
術資料及電腦軟體權利相關法令之規範，ＤＦＡＲＳ 252-
227-7013(C)(1)(ii)(October 1988)。Oracle Corp.
500 Oracle Pkway., Redwood City, CA 94065。
送往國防部以外的美國政府機關之一般資料權利見ＦＡＲ
52.227-14之規定，包括依Alternate III (1987年6月版)
定義而交付之"限制權利"。

顧客應遵守美國及其它國家的法律及規定（"出口法律"）
，以確保無論本程式或任何直接產品皆不會 出口時直接或
間接地違反出口法律，或 為出口法律所禁止之任何目的所
使用，包括（但不限於）為核子的、化學的或生化武器擴散
之目的而使用之。本授權及所有相關行為應適用加州法律。
Ｏｒａｃｌｅ可以稽核顧客對程式的使用。任何顧客的購買文件或
其訂貨文件所載條款應為本授權所取代。

程式使用證之定義：

> 同步裝置／同步使用：在一定時間內使用程式，輸入
> 設備的最大數量。如果
> 使用多用途軟體或硬體
> （如：ＴＰ螢幕），這個
> 數量必須在多數前端末
> 點測量。

> 客戶：電腦一次僅由一個人使用，且在當地記憶體執
> 行Ｏｒａｃｌｅ軟體或儲存軟
> 於當地之儲存裝置。

> 使用者：由顧客授權使用程式的個人，不論此人是否
> 於一定的時間內使用。

> 電子郵箱：電子信件發生或收受之點；當使用者之檔
> 案或有關之申請業已建
> 立於Ｏｒａｃｌｅ辦公室而產
> 生。

Česky/Česka

PODMÍNKY LICENCE NA PROGRAM ORACLE

UPOZORNĚNÍ: PO OTEVŘENÍ BALENÍ NEBO POUŽITÍ PŘILOŽENÉHO SOFTWARU SE UPLATŇUJÍ NÁSLEDUJÍCÍ PODMÍNKY. POKUD NEBUDOU TYTO PODMÍNKY NEBO SOFTWARE PRO VÁS PŘIJATELNÉ, VRAŤTE SOFTWARE DO 30 DNŮ SPOLEČNOSTI, KTERÁ VÁM SOFTWARE DODALA. ČÁSTKA UHRAZENÁ ZA SOFTWARE VÁM BUDE NAVRÁCENA.

SPOLEČNOST ORACLE CZECH S.R.O. ("ORACLE") VÁM ("ZÁKAZNÍK") UDĚLUJE LICENCI NA POUŽITÍ PŘILOŽENÉHO SOFTWARU A DOKUMENTACE ("PROGRAMY") PODLE DÁLE UVEDENÝCH PODMÍNEK.

LICENCE: Zákazník je oprávněn používat program Oracle na Území pro operační prostředí definované společností Oracle, v rozsahu stanoveném v objednacím dokumentu Oracle nebo potvrzení o právu užívat program ("Povolení užívat"), které budou distribuovány zákazníkovi společností Oracle nebo jejím distributorem. Pokud nejsou v Povolení identifikována práva na použití, tato licence se uděluje jednomu uživateli pro jeden počítač. Zákazník smí používat programy výhradně pro interní zpracování dat. Zákazník má právo pořídit si jednu záložní kopii každého licencovaného programu; případná práva na další kopie musí být uvedena v každé objednávce nebo v Povolení užívat. Bez předchozího písemného souhlasu společnosti Oracle nemohou být pořizovány další kopie. Zákazník nesmí: 1. odstranit z programů žádné informace týkající se identifikace výrobku, autorských práv a omezení vlastnických práv anebo jiné informace; 2. používat Programy v obchodním provozu na počítači sdíleném s jinými subjekty, půjčovat programy nebo je používat v servisní kanceláři; 3. předávat, prodávat, postupovat nebo jiným způsobem převádět programy jiné straně bez předchozího písemného souhlasu společnosti Oracle; 4. zapříčinit nebo dovolit provedení technických změn na Programech, jejich demontáž nebo dekompilaci; 5. bez předchozího písemného souhlasu společnosti Oracle informovat o výsledcích výkonnostních testů jakéhokoliv Programu třetí stranu. Zákazník je oprávněn užívat pouze programy, které jsou v tomto balení a které jsou specifikovány v objednávacím dokumentu Oracle nebo v Povolení užívat.

Autorská práva/Vlastnictví programů: Programy jsou majetkem firmy Oracle a jsou chráněny zákonem o autorských právech a ostatními relevantními zákony. Zákazník nabývá pouze právo na použití Programů specifikovaných v této licenci, a nenabývá žádná vlastnická práva, explicitně ani implicitně, k Programům nebo nosičům Programů. Společnost Oracle nebo její zástupce udělující licenci si po celý čas podrží veškerá práva včetně autorských práv, vlastnictví a zájmy týkající se programů a příslušných médií.

Záruky/nároky z vad zboží: Společnost se zaručuje, že po dobu 90 dnů od data dodání Zákazníkovi: 1. se při běžném použití neprojeví na přiložených nosičích žádné závady z hlediska materiálu a provedené práce; a 2. Programy, na kterých nebudou provedeny žádné změny, budou v podstatě fungovat podle popisu v dokumentaci poskytnuté společností Oracle, pokud budou používány na určeném počítači a s určeným operačním systémem.

Společnost Oracle nezaručuje: - že programy budou splňovat požadavky Zákazníka; - že Programy budou fungovat v kombinaci s jinými programy podle výběru zákazníka; - že provoz Programu bude bez chyb a přerušení; - že veškeré chyby v programech budou opraveny. Tyto záruky jsou vyhrazené a nahrazují veškeré jiné záruky, ať už vyslovené nebo implicitní, včetně implicitních záruk prodejnosti nebo vhodnosti pro konkrétní použití. Jestliže Zákazník oznámí do devadesáti dnů závadu v Programech, společnost Oracle podle svého uvážení závadu opraví, nebo poskytne Zákazníkovi informaci o přiměřeném způsobu, jak závadu odstranit, anebo po vrácení Programů společností Oracle Zákazníkem mu refunduje poplatky za licenci. Společnost Oracle vymění bezplatně jakékoliv vadné nosiče, pokud jí budou vráceny do devadesáti dnů. Toto jsou jediné a výhradní nároky z vad zboží, které může Zákazník uplatňovat při jakémkoliv porušení záruky. Tato limitovaná záruka poskytuje Zákazníkovi určitá zákonná práva.

OMEZENÍ ODPOVĚDNOSTI: SPOLEČNOST ORACLE NENESE ODPOVĚDNOST ZA ŽÁDNÉ NEPŘÍMÉ NAHODILÉ SPECIÁLNÍ NEBO NÁSLEDNÉ ŠKODY NEBO ZA ŽÁDNÉ ŠKODY SPOJENÉ SE ZTRÁTOU ZISKU, PŘÍJMU, DAT NEBO Z POUŽITÍ DAT, KTERÉ VZNIKNOU ZÁKAZNÍKOVI NEBO JAKÉKOLIV TŘETÍ STRANĚ, AŤ JAKO VÝSLEDEK ČINNOSTI NA ZÁKLADĚ SMLOUVY NEBO JAKO DŮSLEDEK PORUŠENÍ ZÁKONA A TO ANI V PŘÍPADĚ, ŽE ORACLE NEBO JINÁ OSOBA BYLI INFORMOVÁNI O MOŽNOSTI VZNIKU TAKOVÉ ŠKODY. V ŽÁDNÉM PŘÍPADĚ NEPŘESÁHNE ODPOVĚDNOST ZA ŠKODY ZE STRANY SPOLEČNOSTI ORACLE ČÁSTKU, KTEROU ZÁKAZNÍK UHRADIL ZA UDĚLENÍ LICENCE.

Území: "Územím" se rozumí Česká republika, pokud nebude uvedeno jinak v objednávce nebo v Povolení užívat.

Zákazník se zavazuje, že: 1. bude plně dodržovat veškeré zákonné předpisy a opatření k zajištění toho, aby ani programy ani jakýkoliv jiný přímý produkt těchto Programů, nebyl přímo nebo nepřímo nezákonně exportován. 2. programy nebudou použity pro účely zakázané exportními zákony USA včetně použití k vývoji jaderných, chemických a biologických zbraní. Tato dohoda se řídí českými zákony. Veškeré podmínky uvedené v Zákazníkově objednávce jsou nahrazeny touto licencí.

Definice pojmů v Povolení užívat:

Současný přístup: maximální počet vstupních zařízení pracujících s Programem Oracle, v kterémkoliv časovém okamžiku. Je-li použito multiplexní zařízení, toto číslo je zjišťováno na vstupu multiplexního zařízení (ať už programového nebo fyzického).

Klient: počítač, který je používán pouze jednou osobou v daném čase a vykonává Program Oracle v místní paměti nebo ho ukládá na místním pamět'ovém médiu.

Uživatel: osoba autorizovaná zákazníkem k použití Programu Oracle bez ohledu na to, zda v daném čase program aktivně používá.

Poštovní schránka: místo, odkud je odesílána a kde je přijímána elektronická pošta. Poštovní schránka je vytvářena při definici uživatele nebo uživatelské aplikace v programu Oracle Office.

Dansk/Danmark

ORACLE PROGRAMMELLICENS

ADVARSEL - HVIS DE ÅBNER DENNE PAKKE ELLER ANVENDER DET HERI INDEHOLDTE PROGRAMMEL, FINDER NEDENSTÅENDE BETINGELSER ANVENDELSE. SÅFREMT DE IKKE KAN ACCEPTERE PROGRAMMELLET ELLER NEDENSTÅENDE BETINGELSER, BEDES DE RETURNERE PROGRAMMELLET INDEN 30 DAGE TIL DET FIRMA, HVORFRA PROGRAMMELLET ER BLEVET LEVERET, HVOREFTER DEN ERLAGTE BETALING VIL BLIVE RETURNERET.

ORACLE DANMARK A/S ("Oracle") GIVER DEM ("Kunden") LICENS TIL AT ANVENDE INDEHOLDTE PROGRAMMEL OG DOKUMENTATION ("Programmel") I HENHOLD TIL NEDENSTÅENDE BETINGELSER.

LICENS: Kunden har ret til at anvende Programmellet i det driftsmiljø, der er defineret af Oracle enten (a) i henhold til de relevante ordre-dokumenter eller et Bruger-Certifikat, som Kunden modtager fra Oracle eller Oracles distributør, eller (b) såfremt det ikke er specificeret for én enkelt bruger på én computer. Kunden må kun anvende Programmellet til intern databehandling. Kunden har ret til at kopiere Programmellet til back-up. Såfremt Kunden har erhvervet ret til at tage yderligere kopier, er dette angivet i ordre-dokumentet eller Bruger-Certifikatet. Kunden har ikke ret til at tage andre kopier uden Oracles forudgående skriftlige godkendelse. Kunden må ikke: (a) fjerne produktidentifikation, copyright-notater, eller andre notater eller immaterialretlige angivelser fra Programmellet; (b) anvende Programmellet til time-sharing, udlejningsformål eller i forbindelse med servicebureau virksomhed; (c) overdrage, videresælge eller på anden måde videregive Programmellet til tredjemand uden Oracles forudgående skriftlige godkendelse; (d) foretage eller tillade reverse engineering, rekonstruktion eller dekompilering af Programmellet, medmindre Kunden inden for rimelig tid efter Kundens skriftlige anmodning herom til Oracle ikke har modtaget fra Oracle den information, som Oracle er i besiddelse af og som er nødvendig for at producere edb-programmer, som kan fungere sammen med Programmellet, men som ikke krænker Oracles immaterielle rettigheder, samt (e) meddele resultater af benchmark tests for Programmellet til tredjemand uden Oracles forudgående skriftlige godkendelse. Overflytning af Programmel til et andet driftsmiljø er underlagt Oracles regler og afgifter for overflytning af Programmel. Kunden har kun ret til at anvende Programmellet i denne pakke i det omfang, det er angivet i ordre-dokumentet eller Bruger-Certifikatet.

IMMATERIELLE RETTIGHEDER/EJENDOMSRET: Oracle er indehaver af ophavsretten og andre immaterielle rettigheder til Programmellet, og Programmellet er beskyttet af den gældende ophavsretlige lovgivning. Kunden erhverver kun ret til at anvende Programmellet, og erhverver således ingen udtrykkelige eller underforståede rettigheder til Programmellet eller det medie, som indeholder Programmel, der ikke er specificeret under nærværende licens. Ejendomsretten og alle immaterielle rettigheder til Programmellet og medie forbliver i alle henseender Oracles eller Oracles underleverandør.

BEGRÆNSNINGER AF GARANTIER/MISLIGHOLDELSESBEFØJELSER: Oracle garanterer i en periode på 90 dage fra leveringstidspunktet til Kunden, at (a) det leverede medie ved normal brug er uden fabrikationsfejl, og at (b) Programmellet, medmindre det er modificeret af Kunden, i al sin væsentlighed kan opfylde den funktionalitet, der er beskrevet i dokumentationen ved drift på den relevante computer med tilhørende operativsystem. Oracle yder ingen garanti for, at Programmellet svarer til Kundens behov, at Programmellet kan anvendes i specifikke kombinationer, som Kunden måtte vælge, at driften vil være uden afbrydelser og fejlfri, eller at alle fejl i Programmellet vil blive rettet. Kun de ovenfor udtrykkeligt angivne garantier er gældende for Programmellet. Andre garantier, som måtte følge af deklaratorisk lovgivning eller af sædvane og kotume, er hermed tilsidesat. Såfremt Kunden rapporterer en fejl i Programmellet inden udløbet af den ovenfor angivne 90 dages garantiperiode for Programmellet, kan Oracle vælge enten at udbedre fejlen, eller at anvise Kunden en rimelig måde, hvorpå fejlen kan omgås, eller såfremt Kunden returnerer Programmellet til Oracle, at tilbagebetale Kunden licensafgiften for Programmellet. Oracle vil ombytte defekte media uden omkostninger for Kunden, såfremt de returneres til Oracle inden udløbet af den ovenfor angivne periode på 90 dage. Ovenstående er de eneste misligholdelsesbeføjelser, som Kunden kan påberåbe sig i forbindelse med Oracles misligholdelse af Oracles garantiforpligtelser.

ANSVARSBEGRÆNSNING: I INTET TILFÆLDE ER ORACLE ANSVARLIG FOR INDIREKTE TAB, FØLGESKADER, TABT AVANCE, DRIFTTAB, TABTE DATA ELLER LIGNENDE TAB, SOM KUNDEN ELLER TREDJEMAND PÅDRAGER SIG, UANSET OM ORACLE AF KUNDEN ELLER AF TREDJEMAND MÅTTE VÆRE BLEVET INFORMERET OM MULIGHEDEN FOR AT SÅDANNE TAB KUNNE OPSTÅ. ORACLES ERSTATNINGSANSVAR SKAL I INTET TILFÆLDE OVERSTIGE DE LICENSBETALINGER, SOM ORACLE HAR MODTAGET FRA KUNDEN FOR PROGRAMMELLET.

Kunden accepterer at overholde alle relevante love og offentlige foreskrifter i Danmark og USA eller andre lande i forbindelse med, at Kunden måtte (1) gøre Programmellet, et direkte produkt heraf eller tekniske data om Programmellet til genstand for direkte eller indirekte eksport, eller (2) måtte anvende Programmellet til formål i forbindelse med spredning af nukleare, kemiske eller biologiske våben i strid med eksportlovgiv-ningen. Nærværende aftale samt aspekter herunder er undergivet dansk ret og alle uoverensstemmelser herunder henvises til Sø- og Handelsretten i København. Oracle har ret til at kontrollere Kundens brug af Programmellet. Nærværende aftale har forrang for alle betingelser i Kundens indkøbsrekvisition eller andet dokument.

BRUGER-CERTIFIKAT DEFINITIONER:
Samtidige Brugere: Det maksimale antal indlæsningsenheder, som på ethvert tidspunkt anvender Programmellet samtidigt. Såfremt multiplexer-software eller -hardware (f.eks. en TP-monitor) anvendes, opgøres antallet af Samtidige Brugere ved multiplexer-indgangen.

Klient: En computer, (1) der kun anvendes af én bruger ad gangen, og (2) som afvikler Programmellet i en lokal hukommelse eller gemmer Programmellet i et lokalt fast lager.

Bruger: En individuel person som af Kunden har fået tilladelse til at bruge Programmellet uanset om en sådan faktisk anvender Programmellet på et givent tidspunkt.

Mailbox: Et punkt hvorfra elektronisk post sendes og modtages. En mailbox opstår, når et bruger-id eller en applikation bliver oprettet i Oracle*Office.

Nederlands/België, Luxemburg, Nederland

ORACLE SOFTWARE GEBRUIKSRECHT VOORWAARDEN

ATTENTIE: DOOR HET OPENEN VAN DEZE VERPAKKING OF HET GEBRUIK VAN DE INGESLOTEN SOFTWARE GAAT U ERMEE ACCOORD GEHOUDEN TE ZIJN AAN DE NAVOLGENDE VOORWAARDEN. INDIEN U NIET ACCOORD GAAT MET DE GELEVERDE SOFTWARE DAN WEL DE VOORWAARDEN, DIENT U DE VERPAKKING EN DE SOFTWARE BINNEN 30 DAGEN TE RETOURNEREN AAN HET BEDRIJF VAN WIE U DIT ONTVANGEN HEEFT WILT U IN AANMERKING KOMEN VOOR TERUGBETALING VAN DE BETAALDE VERGOEDING.

ORACLE CORPORATION DAN WEL HAAR DOCHTERONDERNEMING ("ORACLE") VERLEENT U ("CLIËNT") HET RECHT DE INGESLOTEN SOFTWARE EN DE DOCUMENTATIE ("PROGRAMMA'S") TE GEBRUIKEN ONDER DE VOLGENDE VOORWAARDEN:

GEBRUIKSRECHT: Cliënt heeft het recht de Programma's te gebruiken op a) de door Oracle aangegeven hardware/besturingssysteem combinatie als aangegeven in een order document of het 'Program Use Certificaat' verstrekt aan Cliënt door Oracle of haar distributeurs of b) indien de gebruiksrechten niet nader zijn gespecificeerd voor een enkele gebruiker op een enkele computer. Cliënt mag de Programma's uitsluitend gebruiken voor het verwerken van zijn eigen interne data. Cliënt mag één kopie van ieder gelicentieerd Programma maken ten behoeve van back-up doeleinden; het recht om meerdere kopiëen te maken kan evenwel op de order of op het Program Use Certificaat zijn vermeld. Additionele kopiëen zullen slechts kunnen worden gemaakt na voorafgaande schriftelijke toestemming van Oracle. Het is Cliënt niet toegestaan: (a) aanduidingen van produkt identificatie, eigendom, titel, handelsmerken en overige rechten van intellectuele eigendom van de Programma's te verwijderen; (b) de Programma's te gebruiken voor commerciële time-sharing, verhuur of als service bureau; (c) de Programma's te verkopen, vervreemden, in zekerheid overdragen of op welke wijze dan ook ter beschikking van enige derde te stellen zonder voorafgaande schriftelijke toestemming van Oracle; (d) de Programma's te "reverse engineeren", decompileren of te disassembleren, behoudens in die gevallen, waarin Cliënt, na een schriftelijk verzoek daartoe, niet binnen een redelijke termijn van Oracle de beschikbare informatie heeft ontvangen die benodigd is om software te ontwikkelen die kan werken in samenhang met het Programma van Oracle, maar die geen inbreuk maakt op de intellectuele eigendomsrechten van Oracle; en (e) resultaten van benchmark-tests vrij te geven zonder voorafgaande schriftelijke toestemming van Oracle. Iedere overzetting van Programma's is onderworpen aan de transfer-policy en - vergoeding zoals door Oracle gehanteerd. Cliënt verkrijgt uitsluitend het gebruiksrecht op de Programma's in deze verpakking welke zijn gespecificeerd in het order document of het Program Use Certificaat.

AUTEURSRECHT/EIGENDOM VAN DE PROGRAMMA'S: De Programma's zijn eigendom van Oracle en worden beschermd door auteurs- en overige intellectuele eigendomsrechten. Cliënt verkrijgt uitsluitend het recht de Programma's te gebruiken en verkrijgt noch uitdrukkelijk noch stilzwijgend andere rechten op de Programma's en de media waarop de Programma's worden verstrekt dan die aangegeven in deze voorwaarden. Alle rechten, eigendom en overige belangen, intellectuele eigendomsrechten daaronder begrepen, in of op het Programma en de media blijven voorbehouden aan Oracle of diens licentiegever.

GARANTIE EN GARANTIEBEPERKINGEN: Oracle garandeert gedurende een periode van 90 dagen vanaf de afleverdatum dat (a) tapes, diskettes of andere gegevensdragers, bij normaal gebruik, vrij zijn van gebreken in materiaal en afwerking; en (b) dat de Programma's, mits ongewijzigd, in hoofdzaak functioneren overeenkomstig de functies beschreven in de bijbehorende door Oracle geleverde documentatie, mits gebruikt op de aangewezen hardware/besturingssysteem combinatie. Oracle garandeert niet dat de Programma's voldoen aan de eisen van Cliënt, voldoen in alle combinaties die Cliënt voor gebruik selecteert, dat de werking van de Programma's ononderbroken of vrij van onvolkomenheden zal zijn, of dat alle onvolkomenheden zullen worden hersteld. Deze garanties zijn uitputtend beschreven en alle overige garanties, uitdrukkelijk dan wel stilzwijgend, zijn uitgesloten. Indien Cliënt een onvolkomenheid in een Programma rapporteert binnen de garantieperiode van 90 dagen, zal Oracle, te harer beoordeling deze onvolkomenheid herstellen, danwel Cliënt voorzien van een redelijke "workaround" procedure, of, nadat Cliënt het Programma aan Oracle heeft geretourneerd, de betaalde licentievergoeding terugbetalen. Oracle zal gebrekkige media kosteloos vervangen mits deze media aan Oracle is geretourneerd binnen de garantieperiode van 90 dagen. De hier omschreven oplossingen vormen een uitputtende opsomming van de aan Cliënt toekomende rechten uit hoofde van garantie.

BEPERKING VAN AANSPRAKELIJKHEID: De aansprakelijkheid van Oracle voor door Cliënt geleden directe schade krachtens enige bepaling van deze voorwaarden zal zijn beperkt tot ten hoogste het bedrag van de licentievergoeding die Oracle uit hoofde van deze voorwaarden van Cliënt ontving. Oracle zal in geen geval aansprakelijk zijn voor enige indirecte-, of gevolgschade, daaronder begrepen gederfde winst of verlies van verwachte omzet, verlies van data of verlies van gebruik van data, geleden door Cliënt of enige derde, uit hoofde van een actie uit onrechtmatige daad of wanprestatie, afgezien van het feit of Oracle of enig andere persoon op de hoogte was van de mogelijkheid tot het ontstaan van dergelijke schade. Iedere verdere aansprakelijkheid van Oracle is uitgesloten, tenzij sprake is van opzet of grove schuld van de zijde van Oracle. Cliënt zal zich houden aan alle toepasselijke wettelijke voorschriften en regels met betrekking tot (a) het direct of indirect exporteren van de Programma's danwel direct daarvan afgeleidde producten; en (b) het gebruik van de Programma's voor een doel verboden door de export wetgeving zoals onder andere doeleinden betrekking hebbende op nucleaire, chemische of biologische wapens. Deze Voorwaarden worden beheerst door Nederlands Recht. Alle geschillen voortvloeiende uit deze Voorwaarden zullen worden beslecht door de daartoe bevoegde rechter te Utrecht. Alle bepalingen van inkooporders of andere documenten waarvan Cliënt zich bij het bestellen van produkten of diensten bedient, zullen worden vervangen door deze voorwaarden.

DEFINITIES IN HET PROGRAM USE CERTIFICAAT:
Concurrent Device/Concurrent Accesses: het maximale aantal invoersystemen dat de Programma's op ieder gegeven moment gelijktijdig mag benaderen. Indien multiplexing software of hardware (zoals bijvoorbeeld een TP monitor) wordt gebruikt wordt het aantal gemeten aan het 'front end' van de multiplexer.

Cliënt: één computer die (1) tegelijkertijd slechts door een persoon wordt gebruikt, en; (2) Oracle software opgeslagen in een lokaal geheugen gebruikt danwel de software opslaat op een lokale opslag apparatuur.

Gebruiker (User): een individu die door de klant is geauthoriseerd om de Programma's te gebruiken, los van het feit of die individu de Programma's op enig moment ook actief gebruikt.

Mailbox: een punt waarvandaan electronische mail wordt ontvangen of verzonden: een dergelijk punt wordt gecreeerd wanneer een gebruikers account of een applicatie wordt aangemaakt in Oracle*Office.

English

English/Canada

ORACLE PROGRAM LICENSE TERMS

CAUTION: IF YOU OPEN THIS PACKAGE AND USE THE ENCLOSED SOFTWARE THE FOLLOWING TERMS APPLY. IF THE SOFTWARE OR THESE TERMS ARE NOT ACCEPTABLE TO YOU. RETURN THE SOFTWARE WITHIN 30 DAYS TO THE COMPANY FROM WHICH YOU RECEIVED IT FOR REFUND.

ORACLE CORPORATION CANADA INC. ("ORACLE") GRANTS YOU ("CUSTOMER") A LICENSE TO USE THE ENCLOSED SOFTWARE AND DOCUMENTATION ("PROGRAMS") AS INDICATED BELOW.

LICENSE: Customer shall have the right to use the Programs in the operating environment identified by Oracle, either (a) to the extent specified in an ordering document or Program Use Certificate distributed to Customer by Oracle or its distributor, or (b) if not specified, for a single user on a single computer. Customer may use the Programs solely for its own internal data processing operations. Customer may make one copy of each licensed Program for backup; rights to make additional copies, if any, may be specified in an ordering document or Program Use Certificate. No other copies shall be made without Oracle's prior written consent. Customer shall not: (a) remove any product identification, copyright notices, or other notices or proprietary restrictions from Programs; (b) use Programs for commercial timesharing, rental or service bureau use; (c) transfer, sell, assign or otherwise convey Programs to another party without Oracle's prior written consent; (d) cause or permit the reverse engineering, disassembly, decompilation,of Programs: or (e) disclose results of any benchmark tests of Programs to any third party without Oracle's prior written approval. All Program transfers are subject to Oracle's transfer policies and fees. Customer shall have the right to use only the Programs in this package that are specified in an ordering document or Program Use Certificate.

COPYRIGHT/OWNERSHIP OF PROGRAMS: Programs are the proprietary products of Oracle or its licensor and are protected by copyright and other intellectual property laws. Customer acquires only the right to use Programs and does not acquire any rights, express or implied, in Programs or media containing Programs other than those specified in this License. Oracle, or its licensor, shall at all times retain all rights, title, interest, including intellectual property rights, in Programs and media.

LIMITED WARRANTIES/EXCLUSIVE REMEDIES: Oracle warrants that for 90 days from date of delivery to Customer: (a) enclosed media is free of defects in materials and workmanship under normal use; and (b) unmodified Programs will substantially perform functions described in documentation provided by Oracle when operated on the designated computer and operating system. Oracle does not warrant that: Programs will meet Customer's requirements, Programs will operate in combinations Customer may select for use, operation of Programs will be uninterrupted or error-free, or all Program errors will be corrected. These warranties are exclusive and in lieu of all other warranties and conditions, whether express or implied warranties or conditions of merchantability or fitness for a particular purpose. If Customer reports an error in a Program within the 90 day period, Oracle shall, at its option, correct the error, provide Customer with a reasonable procedure to circumvent the error, or, upon return of the Programs to Oracle by Customer, refund the license fees paid. Oracle will replace any defective media without charge if it is returned to Oracle within the 90 day period. These are Customer's sole and exclusive remedies for any breach of warranty. This limited warranty gives you specific legal rights. You may have others, which vary from state to state and/or province to province.

LIMITATION OF LIABILITY: ORACLE SHALL NOT BE LIABLE FOR ANY INDIRECT, INCIDENTAL, SPECIAL OR CONSEQUENTIAL DAMAGES, OR DAMAGES FOR LOSS OF PROFITS, REVENUE, DATA OR DATA USE, INCURRED BY CUSTOMER OR ANY THIRD PARTY, WHETHER IN AN ACTION IN CONTRACT OR TORT, EVEN IF ORACLE HAS BEEN ADVISED OF THE POSSIBILITY OF SUCH DAMAGES. ORACLES LIABILITY FOR DAMAGES HEREUNDER SHALL IN NO EVENT EXCEED THE FEES PAID BY CUSTOMER FOR THIS LICENSE.

Customer shall comply fully with all laws and regulations of Canada ("Export Laws") to assure that neither the Programs, nor any direct products thereof are (1) exported, directly or indirectly, in violation of Export Laws, or (2) are used for any purpose prohibited by Export Laws, including, without limitation, nuclear, chemical, or biological weapons proliferation. Oracle may audit Customer's use of the Programs. All terms of any Customer purchase order or other Customer ordering document shall be superseded by this License.

The law governing this License and all related actions will be those laws in force in the province or Ontario, Canada.

TERRITORY: Programs may only be used by Customer in Canada. Customer agrees to ensure that neither the programs, nor any direct product there of is exported; directly or indirectly, from Canada without prior written consent of Oracle.

PROGRAM USE CERTIFICATE AND ORDERING DOCUMENT DEFINITIONS:
Concurrent Devices/Concurrent Accesses: the maximum number of input devices accessing the Programs at any given point in time. If multiplexing software or hardware (e.g. a TP monitor) is used, this number must be measured at the multiplexing front end.

Client: a computer which (1) is used by only one person at a time, and (2) executes Oracle software in local memory or stores the software on a local storage device.

User: an individual authorized by Customer to use the Programs, regardless of whether the individual is actively using the Programs at any given time.

Mailbox: a point from which electronic mail is sent or received; it is created when a user account or application is established in Oracle*Office.

English/United Kingdom

ORACLE PROGRAM LICENCE TERMS

CAUTION: IF YOU OPEN THIS PACKAGE AND USE THE ENCLOSED SOFTWARE THE FOLLOWING TERMS APPLY. IF THE SOFTWARE OR THESE TERMS ARE NOT ACCEPTABLE TO YOU RETURN THE SOFTWARE WITHIN 30 DAYS TO THE COMPANY FROM WHICH YOU RECEIVED IT FOR REFUND.

ORACLE CORPORATION UK LIMITED ("Oracle") GRANTS YOU ("Customer") A LICENCE TO USE THE ENCLOSED SOFTWARE AND DOCUMENTATION ("Programs") AS INDICATED BELOW.

LICENCE: Customer shall have the right to use the Programs in the operating environment identified by Oracle, either (a) to the extent specified in an ordering document or Program Use Certificate distributed to Customer by Oracle or its distributor, or (b) if not specified, for a single user on a single computer. Customer may use the Programs solely for its own internal data processing operations. Customer may make one copy of each licensed Program for backup; rights to make additional copies, if any, may be specified in an ordering document or Program Use Certificate. No other copies shall be made without Oracle's prior written consent. Customer shall not: (a) remove any product identification, copyright notices, or other notices or proprietary restrictions from Programs; (b) use Programs for commercial timesharing, rental or service bureau use; (c) transfer, sell, assign or otherwise convey Programs to another party without Oracle's prior written consent; (d) cause or permit the reverse engineering, disassembly, decompilation, translation or adaptation of the Programs except where Customer shall not have received from Oracle within a reasonable time after written request such information as is available to Oracle and as is necessary to create programs which are interoperable with the Programs but which do not infringe Oracle's intellectual property rights; or (e) disclose results of any benchmark tests of Programs to any third party without Oracle's prior written approval. All Program transfers are subject to Oracle's transfer policies and fees. Customer shall have the right to use only the Programs in this package that are specified in an ordering document or Program Use Certificate.

COPYRIGHT/OWNERSHIP OF PROGRAMS: Programs are the proprietary products of Oracle and are protected by copyright and other intellectual property laws. Customer acquires only the right to use Programs and does not acquire any rights, express or implied, in Programs or media containing Programs other than those specified in this Licence. Oracle, or its licensor, shall at all times retain all rights, title, interest, including intellectual property rights, in Programs and media.

WARRANTIES/EXCLUSIVE REMEDIES: Oracle warrants that for 90 days from date of delivery to Customer: (a) the enclosed media is free of defects in materials and workmanship under normal use; and (b) unmodified Programs will substantially perform functions described in documentation provided by Oracle when operated on the designated computer and operating system. Oracle does not warrant that: Programs will meet Customer's requirements, Programs will operate in combinations Customer may select for use, operation of Programs will be uninterrupted or error-free, or all Program errors will be corrected. These warranties are exclusive and in lieu of all other warranties and conditions ,whether express or implied in law, including implied conditions of merchantability or fitness for a particular purpose. If Customer reports an error in a Program within the 90 day period, Oracle shall, at its option, correct the error, provide Customer with a reasonable procedure to circumvent the error, or, upon return of the Program to Oracle by Customer, refund the licence fees paid. Oracle will replace any defective media without charge if it is returned to Oracle within the 90 day period. These are Customer's sole and exclusive remedies for any breach of warranty.

LIMITATION OF LIABILITY: Oracle shall indemnify Customer for personal injury or death caused by the negligence of Oracle or its employees. Subject thereto Oracle shall not be liable whether in contract, tort or otherwise and whether or not Oracle has been advised of the possibility of such loss for (a) consequential or indirect loss; and/or (b) loss of profits; and/or (c) loss of revenue; and/or (d) loss of business or goodwill; and/or (e) loss of, damage to or corruption of data; and/or (f) loss of availability, and Oracle's liability otherwise for direct loss or damage hereunder shall in no event exceed a total aggregate limit of liability of £250,000 sterling.

VERIFICATION: At Oracle's written request, Customer shall furnish Oracle with a signed statement: (a) verifying that the Programs and documentation are being used pursuant to the provisions of this Licence including any User limitations; and (b) listing the locations, type and serial number of any and all computer hardware on which the Programs are being utilised. Customer agrees to grant Oracle access, upon reasonable prior notice, in order to audit the use of the Programs and documentation. If such audit establishes Customer has unauthorised copies of the Programs or documentation, without prejudice to Oracle's other rights and remedies, Oracle shall have the right to charge Customer for the costs of performing the audit, in addition to recovering charges which would have been due to Oracle had Oracle licensed such copies for use.

TERRITORY: the Programs may be used by Customer within the European Union.

All terms of any Customer purchase order or other Customer ordering document shall be superseded by this Licence. Customer agrees to ensure that neither the Programs, nor any direct product thereof, is exported, directly or indirectly, from the United Kingdom without complying with all regulations relating to such export issued by the United States and United Kingdom Governments. This Licence is governed by English Law and the parties agree to submit to the exclusive jurisdiction of the English Courts.

PROGRAM USE CERTIFICATE DEFINITIONS:
Concurrent Devices/Concurrent Accesses: the maximum number of input devices accessing the Programs at any given point in time. If multiplexing software or hardware (e.g. a TP monitor) is used, this number must be measured at the multiplexing front end.

Client: a computer which (1) is used by only one person at a time, and (2) executes Oracle software in local memory or stores the software on a local storage device.

User: an individual authorised by Customer to use the Programs, regardless of whether the individual is actively using the Programs at any given time.

Mailbox: a point from which electronic mail is sent or received; it is created when a user account or application is established in Oracle*Office.

Finsk/Finland

SOPIMUS ORACLE-OHJELMAN KÄYTTÖOIKEUDESTA

VAROITUS: TÄMÄN PAKKAUKSEN AVAAMISELLA TAI OHJELMIEN KÄYTTÄMISELLÄ ILMOITATTE YMMÄRTÄVÄNNE JA HYVÄKSYVÄNNE SEURAAVAT EHDOT. LUKEKAA EHDOT HUOLELLISESTI LÄPI ENNEN PAKKAUKSEN AVAAMISTA: ELLETTE HYVÄKSY EHTOJA TAI OHJELMIA, PALAUTTAKAA PAKKAUS AVAAMATTOMANA MYYJÄLLE 30 PÄIVÄN KULUESSA, JOLLOIN TEILLE PALAUTETAAN MAKSAMANNE KAUPPAHINTA.

ORACLE FINLAND OY ("Oracle") MYÖNTÄÄ TEILLE ("asiakas") KÄYTTÖOIKEUDEN OHEISIIN OHJELMISTOTUOTTEISIIN JA DOKUMENTAATIOON ("ohjelmat") SEURAAVIEN EHTOJEN MUKAISESTI.

KÄYTTÖOIKEUS: Asiakkaalla on oikeus käyttää ohjelmia Oraclen määrittelemässä käyttöympäristössä joko (a) Oraclen tai sen jakelijan kanssa sopimassaan laajuudessa tai (b) ellei käyttöoikeudesta ei ole muuta sovittu, yhdellä käyttäjällä yhdellä tietokoneella. Asiakas saa käyttää ohjelmia ainoastaan omiin sisäisiin tietojenkäsittelytarkoituksiinsa. Asiakas saa tehdä niistä ohjelmista, joita hänellä on oikeus käyttää, yhden varmistuskopion. Lisävarmistuskopioista on sovittava myyjän kanssa. Muita kopioita ei saa tehdä ilman Oraclen etukäteen antamaa kirjallista suostumusta. Asiakas ei saa: (a) poistaa ohjelmista mitään tuotemerkkiä, tekijänoikeusmerkintää eikä muita oikeuksia määrittäviä tai muita merkintöjä, (b) käyttää ohjelmia kaupalliseen osituskäyttöön, vuokraukseen tai palvelutoimistokäyttöön, (c) siirtää, myydä, luovuttaa tai muutoin saattaa ohjelmaa kolmannelle osapuolelle ilman Oraclen etukäteen antamaa kirjallista suostumusta, (d) aiheuttaa tai sallia ohjelmien konekielisen koodin purkamista tai sen muuttamista selväkieliseksi eikä (e) paljastaa ohjelmien suorituskykytestin tuloksia kolmannelle osapuolelle ilman Oraclen etukäteen antamaa kirjallista hyväksyntää. Ohjelman siirrossa noudatetaan Oraclen siirtokäytäntöjä ja -maksuja. Asiakas saa käyttää ainoastaan niitä ohjelmia, joiden käyttöoikeudesta on sovittu,. riippumatta siitä, että tämä paketti muita ohjelmia.

OHJELMIEN TEKIJÄNOIKEUS/OMISTUSOIKEUS: Ohjelmat ovat Oraclen omaisuutta ja suojattu tekijänoikeudella ja muilla aineettomilla oikeuksilla. Asiakas saa ohjelmiin vain käyttöoikeuden. Oracle tai sen lisenssinhaltija pidättävät itsellään kaikkina aikoina kaikki oikeudet ohjelmiin ja tallennusvälineiseen.

RAJOITETUT TAKUUT JA TAKUUHYVITYKSET: Oracle vastaa tuotteiden toimituspäivästä lukien 90 päivän ajan (a) siitä, ettei oheisissa tallennusvälineissä ole materiaalista eikä ammattitaidosta johtuvia virheitä normaalissa käytössä sekä (b) siitä, että muuttamattomat ohjelmat suoriutuvat olennaisin osin niistä toiminnoista, jotka on kuvattu Oraclen toimittamassa dokumentaatiossa, kun ohjelmia käytetään sovitussa tietokoneessa ja käyttöjärjestelmässä. Oracle ei takaa, että ohjelmat vastaavat asiakkaan vaatimuksia, että ohjelma toimii kaikissa niissä yhdistelmissä, joita asiakas haluaa käyttää, että ohjelman toiminta on keskeytymätöntä tai virheetöntä tai että kaikki ohjelmavirheet korjataan. Edellä mainitut takuut ovat ainoat Oraclen myöntämät takuut ja korvaavat kaikki muut nimenomaiset tai hiljaisesti sovitut ehdot toimivuutta tai soveltuvuutta koskevasta takuusta. Jos asiakas ilmoittaa 90 päivän kuluessa Oraclelle ohjelmavirheestä, Oracle voi harkintansa mukaan joko korjata virheen, neuvoa asiakkaalle kohtuullisen keinon, jolla virhe voidaan kiertää, tai palauttaa asiakkaalle tämän maksamat käyttöoikeusmaksut maksut asiakkaan palautettua ohjelmat Oraclelle. Oracle vaihtaa virheelliset tallennusvälineet maksutta, jos ne toimitetaan Oraclelle edellä määritetyn 90 päivän kuluessa. Edellä mainitut ovat asiakkaan ainoat ja yksinomaiset hyvitystavat takuutilanteissa. Tässä ilmoitetun lisäksi asiakkaalla saattaa olla muita pakottavasta lainsäädännöstä johtuvia oikeuksia, jotka vaihtelevat kussakin maassa sovellettavan lainsäädännön mukaan.

VASTUUNRAJOITUS: ORACLE EI OLE VASTUUSSA MISTÄÄN EPÄSUORISTA EIKÄ VÄLILLISISTÄ VAHINGOISTA EIKÄ ASIAKKAAN TAI MAHDOLLISEN KOLMANNEN OSAPUOLEN KÄRSIMISTÄ VOITON, TULOJEN, TIETOJEN TAI TIETOJENKÄYTÖN MENETYKSISTÄ, JOHTUIVATPA NE SOPIMUKSEN MUKAISESTA TOIMINNASTA TAI RIKKOMUKSESTA, RIIPPUMATTA SIITÄ, ONKO ASIAKKAALLE TAI MUULLE HENKILÖLLE OLISI ILMOITETTU TÄLLAISTEN VAHINKOJEN MAHDOLLISUUDESTA. ORACLEN TÄMÄN SOPIMUKSEN MUKAINEN VAHINGONKORVAUSVELVOLLISUUS EI MÄÄRÄLTÄÄN MISSÄÄN TILANTEESSA YLITÄ ASIAKKAAN TÄSTÄ KÄYTTÖOIKEUDESTA MAKSAMIA MAKSUJA.

Asiakas sitoutuu noudattamaan kaikkia vientilakeja ja -määräyksiä varmistaakseen, ettei ohjelmia tai mitään niistä suoranaisesti johtuvaa tuotetta viedä maasta lainvastaisesti, suoraan tai epäsuorasti, mukaanlukien ydin-, kemiallisten ja bilogisten aseiden leviämisen rajoittamista koskevat säännökset. Tähän sopimukseen sovelletaan Suomen lakia. Oraclella on oikeus tarkastaa ohjelmien sopimuksenmukainen käyttö. Tämän sopimuksen määräykset ovat ensisijaisia asiakkaan myyjän kanssa mahdollisesti sopimiin käyttöoikeusehtoihin nähden.

OHJELMIEN KÄYTTÖÄ KOSKEVIA MÄÄRITTELYJÄ: Yhtäaikainen käyttäjä/pääte: ohjelmaan tiettynä hetkenä yhteydessä olevien syöttölaitteiden enimmäismäärä, kanavointiohjelmistoa tai -laitteistoa käytettäessä (TP-monitori) kanavointia käyttävien syöttölaitteiden päästä laskettuna; Asiakas (v. palvelin): tietokone, (1) jota käyttää tiettynä hetkenä vain yksi henkilö ja (2) joka ajaa Oracle-ohjelmistoa omassa muistissaan tai säilyttää ohjelmistoja paikallisella varastointipäätteellä; Käyttäjä: henkilö, jonka asiakas on valtuuttanut käyttämään Oracle-ohjelmia riippumatta siitä, käyttääkö hän ohjelmia tiettynä hetkenä; Postilaatikko: paikka, josta sähköpostia lähetetään tai johon sitä vastaanotetaan, ja joka luodaan, kun käyttäjätili tai sovellus perustetaan Oracle*Office-ohjelmistoon.

Français/Belgique, Luxembourg, Pays-Bas

CONTRAT D'UTILISATION DU LOGICIEL ORACLE

ATTENTION: L'OUVERTURE DE CET EMBALLAGE OU L'UTILISATION DU LOGICIEL INCLUS, IMPLIQUE L'ACCEPTATION DES CONDITIONS DE CE CONTRAT. AU CAS OÙ VOUS N'ACCEPTEZ PAS LE LOGICIEL OU LES CONDITIONS CI-DESSOUS, VEUILLEZ RETOURNER LE LOGICIEL ET SON EMBALLAGE À VOTRE FOURNISSEUR DANS LES 30 JOURS SI VOUS SOUHAITEZ LE REMBOURSEMENT DES FRAIS DE LICENCE PAYÉS.

ORACLE CORPORATION OU SA FILIALE ("Oracle") VOUS ("Client") OCTROIE LE DROIT D'UTILISATION DU LOGICIEL ET DE LA DOCUMENTATION ("Programmes") SELON LES CONDITIONS SUIVANTES:

LICENCE: Le Client aura le droit d'utiliser les Programmes (a) sur la combinaison hardware/système opératoire telle que stipulée dans le document de commande ou le "Certificat d'Utilisation du Logiciel" octroyé au Client par Oracle ou ses distributeurs ou (b) si les conditions d'utilisations ne sont pas plus explicites, pour un seul utilisateur sur un seul ordinateur. Le Client peut utiliser les Programmes uniquement pour les opérations de traitement de données internes. Le Client aura le droit de faire 1 (une) copie à des fins de sauvegarde, cependant le droit de faire plusieurs copies peut être specifié dans la Commande ou dans le "Certificat d'Utilisation du Logiciel". Aucune copie additionnelle n'est permise sans l'accord écrit préalable d'Oracle. Il n'est pas permis au Client de: (a) enlever toute notice d'identification du produit, de droit d'auteur, de propriété, de marque ou tout autre droit de propriété intellectuelle; (b) utiliser les Programmes à des fins de "time-sharing" commercial, de location ou de bureau de services; (c) vendre, céder ou transférer les Programmes ou de toute autre manière mettre les Programmes à disposition de tiers sans l'accord écrit préalable d'Oracle; (d) pratiquer le "reverse-engineering", la décompilation ou le désassemblage des Programmes, sauf dans le cas où le Client, après une demande écrite, n'a pas reçu d'Oracle dans délai raisonnable les informations disponibles qui sont nécessaires pour développer le logiciel compatible avec les Programmes d'Oracle mais qui ne constitue pas une violation des droits de propriétés intellectuelle d'Oracle; (e) publier les résultats de tests de Benchmark sans l'accord écrit préalable d'Oracle. Tout transfert de Programme est soumis aux politiques et frais de transfert tels que pratiqués par Oracle. Le Client reçoit le droit d'utilisation pour les Programmes inclus dans cet emballages qui sont mentionnés sur le document de commande ou le "Certificat d'Utilisation du Logiciel".

DROITS D'AUTEUR: Les Programmes sont la propriété d'Oracle et sont protégés par les réglementations en matière de droits d'auteur ainsi que toutes les autres législations applicables en matière de droit de propriété intellectuelle. Le Client reçoit exclusivement le droit d'utilisation des Programmes et ne reçoit aucun droit de propriété des Programmes ou du média sur lequel les Programmes sont distribués. Tout droit, propriété ou intérêt, y compris le droit de propriété intellectuelle, dans ou sur les Programmes reste à tout moment réservé à Oracle ou ses représentants légaux.

GARANTIE ET LIMITE DE LA GARANTIE: Oracle garantit pendant une période de 90 (nonante) jours après la date de livraison: (a) que les bandes, disquettes ou autres supports d'information ne contiennent, pour un usage normal, aucun défaut matériel ou de traitement; et (b) que le fonctionnement du logiciel, s'il reste inchangé, corresponde aux fonctions décrites dans la documentation annexe, à condition qu'il soit utilisé sur l'Unité Centrale de Traitement mentionné dans la commande. Oracle ne garantit pas que les Programmes répondront aux exigences du Client, conviendra à toutes les situations sélectionnées par le Client, ou que le fonctionnement des Programmes se fera sans interruption ou sans erreurs et imperfections, ou que toutes les fautes et imperfections seront réparées. Ces garanties sont decrites ici de manière exhaustive à l'exclusion de toute autre garantie expresse ou tacite. Au cas où le Client rapporte une erreur dans les Programmes pendant la période de garantie de 90 jours, Oracle réparera cette erreur à ses frais, ou trouvera une solution "workaround"raisonnable, ou remboursera les redevances de Licence payées par le Client pour autant que le Client ait retourné les programmes à Oracle. Oracle remplacera gratuitement tout média défectif pour autant que celui-ci soit retourné à Oracle dans la période de garantie des 90 jours. Les solutions ci-dessus décrivent de manière exhaustive la totalité des droits du Client en matière de garantie.

LIMITE DE LA RESPONSABILITE: La responsabilité d'Oracle pour tout dommage direct subi par le Client suite à l'une des clauses de ce contrat sera limitée à un maximum équivalent au montant des redevances de Licence reçues du Client par Oracle dans le cadre de ce contrat. Oracle ne sera en aucun cas responsable de tout dommage indirect ou consecutif, y compris le manque à gagner ou la perte de chiffre d'affaire attendu, la perte de données ou d'usage, subi par le Client ou un tiers, découlant d'une action à tort ou insuffisante, que Oracle ait été informé ou non de cette possibilité de dommage. Toute autre responsabilité d'Oracle est exclue, sauf en cas de faute grave ou intentionnelle de la part d'Oracle. Le Client se conformera à toutes les prescriptions et réglementations légales applicables concernant (a) l'exportation directe ou indirecte des programmes ou d'un produit dérivé des Programmes; (b) l'utilisation des Programmes à des fins interdites par les lois de l'exportation y compris mais non exclusivement la prolifération des armes nucléaires, chimiques ou biologiques. Ces conditions sont régies par le droit des Pays-Bas. Tout litige découlant de ces conditions sera réglé par le tribunal de Utrecht, pour autant que ce tribunal est compétent. Toutes les dispositions de bon de commande ou autre document dont le Client fait usage pour commander des produits ou services, sont remplacées par le présent contrat.

DEFINITIONS DU CERTIFICAT D'UTILISATION DE PROGRAMME:
Concurrent Device/Concurrent Access: Le nombre maximum de systèmes d'entrées de données qui peut accéder au Programme à un Programme donné. S'il s'agit de Software ou Hardware "multiplexing" (par exemple un moniteur TP), le nombre sera mesuré au "front-end" du multiplexer.

Client: Un ordinateur qui: (1) est utilisé par une personne à la fois, et (2) utilise le Software Oracle en mémoire locale, ou archive le Software sur un appareil d'archivage local.

User: Un individu autorisé par le Client à utiliser les Programmes, que l'individu utilise activement ou non les Programmes à un moment donné dans le temps.

Mailbox: Un point à partir duquel du courrier électronique est envoyé ou reçu: ce point est crée lorsqu'un compte d'utilisateur est établi dans Oracle Office.

Français canadien/Québec

CONDITIONS D'UTILISATION DE LICENCE ORACLE

AVERTISSEMENT: L'OUVERTURE DE CET EMBALLAGE OU L'UTILISATION DU LOGICIEL CONTENU À L'INTÉRIEUR ENTRAÎNE VOTRE CONSENTEMENT CONTRACTUEL AUX CONDITIONS ÉNONCÉES CI-DESSOUS. SI VOUS N'ÊTES PAS SATISFAIT DU LOGICIEL OU DES CONDITIONS DE SON UTILISATION, RETOURNEZ-LE AU FOURNISSEUR DANS LES TRENTE (30) JOURS POUR OBTENIR UN REMBOURSEMENT.

LA SOCIÉTÉ D'INFORMATIQUE ORACLE DU QUÉBEC INC. ("ORACLE") CONCÈDE À VOUS (LE "CLIENT") UNE LICENCE D'UTILISATION DES PROGRAMMES ET DE LA DOCUMENTATION CI-JOINTS SELON LES CONDITIONS SUIVANTES:

LICENCE: Le client a le droit d'utiliser les programmes dans le contexte d'exploitation identifié par Oracle, soit: (a) conformément aux conditions stipulées dans le bon de commande ou le certificat d'utilisation des programmes distribués au client par Oracle ou son distributeur; ou (b), sauf indication contraire, pour un seul utilisateur sur un seul ordinateur. L'utilisation des programmes est réservée exclusivement aux opérations internes de traitement informatique effectuées par le client. Le client peut faire une copie de sauvegarde de chaque programme sous licence; les droits d'effectuer des copies additionnelles, le cas échéant, sont indiqués dans le bon de commande ou le certificat d'utilisation des programmes. Aucune autre copie ne peut être faite sans l'accord préalable écrit d'Oracle. Le client n'est pas autorisé à supprimer les identifications du produits, les avis relatifs aux droits d'auteur ou tous autres avis ou restrictions concernant la propriété intellectuelle des programmes. Le client ne peut se servir des programmes pour une utilisation commerciale en temps partagé. De plus, le client ne peut pas louer les programmes ou les utiliser dans un contexte d'impartition. Il ne peut en effectuer le transfert, la vente ou la cession sous quelque que forme que ce soit à des tiers sans l'accord préalable écrit d'Oracle. Le client s'engage à ne pas causer ou permettre l'utilisation de techniques de désassemblage, de décompilation ou de rétroconception pour les programmes. Le client ne peut divulguer les résultats d'essais sur les programmes à des tiers sans l'accord préalable écrit d'Oracle. Le transfert des programmes est assujetti à la politique et aux frais de transfert établis par Oracle.

DROITS D'AUTEUR ET DE PROPRIÉTÉ: Les programmes sont la propriété d'Oracle ou son concédant de licence et sont protégés par le droit d'auteur et les autres droits de propriété intellectuelle. Le client bénéficie seulement d'un droit d'utilisation et n'acquiert aucun droit relatif à ces programmes ou à leur support, que ce soit expressément ou tacitement, que ceux qui lui sont accordés par la présente licence. Oracle, ou son concédant de licence, conserve tout titre, tout droit d'auteur ou tout autre droit de propriété, y compris la propriété intellectuelle, sur les programmes ou leur support.

GARANTIES LIMITÉES ET RECOURS EXCLUSIFS: Oracle garantit, pour une période de 90 jours à compter de la date de livraison des programmes au client, que les programmes utilisés de façon normale sont exempts de défaut de fabrication et assume durant cette période les frais de main-d'oeuvre; que les programmes, à moins qu'ils n'aient été modifiés par l'utilisateur, permettent d'exécuter les fonctions décrites dans la documentation fournie par Oracle, lorsqu'ils sont utilisés sur le système désigné. Oracle ne garantit pas que les programmes respecteront les exigences du client, que les programmes pourront être utilisés dans les combinaisons que le client pourra choisir, que l'utilisation des programmes se fera de façon ininterrompue ou sans erreur, ou que toutes les erreurs des programmes seront corrigées. **Les garanties susmentionnées constituent les seules garanties offertes par Oracle. Elles annulent et remplacent toute autre garantie ou condition expresse ou tacite, y compris les garanties ou conditions relatives à la valeur marchande ou les garanties de satisfaction en ce qui concerne un but particulier.** Si le client signale une erreur dans les 90 jours, Oracle se réserve le droit de corriger l'erreur ou de proposer à défaut une procédure de contournement ou, sur réception des programmes, remboursera le client. Oracle remplacera tout support défectueux sans frais s'il est retourné dans les 90 jours. **Ces recours sont les seules garanties contractuelles données par Oracle.**

LIMITATION DE RESPONSABILITÉ: ORACLE NE POURRA ÊTRE TENUE RESPONSABLE DE TOUT DOMMAGE INDIRECT, ACCIDENTEL, SPÉCIAL OU ACCESSOIRE, NI DES DOMMAGES RÉSULTANT DE LA PERTE DE PROFIT, DE REVENU, DE DONNÉES OU D'UTILISATION, ENCOURUS PAR L'UNE OU L'AUTRE DES PARTIES OU PAR UNE TIERCE PARTIE, RÉSULTANT DIRECTEMENT OU INDIRECTEMENT DE L'UTILISATION DES PROGRAMMES, MÊME SI L'AUTRE PARTIE OU TOUTE AUTRE PERSONNE A ÉTÉ AVISÉE DE LA POSSIBILITÉ DE TELS DOMMAGES. LA RESPONSABILITÉ D'ORACLE POUR LES DOMMAGES N'EXCÉDERA EN AUCUN CAS LE MONTANT PAYÉ PAR LE CLIENT À ORACLE EN VERTU DE LA PRÉSENTE LICENCE.

EXPORTATION: Le client doit se conformer entièrement aux lois et règlements en vigueur au Canada (lois sur l'exportation) afin de s'assurer qu'aucun programme ou produit direct associé ne soit: (1) exporté, directement ou indirectement, en violation des lois sur l'exportation, ou (2) ne soit utilisé à des fins prohibées par les lois sur l'exportation, notamment celles concernant la prolifération des armes nucléaires, chimiques ou biologiques. La présente licence et tout ce qui en découle doivent être assujettis aux lois en vigueur dans la province du Quebec. Oracle se réserve le droit de vérifier l'utilisation des programmes par le client. La présente licence annule et remplace les conditions relatives à tous bons ou documents de commande détenus par le client.

EXPORTATION: En aucun cas, le Client ne fera l'exportation a l'extérieur du Canada de façon directe ou indirecte, des Programmes ou de toute donnée technique en rapport avec les Programmes sans une autorisation au préalable ecrit d'Oracle.

DÉFINITIONS DES CERTIFICATS D'UTILISATION DES PROGRAMMES:
Unités concurrentes/Accès concurrents: Le nombre d'unités concurrentes équivaut au nombre maximal de terminaux et d'unités d'entrée utilisés pour accéder au système désigné à un moment donné. Si des logiciels ou de l'équipement de multiplexage (par exemple, un moniteur de traitement de transactions) sont utilisés avec le système désigné, le nombre d'unités concurrentes doit correspondre au nombre de terminaux et d'unités d'entrée qui sont reliés aux unités de multiplexage.

Client: Ordinateur qui est utilisé que par une seule personne à la fois et qui exécute un logiciel Oracle en mémoire locale ou stocke le logiciel dans une unité de mémoire locale.

Utilisateur: désigne une personne autorisée par le client à utiliser les programmes installés sur les systèmes désignés.

Boîte aux lettres: Emplacement à partir duquel du courrier électronique est expédié ou est reçu; elle est créée au moment de la mise sur pied d'un compte d'un client ou d'une application dans Oracle*Office.

Français/France

CONTRAT D'UTILISATION DU LOGICIEL ORACLE

ATTENTION: L'ouverture de cet emballage ou l'utilisation du Logiciel inclus implique l'acceptation des conditions de ce contrat. Au cas où vous n'accepteriez pas les Programmes ou les conditions ci-dessous, retournez-le dans son emballage d'origine au fournisseur dans les 30 jours de la date d'acquisition pour être remboursé.

Oracle France (« Oracle ») concède à la personne en ayant fait l'acquisition (le « Client ») une licence d'utilisation des programmes d'ordinateur ci-inclus et leur documentation (le « Logiciel ») dans les conditions suivantes:

LICENCE: Le Client aura le droit d'utiliser le Logiciel dans l'environnement d'exploitation (matériel et système d'exploitation) identifié par Oracle, (a) dans la mesure stipulée soit dans le document de commande, soit dans le Certificat d'Utilisation de Logiciel émis par Oracle ou son distributeur ou (b) pour un seul utilisateur sur un seul ordinateur, à défaut de stipulations contraires. L'utilisation du Logiciel est réservée exclusivement aux opérations de traitement de données internes. Le Client aura le droit de faire une copie de sauvegarde des programmes sous licence; le droit de faire des copies additionnelles est, s'il existe, stipulé dans le document de commande ou le Certificat d'Utilisation de Logiciel. Aucune copie additionnelle n'est permise sans l'accord écrit et préalable d'Oracle. Le Client n'est pas autorisé à supprimer les identifications du Logiciel, les mentions relatives au droit d'auteur ou tous autres avis ou restrictions concernant la propriété intellectuelle du Logiciel; ni à utiliser le Logiciel à des fins de temps partagé, de location ou de service bureau; ni à vendre, céder, ou transférer le Logiciel à des tiers sous quelque forme que ce soit sans l'accord écrit et préalable d'Oracle; ni à pratiquer ou autoriser l'ingénierie à rebours, la décompilation ou le désassemblage des programmes, si ce n'est dans la mesure indispensable pour développer des programmes compatibles avec le Logiciel mais n'enfreignant pas la propriété intellectuelle qui y est attachée, et cela dans le seul cas où le Client après demande écrite à Oracle n'aurait pas reçu dans un délai raisonnable les informations disponibles et nécessaires aux fins ci-dessus; ni de diffuser ou communiquer à un ou des tiers les résultats d'essais effectués sans l'accord écrit et préalable d'Oracle. L'éventuel transfert du Logiciel sera soumis aux politiques et frais de transfert établis par Oracle. Les droits d'utilisation sont concédés au Client uniquement pour le Logiciel mentionné sur le document de commande ou le Certificat d'Utilisation de Logiciel.

DROITS D'AUTEUR: Le Logiciel est protégé par les lois relatives au droit d'auteur et aux droits de propriété intellectuelle. Le Client n'acquiert sur le Logiciel aucun droit autre que ceux expressément concédés au titre des présentes. Oracle, ou son donneur de licence, conservent tout titre, droit d'auteur ou autre droit de propriété, y compris la propriété intellectuelle, relatifs au Logiciel et son support.

GARANTIES LIMITEES ET LIMITATION DES RECOURS: Oracle garantit, pour une période de quatre-vingt-dix jours à compter de la livraison que (a) le support d'information sur lequel le Logiciel est enregistré est, en utilisation normale, exempt de défauts de fabrication; et (b) un Logiciel non modifié remplit ses fonctionnalités documentées dans l'environnement d'exploitation désigné. Oracle ne garantit pas que le Logiciel répondra aux exigences du Client, conviendra à toutes les combinaisons que le Client pourra choisir, sera utilisable sans interruptions ou erreurs, ni que toutes les erreurs puissent être corrigées. Ces garanties constituent les seules garanties offertes par Oracle, et excluent toute autre garantie explicite ou implicite. Si le Client notifie une erreur pendant la période de garantie, Oracle corrigera l'erreur ou, à défaut, proposera une procédure de contournement ou, sur réception du Logiciel, remboursera la Client. Oracle remplacera tout support défectueux sans frais s'il est retourné dans les 90 jours. Ces recours sont les seules garanties contractuelles données par Oracle.

LIMITATION DE RESPONSABILITE: Oracle ne pourra être tenue pour responsable d'aucun dommage indirect ou accessoire, y compris la perte de profits, revenus, données ou utilisation, subis par le Client ou un tiers et résultant de l'utilisation du Logiciel, qu'Oracle ait été informé ou non de la possibilité de tels dommages. Oracle sera responsable des dommages directs qui lui seraient imputables dans la limite du prix payé par le Client dans le cadre de la présente licence.

VERIFICATION: Sur demande écrite d'Oracle, le Client lui fournira une déclaration (a) attestant que l'utilisation faite du Logiciel est conforme au présent contrat, y compris quand au nombre maximum d'utilisateurs et (b) listant le(s) site(s), type(s) et numéro(s) de série des matériels sur lesquels ils sont utilisés. Le Client fournira à Oracle une possibilité raisonnable de vérification des conditions d'utilisation.

TERRITOIRE: Le Client s'assurera que le Logiciel ne puisse être exporté si ce n'est en stricte conformité avec les dispositions applicables françaises et des Etats Unis d'Amérique ou utilisé à des fins interdites par ces dispositions, telles que la prolifération des armes nucléaires, chimiques ou biologiques. Ces dispositions s'appliquent sous la loi et le droit international privé français. La compétence revient aux tribunaux français. En cas de conflit entre ce contrat et des conditions générales associées au document de commande, ce contrat prévaudra.

DEFINITIONS DU CERTIFICAT D'UTILISATION DE LOGICIEL

Poste Concurrent / Accès Concurrent: le nombre de postes concurrents équivaut au nombre maximum d'organes d'entrée de données qui peuvent accéder au Logiciel à un moment donné. Si des programmes ou matériels de multiplexage (par exemple un moniteur transactionnel) sont utilisés, le nombre de postes concurrents équivaudra au nombre d'organes d'entrée de données reliés audit programme ou matériel de multiplexage.

Client: ordinateur utilisé par une seule personne à la fois et qui exécute un Logiciel en mémoire locale ou stocke un Logiciel en mémoire locale.

Utilisateur: personne autorisée par le titulaire de la présente licence à utiliser le Logiciel dans l'environnement d'exploitation désigné.

Boîte aux Lettres: Emplacement à partir duquel du courrier électronique est expédié ou reçu. Elle est créée au moment de l'ouverture d'un compte au profit d'un Utilisateur ou d'une application dans Oracle*Office.

Deutsch/Österreich, Deutschland, Schweiz

ORACLE PROGRAMM LIZENZ BEDINGUNGEN

VORSICHT: WENN SIE DIESE VERPACKUNG ÖFFNEN ODER DIE BEIGEFÜGTE SOFTWARE NUTZEN, GELTEN DIE FOLGENDEN BESTIMMUNGEN. WENN SIE MIT DER SOFTWARE ODER DIESEN BESTIMMUNGEN NICHT EINVERSTANDEN SIND, GEBEN SIE DIE SOFTWARE INNERHALB VON 30 TAGEN ZURÜCK AN IHREN VERKÄUFER GEGEN RÜCKERSTATTUNG DES PREISES.

ORACLE GEWÄHRT IHNEN ("KUNDE") EINE LIZENZ, DIE BEIGEFÜGTE SOFTWARE UND DOKUMENTATION ("PROGRAMME") WIE FOLGEND AUFGEZEIGT ZU NUTZEN.

LIZENZ: Der Kunde hat das Recht, die Programme in der von Oracle bestimmten Betriebsumgebung entweder (a) in dem Umfang zu nutzen, wie in einem Auftragsformular oder in einem Programm-Nutzungs-Zertifikat einzeln angegeben ist, das von Oracle oder ihrem Distributor erteilt wird, oder (b) sofern keine Angaben erfolgt sind, die Programme für einen einzelnen Anwender auf einem einzelnen Computer zu nutzen. Der Kunde darf die Programme nur für Zwecke der eigenen internen Datenverarbeitung nutzen. Der Kunde darf eine Kopie der Programme als Backup anfertigen; das Recht zusätzliche Kopien anzufertigen muß im Auftragsformular oder im Programm-Nutzungs-Zertifikat festgelegt werden. Ohne schriftliche Genehmigung von Oracle dürfen keine weiteren Kopien angefertigt werden. Der Kunde ist nicht berechtigt: (a) Produktbezeichnungen, Urheberrechtsvermerke oder andere Vermerke sowie Eigentumsbeschränkungen in den Programmen zu entfernen; (b) die Programme für kommerzielles Timesharing, für Miete oder ein Rechenzentrum zu nutzen; (c) die Programme zu übertragen, zu verkaufen, Rechte daraus abzutreten oder sonstwie einem Dritten zu übertragen, es sei denn, Oracle genehmigt dies vorher schriftlich; (d) Dekompilierung, Dissassemblierung oder Reverse Engineering der Programme durchzuführen oder zu gestatten oder (e) Ergebnisse von Benchmark-Tests eines Programms einem Dritten offenzulegen, es sei denn, Oracle genehmigt dies vorher schriftlich. Alle Übertragun der Programme richten sich nach den Transfer Regeln und Gebühren von Oracle. Der Kunde hat das Recht, nur die Programme in dieser Verpackung zu nutzen, die in einem Auftragsformular oder einem Programm-Nutzungs-Zertifikat einzeln angegeben sind.

URHEBERRECHT: Oracle ist Rechtsinhaberin der urheberrechtlich und in anderen gewerblichen Schutzrechten geschützten Programmen. Der Kunde erwirbt Nutzungsrechte nur für diejenigen Programme, die einzeln in dieser Lizenz angegeben sind. Er erwirbt keine Nutzungsrechte an solchen Programmen oder Datenträgern, die in dieser Lizenz nicht einzeln angegeben sind. Oracle bleibt jederzeit alleinige Rechtsinhaberin aller Immaterialgüterrechte an den Programmen und den Datenträgern.

GEWÄHRLEISTUNG: Oracle gewährleistet für die Dauer von 90 Tagen ab dem Datum der Lieferung: (a) daß der beiliegende Datenträger bei gewöhnlichem Gebrauch nicht mit Material- und Herstellungsfehlern behaftet ist und (b) daß die unveränderten Programme die in der zugehörigen Dokumentation beschriebenen Funktionen auf dem genau bezeichneten Computer und Betriebssystem im wesentlichen erfüllen und nicht mit Fehlern behaftet sind, die die Tauglichkeit aufheben oder mindern. Eine unerhebliche Minderung bleibt außer Betracht. Oracle kann nicht zusichern, daß die Programme alle Anforderungen des Kunden erfüllen oder daß die darin enthaltenen Funktionen in einer vom Kunden ausgewählten Kombination ununterbrochen und fehlerfrei ablaufen oder alle Programmfehler behoben werden. Die Gewährleistung für nicht erkennbare Mängel aufgrund von Hardware- bzw. Betriebssystemfehlern und für solche Programme, die der Kunde ändert oder in die er sonstwie eingreift, ist ausgeschlossen, es sei denn, der Kunde weist im Zusammenhang mit der Fehlermeldung nach, daß ein solcher Fehler oder Eingriff für den Mangel nicht ursächlich ist. Falls der Kunde innerhalb von 90 Tagen einen Programmfehler meldet, kann Oracle wahlweise den Fehler beheben, dem Kunden eine Fehlerumgehung liefern oder dem Kunden nach Rücksendung der Programme an Oracle die Lizenzgebühren zurückerstatten. Oracle ersetzt kostenlos jeden nachgewiesenen fehlerhaften Datenträger, wenn der Datenträger innerhalb der Frist von 90 Tagen an Oracle zurückgeschickt wird.

HAFTUNGSBESCHRÄNKUNG: Oracle haftet dem Kunden, gleichgültig aus welchem Rechtsgrund, für die selbst oder durch Erfüllungsgehilfen vorsätzlich oder grob fahrlässig verursachten Schäden. Eine Haftung für leichte Fahrlässigkeit besteht nur bei der Verletzung wesentlicher Vertragspflichten. In diesem Fall wird die Haftung für vertragsuntypische Schäden ausgeschlossen. Für einen einzelnen Schadensfall ist die Haftung auf maximal DM 500.000, – bzw. den entsprechenden Betrag in österreichischer oder schweizerischer Währung begrenzt. Als einzelner Schadensfall gilt die Summe der Schadensersatzansprüche aller Anspruchsberechtigten, die sich aus einer einzelnen, zeitlich zusammenhängend erbrachten, abgrenzbaren und insoweit einheitlichen Leistung ergibt.

EINGESCHRÄNKTE RECHTE: Der Kunde verpflichtet sich, die Bestimmungen und Vorschriften des Exportverwaltungsgesetzes der USA sowie die einschlägigen deutschen Ausfuhrbestimmungen zu beachten ("Export- Gesetze") und stellt sicher, daß weder die Programme noch direkte Produkte davon (1) direkt oder indirekt unter Verletzung der Export- Gesetze exportiert werden oder (2) zu dem Zwecke eingesetzt werden, den Export- Gesetze verbieten, insbesondere zur Verbreitung von Kernwaffen, chemischen oder biologischen Waffen. Es gilt das Recht der Bundesrepublik Deutschland mit Ausnahme des UN-Kaufrechts. Oracle ist berechtigt, die Nutzung der Programme durch den Kunden zu überprüfen. Diese Bedingungen haben Vorrang vor allen Geschäfts- und Einkaufsbedingungen des Kunden.

Das anwendbare Recht für diese Lizenz und alle im Zusammenhang damit stehende Handlungen bestimmt sich nach der Lieferung der Programme an den Kunden: (a) Schweizer Recht, sofern die Lieferung in der Schweiz erfolgte; (b) Deutsches Recht mit Ausnahme des UN- Kaufrechts, sofern die Lieferung in der Bundesrepublik Deutschland erfolgte; (c) Österreichisches Recht mit Ausnahme des UN-Kaufrechts, sofern die Lieferung in der Republik Österreich erfolgte.

DEFINITION DES PROGRAMM-NUTZUNGS-ZERTIFIKATS:
Concurrent Devices/Concurrent Accesses: Maximale Anzahl von Eingabegeräten, die auf die Programme zu einem bestimmten Zeitpunkt zugreifen. Sofern Multiplexe Software oder Hardware (d.h. TP Monitor) eingesetzt wird, wird die Zahl vor dem Multiplexer bestimmt.

Client: Ein Computer, der (1) nur von einer Person zu einem Zeitpunkt genutzt wird und (2), der die Oracle Software im lokalen Speicher ausführt oder die Software in lokale Eingabegeräte speichert.

User: Eine Einzelperson, die vom Kunden zur Nutzung der Programme berechtigt wird, unabhängig davon, ob die Einzelperson die Programme zu irgendeinem Zeitpunkt tatsächlich aktiv nutzt.

Mailbox: Sendet und empfängt Nachrichten; sie wird angelegt, wenn ein User oder eine Anwendungsprogramm für Oracle*Office errichtet wird.

Ελληνικά/Ελλάδα

ΠΡΟΣΟΧΗ!!! ΠΑΡΑΚΑΛΩ, ΜΗΝ ΑΝΟΙΞΕΤΕ ΤΟ ΠΑΚΕΤΟ ΑΥΤΟ ΟΥΤΕ ΝΑ ΧΡΗΣΙΜΟΠΟΙΗΣΕΤΕ ΤΑ ΠΡΟΪΟΝΤΑ ΛΟΓΙΣΜΙΚΟΥ ΚΑΙ ΤΗΝ ΤΕΚΜΗΡΙΩΣΗ ΠΟΥ ΕΣΩΚΛΕΙΟΝΤΑΙ, ΠΑΡΑ ΜΟΝΟΝ ΑΦΟΥ ΕΧΕΤΕ ΔΙΑΒΑΣΕΙ ΠΡΟΣΕΚΤΙΚΑ ΚΑΙ ΑΠΟΔΕΧΤΕΙ ΤΟΥΣ ΠΑΡΑΚΑΤΩ ΟΡΟΥΣ. ΤΟ ΑΝΟΙΓΜΑ ΤΟΥ ΠΕΡΙΤΥΛΙΓΜΑΤΟΣ ΙΣΟΔΥΝΑΜΕΙ ΜΕ ΑΠΟΔΟΧΗ ΤΩΝ ΠΙΟ ΚΑΤΩ ΟΡΩΝ ΧΡΗΣΕΩΣ ΤΟΥ ΛΟΓΙΣΜΙΚΟΥ

ΣΥΜΒΑΣΗ ΠΑΡΟΧΗΣ ΑΔΕΙΑΣ ΧΡΗΣΗΣ ΛΟΓΙΣΜΙΚΟΥ

ΜΕΤΑΞΥ: Αφενός, της ORACLE ΕΛΛΑΣ Α.Ε.Ε., που εδρεύει στην Αθήνα (11361), οδός Φωκίωνος Νέγρη 30 (στην συνέχεια η ORACLE), και

Αφετέρου, του ΠΕΛΑΤΗ. Ως "ΠΕΛΑΤΗΣ" νοείται ο αγοραστής, με τους πιο κάτω περιορισμούς, του παρόντος πακέτου.

Η εταιρία ORACLE παρέχει με το παρόν στον "ΠΕΛΑΤΗ" μόνο την άδεια χρήσης του λογισμικού και της τεκμηρίωσης που εσωκλείονται στο παρόν πακέτο και τα οποία στη συνέχεια θα αναφέρονται ως "Προγράμματα", με τους ακόλουθους όρους:

ΑΔΕΙΑ ΧΡΗΣΗΣ: Ο ΠΕΛΑΤΗΣ έχει το δικαίωμα να χρησιμοποιεί τα προγράμματα σε λειτουργική μονάδα που έχει καθορισθεί από την ORACLE είτε α) κατά τον τρόπο που καθορίζεται στο έντυπο παραγγελίας ή στην Εξουσιοδότηση Χρήσης του Προγράμματος, την οποία έχει δώσει στον πελάτη η ORACLE ή ο διανομέας της, είτε β) αν δεν έχει καθορισθεί, τα προγράμματα θα χρησιμοποιούνται από έναν μόνο χρήστη σε ένα μόνο ηλεκτρονικό υπολογιστή. Ο ΠΕΛΑΤΗΣ μπορεί να χρησιμοποιεί τα προγράμματα αποκλειστικά και μόνο για την επεξεργασία των δικών του δεδομένων. Ο ΠΕΛΑΤΗΣ μπορεί να αντιγράψει μόνο μία φορά το πρόγραμμα για το οποίο παραχωρήθηκε άδεια χρήσης, για εφεδρία (backup). Το τυχόν δικαίωμα του ΠΕΛΑΤΗ να κάνει περισσότερα αντίγραφα του προγράμματος πρέπει να προσδιορίζεται στο έντυπο παραγγελίας ή στην Εξουσιοδότηση Χρήσης του προγράμματος. Απαγορεύεται να γίνουν άλλα αντίγραφα χωρίς την προηγούμενη έγγραφη άδεια της ORACLE. Ο ΠΕΛΑΤΗΣ απαγορεύεται να προβαίνει στις εξής ενέργειες: α) να αφαιρεί από το προγράμματα τα διακριτικά του, τις ενδείξεις πνευματικής ιδιοκτησίας και κάθε άλλη ένδειξη ή περιορισμό σε σχέση με τα αποκλειστικά δικαιώματα της ORACLE, β) να εκμαθαίνει τα προγράμματα με εμπορική χρονικομετρική ή μη μίσθωση, ή ως επιχείρηση παροχής υπηρεσιών, γ) να μεταβιβάζει, πωλεί, παραχωρεί ή με οποιοδήποτε άλλο τρόπο εκχωρεί τα προγράμματα σε τρίτον χωρίς την προηγούμενη έγγραφη συναίνεση της ORACLE, δ) ο ΠΕΛΑΤΗΣ υποχρεούται να μην προβαίνει, ούτε να επιτρέπει την αντίστροφη μεταγλώττιση (αποσυμπίληση), αποσυναρμολόγηση, αποκωδικοποίηση, μετάφραση, προσαρμογή ή διασκευή των προγραμμάτων, με εξαίρεση την περίπτωση κατά την οποία ο ΠΕΛΑΤΗΣ δεν έχει λάβει από την ORACLE μέσα σε εύλογο χρονικό διάστημα, ύστερα από έγγραφη αίτησή του, τις πληροφορίες που διαθέτει η ORACLE και οι οποίες είναι αναγκαίες για τη διαλειτουργικότητα προγραμμάτων που δημιουργεί ο ΠΕΛΑΤΗΣ με τα προγράμματα των οποίων παραχωρείται η άδεια χρήσης με το παρόν, αλλά δεν παραβιάζοντας τα δικαιώματα πνευματικής ιδιοκτησίας της ORACLE και ε) να αποκαλύπτει σε τρίτους χωρίς την προηγούμενη έγγραφη έγκριση της ORACLE τα αποτελέσματα δοκιμών του προγράμματος. Για κάθε μεταβίβαση του προγράμματος ισχύει η διαδικασία μεταβίβασης και οι αμοιβές που έχουν καθορισθεί από την ORACLE. Ο ΠΕΛΑΤΗΣ έχει δικαίωμα να χρησιμοποιεί από τα προγράμματα που εσωκλείονται στο παρόν πακέτο μόνο εκείνα τα οποία καθορίζονται στο έντυπο παραγγελίας ή στην Εξουσιοδότηση Χρήσης του Προγράμματος.

ΠΝΕΥΜΑΤΙΚΗ ΙΔΙΟΚΤΗΣΙΑ/ΚΥΡΙΟΤΗΤΑ ΠΡΟΓΡΑΜΜΑΤΩΝ: Τα προγράμματα είναι προϊόντα της αποκλειστικής κυριότητας της ORACLE και προστατεύονται από το νόμο περί πνευματικής ιδιοκτησίας.

Ο ΠΕΛΑΤΗΣ αποκτά μόνο το δικαίωμα να χρησιμοποιεί τα προγράμματα και κανένα άλλο δικαίωμα, ρητό ή σιωπηρό, επί των προγραμμάτων αυτών ή επί των μέσων (υλικών φορέων) στα οποία τα προγράμματα έχουν ενσωματωθεί εκτός από αυτό που καθορίζεται στην παρούσα άδεια. Η ORACLE ή ο παρέχων σε αυτήν άδεια χρήσης λογισμικού διατηρεί πάντοτε την κυριότητα και κάθε άλλο δικαίωμα και έννομο συμφέρον, συμπεριλαμβανομένων των δικαιωμάτων πνευματικής ιδιοκτησίας, στα προγράμματα και στα μέσα.

ΕΓΓΥΗΣΕΙΣ/ΑΠΟΚΛΕΙΣΤΙΚΟΙ ΤΡΟΠΟΙ ΑΠΟΚΑΤΑΣΤΑΣΗΣ: Η ORACLE εγγυάται ότι για έξι (6) μήνες από την ημερομηνία παράδοσης στον πελάτη: α) τα μέσα (media) που εσωκλείονται στο παρόν πακέτο είναι απαλλαγμένα από ελαττώματα ποιότητας υλικού και επεξεργασίας κατά τη διάρκεια κανονικής χρήσης τους και β) τα προγράμματα, εφόσον δεν έχουν τροποποιηθεί και λειτουργούν στον καθορισμένο ηλεκτρονικό υπολογιστή και λειτουργικό σύστημα, θα εκτελούν ουσιαστικά τις λειτουργίες που περιγράφονται στην τεκμηρίωση που παρέχεται από την ORACLE. Η ORACLE δεν εγγυάται, ότι το πρόγραμμα θα ανταποκρίνεται στις απαιτήσεις του ΠΕΛΑΤΗ, ότι θα λειτουργεί σε συνδυασμό (με άλλα προγράμματα) που μπορεί να επιλέξει προς χρήση ο ΠΕΛΑΤΗΣ, ότι η λειτουργία του προγράμματος θα είναι αδιάκοπη ή απαλλαγμένη από σφάλματα, ούτε ότι όλα τα σφάλματα του προγράμματος θα επιδέχονται διόρθωση. Οι εγγυήσεις αυτές αποκλείουν (κάθε άλλη ευθύνη ή υποχρέωση) της ORACLE) και υποκαθιστούν οποιαδήποτε άλλη εγγύηση ή όρο ρητό ή σιωπηρό, συμπεριλαμβανομένων ακόμη και των σιωπηρών εγγυήσεων για την εμπορικότητα και καταλληλότητα του προγράμματος για τον συγκεκριμένο σκοπό που το προσφέρει ο ΠΕΛΑΤΗΣ. Εάν ο ΠΕΛΑΤΗΣ μέσα στο χρονικό διάστημα των έξι (6) μηνών αναφέρει στην ORACLE την ύπαρξη ελαττώματος στο πρόγραμμα, η ORACLE θα μπορεί κατά την κρίση της, να διορθώνει το σφάλμα, να υποδεικνύει στον ΠΕΛΑΤΗ τον εύλογο κατά τις συνθήκες τρόπο για να ξεπεράσει το σφάλμα, ή, εφόσον ο ΠΕΛΑΤΗΣ επιστρέφει το πρόγραμμα στην ORACLE, αυτή να του επιστρέφει την αμοιβή που έχει εισπράξει για την άδεια χρήσης. Η ORACLE θα αντικαθιστά δωρεάν όλα τα ελαττωματικά μέσα (media) εφόσον επιστραφούν στην ORACLE μέσα σε χρονικό διάστημα έξι (6) μηνών. Η ευθύνη της ORACLE σε περίπτωση παράβασης των όρων εγγύησης περιορίζεται αποκλειστικά στις πιο πάνω υποχρεώσεις απέναντι στον ΠΕΛΑΤΗ.

ΠΕΡΙΟΡΙΣΜΟΣ ΕΥΘΥΝΗΣ: Η ORACLE σε καμμία περίπτωση δεν θα ευθύνεται για άμεσες ή έμμεσες ζημίες, θετικές ή αποθετικές, τυχηρά, ανωτέρα βία ή για περαιτέρω ζημίες συμπεριλαμβανομένου του διαφυγόντος κέρδους και τις απώλειας δεδομένων ή χρήσης δεδομένων, που προκλήθηκαν στον ΠΕΛΑΤΗ ή σε τρίτον στα πλαίσια συμβατικής ή αδικοπρακτικής ευθύνης ακόμη και εάν η ORACLE ή οποιοδήποτε άλλο πρόσωπο είχε ενημερωθεί για τη δυνατότητα επέλευσης των ζημιών αυτών. Η ευθύνη της ORACLE για ζημίες σε καμμία περίπτωση δεν θα υπερβαίνει τις αμοιβές που κατέβαλε ο ΠΕΛΑΤΗΣ για την παρούσα άδεια χρήσης.

Το παρόν συμφωνητικό υπερέχει των όρων προμηθείας του ΠΕΛΑΤΗ, καθώς και κάθε άλλου εντύπου παραγγελίας. Ο ΠΕΛΑΤΗΣ συμφωνεί να τηρεί πλήρως όλους τους νόμους και κανονισμούς προκειμένου να εξασφαλισθεί ότι ούτε το πρόγραμμα ούτε κανένα άμεσο προϊόν αυτού θα εξάγεται από την Ελλάδα άμεσα ή έμμεσα κατά παράβαση του νόμου.

Ο ΠΕΛΑΤΗΣ είναι υποχρεωμένος να τηρεί πλήρως τους νόμους και κανονισμούς που ισχύουν στις Ηνωμένες Πολιτείες και στην Ελλάδα και αναφέρονται στην εξαγωγή προϊόντων, προκειμένου να εξασφαλισθεί 1) ότι τα προγράμματα ή άλλα άμεσα προϊόντα αυτών δεν θα εξάγονται στην αλλοδαπή άμεσα ή έμμεσα, κατά παράβαση των ανωτέρω νόμων και διατάξεων και 2) ότι αυτά δεν θα χρησιμοποιούνται για σκοπό που απαγορεύεται από τους πιο πάνω νόμους και διατάξεις, συμπεριλαμβανομένης, ενδεικτικά, της εξάπλωσης των πυρηνικών, χημικών ή βιολογικών όπλων. Η παρούσα σύμβαση και κάθε άλλη συναφής συμφωνία ή ενέργεια, δικαστική ή εξώδικη θα διέπεται από το Ελληνικό δίκαιο. Η ORACLE μπορεί να ελέγχει τη χρησιμοποίηση προγραμμάτων από τον ΠΕΛΑΤΗ. Η σύμβαση αυτή υπερισχύει των όρων παραγγελίας αγοράς ή οποιουδήποτε άλλου εντύπου παραγγελίας του ΠΕΛΑΤΗ.

ΕΝΝΟΙΑ ΟΡΩΝ ΣΤΗ ΕΞΟΥΣΙΟΔΟΤΗΣΗ ΧΡΗΣΗΣ ΠΡΟΓΡΑΜΜΑΤΟΣ

Ταυτόχρονα συνδεδεμένες με το σύστημα διατάξεις/Ταυτόχρονες προσβάσεις: είναι ο ανώτατος αριθμός διατάξεων εισόδου στο σύστημα, οι οποίες έχουν πρόσβαση στα προγράμματα σε μία δεδομένη χρονική στιγμή. Εάν χρησιμοποιείται λογισμικό ή ηλεκτρονικό υλικό που επιτρέπει την πολυσύνδεση (π.χ. TP monitor), ο ανωτέρω αριθμός πρέπει να υπολογίζεται πριν από την πολυσύνδεση.

Εξυπηρετούμενος υπολογιστής: είναι ο ηλεκτρονικός υπολογιστής ο οποίος 1) χρησιμοποιείται από ένα μόνο πρόσωπο κάθε φορά και 2) εκτελεί το λογισμικό της ORACLE στην τοπική μνήμη ή αποθηκεύει το λογισμικό σε μια τοπική διάταξη αποθήκευσης.

Χρήστης: είναι το φυσικό πρόσωπο το οποίο έχει εξουσιοδοτηθεί από τον ΠΕΛΑΤΗ να χρησιμοποιεί τα προγράμματα, ανεξάρτητα εάν το φυσικό αυτό πρόσωπο χρησιμοποιεί πράγματι τα προγράμματα αυτά ή όχι σε μία δεδομένη χρονική στιγμή.

Γραμματοθυρίδα: είναι η περιοχή από την οποία στέλνονται ή η οποία λαμβάνει μηνύματα ή δεδομένα με σύστημα ηλεκτρονικού ταχυδρομείου (electronic mail) και η οποία δημιουργείται όταν λογαριασμός ή η εφαρμογή του χρήστη εγκαθίσταται στο Oracle® Office.

ΔΩΣΙΔΙΚΙΑ ΚΑΙ ΑΡΜΟΔΙΟΤΗΣ: Για κάθε διαφορά που θα προκύψει σε σχέση με το κύρος, την ερμηνεία ή την εκτέλεση του παρόντος, αποκλειστικά αρμόδια θα είναι τα Δικαστήρια της Αθήνας κάθε βαθμού και δικαιοδοσίας.

Magyar/Magyarország

AZ ORACLE PROGRAMOK LICENC FELTÉTELEI

FIGYELEM: HA KINYITJA EZT A DOBOZT VAGY HASZNÁLJA A BENNE TALÁLHATÓ SZOFTVERT, ÉLETBE LÉPNEK AZ ALÁBBI KIKÖTÉSEK. HA EZEK A FELTÉTELEK NEM ELFOGADHATÓK AZ ÖN SZÁMÁRA, KÉRJÜK, JUTTASSA VISSZA A SZOFTVERT A MEGFIZETETT DÍJ VISSZATÉRÍTÉSE ELLENÉBEN ANNAK A CÉGNEK, AMELYTŐL BESZEREZTE.

AZ ORACLE HUNGARY KFT. (A TOVÁBBIAKBAN: „ORACLE") ÖNT (A TOVÁBBIAKBAN: „VEVŐ") JELEN SZOFTVER LICENCCEL FELHATALMAZZA ARRA, HOGY A MELLÉKELT SZOFTVERT ÉS DOKUMENTÁCIÓT (EGYÜTTESEN: „PROGRAMOK") AZ ALÁBBIAKNAK MEGFELELŐEN HASZNÁLHASSA.

LICENC: A Vevő a Programok használatára az adott földrajzi Területen, kizárólag az Oracle által megadott üzemeltetési környezetben jogosult, mégpedig vagy (a) az ORACLE vagy annak disztribútora által a Vevőnek átadott megrendelési bizonylat vagy használatbavételi engedély által meghatározott mennyiségi kereteken belül, vagy (b) konkrét előírások hiányában egy számítógépen, egy felhasználóval. A Vevő a Programokat kizárólag saját belső adatfeldolgozási igényeinek kielégítésére használhatja. A Vevő biztonsági célból egy másolatot készíthet magának minden licencbe adott Programról; a további másolatok készítésének jogáról a megrendelési bizonylatban vagy a használatbavételi engedélyben történhet rendelkezés. A Programokról további másolatok az Oracle előzetes írásos beleegyezése nélkül nem készíthetők. A Vevő: (a) nem távolíthat el semmilyen megkülönböztető termékjelzést, a szerzői jogra vonatkozó jelzést, vagy egyéb megkülönböztető vagy a szellemi tulajdonhoz kapcsolódó korlátozó jelzést a Programokból; (b) nem használhatja a Programokat többfelhasználós időosztásos üzemmódban, ha ez kereskedelmi céllal történik, illetve nem adhatja bérbe és nem használhatja számítóközpontban bérfeldolgozásra; (c) nem adhatja át, nem adhatja el, nem engedményezheti vagy semmilyen egyéb módon nem ruházhatja át a Programokat harmadik fél részére az Oracle előzetes, írásos beleegyezése nélkül; (d) nem fejtheti vissza a Programok működését, nem fejtheti vissza őket gépi kódra disassembler segítségével, nem fordíthatja őket vissza, illetve ezen tevékenységek egyikét sem engedheti meg; és (e) az Oracle előzetes írásos beleegyezése nélkül a Programok teljesítményértékelő tesztjeinek eredményeit harmadik féllel nem közölheti. A Programok átruházása csakis az Oracle idevonatkozó rendelkezései és díjai alapján történhet. A Vevő kizárólag az ebben a dobozban lévő, a használatbavételi engedélyen meghatározott Programok használatára jogosult.

SZERZŐI JOG: A Programok az Oracle szellemi termékei, és a szerzői jogi, valamint a szellemi tulajdonra vonatkozó egyéb törvények védelme alá esnek. A Vevő kizárólag a Programok felhasználásának jogát szerzi meg, és nem szerez a Programokhoz vagy a Programokat tartalmazó adathordozókhoz fűződő semmilyen kifejezett vagy hallgatólagos jogot a jelen licencfeltételekben meghatározott jogokon kívül. Az Oracle vagy az Oracle licencbe adója mindenkor fenntart minden, a Programokhoz és az adathordozóhoz fűződő jogot, jogcímet és érdekeltséget, ideértve a szellemi tulajdonra vonatkozó jogokat is.

KORLÁTOZOTT SZAVATOSSÁG/KIZÁRÓLAGOS JOGORVOSLAT: Az Oracle szavatolja, hogy a Vevő részére történő átadástól számított 90 napig (a) a mellékelt adathordozó rendeltetésszerű használat esetén kivitelezési és anyaghibától mentes, és hogy (b) a Programok, amennyiben azokat nem módosítják, az Oracle által adott dokumentációban leírt funkciók végrehajtására lényegileg képesek lesznek, feltéve, ha az előírt számítógépen és operációs rendszerrel használják azokat. Az Oracle nem szavatolja, hogy a Programok megfelelnek a Vevő igényeinek, hogy a Programok a Vevő által esetleg kiválasztott összetételben működni fognak, hogy a Programok megszakítatlanul vagy hibamentesen fognak működni, valamint azt sem, hogy a Programok valamennyi hibáját kijavítják. Mindezen szavatossági előírások kizárólagosak, és helyettesítenek minden egyéb szavatosságot, legyen az vagy hallgatólagos (jogszabályi), beleértve a kereskedelmi forgalmazhatóságért való és a meghatározott célra történő alkalmasságért való szavatosságot. Ha a Vevő 90 napon belül bejelenti a Program valamilyen hibáját, az Oracle belátása szerint vagy kijavítja a hibát, vagy a hiba megkerüléséhez megfelelő eljárást biztosít a Vevő részére, vagy a Vevő által visszaadott Programok ellenében megtéríti a Vevő által fizetett licencdíjat. Az Oracle ellenszolgáltatás nélkül kicserél minden hibás adathordozót, ha azt 90 napos időtartamon belül részére visszaszolgáltatják. A fent felsoroltak a Vevő egyedüli és kizárólagos jogai bármilyen szavatossági probléma esetében. Ez a korlátozott szavatosság határozza meg az Ön jogait.

A FELELŐSSÉG KORLÁTOZÁSA. AZ ORACLE NEM TARTOZIK FELELŐSSÉGGEL SEMMILYEN KÖZVETETT, ESETLEGES, KÜLÖNÖS VAGY KÖVETKEZMÉNYES KÁRÉRT, SEM A VEVŐ VAGY HARMADIK SZEMÉLY ÁLTAL ELSZENVEDETT, HASZON, JÖVEDELEM, ADAT VAGY ADATHASZNÁLAT ELVESZTÉSÉBŐL EREDŐ KÁRÉRT, TEKINTET NÉLKÜL ARRA, HOGY EZ SZERZŐDÉSES VAGY SZERZŐDÉSEN KÍVÜLI IGÉNY, AKKOR SEM, HA AZ ORACLE-T VAGY BÁRMELY MÁS SZEMÉLYT TÁJÉKOZTATTÁK AZ ILYEN KÁROK LEHETŐSÉGÉRŐL. AZ ORACLE JELEN SZERZŐDÉS SZERINTI, KÁROKOZÁSÁBÓL EREDŐ FELELŐSSÉGE SEMMILYEN ESETBEN SEM HALADHATJA MEG A VEVŐ ÁLTAL A JELEN LICENCÉRT FIZETETT DÍJAT.

TERÜLET: a „Terület" Magyarországot jelenti, kivéve, ha ezt megrendelési bizonylat vagy használatbavételi engedély másként határozza meg.

A VEVŐ beleegyezik, hogy az Amerikai Egyesült Államok és más államok összes törvényét és előírását („Exportszabályozás") teljes mértékben betartja annak biztosítására, hogy sem a Programok, sem a Programok, sem a közvetlenül segítségükkel készült termékek (1) sem közvetlen, sem közvetett módon nem kerülnek exportálásra az Exportszabályozást megsértő módon, és (2) nem kerülnek felhasználásra az Exportszabályozás által tiltott célokra, beleértve többek közt a nukleáris, vegyi és biológiai fegyvereket korlátozó rendelkezések hatókörébe eső tevékenységeket. Jelen megállapodás és minden hozzá kapcsolódó tevékenységre a Magyar Köztársaság törvényei vonatkoznak. Az Oracle fenntartja a jogát, hogy a Program használatát a Vevőnél ellenőrizze. Jelen szoftver licenc a Vevő minden esetleges korábbi megrendelésének és megrendelési bizonylatának kikötéseit felülbírálja.

A HASZNÁLATBAVÉTELI ENGEDÉLYBEN SZEREPLŐ FOGALMAK MEGHATÁROZÁSA:
Egyidejű eszközhasználat/egyidejű hozzáférések: a programhoz egy adott időpontban egyszerre hozzáférő adatbeviteli eszközök száma. Ha multiplexer hardvert vagy szoftvert (pl. TP monitort) használnak, a felhasználók számát a multiplexer bemenetén kell mérni.

Ügyfél (kliens): olyan számítógép, amelyet (1) egyidőben csak egy személy használ, és (2) az Oracle szoftvert saját memóriájában futtatja és saját háttértárolóján tárolja.

Felhasználó: a Vevő által a Programok használatára feljogosított személy, függetlenül attól, hogy egy adott időpontban a programot ténylegesen használja-e vagy sem.

Postaláda (mailbox): olyan pont, amelyről/amelyre elektronikus levél továbbítható vagy fogadható: akkor keletkezik, amikor egy új felhasználó vagy alkalmazás hozzáférési jogosultságot kap az Oracle*Office-hoz.

Italiano/Italia

LICENZA D'USO DI PROGRAMMA ORACLE

ATTENZIONE: SE APRITE QUESTO PACCHETTO O USATE IL SOFTWARE IVI CONTENUTO, SI APPLICHERANNO I SEGUENTI TERMINI E CONDIZIONI. SE NON ACCETTATE IL SOFTWARE O I PREDETTI TERMINI E CONDIZIONI, RESTITUITE IL SOFTWARE - ENTRO 30 GIORNI - ALLA SOCIETÀ DA CUI LO AVETE RICEVUTO PER IL RIMBORSO.

ORACLE ITALIA S.p.A. ("ORACLE") CONCEDE A VOI ("CLIENTE") UNA LICENZA D'USO DEL SOFTWARE E DELLA DOCUMENTAZIONE CONTENUTI NEL PACCHETTO ("PROGRAMMI") COME INDICATO OLTRE.

LICENZA: il Cliente avrà il diritto di usare i Programmi, nell'ambiente operativo identificato da Oracle: (a) nei limiti specificati in un documento di ordine o in un Certificato di Uso di Programma distribuito al Cliente da Oracle o da un suo Distributore; o (b) se non specificati, per un singolo utente su un singolo computer. Il Cliente potrà usare i Programmi unicamente per l'elaborazione propria di dati interni. Il Cliente potrà trarre n.1 copia per il caso di guasti, detta copia di backup, di ciascun Programma licenziato; eventuali diritti di trarre copie ulteriori, se del caso, saranno specificati in un documento d'ordine o in un Certificato di Uso di Programma. Non potranno essere tratte altre copie senza la previa autorizzazione scritta di Oracle. Il Cliente non potrà: (a) eliminare dai Programmi i dati identificativi del Prodotto, i dati di copyright, e ogni indicazione dei diritti di proprietà riservata; (b) commercializzare i Programmi, noleggiarli, usarli per erogare servizi a terzi, condividerne l'uso con terzi, concedere anche parzialmente l'uso a terzi e/o temporaneamente l'uso a terzi a qualsivoglia titolo; (c) cedere, assegnare o altrimenti trasferire, a qualsivoglia titolo, i Programmi a terzi senza il previo consenso scritto di Oracle; (d) effettuare o far effettuare la compilazione a ritroso, detta reverse engineering, il disassemblaggio, la decompilazione dei Programmi, salvo che nonostante la propria richiesta scritta, non abbia ricevuto da Oracle entro un termine ragionevole le informazioni, di cui Oracle medesima avesse la disponibilità, necessarie perché altri programmi possano essere resi interattivi con i Programmi, senza peraltro violare diritti di proprietà intellettuale di Oracle; (e) rivelare i risultati di eventuali test prestazionali di alcun Programma, senza la previa approvazione scritta di Oracle. Ogni trasferimento di Programma è soggetto alle politiche e ai corrispettivi Oracle per il trasferimento. Il Cliente avrà il diritto di usare unicamente i Programmi all'interno di questo pacchetto specificati in un documento d'ordine o in un Certificato di Uso di Programma.

COPYRIGHT E PROPRIETÀ DEI PROGRAMMI: i Programmi sono di proprietà di Oracle e sono protetti dalle leggi sul copyright e sui diritti di proprietà intellettuale. Il Cliente acquisisce unicamente il diritto di usare i Programmi, con esclusione di qualunque diritto, esplicito o implicito, sui Programmi e sui supporti materiali che li contengono, diverso da quelli specificati nella presente Licenza. Oracle o il suo licenziante conserveranno sempre ogni diritto, titolo, interesse, inclusi i diritti di proprietà intellettuale, sui Programmi e i supporti materiali.

GARANZIE, LIMITAZIONI/RIMEDI ESCLUSIVI: Oracle garantisce per il periodo di 90 giorni dalla data di invio al Cliente che: (a) il supporto materiale è esente da difetti dei materiali e di fabbricazione, se correttamente utilizzato secondo il suo normale uso; (b) i Programmi nello stato in cui sono stati consegnati sono sostanzialmente in grado di eseguire le funzioni descritte nella documentazione fornita da Oracle, se installati sul computer e sul sistema operativo designati. Oracle non garantisce che i Programmi risponderanno alle esigenze o aspettative del Cliente, né che opereranno in qualunque combinazione scelta dal Cliente per l'uso, né che le operazioni dei Programmi saranno ininterrotte o esenti da errori, né che ogni errore dei Programmi potrà essere corretto. Qualora entro il predetto termine di 90 giorni il Cliente dia comunicazione ad Oracle di un errore di un Programma, Oracle, a propria discrezione, correggerà l'errore, o provvederà a fornire al Cliente una procedura adeguata per superare il problema tecnico rilevato, o, dietro restituzione dei Programmi ad Oracle da parte del Cliente, rimborserà a questi l'importo pagato per la licenza d'uso. Oracle sostituirà gratuitamente eventuali supporti materiali difettosi che le fossero restituiti entro il medesimo termine di 90 giorni. Quanto precede limita ed esaurisce, definitivamente e senza residui, ogni obbligo di Oracle in materia di garanzie, esplicite ed implicite, incluse le garanzie di buon funzionamento, adeguatezza legale e/o contrattuale ad un particolare scopo, ai sensi degli artt. 1490 e segg. e 1512 Cod. Civ. Il Cliente prende atto che il regime della garanzia può variare da Paese a Paese.

LIMITI DI RESPONSABILITÀ: L'EVENTUALE RESPONSABILITÀ CONTRATTUALE E/O EXTRACONTRATTUALE DI ORACLE NON COMPRENDERÀ IN ALCUN CASO DANNI INDIRETTI O CONSEQUENZIALI, DANNI PER PERDITA DI PROFITTI, RICAVI, DATI, USO DI DATI. PER TUTTI TALI TITOLI, PERTANTO, IL CLIENTE NON POTRÀ DOMANDARE NÈ OTTENERE RISARCIMENTO DI SORTA DA ORACLE. FERMO QUANTO SOPRA, LA RESPONSABILITÀ DI ORACLE PER DANNI E PREGIUDIZI DI QUALSIASI TIPO DERIVANTI O CONNESSI CON LA PRESENTE LICENZA D'USO NON POTRÀ IN NESSUN CASO SUPERARE L'IMPORTO PAGATO DAL CLIENTE PER LA LICENZA MEDESIMA. Il Cliente si impegna a rispettare pienamente tutte le leggi ed i regolamenti in materia di esportazione emanati dagli Stati Uniti d'America, dallo Stato Italiano e dagli altri Paesi in cui il Cliente medesimo abbia ad esportare i Programmi ("Leggi sull'Esportazione") e garantisce che né i Programmi, né i prodotti da essi derivati saranno direttamente o indirettamente esportati in violazione delle Leggi sull'Esportazione, o utilizzati per scopi proibiti dalle Leggi sull'Esportazione, inclusa, senza limitazioni, la proliferazione di armi nucleari, chimiche o biologiche. La legge applicabile alla presente Licenza d'uso e alle eventuali azioni ad essa relative è quella italiana. Oracle potrà effettuare verifiche sull'uso dei Programmi da parte del Cliente. Le disposizioni di cui alla presente Licenza prevarranno su tutte le condizioni eventualmente contenute nell'ordine di acquisto o in altri documenti d'ordine del Cliente.

DEFINIZIONI DEL CERTIFICATO DI USO DI PROGRAMMA:
Dispositivi Concorrenti/Accessi Concorrenti: il numero massimo di dispositivi di immissione dati che accedono ai Programmi in un determinato momento. Se vengono utilizzati un software o un hardware di gestione multipla dell'accesso (ad es. un TP monitor), il predetto numero viene determinato con riguardo al numero consentito di accessi simultanei.

Client: un computer che viene usato da una sola persona alla volta, e che esegue il sotware Oracle in memoria locale o archivia il software in un dispositivo di archiviazione locale.

Utente: un individuo autorizzato dal Cliente ad usare i Programmi, senza riguardo al fatto che tale individuo utilizzi attivamente i Programmi in un determinato momento.

Mailbox: un punto da cui viene inviata o ricevuta la posta elettronica; è creato quando un utente o un'applicazione sono connessi ad Oracle*Office.

Oracle Italia S.p.A., sede legale in Roma, Via Laurentina 756, iscritta al Registro delle Societa' del Tribunale di Roma al n. 3277/93, Capitale Sociale Lit. 20.000.000.000.= i.v., cod. fisc. 01603630599, p. IVA 04491561009.

日本語／日本

オラクル プログラム ライセンス条件

注意:このパッケージに含まれているディスケットの梱包を開封し、又は対象プログラムを使用した場合には、お客様が以下の「使用権許諾書」の条項を全て理解し、同意したこととさせて頂きます。以下の条項をお読みになり、同意できない場合には、包装をあけずにお買い上げの日から30日以内に販売会社にお返し下さい。その場合、お支払い済みの代金をお返し致します。

日本オラクル株式会社（以下オラクルといいます）はお客様に以下に定められたプログラム及びドキュメント（以下併せて対象プログラムといいます）を使用するライセンスを付与します。

ライセンス：お客様は、(a)注文書、又はオラクル若しくはその販売会社がお客様に配布致しましたプログラム使用証明書に規定される範囲内という条件にて、又 (b) それらに規定なき場合は、単一コンピューター上で単一ユーザーという条件にて、オラクルが確認した動作環境下で対象プログラムを使用する権利を有します。お客様は自己の内部データを処理するためにのみ対象プログラムを使用できます。お客様はバックアップを目的として、各々の対象プログラムを一部複製することができます。一部を超える複製権が許諾される場合には、注文書又はプログラム使用証明書に規定されることになります。オラクルの事前の書面による承諾なく、ここで定める以上に複製を行ってはなりません。お客様は次の(a)から(e)に定めることを行ってはなりません。(a)製品表示、著作権表示又はその他の注意文言あるいは専有権に基づく制限事項を抹消すること、(b)商用のタイムシェアリング、貸与又はデータセンター用に対象プログラムを使用すること、(c)オラクルの事前の書面による承諾なく、対象プログラムを第三者に対して移転、販売、譲渡その他処分すること、(d)対象プログラムをリバース・エンジニアリング、逆アセンブル、逆コンパイルしたり、または第三者にそれらの行為を行わせること、又は(e)オラクルの事前の書面による承諾なく、対象プログラムのベンチマークテストの結果を第三者に開示すること。対象プログラムの譲渡は全て、オラクルの基準と料金に従って為されるものとします。お客様は注文書又はプログラム使用証明書に規定されているこのパッケージ内の対象プログラムのみ使用する権利を有します。

著作権：対象プログラムは日本オラクル株式会社の親会社である米国オラクル・コーポレーション（以下「米国オラクル」といいます。）が専有する製品であり、著作権及びその他の知的財産権に関する法律によって保護されております。お客様は対象プログラムを使用する権利を付与されたに過ぎず、この使用権許諾書に定める以外に、対象プログラム又はそれを含んだ媒体に係る一切の権利を明示的に、付与されたわけではありません。オラクル、米国オラクル又はそのラインセンサーは、いかなる時に於いても、対象プログラム又は媒体に係る知的財産権を含む一切の権限、権利を保持するものとします。

限定保証：オラクルは、対象プログラムに関し、それをお客様が変更しない限り、引渡時に指定されたシステムで所期の環境において操作された場合には、それがドキュメントに記載された機能を当該引渡時点で発揮することを保証いたします。オラクルは、報告されたエラーを是正する最善の努力をいたします。

2.オラクルは、このパッケージが引渡された日から90日以内にお客様よりオラクルに返却された物理的な不具合のある対象プログラムの媒体につき、交換又は修理を保証いたします。

3.前二項の保証が、法定の瑕疵担保責任を含め、オラクルの保証内容の全てであり、オラクルは対象プログラムの商品性や特定目的への適合性については保証いたしかねます。又、対象プログラムがいかなるコンピューター・ハードウェア及び（又は）オペレーティングシステムでも適切に機能すること、お客様の要求に合致しもしくはお客様が使用するために選択できる組み合わせで作動すること、動作が中断せずもしくはプログラミング上の誤りが皆無であること、又はそれが完全に是正されることについても同様の取扱いとします。

責任範囲：いかなる場合でもオラクルは契約上の行為による損害を問わず、間接的、結果的、特別もしくは付随的損害、逸失利益、使用不能であったこと、又は信用毀損について、たとえオラクルがかかる損害発生の可能性について知らされていた場合でも、お客様ないし第三者が被ったそれらの損害に対し、なんら責任を有しないものとします。又、データのバックアップを確保する責任はお客様にあるものとし、対象プログラムや技術サポートの提供に起因するデータの喪失について、オラクルは一切の責任を負わないものとします。

2. 前項にかかわらず、オラクルのお客様に対する損害賠償責任は、債務不履行、法律上の瑕疵担保責任、不当利得、不法行為、その他請求原因、訴訟形態の如何にかかわらず、本契約の不履行に起因して発生した損害について、オラクルに賠償責任があるものと裁判所が認定した場合においても、オラクルの履行は不履行の直接的結果として現実に発生した通常の損害についてのみ、お客様はオラクルにその賠償を請求できるものとします。かかるオラクルのお客様に対する損害賠償責任は、このライセンスに関してお客様が支払った金額を限度とします。

制限された権利：お客様が米国政府の防衛局 (U.S. Defense Dept.) である場合は、次の規定が適用されるものとします。
Restricted Rights Legend; Use, duplication or disclosure by the Government is subject to restrictions as currently set forth in subparagraph (c)(1)(ii) of DFARS 252-227-7013, Rights in Technical Data and Computer Software (October 1988).
Oracle Corporation, 500 Oracle Parkway, Redwood City, CA, 94065.

お客様が米国政府の防衛局 (U.S. Defense Dept.) 以外の政府機関である場合は、対象プログラムは、FAR 52.227-14, Rights in Data-General, including Alternate III (June 1987) に定める「Restricted Rights Legend」により提供されるものとします。

お客様は、対象プログラム又はその直接的製品を (1) 直接的、間接的を問わず、日本国、米国及びその他の国の全ての法律・規則(以下「輸出管理法」といいます。) に違反して輸出しないこと、又 (2)核兵器、化学兵器、生物兵器の拡散防止に関する規定を含む輸出管理法によって禁じられている用途で使用しないことを保証すると共に、それらの諸規制等を遵守する義務があります。

本ライセンスは日本国の法律に準拠し、これに従って解釈されます。本ライセンス条件により生ずる紛争については、東京地方裁判所のみを専属的に第一審の管轄裁判所とします。オラクルはお客様の対象プログラム使用状況を監査できます。このライセンス条件はお客様の注文書又はその他の注文ドキュメントの条件に優先します。

한국어/한국

오라클 프로그램 라이센스 계약조건

주의 사항: 귀하께서 이 패키지를 개봉하시거나 동봉된 소프트웨어를 사용하실 경우, 하기 계약조건이 적용됩니다. 귀하께서 소프트웨어나 이 계약조건을 수락하지 않으실 경우에는 귀하께서 소프트웨어를 인도받은 회사로 반환하시고 대금을 환급받으시기 바랍니다.

오라클 코퍼레이션과 그 자회사("오라클")는 귀하("고객")께 동봉된 소프트웨어 및 문서("프로그램")를 사용할 수 있는 라이센스를 아래 기재된 바와 같이 부여합니다.

라이센스: 고객은 오라클이 지정하는 운영환경에서 프로그램을 사용하되, (가) 오라클 또는 그 대리점이 고객에게 제공하는 주문서나 프로그램 사용증서에 명시된 범위 내에서 사용하거나, 또는 (나)명시되어 있지 않은 경우, 단일 컴퓨터 위에서 단인 사용자용으로 사용할 수 있는 권리를 갖는다. 고객은 프로그램을 오직 자신의 내부 자료 처리 작업을 위해서만 사용할 수 있다. 그 이상의 복제 본을 만들 수 있는 권리가 있을 경우에는 주문서나 프로그램 사용증서에 명시된다. 그 밖의 여하한 복제 본도 오라클의 사전 서면 동의없이 만들 수 없다. 고객은 (가) 제품 인식표, 저작권 표시, 기타 독점권 관련 제한사항을 프로그램에서 제거하지 못하고, (나) 상업적 시 분할, 임대 .서비스국 용도로 프로그램을 사용하지 못하고, (다) 오라클의 사전 서면 동의없이 프로그램을 타인에게 이전, 매각, 양도, 기타의 방법으로 전달하지 못하고, (라) 프로그램의 리버스엔지니어링, 디스어셈블리, 디콤파일레이션 작업을 시키거나 허락하지 못하고, (마) 오라클의 사전 서면 동의 없이 프로그램의 벤치마크 테스트 결과를 제 3자에게 공개하지 못한다. 프로그램의 양도는 양도에 관한 오라클의 방침과 요금의 규제를 받는다. 고객은 이 패키지에 동봉된, 주문서나 프로그램 사용증명서에 명시된 프로그램만 사용할 수 있는 권리를 갖는다.

프로그램 저작권/소유권: 프로그램은 오라클의 재산에 속하는 제품으로서 저작권 및 기타 지적재산권에 관한 법률에 의해 보호된다. 고객은 프로그램을 사용할 수 있는 권리를 취득할 뿐이며, 명시적으로든 묵시적으로든. 프로그램 또는 프로그램이 수록된 매체에 대해서는 이 라이센스계약에 명시된 것을 제외하고는 아무런 권리도 취득하지 않는다. 오라클 또는 오라클에 대한 라이센스 허여자는 프로그램 및 매체에 대해 항상 지적 재산권을 포함한 일체의 권리, 소유권, 이권을 보유한다.

제한적 보증/배타적 구제수단: 오라클은 고객에게 인도한 날로부터 90일 동안 (가) 동봉된 매체가 정상적으로 사용될 때 자재 및 가공 상의 결함을 나타내지 않을 것이며 (나) 수정을 가하지 않은 상태의 프로그램이 지정된 컴퓨터 및 운영환경에서 작용될 경우 대체로 오라클이 제공한 문서에 서술되어 있는 기능을 수행할 것임을 보증한다. 오라클은 프로그램이 고객의 요구를 충족한다거나, 프로그램이 고객의 용도에 맞는 선택과 결합하여 작동한다거나, 프로그램의 작동에 중단이 없고 오류가 발생하지 않는다거나, 또는 모든 프로그램 오류가 교정될 것임을 보증하지는 않는다. 이 보증은 상품성에 대한 보증이나 특정 목적에 부합한다 는 보증. 명시적이거나 묵시적인, 그 밖의 모든 보증을 배제하고 갈음한다. 고객이 90일 이내에 오류를 신고할 경우, 오라클은 그 선택에 의해, 오류를 교정해 주거나, 고객에게 오류를 극복하기 위한 합리적인 절차를 제시해 주거나, 또는 고객이 프로그램을 오라클에 반환하는 즉시 라이센스 요금을 환급해 준다. 오라클은 결함이 있는 매체가 90일의 기간 이내에 오라클에 반환되면 대가 없이 교환해 준다. 이는 보증 위반의 경우 고객이 갖는 유일하고 배타적인 구제수단이다. 이 제한적 보증은 귀하에게 특정의 법적 권리를 부여한다.

책임 제한: 오라클은 고객 또는 제 3자가 입은 간접적 손해, 부수적 손해, 특별 손해, 결과적 손해 또는 일심 이익, 일실 수입, 자료 상실 또는 자료사용 상실로 인한 손해에 대해서는, 계약 소송이나 소송에 있어서 든 불법행위 소송에 있어서 든, 설령 오라클이 그와 같은 손해의 가능성에 대해 고지 받은 경우라고, 아무런 책임도 지지 않는다. 이 계약에 따른 오라클의 손해배상 책임은 여하한 경우에도 고객이 라이센스의 대가로 지급한 요금을 초과하지 않는다.

제한적 권리: 미국 국방성으로 인도되는 프로그램은 제한적 권리와 함께 인도되며 다음 규정이 적용된다. "제한적 권리 문구: 정부의 사용, 복제 또는 공개 행위에 대해서는 DFARS 252-227-7013, Rights in Technical Data and Computer Software (October 1988), Oracle Corp. 500 Oracle Pkway, Redwood City, CA 94065의 (c)(1)(ii)항에 현재 규정되어 있는 제한 사항이 적용된다. 국방성에 속하지 않는 미국 정부 기관으로 인도되는 프로그램은 FAR52.227-14.
Rights in Data - General, including Alternate III (June 1987)에 정의된 "제한적 권리"와 함께 인도된다."

고객은 미합중국 및 다른 나라들의 모든 법령("수출법")을 완벽히 준수함으로써 프로그램이나 그 직접적 산물이 (1) 직접적으로든 간접적으로든 수출법에 위반하여 수출되지 않도록 하고, (2) 화생방 부기 확산 등 수출법이 금하는 목적에 사용되지 않도록 하여야 한다. 이 라이센스 계약 및 모든 관련 사항은 캘리포니아 법률에 의해 규율된다. 오라클은 고객의 프로그램 사용을 감사할 수 있다. 이 라이센스 계약은 고객의 구매 주문서 또는 고객의 기타 주문서의 모든 조건에 우선한다.

프로그램 사용 증서 정의:

동시 장치/동시 접속: 주어진 시점에 프로그램에 접속되어 있는 최대 수의 입력장치. 다중 송신 소프트웨어 또는 하드웨어(예: TP 모니터)가 사용될 경우, 이 숫자는 다중 송신 전단에서 측정하여야 한다.

클라이언트: (1) 한 시점에 한 명에 의해서만 사용되고, (2) 로컬 메모리에 들어 있는 오라클 소프트웨어를 실행하거나 로컬 저장 장치에 소프트웨어를 저장하는 컴퓨터.

사용자: 고객이 프로그램을 사용할 수 있도록 권한을 부여한 개인. 그 개인 이 어진 시점에 적극적으로 프로그램을 사용하고 있는지 여부를 불분한다.

우편함: 전자우편을 보내거나 수령하는 지점: 오라클 오피스에 사용자의 계정 또는 신청이 설치될 때 생긴다.

Norsk/Norge

ORACLE PROGRAM LISENS

ADVARSEL - HVIS DE ÅPNER DENNE PAKKEN ELLER BRUKER PROGRAMMET SOM ER I DENNE PAKKEN, ER BRUKEN UNDERLAGT BETINGELSERNE I DENNE AVTALEN. DERSOM DE IKKE KAN AKSEPTERE PROGRAMMET ELLER NEDENFORSTÅENDE BETINGELSER, BES DE OM Å RETURNERE PROGRAMMET INNEN 30 DAGER TIL DET FIRMA, FRA HVOR DE FIKK LEVERT PROGRAMMET, DERETTER VIL DE BLI REFUNDERT BETALINGEN DE MÅTTE HA GJENNOMFØRT FOR PROGRAMMET.

ORACLE NORGE AS ("Oracle") GIR DEM ("Kunden") LISENS TIL Å ANVENDE DE VEDLAGTE PROGRAM OG DOKUMENTASJON ("Program") I HENHOLD TIL NEDENFORSTÅENDE BETINGELSER.

LISENS: Kunden har rett til å bruke Programmet i det driftsmiljø, som er definert av Oracle enten (a) i henhold til de relevante ordre-dokumenter eller et Bruker sertifikat, som Kunden mottar fra Oracle eller Oracles distributør eller (b) såfremt det ikke er spesifisert gjelder denne lisensen for en enkelt bruker på en computer. Kunden må kun anvende Programmet til intern databehandling. Kunden har rett til å kopiere Programmet til backupformål. Hvis kunden har fått rett til å ta ytterligere kopier, er dette angitt i ordre-dokumentet eller Bruker-Sertifikat. Kunden har ikke rett til å ta andre kopier uten at Oracle først har gitt en skriftlig tillatelse til dette. Kunden må ikke (a) fjerne produktidentifikasjon, copyright-notater, eller andre notater eller andre immaterielle angivelser av Programmet; (b) anvende Programmet til timesharing, utleie eller service byråvirksomhet; (c) overdra, videreselge eller på annen måte overlate Programmet til en tredje person uten at Oracle på forhånd skriftlig godkjenner dette; (d) gjøre eller tillate andre å gjøre reverse engineering, rekonstruksjon eller dekompilering av Programmet, med mindre Kunden innen for rimelig tid etter Kundens skriftlige henvendelse til Oracle ikke har mottatt denne informasjon fra Oracle, som Oracle er i besittelse av og som er nødvendig for å lage et EDB-program som kan fungere sammen med Programmet, men som ikke bryter Oracle's immaterielle rettigheter; samt (e) meddele resultater fra benchmark testing av Programmet til en tredje person uten at Oracle på forhånd har gitt en skriftlig tillatelse til dette. Overflytting av Programmet til et annet driftsmiljø er underlagt Oracles regler og avgifter for overflytting av Programmet. Kunden har kun rett til å bruke Programmet i denne pakken i det omfang, som er angitt i ordre-dokumentet eller Bruker-Sertifikatet.

IMMATERIELLE RETTIGHETER/EINDOMSRETT: Oracle er innehaver av opphavsretten og andre immaterielle rettigheter til Programmet og Programmet er beskyttet av den gjeldende opphavsrettige lovgivningen. Kunden erhverver kun rett til å bruke Programmet, og erhverver således ingen utrykkelige eller underforståtte rettigheter til Programmet eller det media, som inneholder Programmet, som ikke er spesifisert under denne avtalen. Eiendomsretten og alle immaterielle rettigheter til Programmet og media forblir i alle henseender Oracles eller Oracles underleverandør.

BEGRENSNINGER AV GARANTIER/MISLIGHOLDSFORFØYNINGER: Oracle garanterer i en periode på 90 dager fra leveringstidspunkt til Kunden, at (a) det leverte media ved normal bruk er uten fabrikasjonsfeil, og at (b) Programmet, medmindre det er modifisert av Kunden, i all sin vesentlighet kan oppfylle den funksjonalitet, som er beskrevet i dokumentasjonen ved bruk på den relevante datamaskin med tilhørende operativsystem. Oracle gir ingen garanti for, at Programmet svarer til Kundens behov, at Programmet kan brukes i spesifikke kombinasjoner, som Kunden måtte velge, at driften vil være uten avbrytelser og /eller feilfri, eller at feil i Programmet vil bli rettet. Kun de ovenfor uttrykkelig angitte garantier er gjeldende for Programmet. Andre garantier, som måtte følge av deklatorisk lovgivning eller av sedvane og kotyme, er ved dette tilsidesatt. Såfremt Kunden rapporterer en feil i Programmet innen utløpet av den angitte 90 dagers garantiperiode for Programmet, kan Oracle velge enten å utbedre feilen, eller å informere Kunden om en rimelig måte, hvordan feilen kan omgås, eller såfremt Kunden returnerer Programmet til Oracle, å tilbakebetale Kunden lisensavgiften for Programmet. Oracle vil bytte defekte media uten omkostninger for Kunden, såfremt de returneres til Oracle innen utløpet av den ovenfor angivne periode på 90 dager. Overstående er de eneste misligholdsforføyninger, som Kunden kan påberope seg i forbindelse med Oracles misligholdelse av Oracles garantiforpliktelser.

ANSVARSBEGRENSNING: IKKE I NOE TILFELLE ER ORACLE ANSVARLIG FOR INDIREKTE TAP, FØLGESKADER, TAP AV FORTJENESTE, DRIFTSTAP, TAPTE DATA ELLER LIKNENDE TAP, SOM KUNDEN ELLER TREDJEMANN PÅDRAR SEG, UANSETT OM ORACLE AV KUNDEN ELLER AV TREDJEMANN MÅTTE VÆRE BLITT INFORMERT OM MULIGHETEN FOR AT SÅDANNE TAP KUNNE OPPSTÅ. ORACLES ERSTATNINGSANSVAR SKAL IKKE I NOE TILFELLE OVERSTIGE DE LISENSBETALINGER SOM ORACLE HAR MOTTATT FRA KUNDEN FOR PROGRAMMET.

Kunden aksepterer å overholde alle relevante lover og offentlige forskrifter i Norge og USA eller andre land i forbindelse med, at Kunden måtte (1) gjøre Programmet, et direkte produkt herav eller tekniske data om Programmet til gjenstand for direkte eller indirekte eksport. eller (2) måtte anvende Programmet til formål i forbindelse med spredning av atom, kjemiske eller biologiske våpen i strid med eksportlovgivningen. Denne avtalen samt tilhørende forhold er undergitt norsk rett og alle uoveren-stemmelser herunder henvises til Asker og Bærum Herredsrett. Oracle har rett til å kontrollere Kundens bruk av Programmet. Denne avtalen har prioritet for alle betingelser i Kundens inkjøpsrekvisisjon eller annet dokument.

BRUKER-SERTIFIKAT DEFINISJONER:
Samtidige Tilganger: Det maksimale antall påloggingsenheter som på ethvert tidspunkt bruker programmene samtidig. Dersom multiplexersoftware eller - hardware (f.eks. en TP-monitor) benyttes, beregnes antallet Samtidige Tilganger ved multiplexerinn-gangen.

Klient: En computer som (1) kun brukes av en person ad gangen, og som (2) utfører Oracle software i lokal hukommelse eller lagrer programmet på en lokal hukommelse eller lagrer programmet på en lokal lagringsenhet.

Bruker: En individuell person som er autorisert av Kunden til å bruke Programmet uansett om individet bruker programmet aktivt til enhver tid.

Mailbox: Et punkt hvorfra elektronisk post er sendt eller mottatt. En mailbox oppstår når en Brukerkonto eller applikasjon opprettes i Oracle*Office.

Polski/ Polska

WARUNKI LICENCJI NA PROGRAM ORACLE

UWAGA: JEŻELI TO OPAKOWANIE ZOSTANIE OTWARTE LUB ZAWARTE W NIM OPROGRAMOWANIE UŻYTE, BĘDZIE TO RÓWNOZNACZNE Z ZAAKCEPTOWANIEM PONIŻSZYCH WARUNKÓW. JEŻELI ZAŚ OPROGRAMOWANIE LUB PONIŻSZE WARUNKI SĄ NIE DO PRZYJĘCIA PROSZĘ ZWRÓCIĆ TO OPROGRAMOWANIE W CIĄGU 30 DNI DO FIRMY, KTÓRA JE DOSTARCZYŁA CELEM ZWROTU ZAPŁATY.

ORACLE POLSKA SP. Z O.O. («ORACLE») UDZIELA NABYWCY («KLIENT») LICENCJĘ NA KORZYSTANIE Z ZAŁĄCZONEGO OPROGRAMOWANIA ORAZ DOKUMENTACJI («PROGRAMY») ZGODNIE Z PONIŻSZYMI WARUNKAMI.

LICENCJA. Klientowi przysługuje prawo do korzystania z Programów na obszarze Terytorium w środowisku operacyjnym zidentyfikowanym przez Oracle albo (a) w zakresie określonym w dokumentach zamówienia lub Świadectwie Prawa Użytkowania dostarczonych Klientowi przez Oracle bądź jego dystrybutorów, albo (b) jeśli nie określono inaczej, licencja zostaje udzielona pojedynczemu użytkownikowi na pojedynczy komputer. Klient może używać Programów jedynie w celu przetwarzania danych dla własnego użytku. Klient może sporządzić jedną kopię każdego licencjonowanego Programu jako kopię zapasową; Klientowi nie przysługuje prawo sporządzania dodatkowych kopii, o ile nie jest to określone w dokumentach zamówienia lub Świadectwie Prawa Użytkowania. Klient nie może sporządzać innych kopii bez uzyskania uprzedniej pisemnej zgody Oracle. Klient nie jest uprawniony do: (a) usuwania z Programów jakichkolwiek ich cech identyfikacyjnych, ostrzeżeń o prawach autorskich lub innych zawiadomień lub ograniczeń odnośnie własności; (b) zezwalania osobom trzecim na korzystanie z Programów za odpłatnością, wynajmowania programu lub wykorzystywania Programów dla świadczenia usług biurowych; (c) przenoszenia, sprzedaży, cesji lub zbywania Programów w inny sposób na rzecz osoby trzeciej bez uprzedniej pisemnej zgody Oracle; (d) podejmowania lub zezwalania na podjęcie czynności mających na celu odtworzenie kodu źródłowego Programów (reverse engineering), rozłożenia, lub dekompilacji Programów oraz (e) ujawniania osobom trzecim rezultatów jakichkolwiek testów wydajnościowych (bench mark tests) jakiegokolwiek Programu bez uprzedniej pisemnej zgody Oracle. Klient ma prawo do korzystania tylko z Programów komputerowych w tym opakowaniu, które są wyspecyfikowane w dokumentach zamówienia lub Świadectwie Prawa Użytkowania.

PRAWA AUTORSKIE/WŁASNOŚĆ PROGRAMÓW. Programy są własnością Oracle i podlegają ochronie prawa autorskiego i innych intelektualnych praw własności. Klient nabywa tylko prawo do korzystania z Programów i nie nabywa jakichkolwiek praw, wyrażonych lub oznaczonych, w Programach lub nośnikach, zawierających Programy inne niż te określone w niniejszej licencji. Oracle lub jej licencjodawca przez cały czas zachowuje wszelkie prawa i tytuł, łącznie z intelektualnymi prawami własności, do Programów i nośnika.

OGRANICZONA GWARANCJA/WYŁĄCZNE ZASPOKOJENIE ROSZCZEŃ. Oracle gwarantuje, że w okresie 90 dni od daty dostarczenia Programu do Klienta: (a) dostarczony nośnik jest wolny od wad w materiale i w wykonaniu w warunkach normalnego korzystania z niego; oraz (b) nie zmieniony Program będzie zasadniczo wykonywać funkcje opisane w dokumentacji dostarczonej przez Oracle, o ile będzie wykonywać operacje na określonym komputerze i przy użyciu określonego systemu operacyjnego. Oracle nie gwarantuje, że: Program spełni oczekiwania Klienta, będzie działać w kombinacjach, które Klient może wybrać dla jego używania, operacje Programu będą nieprzerwane lub wolne od błędów lub że wszystkie błędy w Programie będą usunięte. Gwarancje powyższe są gwarancjami wyłącznymi i zastępują wszelkie inne gwarancje zarówno udzielone wyraźnie jak i zrozumiane, włączając w to zrozumiane gwarancje handlowe oraz gwarancje, że Program jest przydatny do danego celu. Jeżeli Klient zgłosi błąd w Programie w okresie 90 dni, Oracle w zależności od swojego uznania może błąd usunąć, zapoznać Klienta z odpowiednią procedurą dla ominięcia błędu lub, pod warunkiem zwrotu Programu Oracle przez Klienta, zwrócić opłatę licencyjną. Oracle wymieni wadliwe media bez dodatkowej opłaty jeśli zostaną one zwrócone w ciągu 90 dni. Powyższe prawa Klienta są jego jedynymi i wyłącznymi prawami z tytułu naruszenia gwarancji. Ta ograniczona gwarancja daje Klientowi określone prawa.

OGRANICZENIA ODPOWIEDZIALNOŚCI. ORACLE NIE BĘDZIE PONOSIŁ ODPOWIEDZIALNOŚCI ZA JAKĄKOLWIEK POŚREDNIĄ, WYPADKOWĄ, SPECJALNĄ BĄDŹ NASTĘPCZĄ SZKODĘ LUB SZKODY ZA UTRATĘ ZYSKÓW, PRZYCHODÓW, DANYCH BĄDŹ BRAKU MOŻLIWOŚCI KORZYSTANIA Z DANYCH PONIESIONĄ PRZEZ KLIENTA LUB JAKĄKOLWIEK OSOBĘ TRZECIĄ ZARÓWNO Z TYTUŁU UMOWY LUB CZYNU NIEDOZWOLONEGO RÓWNIEŻ W PRZYPADKU GDY ORACLE LUB JAKAKOLWIEK INNA OSOBA BYŁY POINFORMOWANE O MOŻLIWOŚCI WYSTĄPIENIA TAKICH SZKÓD. W KAŻDYM PRZYPADKU ODPOWIEDZIALNOŚĆ ORACLE ZA POWYŻSZE SZKODY NIE PRZEKROCZY WYSOKOŚCI OPŁAT ZAPŁACONYCH PRZEZ KLIENTA ZA NINIEJSZĄ LICENCJĘ.

TERYTORIUM: «Terytorium» oznaczać będzie Polskę, chyba że inaczej zostało to określone w dokumentach zamówienia lub Świadectwie Prawa Użytkowania.

Klient wyraża zgodę w pełni przestrzegać postanowień prawa i innych regulacji Stanów Zjednoczonych i innych krajów («Prawo Eksportowe») dla zapewnienia, że ani Programy, ani jakiekolwiek produkty bezpośrednio z nich powstałe (1) nie są wyeksportowane, bezpośrednio lub pośrednio, z naruszeniem Prawa Eksportowego, lub (2) są używane dla innych celów zastrzeżonych przez Prawo Eksportowe, włączając bez żadnych ograniczeń, rozprzestrzenianie broni nuklearnej, chemicznej i biologicznej. Oracle może skontrolować używanie Programów przez Klienta. Wszystkie warunki jakiegokolwiek zamówienia Klienta lub innego dokumentu zamówienia zostają zastąpione przez postanowienia niniejszej Licencji.

DEFINICJA ŚWIADECTWA PRAWA UŻYTKOWANIA

Urządzenia jednoczesne/Dostępy jednoczesne: maksymalna liczba urządzeń mających dostęp do Programów w dowolnym momencie. Jeśli dostęp do oprogramowania lub komputerów zostaje zwielokrotniony (np. poprzez monitor TP), to tę zwielokrotnioną liczbę należy uważać za faktyczną maksymalną liczbę urządzeń, mających dostęp do Programów w dowolnym momencie.

Klient: komputer, który (1) jest używany tylko przez jedną osobę w danym momencie i (2) w którego lokalnej pamięci operacyjnej działa oprogramowanie Oracle lub jest ono składowane w lokalnej pamięci masowej.

Użytkownik: osoba upoważniona przez Klienta do używania Programów niezależnie od tego, czy osoba ta w danym momencie faktycznie ich używa.

Skrzynka Pocztowa: punkt, z którego poczta elektroniczna jest wysyłana lub otrzymywana; jest tworzony w momencie założenia użytkownikowi konta w Oracle*Office.

Português/Brasil

CONDIÇÕES DA LICENÇA DOS PROGRAMAS ORACLE

ATENÇÃO: CASO ABRA ESTA EMBALAGEM OU UTILIZE O PROGRAMA DE COMPUTADOR NELA CONTIDO, VOCÊ ESTARÁ SUJEITO(A) ÀS CONDIÇÕES ESPECIFICADAS A SEGUIR. CASO O PROGRAMA DE COMPUTADOR OU ESSAS CONDIÇÕES NÃO SEJAM ACEITÁVEIS PARA VOCÊ, QUEIRA DEVOLVER ESTE PROGRAMA DE COMPUTADOR, EM ATÉ 30 (TRINTA) DIAS, À EMPRESA DA QUAL O RECEBEU, PARA REEMBOLSO.

A ORACLE DO BRASIL SISTEMAS LTDA. ("ORACLE"), DÁ A VOCÊ ("CLIENTE") UMA LICENÇA PARA UTILIZAÇÃO DO PROGRAMA DE COMPUTADOR AQUI CONTIDO E DE SUA RESPECTIVA DOCUMENTAÇÃO ("PROGRAMAS"), CONFORME INDICADO ABAIXO.

LICENÇA: O Cliente terá o direito de usar os Programas no ambiente operacional identificado pela Oracle, ou (a) na extensão especificada em um pedido de compra, no Certificado para Uso do Programa distribuídos ao Cliente pela Oracle ou por sua distribuidora, ou, na Nota Fiscal que acompanha os Programas; ou (b) se não houver especificação, para uso de um único usuário em um único computador. O Cliente poderá usar os Programas apenas e tão somente para suas próprias e internas operações de processamento de dados. O Cliente poderá fazer uma cópia de cada Programa licenciado para efeitos de salvaguarda (backup); direitos de fazer cópias adicionais, caso haja, estarão especificados em um pedido de compra, no Certificado para Uso do Programa, ou, na Nota Fiscal que acompanha os Programas. Nenhuma outra cópia poderá ser feita sem o prévio consentimento por escrito da Oracle. O Cliente não poderá: (a) remover qualquer identificação do produto, avisos de direitos autorais, ou outros avisos ou restrições referentes à propriedade intelectual dos Programas; (b) usar os Programas para compartilhamento comercial de tempo, locação, ou utilização em bureau de prestação de serviços; (c) transferir, vender, ceder ou de qualquer outra forma transmitir os Programas a quaisquer terceiros, sem o prévio consentimento por escrito da Oracle; (d) promover ou permitir engenharia reversa, desmontagem ou decompilação dos Programas; ou (e) divulgar resultados de testes de desempenho de qualquer Programa para quaisquer terceiros sem a aprovação prévia por escrito da Oracle. Todas as transferências de Programas estão sujeitas às condições e às taxas convencionais de transferência praticadas pela Oracle. O Cliente terá o direito de usar somente os Programas contidos nesta embalagem que estiverem especificados em um pedido de compra, Certificado para Uso do Programa, ou, na Nota Fiscal que acompanha os Programas.

DIREITOS AUTORAIS/TITULARIDADE DOS PROGRAMAS: Os Programas são produtos de propriedade da Oracle Corporation e estão protegidos pela lei de direitos autorais, bem como por outras leis de proteção à propriedade intelectual. O Cliente adquire somente o direito de usar os Programas, e não adquire quaisquer outros direitos expressos ou implícitos, sobre os Programas ou meios físicos contendo os Programas, além dos que não os especificados nesta Licença. A Oracle Corporation, ou sua licenciadora, detém e deterá durante todo o tempo, todos os direitos, incluindo os direitos de propriedade intelectual, a titularidade e os interesses sobre os Programas e sobre os meios físicos.

GARANTIAS LIMITADAS/RECURSOS EXCLUSIVOS: A Oracle garante que durante 90 dias a contar da data de entrega ao Cliente: (a) os meios físicos aqui incluídos estarão livres de defeitos nos materiais e qualidade de trabalho em condições normais de uso; e que (b) Programas que se encontram inalterados irão substancialmente desempenhar as funções descritas na documentação fornecida pela Oracle quando operados no computador e sistema operacional designado. A Oracle não garante que: os Programas irão atender aos requisitos do Cliente, que os Programas irão operar nas combinações que o Cliente possa vir a selecionar para uso, que a operação dos Programas seja ininterrupta ou livre de erros, ou que todos os erros dos Programas serão corrigidos. **Essas garantias são exclusivas e substituem todas e quaisquer outras garantias, sejam estas expressas ou implícitas em lei.** Caso o Cliente comunique um erro existente em um Programa dentro do período de 90 dias, a Oracle deverá, a seu critério, corrigir o erro, fornecer ao Cliente um procedimento razoável para que corrija esse erro, ou, por ocasião da devolução dos Programas à Oracle pelo Cliente, devolver a este último as remunerações pagas pela licença. A Oracle substituirá qualquer meio físico defeituoso, sem custo, se este for devolvido à Oracle dentro do período de 90 dias. Estes são os únicos e exclusivos recursos do Cliente por qualquer descumprimento da garantia dada. **Esta garantia limitada dá a você direitos jurídicos específicos. Você pode ter outros, previstos em lei.**

LIMITAÇÃO DE RESPONSABILIDADE: A ORACLE E/OU A ORACLE CORPORATION NÃO SERÁ RESPONSÁVEL POR QUAISQUER DANOS INDIRETOS, INCIDENTAIS, ESPECIAIS OU CONSEQÜENTES, OU RELATIVOS A LUCROS CESSANTES, OU PERDA DE RECEITA, DE DADOS OU DE USO DE DADOS, INCORRIDOS PELO CLIENTE OU POR QUAISQUER TERCEIROS, SEJA POR AÇÃO COM BASE EM CONTRATO OU POR ATO ILÍCITO, MESMO QUE A ORACLE E/OU A ORACLE CORPORATION TENHA SIDO ADVERTIDA ACERCA DA POSSIBILIDADE DA OCORRÊNCIA DE TAIS DANOS. A RESPONSABILIDADE DA ORACLE E/OU DA ORACLE CORPORATION POR QUAISQUER DANOS EM DECORRÊNCIA DESTA LICENÇA NÃO DEVERÁ, EM NENHUMA CIRCUNSTÂNCIA, EXCEDER A IMPORTÂNCIA DAS REMUNERAÇÕES PAGAS PELO CLIENTE POR ESTA LICENÇA.

DIREITOS RESTRITOS: O Cliente deverá obedecer todas as leis e regulamentos dos Estados Unidos da América do Norte e de outros países ("Leis de Exportação") para assegurar que nem os Programas, nem quaisquer produtos diretos deles decorrentes, sejam (1) exportados, direta ou indiretamente, de forma a infringir as Leis de Exportação ou (2) sejam usados para finalidades proibidas pelas Leis de Exportação, incluindo, sem limitação, proliferação de armas nucleares, químicas ou biológicas. Esta Licença e todas as ações a ela relativas serão regidas pela legislação local. A Oracle poderá auditar o uso dos Programas pelo Cliente. **Todos os termos de qualquer pedido de compra ou qualquer outro documento de pedido do Cliente são superados por esta Licença. Este contrato é regido pelas leis da República Federativa do Brasil**

DEFINIÇÕES DO CERTIFICADO DE USO DE PROGRAMA:

Dispositivos Simultâneos/Acessos Simultâneos: o número máximo de dispositivos de entrada de dados que acessam os Programas em qualquer momento determinado. Caso um programa de computador ou equipamento multiplexador esteja sendo usado (por exemplo, um monitor TP), este número deverá ser medido na saída multiplexora frontal.

Cliente: um computador que (1) é utilizado por uma só pessoa de cada vez, e (2) que roda o programa de computador da Oracle em memória local, ou armazena o programa de computador em um dispositivo de armazenamento local.

Usuário: uma pessoa autorizada pelo Cliente a usar os Programas, independentemente de estar essa pessoa usando ou não os Programas em qualquer momento determinado.

Caixa Postal: um ponto a partir do qual se envia ou recebe mensagens por correio eletrônico; a caixa postal é criada quando uma conta ou aplicação de usuário é estabelecida/cadastrada no programa Escritório Oracle (Oracle *Office).

Português/Portugal

CONTRATO DE LICENÇA DE PROGRAMA ORACLE

AVISO: Não abra este pacote nem utilize o software nele contido, salvo se previamente tiver analisado e aceite os termos que se seguem.Em caso de não aceitação do software incluso e respectivos termos gerais então deverá devolver, no prazo de 30 (trinta) dias, este pacote à empresa que lho enviou.

A ORACLE PORTUGAL ("Oracle") CONCEDE-LHE ("Cliente") UMA LICENÇA DE UTILIZAÇÃO DE SOFTWARE E RESPECTIVA DOCUMENTAÇÃO ("Programa") INCLUÍDOS NO PRESENTE PACOTE, CONFORME A SEGUIR INDICADO.

LICENÇA: O Cliente terá o direito de utilizar os Programas de acordo com o especificado na documentação de encomenda ou no Certificado de utilização dos Programas ("Autorização de Utilização") distribuído ao Cliente pela Oracle ou pelo seu Distribuidor. Se os direitos de utilização da licença não vierem especificados e explícitos numa Autorização de Utilização então esta licença deverá ser considerada como válida para um único utilizador num único computador. O Cliente poderá fazer uma cópia do Programa para efeitos de segurança; o direito à reprodução de outras cópias deverá constar da encomenda e da Autorização de Utilização. Não poderão ser efectuadas outras cópias sem o consentimento prévio escrito da Oracle. O Cliente: a)não retirará qualquer identificação do produto, avisos de direitos de autor ou outros avisos ou restrições de propriedade do Programa; b)não cederá o Programa em aluguer, locação periódica, ou service bureau; c)não transferirá, venderá, atribuirá ou cederá de qualquer forma os Programas sem o prévio acordo escrito da Oracle; d) não efectuará ou autorizará reverse engineering, dessassemblagem ou descompilação de Programas sempre que o Cliente tenha recebido da Oracle, num prazo razoável e após pedido por escrito, a informação necessária para a criação de programas de software interoperáveis com o Programa, mas que não infrinjam os direitos de propriedade intelectual da Oracle, tal como é permitido e disponível à Oracle; e)não revelará a terceiros os resultados de quaisquer testes de benchmark de Programas, salvo mediante prévio acordo escrito da Oracle. O Cliente terá o direito de utilizar apenas os Programas especificados numa Autorização de Utilização para este pacote.

DIREITOS DE AUTOR: O Programa é propriedade da Oracle e está protegido por direitos de autor. O Cliente adquire apenas o direito de utilizar o Programa não adquirindo quaisquer outros direitos de propriedade sobre este ou sobre os suportes físicos em que este se encontre reproduzido. A Oracle ou o seu licenciador manterão a todo o tempo a totalidade dos direitos, título e interesses sobre o Programa e suportes físicos.

GARANTIAS/REPARAÇÕES EXCLUSIVAS: A Oracle garante ao Cliente pelo período de 90 dias a contar da data de entrega a este: a)que os suportes magnéticos incluídos se encontram isentos de defeitos físicos e de fabrico e em condições normais de utilização ; b)que os Programas que não tenham sofrido alterações desempenharão as funções descritas na documentação fornecida pela Oracle se forem executados no computador e sistema operativo designados.A Oracle não garante: que o Programa cumprirá os requisitos do Cliente; que o Programa operará em combinações seleccionadas pelo Cliente, que a operação dos programas seja ininterrupta ou isenta de erros, ou que todos os erros do Programa sejam corrigidos. As presentes garantias são exclusivas e substituem quaisquer outras, expressas ou implícitas, incluindo garantias implícitas de comercialização e adequação para fins específicos. A Oracle substituirá quaisquer suportes físicos defeituosos, livre de encargos, se estes forem devolvidos à Oracle no prazo de 90 dias. Se o Cliente comunicar um defeito à Oracle dentro do referido período de 90 dias, esta optará por: corrigir o defeito, fornecer ao Cliente processos razoáveis para que este possa resolver o defeito ou, devolver as taxas de licença pagas por este, mediante a devolução do Programa pelo Cliente. Estas são as únicas e exclusivas reparações garantidas ao Cliente por qualquer quebra de garantia.

LIMITAÇÃO DE RESPONSABILIDADE: A ORACLE NÃO SERÁ RESPONSÁVEL POR QUAISQUER DANOS INDIRECTOS, ACIDENTAIS, ESPECIAIS OU EMERGENTES, OU POR DANOS POR PERDAS DE LUCROS, RECEITAS, DADOS OU UTILIZAÇÃO DE DADOS, SOFRIDOS PELO CLIENTE OU POR TERCEIROS, CONTRATUAL OU EXTRACONTRATUALMENTE, MESMO QUE O CLIENTE OU QUALQUER OUTRA PESSOA TENHA SIDO AVISADA DA POSSIBILIDADE DE OCORRÊNCIA DE TAIS DANOS, A RESPONSABILIDADE DA ORACLE POR DANOS NO ÂMBITO DO PRESENTE NÃO EXCEDERÁ EM CASO ALGUM AS TAXAS DEVIDAS PELAS LICENÇAS E PAGAS PELO CLIENTE.

DIREITOS RESTRITOS: Se o Programa for enviado ao Departamento de Defesa dos E.U.A., sê-lo-à com Direitos Restritos aplicando-se a seguinte menção: "utilização da Legenda de Direitos Restritos, a reprodução ou divulgação pelo Governo está sujeita às restrições à altura mencionadas no subparágrafo c) (1) (ii) do DFARS 252-227-7013, Direitos sobre Dados Técnicos e Software para Computador (Outubro de 1988). Oracle Corp 500 Oracle Pkwy., Redwood City, CA, 94065. Se o Programa for enviado a um Departamento do Governo dos E.U.A que não o da Defesa, sê-lo-à com os Direitos Restritos conforme definido no FAR 52.227-14, Direitos sobre Dados-Geral, incluindo Alternate III (Junho de 1987)". O Cliente acorda no cumprimento integral de todas as leis e regulamentos dos Estados Unidos da América e de Portugal destinados a garantir que o Programa ou qualquer produto dele resultante (1) não será exportado, directa ou indirectamente, em violação da lei (2) é usado para qualquer fim proibido pelas leis e regulamentos de Exportação, incluíndo, mas não limitado, ao uso com fins de proliferação de armas nucleares, químicas ou biológicas. O presente Contrato é regulado pela Lei Portuguesa. O presente Contrato substitui na íntegra os termos de qualquer encomenda de Cliente ou outro documento de encomenda.

AUTORIZAÇÃO DE UTILIZAÇÃO - DEFINIÇÕES:
Dispositivos Concorrentes ou Acessos Concorrentes: máximo número de dispositivos em modo input que acedem aos Programas em qualquer momento de tempo. Se for utilizado software ou hardware multiplexing (i.e a monitor transaccional) este número deve ser medido no multiplexing front end.

Cliente: um computador que (1) é usado apenas por um utilizador de cada vez, e (2) executa software Oracle na memória local ou arquiva/guarda o software num mecanismo local de guarda ou arquivo.

Utilizador: um indivíduo autorizado pelo cliente a usar os Programas, independentemente de os estar a utilizar activamente ou não num qualquer momento de tempo.

MailBox ou Caixa de Correio: um ponto a partir do qual correio electrónico é enviado ou recebido; é criado quando uma conta ou aplicação de utilizador é criada no Oracle*Office.

Русский/Россия

УСЛОВИЯ ЛИЦЕНЗИИ НА ПРОГРАММЫ "ORACLE"

ВНИМАНИЕ! ЕСЛИ ВЫ ВСКРОЕТЕ ЭТОТ ПАКЕТ ИЛИ БУДЕТЕ ИСПОЛЬЗОВАТЬ НАХОДЯЩЕЕСЯ В НЕМ ПРОГРАММНОЕ ОБЕСПЕЧЕНИЕ, ТО ВСТУПАЮТ В СИЛУ НИЖЕСЛЕДУЮЩИЕ УСЛОВИЯ. ЕСЛИ ВЫ НЕ СОГЛАСНЫ С ЭТИМИ УСЛОВИЯМИ, ПОЖАЛУЙСТА, ВЕРНИТЕ В ТЕЧЕНИЕ 30 ДНЕЙ ПРОГРАММНОЕ ОБЕСПЕЧЕНИЕ В КОМПАНИЮ, ГДЕ ВЫ ЕГО ПРИОБРЕЛИ, ДЛЯ ВОЗВРАТА ДЕНЕГ.

КОМПАНИЯ "ORACLE AG" (ДАЛЕЕ - "ОРАКЛ") ПРЕДОСТАВЛЯЕТ ВАМ ("ЗАКАЗЧИКУ") ЛИЦЕНЗИЮ НА ИСПОЛЬЗОВАНИЕ ПРИЛАГАЕМЫХ ПРОГРАММНЫХ СРЕДСТВ И ДОКУМЕНТАЦИИ (ДАЛЕЕ - "ПРОГРАММЫ") В СООТВЕТСТВИИ С НИЖЕПРИВЕДЕННЫМИ УСЛОВИЯМИ.

ЛИЦЕНЗИЯ. Заказчик имеет право использовать Программы в пределах Территории и в операционной среде, указанной "Оракл" в объеме, (а) указанном в заявочном документе или Сертификате на Использование Программы, переданных Заказчику "Оракл" или дистрибьютором "Оракл", или, (б) если это не оговорено, настоящая лицензия предоставляет право использования Программ одним пользователем на одном компьютере. Заказчик имеет право использовать Программы исключительно для внутренней обработки своих данных.

Заказчик имеет право создать одну копию каждой из лицензированных Программ в качестве резервной копии; права на создание дополнительного количества копий должны оговариваться в заявочном документе или Сертификате на Использование Программы. Запрещается создавать другие копии без предварительного письменного разрешения "Оракл". Заказчик не имеет права: (а) удалять из Программ любые обозначения продукта, предупреждения об авторских правах и иные предупреждения или ограничения на использование информации, составляющей предмет собственности; (б) использовать Программы в системах разделения времени на коммерческой основе, сдавать их в аренду и использовать в сфере обслуживания; (в) передавать, продавать, переуступать Программы другому лицу и иным образом распоряжаться ими в пользу другого лица без предварительного письменного разрешения "Оракл"; (г) выполнять или разрешать восстановление исходного кода, дизассемблирование или декомпилирование Программ; или (д) разглашать результаты любых тестов производительности Программ каким-либо третьим лицам без предварительного письменного разрешения "Оракл". Все переносы Программы выполняются в соответствии с правилами "Оракл" и за определенную плату. Заказчик имеет право использовать только те программные средства из комплекта поставки, которые указаны в заявочном документе или Сертификате на Использование Программы.

АВТОРСКИЕ ПРАВА/ПРАВА СОБСТВЕННОСТИ. Программы являются продуктом, составляющим предмет собственности "Оракл", и защищены законодательством об авторских правах и другими законами об интеллектуальной собственности, в частности (не ограничиваясь этим), российским Законом об авторских правах 1993г. и Законом о правовой защите компьютерных программ и баз данных 1992г. Заказчик приобретает только права на использование Программ, не получая при этом никаких прав, прямо выраженных или подразумеваемых, на Программы и носители, на которых они записаны, кроме указанных в лицензии. "Оракл" и ее лицензиары всегда сохраняют за собой все права, титул и вещноправовой интерес, включая права на интеллектуальную собственность, на Программы и носители.

ОГРАНИЧЕННЫЕ ГАРАНТИИ И ИСКЛЮЧИТЕЛЬНЫЕ СРЕДСТВА ЗАЩИТЫ. "Оракл" гарантирует, что в течение 90 дней с даты поставки Заказчику: (а) поставляемые носители, при их нормальном использовании, не проявят дефектов, связанных с материалами и изготовлением; и (б) функциональные характеристики неизмененных Программ в основном будут соответствовать указанным в документации, предоставленной "Оракл", при условии использования Программ на указанном компьютере в указанной операционной среде. "Оракл" не гарантирует: что Программы отвечают потребностям Заказчика; что Программы будут работать в комбинации с другими программами по желанию Заказчика; что работа Программ будет бесперебойной или безошибочной, и что все ошибки, обнаруженные в Программах, будут исправлены. Указанная гарантия является исключительной и заменяет собой все иные прямо выраженные и подразумеваемые гарантии, в том числе подразумеваемые гарантии товарности или пригодности для конкретного применения. Если в течение 90-дневного срока Заказчик сообщит о наличии ошибок в Программах, "Оракл", по своему усмотрению, либо устранит ошибку, либо укажет Заказчику порядок обхода ошибки, либо, по получении Программ от Заказчика, вернет Заказчику лицензионную плату. "Оракл" заменит любой дефектный носитель бесплатно, если он возвращен "Оракл" в течение 90 дней с даты поставки. Указанные положения содержат единственные и исключительные средства защиты Заказчика в случае нарушения гарантии. Настоящая ограниченная гарантия предоставляет Вам особые юридические права.

ОГРАНИЧЕНИЕ ОТВЕТСТВЕННОСТИ. "ОРАКЛ" НЕ НЕСЕТ ОТВЕТСТВЕННОСТИ НИ ЗА КАКИЕ КОСВЕННЫЕ, СЛУЧАЙНЫЕ, СПЕЦИАЛЬНЫЕ И ПОБОЧНЫЕ УБЫТКИ, А ТАКЖЕ ЗА УПУЩЕНИЕ ПРИБЫЛИ ИЛИ ВЫГОДЫ, УТЕРЮ ДАННЫХ ИЛИ ВОЗМОЖНОСТИ ИСПОЛЬЗОВАНИЯ ДАННЫХ, ПОНЕСЕННЫЕ ЗАКАЗЧИКОМ ИЛИ ЛЮБОЙ ТРЕТЬЕЙ СТОРОНОЙ, БУДЬ ТО В РЕЗУЛЬТАТЕ НАРУШЕНИЯ КОНТРАКТНЫХ ОБЯЗАТЕЛЬСТВ ИЛИ ГРАЖДАНСКО-ПРАВОВОГО НАРУШЕНИЯ, ДАЖЕ ЕСЛИ "ОРАКЛ" БЫЛ ИЗВЕЩЕН О ВОЗМОЖНОСТИ ТАКИХ УБЫТКОВ. РАЗМЕР ОТВЕТСТВЕННОСТИ "ОРАКЛ" ПО НАСТОЯЩЕЙ ЛИЦЕНЗИИ НИ В КОЕМ СЛУЧАЕ НЕ ПРЕВЫШАЕТ РАЗМЕР ЛИЦЕНЗИОННОЙ ПЛАТЫ, ВЫПЛАЧЕННОЙ ЗАКАЗЧИКОМ ЗА ЭТУ ЛИЦЕНЗИЮ.

ТЕРРИТОРИЯ. Если иного не указано в заявочном документе или Сертификате на Использование Программы, "Территория" означает Россию.

Заказчик обязуется в полном объеме соблюдать все законы и постановления Соединенных Штатов Америки и других стран (далее - "Экспортное Законодательство") и гарантирует, что ни Программы, ни их любая прямая продукция, (1) не будут экспортироваться напрямую или косвенно в нарушение Экспортного Законодательства или (2) использоваться в любых целях, запрещенных Экспортным Законодательством, включая, но не ограничивая, распространение ядерного, химического или биологического оружия. Действие настоящей Лицензии регулируется законодательством штата Калифорния, США. "Оракл" может проводить инспекцию порядка использования Программ. Настоящая Лицензия имеет преимущественную силу над всеми условиями любого заказа на покупку Заказчика.

ОПРЕДЕЛЕНИЯ:

Одновременные пользователи/Одновременные соединения: максимальное число устройств ввода, имеющих доступ к Программам в любой выделенный момент времени. В случае использования мультиплексных программных или аппаратных средств это число должно быть определено на входе мультиплексора.

Клиент: компьютер, который (1) используется одним пользователем в каждый момент времени и (2) исполняет программное обеспечение "Оракл" в локальной памяти или хранящий программное обеспечение на локальном диске.

Пользователь: лицо, уполномоченное Заказчиком использовать Программы вне всякой зависимости от степени активности использования Программ в любой выделенный момент времени.

Почтовый ящик: место, в котором электронная почта получается или из которого отправляется: он создается когда в Oracle*Office заносится информация о пользователе или приложении.

Español/América Latina (excepto Brasil)

TÉRMINOS DE LA LICENCIA DEL PROGRAMA DE ORACLE

ADVERTENCIA: SI ABRE ESTE PAQUETE O USA EL SOFTWARE AQUÍ INCLUIDO, REGIRÁN LOS SIGUIENTES TÉRMINOS. SI NO ESTÁ DE ACUERDO CON DICHO SOFTWARE O TÉRMINOS, DEVUELVA EL SOFTWARE DENTRO DE LOS 30 DÍAS A LA COMPAÑÍA QUE SE LO ENVIÓ PARA OBTENER UN REEMBOLSO.

ORACLE CORPORATION O SU SUBSIDIARIA LOCAL (DE AQUÍ EN ADELANTE DENOMINADA "ORACLE") LE OTORGA A USTED (DE AQUÍ EN ADELANTE DENOMINADO CLIENTE) UNA LICENCIA PARA USAR EL SOFTWARE Y LA DOCUMENTACIÓN INCLUIDOS EN ESTE PAQUETE (DE AQUÍ EN ADELANTE DENOMINADOS PROGRAMAS), COMO SE ESPECIFICA A CONTINUACIÓN.

LICENCIA: El Cliente tendrá el derecho de utilizar los Programas en el entorno operativo identificado por Oracle, ya sea (a) tal como se especifica en un documento de pedido o en un Certificado para el Uso del Programa que Oracle o su distribuidor distribuya al Cliente, o (b) en caso de no especificarse, para un solo usuario en una sola computadora. El Cliente puede usar los Programas solamente para sus propias operaciones internas de procesamiento de datos. El Cliente puede hacer una copia de cada Programa licenciado a los fines de conservar una copia de respaldo. Los derechos para realizar copias adicionales, si las hubiere, se detallarán en un documento de pedido o Certificado para el Uso del Programa. No se podrá realizar ningún otro tipo de copias sin el consentimiento previo por escrito de Oracle. El Cliente no deberá: (a) quitar ninguna identificación del producto, notificaciones de derechos de autor, u otras notificaciones o restricciones de propiedad de los Programas; (b) usar los Programas con propósitos de compartimiento temporario comercial, alquiler o prestación de servicios de procesamiento de datos; (c) transferir, vender, ceder o de otra manera otorgar Programas a otra parte sin el consentimiento previo por escrito de Oracle; (d) realizar o permitir la ingeniería reversa, desmontaje o descompilación de los Programas; o (e) divulgar a terceros los resultados de cualquier prueba de conjuntos representativos de datos (benchmark tests) realizados a cualquier Programa sin la autorización previa por escrito de Oracle. Todas las transferencias de los Programas están sujetas a las tarifas y políticas de transferencia de Oracle. El Cliente tendrá el derecho de usar solamente los Programas contenidos en este paquete que estén especificados en un documento de pedido o Certificado para el Uso del Programa.

DERECHOS DE AUTOR/PROPIEDAD EXCLUSIVA DE LOS PROGRAMAS: Los Programas son productos de propiedad exclusiva de Oracle y están protegidos por la ley de derechos de autor y otras leyes de propiedad intelectual. El Cliente adquiere solamente el derecho de usar los Programas y no adquiere ningún derecho, expreso o implícito, sobre los Programas o medios que contengan Programas que no sean los especificados en esta Licencia. Oracle o su licenciante conservará, en todo momento, todos los derechos, titularidad y participación -incluyendo los derechos de propiedad intelectual- en los Programas y los medios.

GARANTÍAS LIMITADAS/RECURSOS LEGALES EXCLUSIVOS: Oracle garantiza que, por un período de 90 días a partir de la fecha de envío al Cliente: (a) los medios incluidos en este paquete no poseen defectos en los materiales o en su fabricación en condiciones de uso normales; y (b) los Programas no modificados ejecutarán substancialmente las funciones descriptas en la documentación provista por Oracle cuando se ejecuten en el sistema operativo y computadora designados. Oracle no garantiza que: los Programas reunirán los requisitos del Cliente, que los Programas funcionarán en las combinaciones que el Cliente seleccione para su uso, que la ejecución de los Programas será ininterrumpida o libre de errores, o que todos los errores de los Programas serán corregidos. **Estas garantías son exclusivas y se otorgan en lugar de todas otras garantías, ya sean expresas o implícitas por la ley.** Si el Cliente notifica a Oracle acerca de un error en un Programa dentro del período de los 90 días, Oracle habrá de, según su elección, corregir el error, ofrecer al Cliente un procedimiento razonable para solucionar el error habilidosamente, o reembolsar al Cliente por las tarifas de licencia una vez que el Cliente devuelva los Programas a Oracle. Oracle reemplazará cualquier medio defectuoso, sin cargo, si éste se devuelve a Oracle dentro del período de los 90 días. **Estos son los recursos legales absolutos y exclusivos del Cliente ante cualquier violación de las garantías. Esta garantía limitada le otorga derechos legales específicos. Usted podrá poseer otros.**

LIMITACIÓN DE LA RESPONSABILIDAD: ORACLE NO SERÁ RESPONSABLE POR DAÑOS Y PERJUICIOS INDIRECTOS, ACCESORIOS, ESPECIALES O CONSECUENCIALES, O DAÑOS Y PERJUICIOS POR PÉRDIDA DE GANANCIAS, INGRESOS TOTALES, DATOS O USO DE DATOS, INCURRIDOS POR EL CLIENTE O POR UNA TERCERA PARTE, YA SEA A TRAVÉS DE UNA ACCIÓN CONTRACTUAL O EXTRACONTRACTUAL, AUN EN EL CASO EN QUE SE HAYA ADVERTIDO A ORACLE O CUALQUIER OTRA PERSONA ACERCA DE LA POSIBILIDAD DE DICHOS DAÑOS Y PERJUICIOS. LA RESPONSABILIDAD DE ORACLE POR DAÑOS Y PERJUICIOS EN VIRTUD DEL PRESENTE NO EXCEDERÁ, BAJO NINGUNA CIRCUNSTANCIA, LAS TARIFAS ABONADAS POR EL CLIENTE PARA ESTA LICENCIA.

El Cliente deberá acatar en su totalidad todas las leyes y reglamentos de los Estados Unidos de América y otros países (de aquí en adelante denominadas Leyes de Exportación) para asegurar que ni los Programas, ni ningún producto directo de los mismos, se (1) exporten, directa o indirectamente, en violación de las Leyes de Exportación o (2) sean utilizados con fines prohibidos por las Leyes de Exportación, incluyendo, pero sin limitarse a, la proliferación de armas nucleares, químicas o biológicas. Esta Licencia y todas las actividades relacionadas se regirán por las leyes locales. Oracle puede auditar el uso que el Cliente haga de los Programas. Esta Licencia anula y reemplaza todos los términos de cualquier orden de compra del Cliente o cualquier otro documento de pedido del Cliente.

DEFINICIONES DEL CERTIFICADO PARA EL USO DEL PROGRAMA:
Dispositivos Simultáneos/Acceso Simultáneo: La cantidad máxima de dispositivos de entrada con acceso a los Programas en un momento determinado. Si se utiliza software o hardware de multiplexión (por ejemplo un monitor TP), esta cantidad debe medirse en el extremo frontal de multiplexión.

Cliente: Una computadora que (1) es utilizada por una sola persona a la vez y (2) ejecuta software Oracle en la memoria local o almacena el software en un dispositivo de almacenamiento local.

Usuario: Un individuo a quien el Cliente autoriza a usar los Programas, independientemente de que el individuo esté utilizando los Programas en forma activa en algún momento.

Buzón: Un lugar desde donde se envía o recibe el correo electrónico: se crea cuando se establece una aplicación o cuenta del usuario en Oracle" Office.

Español/España

Si Vd. ha adquirido su producto ORACLE en España, el presente Contrato de Licencia será de aplicación

ADVERTENCIA: SI VD. ABRE ESTE PAQUETE O UTILIZA EL SOFTWARE ADJUNTO, LOS SIGUIENTES TERMINOS DE CONTRATO DE LICENCIA SERAN DE APLICACION. SI EL REFERIDO SOFTWARE O LOS PRESENTES TERMINOS CONTRACTUALES NO SON ACEPTABLES PARA VD., DEVUELVA EL SOFTWARE DENTRO DE 30 DIAS A LA COMPAÑIA DE QUIEN LO ADQUIRIO PARA EL REEMBOLSO DE SU IMPORTE.

ORACLE CORPORATION O SU FILIAL, ORACLE IBÉRICA, S.A. (EN ADELANTE "ORACLE"), LE CONCEDE (EN LO SUCESIVO "CLIENTE") UNA LICENCIA PARA USAR EL SOFTWARE ADJUNTO Y SU DOCUMENTACION ("PROGRAMAS") EN LA FORMA QUE A CONTINUACIÓN SE DETALLA.

LICENCIA: El Cliente tendrá el derecho de utilizar los Programas en el entorno operacional identificado por Oracle (a) hasta el grado de extensión especificado en la documentación de pedido o en el Certificado de Uso de Programa entregado al Cliente por Oracle o por su distribuidor, o, (b) en ausencia de especificación al respecto, por un único usuario y en un único ordenador. El Cliente sólo podrá utilizar los Programas para operaciones de procesamiento de sus propios datos internos. El Cliente podrá efectuar una copia de cada Programa licenciado para fines de seguridad o "backup"; los derechos para ejecutar copias adicionales, en su caso, pueden quedar especificados en la documentación de pedido o en el certificado de Uso de Programa. No se realizará ninguna otra copia sin el previo consentimiento por escrito de Oracle. El Cliente se abstendrá de: (a) eliminar cualesquiera identificaciones de producto, advertencias de copyright o de restricciones de propiedad de los Programas; (b) utilizar los Programas para fines de "timesharing" o venta por tiempo compartido, préstamo, alquiler o servicios comerciales de procesamiento de datos ("service bureau"); (c) transferir, vender, ceder o transmitir en cualquier forma los Programas a otra parte sin el previo consentimiento por escrito de Oracle; (d) realizar o permitir la realización de actividades de ingeniería inversa ("reverse engineering"), desensamblaje o descompilación de los Programas cuando el Cliente haya recibido de Oracle, dentro de un plazo de tiempo razonable a contar desde su requerimiento por escrito en tal sentido, la información suficiente, en cuanto ésta sea disponible para Oracle y en la medida de que sea necesaria para la creación de programas que sean interoperables con los Programas sin infringir los derechos de propiedad intelectual de Oracle, y; (e) revelar los resultados de cualesquiera tests "benchmark" o de banco de pruebas de cualquier Programa a cualquier tercera parte sin el previo consentimiento por escrito de Oracle. El Cliente sólo tendrá el derecho de utilizar los Programas contenidos en este paquete que aparezcan especificados en la documentación de pedido o en el Certificado de Uso del Programa.

COPYRIGHT/PROPIEDAD DE LOS PROGRAMAS: Los Programas son un producto propiedad de Oracle o de su licenciante y están protegidos por las Leyes de Copyright y otras de Propiedad Intelectual. El Cliente sólo adquiere el derecho de utilizar los Programas y no adquiere derecho alguno de propiedad sobre los mismos o sobre la media o soporte físico en el que aquéllos se contienen distinto de los especificados en el presente contrato. Oracle, o su licenciante, retendrán en todo momento toda titularidad, derechos e intereses, incluyendo los derechos de propiedad intelectual sobre los Programas y la media o soporte físico.

GARANTÍAS/RECURSOS EXCLUSIVOS: Oracle garantiza que durante un período de doce meses a contar desde la fecha de entrega al Cliente: (a) la media o soporte físico adjunto estarán libres de defectos de fabricación y material bajo un uso normal; y (b) los Programas, a menos que sean modificados, desarrollarán substancialmente las funciones descritas en la documentación entregada por Oracle cuando sean operados en el ordenador y sistema operativo designados. Oracle no garantiza que: los Programas cumplan los requerimientos del Cliente, que los Programas operen en todas las combinaciones que el Cliente pueda seleccionar para su uso, que la operación de los Programas sea ininterrumpida o libre de errores ni que todos los errores sean corregidos. Estas garantías, en la extensión permitida por la ley, son exclusivas y sustituyen a cualquier otro tipo de garantías, expresas o implícitas. Si el Cliente avisa de un defecto en los Programas dentro del período de doce meses, Oracle, a su elección, corregirá tales defectos o proveerá al Cliente con un procedimiento razonable para salvar el defecto o, contra la devolución por el Cliente de los Programas a Oracle, devolverá las tarifas de licencia. Oracle reemplazará sin cargo alguno cualquier media o soporte físico defectuoso si el mismo es devuelto a Oracle en el plazo de doce (12) meses a contar desde la fecha original de entrega. Estos constituyen los únicos y exclusivos recursos de que dispondrá el Cliente para el caso de incumplimiento de la garantía.

LIMITACIÓN DE RESPONSABILIDAD: ORACLE NO SERÁ RESPONSABLE POR CUALESQUIERA DAÑOS INDIRECTOS (INCLUYENDO DE FORMA NO LIMITATIVA LA PÉRDIDA DE BENEFICIOS, INGRESOS, DATOS O USO) EN QUE INCURRA EL CLIENTE O CUALQUIER TERCERA PARTE, SEA EN EL CURSO DE UNA RECLAMACIÓN CONTRACTUAL O POR DAÑOS, INCLUSO SI ORACLE HUBIERA SIDO ADVERTIDA DE LA POSIBILIDAD DE TALES PÉRDIDAS. LA RESPONSABILIDAD DE ORACLE POR DAÑOS Y PERJUICIOS DE CUALQUIER TIPO DERIVADOS DEL PRESENTE CONTRATO NO EXCEDERÁ EN NINGUN CASO DE LAS TARIFAS SATISFECHAS POR EL CLIENTE PARA ESTA LICENCIA. LOS PRECIOS DE ORACLE REFLEJAN LA DISTRIBUCIÓN DEL RIESGO Y LA LIMITACIÓN DE RESPONSABILIDAD AQUI CONTENIDA.

El Cliente consiente en cumplir enteramente con la normativa aplicable sobre exportación emitida por los Gobiernos Español o de los Estados Unidos de América ("Normativa de Exportación") a fin de asegurarse de que los Programas, Documentación o cualquier producto directo de los mismos (a) no son exportados, directa o indirectamente, en violación de dicha Normativa de Exportación, ni (b) son utilizados para cualquier finalidad prohibida por la Normativa de Exportación, incluyendo de forma no limitativa, la proliferación de armamento nuclear, químico o biológico. Este contrato quedará sujeto a las leyes españolas. El presente contrato prevalecerá sobre todos los términos contenidos en cualesquiera órdenes de compra del Cliente o cualesquiera otros documentos de Pedido en contradicción con los presentes términos.

DEFINICIONES DEL CERTIFICADO DE USO DE PROGRAMA:
Dispositivos Concurrentes/Accesos Concurrentes: el número máximo de dispositivos de entrada accediendo a los Programas en cualquier momento dado del tiempo. Si se utiliza software o hardware multiplexador (como por ejemplo, un monitor TP), este número debe ser medido al multiplexador "front end"

Cliente: un ordenador el cual (1) es utilizado por una sola persona al tiempo y (2) ejecuta software Oracle en su memoria local o almacena el software en un dispositivo de almacenaje local.

Usuario: un individuo autorizado por el Cliente para utilizar los programas, con independencia de si el individuo en cuestión está utilizando activamente o no los Programas en un momento dado en el tiempo.

Buzón ("Mailbox"): un punto desde el cual se puede enviar o recibir correo electrónico y que es creado cuando una cuenta de usuario o una aplicación es establecida en Oracle Office.

Svenska/Sverige

ORACLE PROGRAMVARULICENS

V I K T I G T - OM NI ÖPPNAR DENNA FÖRPACKNING ELLER ANVÄNDER DEN MEDFÖLJANDE PROGRAMVARAN GÄLLER NEDAN ANGIVNA VILLKOR FÖR DESS ANVÄNDANDE. ACCEPTERAR NI INTE PROGRAMVARAN ELLER VILLKOREN, VAR VÄNLIG ÅTERLÄMNA PROGRAMVARAN INOM 30 DAGAR TILL DET FÖRSÄLJNINGSSTÄLLE VARIFRÅN NI ERHÅLLIT PROGRAMVARAN. ÅTERBETALNING KOMMER DÅ ATT SKE.

ORACLE SVENSKA AB, NEDAN KALLAT ORACLE, UPPLÅTER OCH TILLHANDAHÅLLER TILL ER, NEDAN KALLAD KUNDEN, EN LICENS TILL BILAGDA PROGRAMVARAN OCH DESS DOKUMENTATION, NEDAN KALLAD PROGRAMVARAN, PÅ NEDAN ANGIVNA VILLKOR.

LICENSEN: Kunden har rätt att använda Programvaran i den driftsmiljö, som definierats av Oracle antingen (a) i ett beställningsdokument eller Programanvändarcertfikat, som kunden mottagit av Oracle eller Oracles distributör, eller (b) om inte annat specificerats, innefattar licensen rätt för en användare att nyttja Programvaran på en dator. Kunden får endast använda Programvaran för intern databehandling. Kunden har rätt att göra en kopia av Programvaran för back-up-ändamål. Endast för det fall det framgår av beställningsdokumentet eller Programanvändartillståndet äger Kunden rätt att göra ytterligare kopior. Därutöver har Kunden ej rätt att kopiera Programvaran utan att Oracle dessförinnan skriftligen lämnat sitt medgivande därtill. Kunden skall (a) bibehålla og ej förändra märkning, uppgift om förekommande patent, upphovsrätt eller copyrightmärkning på eller i Programvaran eller på medium med vilket Programvaran göres tillgängligt för Kunden, (b) inte använda Programvaren för uthyrning, utlåning, servicebyråverksamhet eller på annat sätt tillhandahållas för användning av tredje man, (c) får inte överlåta, sälja eller på annat sätt låta annan disponera eller i övrigt förfoga över Programvaran utan att Oracle dessförinnan skriftligen lämnat tillstånd därtill, (d) inte Dekompilera Programvaran annan omfattning än vad som är nödvändigt för att åstadkomma samverkansförmåga med andra programvaror, (e) inte göra resultat av prestandamätningar "bench mark test" tillgängliga för tredje man utan Oracles skriftliga godkännande. Vid överflyttning av Programvaran till annan driftsmiljö gäller Oracles regler och avgifter för överflyttning av programvaror. Kunden har endast rätt att använda Programvaran i förpackningen som är angivna i beställningsdartill-ståndet.

IMMATERIELLA RÄTTIGHETER/ÄGANDERÄTT: Oracle innehar upphovsrätt och andra immateriella rättigheter till Programvaran, och Oracles rättigheter är skyddade enligt gällande immateriellrättslig lagstiftning och lagstiftning om äganderätt. Kunden förvärvar endast rätten att använda Programvaran och förvärvar sålunda inte någon rätt, uttryckligt eller underförstått, till Programvaran eller medium, som innehåller Programvaran, om inte annat specificerats i nuvarande licens. Äganderätten och alla immateriella rättigheter till Programvaran och media tillhör i alla hänseenden Oracle eller dess underleverantör.

BEGRÄNSNINGAR AV GARANTIER/RÄTT ATT AVHJÄLPA FEL: Under en period om 90 dagar från och med det datum som Programvaran levererats till Kunden garanterar Oracle att (a) media såsom band, disketter, som tillhandahålles av Oracle, vid normalt användande ej innehåller materialfel eller andra fel, och att (b) levererad Programvara i allt väsentligt har de funktioner som angivits i dokumentationen under förutsättning att Programvaran inte modifierats och att den använts på därför avsedd dator med tillhörande operativsystem. Oracle garanterar inte att Programvaran och/eller dokumentationen motsvarar Kundens alla behov eller att programvarudokumentationen alltid kommer att fungera under sådana förhållanden där Kunden vill nyttja den. Oracle garanterar inte att Programvaran alltid fungerar felfritt, att alla fel kan avhjälpas, att Programvaran fungerar utan avbrott, att den är felfri eller att alla fel kommer att bli rättade. Oracle har inget ansvar för fel eller brister utöver vad som uttryckligen angivits i detta avtal. För det fall Kunden meddelar Oracle att fel föreligger i Programvaran innan utgången av ovan angivna garantiperiod om 90 dagar, äger Oracle rätt att välja om Oracle skall åtgärda felet, eller tillhandahålla Kunden annan rimlig möjlighet att undgå felet, eller för det fall Kunden returnerar Programvaran till Oracle, återbetala de licensavgifter som har erlagts av Kunden. Under förutsättning att Kunden returnerat defekt media till Oracle inom utgången av angivna garantiperiod om 90 dagar, byter Oracle ut media som är felaktiga utan kostnad för Kunden. Kunden äger ej rätt till någon annan form av avhjälpande eller gottgörelse än vad som ovan angivits.

ANSVARSBEGRÄNSNING: ORACLE SVARAR INTE UNDER NÅGRA OMSTÄNDIGHETER FÖR INDIREKT FÖRLUST, FÖLJDSKADOR, UTEBLIVEN VINST, DRIFTSFÖRLUST, FÖRLORAD DATA ELLER LIKNANDE FÖRLUST SOM KUNDEN ELLER TREDJE MAN ÅDRAGIT SIG OAVSETT OM ORACLE AV KUNDEN ELLER AV TREDJEMAN BLIVIT INFORMERAD OM RISKEN FÖR ATT SÅDAN FÖRLUST SKULLE KUNNA UPPSTÅ. ORACLES ERSÄTTNINGSANSVAR SKALL ALDRIG ÖVERSTIGA ETT BELOPP MOTSVARANDE STORLEKEN AV DE LICENSAVGIFTER SOM KUNDEN ERLAGT FÖR PROGRAMVARAN.

Kunden skall var helt införstådd med att alla lagar och förordningar i Sverige och USA samt andre länders efterlevs för att försäkra sig om att varkan program eller andra produkter härav (1) exporteras direkt eller indirekt i strid med exportlagarna eller (2) används i något syfte som strider mot exportlagarna, vilket inkluderar utan begränsningar, spridning av kärnvapen, kemiska- eller biologiska vapan. Denna licens och alla berörda handlingar skall lyda under svensk lag. Oracle har rätt att granska Kundens användning av Programmen. Alla villkor som berörs av en inköpsorder eller annat orderdokument från Kunden skall ersättas av denna licens.

DEFINITIONER FÖR PROGRAMANVÄNDARTILLSTÅND

Samtidiga användare: Det maximala antalet inläsningsenheter, som på en given tidpunkt använder Programvaran samtidigt. Om multiplexer program- eller hårdvara användes, avgörs antalet samtidiga användare vid multiplexer-ingången.

Klient: En dator (1), som används av endast en person åt gången och (2) exekverar Oracles Programvara i ett lokal minne och lagrar Programvaran i en lokal minnesenhet.

Användare: En individuell person, som har Kundens tillstånd att använda Programvaran oavsett om det sker på en given tidpunkt.

Mailbox: En punkt varifrån elektronisk post skickas och mottages. En "mailbox" uppstår, när ett användar-id eller en applikation har upprättats i Oracle*Office.

Türkçe/Türkiye

ORACLE PROGRAM LİSANSI ŞARTLARI

UYARI: BU PAKETİ AÇAR VEYA İÇİNDEKİ BİLGİSAYAR PROGRAMINI ("YAZILIM") KULLANIRSANIZ, AŞAĞIDAKİ HÜKÜMLERE TABİ OLURSUNUZ. YAZILIMI VEYA BU HÜKÜMLERİ KABUL EDİLEMEZ BULUYORSANIZ, YAZILIMI 30 GÜN İÇİNDE ŞİRKETE GERİ GETİRİNİZ, BU DURUMDA YAZILIM GERİ ALINACAK VE PARANIZ İADE EDİLECEKTİR.

ORACLE BİLGİSAYAR SİSTEMLERİ LTD. ŞTİ. ("ORACLE") AŞAĞIDA BELİRTİLEN SINIRLAR DAHİLİNDE SİZE ("MÜŞTERİ") İLİŞİKTEKİ YAZILIMIN VE DOKÜMANTASYONUN ("PROGRAMLAR") KULLANMA LİSANSINI VERİR.

LİSANS: Müşteri (a) sipariş formunda veya Oracle yahut Oracle yetkili dağıtıcısı tarafından Müşteriye verilmiş bulunan Program Kullanma Sertifikası'nda tanımlanan sınırlar içinde veya, böyle bir tanım yoksa (b) tek bir kullanıcı tarafından ve tek bir bilgisayarda kullanılmak üzere Oracle tarafından tesbit edilmiş olan iletim sisteminde ve Ülke içinde Programları kullanma hakkına sahiptir. Müşteri, Programları sadece kendi veri işleme işlemlerinde kullanabilir. Müşteri her bir Lisanslı Programın yedekleme amacıyla sadece bir kopyasını çıkartabilir; eğer verilmişse, ek kopyalar çıkartabilmek hakkı, sipariş formunda veya Program Kullanma Sertifikası'nda mutlaka yer almalıdır. Oracle'ın açık olarak yazılı izni alınmadıkça başkaca kopya yapılamaz. Müşteri, (a) Programlardan herhangi bir ürün tanımlamasını, telif hakkı uyarısını, diğer her türlü uyarıyı veya mülkiyet kısıtlamalarını kaldıramaz, (b) Programları ticari zaman paylaşımlı sistemlerde kiralama yoluyla veya servis büro işlemlerinde kullanamaz, (c) Oracle'ın önceden yazılı kabulünü almaksızın Programları başka herhangi bir kişiye veremez, satamaz, nakledemez ya da başkaca herhangi bir şekilde devredemez, (d) Programları ters mühendislik (reverse engineer) kod formunun çevirisi (decompile) veya derlenmiş kodu çözme işlemlerine tabi tutamaz, (e) Oracle'ın önceden yazılı onayını almaksızın her türlü üçüncü kişiye herhangi bir Programın herhangi bir kontrol testi (benchmark test) sonucunu açıklayamaz. Programların devirleri Oracle'ın devir politikası ve devir ücretlerine uygun olarak yapılacaktır. Müşterinin tek ve yegane hakkı, bu paketteki Programları sipariş belgesinde veya Program Kullanma Sertifikası'nda yer aldığı şekilde kullanmaktır.

oracle/shrinkwrap.lic

TELİF HAKKI/PROGRAMLARIN MÜLKİYETİ: Programlar Oracle'ın malik olduğu ürünlerdir ve Fikir ve Sanat Eserleri Kanunu ile diğer fikri mülkiyet kanunları uyarınca korunurlar. Müşteri sadece Programları kullanmak hakkını edinmekte ve bunun dışında Programlar veya Programların yer aldığı ortam ("Ortam") üzerinde işbu Lisansta yer alanlar dışında hiçbir ne şekil ve surette olursa olsun herhangi bir hak elde etmemektedir. Oracle veya onun adına lisans verenler, Programlar ve Ortam üzerindeki fikri mülkiyet hakları da dahil olmak üzere ürün ve onun semereleri üzerindeki tüm haklara daima sahip olmaya devam edeceklerdir.

SINIRLI GARANTİ/TANINAN İMKANLAR: Oracle, Müşteriye teslimden sonraki 90 günlük süre için (a) normal kullanım halinde Programların yer aldığı ortamın malzeme ve işçilik kusuru taşımadığını ve (b) değiştirilmemiş Programların uygun bilgisayar ve işletim sistemi altında çalıştırılmak şartıyla Oracle tarafından sağlanan dokümantasyonda genel olarak tanımlanan işlevleri yerine getireceğini garanti eder. Oracle hiçbir şekilde, Programların Müşterinin ihtiyacını tam ve uygun olarak karşılayacağını, Programların Müşteri tarafından kullanılan diğer Programlarla birlikte çalışacağını, Programların çalışmasının kesintisiz, hatasız olacağını ve Programların tüm hatalarından arındırılmış olduğunu garanti etmez. Oracle tarafından verilen garantiler bu sayılanlarla sınırlı olup ticari değer veya özel bir amaca uygunluk garantisi de dahil olmak üzere kanun tarafından veya başka bir şekilde tanınan ister sarih ister zımni her şekil ve suretteki garanti ve hükmün yerine geçer. Eğer Müşteri 90 günlük süre içinde Programlarda bir hatanın bulunduğunu bildirirse, Oracle seçim hakkı kendisinde kalmak üzere hatayı giderebilir, Müşteriye hatanın giderilmesi için bir yol önerebilir veya Programların Oracle'a teslimi şartı ile lisans bedelini geri ödeyebilir. Oracle hatalı ortamı 90 günlük süre için kendisine teslim edilmiş olması koşuluyla ücretsiz olarak değiştirecektir. Tüm bunlar herhangi bir garanti ihlali durumunda Müşterinin sahip olabileceği tek ve yegane imkandır.

SORUMLULUĞUN SINIRLANMASI: ORACLE, İSTER SÖZLEŞMEDEN VEYA HAKSIZ FİİLDEN KAYNAKLANSIN, İSTER MÜŞTERİ VEYA DİĞER KİŞİNİN BÖYLE BİR ZARARA UĞRAYABİLECEĞİ ORACLE VEYA HERHANGİ BİR ÜÇÜNCÜ KİŞİ TARAFINDAN KENDİSİNE BİLDİRİLMİŞ OLSUN HER TÜRLÜ DOLAYLI, TESADÜFİ, ÖZEL VEYA ÖNEMLİ HASARLARDAN VEYA MÜŞTERİ YAHUT ÜÇÜNCÜ BİR KİŞİNİN UĞRADIĞI KAZANÇ VEYA GELİR, VERİ VEYA KULLANILAN VERİ KAYBINDAN KAYNAKLANAN HASARLARDAN SORUMLU DEĞİLDİR.

ORACLE'IN BU TÜRDEKİ HASARLARDAN SORUMLULUĞU HİÇBİR ŞEKİLDE BU LİSANS DOLAYISIYLA MÜŞTERİ TARAFINDAN ÖDENMİŞ LİSANS BEDELİNDEN FAZLA OLMAYACAKTIR.
Ülke: "Ülke" aksi açık bir şekilde sipariş belgesinde veya Program Kullanma Sertifikası'nda belirtilmediği sürece Türkiye Cumhuriyeti anlamına gelecektir.

Müşteri, Amerika Birleşik Devletleri ve Türkiye Cumhuriyetinin tüm gümrük ithalat ve ihracat mevzuatına ("Mevzuat") tamamıyla uyacaktır ve ne Programları ne de bunlardan faydalanılarak oluşturulan her türlü ürünlerin (1) Mevzuata aykırı olarak doğrudan veya dolayısıyla ihraç edilmeyeceğini veya (2) sayılanlarla sınırlı olmaksızın, nükleer, kimyasal veya biyolojik silahların yayılması da dahil olmak üzere mevzuat tarafından yasaklanmış her türlü amaçla kullanılmayacağını taahhüt etmektedir.

İşbu sözleşme ve ilgili tüm işlemler Türkiye Cumhuriyeti kanunlarına tabiidir. Oracle, Müşterinin Programları kullanmasını denetleyebilir. Müşteri tarafından verilen ürün siparişi formları veya sair Müşteri Sipariş dokümanları bu lisansın ayrılmaz parçasını oluşturur.

PROGRAM KULLANMA SERTİFİKASI TANIMLARI:

Aynı Anda Erişen Aygıt/Aynı Anda Gerçekleşen Erişimler: Herhangi bir zamanda Programlara erişen girdi aygıtlarının sayısı. Eğer çok evreli yazılım veya donanım (örneğin TP ekranı gibi) kullanılıyorsa, bu sayı çok evrelenmiş uçların sayısına göre hesaplanacaktır.

Müşteri Bilgisayar: (1) herhangi bir zamanda sadece bir kişi tarafından kullanılan ve (2) belleğinde Oracle yazılımını çalıştıran veya yazılımı iç saklama ünitesinde bulunduran bir bilgisayar,

Kullanıcı:herhangi bir zamanda Programları kullanıp kullanmadığına bakılmaksızın Programları kullanmak üzere Müşteri tarafından yetkili kılınmış kişi

Posta Kutusu: Bir kullanıcı veya Oracle Ofisinde kurulmuş bir uygulama tarafından yaratılmış elektronik postanın gönderildiği veya alındığı nokta;

Oracle WebServer Trial License

Oracle Corporation ("Oracle") giver hermed Kunden en vederlagsfri testlicens til i 60 dage regnet fra leveringsdagen at anvende Oracle WebServer Programmellet på en enkelt afviklingsmaskine med tilhørende operativsystem, hvortil Programmellet er leveret, udelukkende med henblik på evaluering af Programmellet, i overensstemmelse med de licensvilkår (Oracle Program License Terms), som er leveret sammen med dette Oracle WebServer Programmel. Programmellet er ikke til anvendelse i produktionsmiljø eller tiltænkt anvendelse i forbindelse med "live" data. Efter ovennævnte 60 dages testperiode, skal Kunden enten betale Oracle for en produktionslicens eller ophøre med at anvende og returnere eller destruere alle eksemplarer af Programmellet. Oracle leverer Programmellet "as is" uden garanti af nogen art og fraskriver sig således enhver udtrykkelig eller implicit garanti, herunder garanti for egnethed til et specifikt formål.

Oracle Corporation ("Oracle") verleent de Cliënt een kosteloze proeflicentie voor het gebruik van Oracle WebServer Programma op één enkele computer voor de Operationele Verwerkingsomgevingen waarvoor het programma verzonden is en slechts voor beoordelingsdoeleinden gedurende een periode van 60 dagen, te beginnen op de datum van levering overeenkomstig de Licentievoorwaarden van Oracle software die gedistribueerd zijn bij Oracle WebServer Programma. Het programma is niet voor productiegebruik of bedoeld voor gebruik met "live" gegevens. Na een proefperiode van 60 dagen betaalt de Cliënt Oracle óf voor een licentie voor productiegebruik óf houdt hij op met het gebruik en retourneert of vernietigt alle kopieën van het programma. Oracle biedt deze licentie op basis van de huidige conditie zonder enige vorm van garantie; Oracle wijst alle uitdrukkelijke en stilzwijgende garanties af, met inbegrip van stilzwijgende garanties van verkoopbaarheid of geschiktheid voor een bepaald doel.

Oracle Corporation ("Oracle") grants Customer a no-charge trial license to use the Oracle WebServer Program on a single computer for the Operating Environments for which the Program is shipped solely for evaluation purposes for a period of 60 days beginning on the date of delivery, in accordance with the Oracle Program License Terms distributed with this Oracle WebServer Program. The Program is not for production use or intended for use with "live" data. After the 60 day trial period, Customer shall either pay Oracle for a production use license or cease using, and return or destroy all Program copies. Oracle is providing this license on an "as is" basis without warranty of any kind; Oracle disclaims all express and implied warranties, including the implied warranties of merchantability or fitness for a particular purpose.

Oracle Corporation myöntää Asiakkaalle veloituksetta koekäyttöoikeuden Oracle WebServer -ohjelmaan. Koekäyttöoikeus on voimassa yhdessä tietokoneessa niissä käyttöympäristöissä, joihin ohjelma on toimitettu, ja ohjelmaa voidaan käyttää ainoastaan arviointitarkoitukseen. Koekäyttöoikeus on voimassa 60 päivää toimituksesta. Käyttöoikeusehdot ovat ohjelmatoimituksen mukana. Ohjelma ei ole tarkoitettu tuotantokäyttöön eikä käytettäväksi "todellisella" datalla. 60 päivän koekäyttöjakson jälkeen Asiakas voi joko maksaa Oraclelle tuotantokäyttölisenssistä tai lopettaa käytön ja palauttaa tai tuhota ohjelmakopiot. Oracle myöntää tämän käyttöoikeuden "as is" -periaatteella eikä myönnä ohjelmalle mitään takuuta; Oracle kumoaa kaikki mahdollisesti hiljaisesti tai nimenomaisesti annetut takuut mukaan lukien takuut kaupattavuudesta tai sopivuudesta tiettyyn tarkoitukseen.

Oracle France (« Oracle ») concède à la personne l'ayant commandée (le « Client ») une licence gratuite d'évaluation du Programme Oracle WebServer, sur une seule unité centrale, pour l'Environnement d'Exploitation pour lequel le Programme a été livré. Cette licence a une durée de 60 jours à compter de la date de livraison, et est sujette aux termes et conditions de la Licence de Programme Oracle livrée avec le dit Programme. Le Programme n'est pas destiné à un usage en production ni adapté au traitement de données « live ». A l'expiration de la période d'évaluation de 60 jours, le Client paiera à Oracle le prix d'une licence de production, ou cessera l'utilisation du Programme et retournera à Oracle ou détruira toutes copies du Programme. Oracle fournit le Programme dans l'état ou il se trouve (« as is ») sans garantie d'aucune nature, explicite ni implicite, y compris les garanties d'utilisation commerciale ou aptitude à satisfaire un quelconque besoin particulier.

Oracle Corporation ("Oracle") udziela Klientowi bezpłatną licencję na okres próbny na korzystanie z Programu Oracle WebServer na pojedynczym komputerze w Środowiskach Operacyjnych, dla których Program jest przeznaczony wyłącznie dla celów poznawczych, na okres 60 dni rozpoczynający się w dacie dostawy zgodnie z Warunkami Licencji Programu Oracle dostarczonymi wraz z niniejszym Programem Oracle WebServer. Program nie służy do użytku produkcyjnego ani nie jest przeznaczony do korzystania z danymi rzeczywistymi. Po upływie próbnego okresu 60-dniowego Klient powinien zapłacić Oracle opłatę za licencję na produkcyjne korzystanie z Programu, bądź zaprzestać dalszego korzystania i zwrócić, bądź zniszczyć wszelkie kopie Programu. Oracle udziela niniejszej licencji tylko wyłącznie na ten Program, który został dostarczony i w postaci w jakiej został dostarczony bez udzielania gwarancji i rękojmii jakiegokolwiek rodzaju. Oracle wyłącza wszelkie przewidziane przepisami prawa bądź dorozumiane gwarancje i rękojmie, włączając w to dorozumianą rękojmię wartości handlowej lub przydatności dla określonego celu.

A Oracle Corporation (Oracle) concede ao Cliente uma licença temporária grátis para uso do Programa Oracle WebServer num único computador para o ambiente operativo designado. Este Programa só é válido para efeitos de avaliação e teste para um período de 60 (sessenta) dias contados a partir da data de entrega, de acordo com os Termos Gerais e Condições de Licenciamento de Programas Oracle distribuídos com este Programa. Este Programa não é válido para correr em ambientes de "produção" nem deverá ser utilizado com dados "reais". No término do período de avaliação e/ou teste o Cliente poderá (i) pagar à Oracle uma licença de uso completa ou (ii) deixar de utilizar os Programas pelo que os deverá devolver ou destruir. A Oracle concede esta licença numa base "no estado actual dos programas" sem qualquer garantia de qualquer espécie; a Oracle rejeita qualquer garantia implícita ou explícita, incluindo as garantias implícitas de mercantibilidade ou adequação a um fim particular.

Корпорация Оракл ("Оракл") предоставляет Заказчику бесплатную лицензию на тестирование для использования Программы Oracle WebServer на одном компьютере в операционных средах, для которых Программа была приобретена, только для целей оценки на срок 60 дней, начиная с даты поставки, в соответствии с Условиями Лицензии на программы Оракл, распространяемыми с Программой Oracle WebServer. Программа не предназначена для промышленного использования, а также для использования с реальными данными. По окончании периода тестирования в 60 дней, Заказчик должен либо уплатить Оракл за лицензию на промышленное использование либо прекратить использование, вернуть или уничтожить все копии Программ. Оракл предоставляет настоящую лицензию на условиях "как есть" без каких-либо гарантий; Оракл отказывается от всех прямовыраженных и подразумеваемых гарантий, в том числе подразумеваемых гарантий товарности или пригодности для конкретной цели.

Корпорация Оракл ("Оракл") предоставляет Заказчику бесплатную лицензию
на тестирование для использования Программы Oracle WebServer на одном
компьютере в операционных средах, для которых Программа была приобретена,
только для целей оценки на срок 60 дней, начиная с даты поставки, в соответствии
с Условиями Лицензии на программы Оракл, распространяемыми с Программой
Oracle WebServer. Программа не предназначена для промышленного использования,
а также для использования с реальными данными. По окончании периода
тестирования в 60 дней, Заказчик должен либо уплатить Оракл за лицензию
на промышленное использование либо прекратить использование, вернуть или
уничтожить все копии Программ. Оракл предоставляет настоящую лицензию
на условиях "как есть" без каких-либо гарантий; Оракл отказывается от всех
прямовыраженных и подразумеваемых гарантий, в том числе подразумеваемых
гарантий товарности или пригодности для конкретной цели.

Oracle Svenska AB ("Oracle") upplåter till Kunden en kostnadsfri lånelicens för användning
av Oracle WebServer Programvara på en enstaka dator för den Plattform på vilken
Programvaran levererats. Lånelicensen innebär endast rätt att testa Programvaran för en tid av
60 dagar från leverans, i enlighet med Licensvillkoren som medföljer WebServer Programvara.
Programvaran får icke användas i produktion eller på annat sätt användas för "live-data". Vid
låneperiodens upphörande skall Kunden antingen betala till Oracle för en produktionslicens
enligt gällande prislista, alternativt omedelbart upphöra med användningen och återsända
eller förstöra samtliga kopior av Programvaran. Lånelicensen upplåts i befintligt skick utan
garantier av något slag, vare sig uttryckliga eller underförstådda. Oracle har inte heller i övrigt
något ansvar för användningen av Programvaran.

Oracle şirketi, "Oracle WebServer" programı ile verilen. Oracle Programı lisans şartlarına
uygun olarak, teslim tarihinden başlamak üzere 60 günlük süre ile, Oracle WebServer
programını tek bir bilgisayarda ve işletim çevresinde, programı değerlendirmek amacı ile
kullanılması için Müşteri'ye ücretsiz bir deneme lisansı verir. Program üretim amacı ile
veya canlı veriler ile kullanılamaz. 60 günlük deneme süresi sonunda Müşteri, Oracle'a
ya lisans bedelini ödeyecek, veya programı kullanmayı durdurarak iade, ya da programın
bütün kopyalarını imha edecektir. Oracle, bu lisansı "Olduğu gibi", ve olması gerektiği
şekle ilişkin herhangi bir taahhütte bulunmadan vermektedir; Oracle, ticarete uygunluk
veya özel bir amacı karşılama halleri de dahil olmak üzere, hiçbir açık veya üstü örtülü
taahhüdü peşinen kabul etmemektedir.

Oracle Italia (« Oracle ») concede a voi (« Cliente ») una licenza gratuita per l'uso del
Programma Oracle WebServer su un singolo elaboratore allo scopo di prova ed evaluazione
esclusivamente, nel Ambiente Operativo per il quale il Programma viene consegnato,
per 60 giorni dalla data di consegna, e sotto i termini e condizioni della Licenza di
Programma Oracle consegnata con il Programma stesso. Il Programma non è adatto
per l'uso in produzione ne per l'elaborazione di dati « live ». Al termine del periodo di
evaluazione di 60 giorni di cui sopra, il Cliente sarà tenuto di pagare alla Oracle una licenza
di produzione, o cessare l'uso del Programma e restituire alla Oracle o distrurre ogni copia
dello stesso. Il Programma è fornito « as is », senza garanzia di nessun genere; Oracle non
fornisce garanzie esplicite ne implicite, incluse le garanzie di qualisiasi adeguatezza
commerciale o a uno scopo particolare.

오라클 번인 회사 ("오라클") 는 소비자에게 운영 환경에 적합한 단독 컴퓨터에서 사용할 수 있도
록 오라클 웹서버 프로그램에 대한 비판매 시범 라이센스를 부여한다. 본 라이센스는 단지 제공한
프로그램을 평가할 목적으로만 사용되어야 하며, 배달된 날로부터 60일간만 사용할 수 있다. 본
오라클 웹서버 프로그램의 사용은 본 프로그램에 함께 첨부된 오라클 프로그램 라이센스 계약 조
건에 준한다. 본 프로그램은 생산 목적으로 사용되어서도 안되며, "실지" 데이터와 함께 사용되어
서도 절대 안된다. 60일간의 시범 기간이 끝나면, 소비자는 제품 사용 라이센스비를 오라클에게 지
불한다. 그렇지 않으면, 본 제품의 사용을 중단하고 모든 프로그램의 복사품을 파기하거나 오라클
에 되돌려주어야 한다. 오라클은 본 라이센스를 어떠한 종류의 보증 없이 "현 상태 그대로" 제공
한다. 오라클은 상품성에 대한 묵시적 보증과 특정 목적에의 부합성을 포함한 어떠한 명시적 또는
묵시적 보증을 하지 않는다.

Oracle gir med dette Kunden en begrenset bruksrett til programvaren Oracle WebServer Program, som følger: Programvaren kan bare anvendes på en enkelt prosessor, og bare for det formål å teste og evaluere programvaren. Varighet av bruksrett: 60 dager fra mottak. Programvaren kan ikke anvendes på annen plattform (operasjonssystem og maskinutstyr) enn som det fremgår av leveransen. Vedlagte lisensbetingelser er gjeldende. Programvaren kan ikke anvendes til produktiv bruk, inklusive bruk av aktuelle produksjons- eller driftsdate. Efter utløp av den 60 dager lange testperioden kan Kunden velge enten å betale Oracle full lisensavgift for programvaren og derved få rett til fortsatt bruk, eller opphøre med bruken og makulere alt mottatt materiell. Programvaren leveres i den stand den befinner seg. Det gis således ingen garanti forat programvaren er feilfri eller at eventuelle feil eller mangler vil bli rettet.

Η Εταιρία Oracle παρέχει στον Πελάτη χωρίς επιβαρύνσεις την άδεια να χρησιμοποιήσει δοκιμαστικά το Πρόγραμμα WebServer, σε ένα μόνο ηλεκτρονικό υπολογιστή, στο Περιβάλλον των Λειτουργικών Μονάδων για τις οποίες το Πρόγραμμα αυτό εστάλη, αποκλειστικά και μόνο προκειμένου να το αξιολογήσει, για χρονική περίοδο 60 ημερών, η οποία αρχίζει από την ημερομηνία της παράδοσης, σύμφωνα με τους όρους παροχής άδειας χρήσης του προγράμματος, οι οποίοι διανέμονται μαζί με το Πρόγραμμα WebServer. Το Πρόγραμμα αυτό δεν μπορεί να χρησιμοποιηθεί για παραγωγικούς σκοπούς ούτε παρέχεται με σκοπό να χρησιμοποιηθεί με πραγματικά δεδομένα. Μετά την παρέλευση της δοκιμαστικής περιόδου των 60 ημερών, ο Πελάτης έχει τη δυνατότητα είτε να καταβάλει στην Oracle αμοιβή για την παροχή άδειας χρήσης του προγράμματος για παραγωγικούς σκοπούς είτε να σταματήσει να το χρησιμοποιεί και να επιστρέψει ή να καταστρέψει όλα τα αντίγραφα του Προγράμματος. Η Oracle προμηθεύει την εν λόγω άδεια "όπως είναι" χωρίς καμμία εγγύηση οποιασδήποτε φύσης. Η Oracle απαλλάσσεται από κάθε ρητή ή σιωπηρή εγγύηση συμπεριλαμβανομένων ακόμη και των σιωπηρών εγγυήσεων για την εμπορικότητα ή την καταλληλότητα του πογράμματος για ένα συγκεκριμένο σκοπό.

Az Oracle Corporation (továbbiakban "Oracle") feljogosítja a felhasználót az ingyenes próbalicensz alapján, hogy az Oracle WebServer programot egyetlen számítógépen használja, abban a környezetben amelyre az készült, kizárólagosan kiértékelési céllal, a szállítás napjától kezdve 60 napos időszakban, az Oracle WebServer programmal együtt szállított "Az Oracle programok licensz feltételei"-nek megfelelően. A program nem használható "éles" adatokkal. A 60 napos próbaidőszak lejárta után a felhasználó vagy kifizeti az Oracle-nek a termék használati licenszdíját vagy a továbbiakban nem használja a programot és visszadja vagy megsemmisíti a program minden másolatát. Az Oracle ezt a próbalicenszet bárminemű felelősségvállalás nélkül adja, nem vállal semmiféle közvetlen vagy közvetett szavatosságot, nem szavatolja, hogy adott célra a program felhasználható.

Oracle公司授权客户在为环境运作服务的单一电脑上免费试用 Oracle WebServer 软件。此软件供客户在交货后六十天内仅作功能评估之用，须受所附授权条件的约束。此软件不可用于正式业务运作，也不得与日常运作数据资料混同使用。客户应于六十天试用期满后，向本公司付款购买此软件的正式使用权，否则应停止使用此软件，并退还或销毁该软件的一切版本。本公司仅按软件现有实际情况提供使用权，不作任何形式的担保，不承担任何明示或隐含的担保，其中包括关于软件之适售性或特定用途适应性之任何隐含的担保。

本公司授權台端於乙部電腦上免費使用內附之 Oracle WebServer 軟體試用版。此軟體乃供台端於付運後六十天內作免費試用及評估用途，一切軟體之使用均受內附授權合約之約束。此軟體不可作生產用途，亦不得與現行數據一併使用。台端應於六十天試用期後，向本公司付款購買此軟體之生產版，否則應停止使用此軟體，并退還或銷毀所有軟體樣本。本公司不為其他明示或暗示擔保，其中包括軟體之通售性或符合特定使用此授權合約目的之默示。

Společnost Oracle ("Oracle") uděluje Zákazníkovi bezplatnou zkušební licenci k použití Programu Oracle WebServer na jednom počítači pro operační systémy, pro které je Program dodáván. Tato licence se uděluje výhradně za účelem vyhodnocení na období 60 dnů počínaje datem doručení, v souladu s Podmínkami licence Programu distribuovanými společně s daným Programem Oracle WebServer. Program není určen k provoznímu použití nebo použití se "skutečnými daty." Po uplynutí lhůty 60 dnů je Zákazník povinen buď zaplatit za licenci k použití Programu, přestat Program používat nebo vrátit a zničit všechny kopie Programu. Oracle tuto licenci uděluje na Program "ve stávajícím stavu" bez jakékoli záruky. Oracle se zříká veškerých záruk, ať už vyslovených nebo implicitních, včetně implicitních záruk prodejnosti nebo vhodnosti pro konkrétní použití.

ORACLE®

Oracle Corporation
World Headquarters
500 Oracle Parkway
Redwood Shores, CA 94065
USA

Worldwide Inquiries:
Phone +1.415.506.7000
Fax +1.415.506.7200
http://www.oracle.com/

Americas Headquarters
Phone +1.415.506.7000
Fax +1.415.506.7200

Asia/Pacific Rim/India
Headquarters
Phone +65.220.5488
Fax +65.227.4098

Europe/Middle East/Africa
Headquarters
Phone +31.34.069.4211
Fax +31.34.066.5603

Japan Headquarters
Phone +81.3.5213.6666
Fax +81.3.5213.6600

To offer our customers the most complete and effective information management solutions, Oracle Corporation offers its products, along with support, education, and consulting, in more than 90 countries.

Oracle is a registered trademark of Oracle Corporation.

Printed in the U.S.A.
9317.1095.50K

A43753-1

Get Your **FREE** Subscription to Oracle Magazine

Stay informed and increase your productivity with every issue of *Oracle Magazine*. Inside each FREE, bimonthly issue, you'll get:

- Up-to-date information on the Oracle RDBMS and software tools
- Third-party software and hardware products
- Technical articles on Oracle platforms and operating environments
- Software tuning tips
- Oracle client application stories

Three easy ways to subscribe:

1 **MAIL:** Cut out this page, complete the questionnaire on the back, and mail to: *Oracle Magazine*, 500 Oracle Parkway, Box 659952, Redwood Shores, CA 94065.

2 **FAX:** Cut out this page, complete the questionnaire on the back, and and fax the questionnaire to **+ 415.633.2424.**

3 **WEB:** Visit our Web site at **www.oramag.com.** You'll find a subscription form there, plus much more!

If there are other Oracle users at your location who would like to receive their own copy of *Oracle Magazine*, please photocopy the form on the back, and pass it along.

You must answer all eight of the questions below.

1 What is the primary business activity of your firm at this location?
(circle only one)
01. Agriculture, Mining, Natural Resources
02. Communications Services, Utilities
03. Computer Consulting, Training
04. Computer, Data Processing Service
05. Computer Hardware, Software, Systems
06. Education—Primary, Secondary, College, University
07. Engineering, Architecture, Construction
08. Financial, Banking, Real Estate, Insurance
09. Government—Federal/Military
10. Government—Federal/Nonmilitary
11. Government—Local, State, Other
12. Health Services, Health Institutions
13. Manufacturing—Aerospace, Defense
14. Manufacturing—Noncomputer Products, Goods
15. Public Utilities (Electric, Gas, Sanitation)
16. Pure and Applied Research & Development
17. Retailing, Wholesaling, Distribution
18. Systems Integrator, VAR, VAD, OEM
19. Transportation
20. Other Business and Services ____

2 Which of the following best describes your job function? *(circle only one)*
CORPORATE MANAGEMENT/STAFF
01. Executive Management (President, Chair, CEO, CFO, Owner, Partner, Principal, Managing Director)
02. Finance/Administrative Management (VP/Director/Manager/Controller of Finance, Purchasing, Administration)
03. Other Finance/Administration Staff
04. Sales/Marketing Management (VP/Director/Manager of Sales/Marketing)
05. Other Sales/Marketing Staff ____
TECHNICAL MANAGEMENT/STAFF
06. Computer/Communications Systems Development/ Programming Management

07. Computer/Communications Systems Development/ Programming Staff
08. Computer Systems/Operations Management (CIO/VP/Director/ Manager MIS, Operations, etc.)
09. Consulting
10 DBA/Systems Administrator
11. Education/Training
12. Engineering/R&D/Science Management
13. Engineering/R&D/Science Staff
14. Technical Support Director/Manager
15. Other Technical Management/Staff

_____

3 What is your current primary operating system environment?
(circle all that apply)
01. AIX
02. HP-UX
03. Macintosh OS
04. MPE-ix
05. MS-DOS
06. MVS
07. NetWare
08. OpenVMS
09. OS/2
10. OS/400
11. SCO
12. Solaris/Sun OS
13. SVR4
14. Ultrix
15. UnixWare
16. Other UNIX
17. VAX VMS
18. VM
19. Windows
20. Windows NT
21. Other ____

_____

4 What is your current primary hardware environment? *(circle all that apply)*
01. Macintosh
02. Mainframe
03. Massively Parallel Processing
04. Minicomputer
05. PC (IBM-Compatible)
06. Supercomputer
07. Symmetric Multiprocessing
08. Workstation
09. Other ____

5 In your job, do you use or plan to purchase any of the following products or services
(check all that apply)

SOFTWARE	Use	Plan to buy
01. Accounting/Finance	☐	☐
02. Business Graphics	☐	☐
03. CAD/CAE/CAM	☐	☐
04. CASE	☐	☐
05. CIM	☐	☐
06. Communications/ Networking	☐	☐
07. Database Management	☐	☐
08. Education	☐	☐
09. File Management	☐	☐
10. GIS	☐	☐
11. Image Processing	☐	☐
12. Laboratory Control	☐	☐
13. Materials Resource Planning (MRP, MRP II)	☐	☐
14. Multimedia Authoring Tools	☐	☐
15. Office Automation	☐	☐
16. Order Entry/ Inventory Control	☐	☐
17. Programming/Systems Development	☐	☐
18. Project Management	☐	☐
19. Scientific and Engineering	☐	☐
20. Spreadsheets/ Financial Planning	☐	☐
21. Systems Management Products	☐	☐
22. Workflow	☐	☐
HARDWARE		
23. Macintosh	☐	☐
24. Mainframe	☐	☐
25. Massively Parallel Processing	☐	☐
26. Minicomputer	☐	☐
27. PC (IBM-Compatible)	☐	☐
28. Supercomputer	☐	☐
29. Symmetric Multiprocessing	☐	☐
30. Workstation	☐	☐
PERIPHERALS		
31. Bridges/Routers/ Hubs/Gateways	☐	☐
32. CD-ROM Drives	☐	☐
33. Disk Drives/Subsystems	☐	☐
34. Tape Drives/Subsystems	☐	☐
35. Video Boards/Other Multimedia Peripherals	☐	☐
NETWORK/COMMUNICATIONS		
36. Communications Controllers	☐	☐
37. Local Area Networks	☐	☐
38. Modems	☐	☐
39. Wide Area Networks	☐	☐
SERVICES		
40. Computer-Based Training	☐	☐
41. Education/Training	☐	☐
42. Maintenance	☐	☐
43. Online DatabaseServices	☐	☐
44. Support	☐	☐
45. **None of the above**	☐	☐

6 What Oracle products are in use at your site? *(circle all that apply)*
SERVERS
01. Oracle7
02. Oracle Media Server
03. Oracle7 Workgroup Server
04. Personal Oracle7
05. Oracle Rdb
TOOLS
06. Designer/2000 (CASE)
07. Developer/2000 (CDE, Forms, Reports, Graphics)
08. Oracle Media Objects
09. Oracle Power Objects
APPLICATIONS
10. Oracle Financials
11. Oracle Human Resources
12. Oracle Manufacturing
13. Other ____
14. **None of the above**

7 What other database products are in use at your site? *(circle all that apply)*
01. CA-Ingres
02. DB2
03. DB2/2
04. DB2/6000
05. dbase
06. Gupta
07. IMS
08. Informix
09. Microsoft Access
10. Microsoft SQL Server
11. Progress
12. Sybase System ˡ
13. Sybase System
14. Sybase SQL Ser
15. VSAM
16. Other ____
17. SAP
18. Peoplesoft
19. BAAN
20. **None of the abo**

8 During the next 12 months, how much do you anticipate your organization will spend on computer hardware, software, peripherals, and services for your location? *(circle only one)*
01. Less than $10,000
02. $10,000 to $49,999
03. $50,000 to $99,999
04. $100,000 to $499,999
05. $500,000 to $999,999
06. $1,000,000 and over

About the CD-ROM

Inside the back cover is the accompanying CD for *Oracle Web Application Server Handbook,* by Dynamic Information Systems, LLC.

This CD contains a demo version of Oracle's Web Application Server, version 3.0 for Windows NT.

To install the Oracle Web Application Server from the CD-ROM, insert the CD-ROM and launch the setup.exe application. For installation instructions and release notes, open the welcome.html file in the root directory of the CD-ROM.

The Oracle Program is distributed according to the terms of the Trial License and Global License Terms included. They are distributed "as-is," and Oracle shall not be liable for any damages resulting from use of the CD-ROM or this Program, including direct, indirect, incidental, special or consequential damages, or damages for loss of profits, revenue, data, or data use. This is the Export Version of the Oracle Program.